ENJOYMENT
OF
LIVING

By MAX EASTMAN

HARPER & BROTHERS *Publishers*
New York and London

3-8

ENJOYMENT OF LIVING

FIRST EDITION

B-X

ENJOYMENT

OF

LIVING

Books by the Same Author

ENJOYMENT OF POETRY

JOURNALISM VERSUS ART

UNDERSTANDING GERMANY

THE SENSE OF HUMOR

SINCE LENIN DIED

LEON TROTSKY, THE PORTRAIT OF A YOUTH

MARX AND LENIN, THE SCIENCE OF REVOLUTION

VENTURE, A NOVEL

THE LITERARY MIND, ITS PLACE IN AN AGE OF SCIENCE

ARTISTS IN UNIFORM

ART AND THE LIFE OF ACTION

ENJOYMENT OF LAUGHTER

THE END OF SOCIALISM IN RUSSIA

STALIN'S RUSSIA AND THE CRISIS IN SOCIALISM

MARXISM, IS IT SCIENCE?

HEROES I HAVE KNOWN

Poetry

CHILD OF THE AMAZONS AND OTHER POEMS

COLORS OF LIFE

KINDS OF LOVE

LOT'S WIFE, A DRAMATIC POEM

Translations

THE REAL SITUATION IN RUSSIA by Leon Trotsky

GABRIEL by Pushkin

THE HISTORY OF THE RUSSIAN REVOLUTION by Leon Trotsky

THE REVOLUTION BETRAYED by Leon Trotsky

Edited

CAPITAL AND OTHER WRITINGS by Karl Marx

TABLE OF CONTENTS

❧❦❧

CONTENTS

List of Illustrations

A group of portraits and photographs follow page 302.

Pictures from *The Masses* appear in the latter part of the book, Chapters 50-52

Credit should be given for the following photographs: The photographs of Dr. John George Gehring and Amos Pinchot are copyright by Underwood & Underwood; those of John Dewey, William James and Mother Jones are by Brown Brothers; J. McKeen Cattell by Press Association, Inc.; Mrs. Emmeline Pankhurst, Mrs. O. H. P. Belmont, Max Eastman at Union Square, and the pictures of Max Eastman and Ida Rauh, Carlo Tresca, Elizabeth Gurley Flynn and Bill Haywood by European Picture Service; Inez Milholland by Rochlitz Studio; Boardman Robinson and Rosalinde Fuller by Culver Service; E. W. Scripps and Jack London by Acme News Pictures; Floyd Dell by Marjorie Jones; Art Young by Frederick Hier, Jr.; Florence Deshon by Margareth Mather.

Invitation

Come let us be friends
If you have the leisure to be.
   Climb the wall and come over,
   Come straight through the clover,
And walk in my fields with me.

   I cherish no ends
In our converse except to set free
   In the realm of your spirit,
   If you will so share it,
A craving more largely to be.

   Not to cleanse or uplift
Or embellish, but only extend,
   Through your knowing and seeing,
   The range of my being
Which soon and so humbly must end.

   So give me the gift
Of unemulous friendship: I'll give—
   That pride shall not alter,
   Nor shame cause to falter,
One line of the life I relive.

   We will grandly dismiss
This beggarly question of place,
   This who gets the better,
   Who wears the big letter,
That nags at the soul of our race.

   Shall we shake hands on this?
However unseemly, uncouth,
   Unlike what men peddle,
   Least like a gold medal,
The aim of our meeting is truth.

And thus when we part,
Having finished the gift you began,
As you plod through the clover,
And climb the wall over,
And leave me a greater man,

You may have in your heart,
If you love to be growing too,
Some grain of my reaping
Worth thoughtfully keeping
As seed toward the harvest of you.

Foreword

I BEGAN life, to go back to the very pinpoint of commencement, as a gloom in a minister's family. If my mother had known what I know, I would never have been born. Nothing more inopportune than that abrupt damming of her blood-tides in the spring of 1882, which gave notice of my separate and impetuous plasma, could have been invented by a malign deity. I was, in all humbleness, a momentous catastrophe.

My mother did not want me, and worse than that, she did not want any more of the experience which produced me. My coming marked the end of my parents' physical relations and the beginning of a series of calamities that well-nigh broke up our whole family. Little could have been said in justification of my solemn-eyed arrival on the basis of the existing data. And yet I made good and lived to hear my mother use me as an argument against birth control.

By "made good" I mean that I had a good time and was useful to some ends beyond myself. I take a matter-of-fact view of what is worth while to a parcel of humans riding round the sun on a small planet. If the planet were smaller, and we fewer, and the ride briefer —if there were six of us going three times round—we should see clearly what the central problem is. We should see that we can never arrive at absolutes on such a journey, and that the chief thing is to have a good time ourselves and be gallant and, where possible, generous in promoting the enjoyments of others.

Perhaps I have put this a little crudely. There is something self-defeating in the too conscious pursuit of pleasure. Epicurus sits on a low stool a little removed from the august philosophers. His system is too easy—and besides it is bad manners to be so frank. He is right, however, that conduct begins in a recoil from painful stimuli and a swimming toward pleasant ones. That is the basic discrimination through which life survived; it is life's way of fitting into inorganic matter. And when we leave it too far in our moral and intellectual excursions, we are in danger. So are those around us.

A million crimes and insanities, whole ages of fanatic cruelty and woe, have been caused by the loss or burial under various kinds of ideological top-hamper of this simple standard of choice. If we say happiness instead of pleasure, or speak of living a rich and rewarding life as the true end of man, we shall do justice to the mind as well as the body—to Plato as well as Epicurus. And we shall have built our house of morals on a fact that will stand long after those august philosophers have passed into the mist with voodoo gods and superstition.

I, at any rate, have always had a strong and shameless interest in having a good time. I have felt that something was profoundly the matter, and that desperate measures should be taken, if I was not happy. The same thing is true of my sister Crystal, who was a devoted idealist, a "great leader," as an editorial in the *Nation* described her when she died. She was even more intolerant of woe than I, for I was afflicted from babyhood with timid melancholy, and was habituated to it and could not wholly escape it try as I would. But she was bold and joyful-tempered, and as impatient of anything that deprived her of the right to "have fun living" as anyone I have known.

Of course the variety of motives in any character is vast, and when I speak of my days as dedicated to the enjoyment of living, that is a reckless simplification. I have been tossed by conflicting impulses, yet more by external circumstances, sheer accident usually deciding which of many things I did. I felt in boyhood that I could be any kind of person I wanted to, that with a principle to stand on I could choose a character as well as a career. But I did not find any principle. I did not make any choice. I have, in a very honest sense, no character. Therefore, when I present myself as having diligently endeavored to enjoy my share of life and make it richer than the common run, I am deceiving you as to my force and circumspection. I have been no such soldier as that.

Nevertheless, the idea and the purpose to live my earthly life to the full has been the one steady and arrogant and implacable thing in my breast. It has been the legislator, court of last resort, and king among my motives, holding the same place the Bible of Jehovah held in those I stem from, and commanding the same devout and dangerous passions. Wherever the story wanders, though it faints on cliffs or starves in deserts of sterility and gloom, that is the theme of it. That is where it is going.

It is the story of how a pagan and unbelieving and unregenerate, and carnal and seditious and not a little idolatrous, epicurean revolutionist emerged out of the very thick and dark of religious America's deep, awful, pious, and theological zeal for saving souls from the flesh and the devil. It is, and will be to the end, I hope, a story of growth. For after the axiom that happiness is the chief end of man, the next truth of natural ethics is that the chief way to be happy is to grow.

I have been unusually candid in telling this story, and in many points it involves my relations with other people. I must therefore remind the reader that mine is only one side of it. Others would remember differently. I give but my own experience of life as it survives in my own records and memory.

Before telling the story, I will indulge in a little genealogy, or that branch of etymology commonly so called. I do not confuse my ancestors with my attributes, but I think of this book sometimes as a chapter in the history of American idealism; and the adventures through which the name Eastman came to me, and the name Ford to my mother, provide a "summary of preceding chapters" that could hardly be improved.

ENJOYMENT

OF

LIVING

PART I

MY LOAD OF VIRTUES

Chapter 1

New England Piety

EARLY America, as is well known, was the most virtuous country in history. No such crowds of people enthusiastically interested in being good ever gravitated to one place before. Duty and the deity were never more closely united. And, moreover, if you make a moral and religious map of the United States, you will find the heavy shading, or high points of elevation—the center of gravity, so-to-speak, for a grave business it was—in eastern Massachusetts and southeastern Pennsylvania. I draw from these two regions not only the blood in my body, but the atmosphere of my early home, the pap on which my soul was fed. No one so mixed of Christian moralism and pagan revolt against it could have originated anywhere else.

The name Eastman, so far probably as it occurs in this country, derives from the Puritan Roger Eastman, who sailed here from Southampton in the good ship *Confidence* in 1638 to "worship God and prepare himself for heaven." He came from Langford, County of Wilts, in the west of England, and was entered in the ship's papers as a servant. "It is believed," say the family records, "that on account of emigration laws, or for political reasons, his real rank was higher than appears." Just why this is believed, except that it seems im-

1

proper for the seeds of a proud family to be planted by a servant,
I do not know. These fine points of propriety are hardly ever
borne in mind when planting the seeds of a family, and I am disposed to assume that Roger was correctly entered in the books. At any
rate he settled with a wife, Sarah, in Salisbury, Massachusetts, and
begot Joseph, who fought in King Philip's War. Joseph moved up
to Hadley, Massachusetts, and married Mary, the daughter of
Deacon Peter Tilton, the big man of Hampshire County, and became a big man and a deacon himself.

Joseph and Mary begot Peter Eastman, who married Mehitabel
Root of Deerfield, Massachusetts, and moved first to Morristown,
New Jersey, then to New Fairfield, Connecticut. Peter begot Ben-
jamin, who moved to New Milford, Connecticut, married Mary
Hitchcock, moved again to Arlington, Vermont, and begot Abihue.
Abihue moved to Fairfield, Herkimer County, New York, married
Bathsheba Gardner, begot Morgan Lewis, moved to St. Lawrence
County, and was drowned in the Oswegatchie River. Morgan Lewis
married Evelina Thorpe of Ogdensburg and begot Samuel Elijah.
Samuel Elijah married Annis Bertha Ford of Peoria, Illinois, and
begot Morgan, Anstice, Crystal, and Max.

The reason I call this etymology is that it gives the history of my
name only. So far as the genes go, Roger Eastman was no more my
ancestor than 127 of his contemporaries.

My grandfather Eastman used to say that one of his maternal
ancestors was an Indian, and this is not hard to believe. For a portrait
of him and his eight grown children, eagle-eyed, dark-skinned, tall,
lean, scrawny, with high cheekbones, and wide slim mouths, would
certainly look, if you dressed them in feathers, like the last, the very
last, of the Mohicans. On the other hand, I learn from a life of
Daniel Webster that our original ancestors, his mother's family,[1]
were called "the black Eastmans," and I have rarely seen a man, or
a picture of a man, named Eastman who was not large-mouthed and
dark.

Spiritually old Deacon Peter Tilton seems to have set the pace for
our branch of the family. He had the two strains in him whose conflict kept so many of us tense and excited—the devout· Christian
and the insolent rebel. How devout he was, and how sure that the
Infinite Sovereign of the Universe had elected him to a seat in
Paradise, may be seen in this sentence from his will, which he made
for the purpose of "preventing sin and trouble":

[1] Besides Joseph, the original Roger Eastman begot John; John begot John 2d; John
2d begot Roger 2d; Roger 2d begot Abigail, and Abigail was Daniel Webster's mother.

"Committing my whole self, Soulle and Body, into ye hands of my most gracious God and Merciful Father in Jesus Christ, and of Him my dear Redeemer who I trust hath bought me with his most precious blood, and of ye Blessed Comforter, the Holy Ghost, I therefore most gladly leave myself, hoping and looking for His mercy unto Eternal Life."

Notwithstanding his readiness to "leave himself" on these humble terms to the Heavenly Powers, the Worshipful Deacon Peter was in matters of earthly church government an obstreperous democrat— or "strict Congregationalist," as they said then—and in politics a traitor and a state criminal. While himself an officer in the government of King Charles II he gave shelter to Cromwell's generals, Goffe and Whalley, members of the court that condemned Charles I to death, who, notorious as "the regicides," were hunted through New England by the new king's loyal officers for fourteen years. Throughout those years General Goffe lived in Peter Tilton's attic. There is a tradition in Hadley that once while the citizens were attending a town meeting, a band of Indians stole against the town. General Goffe, seeing them from his high window, rushed out and gave the alarm, led the citizens into battle, routed the Indians, and disappeared as suddenly as he had come. The citizens decided that he was a white-haired angel sent by God to save them, and Deacon Peter never disillusioned them.

If you doubt all this, you can go to the public square in Hadley and see it printed, as the Ten Commandments were, on blocks of stone:

HON. PETER TILTON
DIED JULY 1 1696
HE WAS ONE OF THE FOUNDERS OF HADLEY
A MAN OF GREAT INFLUENCE IN CHURCH AND STATE
HE WAS ALSO ONE OF THOSE WHO ASSISTED IN
CONCEALING THE REGICIDES

JOSEPH EASTMAN
BORN JAN. 8 1651
MARRIED MARY TILTON 1682
DIED APRIL 4 1692

ERECTED BY THEIR DESCENDANTS
AUGUST 9 1910

A quotation from the oratory at the unveiling of the monument will show in what ways Peter set the pace for our family. It was not a martial pace. "We do not find his name," says the orator, "among the military leaders of the settlement, nor among the soldiers who went out to the Indian wars. He was a man well equipped for the affairs of peace. . . . First and best of all, he was a deacon in the church." And last but not least of all: "He occupied from time to time all the offices which were at the disposal of the town."

If it puzzles you to know why Joseph Eastman should be immortalized just for marrying another man's daughter—an heroic deed, to be sure, but not unique—it is perhaps because you have a too retrospective view of the mechanics of immortality. In marrying Mary Tilton and producing a son Peter, Joseph became not only my ancestor, a feat that would hardly have got his name on a monument, but the ancestor of the Eastman Kodak Company.[2]

In Joseph's son Peter, as in the age in which he lived, the Yankee soon prevailed over the Puritan. He went out to Morristown, New Jersey, "attracted by the deposits of iron ore," and bought three hundred acres of land, thirty acres of it laid out to accommodate an iron works. He is described in the debenture as a yeoman, but he did so well out there that when he moved back east he joined the landed gentry. Besides buying ample acres in New Fairfield, Connecticut, he absorbed real estate as far north as Cornwall, where he is credited in the village history with building the first house. The estate in New Jersey he sold for four hundred pounds to his "beloved son" Benjamin, who had settled in New Milford. Benjamin appears also to have been "a man well equipped for the affairs of peace." At least his sole act in the family records was to "move up to Vermont shortly before the revolution," and if he was anything like me, he did not move up there because he thought the principal battles were going to be fought in the Green Mountains. I am afraid the sad fact is that, as a wealthy landholder and absentee iron magnate, Benjamin had become a small colonial imitation of a big British squire. I doubt if he knew that his great-grandfather had concealed the regicides, and if he did, he probably kept it under his hat. His eldest son fought against Washington with the soldiers of the crown, and his youngest son, Abihue, my great-grandfather, was

[2] My father once went up to Rochester and asked George Eastman, on the rather tenuous basis of this common great-great-great-grandfather, to contribute to the endowment of Starkey Seminary, of which he was a trustee, and got turned down. That is the nearest our branch of the family ever came to any substantial sums of money.

a member of the Anglican church. The "ideological superstructure," as Marx would say, had shifted to fit the economic facts.

The economic facts shifted again, however—and so did the ideology. The lands of the Tories being confiscated by the new government, Abihue and his father, destitute, moved west along the Mohawk to carve them a new farm out of the wilderness. They became pioneers again, like Deacon Peter. And young Abihue liked the pioneer life; he liked the American republic. When his Tory brother came back from Canada, whither he had fled after the Battle of Saratoga, and offered him a fine farm if he would move up there and share a new-found prosperity, he stubbornly refused to go. At the age of forty, while his old father was still alive, and I suppose still arguing about the Revolution, he decided to restore the family honor, and end the argument, by enlisting as a soldier in the War of 1812. That put him with the "democrats" against the "Federalists." And I strongly suspect he enlisted for that reason. He transmitted little but a few warlike metaphors to my grandfather, Morgan Lewis, who was again a man well equipped for the affairs of peace. He was also—that the gospel according to Marx might be fulfilled—a "strict Congregationalist."

Chapter 2

My Worshipful Grandfather

TO MORGAN LEWIS EASTMAN his origin was a complete mystery. "I know no more about my grandfather's birthplace than Melchisedek's," he wrote. "Neither do I know my own father's. He was drowned when I was thirteen and no record kept but an entrance in a little paper-covered primer—Abihu Eastman." That little primer was enough, as you have seen, to place my grandfather in a significant history.

Abihue taught his son to read and write and try to talk like the Book of Common Prayer. But Morgan Lewis had less than six months' schooling, and was hard at work long before his father died. By eighteen he had acquired a reputation among his neighbors along the St. Lawrence as a prodigious worker and a great athlete, and was convinced in his own impressionable mind that he had lived a wild life and was something of a rake. Amid the wave of revivalism that passed over the country in 1830-32, he was drawn into a neighborhood prayer meeting and "got religion" in a form less elegant and more fervid than one gets it from the Episcopal Prayer Book. He consecrated himself straight off without fuss or hesitation to the service of the Lord, and turned his brilliant mind loose on the Bible, which he soon had pretty well by heart.

For fifteen years he functioned as an "itinerant minister," one of those unlicensed and irregular saints who scandalized the respectable churches by riding about preaching and teaching and doing good works without any refined discrimination. His eloquence and beloved character finally drew him a call to the Congregational Church in Lisbon Center near Ogdensburg. He accepted the call and was ordained there at the age of thirty-eight. From that point of vantage he continued his career as a horseback evangelist, doing more or less regular service in twenty-five churches throughout St. Lawrence and

6

Jefferson counties. He became, I am told, a kind of unofficial priest and pastor for that whole section of the country.

In these labors he was loyally supported by my plump and stead-fast grandmother, Evelina, the daughter of a Dutch blacksmith named Daniel Thorpe.[1] Evelina had the one thing Morgan Lewis lacked, calmness of spirit. She took life as the anvil takes the hammer. She said little and did much; what she said was pious, and what she did was kind. The fame of her cookies survives to this day—also the memory of her walking six miles to prayer meeting with a baby in her arms. There survives also the fame, or rumor, that she was in-clined to give her husband the cream and bring up her children on skim milk. I suspect the truth underlying this rumor is that Evelina was not entirely buffaloed by the mother-instinct—it is one of the best traits of the women in our family that they were not—and that she could plainly see which member of the household was burning up the most energy.

At any rate, I am going to erect here a little monument to Evelina inscribed with a tribute paid to her in a letter by her husband:

"Yes, I remember well those verses you all used to sing when returned from y'r schools, or distant employments, on a visit; one at the organ—the others around her, and Dear Ma sitting in State, queenly, grand, quiet, majestic, calm, sweet, Princess, unpretentious —dignified, yet unconscious of her greatness while you sang. . . ."

From these quotations you can see what a load of virtue I in-herited from this one grandmother alone. I must add that I inherited my grandfather's gift of intemperate admiration, a gift which has brought me life's sweetest pleasures and some very bitter pain.

In 1869, following a trek of his parishioners, Morgan Lewis moved to Royalton, Wisconsin, where he continued the life of a ministerial circuit-rider, serving three churches as pastor with a salary of two hundred dollars a year, preaching frequently in eleven more, and still supporting his large family as a farmer. He lived life like a river at the flood.

[1] I was told recently that Evelina Thorpe's mother was Miriam Chapin, daughter of John Chapin, "pioneer of Ogdensburg," and he in turn a direct descendant of Deacon Samuel Chapin, patriarch of Springfield, Massachusetts. But I have long ceased to be surprised at the discovery of deacons in my blood. A more interesting piece of history is that when St. Gaudens made the famous statue of Samuel Chapin, to be seen now both in Springfield and in Lincoln Park, Philadelphia, he borrowed the deacon's actual peaked hat and flowing cape to get a good likeness, and left them kicking around his studio until they got swept out with the rubbish.

"Have three preaching stations," he wrote to my father, "Seymour the centre, Angelica north 12 miles, Osborn south 4 miles. . . . This before me after preaching evenings all winter, and twice on Sab. and sometimes 3 times. This will need some physical grace, if there be such . . .

"The corn and potatoes, oats and pumpkins are all brought in, and the oxen and cows turned into the green and fresh feed this morning before breakfast. The wheat field is a beautiful scenery; about 3 inches high, and the ground covered. O, Samuel! to stand in the wood-shed door, and look over to it is captivating, and inspires the purest gratitude to Our Great and Loving Father in heaven."

His economic independence as a farmer gave my grandfather a freedom of expression that any artist must envy, and that he especially required. For he was as impulsive as a child and recklessly unrestrained by convention. "He could outrun, outswim, outwrestle and outshoot any man in St. Lawrence County." So runs the family tradition (from which you may be absolutely sure that he knew how to swim and could load a gun), and I have it in a letter of my father's that he was forty-seven before he ever failed to "jump a fence at one bound." And all this physical power and agility came into play in the pulpit. I do not mean that he put on a show, for he had both dignity and intellect; he wrote his sermons out with thoughtful care. But he was all there and all in motion when he talked. If his cuffs came loose, he would strip them off, set them on the pulpit, and go to work again free of encumbrances. One Sunday a family that he loved were missing from the church, and looking out the window in the midst of his sermon, he suddenly exclaimed:

"Here come the Ritchies, God bless them!"

On another occasion, when reading a passage of scripture containing the word belly, he stopped abruptly and shouted:

"Some people are afraid to say belly, but I'm not—belly, *belly*, BELLY!"

My father once went to New York with him, and they ate lunch in the restaurant of the old Grand Central Hotel. Morgan Lewis got up from his chair when his plate came, rapped commandingly on the table, and said:

"Friends, we will ask the blessing of God upon this food!"

There were no snickers—the whole restaurant bowed their heads.

Morgan Lewis had a gift for pouring out large tears on abstract subjects, and no shame or modesty about it. Indeed he loved nothing better than to conduct funerals and send all the mourners home wet and red-eyed for the good of their souls. Emotion was so much the essence of his genius that, like a poet, he felt bound only to give it fluent words. The prayers he sent to heaven, standing there in those little rural pulpits looking up into a white plaster ceiling, his bright dark eyes streaming, his mellow voice broken, his beautiful strong frame shaken with the woes and sins of all humanity, would have melted any God that had a heart. A letter written to my father in 1869 suggests his eloquence in this declining art:

"Dear Son S.:

"Your last letter informing us of your fearful cough, filled my heart with sorrow, and my eyes with tears. I could not help weeping, when I thought, perhaps this cough might so rend your lungs as to result in that stealthy, and much dreaded disease, consumption, and end all my fond hopes, and pleasing anticipations of some day hearing my son preach the unsearchable richness of Christ. O my Son! How are you while you read this? Dear Saviour, canst thou hear me pray, and heal my son, or have I provoked a chastisement from thee that will make my heart-strings break, and my soul quiver under thy hand? Samuel, I cannot write you about any of the Autumnal joys and pleasures; the work accomplished, the golden leaves rustling to the ground, and the wheat field's green garb, the cellar wall all beautifully reared in lime mortar, and laid by a line in the hand of a cunning workman, 50 bushels of potatoes in the cellar and about 24 more to dig, and about 30 baskets of corn husked, and plenty more to husk;—for you are sick, and it all fades in its otherwise gratifications, and I am sorrowful . . ."

There was pity but often also a warlike glitter in my grandfather's tears. They were a part of the ammunition with which God equips those who fight his battle for souls. The old man had, in general, a somewhat belligerent conception of his labors in the cause of Christian love.

"Your letter made me weep," he writes again to my father. "I wondered if I should live to see you through the schools and out on the white and whitening fields with sickle in hand helping to gather in the wasting grain! My yearnings are irrepressible to live and have you live to be by my side, and with the mighty blows the school acquisitions help to strike, you could act as a battery over my defenseless head, while I filled the enemy's ranks with small shot . . ."

Not a strictly pastoral way of gathering in the grain!

Even before God Himself, Morgan Lewis stood his ground in a

rather bellicose fashion: "Just forgive me, my Son, that's what God has to do all the time, or let the Arm of terrible justice fall on me, and that he can't well do, because I cling to Christ. He smote Christ once for sinners, He can't and don't want to do it again, and He can't smite me without hitting Christ, because I cling to him so tight."

Morgan Lewis was very sure that at some not distant day the Catholics would make an effort to kill all the Protestants, and I gather from his metaphors that he had not cast himself for the role of lamb-at-the-slaughter when the day came. He was a most pitying and tender person, with a veritable genius for love. But he had wrath as well as love in him, and a fearless loyalty to what he believed true that makes him remembered up there in St. Lawrence County after seventy years, as villages in India remember an old lion that haunted them.

"He was terrible," a frail old lady in a wheel chair told me. "He would speak out the naked truth to anybody anywheres."

She recalled how he once walked down the road with farmer Shattuck, and when they came to the crossroads, Shattuck said:

"Well, parson, our ways part."

"Shattuck," he said, "they parted long ago—mine goes to heaven and yours to hell."

But Morgan Lewis had joy and humor in him too. He laughed as easily as he cried, and often very soon after. And he had imagery for all his moods.

"This morning's mail bro't y'r communication and to my waiting heart a tidal wave of sweet and tranquil joy. Oh! what volumes of pure, crystal, thrilling memories came rushing into my soul like a full-freighted commercial ship, proudly heading into port with its endless variety of richest treasures for unlading and disbursement among waiting merchant men."

"How we as a family have been driven out of our sweet cozy nests, forced to the use of our wings reluctantly perhaps, at times, and how when ignorant of their use, and apparently gravitating desponding or despairing-ward, God has glided under us quickly with broadened wings, bearing us on . . ."

He played the snare drum and fervently enjoyed a cockfight. He was a connoisseur of pretty girls. He loved to tilt his chair against a wall on the back porch and play the jew's-harp, or sing the endless story-folksongs of the pioneers. At "sugarings-off" in his maple grove he was always gay. Among the guests at one of these festivities was the local strong man, a teacher, who was showing off by laying out his pupils in bunches as they would pounce on him and try to get him down.

"Why don't you take somebody your size?" Morgan Lewis asked him.

"I only wish you were twenty-five years younger, I'd take you on," the young man answered.

"Never mind the twenty-five years," Morgan Lewis said, removing his coat.

He was then in his late fifties, and he laid the young man in the grass three times—to the delight of his parishioners.

He was once called upon to preach in one of the large metropolitan churches, and was pretty nervous about the outcome.

"I laid three sermons on a chair," he said, "and kneeling before them asked God to tell me which one to preach. He told me pretty quickly too."

"What did he say?"

"He told me to preach whichever one I'd a mind to."

It was printed of him after he died that "there were flights of grandeur in his sermons reached by few and surpassed by none." And after coming under the spell of his eloquent letters, I can almost believe this to have been true. His lack of schooling, together with an infinite regretful humbleness about it, kept him from high advancement.

"I am going down to the grave," he wrote, "and shall go, mourning because I did not secure a preparation in the schools for the ministry. I shall gasp my last with a tear on my cheek over this."

Another obstacle to larger fame was his own wish. He was a pioneer; he hated town and city life. He made the long move to Wisconsin because life was getting too civilized for him—in 1869!— along the banks of the St. Lawrence. He loved to be on a horse plunging ahead on rough roads and through black forests in the service of the Lord. He must have known implicitly, as one knows with the tendrils of pure feeling, that death to his whole faith, labor, and rapture was contained in those advancing industries and cities. He fled wisely to the frontier.

I smile sometimes as though he were the younger at the odd way in which a bit of totally un-God-inspired horse sense will push through my grandfather's theological lyricism and peek out in a parenthesis—or how, other times, God Himself will get but a parenthesis in which to sanction some piece of mundane sagacity.

"Our mortar lies in the bin where it was mixed, have to water it every day or two to keep it from spoiling, the house to be lined up inside with two thicknesses of $\frac{1}{2}$ inch stuff, and to be lathed before we can use the mortar, the crops have had to be put in, visiting has had to be done, sermons have had to be studied and prayed over; and floods of letters from St. Lawrence and Jefferson Counties to be answered, &c., &c., and nobody to do all this but your brother and I (God helps us of course) but human muscles I mean."

His advice to my father when considering his first call to a church in St. Lawrence County is also characteristic:

"Go if God bids you. But don't flatter yourself that they are angels. Watch every man till you know his deep, underlying shrewdness, and what he unreasonably expects from ministers. Lay down and take a good sleep any time, and anywhere, when you think you need it. Ask for a sofa, bed, or something, without blushing or mortification. Brothers H. and Ashley, and their families, like frequent calls, and want fresh, tender, sympathetic prayers—that touch every muscle, nerve and sinew in the family, and in the church. God will take care of that—if He don't, you can't certainly . . ."

In me the idea of going into a strange village, looking up Brothers H. and Ashley, and proposing that they kneel down on the floor and join me in a fresh, tender, and sympathetic prayer, evokes a feeling of embarrassment that drowns all other sentiment. I do not quite see how a young man just out of college could do it or contemplate it. That shows only that I have wandered from the faith of my fathers, however, not from their folly. I did go round the country begging rich businessmen to give money to a magazine dedicated to proletarian revolution—a thing almost as embarrassing and alien to my nature, a thing that I never for one moment *wanted* to do. It seems to me there is a biological impulse in men to deny themselves what they most want and do what is most painful to them. Puritanism is not primarily cultural; it has its basis in our physiology. If you attach a hypertrophied cerebrum to a sound animal, it just seems to produce this rather morbid effect.

My wandering from the Faith has been upon the whole a smooth process. I can distinguish several stages between my believing grandfather and my infidel self, my father taking some slight steps in heresy and my mother several more. But there has been no sudden change. Nobody has broken away, or abjured, or renounced, or done any melodramatic thing. There is in consequence a certain calmness about my unreligion. It is not central to my mind as it was to so many freethinkers before me, men like Robert Ingersoll or Clarence Darrow or James Harvey Robinson, or even James Joyce, who on the calendar belonged with me. Their whole thinking life was polarized by the revolt against the Divine Father. That negation had been so aggressive and passionate that it seemed a positive philosophy of life. They "rested," as the lawyers say, and never took any real position beyond that about anything.

To me the change has been genial, an extension of the realm of humor rather than a mutiny against the rule of faith. Morgan Lewis used to tell how one day when he had been making pastoral calls and was tired enough to go home, he saw a house at the top of a long hill and became possessed of the idea that God wanted him to visit the people in that house. He wrestled with his weariness awhile, and finally toiled up the hill in obedience to God's command. He found the house vacant. He loved to tell the story, and draw the obvious moral: "It shows that God loves a joke as well as any of us." We loved to tell the story, too, but with us the moral was a part of the joke.

ENVOI

In 1938 when I was conducting "The Word Game" for the Columbia Broadcasting System, I received the following remarkable letter from Sidney, Ohio:

"Dear Mr. Eastman:

"Fifty-two years ago, when I was five years old, I visited an aunt in the little village of Royalton, Wisconsin. She took me to church where an elderly minister with a long white beard preached a sermon. It was the first time I remember going to church and the first time I heard a sermon.

"Down through the years that event has been remembered, chiefly, I think, because the minister looked straight at me much of the time. At other times he looked upward and talked with great earnestness. I never comprehended what the sermon was about; but it has followed me through more than half a century and given me the very distinct impression that he was a great and good man. . . .

"The first time I heard your radio program I tuned in late and the first voice I heard was yours. Strange as it may seem, I instantly pictured you as an elderly, somewhat spare man with a long white beard and a clerical coat. When your name was mentioned at the end of the program, my memory flashed back to the little church in Royalton.

"There is something about your voice that reminds me of this man. His name was Eastman. Perhaps he was your grandfather. . . .

Yours truly,
John Whitney"

Chapter 3

My Sainted Father

M Y FATHER had a thin keen handsome face, straight-lipped yet gentle. He was admired extravagantly by his parishioners and by many fellow citizens not of his parish. He was in his later years something of a patriarch, a First Citizen of Elmira, New York. Professor John R. Tuttle, who taught philosophy at Elmira College, describes him as "one of the great spirits of our time," and ranks him with Thorstein Veblen and Dean Creighton of Cornell as the most impressive of his teachers. He was certainly an anchoring ground to hundreds of people, and seemed to them not only a moral but an intellectual leader of high force and independence.

Notwithstanding the dignity and nobility of his public character, there was to us who knew him intimately—and only his wife and children knew him intimately—a pathos about my father that often brought tears to our eyes. "I wonder why it is," my sister wrote, "that Dad always makes me want to cry. In childhood I used to burst out sobbing wildly just at the thought of him." And like all things that have pathos in solemn moments, his character seemed funny to us when we were hilarious. I can see him sitting there at the dining-room table, gently austere and a little bewildered, while we roared and rocked at something he could not perceive as ludicrous.

"Now you are getting into a gale!" he would invariably say.

And that phrase, having come to contain and symbolize what in him was inelastic and unadapted to the nimble tricks of social intercourse, would set us all roaring and rocking again, until frequently one or two would get up and stagger from the room in sheer incapacity to contain so much mirth. Humor is close to the heart of friendship, and by this divergence in sensing the laughable our family was very definitely divided—although the tears are still close to my eyes when I say it—into two camps of congeniality, with Dad alone in one camp and the rest of us in the other.

His solitude was really less painful to him than it was pathetic to us, for he was serenely extrovert. His attention was almost always upon things outside him; when he did contemplate himself, it was apt to be with a feeling of complacence. In the family circle, he could not forbear to brag a little about evidences of the esteem in which he was held—though that was not so much vanity as a lack of sensitivity. We all would brag if we thought it paid, but seeing we lose more esteem by recounting our exploits than we gain by performing them, most of us try to hold in. Dad did not try very hard to hold in— that was all. And I must say it was a humble sort of bragging, often a mere attempt to keep his end up in a family of rather overwhelming children.

That shifting back and forth between matter-of-fact and matter-of-theology, so spontaneous in my grandfather, had become in my father almost a deliberate art. I suppose it happened in all ministers who clung to their faith yet kept abreast of the advancing wave of knowledge. He was boldly heretical about things like Sunday baseball and the divorce laws, and he was often in a minority of one at the Ministers' Club. He had social courage. But he had not the temperament of a rebel. There was a touch of the Colonel House in him, a gift of seeing your point of view that might for amity's sake extend to the point of deceiving you about his own. People invariably felt better after a talk with him. No one was ever afraid of what he might say. He was too "approbative" for that; he too well enjoyed being liked. So do I, and that is why I discourse of this so fluently. Both my mother and sister had something angular in their characters, something like the edge of a crystal, which stayed clear while they were talking to people. I have it in some degree when I am alone, and I sometimes retire deliberately to recover it. But unless fortified by anger or deliberate resolution, I am apt to be pretty weak soup in contact with people. *Anything to avoid a harsh scene* is the motto of my instincts, and it was of my father's.

Aside from these frailties, it is hard to name a trait in his character that was not a virtue. He was kind, reasonable, patient, courageous, sweet-tempered, generous, truthful, just, temperate. He was more than temperate; he was abstemious. In contrast to old Morgan Lewis, who would have his chaw of tobacco now and then Christ or no

Christ, he never touched the poisoned leaf, or breathed a breath of its seducing incense. No drop of liquor ever passed his lips.

Mark Twain once contrasted my father with his own wife Olivia, saying that she had been born a saint, but he had come to it by hard struggle. The fact is that sainthood was wished upon him about ten minutes after his birth. He was, in the opinion of the midwife, still-born, and was wrapped up in a blanket and laid away in a bedroom to await the undertaker. His aged grandmother ambled in there to have a look at him, and brought him back into the kitchen where it was warm.

"What are you talking about?" she said. "This child is alive!"

My grandfather went down on his knees then and there and dedicated the child to God, and with two pious old women working on him and a tear-stained evangelist praying above him, he was dragged back from limbo by main force and with the express under-standing that if the effort were successful, he was to be dedicated to God.

Thus he never really had a chance to be anything but a saint, and I doubt if any project to the contrary ever entered his head. I have a tiny notebook full of pressed flowers and petals, entitled on the flyleaf SAMUEL EASTMAN, JOURNAL, YEAR 1852, SUNDAY. He was then six years old, and here is the first entry:

Jenuary 1, 1852
Now i comence my diree. We are habeing a reviveoal to the church lisbon an now i am keeping a record of the siners that ar convirted

|||||||||||||||||||||||||||||||||||||||||||||||||

Thirty-six of them by actual count, and all from that date for-ward, his father assured him, safe in the arms of Jesus. For Morgan Lewis was of the "New School of Theology," who tempered their Calvinism not only with a belief in the miracle of conversion—Jonathan Edwards' one little weakness—but with the imputation of love to God, free will to man, and salvation power to the act of belief. He could not have preached a cold-hearted religion.

Notwithstanding the love, and the duty of love, that sat in the place of philosophy at his fireside, Samuel Elijah spent the years from 1861 to 1865 yearning to go south and shoot the rebels. And in 1865, at the age of eighteen, he did manage to enlist in the army. His mood still lives in a faded clipping that I find in his soldier's wallet:

"The Death of Warren

"On the day of the memorable engagement at Bunker Hill, General Joseph Warren, then in the prime of life, joined the American ranks as a volunteer.

"'Tell me where I can be useful,' said he, addressing General Putnam.

"'On to the redoubt,' was the reply. 'You will there be covered.'

"'I came not to be covered,' returned Warren. 'Tell me where I shall be in most danger—tell me where the action will be hottest.'"

My father succeeded in getting where the action was hottest, at Cold Harbor, in the last battles around Richmond, and he staggered straight into the bullets as he had promised himself he would. He staggered because he was sick with typhoid pneumonia, and he fell on the battlefield, not wounded but unable to stand, and was sent to the rear by an officer who felt his pulse. After lying eight weeks in a fly tent at City Point Hospital with a fever in which his left lung was all but consumed, he was shipped home—thin, tottering, hollow-voiced, hollow-chested, a pale and half-obliterated copy of the lusty boy he had been.

He was still only eighteen years old. The life dedicated to God was yet to be accomplished. His was to be, moreover, no amateur dedication, no "incoherent, uncultured, unscientific, illogical, awkward scribbling," to quote the adjectives Morgan Lewis applied to his own sermons.

Thus, while recovering what strength he could with that withered lung, Samuel Elijah taught for two years in a little red schoolhouse, studying at night and saving to pay his way to Oberlin.

Chapter 4

Pennsylvania Goodness

TO GET the full weight of my native load of virtue, you must now turn back to those pietistic pilgrims who came over in the wind of William Penn's evangelical advertising campaigns and settled in southeastern Pennsylvania. They had a pleasanter kind of virtue than the Puritans had; they meant something by freedom besides having their own way. But they had the same fearful preoccupation with being good. If you travel over that region from the Cumberland Valley to the Delaware even now, you can see in the shapes of the houses and the trim thrifty look of the fences and farm lands—even in the way the chickens cross the road—the same bracing and yet depressing evidence of austere self-discipline that you see in New England.

Henry Ford was a man of money and a public-spirited citizen, as Henry Fords logically must be, in the village of Harrisburg, Pennsylvania. On January 1, 1785, he contributed £7 4s. toward the purchase of a milldam that the town wanted to condemn and destroy as the probable cause of an epidemic fever. He also contributed £6 6s. toward the new court house.

That is all I know about Henry, except that he begot John—and even of that I am not quite sure.[1] John begot George. George married Catherine Stehley, moved to Peoria, Illinois, and begot Annis Bertha Ford, my mother. The Fords were Scotch-Irish, which does not mean, I am sorry to say, that they had Irish blood in them. The

[1] The memory of my family goes back to John, and the *Annals of Harrisburg* by George H. Morgan tell me about Henry, but the relation between them is my guess. Of John and all his trembling hardihoods and excitements, one fact alone remains in memory. When my mother was born, he was a deaf old man lost in a growth of whiskers. They brought the new baby in to show him, and he inquired her name.

"Annis Bertha," they shouted.

"Amus Bertle—well, well!" he said.

Scotch-Irish were pure Scotch and pure Presbyterian. A vigorous population "distinguished by thrift, industry and endurance," they fled to Ulster in the seventeenth century to escape taxation and religious persecution under the Stuarts; and they fled to America in the eighteenth century for similar reasons. The term Scotch-Irish is a misnomer, and a purely American one. "First used as a term of reproach," says W. F. Egle in his *History of Dauphin and Lebanon Counties,* "it has become a synonym of enterprise, intelligence, patriotism"—you see how the virtues are piling up again—"and religious fervor."

George Ford inherited all these virtues, and by paying his bills with absolute regularity once a year, he acquired, besides, the nickname of "Honest." Honest George Ford was a gunsmith, and made such fine rifle barrels that he had a little reputation all his own among huntsmen in the Middle West. He also had a violent temper, and one that did not die down after wrecking everything like a storm at sea, but kept right on raging over the wreckage for years.

George conceived himself around the family hearthstone as a big male boss, and he put this over to the extent that every one of his five handsome daughters grew up an ardent advocate of woman's rights, and his scions by and large made no small contribution to the feminist movement in America. After making her nest on the ledges of his tyranny for some thirty years, Catherine Stehley one day took it into her head to visit her relatives in Harrisburg. As usual, George said *no!* But the children were grown now—the labors of her life were done.

Catherine said: "Well, I'm going."

George said: "If you go, you can't come back."

And having said that in a rage, he stuck to it—in a rage—for the rest of his life. Whisky, already a warm friend, soon took the whole place of gentle and temperate Catherine Stehley, and George did not live very long. He died, my mother always said, "of melancholy." He just put his head down in his arms on the table in his lonely home and died.

No such lapse from virtue is to be found among the Stehleys. They were Pennsylvania Dutch—which also does not mean that they had Dutch blood in them. The Pennsylvania Dutch were German Protestants who fled like the Scotch-Irish from religious oppression and other more worldly afflictions. They comprised a variety of sects, all more or less akin to the Quakers in religion and in that discipline of friendliness which is about the best thing religion ever produced. They were like Quakers, too, in the virtues which swarm around and speckle every page on which their names are mentioned: "industrious," "thrifty," "staid," "frugal," "patient," "temperate," "pious" . . .

Ulrich Stehley of Bethel Township died in 1766, leaving eight children, among them Jacob. Jacob, another man "well equipped for the affairs of peace," fought in the War of Independence, and rose to the rank of deacon in the Dutch Reformed Church, the first church built in Harrisburg. He died in 1793, leaving a widow who contributed two pounds more than Henry Ford did to purchase the sinister milldam "and with Divine favor, restore the borough to its former state of health and prosperity."

Jacob's son George married Sarah King, my great-grandmother, whose portrait is in this book. She was not a Quaker, but loved the Quaker costume and wore one like it for that reason. Sarah's mother was Charlotte Pancake—Pfannekake, I believe, if she wanted to be fancy about it, but she didn't—and Charlotte was something of a heroine in the early days in Harris's Ferry. She married Sebastian Crevous in 1762 and moved with him far up into Northumberland County. He was among the first voluteers in the War of Independence, was wounded and taken prisoner in the Battle of Long Island, and died soon after in the hands of the British. Charlotte continued to live there in the wilds until 1778, when she was warned by a friendly Indian of the approaching Wyoming Massacre. She grabbed her three children and an armful of provisions, leaped into a small boat on the Susquehanna and paddled downstream through seventy miles of forest to Harris's Ferry. John Harris gave her shelter, and there she subsequently married Richard King and had one more daughter. The daughter was Sarah King, my great-grandmother.

So Catherine Stehley was not the first woman of her tribe who could take action in a crisis—not the first to arrive home in Harrisburg after an act of will! I think that the women in our family owed much of their force of character, their arrant independence, to this strain that came down from the "staid" Quakerish Germans who settled Harrisburg. I know too, from what my mother told me, that my grandmother Stehley had much of the same poiseful humor, a kind of perpetual inward half-acknowledged mirth about the absurdity of one's being what one is, and being stubborn about it, which made my mother and sister such a source of joy. And I know from a fragment in her handwriting preserved for me by my mother that she battled for a lifetime with religious doubt:

"This is the eve of my birthday. How many I have seen. How good God has been to me. How many comforts I have had. But what poor returns I have made for all the blessings I enjoy. Filled with doubt and unbelief I can only cry God have mercy on me a sinner. Unbelief is my worst foe."

My grandmother lived long enough to name me Max, a name I think she found on a dog, and died about the time I was born. I long ago forgave her this offense to my dignity, and I commend her serene, strong, gentle face to your affection.

Chapter 5

My Heroic Mother

MY MOTHER was of medium height, with light-brown hair and green-blue eyes, a gently curving beauty both of face and figure. Like my father she was a Christian minister, one of the first women ordained in the Congregational church. Unlike him, she struggled all her life with doubt. She inherited from Catherine Stehley that sense of hard fact and that terrible honesty which makes unbelief an almost inconquerable foe. And she inherited some also of the devils and darkness in George Ford's impetuous disposition. She was not loved with a civic affection by the city of Elmira as my father was, although more eloquent, more celebrated beyond the city, and more personally and deeply loved by those who loved her. To her children she seemed more heroic than he. She seemed to struggle harder toward her vision, and keep pushing her vision farther from her.

"I am trying to improve every day," she would say jokingly when anything went wrong in her admirably conducted household. We would laugh, because she voiced it like a child, but it was true.

Within the demands life made upon him as husband, father, citizen, and minister of the gospel, my father was unfailing and unfaltering in his goodness. But the Christian ideal, if you really mean it, demands more of you than "life" does. It demands that life itself, as we live it, be transcended and superseded and changed. It is a utopian ideal, and ethically, at least, revolutionary. That is what St. Francis, George Fox, Tolstoy, John Humphrey Noyes, and others so sincerely Christian that they had to renounce the existing forms of Christianity realized. And that my mother realized. In her simple and unself-conscious way, without zealotry—for she had too much humor for that—but with constant inward struggle, she tried to live a life the core of which was doing, and not just being, good.

23

She adopted one waif after another into our overcrowded and far from prospering family, took them in and brought up and educated them on a shoestring. I can not remember a time when there was not some boy or girl living in our house because he had nowhere else to live.

And these were only the large chunks of her benevolence. She was always secretly putting herself through some discipline of sacrifice and generosity. I remember one which occurred during a period when, besides running the church, she was cooking three meals a day and helping us children with the dishes. A lonely old lady, who rode in five miles from the country every Sunday to hear her preach, was stricken with paralysis and went blind. My mother got on a streetcar and traveled out to see her. When she came back she said:

"Max, Mrs. L—— tells me that my sermons were the only thing that gave her courage to live. She has absolutely nothing left, you know. I told her I would come out every week and read my sermon to her. I'll read her a novel too—that will do her more good."

I was old enough to be appalled. "Can't you send the sermon and let someone else read it to her?" I urged.

"You know that isn't what she wants," my mother said.

Every Thursday afternoon as long as the woman lived my mother took that tiring trolley ride out into the country. No worry and no weariness could deter her from this almost wanton regimen of kindness, about which no murmur of complaint or complacence ever crossed her lips.

In a person shrouded in solemnity this goodness might not seem so beautiful, but she carried a gay, unmasking humor with her everywhere. One of her parishioners who believed in spiritism once persuaded her to visit a medium. It required a long walk, and when they arrived in the seance chamber my mother sank rather eagerly into a comfortable chair. The medium started forward in agitation.

"Oh, you mustn't take that chair—George is sitting there!"

"Well, I wish you'd ask him to move," she said. "I'm tired!"

She had an amused sensitivity to those distinctions of pecuniary caste which prevail in a democratic society, and the minister's peculiar relation to them. She took five dollars out of a lecture fee once and firmly announced to the family that, come what may, she was going to buy a silk umbrella.

"There's nothing in this world," she said, "that sustains a woman when she walks along the street like knowing she's carrying a silk umbrella."

I borrowed that umbrella one morning about a week after it was purchased and came back home at night without it. After retracing my steps and making every effort to discover its hiding place, I had finally to bring her the sad news that I had lost it.

"Max, you've destroyed my sole claim to respectability!" she said. "However, I knew it was a false claim—no silk umbrella ever really belonged to me!"

Not only in extending the boundaries of kindness but in advancing the frontiers of knowledge, in stating publicly and boldly what her study and meditation led her to accept privately as true, my mother seemed heroic. She was sometimes uncontrolled, unreasonable, impatient; she was physically timid; she was melancholic to the point of moody madness. But she was as selfless as she was clearheaded in her devotion to truth and the ideal of Christian character. No trace in her of vanity, no trace of self-deception. She took other people's woes into her heart and cared about them deeply, and she rejoiced in other people's joys as though she were their mother.

Her genius for speech and writing was as serene as her character was turgid. It was too serene, indeed, too facile to impel her to great efforts. From girlhood she could sit down any time and pour off an essay in fine and fluent English on any topic you proposed. In Peoria, according to a schoolmate, Bertha Ford commonly wrote themes for "about half the girls in school." Once a stupid little girl in the class above her went around crying because she wasn't going to be promoted at the end of the year, and was going to get licked for it, too, in the warmth of the home circle. My mother said:

"I tell you what we'll do. I'll write a theme for you to read in English, and make it so good they'll just have to promote you."

It was about the time they opened the famous park in St. Louis which goes by the name of Shaw's Garden, and my mother, adopting that title, penned a glowing description of the delights of nature in the midst of a great city she had never seen, and carefully rehearsed the little girl in the reading of it. She neglected, however, to rehearse her in the title, and the paper was read, with tremulous solemnity, as an original composition on the subject of *Shaw's Gander*.

Another memory of the schoolgirl Bertha Ford is that on the occasion of a woman's rights convention in Peoria she introduced Susan B. Anthony. She did it so eloquently that, according to a newspaper clipping in my possession, the whole town was talking about her the next day. What George Ford said on that day is not recorded.

I do not know how much ambition Bertha's gifts awakened in her. Her graduation essay when she came out of Peoria High School in 1870 was entitled "Oh, Femina, Femina!" I am sure it expressed the smiling wish that women would buck up and *be something,* and the opinion that it was their own fault and men's loss as well as theirs if they didn't. It was this at least in after years that made her feminism so uniquely persuasive and undidactic. I know from her correspondence that she went to college with a definite determination to be economically independent—to "earn her living in competition with men."

Chapter 6

Oberlin Purity

THE two streams of pious virtue that produced me had their confluence in Oberlin, Ohio, probably the sole point west of the Alleghenies where people were as concerned about being good as they were in New England and eastern Pennsylvania.

"Lamenting the degeneracy of the church and the deplorable condition of our perishing world, we pledge ourselves to remove into Oberlin Colony, and there fix our residence for the express purpose of glorifying God in doing good to men. . . . That we may have time and health for the Lord's service, we will eat only plain and wholesome food, renouncing all bad habits and especially the smoking and chewing of tobacco . . . and deny ourselves all strong and unnecessary drinks, even tea and coffee . . . and everything expensive that is simply calculated to gratify the palate . . . and all the world's expensive and unwholesome fashions of dress, particularly tight dressing and ornamental attire . . ."

So reads the Oberlin Covenant on which the community was founded in the early thirties. Under the brilliant and benign evangelist, Charles G. Finney, it became the seat of a life of religious emotion so intense as to have seemed to many Americans dangerous and crazy.

"The Sunday services were solemn in the extreme, nor less the gatherings for social worship during the week. Nor was it uncommon for recitation hour to be occupied with religious exercises. On special occasions all literary work would be set aside for several days that the fundamental theories of the gospel might be pressed home to the hearts and consciences of all . . ."[1]

Like Deacon Peter Tilton, Oberlin's Christians combined their

[1] D. L. Leonard, *The Story of Oberlin.*

rapt gaze toward heaven with a very radical urge to fix things right in "this perishing world." Under the slogan, "Glorify God in doing good to men," backed up by Finney's personal doctrine of "benevolence the sum of virtue," the college took an advanced post in the moral and mental life of the country. It introduced a century ago many of the reforms now called modern education, abandoning required attendance at classes, adopting the honor system, assuming that free thought, free agency, free expression are essential to the growth of a Christian soul. It was the first college to give a diploma to a woman, the first coeducational college, a pioneer in admitting Negroes to higher education. It became a station on the "underground railroad," and President Finney's attic a center of the station. In 1858 a runaway slave named Littlejohn was captured in Oberlin by a United States marshal. He was recaptured ten miles south by a band of embattled students and professors, thirty-seven of whom were arrested and imprisoned—probably the largest single phalanx of the intelligentsia that ever really did anything in the whole history of our country.

For these and similar virtues Oberlin suffered its good share of denunciation and ridicule. Its graduate ministers were boycotted in the forties by both Congregational and Presbyterian pulpits; a special convention was called at Cincinnati to proscribe its heresies. "Oberlinisms" were singled out, along with free love, woman's rights, and "Osawatomie Brown" for some of the most reactionary kidding that we have from the pen of Artemus Ward.

"Oberlin is a grate plase. The College opens with a prayer, and then the New York *Tribune* is read. A kolleckshun is then taken up to buy overkoats with red horn buttons onto them for the indignant cullered peple of Kanady. At the Boardin House the cullered peple sit at the first table. What they leeve is maid into hash for the white peple. As I don't like the idee of eatin my vittles with Etheopians I sit at the secking table, and the konsequence is I've devowered so much hash that my innards is in a hily mixt up condishun. Fish bones had maid their appearance all over my body and pertater peelins air a springin up through my hair."

My grandfather knew all these things and rejoiced in Oberlin's militant and good sense as well as its evangelical ecstasy. He sent his dedicated son there with boundless hopes. When the boy withdrew to teach school during his first vacation, his father wrote:

"We necessarily conclude that you have become invulnerable to ignorance, and sin, or temptation. Darkness cannot exist within the limits of the sun's rays, nor vice survive in the atmosphere of Oberlin purity. Neither can a few months' absence from the Holy Land dim the lustre of an Oberlin sun, scientifically, or religiously, after its penetrating beams have shot a man through and through for seven or eight months. You must have created around you a perfect globe of light, so large in circumference, and consequently so far across in diameter, its center, the vital point, your heart, cannot be reached by adverse elements . . ."

The evangelical ecstasy was dying down a little when my father entered Oberlin in 1867. The last "remarkable visitation of heavenly grace," followed by "an accession of 108 members to the church," occurred in 1866, and in the same year President Finney resigned and was succeeded by a less incandescent teacher of Christ's ethics, James G. Fairchild. Therefore, in entering just when he did, my father took unknowingly a first step away from that naïve universe in which Morgan Lewis was spending his days galloping along the banks of the St. Lawrence and through the solemn forests, herding lost souls in between the gates of paradise. He was not destined to be at all the kind of prophet the old man had in mind.

And Morgan Lewis was not insensitive to this. He urged his boy not to neglect any opportunity of association with ex-President Finney.

"My son! better for you had you not been born, than to fail of feeling in some degree at least, that man's mantle falling on you! Watch that great man of God."

And he wrote later:

"I have often a powerful exercise in prayer for Oberlin. And then feel ashamed that I had the audacity to pray for a place and people so far above me in faith, piety and intelligence, and hang my head *Down*, and think I won't do it again. Then it will come on to me with greater pressure than ever, and I am at it again on my knees, bathed in a flood of tears."

These tears and wrestlings for the soul of Oberlin were rendered a little irrelevant by the fact that my beautiful mother came just then for a drink of knowledge and virtue at the same fountain. It was from her rather than Charles G. Finney that Samuel Elijah took flame. Her more genial Pennsylvania pieties, and more joyful native sense of what goodness means, in the long run determined the kind of prophet he would be.

I have a little package of essays they both wrote in the year of their meeting. My father's were on such topics as: Kindness, A Test of Christianity; A Free Mind; Incompleteness; Temperance; Purity Essential to the Highest Intellectual Culture. My mother wrote about: Christmas; Hobbies; Unfinished Work; Egotism; Things that Used to Delight Us.

A comparison of my father's oration on "Purity," delivered at the age of twenty-six, with my mother's thoughts at eighteen on "Things that Used to Delight Us" will reveal the contrast of their characters. My father, obsessed by Christian virtue and yet more carried away by logical arrangement, thus expounds the psycho-physiology of culture:

"He who would attain the highest mental culture must keep pure. *First*, he must keep his hands clean, not in figure, but *literally* clean, washed clean. The reason is plain. The mind in its earliest development is entirely dependent upon bodily organs . . .

"Again, he must speak only pure clean words. The circumstances cannot be conceived which would make it possible in jest or earnest to utter a single impure word without staining indelibly the whole mind, and the reason is plain. It is the intimate relation of language and thoughts . . .

"Once more. He must think only pure clean thoughts. An evil thought is not superadded to the mind and thus distinct from it. It permeates the whole soul . . .

"Finally, every simple emotion, every desire and every affection must be clean and clear of everything that defiles. The reason may be seen in the fact that in the feelings rests the motive power. Their influence upon the intellect none can estimate . . ."

My mother thus concludes her juvenile reflection on the changing objects of man's pleasure:

"Blessed be Hope and Joy and Delight! We cannot live a day, take all it brings, and then leave it behind us. Something in it has become a part of us, is written in our hearts and on our faces. Why not write there some of the beautiful sights we see, the memory of a sunset, the laugh of a child, the joy of a meeting; not so much of the sorrow and sighing, the storms and dirges, the sad partings? O, for a heart to sympathize, to *enter in* to every joy of one human life—to be a child with children, not awkwardly, a man among men heartily, old among the aged, reverently!

"Is it not something in this sense that the Great Heart, though above all, is yet through all and in us all?"

MY FRIGHTENED CHILDHOOD

Chapter 7

A Nineteenth Century Love

WITH this rare and original feeling, this Epicurean piety, Bertha Ford arrived in Oberlin the year that Samuel Eastman graduated from the college and entered the Divinity School. She had funds for only a year's study. "A breath of fresh air in this quaint godly town," she called it.

I do not know whether anyone has ever told the love story of his parents. I am not sure this can be accurately done. But the color of the relation between my father and mother was so woven into me in infancy that without it I could not pretend to give the record of my life.

They met in a boarding house where students took their meals around a common table. Little passed between them there—a glance, a conversation, a daily smile of welcome. But when, after the year's study, she went away to teach school, he was lonesome for that little. She had gone, he knew, to the small village of Erie just over the line in Pennsylvania. He wrote her there in April 1873, a very diffident letter. Remembering that April 12 would be her birthday, remembering it a few days' wrong, he told her that he wished they might celebrate the day together. She refrained from reminding him in her answer that the date was April 24.

"Dear Friend,

" 'Tis sweet to be remembered.' Yes, I am glad you have told me the beautiful plan, though the tears *did* come to my eyes as I read. I am less brave at 'seven times three' than I was at 'seven times one' for I remember that it rained on my party day then, and I did not cry.

"On the morning of the twelfth I shall try to think we are going: shall see in imagination our happy faces as we leave the Hall; enjoy the drive to Elyria and the sight-seeing there: then the row down the lake—let us take a row boat—after that our picnic— Shall we make a fire and have some coffee? . . .

"My work is delightful. My girls and boys are little folks—some of them have never been to school before. And to think that they tell me some of their first fresh thoughts! Oh, I am learning so much from them all every day!

"Thank you for your kind letter. The remembrance of a friend does strengthen us for duty, don't you think so?

"Goodbye, Mr. Eastman . . ."

There is no sweeter joy than to admire those we love. And all that Sam Eastman longed to admire in a girl was in this letter: feeling, imagination, industry, human kindness, aspiration, ethics. Above all, ethics! Bertha may not have been quite so naïve as she sounds in that sentence about duty. She had not dwelt in the well-springs of the Sanctification Theology for nine months without learning what to say when she wanted something. And Sam Eastman was not only chemically pure in hands, boots, linen, language, thought and feeling, and on that basis out for the highest intellectual culture. He was unusually handsome, and, notwithstanding his frailty—acquired after all on the battlefield—possessed of a diffused attractiveness to women which some observers have been disposed to class with the mysteries of gravitation. His answer came in a very few days:

"My friend, Bertha,

"My boldness in writing to you before surprised me and now that I did not get a rebuke nor even a censure from you but a kind little letter in reply, I am still bolder. . . .

"I enjoyed your letter, Miss Ford. And this is written that I may hear from you once more, and then again and again, that we correspond, you and I. . . . But if my letters were to come between you and a *friend*, or the correspondence were not to be a *pleasure* to *you* as well as to me, then I do not wish it.

"You'll tell me, please, Miss Bertha. Excuse me, for that name is so beautiful . . .

> Unforgetfully,"

Only those two letters survive from that springtime when the problem of my being was in such reckless and unwarrantable suspension. I know, however, that on June 28 he went to Erie, which for all her tears was not a million miles away, and together in a red sunset they drove down through blossoming fields of clover to the shore of the Great Lake. There, sitting against an old log under a tree watching the moon on the water, they plighted their troth. His next letter begins "My Heart's Own Bertha," and anticipates her visit to Oberlin on her way home for the summer.

"There is so much I want to talk to you about during the short week. I shall be awful selfish of your time. I shall want to visit you every evening sure, and perhaps oftener, if I can possibly get the time. . . . Shall I speak to Mrs. J. about seeing you after eight o'clock or do you want to do it?

"Since you expect to study here next year, it might be pleasanter for you, probably would be pleasanter, not to have it generally known that you were engaged. It would make some difference, wouldn't it, in the attention you would receive from the young men? I would not like you to live a kind of hermit life while I am away all the next year. I am not fogyish or prudish or jealous, at least I hope I am not. So I know, as I do know, that my Bertha loves me, and lives in my heart and works and studies and thinks with me, together all the time though miles be between, I would hate myself to death for any of those miserable jealous feelings that come to some small souls.

"How we will talk next week! Happy, happy week!

> Your loving, unforgetting,
>> Sam."

To him it was all happiness, for he was so simple. But to her, partly for that very reason, there was sadness in the beginnings of love. I understand this, but I find all the words harsh in which I think to set it down. My mother was aesthetic; her strings were strung tight; her perception of differences was very fine; she was subtly and variously sensitive, and therefore also, having a quick intelligence and a witty humor, possessed of natural sophistication. My father was clumsy-hearted and rustic, and would be so forever.

There is always sorrow in love to an imaginative person. Love dwells in the sky with perfection; to bring it down and attach it to some concrete object is painful while our eyes are open. Only blind men climb down Plato's ladder, and it takes some time for love to make us blind. In my mother's case it took two years for this miracle to happen. She had been in rapture that evening by the lake shore; she had been lifted up into a joy that seemed of its own nature, even though it vanish in a year, eternal. But she was not swept along through all the minutes of each day and night by this eternal joy. In those quick rays of wishful thinking, which like the ghostly pencils of the northern lights both are and are not, though they do contain and constitute our selves, she was not his. She was not giving with a constant lavish hand her life to him.

It is not only to the blemishes of a single object that love must blind us, but also to the beauties of an infinitude of dreams. It is those beauteous and free dreams, bound up with the concept of ourselves or the universe—for these in youth are not two entities—which make it hard for us to give our hearts away. Bertha Ford, although so feminine and even timid in her charm, possessed the robust desire to make an impact on the world. She not only believed that women ought to "be something," she felt in herself the wish and power to achieve it. She had more force, and was destined, besides bearing and rearing children, to exercise more force upon the world than Samuel Eastman would. To that fact also she had to become a little blind in order to love him in the manner they conceived of love. The struggle, which in her mind took often the form of self-reproach and almost of a wrestling match with demons to make herself worthy of this man of God, made her a little sadly serious. It checked her romping gaiety and marred her vigorous good nature with fits of irritability.

She sent him some pictures after their week together in Oberlin.

"They are so true," he wrote, "and they look right at me so steadily and so lovingly. Do you know the artist caught the expression of love that has been on your features since the wonderful time? I wonder if it is that that C. S. sees and calls sad. I almost know it is."

He did not know the truth of the look, and he would not know unless she told him. Yet he was troubled; he recurred to the problem:

"Did C. S. look for a mirthful face? Love is not mirthful. Nor is it sad. Love is *joyful, peaceful, serious, earnest,* and its expression in the face is akin to the expression of sadness and may easily be mistaken for it. Is not that true? Or do I guess at it?"

She could not explain to him what she was going through. She was alone in this so unexpected and yet ancient dismay, this discovery of a fearsome darkness settling down upon her in the name of love.

"You are not nearly so amiable as you used to be," her sister Frances told her. And that was so disturbing that she reported it to him, hoping he would say, or be, something that would lift the gloom.

"Fan *ought not* say such things to you," he wrote. "It was an awful thing to say, and not so at all. I don't mean to say Fan told a lie. She thought so for the moment no doubt . . ."

But that did not help. It was not Fan's moral character that was in question.

What did help most, I think, and in the end most largely cleared her heart of darkness, was the generosity of his admiration for her. There is so much egotism usually in men's love that I wonder how women stand it at all. He adored her for the qualities that were really adorable, and among them, as it must always be, strength. He wanted her to be a great person. And that, if I may suggest a solution of this age-old mystery, is the secret of success with women, a secret few men have it in their size to grasp.

"And I saw in your picture—O, words come to me! How can I tell! I saw all that I saw in you at first that awakened my love—an overflowing sympathy, a delicate sensibility, a mighty will, and above all and around all and through all, a love unspeakable."

When a young man admires in his girl a mighty will, it is something to be remembered. It is a state of mind which, if generalized, would do more to improve the human breed than all the sermons that have been preached. My father's attitude to my mother's genius and her fame—for those were the words we used in the home circle —was as near as any mortal thing I have seen to perfection. It contained no trace either of adulation or envy, no exaggeration of self and no disposition toward self-effacement. It was a level-eyed and level-headed joy in something good and beautiful. He was not a man who had to be propped up by association with inferiors.

Another trait in Samuel Eastman which made it natural for Bertha Ford to love him was his instinctive democracy. With all his hyperpurity there was no priggishness in him. To my rare good fortune those little inward squirts of snobbish feeling which so frequently defile both social sympathy and social judgment in the best of men were left wholly out of both my parents.

Besides that, my father possessed, to make him lovable, a vein of earthly poetry. He loved nature with a child's simplicity; he loved the leaves on the trees. In that he was untheological, unschematic, unobsessed by Godhead; he was mellow, captivating and contagious. And that gave a garment of warm colors to his wooing of her heart.

"I sat down on an old hemlock log literally covered with moss— the parent of all the little ambitious sprouts. Then I took out the letter and the pictures, read it once more and looked while the shadows became dimmer and the rays through the leaves more horizontal, and the sun was disappearing. Then twilight began to fade and the night bird to sing and the moonlight to come coyishly down through the foliage of the tall trees to the mosses and ferns and me. And I pressed the picture of my darling to my lips and cheek and whispered 'Good night, Bertha.'"

She wrote him in her next letter that she had learned a lesson from what Fan said, and was "ready now to live with you always." He answered, still in his strange way abstracted from the dark things passing in her heart:

"You are *ready now*, my Darling, to live with me always. Do you hope to become perfect before you become my wife?"

With such tender, gentle, humble, unselfish, adoring, altogether Christlike obliviousness he would gather her into his arms. It was impossible to go on wishing he could really know her, really touch her heart. It was impossible not to love him. Perhaps men never touch women's hearts. Perhaps this is what love is.

"Your father is so good!" she would say to us. "Your father is so good!"

And how true it was! How often she must have said it to herself before we came to comfort her with our sinfulness and understanding.

But now the passion of young life was in her blood. Desire was stronger than dismay. The much debated picture, as you see for yourself, is hardly very sad. If it took her two years to fall in love with him, that does not mean that she did not love him finally with reckless joy.

"My dear Love,

"I heard every whispered word. I was *very near* to you, *right in your arms*. There were no ugly miles of distance between us. My head lay at rest—such perfect rest—on your breast. I felt your strong heart beating its love for me.

"You are my life, you know. I live and move and have *my being* only in you . . . My doubts must come so long as I am myself, I guess, but they can not live long in the sunshine of love . . ."

In February even the thought of her work grows dim and bewildered in his presence. He is in New England now, finishing his knowledge of God at Andover Theological Seminary. He is studying with intense fervor, wrestling all night with the problem of determinism and free will, which like all young men he did, of course, succeed in solving.

"Erie, Pa., Feb. 20, '75

"Will I interrupt your study, Mr. Eastman? May I just sit here by the window if I won't say anything to attract your attention?

"He studies and I am far from his thought. His eyes do not wander from the page to where I sit alone. Shall I mourn that I am forgotten?

"By and by the book will be closed—

"Then he will come to the window perhaps to tell me something wise and good that has come to him in his study—perhaps to tell me a thought that troubles him—perhaps to look with me at the sunset—perhaps to say 'I love you so, my own Bertha.' The world will be glorified whatever be the words said—and the silences will be golden.

"The hours are slow. But now the light is growing fainter. People are going home. Is there a *work* for me to do? Anywhere in the world is there a work that needs *me*? But I must wait for the book to close. In this one room are my life and my world, my work and *my love* . . ."

In the summer of that year he graduated from Andover and received a call from the Congregational Church in Swampscott, a beautiful town by the sea near Lynn, Massachusetts. They were married in Peoria on August 25, 1875, and their honeymoon was the trip back east to Swampscott, where their lifework and their faithful friendship, and the testing of their love began.

I believe that love's raptures are usually, for those honest enough to perceive it, of comparatively short duration. But some subside quietly, like a river below the rapids, and glide smoothly out into the meadows of friendship. Others have a turbulent and roaring fall and a desperate time finding, if they ever find, those tranquil meadows. Their love was of the latter kind. I can not fix the date when my mother realized that the darkness which descended upon her after she plighted her troth had been a portent of the truth. She wrote enthusiastic letters to not very intimate friends about her lovely home in Swampscott with its great windows looking to the sea, her husband's cozy study, her spacious sitting-room. She told them what fun it was to keep house with fine new furniture and a new range, and "chief beauty in the kitchen, a shiny copper water tank which stands on the range always full of hot water." She even mentioned the word bliss. But to her close friend, Mary Landen— "who was *all* to me in Oberlin"—she wrote begging her to come and live with them, and help her to "feel at home." Being a spinster foreordained of God, and an excellent private tutor, Mary could move where she would. And she did come. She made her home with our family off and on for fifteen years, giving my mother what she so desperately missed in her all-too-perfect husband—a friend of her intuitions and her wit. Without Mary Landen's quick mind and faithful sympathy and ever-helpful laughter, I do not believe Bertha Ford could have endured "the sadness which comes from a contemplation of living on and on, inevitably, with an uncongenial personality."[1]

Beneath this sadness, and too often the very substance of it, was that disappointment in the intimacies of love which was so commonly the lot of women in that day when ignorance was holy. In her the recoil of passion from this disappointment was acute and terrible, and he was grief-stricken by her moods and tempers. His fanatical "purity" became at some moment, as all fanaticisms do, a monstrous unintelligent ineptitude. Her "mighty will" became a dreadful fortress against which only intimate, clever, informed understanding could have prevailed. She said to me once of a sudden, when I was twenty-one: "Max, when you are married, if your wife ever refuses to satisfy you—don't let her *see* your passion!" I was stubbornly silent about such subjects then, but I knew she was opening for me a glimpse back into the very source of her sorrow. It was not in wrath—it could not be—but pity and distaste that her love died away. And for that reason it left in its place not only a pagan despair, the bleak and at times frantic despair of one who had known in her youth, as few have the courage to know, that she had been born for joy. It left also a bitter and Christian remorse, that crippling and sickening conviction of sin from which Christ himself, if He saw what He had done, would die again on the cross to redeem the world.

[1] I quote this description of her sadness from a letter written by my sister, who, when she grew up, replaced Mary Landen as my mother's closest friend.

But after two years their first baby came, a child so saintly-beautiful and of such sweet-tempered poise and precocious sympathy and swift intelligence that God Himself seemed to have set a seal upon their marriage.

"He was the most beautiful child I ever saw," she wrote in after years. "I remember one night when he was about a year and a half old I was rocking him to sleep in my arms beside an open fire. There was no other light in the room and as I looked down at his face with its wonderful eyes that would half close and then start wide open again as he tried to resist the drowsy god, I thought of stars and suns and every shining thing."

They named the baby Morgan after his grandfather of whose genius they were so proud. They named Mary Landen, of course, "Aunt Mary." And there was a "Grandma" now too, for Catherine Stehley, after her parting with George Ford, had come to live with them. So it was home at last.

In the winter after Morgan was born, they moved to a parish in Newport, Kentucky. Bertha went ahead with the baby, stopping with friends in Erie. A mood of contrition that grew slowly, and became at times in after years almost an obsession, is already evident in her letter to him from Erie.

"My dear husband,

"After a successful journey we arrived safely at 3:45. . . .

"Are you very tired? Take good care of yourself and come soon. This is a lovely home. I wish I was a better housekeeper and better wife and all.

"Do you care for me? . . .

"I have seen Joe and her babies and Fan. All are well. I wonder how you are and if you love me yet.

"Everyone seemed to like Baby on the cars . . .

"I'll see you soon. We'll soon have a new home.

"Mother enjoys being here.

"I must stop. I hope you like me.

Bertha."

My father could not find the poise she found in the love of their baby. He tried to deny and drive down his grief, and it took its revenge upon his body. His health mysteriously broke down in Kentucky, and for a time he seemed very near to dying. Remembering his withered lung, they thought the climate disagreed with him, and so before long he was back again in New England, supplying in the pulpits around Andover and looking for a permanent place to preach. Moreover, in that year my mother's sister Elmina died by suicide, and they felt a Christian obligation to take her twin infants, John and Chambers, into their home. One of the worst depressions in our history had prevailed throughout the years of their love and marriage, and the country was barely staggering up again. It was a time of bitter anxiety, and it drew their hearts close together in a new way. She was pregnant with another son when she wrote him from Kentucky.

"Do not be discouraged, dear. God will bring good out of it. It has been hard for me to hear the dismal news of failure every day. It would not be so hard if we were bearing it together—I mean side by side. No matter what happens, so I have you I don't care! We can live on a crust together, can't we, dear? You furnish bread and I'll furnish the water.

Goodbye, my *own dear* husband,"

Their second son was born in December, 1878, and named Anstice Ford—a bisexual invention which its victim subsequently whittled down to Ford Eastman. Soon after his birth they moved to Marlboro, Massachusetts, where my father preached in the handsome Congregational church overlooking the park. Here they stayed long enough to produce another baby, more happily named Crystal, born on June 25, 1881.

In the autumn of that year they came to Canandaigua, New York, where my father was installed as pastor of the First Congregational Church. Canandaigua is a lazy, leaf-abounding village reclining on a green slope with its feet in a lake. It is the seat of Ontario County, a town of four or five thousand (seven now, I am told) consisting mainly of one parklike street, wide enough for eight two-horse teams to drive down to the lake abreast. I think it is the only town in the United States which had room for the automobiles when they came, and I am not sure but an airplane could land in lower Main Street. It is very old, older than its white settlers, and my father's church was founded in 1799. The church dwelt in a remarkable edifice, so unique in its beauty that the Library of Congress recently sent architects to copy its design. It comprised very rich parishioners, the richest in the town. It paid its minister an adequate salary. It provided him a spacious parsonage fronting on a little almost-private grove of trees. My father soon made himself loved in the community, and so did my mother. They had reached an adjustment, based more in equity than joy on either side, but still an adjustment, of their physical relations. It seemed as though after a good deal of tossing here and there a haven had been found.

Anstice had not the exuberant sweetness and rare gift of sympathy that made Morgan seem divine. He was in fact a scowling, stormy little sinful compact of very earthbound energy; but he had an almost precocious mind and memory. Crystal, on the other hand, although not precocious mentally, did have Morgan's gift—so spontaneous and tranquil a gift that in both it seemed like musical or mathematical genius—for loving-kindness.

It was into this harmonious and quite adequate assemblage of elements that I made, on January 4, 1883, what I have described as an untimely intrusion. I do not mean that my mother, because she did not want me, was unaffected by my charms when I arrived. On the contrary, she paid me compliments in the first year of my life that I have never received since. She describes me as a "rollicking baby, with a big sunny curl on the top of his head and with sprouting curls on the sides, with wondrous deep solemn eyes—great wells of wisdom and light." She spoke of "some sturdiness, perhaps *spunkiness*" in me which caused a neighbor to prophesy that I would make my mark in the world. And she observed that I was "very fond of striking" and particularly enjoyed belaboring my brother with a wooden horse.

"Four stages in plastic life are in my hands: the baby lying in his carriage looking up at the bit of bright worsted tied above him —showing already intelligence and will—the little maiden just learning the 'mine and thine' of life's relations, and finding it so hard a fact that all things are not her own. The oldest boy, full of climb and shout and run, and the one who follows hard after him though in himself so different a creature, a leaning, lolling, sprawling boy who wants to touch some human being at some point all the time. Yet not a bit lazy—Morgan says sometimes that he is a 'swamp cinnamon grizzly bear.' "

It was, on the whole, the very picture of a happy family into which I was born, happy to look at even from the inside. Nevertheless, if you wish to know it intimately and understand how that small baby carriage full of "intelligence and will"—full enough at least to look up at a bright piece of worsted—grew up to be just what I am, you will have to remember the story I have told you and feel the underflow of sorrowful yet brave emotion. You can feel it in a letter that my mother wrote to my father in 1884 on the anniversary of their betrothal:

"Dearest and Best of Husbands:—

"I want to use these last rays of daylight to tell you that I remember this day eleven years ago when you first came to Erie to see me—and when we rode up to the Head by the lake shore in the sunset glow.

"I can see the red sky before us as we left the gate—I can smell the clover fields that we passed. I can see the shimmer of the moonlight on the water—the path of light that stretched from our feet to the moon. Ah, how young we were then, and yet how old! Wiser in our young love than we are now with all the experience of these years.

"The future held no terrors for us—poverty looked so easy—and pain borne for each other a thing to be desired. In those days I should not have cared if you had sold the stove for twelve cents, copper tank and all. If wishing would put me back there, how swift I would go—not back in time nor in events of time—but back there in heart and spirit.

"The sense of my failure chokes me tonight and floods my heart. I have started out to go to my husband in this little letter, but ere I have taken three steps I begin to see the winds and waves of the Past, and I sink. Like Peter of old I can only cry out—'Love, save me, I perish!' If I am ever saved—how much shall I owe to the patience and long-suffering of my husband no one but God can know.

"You did not think of the day, nor did I until about tea time. After that I bathed and kissed the children and put them to bed. Now I am on the piazza and the light is fading. It will not be the 28th much longer.

"I want to tell you that I love you—that I wish I had been made better in the beginning, and that I had taken all the gracious discipline of life as God intended it, so that I might have been *truly* a *helpmeet* for you.

"I have another thing to say. Since our talk the other day about your vacation when you said: 'My heart draws me to my old home,' I have been very sorry for my part in the talk. As usual it was the voice of worldliness and selfishness that spoke in me. I am rebuked. I know that

'It is the heart and not the brain—
That to the highest doth attain.'

"I *know* it—I am sure it is so. Go home to your father and mother. *Trust* your *heart*. Oh, don't let me make you hard and calculating—sharp at a bargain—eager to secure your rights—grasping at everything for yourself. *Trust your heart* and lean not to my understanding—for it is a false guide. It is of the earth, earthy.

"I did feel ugly and cross about the stove, but mingled with it all was a little sentimental regard for my copper tank. You had it made for me without telling me. It was one of my young housekeeper *treasures*, and I am really fond of it. Do you understand how that can be? Can you bear with me—such a mixture of bad and good, of hardness and heart—of worldiness and the most painful longings after something better.

"Ah, you have borne with me nearly nine years!

"Think of the children . . . the work in our hands . . . the hosts of friends . . . the home . . . the books . . . the wide world of delight . . . health and strength. Is anything to be desired? If ever we live to be poor and old and feeble and alone—forgotten of the world and with no power to enjoy it—let us remember this rich, this radiant day, when we had all that human life can give, except what you have missed in me. But there are sweet women in the world— women like Mary or Dr. Bevier. There *are*—you must believe it.

"Goodbye—with a heart full of love and a strong desire to be worthy.

Your wife Bertha."

Within two weeks after those lines were written, "Let us remember this rich, this radiant day, when we had all that human life can give," an event happened which brought to the surface all the underlying anguish of my mother's disillusioned love and filled my infancy with terrifying glooms. My mother has recorded this event in a diary she left me, a "History of Morgan, Anstice, Crystal, and Max Eastman." No other event, I am sure, nothing but my heredity, has played so fateful a role in determining my nature and my history. And since its influence was transmitted through her, I am going to let my mother describe it in her own words.

Chapter 8

The Shadow in My Soul

(From my Mother's Diary)

AFTER the last entry—June 18, 1884—I was very busy putting up fruit, making jelly and helping the father to keep up until vacation should come; the boys were both in school, but Morgan was not strong.

It was in July that he and Anstice went to leave a book at Mrs. Granger's where they had a pleasant little visit. When they reached home I was looking for them, for it was growing late and their father was going to take them into the country that evening.

I began asking about the good time they had had and if they had been good boys, and Morgan said: "Don't tell, Anstice! Let's have it a surprise. It's all in the note!"

When I opened the note I read aloud what Mrs. Granger said of them, that they had been perfect little gentlemen. Oh, how his face beamed when I told them how happy it made me! Never before was I so impressed with their beauty, never did I feel so rich and proud in them as that night. Morgan was radiant, and strangely *he* was the talker. His eyes were like stars, and he was overflowing with joy and a desire to make me share it. He offered to tell me a story Mrs. Granger had read to them, and he did tell it all—so clearly and connectedly and sweetly. His own lip quivered when he came to where Hop O'My Thumb and his brothers and sisters are taken far away from home to be deserted by their parents, and when I began to exclaim at the sadness of the story, he cried: "O Mamma, don't let your sorrow rise yet, *they all* get home! *They all* get home!"

And with these words I comfort myself now—"Don't let your sorrow rise, they all get home!"

But soon the buggy came, and after putting on their overcoats and reminding them to be good boys, I saw them drive away, both

44

nearly wild with delight. I turned to the quiet house and the sleeping babies, so glad that Morgan, especially, was to have a few days of real country life.

All the next day I thought of them with much pleasure; but in the evening, just as prayer-meeting bells were ringing, I walked out into the kitchen and saw a horse at the side door. I went to the door to meet Samuel with Morgan in his arms, the child's face pale, and his little head dropped over on his father's breast in that pathetic way which I have never noticed in any other child, and which always made me think instantly of a dead bird.

He had started out full of life and joy in the morning, but had come in about ten complaining of his head. His Papa had him lie down, he grew no better, and by evening he was perfectly willing to be brought home. We both thought it was one of his ordinary sore-throat attacks, and I had medicine in the house. By morning he was much better, and on Friday he got up—for he was so full of play that I thought it safer for him to be dressed than not.

On Saturday he *would* be out to play. Oh! what energy and will dwelt in that feeble frame! At noon he was so tired that I begged him to lie down and he did. The afternoon I do not remember well, but the next morning is as fresh as yesterday to me.

The Reverend Mr. Temple from Hall's Corners was in the house, and Samuel had gone to his pulpit in Hall's Corners. Mr. Temple had brought his oldest son, a lad of nine years, but they had arrived after the children went to bed. In the morning when Morgan came in to my room before dressing I was struck with his pallor, but he begged to be allowed to stay up. While he and Anstice were dressing I told them about the little boy visitor. I said: "Now I want you to go down and go into the parlor and shake hands with him, and tell him you are glad to see him." They started, Anstice ahead as usual. Anstice rushed into the room, but when he reached the lad he was struck dumb and motionless with embarrassment, and stood scowling at him. Morgan in sweet unconsciousness of himself held out his hand and said: "I am glad to see you!"

As we sat down to our pretty breakfast table, my heart leaped with pride in my children, especially in him who sat opposite me, so sweet and beautiful and so polite. But at the first spoonful of his oatmeal, he said:

"Mamma, I'll have to be excused."

I said: "All right, dear, don't stop to fold your napkin, go right up to my bed."

As he left the room, I called: "Shall Mamma go with you?"

"No, it isn't necessary, Mamma!" he replied, and toiled up the weary stairs alone.

When I reached him he was in a chill. His lips were blue and he seemed cold. I covered him closely and sent for a doctor who lived near us, and not for our own Doctor John. The doctor came after the chill had passed, said the boy had no fever, that it was probably a cold, and left me much reassured. All morning Morgan lay on my bed imploring me not to stir him to undress him. I was not well myself, and lay down beside him a long time. He vomited several times during the day, the first time getting up and walking to the urn alone. By night diarrhea had set in, but still the doctor, who called again, said it was probably a cold working off in that way.

I had brought him some of my new jelly, the first jar I opened, and he was fond of it. But he ate nothing. From ten o'clock until morning he suffered much, vomiting at intervals all night. I tried the remedies I had, in despair at last using a few drops of brandy; but that threw him into worse suffering, and at three I sent word to the doctor. He did not come, but sent medicine, which did no good. In the morning Morgan showed signs of catarrh—his old trouble, and this grew worse all day. Still the doctor expressed no anxiety. On Monday night his Papa came home, and he cared for Morgan that night. I had not been well, and slept. Morgan had a restless night, and the diarrhea continued. In the morning the doctor left town, and in the afternoon we sent for our own doctor. Nothing can excuse my stupidity, but I never dreamed of anything worse than an exaggerated cold. His restlessness, so unlike his usual quiet way in sickness, seemed to me to argue that he was not very sick.

Doctor John at once pronounced him very sick indeed, with a raging though masked fever. He discovered a slight rash on his breast, said that he would not pronounce upon the disease, but feared scarlet fever. In the morning Max too was sick, and there was no mistaking Morgan's case: malignant, masked scarlet fever. At noon Crystal came down and by night was very sick indeed. Morgan grew steadily worse. Nothing could be found to stay in his stomach and his strength failed fast. Wednesday night I made him a little meal of Gramm. "That is baby's food, I know," he said. But at my request he took a little.

That night a hired nurse stayed with him. It was a dreadful night. I was suffering with such pain in my back that I could not stand—

could only lie and listen, listen to every sound. Samuel stayed with Crystal, who pleaded every moment for "Water! Water!" In the morning there was no change.

"If he can live the next twenty-four hours, he may pull through!"

His restlessness increased and he still could take no nourishment. We kept ice-cold water on his head and tried to sponge him with tepid water, but he tossed so that we could do little. In the afternoon he wished for a drink of sulphur water from Clifton Springs. When he was given some champagne he said, "That shall stay down!" And it did, and we took heart again.

Dr. Ely of Rochester came in the evening, and Dr. Hayes. When Dr. Ely left, I was by the door, and he said he was sorry for us and hoped the children would get well.

"Can they get well, do you think?" I asked.

"Yes—they can get well, but I should feel very anxious about the little boy."

Once during the evening I went to his room where his Papa sat trying to hold him quiet. His head was off the bed on his father's knees. I bent over him and said:

"Can you give me a kiss, darling?"

"Yes, ma'am," he said so clear and sweet.

His voice was always above his pain when one spoke to him. It was only in the sighing breaths, and the involuntary "Oh, dear!" spoken so often, that his suffering appeared. I bent over and kissed his poor little mouth and he kissed me.

I said, "Thank you, dear."

"You're welcome," he replied.

I was to keep Crystal this night while the nurse kept Max downstairs, but early in the night Morgan called to me in a sharp voice that thrilled me through. I left Crystal with the nurse, and together Samuel and I stood powerless by his bedside. Nothing could keep him still. From one side to the other he threw his weary, wasted body.

Once he said: "I have the best nurse and the best bed in town."

Once, too, he said to his father: "Papa, I wish I could be *excused*."

"Excused from what, dear?"

"Oh, excused from all this!"

The doctor had been very desirous that he should take brandy in his milk, and it always nettled him. He said to me:

"Mamma, if God had meant us to have brandy in milk, he would have put it in the grass that the cows eat."

While I sat by him trying to sponge him, I said: "You know every little helps. Little drops of water, little grains of sand, little deeds of kindness, little words of love, make this earth an Eden like to that above."

I forgot that there was another verse, but he took it right up, with lips sore and quivering in pain: "And the little moments, humble though they be, make the mighty ages of Eternity."

It has been a comfort to me to remember this; it seems somehow to connect our lives. Momently I am drawing nearer to him. I have only to be faithful moment by moment.

Seeing some nasturtiums on the stand, he said to me:

"Aren't those flowers beautiful, Mamma? One seems to be looking right at you."

He never thought of things with reference to himself.

After a while I said: "Bring him in on Mamma's bed."

He signified assent, and his father brought him in. Oh how we tried to get him still—putting heat to his feet, bathing his head, holding his hands. But all was of no avail. He must toss on now until the stillness of Death overtook him.

I spoke of my love and asked him if he loved me. He said "yes." I told him his sufferings would soon be over. He said: "I don't feel sure of that."

Once he murmured: "I wish I could find a shady tree and lie down to rest."

"Bring him to me," I cried, "and let me hold him in my arms. Let him be Mamma's baby again."

He said "yes," and held out his arms.

His father brought him and laid him in my arms, and at that very instant he straightened out and was still, his breath coming only a few seconds longer in painful gasps.

On his own little bed we laid the body, now so still, an hour before so madly tossing. He had asked his father to be taken to his own bed, but his father, afraid to move him, had reminded him how hard it was. He had said:

"Papa, you don't know that little bed as well as I do!"

The next day at five o'clock his little body was carried out for burial. Crystal was then in the first and nervous stages of the fever when she could not be left for a moment. I could only go a few minutes, while Dr. John watched her, to say goodbye to the form I loved so passionately, and to kneel with his father beside the little white casket so soon to be hidden away from mortal sight.

He had on his Sunday suit—the dark blue cloth which was so becoming to him. All about him were the simple flowers he loved, daisies and clover. Oh, the *patient* little hands! The willing feet, the loving guileless lips, the majestic brow, the glorious eyes closed, the sensitive chin, the slight frame! When shall I cease to love you and mourn for you and *long* for you, and *ache* to hold you and rejoice over you again!

Chapter 9

A Sombre Infancy

HAD my mother not been wounded already with a slower grief, she might have recovered, as mothers somehow do, from the heartbreak she has described. But this divine-seeming boy, whom she could speak of when seven years old as "the spiritual prop of the family . . . the blessed, the beautiful, the chosen one, a boy in whom is no guile," was more to her than a first child of love. He was the gift by which God had reconciled her to the bodily death of love. He was the purpose of God in that ghastly tragedy, the sanction and compensation for a lifelong disappointment. For that reason the effect of his loss upon her was almost fatal.

I do not mean that she lost her daytime courage. She sought comfort in brave lines of poetry, and was "minded by the gathered memories of him to try to catch something of the beauty and brightness of the three lives still going on." She laughed out loud in October when Crystal said: "Mamma is going to buy me a muffin to put on my hands." And she was able somehow to endure it when she found Crystal "playing she was a peddlar selling a kind of candy that would make the whole family die together." She was not one to surrender in the open field. But in the lonely dark, the midnight wakings, "black thoughts" began to rule her mind. Mixed thoughts they were of mutinous revolt against what life had brought her, what God had brought her—Is there then a God?—and still blacker thoughts of her own sin in thinking them, her iniquity of unsubmissive, heathen, hard, indignant yearning after joy. Like her own mother she cried to an unbelieved-in God to help her unbelief—the most hollowly echoing of all cries for help. And she cried as vainly for the power to love an unloved husband. Even in sleep she found no true release, it seemed. "Only once," she wrote in her

50

private diary, "has Morgan come to me in a dream. Finding me in trouble, sorrowing, he threw his arms around my neck and with such a radiant face said: 'All four of us, Mamma, all four of us!' "

It is not easy in this sophisticated day to estimate the tension induced by her unregenerate revolt—redoubled since my coming by the dread of pregnancy, and since Morgan's going by the dread of life itself—against the embraces of that gentle husband. Where she concluded her letter, agonizing over his spirit, "There *are* sweet women—Mary, Dr. Bevier—you must believe it," she might today, instructed of his body, exclaim: "There *are* sweet women—go and make love to them, we can live together just the same!" But no such simple speech could rise to her lips. She was a doubter in God's temple, but her doubts never reached down to that groundwork of sexual negation upon which the temple is built. Complete chastity outside the marital bond was a law of the code of Christianity to them both. What storms and horrors this locked them up with I will not imagine. But in the end the sole way out to a fruitful life was to make regnant in their breasts the two most sorrowful of Christian virtues—in him, unflinching resignation; in her, perpetual repentance, a sharp grievous sense of her unworthiness.

Nature of course rebelled against this solution. Not long after Morgan died, my mother was stricken down by an unexplained illness that lasted for more than a year. And from this she recovered only in time to stand firm while my father began, as mysteriously as though sucked by a vampire, to lose his small vigor and fade out into the frail, hollow, weakly gesturing, half-whispering ghost of a minister. It is not hard now to understand these events, but I suppose no doctor then was told about their intimate relations. My mother, challenged by the disaster of his collapse, recovered her own strength completely. But my father's neurasthenia lasted through the years that should have been his prime, and his health came back only as his lustihood declined.

He himself had no inkling of the causal relation this implied. He thought he was still suffering the consequences of his Civil War campaign. And of course my mother had none. She merely saw her husband come home after preaching, weaker each Sunday and slower in his pace, his knees hardly able to straighten up after a step, his eyes wan, his throat aching, his lips set in a thin line of courage. He consulted physicians, went away to sanitariums, took rest cures, tried every way to cling to the dwindling threads of his vigor, but it became each day more evident that the strain of preaching was intolerable—the pathos intolerable, too, of watching him try to preach. She wrote letters for him, wrote prayers, wrote sermons, eased and supported him in every way but one that a woman can. Finally, on August 9, 1886, she wrote for him his resignation.

In her twilight letter to him of June 28, 1884, she had said: "Think of the children—the work in our hands, the hosts of friends, the home, the books, health, strength. Is anything to be desired?" Two years from that date her dearest child and her husband's health and strength were gone, the work was gone, the books were sold, the home completely broken up. Only the host of friends remained.

Thomas Hobbes says in his autobiography, after describing an ominous event which preceded his birth: "My mother conceived such fear that she gave birth to twins, myself and fear together." A similar thing happened to me, except that I can not date so early the emergence of my twin. Both the calendar and my mother's memories attest that fear was added to me in and after my second year, when those black storms were raging in her breast. When she took up again, three years after Morgan's death, the history of her children, I was no longer "sturdy" or "spunky," and was far indeed from "rollicking." She has hardly a word now which does not confirm my own memory that I was constantly and to an almost pathological degree afraid.

"March 14, 1888
"Max is five. He is a very loving boy who can not bear to be away from his mother. He can not bear to have anyone else undress or dress him. He is very shy and suffers a great deal from fear of everything . . ."

"March 25, 1888
"Max is such a clinging kind of boy. Sometimes I weary of his climbing upon me and back of me on the chair, but what would I do if he were not with me?"

"July 1888
"Max is one of the cuddling, caressing children—he likes to put his face right up close to mine, says my face smells so sweet."

"February 1890
"Max is still a baby, though seven—still timid and fearful of everything."

"September 1890
"Max goes to school, is growing braver . . ."

"May 1891

"Max is not very strong but plays hard all the time. He never wishes to rest or read. The only way to win him from play is to ask him to come and snuggle with me in the big chair. He is often tired and half-sick—reminds me more and more of his father who keeps up no matter how tired he is."

What I received at birth, it seems, was an unstable and too sensitive nervous system. At least that has been the opinion of a small army of doctors, and I myself came to believe it only after putting myself through a considerable course of heroics. I regard that early nineteenth century invention, the Artistic Temperament, with contempt. To me it seems shameful for poets to act as though their gifts were an illness. When all the heroics are finished, however—heaving the pick and shovel ten hours a day, sleeping on bare boards, diving off high cliffs, assaulting ruffians against whom I have no grudge—when, in fact, it is safely proven that I am a man, the fact remains that I am an excessively sensitive one. I suffer and toss where others are unaware that anything is the matter. I have gone to sleep many a night by sheer naked resolution knowing there was a pea under the twentieth mattress, conceding that much to the world's standards of hardihood; but I refuse to concede that I was not really and because of my native sensitivity in misery because the pea was there.

Having these extra-naked receptors, I was open as though at the pores to the influence of my mother's moods. Even without her testimony, it would seem obvious that from these moods, so black upon her in my babyhood, I imbibed that irrational emotion which engulfed so much of my early life and upon which my gradually emerging equilibrium, my gestures of courage, my wonderful days of delight, all indeed that I am—even, as I learned in a crisis, my sanity —float rather precariously and on a shallow keel. I am writing a story about joy, but it begins with the rather discordant fact that during my first twelve to fourteen years I was normally, except in moments of tense activity or playful excitement, sad. A vague, remorseful dread, as of some monstrous evil descending around me, was my familiar not only in nightmares but in daytime life. I was full of this feeling if I awoke in the dark, and I rarely opened my eyes in the morning to any thought or prospect that could exclude for some moments a sense of universal doom.

It is difficult to measure quantities of melancholy. Both in my mother's case and mine it would be easy, especially if one dwelt on the hours of physical darkness, to exaggerate the sombre side. To neurotic people the nights are very different from the days. My mother and I used often to greet each other in the morning like two pilgrims who had successfully emerged from a murky tunnel. We would laugh about the goblins in the daylight, but the experiences of the night were no less real. We were "manic-depressive types," I suppose, if the term means anything when applied to the relatively sane. It will serve, at least, to reconcile my story of an underlurking melancholy, which seemed to be a co-conspirator of sleep and hold full sway at midnight, with the indubitable fact that we were both endowed with gaiety, and did very often laugh hilariously together.

There is no gloom in the two images that stayed in my memory from the three-and-a-half years I lived in the Canandaigua parsonage. One was of my own baby carriage, an enormous red-brown institution, which served me, I learned afterward from my mother, in place of a cradle. The other was of my pleasure in a plate of baked potato which had been delightfully buttered by a sort of mother sitting on my right. The "sort of mother" was perhaps my Aunt Mary Landen, who lived so often in our house, and was clothed with the discretion, if that is what you want to call it, of a parent. Or perhaps it was Aunt Mary Antes from the long white house across the street, another gentle and capable spinster, who did a considerable amount of "bringing up" on all of us children. The psychologer who believed that our earliest memory indicates our character-pattern might have found something in this cordial acceptance of benefit from a substitute mother. A determination to make the best of things as they are, instead of conceiving them wishfully or rebelling fanatically against them, has distinguished me from many of my friends both personal and political.

Another fact that interests me in these earliest memories is their accurate localization. I never remember anything without remembering its position. I can always predict the place on a page where I will find a missing quotation, even when I can not remember the book that contained it. I can recall now the exact position in which I sat, and the position in which another person sat in relation to me, when he or she threw a cigaret stub and burned a hole in my sweater, but I can not remember who it was, or where it was, or when it was, or what color the sweater was, or how I felt about it. This keen sense of spatial relations has something to do, I suppose, with my pleasure in putting things in order whether in a room, an essay, or an argument. I am not overconfident of my taste in colors or sounds, but I am always ready to state categorically whether a composition is good. Sometimes in a hotel room I feel so crisscross that I move the bed and bureau into their places before I can go happily to sleep. I suspect that this fact gives a slightly old-maidish —or classical!—limitation to my critical judgments. I believe in chaos, but I have to make a slight effort to appreciate it.

I must further mitigate the gloom in this chapter by stating that my mother was not only stimulated to brave effort by her husband's collapse, but also liberated into her own earlier and more eager self. The maternal instinct has in few girls' breasts such lone sovereignty as certain thin-minded males would like to think. My mother had never sold herself completely into motherhood. She had studied Greek and Latin with her husband, and even theology as long as their patience lasted. She had become vice-president of the Women's Home Missionary Union of New York. An attempt to learn German had been given up only because of her distance from the school: "I must be content with the crown of motherhood." But she was not content. That early yearning to *be something* had never died in her heart. And nothing she saw in the ministerial environment suggested that she lacked the power to achieve it. She soon found out by helping him that she could write a sermon as well as her husband—and how much faster! He had more knowledge than she, and more analytical logic, but far less synthetic intellectual skill. He would pass over to her, as a matter of course, a letter which he could not decipher, and with amused admiration watch her read it like a printed page.

All these things made the challenge of calamity almost welcome to her. By the time she wrote his resignation, she had secured a job teaching history and English at Granger Place School, and had arranged to take my seven-year-old brother to live there with her and attend the school. It was a genteel girl's boarding school, and how this anomalous arrangement was put over remains something of a mystery. To my brother, looking back, it seemed but a natural part of the curse wished on him with that ambiguous name, Anstice. The Misses Granger, Antoinette and Isaphine, were tall, slim, bodiced ladies out of an early Victorian novel. Their grandfather, Gideon Granger, had been Jefferson's campaign manager, postmaster general of the United States for thirteen years, and had erected this mansion for his descendants to live in. But they had moved out and converted Granger Place into a Christian institution of learning. In a pecuniary sense, they were the pillars of my father's church, a tight-laced but sturdy species of caryatid, and they loved my father with a pious and most generous love. If my brother found himself safely folded in as a member of a young ladies' finishing school, he could thank a very drastic kind of generosity that he got folded in anywhere at all.

He rewarded his benefactresses by grabbing the young ladies' hair, jumping out of dark corners at them, snatching their books and running away too fast to catch, and taking his place with an expression of unmeasured scorn at the head of all their classes. There never was a boy less like a girl or less designed by nature to fit into the gentle regimen of a girls' boarding school. I myself, I always thought, could have got along splendidly in that upholstered berth.

But fate had harsher plans for me. My mother, I suppose, did not want a baby, and much less a "clinging" baby, hanging around her skirts while teaching school. So my father took me away with my sister, she four and I three years old, to the Pratts' farm out on the road to Geneva, a mile or so beyond the lake. The memory is harsh to me because of the "Butter" who lived in the great grey barn across the road. This creature was represented as capable of jumping the barnyard fence, or indeed walking right through it, and coming over into my yard and up the front steps and actually—if you can present such a contingency to your imagination—actually butting me! I do not know who inspired in me the feeling that to be "butted" was some sort of absolute catastrophe, terrible enough physically, but in a metaphysical way associated with those large gruesome horrors that lie beyond the edge of doom. I can see now, with some slight effort, that giving Henry Pratt's prize ram the name of "Butter" was a joke. But I can not see it half so plainly as I can see the ram. My brother tells me that I was actually attacked in the barnyard by this ram and saved from destruction by my cousin John Stettinius, who stopped him with a baseball bat. I do not remember that, but I taste to this day a wave of trepidation when the word "butter" brings before me that ominous grey shape moving stealthily behind his too frail bars.

Another frightening thing happened during the year we spent on the Pratts' farm. And these two frights, except for the position of the house and barn and outbuildings, which my brain holds accurately after all these years, are my sole memories of our sojourn there. Crystal and I had climbed up into the corncrib, and Crystal was wearing a straw hat with lovely flowers around the brim. The pigs lived under that corncrib, and there was a square hole in the floor through which the corn could be thrown to them. We were peering with almost excruciating excitement down through that hole at the pigs, and I guess we had thrown down some corn, for they were rooting the mud and grunting and squealing beneath us. Crystal's hat came off and fell right down among those under-monsters, and they nosed it and chewed it and trampled it in the black mud, flowers and all, until you could no longer see what it looked like. That is my earliest memory of anguish. I had feared that such things might happen—my fears have always exceeded the evil in my life—but now I knew they could.

Henry Pratt was an excellent farmer. His lands were wide, his barns ample, his rows straight, and his meadows level both at high grass and harvest. And Henry's sisters, Anna and Minnie and Puss, were generously loving like the Grangers, and yet not so tall or slim or insulated with gentility. I always took their generosity to us for granted. Up to this moment I do not believe I ever gave them a grateful thought. But as I think back upon it now: we were waifs, we had nowhere to go, and we found ourselves in this homelike white house in an atmosphere of tender and intelligent affection.

I can not remember, perhaps because I was too terrified, any sense of separation from my mother in this period, but Crystal felt bitterly the breaking up of her much brooded-over family. "What a heart-breaking experience it was," my mother wrote, "to visit my babies and stay over night. And how Crystal suffered with her dear loving heart. Once she said to me: 'Before you go, won't you and Anstice and Papa and Max come up into our room a little while?' I asked her what for, and she said, with quivering lips: 'Oh, so we can have our *family* all together!' "

In 1928, the day after Crystal died in my brother's house in Erie, Pennsylvania, I drove home through Canandaigua, reaching there at twilight. I wanted to go down to our real home, Glenora, on the shore of Seneca Lake, and on the way I passed what used to be the Pratts' farm. A sign on the porch said TOURISTS, as I almost knew it would. I went in and took a room and spent the sad night there where Crystal and I had been baby friends together, and I had seen those monsters trample and destroy her lovely hat. I did it for the same reason, I suppose, that one writes a poem.

Chapter 10

Farmer's Boy

DURING our year on the Pratts' farm my father, despite his weakness, went into the business of buying live ducks, calves and chickens, killing and dressing them, and peddling them through the parish. His parishioners found it almost as painful to have this thin and frail-voiced saint arrive at their back doors with a dead chicken in his hands and a gentle smile in his eyes, as it had been to watch him try to preach. Many a housewife would fold back the neck of some tender fowl and stow it away in her icebox with tears welling in her eyes.

It was, of course, a temporary expedient, a matter of doing the first work that offered itself. In the depth of my father's heart there lurked all through this anxious and calamitous period a very particular hope. He might, without getting well enough to preach, get well enough to run a farm! Farming was the meat of life to him, his art, his science, his one unfailing passion. I can see him in his old blue overalls—indeed, I always see him so—with a hoe over his shoulder, or carrying a whiffletree or some earth-dripping basket of plants, or perhaps a forkful of manure, glowing with the joy of life, and pausing as we met to smile into my eyes: "Max, I love to make things grow!"

The old Swart farm way up Main Street at the edge of the town contained forty acres of rich soil, orchards, pasture-lands and meadow, and down by the creek a "muck lot," black as pitch and manifestly inlaid by the Lord God with the thought of celery and carrots. The farm was but half a mile from where my mother taught. It was for sale at $6500, and my father borrowed money and bought it. I do not know where he got the money. His parishioners would have put up twice as much to get that vision of imperturbable virtue away from their back steps. It was a risky move in the state of his

58

health, but the reunion of the family seemed all-important, and he justified the risk by making $1500 the very first year. Inside of three years, he owned twenty head of cattle and a stationary engine, had built the first silo in Ontario County, a tongueless campanile that spread his fame throughout that region, and was, in every respect except health, prospering to the surprise of all good Christians. For who would believe, after all, that a saint could do anything?

My next memory then—for I have told you all I can remember up to the age of five—was of our riding on top of a load of furniture from the Pratts' house down the long hill, past the lake, and up through the main street of Canandaigua to the old Swart farm. That remains, I honestly believe, the most exciting adventure of my life. For Crystal's bed was the very tiptop of that high pile of furniture, and Crystal and I, in our nightgowns, were snugly tucked in bed! Even now, if you'll be honest with yourself, can you imagine anything more exciting? It is one of the blessings I owe to a mother who believed that God Himself is joy.

It was a vast dilapidated drab old wooden house that our family reunited in, a high square object with a cupola and a pillared porch around it, and a driveway that swept rather hastily round a small "pine parlor" in the side yard. It boasted a "bathroom" operated with rain water from a cistern in the attic, and I can remember being initiated into the extraordinary ingenuities of the toilet. I thought it was a momentous invention, and in this I anticipated some very modern sociologists.

The house stood on a hill that sloped up from the road, and in my childhood that slope was nothing less than precipitous. We slid down it in snowtime with exquisite danger to life and limb. Somehow or other it has subsided with the passage of time, and I do not see now how anybody could slide there at all. Growing up is like ascending in a plane; it flattens everything. Moreover, the iron dog and deer are gone from Mr. McKechnie's "estate" opposite, and the iron fence has dwindled, and the house does not stand half far back enough from the road.

Mr. McKechnie was an Episcopalian and owned the "buery" where they deliberately manufactured beer. . . . I pause to say that I had an independent opinion about the word *buery*, and also *Febuary*, and although my brother started heckling me about it when I was six, I stood my ground firmly to the age of twelve. . . . Beer was a sinful substance, and Episcopalians had some indefinable thing the matter with them, and that was enough to extrude the

McKechnies from my intimate life forever. I never went inside those towering iron pickets and I never will. Nevertheless, I imbibed from the unspoken emotions surrounding me a feeling of awe rather than contempt toward those sinful and Episcopal McKechnies, and a sense of the inferiority of our family who, with all their Christian virtues, did not possess an iron dog and deer. That feeling was one of the deepest in me and most unmanageable, a feeling that I belonged to a socially inferior tribe. I later played sometimes with Janet and Isabella McKechnie, nieces of the rich, the deliberately sinful McKechnie. They moved at ease within his iron fence, but I never followed them there. I never was free of a sense of the audacity of my playing with them and a fear that I might do it wrong.

We lived four years on the Old Farm, and throughout those years I cared little about anything in the world except animals. My mother's diary confirms my memory here. "I hardly see Max during the week for he is always off on the farm following the workmen or his Papa or watching the animals." I have no clear image of my brother or sister or even my mother in those days, but I can see the Jersey heifer, Plush, as plainly as these lines before my eyes. I often heard how my father's "health failed," a colorless phrase we used: it moved me as little as it does you. But when the spotted heifer, Beauty, broke loose and wandered up the railroad track and got killed by a locomotive, I knew that the hand of doom had fallen upon the Eastman family. My father let me go with him, and I saw Beauty lying there upside down and awkward in the grass. I see her still.

Each of us three children had a calf to call his own. Crystal's was Daisy, mine Buttercup, and Anstice's Clover. Anstice made Clover a little bridle and used to ride her around the yard, a prodigious feat such as he was always performing and that I would no more think of imitating than of climbing up the sky. I was once carrying water to the cattle in their stanchions, and to reach the farther ones I had to pass my calf, Buttercup, who had grown to be a good-sized heifer then. She was thirsty and would look round at me as I went by with the pail. I told her to stop looking at me when I was busy, and to assert my authority I went out and cut a switch and switched her flank each time she did it. After I had switched her three times she shrank from me as I went by. I broke my switch and threw it on the manure pile, rushed to her head with my pail of water, ran into the forbidden granary and with tears pouring from my eyes brought her a whole peck of bran to eat. I then found an old tub and filling it with water, pail by pail, gave her a complete bath and currying from head to foot. I am sure Buttercup thought the world was coming to an end.

Our handsome little black-and-tan bull, Boniface, is another vivid image from those times, and especially his underparts with which he was said to create calves. It was the hired man, Ownie Clark, for whom I sometimes used to hold the horses while he delivered milk, who undertook to illumine me on this topic. Here, however, I was stubborn and practically impervious to education. I conceded that Boniface might create calves with his testes, for they were large and I could see no other use for them, but I had seen him use the other organ and I knew what it was for.

"I guess you weren't watching carefully," I told Ownie.

"I'll show you which part I mean when we get home," he said.

He did show me, but a careful inspection confirmed my opinion that Ownie lacked the acuity of the true naturalist. It was years before I got this thing straightened out.

The principal sign of promise I revealed during those early years on the Old Farm was an extraordinary gift for playing horse. Any time my mother or one of my Aunt Marys got bored with me, all she had to do was to say, "Whoa, Boy," loop a little string around my neck, and lead me out to the hitching post and tie me up. I would stand there stamping and snorting and whinnying for hours on end. There was a shining harness on me and a four-wheeled carriage behind; I had been told that a good horse under those circumstances would "stand." And so I stood. "I can see you now," my mother wrote long after, "standing there stamping your foot and neighing and shaking your head and chafing the bit. I never saw anyone else so sink his identity in another creature's."

Another way I played horse was to gallop around the yard with halves of barrel hoops. I kept these curved horses each in his own stall in a picket fence, and I would drive or ride them at different paces according to their size and thickness. The flat wooden hoops from apple barrels were Percherons, those made of iron were "Glidesdales," and the slim ones with bark on were Hambletonians. I had more than fifty of these horses on my farm, and I loved them as I have rarely loved anything since.

Some of the child psychologists, following John Dewey in his zeal for obliterating distinctions, say there is really no such thing as play. "Play is merely a name for the activities of children." I do not see how anybody who ever was a child could make such a mistake. I *remember* the difference between play and serious activities. I remember feeling that serious activities were distinctly inferior in charm, and how the moment they were finished I would settle down to "play something" with passionate joy.

My brother, for instance, used to drive a nail backwards into the end of a pole—to this day I do not know how it was done—and go down through the muck lot to the creek and spear bullfrogs. He liked to take me with him, but it seemed to me a serious enterprise, and I preferred to play horse. He also had a tub of polliwogs out in the back yard, and we watched them lose their tails and turn into frogs. It must have been intimated to me that I could "learn something" by watching those polliwogs, for that too I remember as a serious pursuit, to be got through with hastily. (The polliwog enterprise has a special interest, because it was participated in by Tom and Rob and Lottie Smith from down on Bristol Street, and Rob was later known to fame as the comic artist Sidney Smith, inventor of Andy Gump.)

My passion for animals was perhaps the reverse side of an abnormal fear of people. I never dared go out of the yard alone—except when enticed across the hedge with a cookie by our next-door neighbor, Miss Lucy Stowe, another of those gentle spinsters who played a kindly part in my development. It was a considerable adventure to go over into Miss Lucy's yard without Mamma. As for staying alone in the wagon while Ownie dashed into the houses with milk, that was pure heroism. Only the fact that I was "holding real horses" nerved me up to that.

It was not only people I feared, but every strange thing. Once it was the laws of perspective that threw me into a bottomless fright. Crystal and I had walked down to the front gate with Mother and were standing on the sidewalk watching her depart, as usual, for school. As I saw the loved figure growing smaller and smaller, it suddenly came over me, as a matter of mere logic, that she would soon be nothing at all. I opened my mouth wide and dashed down the street after her, shrieking like a fire engine. All the dogs barked, and all the neighbors came running to their doors. The noise I made that morning, and my total inability to explain it, spread widely the opinion, already well established in our family, that I was "a trifle too high-strung."

There was a flavor of mortification in my fears, and it was while on the Old Farm that I developed a habit, vastly irritating to my sister, of stopping every few minutes, whatever I was doing, to pray. I had got from somewhere the idea that people prayed by putting their middle and fore fingers in the corners of their eyes, and murmuring "God help me to be good, God help me to be good, God help me to be good." I went through this ceremony dozens of times a day and always, of course, at the most inappropriate moments. I clearly remember Crystal's public embarrassment and private indignation, and yet her inability to meet in any satisfactory way my question: Didn't she also want to be good?

When I was seven my mother took me to Swampscott to visit "Aunt Kitty Honors," still another of those gentle spinsters with whom my childhood was surrounded. I remember Egg Rock out in the bay; I can see its place and the shape of it. And I remember that Mamma and Aunt Kitty went out one evening after putting me to bed. I awoke in the dark and called out, and was aghast at receiving no answer. A deaf old lady had been in the sitting-room, but she had gone to bed. I was in a small square chamber alone with fear. I was trembling and sweating. I wanted to shriek, but there was no use. I was trapped in a Black Absolute and was beyond help. That experience looms so large and awful in my memory that even now I can not smile with my mother when I read in her diary of my ludicrous efforts on a subsequent evening to keep the old lady awake and entertained.

Another terror came when, at the age of six, they tried to send me to the public school, an ominous blood-red brick building down on Chapel Street. My mother herself took me there and introduced me to the teacher, a plump round female ogre with frizzly black hair, who gave me what she thought was a sweet and cordial smile. It was, I plainly perceived, a leer, and I knew that I was in mortal danger. My heart pumped wildly, and I clung like a crab to my mother's hand. She had to lead me to my seat, which was halfway down the center aisle, and extricate herself by main force. When she had gone, I sat erect in that sea of strange beings, rigid with fright. The teacher began to call out names, and up and down the rows of seats I heard the pupils answer "present!" The word seemed to me to have no relevance to the situation, and I was not sure I heard it correctly. When she came to my name, I was in a panic. "Christmas!" I said. A yell went up, and my memory after that is a blank—until the noon hour came and the school was dismissed. Then I gathered my little pile of books and bolted for the door.

"No, no, Maxie!" the frizzled ogre called out. "You don't take your books home. Just leave them in the desk."

A sudden firmness of character descended into me, as to my

perpetual wonderment it still sometimes does. I said, in tones which admitted of no answer:

"I am not coming back!"

That night I rose out of my bed and came down into the living room, my eyes opened wide in terror, but my mind fast asleep. It took some time to convince me that I was in my mother's arms. The dream which caused me this terror was not definite. Some vastness or darkness was descending round me to occlude me. I do not know quite what "occlude" means, and so it expresses the vagueness of the danger. Those night terrors became a regular part of my life, increasing in violence at the suggestion of sending me to school or indeed anywhere outside the yard alone. In consequence I remained ignorant, even of the alphabet, until I was almost eight years old.

You would think that I might have picked up a little learning around the house. But I was not interested in learning. I was not interested in the house. My home was in the yard and barn. I hated to be read to; I never learned a line of *Mother Goose; Robinson Crusoe* bored me to death. The only book I could tolerate was *Swiss Family Robinson* and that only after I had got in bed, and mainly because there were children in the book who trained wild animals like horses. My mother subsequently recalled those days:

"I used to be so vexed with you on Sunday afternoons when the other children were content to be read to. You never would agree, but would put on that mournful expression and go off to be miserable. You *never* wanted reading. I thought you were going to be unintellectual."

Van Wyck Brooks in an essay directed against my book *The Literary Mind* says that I have "a deep contempt" for my own vocation that "constantly leads one to ask" why I pursue it. I think he completely misunderstands my thesis, but it is a fact that in earliest infancy I regarded books as an enemy of life's real joy. I shied at the hint that I might listen to one, and ran-not-walked to the nearest exit if anybody drew one from the shelf. This attitude survived to manhood in a certain suspicion of literature, and yet more of English professors, and a disposition to keep away from people who make a business of writing. I felt that with few exceptions they would raise a veil between me and the downright experience of life whether in sensation or reflection.

A further cause of my getting so late a start with education was the troubled condition of my health. I was forever feeling tired to the point of sickness, though no doctor ever found out why, except to blame it on the nervous fibre. And moreover during the early part of this period I made it a system to wet my pants every day, and get spanked for it every night. These spankings did not hurt much. My mother used up all her real spanking genius on my healthy and cantankerous brother. The whole thing stands in my memory as a kind of incomprehensible ritual. I did not understand when or how my pants got wet, or why this rather occult phenomenon, when established by a nightly inspection, should entail turning me upside down and stinging my behind before I got in bed. It was just part of the way things were done. The world after all was full of strange procedures. I first got a keen sense that something was the matter when Dr. Walmsley came out and circumcized me, or rather when he washed the wound. On that occasion I confided to my mother that I had "asked God for me not to cry."

Notwithstanding my backwardness in verbal education, I must have been alive those days in my mind. My mother records one or two remarks that seem to prove it.

"July, 1888

"Max came down heavy and lazy with sleep, and I offered to break his bread into the milk for him because he was so tired. He leaned over on me and assented, only adding sleepily, 'Don't eat it for me 'cause I'm so tired."

"Max says that calves look cowish when they are black because of the sharpness of their backs."

"March, 1889

"When I came home this noon Crystal and Max were playing they were very sick. Max said: 'My head came off and I got as close to Jesus as I could.' "

"March, 1891

"Hearing a robin sing, Max said: 'I like one robin singing all alone trying to make the world happy better than a whole lot of robins.' "

Having thoughts has been to me as much a part of life's adventure as having experiences—"thoughts" meaning both ways of conceiving and ways of seeing or saying. I remember having two of these thoughts in my bedroom on the Old Farm. One was that summer nights sound like winter days because of the similarity to sleigh bells of the throbbing of the insects' song. The other was that the smell of castile soap, while very pleasant, is too faint to satisfy, and yet you can not eat the soap, and that this is true of other things you like. In all pleasure, I would put it now, there is unsatisfied desire.

My earliest memory of lust dates also from the Old Farm. It took the form of an intense wish to go into the bedroom where a little brown-haired playmate slept beside my sister, and kiss her in her most secret place. This desire was private to me, and furtive, unrelated to our daytime play, a thing I burned with after I had gone to bed. It seems simple enough now, and my only remorse is that I lacked the dash to do it. But when I reflect what a kiss was then in my childish consciousness, innocent of its erotic uses, my invention of this particular exploit as fit to satisfy the burning thirsts in me seems significant.

Men fumble in the first functioning of the sex instinct as animals do, but they do their fumbling usually in their minds, that being what a mind is for. This gives them, in the false starts they make, a complete freedom of expression. My brother, about the time I was yearning to bestow this tender token at a point so remote from where it belonged, was consumed with an equally occult desire to spank a certain Canandaigua lassie. My brother and I were constantly in conflict, and it will appear, I think, as I go along, that this difference of blundering fancy epitomized the contrast of our characters.

While I was thus irresponsibly feeling out the flavors of experience, my mother and father were confronting a heavy problem. During the first year or so on the farm his health improved, and he was even able to preach sometimes, traveling eight miles to supply a vacant pulpit.

"Am preaching in East Bloomfield," he wrote to his father in 1888. "The people here tell me it is the preaching that keeps me sick all the time, but I do not think so. I become so restless when I do not preach at all. My mind sort of eats itself up. But let me leave the farm on Saturday evening for a preaching engagement and all the week previous I am contented and restful."

To Morgan Lewis, this letter, sad though it seems to me, brought a "tidal wave of sweet and tranquil joy." But soon there was a new sinking, and he received a letter from the Gleason Sanitarium in Elmira, New York. Gradually the old man was forced back from his last hold on sweet and tranquil joy. By 1890 when he himself, at seventy-six, was compelled to cease his labors in "the white and whitening harvest," the lavish sum of his heart's hopes that he had invested in his beloved Samuel Elijah seemed wholly lost.

"I was stung to the center of my being as I read the following clause in y'r letter: 'I am *trying* to *face* the fact that I may never be able to speak continuously in public again!' Dear, dear son: the sting of a scorpion could not have so stirred to its depths the grief of my heart. I fell upon my knees, and cried aloud in my closet, O Lord! spare his Mother's consecrated boy to do the work to which she gave him!"

Meanwhile, however, a thing had happened which could hardly have been dreamed of in any other family, and which old Morgan Lewis, still flexible and free-minded, welcomed with a new wave of joy. My mother has told the story in an essay called "The Making of a Woman Minister," and with your permission I will turn over the next chapter of my book to her.

Chapter 11

"The Making of a Woman Minister"

by Annis Ford Eastman

THE minister soon fell into the habit of talking over his sermons with me early in the week, saying it helped define his thoughts to have to fight for them. I liked those talks, and soon learned to be more gentle and insinuating in my disagreements, and he to be more tolerant of my opinions. . . . Through ten years of domestic and ministerial ups and downs, with sickness and moving and multiplied cares, my interest in the sermons never flagged. And each year I noted with silent satisfaction that the minister knew less about God and more about people, talked less religion and more life. . . .

There came a day when it was no longer possible to conceal the fact that the minister could preach no more. For months he had dissipated in tonics and been eased by exchanges. But when one good sister said to me, "His sermons are just as good, but he makes such a draft on our sympathies by his looks that we can't enjoy coming to church any more," it was evident that he must stop.

Together we faced the situation—three children, one baby of three years, no money, no health, only pride and courage and friends. The story of those years that followed, when all the high counsels of the pulpit were translated into the common deeds of the common day, what need to tell it? It is written in the hearts of the farmers and housekeepers and laboring men, who saw him going about the humblest tasks on the streets of his aristocratic parish with the same simple dignity which had marked his pulpit ministrations. . . .

As the minister lay on his couch one day—which had become as much the center of things as an open fire, and for the same reason— I told him of my recent trip through the churches of the state in the interest of home missions. As I spoke a thought suddenly came to me which I as suddenly expressed, although only in fun: "Sam, I believe *I'll* preach!" It had the effect of a galvanic shock. The minister raised himself right up and said, with almost solemn earnestness, yet with the dazed air of one making a surprising discovery: "It's what you were made for!"

Then came the weeks of consultation with friends, of discouragements from quarters where help was confidently expected, of surprising offers of furtherance from those who had no faith in women preachers, but thought there might be such a thing as a divine leading. . . . For a time it seemed likely that my high resolve to preach was to be frustrated by a counter-resolve on the part of the churches, but at last there came a letter from a home-mission secretary, telling of a little church which had fallen among thieves and robbers, and was left more than half dead. "They have a debt and a leaking roof, several antiquated church quarrels and about twenty-five members. They will have you for one Sunday, but promise nothing after that."

As I walked down the streets of my own town to the station, I felt as much shame and humiliation as if I had been led along by a policeman. Citizens I had always known averted their eyes as they saw me coming; those who spoke to me did so compassionately; children gazed at me wonderingly; and the ticket agent (a woman!) seemed to feel the indelicacy of my buying a ticket to Brookton on Saturday afternoon, and tossed it to me as if she said: "I wash my hands of you!"

At the little station in the solemn hills near Ithaca I was met by a florid gentleman of pleasant countenance, who plainly regarded me as a religious joke. He seemed to divine the ambitious hope I cherished, and as we drove down the hill into the little hamlet, took occasion to tell me the needs of the church.

"We must have here a man"—with pitying emphasis upon the word—"who will come and live among us, a man with a family, I might say." I had the latter requirement, but I said little, for one cannot talk with her heart in her mouth.

I preached twice on Sunday. In the Scripture that I read in the morning were these words: "And the Lord sent Moses and Aaron and Miriam!" I never knew of the coincidence until years afterward, but it was remembered of me as a great stroke of diplomacy. Before the day was over I had begun to feel human again and to realize that the people before me were men and women to whom one might hopefully say, "Come, let us reason together." They were kind people, and waited in the dim light of the smoky kerosene lamps to speak to me.

But oh the dawn of the next morning! Every inch of my body was sore as if I had been beaten. I was one throb of pain from head to foot. "The croakers were right after all," I said. "A woman cannot do a man's work." But I have since decided that a man who had baked and scrubbed for his family all day Saturday, and had prepared everything in the home for Sunday from the minister's white necktie to the smallest tot's clean shirt, and had then taken a plunge into the world to swim against the tide of immemorial custom in a community of strangers—even a man might be sore in spirit and tired in body on Monday morning.

On the way to the station my weary soul and bruised body both were comforted by a change in my escort's manner. I had ceased to be a joke. Would I come next Sunday, and would I consider an engagement for a year? And I took the precious dollars home, the price of my shocked nervous system, and told "him" that they were willing to have me another Sunday. He did not seem as much surprised as I had expected.

For three years I kept my first parish, although at arm's length. We put a new roof on the meeting house, and mended the steps, and cleaned it. Oh, how we did clean it! And the people revealed such beauty of character and grace as I could never have imagined.

After a time my humble friends in the little church called a council to ordain me. It was afterward spitefully called a "picked council," but this was true only in the sense that we picked the biggest and best men we knew in our neighborhood.

Of the work and worship of that day I will not speak, but only tell the dream I had the night before, which was a prophecy. I was at the foot of a high mountain. I knew that on the other side was a company of ministers. I could see them in their long black coats and white ties; they looked very dreary but earnest and dependable. Before me was an indistinct sort of vehicle, which I was to enter and which they were to pull up to the top of the mountain by an attachment of rope and pulleys. I hesitated to get in, for the mountain was high and rocky, and I feared the rope would break or the ministers would not be strong enough. Yet it seemed necessary, and I entered the vehicle finally, although woefully and trembling. As I began slowly to rise, I lifted my fearful eyes to the summit of the mountain, and there appeared the old house which we called home. Light streamed from its open door, and in its upper windows appeared the eager faces of my three children. They were waving their hands and crying: "Don't be afraid, mother. They won't let go! They'll pull you up!"

And they did pull me up, making me a full-fledged minister, with authority to pronounce benedictions and solemnize marriages and join associations—if the associations didn't object. And I have lived happily ever after.

Chapter 12

Petty Bourgeois

THUS from the age of six to nine I was the child of a woman who disappeared every Saturday, and after being a preacher and a pastor for two days, returned Monday to be again my particular mother. It seemed natural enough to me, and worked well, although I suppose the high proportion of Aunt Marys in the environment was an essential factor. My mother was quite as gifted on the home-and-mother side as in the pulpit, a wonderful cook and housekeeper, and she would always gather us together and explain how everything was to be conducted in her absence. On one of these occasions I came forward, always preparing for the worst, with what she considered the one insoluble problem:

"What shall we do if a baby should be born!"

Frances Hossford, in her history of coeducation at Oberlin, says: "It is utterly unreasonable for a woman to attempt to attain eminent success both within and without her home." Perhaps it is, as a general rule, unreasonable; my mother's energy was unusual. But that is what she attempted and what she attained.

In 1891, a year after my mother was ordained, we sold the Old Farm, and my father opened a grocery store. Thus from being a "peasant's son" I became the son of a retail merchant. Fate, I am sure, had in mind to keep me out of the Marxian categories, but my father was moved by a more immediate need. He could not endure any longer the strain of a planned undertaking. Edgar S. Wheaton, his partner in the grocery business, was a younger man, and their agreement was that my father should do nothing active in the store but keep the books. So we sold the cows and horses and the pine parlor and cupola, and moved down to a cheap and shiny little burgher's domicile on West Gibson Street. I felt the shock of seeing my revered parent tucked away at a high desk in a corner behind sugar

72

barrels and sacks of potatoes, but he took this second step downward with the same serene poise as the first. He was disturbed only when a customer one day alluded to him as "the elderly gentleman at the desk." He went home that night and shaved off his side whiskers, an act which greatly improved the aspect of our family, and somewhat, I believe, its moral tone.

My life during our year-and-a-half at West Gibson Street is summed up with masterly brevity in a letter I wrote to grandpa in October, 1891.

"Dear Grandpa—
"I love you and hope you are well. Anstice and I have too rabbits and I go to the union school and I have a lovely teacher I study reading spelling and writing singing I hope Hope is very well this is for you to laugh at goodbye from your dear

Max"

During our last winter at the farm, I had been tactfully enticed into a little private school in Miss Parmelee's house down below Granger Place. There I had learned enough so that now, when almost nine, I entered the second grade at the Union School. I remember my "lovely teacher," who was very tall and slim; I remember making the joke about my cousin Hope Leonard in the letter to my grandfather; and needless to say, I remember the rabbits. I wondered what they were doing when they mounted and clung to each other in such frantic eagerness, and my brother explained that they were doing the same thing Boniface did to the cows. He tried to tell me that human babies were made in the same uncouth fashion, but although I had no contrary hypothesis, I refused to believe it. Human beings, as I understood the thing, were spirits, and this new story of his seemed to me as improbable as that "buery" should be pronounced *brewery*.

Although brave enough to go to school, I was still a 'fraid cat on West Gibson Street. Once while lying in bed in a room upstairs I heard my father go to the door in answer to the bell. A plaintive voice said something to him out of the wintry night, and he answered fiercely:

"If you're not out of this town inside of twenty-four hours, I'll have the police after you!"

He slammed the door, and I shuddered and began to cry. I can still hear his frail tenor voice, too shallow in his throat for such uses. It seemed horrible to me, as unqualified ruthlessness always does, no matter how provoked or why decided upon. To shut off sympathy absolutely against a fellow-being offends me in much the same way as a fallacy in logic. I do not quite see how it *can* be done.

It was my cousin, Chambers Stettinius, who was thus thrust out into the winter when he came, a beggar, to our Christian home. My father and mother had made painful sacrifices for him. It was he and his twin brother John whom my parents took into their home during their first struggle with poverty and failing health. John wonderfully rewarded them. He was a rare workman, and he made possible my father's quick success on the Old Farm by giving him as a present a year's work without wages.

But Chambers was a bad boy. He was worse than that, a bad boy with brains. They prepared him for college, and my father got him a chance at Oberlin to pay his board and lodging by tending the stoves in a private house. One morning he came down from his bedroom late and said:

"I suppose you think I'm going to clean the ashes out of that stove, but I'm not!"

He went back upstairs and got his bag and walked out of the house and down the open road "afoot and lighthearted"—lightheaded, too, alas. He became a first-class bum, and that whine out of the dark at West Gibson Street was but one of his many efforts to come back for another handout from his foster parents. My father saved through all the years a little notebook in which he had jotted down the pathetic sums advanced from his poverty to give Chambers Stettinius a chance at college. I am silenced by its mute testimony. I can say no word against my father's ultimatum now. Nor could I then, for I still thought he represented life the best that it could be. But I was scared to learn that it could be like that.

I must tell one more tale of my early heroism before we leave West Gibson Street. I had arrived now at a point where I could go out of my own yard without company, and was in fact making daily incursions into the territory of my soft and fat friend, Bobby Knapp, who lived across the street. Bobby's mother gave him bread and sugar every afternoon. I was mature enough to know that a mother ought not to allow her child to eat sugar on his bread, and it was with a certain intellectual condescension that I permitted her to prepare a slice for me; but I was there pretty regularly when the bread line formed. I also played with Earl Lee, who lived up on the corner by the railroad track, but I was less at ease with Earl because he was lean and hard and had prowess. Of all excellent virtues, prowess, I need hardly remark, is the one that makes me most uncomfortable.

One day we all took a walk up to the Old Farm to see how it was getting along under the new owner, Mr. Rawlings. The adventure was led by my brother, as all adventures were at that time and long after. Bobby and Earl and I were private troops in his command. We found Mr. Rawlings' calves flourishing in the back pasture, and exactly at the proper age to play crack the whip. I often feel a compassion for boys brought up in the city, and when I reflect that probably city boys feel the same way about me, I look around for some Absolute Good which is intrinsically rural in its nature. In the long run it comes down to this, that city boys never know the pleasure of grabbing a calf's tail in a big pasture and seeing how long they can hang on.

After we had enjoyed this sport to the point of exhaustion, we wandered into the apple orchard and pitched our camp under a red-fruited tree. I was tired out and lay down among the fragrant apples to rest. But I had not more than stretched out completely when my brother, whose energy and invention were inexhaustible, proposed, to my infinite horror, that Earl and I should have a fight. I had got far enough from Mamma's apron strings to know that such a proposal can not be rejected, but not far enough to say to myself, as we all one day have to: "Well, the worst I can do is get killed!" I just thought it was awful—that is the only way to say it—and I went in with both mental and physical reservations. At the first crack from Earl's knotty little fist I put my arms around my face and got down on the ground and cried. It was not that I minded the pain; I was appalled at being hit in the face. It made me feel altogether sick. The fight was over so soon that everybody was a little embarrassed, and I was so ashamed that I pulled my cap over my eyes and lay prostrate, pretending to be badly injured, yet willing that my shame show through the pretense. My brother, who carried in his belligerent breast a special tenderness toward me, and who had moreover had my "frailness" drilled into him since infancy, came over and removed my cap and lifted me up.

"You're all right," he said. "It doesn't matter."

But I knew I was not all right, and it did matter, although I was not yet prepared to do anything about it.

I must have been largely preoccupied then, as since, with the problem how a Mamma's boy could become a man, for my two other vivid memories from West Gibson Street concern this subject. A sewer was being laid across the green lot beyond our back fence, and the big tiles stood on end in a snaky row across the grass. We ran along them, stepping on the edges as you do on railroad ties. I made a misstep, and plunged into a tile, striking my forehead on its edge. I was senseless for some moments, and the gash in my forehead was deep and wide. I climbed out of the tile without tears, however, and ran for home. Just as I was scrambling over the high fence into our back yard, bloody and white, and with two pale little boys and a pale girl helping me, my mother emerged from the kitchen door.

"Oh, my baby, my baby!" she cried, and ran to catch me as I dropped from the fence.

I was poignantly ashamed that my mother should call me her baby in front of those other children, and although the doctor took several stitches in my forehead, I do not remember any other pain in connection with the accident.

Another emotion remembered from those days points the same way. It seems that my unremitting prayers to God to make me good had somewhat impressed Him, for at the end of my first term in the Union School I was singled out for decoration with a blue ribbon tied in a bowknot, a sort of *Croix de guerre* for "excellent deportment." Again I was boy enough to know that being so decorated is a disgrace, but not man enough to tear the ribbon off and throw it in the gutter. I just stood against the wall during the recess with my arms folded over my shame, declining all invitations to play. My "lovely teacher" saw and understood my predicament, and came up and said with a too-knowing smile:

"Don't be ashamed of your ribbon, Maxie. It's an honor to you that you behaved so well."

I unfolded my arms and tried to face it out, but I was in a turmoil. I thought it was wrong of her to come up when she saw my embarrassment and make it worse. I thought further that there was something wrong about the whole business of being good. This thought did not lead to any drastic action; nothing ever did throughout my early years. I merely steered a careful course between being bad and winning any more ribbons. But I also entered upon a series of reflections which culminated eighteen years later in one of my small triumphs, an essay in the *Atlantic Monthly* entitled "The Ignominy of Being Good."

It may seem surprising that a child in the second grade should reflect abstractly about the problem of morals. But my memory of this was confirmed some time after I wrote the above paragraphs by a note discovered in my mother's diary:

"Max's beautiful teacher, Miss Rockwood, gives little blue ribbon badges for good behavior. I missed his one day and asked him about it. 'Oh,' he said, 'Mamma, I don't want to be so awful good—the boys will laugh at me. I have to cut up a little once in a while.' "

After all, I was *old* enough to be in the fifth grade, and I was a meditative child. My parents called me "the philosopher" before I knew what the word meant. I seemed to them as calmly grown-up in my mental life as I was babyish in emotions. It became my trick to sit back listening intently to the violent discussions that raged around our dining table and try to come in at the end with a four-sided conclusion. Especially in the field of morals my family were impressed by my judgment. They rarely disagreed when I said a thing was right or wrong. My grandfather, after a visit to us in 1890, gave me this hearty send-off:

"Thin, peaked Max, tho' slow in learning now, will fetch up by and by like one of those race horses that lag on the start, but reserving their forces for further on, strip by their competitors and seize the prize after all. Push on, Max, y'u are all right; put in y'r best leaps as y'u accumulate strength through the years. Yu'll grow so tall yu'll reach the top of the hill of science and virtue."

What effect these words may have had upon me then, in my struggle toward manhood, I do not know. Today, finding them among my father's letters, I glance up that long hill with a feeling of remorse.

Chapter 13

Country Village

WEST BLOOMFIELD was a little town of two hundred houses straggling along a dirt road—the old stage road, I believe, between Albany and Niagara. The houses stood well back from the road, and so did the sidewalk, leaving space for grass and trees. There was one crossroad, and a few houses strayed each way on that. To the west the land dipped to a "crick," where the small village had a smaller suburb called Factory Hollow. There was a skunk farm and traces of a brick kiln in Factory Hollow, but no factory—only the crumbling walls of a forsaken mill, the broken mill wheel, and the dark deep mill-race overgrown with jewelweed. West Bloomfield was a casual and very rural town. That sidewalk I spoke of would forget itself once in a while and become a loamy path. East Bloomfield was larger, and so was Lima four miles west, and they used to taunt West Bloomfield: "Quite a town—they have a fish pond, a skunk farm, and a woman minister!" A remark of which my mother made delightful use in her lectures.

The red brick church with its trim slate-covered steeple stood, very graceful, on a rise of ground removed from the road by a small grove of trees. The little white schoolhouse squatted low next door. Up the road and across from the church were two general stores with a common hitching rail and dusty hollows where the horses stamped their hoofs. George Ayers' shop where you could buy a milk shake, although in essence it was a barber shop, stood just this side the stores. A little the other side was the Catholic church, a small white frame building, alien as well as insignificant to me. The parsonage was a short way up the hill on the crossroad, and by going through the "clover lot" opposite and sliding in beside the church, I could make a short cut to the stores or to George Ayers' shop to get a milk shake. I remember it all so well because it provides the imagery whenever I read a book or poem about village life.

Moreover, I drove up there a few years ago and confirmed these rather geometrical memories. I found the drowsy village gutted and destroyed, slit from end to end by Route 20, a hard wide cement road along which pours the roaring traffic between Albany and Buffalo. It was a tragedy to find it so, and what machines are doing to mankind *is* in large degree tragic, notwithstanding the utopian hope they hold. The tragedy was mitigated for me by an enormous red sign MILK SHAKE on the new store and post office, and by the fact that after forty-five years George Ayers was still inside that shop shaking milk! I also found Nell Peck sitting on her porch just where she sat when we used to gather down there and play Drop the Handkerchief, and where I once, to my own astonishment, taking a firm stand on the rules of the game, made bold to touch her pale pink-apple cheek with my lips.

Carl Carmer in his *Listen to the Lonesome Drums* speaks of driving over to West Bloomfield "to hear good talk," and it does not surprise me, for West Bloomfield contained in our time an unusual number of thinking people. Book dealers in near by Rochester were aware of the fact, and the spontaneous call to my mother to become pastor of the "big church" is conclusive proof of it. They knew they were getting more brains and eloquence for their money than they could have in a man. Only one objection was raised to extending her the call. That was canny old Deacon Hall's remark: "She won't be permanent—she's too good for us."

My mother's salary was eight hundred dollars a year and a commodious parsonage with natural gas in the kitchen and a barn and garden. My father continued his grocery business in Canandaigua, commuting daily on the "Peanut Line," and bringing home twelve to fifteen dollars a week. This regime began the first Sunday in February 1892, and continued for three years, and those were the years in which I began to taste the world outside my home.

I was still backward in all that had to do with books or ideologies. I never listened in church or learned anything that I could avoid learning in Sunday school. I made the most of my "frailness" and my mother's preoccupation with her sermon by playing up sick every other Sunday. In day school too I was inattentive and my progress slow. My state of literacy at the age of nine is revealed in a letter I wrote to Crystal while she was away on a visit:

"West Bloomfield, N. Y.
July 24, 1892

"Dear Stal,

I miss you very much for I have nobody to teas. I went up the lake to the N. S. C. Fryday and went in swiming but that was about all. A Mr. Sanburn preched here who was pater here 13 years 23 years ago. In the Orchard up to the farm there are quit a fue apples but not ripe.

Just think papa has paid 50 dollars on the peano. Papa is talking to Aunt Mary and evry minute and four quarteres I interupt them to know what to say in this letter. The wind is blowing and when it touches the vines they laugh and nod to it. Papa has mown part of the grass it is spoiling becaus we are to lazey to take it in the barn. Papa didnt go to church nor Sunday school but a nother man tought the Bible class. Decken Peck brought a quart of curents last night and Papa some bananos.

Good by.

Answer soon.
Max."

The only thing I mastered brilliantly was the names of the southern tier of counties in New York state: Chautauqua, Cattaraugus, Allegany, Steuben, Chemung, Tioga, Broome, Delaware, Sullivan, Orange, and Rockland. The reason for this feat of intellect was that Ethel Marble sat in the last seat on the girl's side over by the map, and our white-bearded teacher, Mr. Beebe, used to let a boy go over and sit with a girl to study the map. Ethel had mottled cheeks —a vast unregulated rosy patch on them, I mean—in maddening contrast to her creamy skin. I loved her with romantic love. But the most I dared do about it was to sit beside her in a mute excitement studying that map, upon which nothing was legible from my close seat except the southern tier.

I loved Ethel Marble from the time I saw her until we left West Bloomfield, and I love her still. But I believe I never communicated with her except the momentous once when I handed her a little circle of white peppermint candy stamped with the words: "Will you be my sweetheart?" She brought me back the next day a similar circle of candy, colored with lime, and stamped: "You're too young and too green." It was all ostensibly a joke, and I tried hard to make it so in my heart, but not successfully. There is almost always some single part or feature of a girl upon which your passion concentrates, and those mottled cheeks combining so miraculously with the wondrous beauty of her name—I trust you will have the courtesy to perceive its wondrous beauty—kept me in a state of sad poetics for a long time.

Side by side with that, and not a bit the same, I felt a lustful yearning over Nonnie Marlin. So did every other well-sexed boy in town, for notwithstanding her pimply complexion, there was a great power of attraction in Nonnie. Her round strong shoulders and round breasts and ease of attitude and action made her like a warm animal. She lived in a poor and tiny house four or five doors down the road from ours, and I never went by there without a forlorn casting down of eyes and a rising in me of the hot but hopelessly diffident desire to "put my arm around" Nonnie.

I did not dream that my two feelings toward these different girls might someday be focused upon one, and what a birth of the universe that would produce. A great many American boys of my generation—and boys everywhere, I guess—never do succeed in combining these two feelings, and that is one of the troubles with the life of love.

My memories of West Bloomfield are all colored with a feeling of my own inadequacy and unimportance. I did not dare play baseball in the schoolyard, although I wanted to, because it seemed axiomatic that I was not "good enough." Freckle-faced Gus Brown, whom my mother undertook to inaugurate as my special playmate, I regarded with a feeling not of camaraderie but of humble respect. He did play baseball, and he swam and skated and fought, and in general possessed the thing of whose lack I was intelligently conscious, though I could not name it: self-assurance. I respected him further because his father owned a three hundred-acre farm, which meant that he was rich, whereas I knew well that I was poor.

There were two rather fancy houses in West Bloomfield; at least they had pillared porches with a number of unnecessary curlicues on them. They stood sedately side by side and belonged to Mr. Marvin Peck and Mr. Ainsworth. These two men were the magnates of the village, and as the village was the world to me, they were mighty and portentous persons. Mr. Ainsworth, a tottering octogenarian, had once been a fish breeder and well-known advocate of state conservation in this field. I did not know this then, but I knew that a man who owned a private fish pond was a great man. Mr. Peck was not related to my schoolmate Nell Peck; he was a totally different order of being, one who could walk right into a bank and pick up money. I passed by these two great men's houses with a sentiment of awe, and would as soon have thought of crashing the gate at Buckingham Palace as of turning in for a closer look at those curlicues. I really think I felt more remote in my insignificance from Marvin Peck and Mr. Ainsworth than I did from God. God, after all, if not a member, was a close friend of the minister's family, poor as they were.

As you see from these feelings, I was making small progress with my task of becoming a man. My father brought home a little bay mustang one Saturday afternoon and said if I would ride her he would buy her for me. I remember how beautiful she was, a white star in her forehead, an arching neck, and tense nostrils. And I remember how scared I was. An old nag would have offered no problem, but this was the real thing, a chance for a boy who had *played* horse all his life to make good. There was no escape, nothing to do but clamber into the saddle and say "giddap"—which I did, somewhat gaspingly, and, as nothing happened, my father gave the pony a sharp slap on the flank. She made three leaps forward and stopped short with her head down, whereupon I turned a perfect somersault and landed against the barn in a "highly mixed-up condition." I was thankful to be back on earth in any condition, but I dared not say so. I had to enjoy that horse, since she was real; I could see the logic of that. So I jumped up and came right back, saying "whoa!" in a shaky but masterful voice. I climbed into the saddle and made her take me around the yard, and my father was happily impressed. He thought I was a man after all. But I knew well that I was only pretending. I did not want to ride a real horse again, and I was vastly relieved when my mother decided I was hardly "strong enough" to take such risks.

So Crystal got the little mustang—and got a big slice, at my expense, of the enjoyment of living. (It takes some courage to achieve it.) I envy her now, careening around the town and country on a man's saddle in fluttering vast brown bloomers—very shocking to the public, although those bloomers were spacious enough to hide a hundred legs like hers and ugly enough to frighten a Turk. But it did not bother me then to be inferior in joy to my sister. I was *glad* of those words "not strong enough," which permitted me to go back to my black dog Major,[1] or the kitten, Brownie Busybody

---

[1] For history's sake I must record that Major had to be "put out of the way" because he barked savagely at innocent Christians who came to pay a call upon their pastor. I spoke eloquently in his defense, but in vain—the Christians were, for some reason,

Goldeyes, or Tommie Neal, a little boy neighbor who made no demands whatever upon my character.

Tommie was half my size and hardly a boy at all—little more than a baby. His family were desperately poor, and their place was down at the heels and dirty. The yard, both fore and aft, was a hen and barn yard and a general dump. Cow turds and old tin cans and cast-off wheels and furniture and broken dishware took the place of grass. Tommie himself was dirty, his nose snotty, and his clothes but half attached to his body. A little girl named Minnie Roberts, also much younger than I and not extra-bright, used to come across the road sometimes and play with us. She herself was no paragon of cleanliness, but she arrived one morning, under instructions from her mother, with an ultimatum: She could not play with Tommie any more unless he washed his hands after he went to the water closet. It was a way of getting Tommie to wash his hands at least once a day. I can imagine my own mother's state of mind, for I was nine or ten years old, and this little growthless urchin, to whose undemanding companionship I was absolutely addicted, was hardly past six. My mother's concern to get me off to the other end of town to play with a boy of my own age like Gus Brown, was therefore serious and wise.

It was also unsuccessful—and if you will promise not to be any more embarrassed than I am, I will tell you why. One day Gus and George Leach and I went down to the fish pond where I had learned to swim by dog-paddling with a plank under my stomach. When I got undressed George and Gus put me down in the grass and threatened to perform an operation on my private parts. Their operation did not go much farther than prodding with a piece of grass, but I was frightened to death and, like an opossum, paralyzed instead of angered by the attack. I did not want to growl or show my teeth; I wanted to roll away and go home. My brain, however, was not paralyzed, for I thought of a wonderfully ingenious way to scare them off. I remembered my mysterious affliction and Doctor Walmsley's ministrations, and I said:

"You'd better look out, I've had trouble with that pecker!"

Although I think I have never related this incident before, those words are graven in my consciousness as indelibly as my own name.

---

more important. He would die by chloroform, I was assured, and his death be but a sleep and a forgetting. I got news by the schoolyard route, however, that Bert Shattuck, to whom the task was entrusted, had killed Major with an axe. It made ghastly the already grievous loss of a friend.

It is not only because they succeeded like magic, but because I knew they were ridiculously funny. In my heart I laughed more than I cried on the way home. I wonder if it is true of many shy people that they are leading inwardly a life of subtle and suave perceptions, while still mere babes and boobies in their speech and behavior. It was true of me, and the exploding into social expression of that inward life, on a certain occasion which I shall later recount, was a momentous event in my history.

Chapter 14

Inside the Family

WITHIN the home, of course, I was more free of inhibitions and was growing. I used sometimes when lying awake at night to burst into a cold sweat at the thought that some day I would have to propose to a strange girl—just as I do now at the too vivid image of a public disgrace, or of a shark rising toward me in the water. As a result of this emotion I maintained stoutly for some years that I was going to marry my sister, a fact whose aspects in the unconscious I leave to the authorities on that region. Crystal, at least, was the only playmate besides Tommie with whom I felt at ease. I was abnormally reticent. I was also the most selfish member of my family—a frail child is apt to be—and hence my friendship with Crystal was a little one-sided. She poured magnetic streams of generous love around her all the time, and she loved me with especial warmth. I loved her too, and deeply admired her character, but kept up a catlike aloofness about it all through life, receiving more than I gave. For these reasons, and because of her less sensitive and bolder plunge into experience, I think I was probably growing faster in my play with Crystal than in other relationships in West Bloomfield.

My brother's temperament was not so auspicious for coaxing a mouse out of its hole. He too was bold, although his boldness took the form of raising secret hell rather than openly defying convention. He was rash, reckless, agile and muscular, of prodigious endurance, and, as far as anyone could see, by far the "brightest" of us children. He was ready for college at thirteen, and had to be shipped out to Idaho to work on a ranch for two years to pass the time. To my "thin and peaked," and bashful, and belatedly literate self, he seemed so all-round superior a being that the idea of rivalry between us could not enter my head. All I could do was to get into helpless rages against him, and that was no achievement, for pretty nearly everybody did.

I never altogether understood my big brother, but as he was a kind of thunder god overshadowing my childhood, I want to suggest the outlines of his peculiar nature. He was, in the first place, belligerent. He was just the way he looks in the little four-year-old picture in this book. When he was seven our grandmother died, and his letter of condolence to Morgan Lewis, scrawled in his own hand, begins on this imperious note:

"My dear Grandpa,
"I am sorry for you but Grandma is having a better time than you can think of, you know she is."

My brother, in short, was born with a chip on his shoulder. And this disposition was certainly not mitigated by the fact that his own elder brother, Morgan, had been incomparably gentle and beautiful and adored as a saint by our parents, so that the scowling little Anstice, with his funny-looking knob of a nose, was at first blush distinctly a comedown. He may well have got the habit of lashing out at the world by way of protest.

Underneath that bellicose habit, Anstice was extremely tender and even sentimental, but that was something you often forgot and had to try to remember afterward. On the surface he was all set to pounce on you, and pfff you, and cuff you with his tongue at the slightest hint of stupidity or ineptitude. As a father and a physician he had to learn to curb these impulses, but the process was difficult. His first patient was a young man who came in sniffling and moist around the lip:

"Doctor, I wish you could find out what's the matter with me!"

"I'll tell you one thing that's the matter with you right now," he said. "You need to blow your nose!"

The worst of it from my standpoint was that if you flared up and answered back, Anstice would *enjoy* the resulting clash, enhanced rather than depressed by a quaff of anger. And a few moments later, while you were still weighing the merits of different kinds of murder, he would address you in the friendliest fashion, unaware that anything to mar a perfect day had happened. As I am by nature a peace-breathing animal, and a spell of violent anger puts me to bed pale as though rage had drunk the very red out of my blood, this trait in my big brother was not an unmixed blessing. I never threw an axe at him, but I have thrown shovels, saws and whiffletrees, and if I did not on one occasion throw a horse and wagon, it was not through superior dignity or restraint.

We used to go all-day fishing together in the creek at West Bloomfield. We would take our lunch and, starting way up at the level in the woods where we caught suckers and bullheads, work our way down through Factory Hollow, catching "helgomites" in the rifts and feeding them to the black bass in the still pools and deeper rapids, until we arrived in early evening at the Button-Ball Hole some way the other side of the village. It was a long trudge for me, and there would be one or two fights to increase my weariness. And yet I loved it. Apart from those fights we were happy companions. In his heart as we strode along my brother had a feeling of chivalry toward my lesser strength and knowledge, and no undue pride of his own prowess.

One evening at the Button-Ball Hole he caught sight of a big shadowy bass swimming toward the ripples and cast his line eagerly —or tried to—a little way upstream beyond the fish. I was standing idle, waiting to go home, and the hook caught in my ear. He burst out against me with one of those curt, sneering speeches.

"Say, if you don't want to fish, will you please get your carcass out of the way of my line!"

Then he saw me standing there holding back tears while I wiped the blood. We made up a good deal faster than usual that time. Walking home in the twilight, we made a bargain that we would never fight again. The terms of it were that if either one saw the other getting mad, he would hold up two fingers and say "B" which stood for "bargain," and then the other would have to calm down. It worked for a while—according to my brother's recollection, for a long while.

Those "fights" were a problem not only to us but to our parents, who were troubled about the effect upon me of so many impotent rages. They were right, too, although it was not the impotence, but the certainty that no matter what I said or did I wouldn't get hurt which did me the most harm. My brother's underlying tenderness and generosity thus conspired with his "ugly disposition" and his brilliant abilities to keep me babyish.

My mother and father had as desperate a time handling that disposition as I did, and owing to their semi-Calvinistic moralism they made a mess of it. I find it hard to relate the cruel story of their efforts to whip the "impudence" out of my big brother. There is an unnatural sadism in mankind, a trait not found at least elsewhere in nature, and no idea is more dangerous than one which justifies on moral or political principles conduct which would otherwise be condemned as brutal.

All of my brother's sports, I pause to say, were of the militant sort —spearing bullfrogs, shooting birds and squirrels with an airgun, playing I'm the King of the Castle, dressing up as Lord Nelson or Horatius at the Bridge. Once on the Old Farm he got Crystal and me all rigged out in armor made of smashed apple barrels, with great grim shields and swords and helmets adorned with plumes he borrowed from the Brown Leghorn rooster. We marched down the driveway to greet mother on her way home from school, singing out as she approached the gate:

"We are the dauntless three!"

There was something so absolutely not dauntless about Crystal and me that mother never ceased laughing at that picture of the lopsided characters of her three children.

Besides shooting birds and squirrels one of my brother's early diversions was to post himself behind a knot-hole in the barn and shoot the hired man in the pants when he bent over to pump water for the cattle. For such things he would be invited to go into the orchard and cut a switch—a ceremonial nicety which comes down, I think, with the New England ethics—and he would be licked either by my father or mother until welts stood out on him. My father sometimes dispensed with the preliminaries and did the work with a razor strop, and on one occasion he took his son out in the barn and horsewhipped him. That was when Anstice and Ray Church went down to the creek to spear bullfrogs, and took Crystal with them. Not finding the bullfrogs sufficiently entertaining they all undressed, and after some studies in comparative anatomy, the boys taught Crystal two or three of the forbidden names of things. They swore her to secrecy, of course, and that resulted in her telling mother about the undressing and saying there was "something worse" which she couldn't tell! Mother just went out of her head. She stood Anstice up in front of her naked, and whipped him until he divulged to her also each of those forbidden names and two or three more. And then she took him down in the library and made him sign a paper swearing that he would never again in his life utter a dirty word, and that he would do all things in his power to keep his sister from being contaminated by evil thoughts. When father came home, he decided that the punishment had not been thorough and took Anstice out in the barn and "thrashed" him until the boy lifted his shirt and silently exposed the blood stains on his skin.

There was fear in all this, of course, a very Christian fear, and a mixture of still less relevant passions. My mother and Anstice used to go into surly glooms against each other like two lovers quarreling. For as long as three or four days they would not speak, nor their eyes meet. The house for me during those days would be a place of misery. My feeling was both sad and bewildered. I can not remember that I took sides. I think I saw even then in my mother a little of the same contumaciousness that was so incomprehensible to me in my brother.

One day in West Bloomfield Anstice came down to the noon meal with a new necktie on. My father said in his kindly voice:

"Why, Anstice, are you wearing your best necktie on a weekday?"

"Have you any objection," he spat back, "to my wearing the necktie my mother told me to!"

"Anstice, you may go to your room—and wait there until I come!"

It was an old story. But this time the end was different. The switch had been forgotten; the razor strop was not handy; or perhaps my father was beginning to lose heart. At any rate he used his own hand. When he was about half through he said, not with brilliant originality:

"I hope you realize that this hurts me as much as it does you."

My brother answered with his supremest sneer:

"There's a board over there. Why don't you use that if it hurts your hand?"

My father sank down on his knees and put his head on the bed and cried.

"Anstice, no matter what you do," he said, "I will never strike you again as long as I live!"

That ended the rawest part of this tale of conscientious cruelty, which only added a strain of self-pity to my brother's burden of belligerence. A letter from Morgan Lewis may perhaps have played a part in this change.

"As for Anstice, there can be no doubt but that y'u will be able to 'land him' with God's implored, and effective promised aid. Be careful—pull, but don't jerk the line, lest it break, or tear the gills and y'u lose the fish! I can now retrospect, and see where I jerked, but Jesus forgave, and overruled, and bro't to shore. Y'r dear Mother never jerked."

My brother, in a defensive moment, would have told you that

Crystal and I were sissies and that he was the one live pup in the
litter. It is an aspect which the facts can wear. Crystal was really
good in the large sense, and I was painfully preoccupied with trying
to be. My state of inner righteousness may be inferred from the fact
that for years I made it a point to put on my left shoe first on the
theory that this was the harder task and there must be no evasion of
life's problems. If sometimes when it came my turn to perform a
really heroic task like washing the dishes or digging up the chicory
from the front lawn, I developed symptoms of acute indigestion or
paroxysmal pains in the region of the liver, that is only further evidence of my preoccupation with the moral law. Although by some
inner force destined to reach it, I was as far from a principled belief
in the Enjoyment of Living as the dourest ascetic of the Libyan
desert. The idea of sneaking out at chore time *because of* some fun
to be had elsewhere could not be judged and rejected by me. It had
no way of getting into my mind.

Although my concern with virtue was so constant, it was not, so
far as I can remember, supported by religious thoughts or feelings.
I always tried to have the appropriate emotions when I said my
prayers, just as in other matters I tried with plebeian faithfulness
to be "correct." But I have no memory of any genuine transport
about God or Jesus or the Holy Angels. My mother's diary supports
my recollection that in the act of prayer I was inclined to reflection
and practicality rather than pious fervor.

"When Max knelt down to pray, he said: 'God made us just right,
didn't he?'

" 'How?' I said.

" 'Oh, just the right shape—standing up and all that.' "

"Max's prayer shows the great need of the family: 'Oh God, we
do thank thee for making Papa so much better. Make him better
and better. Make him as well as Mamma. Then make them both
better. Then make us all better.' "

Every Sunday morning from breakfast time to church my father
compelled us three children to learn verses from the Bible by heart,
an exercise which killed the Bible but marvelously trained our
growing brains and tongues. I remember a time when my brother
could recite the three chapters of the Sermon on the Mount in one
minute and forty-two seconds, coming in with a lead of three verses
after giving me a handicap of six Beatitudes. I believe I put in
the first strenuous brain work of my life trying to cut down that lead.

Such facts reveal the somewhat remote and formal nature of my father's impact on us. On Sunday afternoons he would take us walking across the meadows and through the woods. His sweet good humor and love of nature made these walks a treasured memory to my sister, but to me they have carried through the years an undertone of impatient emotion. My father's idea was that the austerity of the Christian Sabbath should relax a trifle in these walks, and a certain fun and playfulness commingle with the love of nature. But I scented the flavor of ceremonial even in this act of relaxation. I did not want a permitted playfulness; I wanted to play. To be specific, I wanted to play horse!

My mother's impatience of these chronological and ritual aspects of righteousness was almost as extreme, I think, as mine. I remember well one breakfast when my father, after reproving one of us for using some dreadful expletive like "goodness gracious!", exclaimed:

"It is time I preached my sermon again on polite swearing. It is long since I have explained to the people what those expressions mean."

"Oh, Sam," mother said, "aren't there enough real troubles in the world without your worrying about whether people say 'goodness gracious'?"

A word from her like that would bring him home to reality, where he wanted to be. But in his own mind he was prone to wander off among these webby relics of theology and still earlier taboos. His influence upon his children, and upon me especially, lay rather in the unfailing example that he set of firmness, honor, patience, fortitude . . . in this, rather than in anything he communicated in speech. His inmost being was, as I have said, strangely insulated.

My mother was by contrast a vivifying mind and voice. Her originality and impulsive candor, the everlasting humorous surprise in her, kept everybody in her neighborhood alert and aware of life to an unusual degree. To us in her household she enriched the world like a perpetual change of seasons. Ideas and people and things, the littlest things, were painted ever in fresh colors by her inexhaustible selfless interest in them. Children especially were instant captives to her charm—her children's sermons were quite famous—and it would be folly to pretend that I am not afflicted with the "mother complex" in its most seizing form. I am afflicted, too, with the fact that I was her youngest child, the last one to be her baby, and I was not well and strong. For the life of me I can not say what my malady was, nor what its symptoms were, the thing being inextricably confused in my memory with the problem of getting out of going to church.

But I must have been ailing, for my sister was asked to give up a long-anticipated trip to Florida with Aunt Mary Landen in order that I might go for my health's sake in her place.

It was my father's family, Aunts Miriam, Luna and Lucy, three of the lank dark Indians, that we visited in Florida. The house and yard in which we lived with Aunt Miriam looms now, a brown mossy ghost, visible only to my cousins and me, in the very center of Daytona's brickiest and busiest block. Aunt Miriam was good to me, and allowed me to eat between meals, a sin which I suspect was the very medicine I needed. With her encouragement, too, I earned my first money selling Sunday papers to the guests in a small hotel a half mile south. In order to reach it I had to pass a shanty around which congregated a gang of pickaninnies. They yelled and threw stones at me and inspired such terror in my heart that the problem of getting to that hotel and back each Sunday morning darkened my existence. I was frightened also one black night when I had to come home alone through the long orange grove behind Aunt Miriam's house. I whistled "Jesus, Lover of My Soul" to keep up my courage, but had enough presence of mind to change the tune when I reflected that "Jesus, Saviour, Pilot Me" would be more appropriate.

Brightest of these memories was a visit to Aunt Lucy and Uncle John in a little solitary cottage over on the great beach that has since grown populous. Those three days hang in my memory like a spacious picture, warm with my gratitude to Aunt Lucy for overcoming my shyness and cool with the blue ocean rocking its cradles out beyond the white breakers. And in the very center of the picture, far out in the blue, a silver tarpon flashes up like a sword in the sunlight.

Aunt Lucy was the beauty and the "genius" of my father's family. After the Civil War she went down south to teach the Negroes, and by way of notification to the enemies of this Christian mission, took along a pistol and practiced daily in the schoolyard until she became a crack shot. She liked the experience so well that she decided to become a doctor-missionary, and went back to Chicago to study medicine. There she cast her lively eyes upon a virile Mr. Brown and married him, but found the marriage "vile." All that remains in history of Mr. Brown is that, on jumping into the cab beside her after the wedding, he shouted: "Now I've got you!" For this crime —and others, I hope, of which it was symbolic—she divorced him promptly, and to signify her own spotless, or very nearly spotless, condition, took the name of "Doctor Ermine." The Missionary Board were not convinced, or would not risk the morals of the heathen in the hands of a divorced Christian, and so Dr. Ermine stayed at home and built a large and lucrative practice in Chicago.

She also found a more spiritual, or more tactfully passionate lover, big burly handsome and warmhearted John Powell, whom she enthusiastically married. Powell was a professional boxer when she met him, one of the trainers, I was told, of Bob Fitzsimmons, but she persuaded him to study medicine and join her in her practice. Death ended her brave life too soon, but not before she had blessed me with a sweet bewilderment, a wondering sense of the superior richness that can be possessed by those upon whom the church looks down with disapproval. She and Uncle John adored each other and were joyous, and led me out boldly laughing into the terrible white surf.

There is a principle in psychology called the "oblivescence of the disagreeable," which like so many psychological principles doesn't work very well. Among my experiences in Florida I find that memory has made a very dispassionate choice of pleasant and unpleasant. Our trip up the Halifax River in a sailboat to Pelican Island, our landing on the island under a suddenly arisen cloud of egrets or ibis, their angry clamor in the sky, their blue eggs and fuzzy scurrying babies under the slim-stemmed trees, are as joyfully exciting a recollection as a northern farmer's boy could have. Yet quite as vivid is the painful moment of our starting, when I had climbed from the little dock into the sailboat, and my sandy-bearded Uncle Hewitt, having loosed the painter, was trying to swing the stern of the boat toward him so that he could get in.

"Shove the tiller over, Max," he shouted.

I had not the slightest idea what a tiller was.

"Be quick about it, man!"

I grabbed at various things, and finally stammered:

"I don't know what you mean."

"Oh, I see you're no good in a sailboat," he said, and climbed in and took his position without looking at me.

There is a disadvantage in being brought up as gently and justly as I was. You dwell ever after in a world whose meanness and illogic are bewildering. I hated my Uncle Hewitt all the way to Pelican Island and all the way back. I hated him with a kind of amazement, for I did not see how a human mind could *possibly* commit the fallacy of inferring that a boy is no good in a sailboat because he has not yet learned the names of its appurtenances.

Still, I do not want you to conclude that I was a spoiled child. I have been spoiled somewhat of late, but I was brought up with a very good mixture of free will and discipline. One of my mother's progressive inventions was to have "children's meals" when grownups were not allowed to talk; but these were offset by grownups' meals, and both regimes were well enforced. Moreover, our household was run on feminist principles. The boys took their turns with the girls at making beds and washing dishes, and the girls took their turns at hoeing the garden and cleaning out the stable for Merrilegs—or "Old Foolish," as my brother dubbed her—a superannuated racing mare that took my mother on her pastoral calls. All such duties were divided, theoretically at least, on a basis of pure justice, and if I got away with anything, it was through assiduous scheming and always with memorable pangs of conscience. In short, I was allowed to know from my earliest years that life consists largely of doing what you don't want to, and for that privilege I am profoundly thankful.

I have two keen memories of my mother's disciplinary tactics. Once she grabbed me as I was about to go upstairs and bit my shoulder until it hurt. I shuddered and looked at her in gruesome terror.

"I just wanted you to know what it felt like," she said, "when you bit Crystal's arm yesterday."

I can truthfully say that that ended my career as a biter.

The other discipline was more subtle. One of my mother's saints in the West Bloomfield church was Deacon Myron Peck, who supplied the parsonage with milk and eggs—not to be confused with the portentous and pecuniary Marvin Peck. The deacon was a gracious and sweet-mannered little man, wrinkled and old and always with a smile behind his whiskers. He sat in our parlor one day waiting for my mother to come downstairs, and I walked through the hallway practicing a newly acquired art of whistling. As I passed the door, balancing on the high bars of "Marching through Georgia," Deacon Peck smiled and bowed graciously and said: "How do you do, Max?"

I also smiled and bowed graciously—extra graciously, I thought, for I made the bow so low that it was not necessary for me to stop whistling. I think if my mother had seen me, she might have understood my fatuous misconception and been more merciful. But she only heard Deacon Peck's friendly salutation die on the air, and me go right on marching through Georgia. She informed me, after he had gone, that I would have to go over to Deacon Peck's house and knock on the door and present my apologies.

There was no appeal from these decrees of hers, and I did go, sick and sweating and wishing I were in the bottom of the creek—pondering too on the injustices, or at least the extreme subtleties, of things. I had intended to be courteous to Deacon Peck—honest I had. Even more than that, I had intended to reveal to him in a particularly graceful way my fine manners.

It occurred to me as I approached the little white door which was to be the scene of my agony that I might have explained this latter point to mother and perhaps have begged off. But no, that wouldn't have done any good. She would have said: "Well, if you were showing off, that only makes it worse!"

So there was nothing else to do, and I came shivering up to the little door and lifted the knocker and knocked about as loud as a rabbit would.

Deacon Peck must have seen me coming, for he opened the door at once, and before I had got six stammering words out of my mouth, he took in the whole situation. He took me in, too—grasped me in his arms and actually *thanked me* for coming!

Of course I knew that he was not grateful to me for coming, nor to my mother for sending me. He wished, as I did, that he were in the bottom of the creek. But he was not thinking of himself. He was thinking of *my feelings!*

That is how I learned that courtesy does not consist of showing off your fine manners. And I learned many gentle wisdoms in the same hard way. No, I was not spoiled—not any more than a "thin and peaked" child inevitably is. My mother was wiser than the modern schools, for she knew how to insert into a general diet of freedom an adequate dosage of discipline.

Chapter 15

City Life

MY MOTHER'S fame grew rapidly in western New York, and she traveled away frequently to preach or lecture. She was, I suppose, the most noted woman minister of the time,[1] and her tiny parish was very proud of her. "Our pride reached its climax," writes a parishioner, "when she was invited to address the World's Parliament of Religions at the Columbian Exposition in Chicago, and our West Bloomfield Church stood, so to speak, alongside of world-wide castes and creeds." The fees my mother received for these lectures were not very large. At least I remember an occasion when some minister, after urging her to edify his flock for nothing, concluded his letter:

"Or are you like Henry Ward Beecher, who was always willing to speak for F-A-M-E, meaning Fifty And My Expenses?"

She answered: "I will speak for Ten And My Expenses, and I call that T-A-M-E."

Her fees were often higher than that, but rarely exceeded twenty dollars.

She wore in the pulpit a simple black robe of her own design which she called a surplice. It was pleated in front and made feminine by a little black lace at the opening at her throat. Her manner in the pulpit was as simple as her gown. She made few gestures and never a motion that was not native to her. She had the two indispensable gifts of the orator, self-possession and a thrilling voice. When she rose to speak, you knew at once that she was in complete command of the situation, and you felt at ease. As there was nothing in the least degree mannish about her, you stopped bothering about whether she was a man or a woman. And when she began to speak,

---

[1] The suffrage leader Anna Howard Shaw was ordained, but was not noted as a minister.

you were taken quiet possession of, first by the tones of her voice, and then by the surprisingly candid and wise and joyous, and often humorous, things that she would say.

My mother's great friend and champion in western New York was the biggest preacher in the region, and one of the biggest men in churchdom anywhere, Thomas K. Beecher of Elmira. He was a half-brother of Henry Ward Beecher, and by contrast to him a very whole man. He headed the council in Brookton which somewhat high-handedly, in view of her rapid flight over theological education, ordained my mother. He said more than once that she had preached the greatest sermons he ever heard. He often invited her to preach and lecture in his famous Park Church, and when he was nearing seventy he proposed that she be called to Elmira as his associate. The wish was general that my father be associated in the call, but he explained that he was "not able to accept the responsibility of a pastorate."

"It will not be worth while for your committee to consider us save with the understanding that Mrs. Eastman would be responsible for the preaching. I think I could be helpful in the executive work, but preaching is too exhaustive for me to think of undertaking."

It was on this basis that the call was extended. The salary was two thousand dollars and, as a parsonage, two corridors of rooms above the church parlors. Thus in July 1894, we moved to Elmira, and my inferiority complex, which had been thriving adequately on my being the son of a woman minister, found additional nourishment in the fact that I lived in a church. It was helped along further by my being clad in a "cutaway" coat and vest with short pants, a sort of legless imitation of a natty grown-up costume, which may perhaps have looked citified in the country but in a city looked ridiculous. My mother used to tell with laughter that, when I came back to our rooms the first Sunday, and she asked me how I liked the famous Park Church Sunday School, I said:

"Well, at least I've got to have a new necktie!"

She little guessed the aching emotion under that remark. I dared not ask for a new suit. My suit, alas, was already new. I was clearly aware that I was a boob and was destined to be one for what seemed an interminable period of time. Nor was I deceived that anything in my face or figure compensated for this handicap. "My, you were an ugly little boy!" is the principal memory of one of my mother's surviving friends. At least I evaded the sad fate of those who are good-looking in childhood and get the habit of knowing it. Throughout my entire youth and young manhood the idea never once occurred to me that I might be attractive to look at. And in those days, I sneaked around Elmira not only as poor, but as industriously unobtrusive, as a church mouse.

Do not despair of me, however. I had my cell in that church decorated with busts and portraits of Abraham Lincoln, John Wilkes Booth, Charles Dickens, Julius Caesar, Charlotte Corday, Robert E. Lee—anybody and everybody who ever did a historic thing, no matter what—and I was sure to explode some day.

I went to school the first year to a very Christian Miss Young, who conducted classes in her private dwelling. I can not remember learning much of anything at Miss Young's school except the phrase *Quelle surprise!* which I had to bring forth, and did bring forth, at exactly the right moment in a little French play. I also learned to tease Eleanor Silsbee, which was quite a step in my development, for Eleanor was both rich and handsome, and teasing implies at the very least a status of equality.

The next year I entered Number 2 School, where again I have no memory of learning anything, but a clear memory of *not* learning English grammar and feeling incapable of it. Particularly I did not grasp the parsing and diagramming of sentences. For the life of me I could not make out why one part of a sentence should be put on a horizontal line across the page and the other parts hitched underneath in little lines that slanted down. Why should they slant? And why should they slant down? And why should they hitch on in one place instead of another? Moreover, what, in all candor and confidence, is the difference between a complex and a compound sentence? And what is the subjunctive mood, and why? An extremely vague and vaporous entity, I thought, to be grasped only by people with a special talent for it—people possessing a certain vim I seemed to lack. With my limited faculties I naturally felt more at ease among numbers, which are clear-cut entities capable of undergoing definite operations—operations, moreover, which produce a result. If you divide 228 by 19, you may have to draw a lot of irrelevant lines on a blackboard, but you get something out of it —namely, unless I have lost the art, 12. But when you have diagrammed a sentence, also with a lot of irrational line drawing, what have you got? Nothing! Nothing at all! I did not feel contemptuous, of course, but bewildered.

I was naturally a good deal concerned, on going over to Number

2 from Miss Young's, with trying to be, or seeming to be, a "regular guy." My mother, with an opposite impulse, had provided me with a becoming blue "blouse" for the occasion. It wasn't what the other boys had on, and that increased my determination to be regular in other respects.

We were seated alphabetically, starting from the rear of the hall, and Mattie Fennell, an Irish saloon-keeper's son from Railroad Avenue, sat right in front of me. Mattie was really a gentlehearted boy, but my blue blouse or my religion or some intuition he had of my interior diffidence challenged his manliness. He had muscles of steel, and he devised the idea of poking his arm back under the desk, grabbing my hand and squeezing the knuckles together until the tears ran down my cheeks. He knew I would not holler. I was too shy to holler.

As my first harsh experience of public school *mores*, this impressed me deeply. I noticed that Mattie was held in high regard among the boys, and I inferred that it must be the thing to pick on somebody and make him miserable. So I decided I would pick on Dean Chadbourne who sat just behind me. Dean pushed me out of line one morning and edged through the school door ahead, and that gave me some pretext for a deed of prowess. It began to seem appropriate, and indeed the more I thought about it logically necessary, taking Mattie's heroism as a premise, for me to "kick Dean in the pants." Without further preliminaries, then, I marched up behind Dean one day during recess and kicked him. . . .

You know sometimes when you kick hard and not quite accurately, it causes you to sit down? Well, that is what happened to me. I sat down. Dean turned around and, instead of jumping on me as the evolution of the drama demanded, asked me what was the matter.

It seemed impossible to make my deed heroic by an explanation from a sitting posture, so I merely said: "Aw, nothing!"

Be yourself, is what I had begun to learn there—a basic principle of life's enjoyment. *Be yourself, and don't kick so hard that you sit down.*

My grand passion in those days was still for animals, but I was also enamored of warriors and battles. I find in a surviving scrapbook that Napoleon Bonaparte, George Washington, General McClellan, General D. C. Buell, and the *Monitor* and *Merrimac* cohabit with Sir Bedevere, King of St. Bernards, the Scotch fantail Queen of Scots, an Indian antelope, the American setter Grousedale, Rosa Bonheur's "Old Monarch," Marco, one of Queen Victoria's favorite spaniels, and other quadrupeds, in the proportion of 14 to 50. I myself possessed a beautiful Irish setter named Ajax, a gift from mother's friends in Swampscott. Ajax was my dearest companion in those first years in Elmira, and if you will glance at our picture among the illustrations and see with what measureless aplomb he faces the world, and what a formless frightened little cell of life I was, you will fully understand the nature of our friendship. I have always thought that if I had in me the principle that causes one dog to trot boldly up to another who is ferociously bristling and snarling, and take a cool and inquiring smell, everything in my life might have prospered. That is really all that is the matter with me—I have a too vivid sense of what is going to happen next.

Besides my friend Ajax, I was warmly occupied with some pigeons that I kept in a small old barn behind the church. They were "fancy" pigeons—pouters, nuns, jacobins, etc.—but I never liked that word, and did not regard myself as a "pigeon fancier." I loved them more than that! I used to climb into the loft and sit for hours peering into their home, watching their impetuous goings and comings and their eager romances, all concerned like ours with either love or precedence. I learned from them that the main question in social relations is not who is actually the stronger—that may never be decided—but who gets the psychological drop on the others. Each individual has two instinctive attitudes, dominance and submission, and it is often settled by chance, or by bluffing, which will function in a given relation.

In this absorbing enterprise I had the companionship of Rodney Day and Bob York, and their real friendship. They were the first boys of my own age that I ever felt close to, and they share altogether—I can hardly say more—the warmth in memory that is enjoyed by my red jacobins: Rodney with his big blue eyes and round wondering expression like a blond owl, and Bob, clear-eyed and curly-headed as a cherub, but tall and lank and with a funny springy walk instead of wings. If I met them today I would experience just such an unbalancing billow of tender emotion as I did not long ago at the Danbury Fair when in a sudden childish frenzy I bought a half-dozen of my most adored breeds of pigeons and put them up in the loft over my study where they bothered me no end with their little pattering feet and all-day cooing.

In 1896, when almost fourteen, I entered high school. If you will recall that my brother had *graduated* from high school at *thirteen*, you will realize that the family were not watching my progress as one watches a meteor in the midnight sky. In a letter of 1897 my mother exclaims: "Max stood 94½ in Algebra, counting exams and class standing. Isn't that fine!"

It was indeed fine, for I did not enjoy algebra, and it shows that I had finally grasped the idea of doing hard work with a book. The following year I stood 100 in the state regents' examination in geometry. I did that without effort or intention, for geometry was the air my mind naturally breathed. I also stood 100 in United States history, but that I well knew was a fluke. History consists mainly of describing the Battle of Gettysburg, and there can be no such thing as 100 percent in describing anything.

Those two high marks did not awaken me to egotism or give me a twinge of intellectual ambition. They only meant that I belonged to the same family as my big brother. If any prouder thought arose, there was always somebody in the immediate vicinity to quash it. Right across the aisle from me at the Elmira Free Academy sat Ross Marvin, a mathematician and mechanical prodigy with a harelip, who subsequently accompanied Lieutenant Peary on the North Pole expedition and got lost on an ice floe—the world news of the moment. Ross used to work out intricate problems in higher mathematics, higher at least than I could reach, and hand them across the aisle for my inspection. Right in front of me sat Frank Easton, another "genius," who could draw pictures of people in any pose and make their eyes look in the right direction. I never saw anybody with a gift like that before, and I treasured almost worshipfully the little drawings Frank would drop back over his shoulder when we were supposed to be studying. I tried to imitate them, and did learn how to make eyes look frontways in a profile and a few other simple facts about perspective. But they remained mental facts to me; they never came down and lived in my fingers as they did in his. I was acutely aware of this inferiority and found here another strong reason to regard myself as a second-rater.

My esteem for Frank was not injudicious, for one Sunday in 1928 I picked up the *New York Times* and saw the reproduction of a landscape by one Frank L. Easton of Denver, Colorado, which had been awarded the first prize in the Associated Amateur Art Clubs exhibit in Chicago. He had become a commercial traveler and lived a long hard push of a life, yet could not quite abandon this gift, which did really almost amount to genius.

Frank and I became devoted and rather lonely friends. He was the son of a physician out on Lake Street—not one of the prominent physicians. Frank was short and had very short legs; but he had clear-cut Greek-statue features upon which sat a sternly belligerent expression, and above which he wore, parted in the middle, a tower of fluffy soft brown hair. Not many liked him. His fluffy hair and haughtiness, the one feminine, the other all too masculine, were appraised in the swift and heartless manner of youth with a simple *thumbs down*. I was keenly aware of this, especially after I diffidently one day proposed him for membership in Jean Clemens' Humane Society. The society was not too humane to blackball Frank with one loud groan, and the resulting problem of loyalty was a sharp one for me. I recognized a validity in those groans. Frank's haughtiness sat as inappropriately on his short legs as his high piled-up hair. With such qualities he could never aspire, as I just barely could, to climb among the "best people."

Nevertheless, I liked Frank Easton. He was, inside these poses, simple, honest, thoughtful, pleasure-loving, and imaginative. His gift of drawing seemed to me more distinguished than anything to be found among the chosen young ladies and gentlemen of the Humane Society, or the Misses Weal's dancing school, or the occasional dancing parties with refreshments. I longed to be at ease in these places; I wanted to "belong." But I was not at ease and did not belong—except in that rather shamefaced *ex officio* manner in which the minister's family rings in on everything. Of all this I was painfully conscious, and there was a tinge of the virtue of necessity in my adhering to Frank Easton. On the other hand, I love ability far better than social polish. I also, in my inner life or life within the family—so largely dominated as it was by spiritual rebels like my mother and Mr. Beecher—felt a certain contempt for dancing-party standards. When my mother said, anent that awful little vesty suit of mine, "It is not what you wear, but what you are that matters," although I think now that she was putting me to a dreadful and too early test, there was in me a chord that genuinely responded.

I was, as you see, keenly aware of the caste distinctions in Elmira and the peculiar relation to them which resulted from my social timidity. I went to the dancing school of the Misses Weal in an upstairs hall just off Baldwin Street, and afterward to that of Miss Curtis on East Church, and there I met and mingled with the children of the "upper bourgeoisie." In these meetings and minglings my shyness was in full force, and I never got anywhere with anybody, boy or girl. I mean I never formed a real comradeship or gave my heart to a romance. I liked Gretchen Fassett better than any other girl in Elmira, but she was too *momentous* for me. Her family were the richest in town, her mother a Crocker of San Francisco, her father a Congressman and a suave and easeful orator, who had run for governor of the state. If I had been of normal poise and confidence, I would have fallen in love with Gretchen. I would have fallen in love with her then, I mean, instead of now when I am only looking back and remembering how beautiful and strongly kind she was, and how she loved to laugh. But in order to fall in love with a girl you have at least to put your arm around her, and I could not even imagine coming close enough to Gretchen for that. She lived in a castle out on West Hill, and I was a serf down in the town below.

On the other hand, when Frank Easton introduced me to Mabel Utley, the comely daughter of a locomotive engineer, who lived out near the railroad yards, I was brave enough to think of her as "my girl," and go and call on her of an evening. I can not say that I ever put my arm around Mabel—that would be boasting—but I do remember sitting beside her on a very narrow piano stool while she played "Drink to Me Only," and exulting, whether more in her warmth or my boldness, I can not tell. The combination was intoxicating.

I was also enamored all one winter of Marian Freeman's wasplike waist, and I used to walk home from high school behind her, yearning over its contours and wishing vainly that I could hasten my steps a little and catch up and say casually: "Hello, Marian, are you going my way?" But I could not do it. If Marian had died from that tight lacing, as in nature's justice she might well have done, it would have been in vain, so far as I, its stricken victim, was concerned. I never spoke to her. I never gave her the reward she earned.

It was my morning chore to go down into the cellar and send up skuttles of coal on a dumb-waiter and empty the ashes from the five or six stoves that heated our "church home," as mother bravely called those two corridors of rooms. My father conducted the upstairs end of his operation, and I was very far away downstairs. That church cellar was a vast cavernous region, a whole block long with hide-outs for an active army of robbers and goblins, and I was often afraid to go down there. I had ways of placing myself in relation to its dark arches which would prevent any creature from unexpectedly jumping on my back while I was shoveling the coal. This I never spoke of in my life.

One evening Anstice and I were drawing pictures of my mother. Mine was the better likeness, and mother must have made some jest about my becoming a great artist, for Anstice said:

"I certainly wouldn't want to be a great man."

I cried out against him: "How can you possibly say such a thing? Why should you be at all, if you don't want to be great?"

He was rather overwhelmed by my ardor, and said: "Well, maybe it is just because I know I can't be. You go ahead. Perhaps you can!"

I had then, at the age of fourteen, read three books, and they were all "Henty books": *In the Reign of Terror, A Young Carthaginian,* and *With Lee in Virginia.* I adored Hannibal, whom I proudly asserted was "the greatest general in history," although inwardly I wondered what a general's greatness really consists of, since he doesn't fight anybody. I still wonder a little about that. Those Henty books probably influenced my formation as much as anything in literature, awakening me to a sense of history and the excitement of being in it. On the other hand, the habit of hero worship nourished by them probably retarded my slow ascent to manhood. While crossing the Alps with Hannibal, I had no pressing need to play hockey with a gang of boys on the Chemung River. And I never did play hockey, although I could skate as fast as they. I stood aside from the rough games of boys as though I were a girl. To put it more accurately, I was pushed aside by a social process with which I could not cope. I would gladly have played those games, and not minded getting hurt, but nobody seemed to believe in my adequacy for it, and I the least of all.

My brother, by contrast, was an accomplished daredevil. He belonged to a gang of four who were pretty constantly occupied with eluding the police. They stopped all the town's trolley cars one day by throwing a wire over the cable in front of the church. They entered at midnight the vacated house of a banker and went over his papers looking for rare stamps. They also entered a fine barn belonging to J. Sloat Fassett, searched his old papers for the same purpose, and helped themselves to some bottles of his imported wine. My brother broke into the tool house of the stone quarry on East Hill, and under the nose of the watchman removed, with the help of lighted matches, eighteen one-pound sticks of dynamite and four or five boxes of fuse. He also took two kegs of blasting powder and rolled them down hill to the river. With these materials he and his three pals spent the small hours of the next night trying to blow up the monument to General Sullivan on a hill out south of the city. They did, in fact, loosen its foundations and blow enough holes in it so that in due course the general got a new monument.

My brother loved my companionship and notwithstanding my exaggerated moralism was forever tempted to let me in on his mischief. He took me down in the church cellar one day and showed me a bottle of whisky concealed under a pile of boards. I was horrified, for "strong drink" was essential sin in my mind, almost as bad as fornication. I threatened to "tell on him," and indeed thought for a time it would be my duty to my ideals to do so. What he may have said in dissuasion is gone from memory, but I remember my choice, a somewhat trembling choice, of sinful loyalty as better on the whole than traitorous virtue.

I had by that time my own lapses into concupiscence, and was, thank God, too clearheaded to play the saint. They mostly concerned a comely girl named Audrey Croons, an orphan whom my mother had adopted into our house and undertaken to educate. In the course of our inventive play together it became necessary for Audrey and me to devise punishments for each other. She would punish me by locking me in my room, and I would punish her by pinching her legs. I pinched them exceedingly high up one evening when we were left alone, In my excitement I pinched them also hard enough to hurt, and she became angry. I was tortured for months by the question whether she was angered because I hurt her or because I touched her too close. But I lacked the force of character—tantalizing as that unresolved question remains—to find out. There came into play that combination of extreme shyness with a morbid concern about being good, the one falling in where the other failed, which kept me in a state of demivirginism to a wastefully advanced age.

We had a hired girl in the church named Rose McLernan, a generously moulded, friendly-hearted Irish girl, possessed of blue-grey eyes and dusky hair. I loved her far better than I did Audrey, or indeed for a long time anybody else in the world. Because of her beauty I loved her with lyric exaltation, but because of her daily and nightly proximity I loved her also with erotic thirst. We often slept alone in the upper corridor of rooms, at one end of which a flight of steps led up to the Romp Room of the church. Beside that entrance was a narrow storage closet illumined by a tiny window that looked down into Rose's bedroom almost from the ceiling.

The closet was never used, and there was no curtain on that window. It offered a discreet yet heavenly view of Rose removing her warmed garments one by one and putting on her cool nightgown before crawling into bed. I am not romancing when I say that this was a ravishing sight, for even my mother's letters from those days speak of Rose's wondrous grace and beauty. Although I thought about it nightly and half the day long for months, I never ensconced myself in that closet and watched the lovely Rose undress. When courage was adequate, conscience would be too strong; when conscience was lulled, I lacked the courage. Whatever may be the mature and moral judgment upon this miserable anticlimax, I do not know. I confess myself too filled with a passion of regret to have any judgment about it.

Chapter 16

The Church I Lived In

WHILE asking some pity as a boy who lived in a church, I must add that that church formed the center of a fruitfully exciting cluster of people and ideas. They happened to be the same people and ideas that Mark Twain had absorbed into himself by marriage twenty-five years before. His wife's family, the Langdons, lived just across the street from the church, and they were not only the central pillars but the foundation stones upon which it had been built. The portrait of Olivia Clemens' mother still hangs over the fireplace in the church parlors, and the memory of her father is one with the church's memory.

Ida Langdon, Olivia's niece, was an adored friend of our family and my sister's boon companion for years. I met Mark Twain himself in the pews of the Park Church and heard him make a speech from my mother's pulpit. Mrs. Clemens' sister, Susan Crane, who lived on Quarry Farm where Mark Twain wrote *Tom Sawyer*, decorated the pulpit with flowers every Sunday morning for half a century; she was one of the people whom my mother loved best. My mother, with Mr. Beecher, officiated at the lonely funeral of Mark Twain's beloved daughter, Suzie, in 1896. My father offered the prayer at the burial of Mark Twain's wife. And when Mark Twain himself died, it was again my father, reading a manuscript which my mother had written for him, who officiated at the funeral. All these facts made that great radical democrat and infidel a considerable influence in my life. But still more significantly I was influenced by those extraordinary "Park Church people" who played so strong a role in moulding him.[1]

Chief among them, of course, was the pastor and creator of the

[1] In an essay called "Mark Twain's Elmira" (*Heroes I Have Known*, p. 105), I went more deeply into this.

church, Thomas K. Beecher, who to begin with did not call himself a minister of the gospel. He called himself "Teacher of the Park Church," and a whole rebel character and thought of life lay behind that choice. His thought was to live and be helpful in the community as a modern Jesus would, a downright, realistic, iconoclastic, life-loving Jesus, with a scientific training, a sense of humor, and a fund of common sense. He was, in fact, a very eloquent preacher, more eloquent to a lucid listener than his famous brother, Henry Ward. But unlike Henry, he did not believe in preaching. When invited to the Park Church in 1854, he replied with a letter laying down in most imperious terms the conditions on which he would serve.

"Do you remember that I do not think good can be done by a preacher's preaching? It must be by Christians working that good is done, if at all. . . . Do you remember this, yes or no?"

One Sunday Thomas substituted for Henry in his famous Plymouth Church, and when he rose in the pulpit a good number of the vast audience got up to go. He stopped them with his hand.

"Those," he said, "who came here to worship Henry Ward Beecher are excused. Those who wish to worship God will remain."

The man was masterful, humorous, poised upon himself although impetuous, and endowed with a supreme contempt for fame, money, and "success." He declined calls to our greatest metropolitan churches because he had "found love" in Elmira and created there a church in his own free-moving and magnanimous image. His first announcement from the pulpit—in 1854—had been this:

"I cannot make pastoral calls. I am not constructed so that I can. But I am yours all times of the day and night when you want anything of me. If you are sick and need a watcher, I will watch with you. If you are poor and need someone to saw wood for you, I will saw wood for you. I can read the paper for you if you need somebody to do that. I am yours, but you must call me the same as you would a physician."

Adhering to that program Mr. Beecher became as much a man-of-all-work as a pastor to his congregation. He was a thoroughly trained mechanic and locomotive engineer, able to build a house and handle and repair anything from a ship to a railroad train, and he served his parishioners as carpenter, painter, paper hanger, clock and sewing-machine mender. For forty years he wound and set the Elmira town clock, keeping it in pace with the sun by means of observations made with his own instruments on East Hill halfway up to Quarry Farm. He preached no doctrine but the fatherhood of God and brotherhood of man, and he walked about Elmira in ordinary and usually very old clothes like a workman, carrying when necessary a sewing machine or even a sofa on his back.

Mr. Beecher was not only a man of all work; he was a man of all play. He was a skilled bowler and cricket player; he joined a whist club and organized a baseball team called the Lively Turtles, which scandalized the churchmen by not even taking baseball seriously. He sang college songs and played them on the church organ. He attended theaters, and played pool and billiards, and even had a pool table in the church parlors. Although the original charter of his church declared for the "unfermented juice of the grape" in communions and affirmed that "no intoxicating liquors shall be used by the members," he strolled into a saloon when he felt like it and took a glass of beer. In fact, he made this a permanent revolution by installing his own private mug in a favorite saloon as others did in barber shops.

* He ran a weekly column in the local paper—a pioneer in this field, too—joining the politicians' battles with a sword of truth that slashed both ways, and like an early Christian Walter Winchell, naming those who scandalized him by their proper names. The prohibitionists scandalized him with their strait-laced lies. Remarking that this country is "too sunshiny and roomy" for all that rant, he took his public stand behind the liquor dealers. Still better, when he changed his mind on this in after years, he said that too. The extreme to which he dared to follow his conception of a Christian life is revealed in his befriending a notorious prostitute, whom he finally, to the horror of his neighbors, took into his house and treated as a daughter until she gained her poise and married and went away.

It is needless to describe the raw hate aroused by these consummate blasphemies among the surrounding Apostles of Christ Jesus. Beecher and his church were regarded as a moral ulcer eating up the harvest of the gospel throughout the whole Chemung and Susequehanna valleys. When his Sunday evening meetings grew too big for the old meeting house, and he crowned his sins by hiring the local theater, actually inviting in vast crowds to offer prayers to God in that Satanic edifice, the storm broke from all sides on this "Opera House preacher." He was expelled from the Ministerial Union and denounced from every pulpit in the city. He made no public answer to the fulminations of the ministers, but embarrassed them in private with an extra-Christlike courtesy.

Jervis Langdon stood behind him like a rock. "My purse is open to you," he had said, "you can do more good with it than I can." And he now headed a movement to buy shares in the Opera House to insure the future of this outrage. Mark Twain himself stood by him—not the Mark Twain you know, but just a well-known wit and travel writer who had married into the Langdon family. "Happy, happy world," he wrote in the *Elmira Advertiser*, "that knows at last that a little congress of congregationless clergymen, of whom it never heard before, have crushed a famous Beecher and reduced his audiences from 1500 down to 1475 in one fell blow!"

Far deeper than these evidences of realistic good sense, two things distinguished Thomas K. Beecher from all other great American ministers. First, he was a man of science. Together with Professor Farrar of Elmira College, he founded an Elmira Academy of Sciences, which corresponded with the Royal Academy in London— with Tyndall, Darwin, Huxley.

The other thing which distinguished Mr. Beecher from all other men in the annals of our pulpit was the scope of his magnanimity, his absolute rejection of all sectarianism whatsoever. He not only invited men of all denominations to become members of his church; he invited the members of his church to leave for no matter what trivial reasons of convenience and go and join some other. In his book *Our Seven Churches* religious tolerance, a rare substance in any solution, is presented in pure essence. It is, so far as my knowledge goes, a unique book, a book similar in spirit as well as in the date upon its flyleaf to Walt Whitman's world-embracing mystic vision, a book that dropped unnoticed into an age absolutely deaf to so lofty and magnanimous an evangel.

It is inadequate to say, although I believe it is true, that the Park Church was the first "institutional church" in the country. It was a great deal more than that. Mr. Beecher himself called it a "home church," and tried to make it a place where Christians of all creeds, or no creed, would feel that they "belonged" as a man belongs at his own fireside. The church had a kitchen equipped with china and silver for two or three hundred, "parlors" available to any who wished to use them, a free public library, pool and billiard tables, a dancing hall and children's Romp Room with a stage and the complete fittings of a theater. All this in 1873! There would be a "picnic supper" every week and a "pay supper" every month.

Every fourth Sunday would be Children's Sunday, and the grown-up folks could stay at home or come and hear a "children's sermon." The rest of the month the Sunday School would meet in the main auditorium following the morning service, and after a preliminary exercise in common, the children would march to gay music on the organ to their separate rooms and places of assembly. Mrs. Beecher remembered a Sunday back in the seventies when they marched to the tune of "Captain Jinx of the Horse Marines," and I remember a day when our eccentric organist, George B. Carter, sent us skipping with a medley composed of "Onward Christian Soldiers" and "There'll Be a Hot Time in the Old Town Tonight." Some shook their heads and smiled, but there was no indignant gossip; nobody was disturbed.

A humorous informalness, a being at ease with your play instincts, was characteristic of all the Beechers—even austere old Lyman having been a brilliant performer of the double shuffle. It was equally characteristic of Mrs. Beecher, a granddaughter of Noah Webster—"my strong, courageous, energetic Julia," as her husband called her. Her vigorous whims and impulses of geniality and dynamic common sense were uncontrollable by any feeling except the fear that she might really hurt somebody's feelings. She and my mother were the closest of friends, their friendship consisting largely of a voyage together, in the company of Emerson and William Morris and Walt Whitman, beyond the confines of churchly ethics and religion. I cherish the image of her sitting by my mother's hammock beside a brook, reading aloud, with an expression of grim and yet joyful determination in her gentle features, the Calamus poems in Walt Whitman's *Song of Myself*.

When I think of Mrs. Beecher, I see always the sweet and faithful firmness of the closure of her lips. And as I look she jumps suddenly up to be on her way in endless labors for the suffering, sick, and ignorant with brisk and selfless energy. An admirer once said to her: "I love to see you pour coffee, because you do it with such indiscriminate fury!" With the same indiscriminate fury she would gather up the dishes after a meal, scrape them, and pile them to save labor for someone in the kitchen. "Your plate!" she would exclaim suddenly, stretching out a commanding arm to the astonished guest.

Mrs. Beecher was quite as headstrong as her husband in smashing through forms and conventions, and her rebellion was not only moral but aesthetic. She bobbed her hair in 1857, anticipating Irene Castle by about sixty years, and imparting to her beauty a quality as startling to her neighbors as though a cherub had alighted in their city.

She invented, one day when she was darning an old stocking, a species of rag doll which became celebrated for its plump and genial superiority to circumstance, and by turning herself into a factory for these "Beecher dolls," kept a lifelong stream of money pouring from her hands to charity. She made sculptures, too, and comic drawings, and queer birds and beasts out of roots, grotesque things that Mark Twain called "jabberwoks." These, too, she would auction off for charity, and on one occasion Mark Twain functioned as the auctioneer. He wrote her:

"My dear Mrs. Beecher:

"I have arranged your jabberwoks and other devils in procession according to number and rank on the piano in the drawing room, and in that subdued light they take to themselves added atrocities of form and expression and so make a body's flesh crawl with pleasure.

"If I come down at midnight (with my usual dose of hot Scotch stowed) I shall very well be able to imagine I see them climbing about the furniture bearing their rigid tails high and inspecting everything with their calm, critical brass eyes."

When I met Mark Twain in the Park Church, a new organ was being installed. There was hardly anybody there but organists and Langdons and Mark Twain and the pastor's family. I was astonished at the princely grace of his greeting when my mother introduced me. I might have been the Lord Mayor instead of a scared kid. My admiration for the man was, and still is, as firm and emotional as though he were the saint of a faith to which I adhere. And in a sense he is, for I do give to humorous intelligence a place in life not unlike that which believing people give to religion.

It has been assumed by Mark Twain's biographers that the influence of his Elmira wife and her family was in all ways a reactionary one. The error has its source in the official biographer, Albert Bigelow Paine, who says: "She sensed his heresy toward the conventions and forms which had been her gospel. . . . She suspected that he might even have unorthodox views about religion."

Olivia's gospel, in so far as she learned it from the church in which her mother and father were the central social and financial force, was one of self-reliant revolt against forms and conventions as such.

She was, undoubtedly, a refining influence, and perhaps a little too refining. I myself, much as I admired and loved her family, was always a little frightened by their refinement. I was tongue-tied and troubled by the discovery that I had hands and feet whenever I entered the serene door of the stately brown mansion where they lived. Clara Clemens has described the "confusion of greetings and exclamations of delight from old and young" when her family would arrive for a visit in that mansion. I find it difficult to imagine confusion there, and I am sure that within its precincts I never summoned up anything so disturbing to the atmosphere as an exclamation. "The hall and spacious living room," Clara says, "were rather dark, which added to their interest and general personality . . . and the wide mahogany staircase belonged in an eventful romance." I, of course, was afraid of the dark, and a wide mahogany staircase could put me in my place about as quickly as anything short of a direct command. So I think it might be well to add my memory and Clara's together and divide by two. Even then you will find the Langdons, and especially the women folk, distinguished so exactly by "refinement," that the contrast between them and the Mark Twain whom the wayward Charlie brought among them in 1867 must have been indeed abrupt and startling.

On the other hand, my extreme timor, and a resulting sensitivity to qualities as well as quantities of social elevation, enables me to testify that the Langdons occupied a somewhat special position in Elmira society. There were richer families there, with staircases which frightened me quite as badly, but most of them were a little raw and conscious of themselves by comparison. Olivia's family were less like an "upper bourgeoisie" than a nobility in Elmira. Their elevation seemed deep and old and spiritual and infinitely removed from snobbishness. They were at once princely and democratic. And so far as concerns social and political attitudes, they were far more "radical" than Mark Twain was when he met them. Mark Twain married in 1870, and the best proof of the liberating influence of the new environment is contained in what he himself said, twenty years later, speaking of what a man learns "while he sleeps":

When I finished Carlyle's *French Revolution* in 1871, I was a Girondin; every time I have read it since, I have read it differently—being influenced and changed, little by little, by life and environment (and Taine and St. Simon) and now I lay the book down once more, and recognize that I am a Sansculotte!—And not a pale, characterless Sansculotte, but a Marat. Carlyle teaches no such gospel; so the change is in *me*—in my vision of the evidences.

Had Mark Twain set out to prove that the unconscious influence of the Park Church circle upon his social outlook had been a liberal and almost a revolutionary one, he could hardly have penned a better argument.

Not only is Olivia slandered by the myth which has been built up to the contrary, but Elmira also, and in general "those upstate towns." They were occupied by some of the finest families in the post-revolutionary American aristocracy, an aristocracy which, deprived of titles and not yet debauched by industrial profits, rested its superiority feelings far more than most dominant classes do upon intellectual culture and genuine moral elevation. Being in political faith "democratic," this aristocracy was hospitable to intellect and talent no matter where they arose. It cherished great literature; it valued bold and iconoclastic thinking. It had much of New England's spirituality, little of its tight-mindedness.

I could write a volume, if I were not so bent on the progress of this book, about the grand people and families, nobles in the true sense, who as friends of my father and mother stood in a relation of godfatherly spur and model to my development, helping to make it spacious. I have spoken of the Grangers in Canandaigua; I could write a chapter about Nanny Miller of Geneva and her innumerable friends, among them my mother and Susan B. Anthony. Her simple and beautiful Camp Fossenvue on the east shore of Seneca Lake was a point of focus for the highest culture of the time. Dr. Gannett, Unitarian poet-minister in Rochester, father of the literary critic Lewis Gannett, was another such focus. There were others in Ithaca, in Auburn, in Utica, in Syracuse, fine-minded and big-hearted friends, eager to welcome in gracious homes my radical mother-minister when she came to preach or lecture. They would come to see us too, and many a nobleman from farther away would pause for a day or a night in our house. (Most vividly I remember the mild, soft-spoken, unpretentious and yet princely manners of Booker T. Washington.) In Elmira I have spoken only of the Beechers, the Langdons and the Fassetts, but I could extend the list until I believe it would show that, in proportion to the total population, the number of highly developed, sensitive, progressive and thinking minds in that upstate town was larger than in the metropolis.

Here I can dwell only upon one who played a direct part in my development. That is Z. R. Brockway, the head of the Elmira Reformatory, memorable in criminology, genial, humane, and agnostic, a high-domed, white-bearded Socrates, who questioned everything and believed only in Reason. He was attacked by a newspaper scandal, one of the old New York *World's* atrocities, as a sadist who delighted in flogging and torturing the young convicts in his charge. In the midst of the nation-wide furor this mad accusation raised, and before any investigation had been made, New York's young governor, Theodore Roosevelt, came to Elmira to attend some celebration at the armory. The venerable head of the reformatory, a veteran of international repute in prison reform, wishing to present his defense to the governor, came up the armory steps to greet him.

"I have no time for you, Mr. Brockway," the governor said, without extending his hand.

As a result of this disgraceful episode I escaped any temptation to idolize Teddy Roosevelt. I also acquired an extraordinary friend. For upon his forced retirement Mr. Brockway moved down into a private house not far from where we lived, and I formed the habit of strolling over there for purely intellectual conversations with this acute and erudite old man. He told me I had a "profound and original mind," a thing I badly needed in those early days to be told.

Chapter 17

The Discovery of a Brain

IN THE summer of 1898 a deep-voiced Roman senatorial giant named William Mann Irvine, principal of Mercersburg Academy, invaded Elmira and took away seventeen young gentlemen from the public high schools. They were the cream of the town from a social, financial, or else athletic point of view, all dressed in exactly the right clothes and possessed of a celestial savoir faire. I went along on special terms as the minister's son. It was an all-day journey, for Mercersburg is on the southern edge of Pennsylvania, and I was gauche and speechless in that easy-mannered crowd. My mother had given me an extra quarter to spend on the way, and that made me feel wildly reckless. Indeed it conditioned me so that to this day I become a spendthrift the minute I go on a journey. But it did not help me find a friend among those elite and jocular young men. I had to pay now for my lonely and slightly déclassé comradeship with Frank Easton.

I do not know how much my timid sense of ineptitude and of not "belonging" was present to the minds of the other boys at Mercersburg. It is my rare good fortune that when chilled with diffidence, I freeze in an attitude suggesting disdain. I thus often appear when most inwardly abased to be a sublime prig, although I think there is not an atom in me even of the innocent ingredients of priggishness. I also do not know to what extent those other boys really possessed that social ease and confidence I saw in them. The one who impressed me most was Ned Graham. Ned was our nimble fielder, and had the sturdy, suavely masterful poses of the born athlete. Not long ago Ned came to see me, still sturdy, still suavely masterful in his poses, and represented himself as a great radio manager, and incidently a formidable tennis player. He got me one engagement as guest-author on the radio, but he could not get his racquet into the vicinity of my serve.

Another young lord, overwhelming to me mainly on account of his clothes and toilet articles, was Henry Radburne, who chanced to be my roommate. Henry and I lived together, it seemed to me, somewhat like a friendly gentleman officer and his equerry. I at least was acutely conscious of my inferior outfit and my poor-boy's ways. To save money, and also because my mother loved to care for me, I would send my laundry home by express to be washed; and that seemed astonishing to Henry, although he was not squeamish about enjoying the soft dark gingerbreads and chocolate cakes that mother would send back with the clean clothes every week. My brush and comb looked as though they had been found in the barn, and my best suit was a light tan which had been dyed black, but, being part cotton, had come home of an all-spice hue with hushed stripes like a hyena. A padded trunk cover that my mother made for me so that I could use my trunk as furniture, another poor man's custom, also embarrassed me, and my weekly allowance of ten cents for luxuries I studiously concealed. With my brother at Princeton and my sister and our cousin Adra in Granger Place School, the family income was so strained that a question of my mother's getting me shoestrings where she did not have to pay for them was twice urgently mentioned in our letters. That problem also, needless to say, was not imparted to my roommate. . . .

A year or so ago I spent the night at a hotel in Greenwich Village, and when I registered, the clerk looked up at me with a quizzical smile.

"Do you remember me?" he said.

"I'm sorry but I don't."

"We roomed together at Mercersburg."

Such incidents lead me to think that I had an exaggerated notion of the lofty status of these boy-gentlemen, their corporate consciousness, and my exclusion from it. Their serious interests I was not excluded from—they would come to me sometimes for help on a mathematical problem or a translation—but I was excluded from their jocularity. I lived among them like a person lacking humor, or too dumb to catch on to the nuances of their wit. And as happens to extremely diffident people, I half-believed—even while inwardly savoring and rather maturely judging their wit—that I was unable to catch on. There is always a slang word in boarding schools for the pupils who, because of some crude lack, are flatly not accepted by the group. In our day they were called "warts," and it seemed to me that I had practically all the warty attributes, including superior ability in the classroom and no ability that I cared to exhibit on the athletic field.

To make you know me, I must offset this glimpse of my external predicament with the vista of an inner life lived wholly above the problems of "indivious distinction," and sustained by my mother in letters as wise and strong and witty and tender as a boy has ever received.

"Do not go with the crowd to do evil," she wrote. "Conformity is beautiful until it requires a sacrifice of principle—then it is disfiguring."

"By this time you have received my letter with $2.00 which I hope relieves your financial embarrassment for the present. If you need more let me know. It wasn't a bit philosophic to be made sick and go to bed about money. Of course you must do your share of the essential things and we must manage it the best we can. I have several chances to lecture this fall which will add a few dollars for the 'extras.' . . . I want you to do your share in all right things. But, dear, I do want you to judge for *yourself* about all matters of behavior. My only fear is a thoughtless going with the crowd. Be an individual—nothing you can gain will make up for the loss of yourself."

"I hope you are not having too hard a time with your exams, and that you are not giving up to melancholy. Fight it hard—it is your deepest danger, and it makes me sad because it is my fatal gift to you."

"*Live out of yourself persistently.* Become interested in all that is going on in the world and train yourself to think about it. It's better to have your own thought, even if it's a mistaken one, than to be always repeating other people's better thoughts."

"I'm glad you like the piece I sent you for speaking. Speak out to the man farthest away and determine to make him *see* it. Make the picture vivid to yourself and it will be vivid to others, and don't be *afraid*. Fear is our greatest enemy. Just forget yourself in the thing you are saying, and try to feel how much greater it is than words can tell."

With such thoughts poured to me so lavishly by that racing pen, it was inevitable that I should, in my inward or thinking life, hold myself *above* those urgent issues of prowess and social prestige which loom so large to the American schoolboy. Externally, however, or in my everyday emotions, they loomed large to me. It was not only with ideal purpose and a natural attraction, but also with pangs of regret and of inferiority that I gravitated toward that group in the school who, instead of athletics and the state of worldly grace —under which term I mean to include toilet articles, clothes, spending money, social ease and humor, loafing gracefully in pool rooms, familiar talk about sex and defecation, and all the rest that goes to make up a boy-of-the-world—chose mental development for their goal. As high marks are rather looked down on by those possessing this grace, I was in certain moods ashamed of my best gifts, ashamed of being a "highbrow"—a peculiarly American state of consciousness which often impedes my speech to this day. However, having resigned myself to the secondary sport of classroom competition, I went in for it with race-horse concentration.

Of course, to acquire knowledge in any field was and still is to me a sustained delight. Although I retain some of my childish impatience about "reading," I really love to study. I can take a textbook on any subject, any time, and all I ask besides is a couch or a comfortable chair, and I can disappear happily for days on end. To this motive was added the pleasure of delighting my mother and father and my whole family by getting high marks. That was a new role for the backward kid brother. Nevertheless, I had no noble purpose and no large ambition. I wrote my mother to "send me all the pictures of eminent men" she could find, and I had my room well-nigh papered with heroes, but I was humble enough in my own outlook to think for a long time that I would become a professor of Greek. The main force lifting me to those high marks was a narrow spirit of competition. I went in for the studious life because I could find no other avenue of local success and distinction.

It all began with my going upstairs to study Greek with "Reuben" Reed. Reuben was a big, lumbering, half-Irish, redheaded rustic— infinitely good-natured and surprisingly strong like a St. Bernard pup. He became a Presbyterian minister—moderator, I see, of the Ohio Presbytery of the Presbyterian Church—so I should call him Robert Rush Reed. He too enjoyed a contest, and we used to make a competitive game of learning the paradigms. I soon discovered that I could learn faster and remember longer than he, though his name had been spoken in Elmira as a boy-wonder destined to be the leader of our class. The discovery set me off on a chase of glory, timed to perfection for the distention of my growing brain cells.

I studied all day long and all evening, and as I have an exorbitant sense of orderly perfection, this resulted in my gathering in every last hanging shred of information relating to each day's lesson and being almost literally perfect in every subject. I used to know by heart both in Latin and English the passages from Cicero or Virgil which we translated, and I can remember lying on my bed without a book expounding the day's lesson to a group of those Elmira boys, who had been too late or lazy to study it themselves. It was balm to my inferiority complex to see their amazement when I would "construe" some horrendous sentence without looking at the book. But I would gladly have exchanged my precious gifts of memory and understanding for that single trait of theirs—again I am puzzled what to call it—of being "on," *au fait,* or "in the swim." It was, and still is, closely associated in my mind with the gift of wit and humor. To have made one remark that would have been greeted by those boys with an uproarious laugh would have been worth all their alien admiration for my "brains."

My rise as a student, once I got started, was very rapid. I entered Mercersburg in the fall of 1898 with no particular hopes pinned on me. My report for December of that year showed a general average of 92. By March I had Reed's place at the head of the class with a general average of 97. By December of the following year I was written up in the local paper: "During the school term just closed Mr. Eastman made the highest grade for scholarship ever known at Mercersburg." At the end of the next year the principal wrote home to my father: "You are to be congratulated. Max's grade of 99 plus is the best ever made in the school. *Max must go to Princeton.* It would be a calamity to send this boy away from Princeton."

I was disappointed in my marks. I wanted to stand 100 in everything. I wanted to make a record mathematically impossible to beat. Short of that I could not enjoy a moment of complacence—Milton or Isaac Newton might have done better! All it takes to keep you humble is *enough* egotism.

I must add that this ego tension soon and often grows tiresome to me; it is egregious but ill-sustained. Even in those exciting days when I discovered my mental ability, something else emerged in my heart that seemed quite as momentous. It was, indeed, more momentous, if growing toward life's full enjoyment was the business in hand. It was born in a friendship I made with another minister's son, a gentle, quiet, deferential, almost wistful boy in my remembrance, who entered from Maryland during my senior year. His name was Bill Seabrook. Bill and I chimed in a mood of rebellion against what was being put over on us by the school authorities and the YMCA, as well as the athletes and well-dressed young gentlemen who set the social tone of the school. The slogan of our rebellion as near as I can name it, was the Adventurous Life. We agreed that almost everybody in the institution was through habit about half dead, and that in general most people in this world miss their chance to live. We went in for busting out of the rut and having sensations.

Our friendship did not last very long, and I can not remember anything more adventurous we did than to sneak up the valley one midnight, steal a chicken from a farmer's coop, and roast and eat it out there in the small hours. The record of our friendship, however, and of its mood and motive, was indelibly stamped upon us both. For in our thirst after the raw taste of being, we got around to the question of torture and fell to wondering what it would be like to be branded. Bill had a scarfpin in the form of a crescent with a dagger through it, and we heated that in the flame of his lamp. The crescent and dagger fell apart, but we took up each one separately between scissors points, heated it white hot, and dropping it on the flesh of our left hand between the thumb and forefinger, pressed it in with the butt end of the scissors.

The last thing I remember of that early friendship, after the smell of fried meat, was our furtive meetings on the campus to compare the progress of two great running sores. Bill has since distinguished himself, aside from his adventurous books, by frank avowals of an erotic interest in pain and cruelty. I have no such specific interest. I was moved by a general thirst of life's experience, and a premonition that, if I was to drink the full cup of it, I must have fortitude.

I said awhile back, discussing my shyness, that the exploding into social expression of my rather maturely humorous inward life was momentous in my history. It occurred on the occasion of my graduation from Mercersburg, and it changed my whole career. I made, of course, the valedictory oration, and I took for my subject—of course—"Unrewarded Heroism." I do not remember what I said, but I said it with a throbbing voice and, according to my own judgment after I sat down, too much unction. But besides that I had been elected, far from unanimously and rather out of respect to my high marks, to a place on the Class Day program. I was the class prophet, and my function was to predict in telling gibes what each member of the class would probably turn out to be. As I had had the whole spring to prepare myself, this gave me a rare chance to uncover that humorous sophistication which my shyness had concealed. I do not mean that I realized this in advance. I was surprised and absolutely swept off my feet by the roars of laughter and almost unintermittent applause which greeted my Class Prophecy. It was the success of the week, and a success in exactly that field in which I had regarded myself as a hopeless dud. Nothing in my life has ever exceeded the joy of that occcasion. All my intellectual achievements, my perfect examination papers, my so well self-criticized oratory, dwindled to nothing. I felt that I was a boy among boys, and would be a man among men, and I cared about nothing else in the world.

Chapter 18

A Taste of Princeton

THE reason I did not go to Princeton was that Mrs. F. F. Thompson, my father's rich parishioner in Canandaigua, offered me a scholarship at Williams. These Thompson scholarships pay the board and tuition of promising poor boys— promising in more than one sense, for they have to sign a paper stating that when they get out into the world and make money, they will hand on the gift to another boy. I do not know how well that works in most cases. I never made any money or intended to, and perhaps for that reason very soon forgot the promise.

I was desperately disappointed when the news came that I was not going to Princeton. I had never heard of Williams, and my brother had already filled me full of "Princeton spirit," having won the Freshman quarter mile down there and being of that nature which prodigiously enjoys "belonging." I dreamed, the night the bad news came, that I had a vivid orange-and-black flag on my wall and came home and found that somebody had stuck up a muddy rag in its place. I told my mother this dream, but also told her that I recognized the financial necessity of accepting the scholarship. We can not know in advance—I added—whether it would prove better for me to go to Williams or Princeton. The difference might be that if I went to Princeton, a brick would fall off a roof and kill me, and if I went to Williams, it wouldn't. My mother loved these "philosophical" remarks of mine, and her answer is characteristic:

"I hope you'll let me come and live with you when I'm old. I know I shall like it best at your house. It will probably be a lovely rambling old house on some beautiful college campus with elm trees full of birds right outside the windows. I have had a very bad time since I wrote to you, for Papa said I ought not to have told you about the Williams offer—that you are working so hard and it would make you sick, etc. . . . I'm almost afraid to go to sleep lest I shall see orange-and-black flags weeping and dirty-colored Williams flags drearily flopping in the breeze!"

As compensation for my good nature, I was allowed to visit my brother in Princeton after my graduation and great awakening in June. I thought I would express my new-found manhood by loafing companionably among his classmates, breathing at ease the "Princeton spirit." I found myself more tongue-tied and abashed than ever. My remarks were an intrusion from the side lines, and with all my art I could not get them into the game. It is one thing to prepare and deliver a humorous speech, to act the part of a sophisticated person; it is a different thing to be one.

I hope the reader knows what I am talking about. It was the struggle of an outsider to get into the human race. My good points stood as much in the way as my bad. My too logical brain, with its queer tendency toward generalized thinking, my extreme sensitivity, my squeamishness about smutty language, troubled me as much as my timidity, self-consciousness, and everlasting worry about being good. An inferiority feeling attached to them all, and I was ready for heroic measures of emancipation. Under influence of the "Princeton spirit" I took my first gulp of spirituous liquor, which I found very hard to stomach, and I chased a lady of easy virtue into the bushes behind the Presbyterian church—where also I was unable to prove myself a man. I was unable, in those crude circumstances, even to desire to. I suppose all imaginative boys, if their erotic life is lived too long in daydreams, have some trouble achieving a "transference" to reality. The first shock of the palpable naked flesh of a woman's body chills instead of exciting them. In me this poetic impotence, if I may so describe it, was reinforced by an overwhelming bashful reticence which stood like a wall between me and the downright act, or even the explicit mention, of sexual union. It closed against me, to my good fortune, that puerile initiation into physical love which for so many gives it a tint of bawdiness never to be washed off.

Lust does not seem to me an evil thing when it is mutual and overmastering. It is taking sex relations in a cheap, flip, facetious, and vulgar fashion that offends my sense of virtue. This seems to me a sacrilege against life's true enjoyment. If the highest point of bliss is flattened, the whole temple is deprived of grandeur. And that desperate concern about chastity which prevailed in Christian parents of my generation tends to beget, in boys at least, this attitude of sacrilege. Boys have often a passing disposition to mock at life and profane it, a mischievous mood that does not matter much or carry far. But when life's most intense and happy raptures are withheld from them as connatural with lying, cheating, cruelty, hypocrisy, perjury, and robbery and murder, they take their revenge by vulgarizing those raptures in a certain permanence. If we can not openly enter your Holy of Holies, they say to their elders, we can at least sneak in and spit upon the altar.

My brother took me down to the running track to show me where he had won the freshman quarter-mile, a victory which had loomed rather large in the pride of our family. We started trotting around the track, and our trot soon extended itself into a quarter-mile race, which to our mutual astonishment I won by several yards. That was an event of importance, which my brother related with generous delight the next morning and indeed never tired of relating throughout his life. It helped me along in what now seems a rather pathetic effort to escape, not only from inferiority feelings, but from my own nature.

My brother also took me to his class in political science to hear a professor whose lectures he said were becoming famous. The class filled a large churchlike auditorium, and the professor delivered his lecture downward from a high platform. I tried dutifully to be impressed, but found his diction too full of fluent abstractions to catch hold of my undeveloped mind. His name was Woodrow Wilson. I heard him several times thereafter, but no matter how much I developed my mind, his diction was always too full of fluent abstractions to catch a good hold of it.

Chapter 19

Cherith Farm

HROUGH all my early life the vital thing, the thing that seemed to *be* my life, was what I did in summer. My home was out-of-doors, and my true friends the wafted air and sunshine. As soon as the windows went shut in autumn and I found myself indoors with conversation and books, I began waiting—in the depth of my soul doing nothing else but waiting—for "next summer." A migratory bird trapped in the autumn just when his wings were lifting for the glad flight south would feel as I did when I had to case myself in fitting clothes and go to school.

Like all wise places of learning, the Park Church laid off for July and August, and the ministers packed up and moved away. As we children from early years were sent to boarding schools in winter, these holidays contained the substance of home life for us. We hardly nested in Elmira, we nested on the shores of lakes: at Sodus Bay, at Keuka, at Fir Tree Point, and then for many years at Glenora on Seneca Lake. In these happy summers I learned under my father's tutelage to dive, and row, and sail, and paddle a canoe. And in my mother's company I learned to call by name the trees and birds and wild flowers which I loved. This latter learning was desultory and did not "stand me in stead" on some memorable occasion, but it gave me joy. I think a great many people who go in for abundant living fail of the goal through not inviting their brain to participate. I can remebember lying all morning under the low shrubs in a glade above the "Fruit House" we lived in on Keuka Lake when I was twelve, watching a pair of catbirds, listening to their softly whispered "phut phut," and feeling akin to them because I knew their markings—particularly their "red rumps," for it had startled me to find that naughty word quite plainly printed in my book.

For the summer of '97 we rented a decaying pale-blue cottage on Fir Tree Point, thirty miles north of Elmira on Seneca Lake. I repainted the front wall, and as the cottage was backed by a wooded slope and flanked on both sides by lilac bushes, my hasty brushwork gave it a wholly slick exterior. An assemblage of furniture from the church cellar and the attics of parishioners, a patient and powerful scrubbing by Rose McLernan—down on her knees all day with willing arms and shoulders—a few new window panes and new curtains made it gay inside. Frank Easton and I took our pirate ship up there that spring, only a flat-bottomed Chemung River punt, but with a centerboard and a genuine mast and sail. I named it *Slim Jim,* and although not allowed to cross the lake, I navigated all the shores in every kind of wind. I fished and swam and fenced, and fought hopeless battles with my brother, and yearned vainly over Rose's ever rounder-swelling breasts. And I picked wagonloads of fruit. We always had to plod up the hill and hire out to the farmers when the fruit was ripe. For life on this planet consists very largely of work, and we were not to forget it!

With Rose's help I nursed old Ajax through his "panting spells" that summer, and left him when fall came, with philosophic thoughts and a great wish for tears, under the leafy mould on the slope behind the cottage. . . .

The next year my father discovered at Glenora, three miles north, a thirty-acre hillside farm which he bought from a tired farmer named Vince Eddington. An all-year laughing stream flowed past the house, and my mother named it Cherith Brook. For the next fourteen years, that sunny hillside was my real home. Although I was thirteen when we moved there, I think of it as my native heath.

Cherith Farm was made mostly of shale, and it tilted from the lake at an angle of about twenty-five degrees. The farmhouse stood some four hundred feet above shore level, and from that height as you look to the lake you see only treetops and the water, for through all that region a strip of young woods borders the shore, and the shore itself is a rock cliff twenty to thirty feet high. That grey cliff is darkened with overhanging oaks and hemlocks and painted all wet shades of green by thick turfy moss from which harebells and columbine and other thin-stemmed flowers spring out and hang down trembling over the lake, and from which in a moist season water drips musically and with answering gleams straight into the waves below. Seneca is not like other big lakes; it is a deep, clear spring that does not freeze in winter or grow weedy-warm in summer. It is so crystal clear that when you paddle a canoe along under that green, soaked, whispering cliff, the cliff goes right on down into the water and meets another sky in its depths. I always say to myself when returning to Glenora: "Remember it was your childhood home and can not possibly be so beautiful as you imagine." And I am always surprised to find it more beautiful than I imagine.

The lake is forty miles long and where we lived a mile and a half wide, a cleft between two far-spreading hills that wear a checked pattern of farm lands, diversified with glades and glens and a visible cataract tumbling toward the shore. From our house on the westward hill, we could see on the opposite horizon a whole county spread before us, sloping upward for a mile and stretching thirty miles to north and south—a simple landscape, in its lines almost austere, and for that reason enduring in its beauty as not all lake regions are.

Watkins Glen, nine miles south, is famous for its thrilling depth and grotesque rock formations. But Cherith Farm is made of the same rock, and the glen a half-mile walk from our back door, although less deep, is quite as lovely as Watkins Glen. Here, again, the forest trees overhang and shadow a grey moist ferny-smelling cliff, or two such cliffs so near together sometimes that the trees from each side mingle overhead and make a dark and dank Avernus forty feet below. At other times they spread out suddenly and let in great shafts of sunshine, heating the flat stone floors as hot as coals. A cool and never-failing stream, spring-born but with experience of meadows, sings through these chasms to the cataract above the lake, and on its way it makes two pools to swim in. The "round pool" is a carved tank of solid rock, a veritable "giant's bathtub," with ledges anywhere from three to thirty feet to dive from. The "square pool" is made gayer and more lightly musical by a spreading waterfall with a shelf across it where you take a shower, or hide behind the spray, or dive in with the foaming water.

Except for play, nothing is more important to the enjoyment of living than work. And I was lucky, I think, in those summers before my own ambition drove me to a desk to be employed with my brother as hired help on Cherith Farm. I did not always appreciate it then; indeed if we had not "laid off" every afternoon and gone over to the glen for a swim and a rendering of the Doxology to the reverberating cliffs, I do not know how I could have got through it at all. Unlike the other members of my family, I do not like hard physical work. I like to play hard and to work hard with my brains. In the intervals, my natural tendency is to hunt for a good place to lie down. Doctors tell me that my muscles lack tone, my nerves lack energy, my blood lacks adrenalin, my food lacks vitamins, my ego lacks integration, and I dare say all these things are true. I am, at any rate, by nature active only when excited, and what has saved me, it seems, from complete degeneration is that I happen to be easily excited by ideas.

I was indeed excited by the idea of doing farm work. I boasted to my sister in the spring of '98 that I was going to plow, and harrow, and dig potatoes, and pick grapes, and "bat berries," and milk the cow, and pitch hay, and clean the stables, and do all those things associated with my notion of an active man. And I did do all those things; I did them for three summers, and got real wages for them, most of the time from my father, at brief periods from a neighboring farmer. But I can not pretend I enjoyed the deed as I did the idea. Exalting as it is, the idea that you are working on a farm becomes a rather feeble source of energy toward the middle of a hot afternoon in a cornfield in the late days of August. Indeed, once you have put in a day on each of the different kinds of work, its connotation, to an undeluded judgment, is about played out.

Thus you may imagine me, during the next three summers, as a rather lazy-fibred and exasperating farmhand, always doing my share of the work in principle—for I was still the soul of Christian virtue—but in practice finding frequent reasons, my well-known "frailty" the chief among them, for being elsewhere when the tiresome work was done. By tiresome I do not mean things like plowing or pitching hay, which involve action in large curves, but hoeing, weeding, and above all, picking berries. I could not convert these labors into competitive games and thus bring egotism to my aid, because my brother was too good for me. He could fill a quart basket with raspberries while I would be covering the bottom of mine. His nimble fingers flew through those bushes like a flock of birds, making me feel not only tired but mortified.

I will quote his good-humored view of the situation from a speech he made years after, introducing me to an audience in Erie, Pennsylvania:

"Somebody once remarked that he had never seen Max standing up when he could be sitting, or sitting when there was a place to lie down. When an opportunity, even an urgent opportunity, arose for physical effort with a utilitarian purpose, Max always met the situation with serene Olympian superiority and the immobility of Gibraltar. On those rare occasions when an irresistible force, in the way of parental authority, made him get busy, a snail is a lightning flash compared with Max's ameboid, glacier-like activity. But there is another side to this laziness. Max always had plenty of enthusiasm for any kind of physical exertion whose satisfactions derive from the effort itself rather than from its result. He used to go into the water from the high springboard in any one of fifty-seven varieties of forward and back dives, somersaults and aerial gyrations . . ."

Besides this lack of zest for hard labor, which marked me as a decadent among Eastmans, I lacked our ancestral interest in "the affairs of peace." Affairs in general, and that includes both politics and economics, failed to catch my attention. I do not mean that I was impractical in a small way. On the contrary, my sister recalled that as a boy I always had a little money on hand from my pigeon enterprises, and always knew just how much I had. But about the business aspect of larger things I was not even curious. After picking and packing grapes or berries all day, we would write on each basket the name of a firm in Baltimore, take them up to the station, and load them one by one into the express car on the evening train south. It struck me as remarkable, considering the number of big stations between Glenora and Baltimore, that this operation should be so simple. But I did not care enough about it to ask my father what kind of a firm it was, where the express charges were paid, how the fruit reached the ultimate consumer, or when and with what medium of exchange it was paid for.

I once drove a wagonload of early potatoes to Watkins and sold them to a grocer for a dollar a bushel. When my father boasted of this big price as due to his superior good sense in planting them while the neighboring farmers still thought it was winter, I reflected that luck probably had more to do with it than good sense. He had gambled on the weather and happened to win. But I did not care enough about the whole question to jar his complacence with this remark. Potatoes as an article of consumption engaged my fervent interest, but potatoes as a commodity left me cold. In view of my subsequent career among opinions, this trait is more significant perhaps than my unEastmanly distaste for physical work.

My brother and I performed our labor in as few clothes as possible —shoes, overalls, and a swimming shirt, or no shirt at all, and much of the time no hat, and we became a rich and coppery brown. An elderly farmer of the region, meeting a Park Church deacon who was summering on the point, said:

"Have you seen them two Indians that's workin' Vince's farm?"

The deacon said: "Why no, those aren't Indians. They're Elmira boys."

"No, they ain't," the farmer answered. "Them's Indians."

The deacon persisted: "Why no, those are the sons of our pastors, Mr. and Mrs. Eastman."

"Don't make no difference—them's Indians."

We thought the designation highly appropriate, in view of our ancestry, and used to go somewhat out of our way to live up to it. My father had bought in a moment of weakness a mettlesome two-year-old whom we named Greylocks. And my brother and I, racing around that tranquil countryside, yelling and slapping the reins on this wildly galloping colt, while balancing on our toes and heels in a light lumber wagon, had more the semblance of a Wild West Show than of agricultural labor.

Even when yoked to a one-horse plow, Greylocks could not bring himself to the tedium of walking. He could stand still if necessary, tossing his bit and looking around fretfully to see what was the trouble. But when the trouble was over, he would draw back and rush into his collar at a racing trot. The gleaming plow point would glide through the shale like a pickerel chasing a spoon, and the poor plowman wave helplessly out behind. And when that gleaming point would catch under a boulder or in the crevice of a ledge, the plowman would be lucky if he did not find himself astride the horse. As only a superman could handle Greylocks and a plow too, it mostly fell to me to hold the long reins while my brother plowed. It also fell to me to bear the brunt of his indignation with the horse, the plow, the hillside, and the laws of gravitation, when those sudden halts occurred. I bore it with no special tact or patience. Thus our first summer at Glenora, thanks largely to that too-beautiful horse, was marred with more than the normal frequency of irrational outbursts on his part and untempered rages on mine. One day down in the lower vineyard, which we were plowing up to plant rye, the plow flew out of the furrow and down the hill, and my brother, straining to drag it back, tried at the same time to tell me what to do with the horse. I objected to his imperious way of telling me. He objected to my objection.

"I guess I know how to drive a horse," I said.

"Well, for Christ's sake, then, will you please do it?"

"I won't do a thing if you're going to use profane language."

"You goddamned little son-of-a-bitch, you'll do what I say or I'll . . ."

I had frozen like a setter sighting a partridge, and he turned and saw my father standing in the saplings twenty feet away.

"Max, you may go up to the house," he said. And that was all. The days of the razor strop were past. But poor Anstice had to wrestle with that rebellious hillside all alone, and I, beneath my wrath and outraged virtue, was extremely sorry for him.

There was an old fruit-basket factory down on Glenora Point, and we contrived when possible to drive down there for baskets just when the big lake steamer landed at the pier. We would put on bathing trunks, board the steamer by the paddle wheel, and dive from the hurricane deck as the boat pulled out. My brother at least would dive, and I would jump or "turn a back flip," for I was under the impression that in order to avoid severe headaches I had to hold my nose when I went under water—still a mollycoddle even though acting with nerve! When the captain objected to these performances and ordered us to keep off the boat, we devised the scheme of hiding under the dock and climbing up the rudder chains while he was busy at the wheel. He countered by throwing pop bottles at us after we were in the water.

It became a feud, and one in which of course we were doomed to defeat. So we selected the Fourth of July excursion landing for a grand finale, inviting the whole town out to the dock to see it—the whole town comprising some twenty people, most of whom disliked the captain. Dressed up in excursion apparel, I in white ducks and a silk necktie, my brother in his western sombrero with a cigar in his mouth, and Claude Bowles, a co-conspirator, in a business suit and derby hat, we paid our fare and got on board as passengers. My brother went up to the hurricane deck, and Claude and I to the middle deck. As the boat pulled away I leaned far out waving good-bye to my friends on the pier, leaned *too* far out, and with a blood-curdling scream did my "back flip" into the water. My brother yelled "Man overboard!" and sailed through the air from above, sombrero and cigar and all; Claude Bowles ran the whole length of the ship yapping in a hysterical manner, jumped up on the rail, and dived off in his derby. In the water we put on a drowning scene, and the passengers almost capsized the steamer crowding to the rail to see it. It all made the captain very unhappy and was a glorious Fourth.

PART III

MY PLUNGE INTO LIFE

Chapter 20

Friendship and Fun

I ENTERED Williams College in the fall of 1900 with one firm and clear ambition: not to lead my class. I had shown what I could do in that line at Mercersburg, and now I was out for higher forms of competition. I was going to show that notwithstanding my brains, once my shell of shyness was broken, I could live life!

In that mood I started keeping an "Experience Book," and for the last five months of freshman year, a diary. The world-shaking ways in which I carried out my resolution are thus, as the historians say, documented.

My success in breaking my shell was due largely to my being taken into a fraternity where twenty-odd students ate their meals around a common table. "When I get to know fellows well, I can have fun even with a big crowd of them," I noted with delight. "Nobody ever likes me until he gets to know me well. . . ." The fraternity I joined was Delta Psi, and that was solely because F. F. Thompson, the banker husband of my benefactress, had been a founder of its Williams chapter, and she recommended me for membership. The Delta Psi fraternity, otherwise known as the St. Anthony Club, is far from plebeian—far too from following in the austere steps of St. Anthony. Its Williams chapter was particularly renowned for wealth and sporty polish, and I came very near bolting when, during the rushing season, I heard it described as snobbish.

My reluctance was overcome not only by the absence of other bids, but by a momentary conversation with a member named Sid Wood. All I recall about that conversation is Sid's powerful frame, his undershot jaw and belligerent lip, and the astounding impact with which his blue eyes looked straight at me while he talked. Sid had the strength of a gorilla and carried himself the same way, his big torso slightly stooped and his very long arms hanging outward and a little forward, and this made the clear spirit in those blue eyes more arresting. No doubt he made some candidly ironical comment on the rushing custom that delighted me, for he was always in laughing revolt against the follies of civilized man. He was, in fact— or rather in the terms of literary sophistication—a romantic of the school of Rousseau. When I met him he had just spent a summer with the Osage Indians, and he would spend years thereafter among the Navajos and Hopis in the Painted Desert, living their semi-savage life because he really liked to live it. He went down to Mexico in 1904 to join the Yaquis in their uprising against Porfirio Diaz, and only escaped a massacre by lifting himself with those apelike arms straight up the side of a canyon where a band of warriors was trapped.

I am not surprised to find in an old letter to my sister that it was "Sid's eyes which made me join the crowd." "The great thing about him," I added, "is his deep perfect enduring sense of humor—seeing funny things everywhere and making you see them." Although he was expelled from Williams a few months after I entered, Sid Wood's influence on me outweighed that of the fraternity or anybody else in it—outweighed, indeed, that of any other person I have known beyond my family.

The season in track athletics began with a cross-country hare-and-hounds run designed to sort out promising material from the incoming class. I loved this race through fields still thick with goldenrod and purple asters and over woodsy hills, the rhythmic jumping of old stone walls, vaulting of high fences, and splashing herdlike through clear mountain streams. I was enough exhilarated, and elastic enough after my summer of farm labor, to get back to the gymnasium first. This gave me a place in Sid's attention, for he was passionately fond of athletics, being himself as agile as he was powerful, and yet prevented by the necessity of wearing glasses from becoming an all-round star. He loved athletes in a Greek manner, as a part of the sunny landscape and the cleansing idea of healthy out-door life. He gave me a good pat on the back, and told me I had an ideal build for the quarter-mile—which was true, the only trouble being that I couldn't go quite fast enough.

During that autumn Sid and a small, quick-minded, wiry classmate of his named Stanley Washburn were conducting a violent McKinley-and-Roosevelt campaign. I do not know why, except that Stanley was the son of a Republican senator from Minnesota, and Sid, with his zeal for the Wild West, naturally adored the colonel of Rough Riders —and they both adored to raise a rumpus. I was and am by instinct a militant mugwump, and out of this grew an incident which made Sid Wood my friend. I described it in a letter to my sister.

"One of the boys asked Sid at dinner: 'What are Bryan's political views anyway?'

"Sid said: 'I don't know—I guess he hasn't any as far as I can see.'

"Whereat I had one of those rushes of speech that come over me occasionally—I had never opened my mouth at the table before— and I up and told him, who was a senior, that he would see a great deal farther if he wouldn't spend his nights poring over the Repub-lican campaign book and his days hitching together speeches out of Republican placards, etc. etc. Somebody finally stopped me and said:

" 'Well, you're a Democrat, are you?'

"And I said: 'I am while Republicans are talking that way.' "

Sid did not make any answer to my diatribe, and I subsided with some embarrassment. After we rose from dinner, however, he came up in front of me and put his hand on my shoulder.

"I like the way you oppose things," he said.

A few evenings later I went down to his room in a truckman's house up a back alley off Spring Street, and we took a cross-country run by moonlight. After we got back he drew out a pot of buck-wheat honey that had been given him by a farmer up toward Peters-burg Mountain, and we regaled ourselves with crackers and honey and long draughts of cool clear water from Walden's Spring near by. Every night or two after that we took those cross-country runs to-gether, coming back to his room to bathe, and eat crackers and honey or maple sugar. He thought he was training me for the track team, and he did get me to the point of high-jumping 5 feet 7 inches and doing the quarter-mile in 55 seconds. But my 55 seconds did not win the race, and I almost fainted after crossing the tape. Since I obviously could not be a great athlete, I decided not to go in for athletic distinction at all.

Fortunately for me Sid Wood, although no student, was a man of ideas and a lover of poetry. On his farthest treks back to savagery he carried with him a volume or two of the English poets. He had himself, as I wrote my sister, "more poetry of the real bursting forth kind in him that anybody else I've known." My life interest in the definition of poetry was born of reflections on his metaphoric ways of talking. I saw him not long ago in a mining town up in Grass Valley, California, where he was digging gold and still living a good deal like an Indian. As we drove back from the mine through hilly pastures, I remarked on the number of new-born lambs to be seen everywhere. "They've been popping in the fields this spring like popcorn," he said. That autumn at college he was cherishing the works of Richard Realf, an American poet of whom I had never heard and have never heard since, but one of whose sonnets I have still by heart:

> O Earth! thou hast not any wind that blows
> Which is not music: every weed of thine
> Pressed rightly flows in aromatic wine;
> And every humble hedgerow flower that grows;
> And every little brown bird that doth sing;
> Hath something greater than itself, and bears
> A living Word to every living thing,
> Albeit it hold the Message unawares.
> All shapes and sounds have something which is not
> Of them: A Spirit broods amid the grass;
> Vague outlines of the Everlasting Thought
> Lie in the melting shadows as they pass;
> The touch of an Eternal Presence thrills
> The fringes of the sunset and the hills.

I remember Sid's reading it to me after we came in from a starlit run over Stone Hill, picking the book up from a clutter of boxing gloves, baseball bats, hockey sticks, spurs, bridles, tomahawks and other unexquisite accoutrements that filled his room. It was exciting to find poetry, which had burned sacredly for me in my life with mother and in my frenzy of learning at Mercersburg, burning here also where I was in manly outburst against these childish things. Thanks largely to Sid Wood, I took poetry and my naïve love of nature with me on my reckless voyage into manhood. And thanks to him and his cross-country runs and brown honey, I acquired, although I did not know it then by name, a very Greek conception of what manhood is.

In that classic conception, as in Rousseau's romantic adoration of the noble savage, there is a vein of strongly democratic feeling. There is at least a dislike for the impediments of elegance, a taste for people who live close to the earth. This vein in Sid was very deep, and it was harsh and arrogant. His best friends at Williams were the farmers in the surrounding hills. He was forever plodding up a lone mountain road to eat dinner with some hermit in a clearing in the woods, or skipping school to help a farmer with his haying, or racing down the Pittsfield Road to join a "sugaring off." He and Stanley Washburn, scorning the dormitories, had gone down into the business end of the town and up an alley, where they took rooms in the house of a chesty truckman named Hi Walden. Here they lived the life of the town as much as of the college, dipping into local politics and local cockfights and boxing matches, and even business problems, coming up to the fraternity house only for their meals, taking their classes on the run, and in general introducing into college life the texture of adult experience that it lacks.

I have no full right, perhaps, to call this departure democratic. Stanley Washburn, who subsequently distinguished himself as a daring correspondent in the Russo-Japanese War and was celebrated in a book by Richard Barry as "The Events Man," later attained a not exactly plebeian renown by conducting Queen Marie of Rumania on her royal advertising tour through our humble republic. But he also, to the dismay of his forebears and all good plutocrats, managed Teddy Roosevelt's Bull Moose campaign in the state of Minnesota. He had in him the same noble distaste Sid had for the dull routine of being a gentleman. He loved reality and downrightness and rough contacts, loved the raw taste of life, and loved above all things adventure. They were neither of them much interested, I think, in doctrines. They were not speculating about life, but living it. And they were living it with their minds on pranks and ructions engineered partly to express revolt against authority, but still more for the sake of laughter at the race of man. I never enjoyed more laughter than I did in those two or three months of my association with Sid Wood.

In this spirit I joined him in the campaign for McKinley and Roosevelt, and our cross-country runs were interrupted by drives over the mountains to exhort the neighboring villages on the horrors of Bryan's Free Silver policy and the glories of the war against the Filipinos. Here is a sample of my eloquence at a mass-meeting in East Greenbush near Albany:

"In his theoretical ravings, this crafty speaker cries, 'Did not our ancestors deserve their freedom and independence? Shall we deny it to these people?' Are our heroic forefathers who left the country from which they demanded their freedom because they had advanced beyond it in their beliefs, and who demanded self-government because they were capable of it, they were the peers of their masters —are they to be compared to these hordes of ignorant barbarians, who prefer to wallow in the filth and gore of fruitless war rather than to come forth from their state of uncivilized stagnation and learn to govern and to be governed? . . ."

To me it was a pure lark, and I wrote my sister: "Wasn't that a great experience, to get up before this roomful of Reubs and spout forth far-fetched figures and absurd similes after the fashion of the regular stump speaker?"

Crystal fully shared my zeal for "great experiences." "I love nothing better," she replied, "than to get into a certain situation, funny, solemn, romantic, sentimental, or just unusual, and *feel* myself in it with a kind of exulting joy." But she did mildly suggest that I might have had just as much fun if I had been on the right side.

Sid wound up his campaign with a great bonfire and mass meeting on the campus, at which he distributed a publication called *The Williams College Sound Money Advocate*. It contained telegrams of congratulation from McKinley (sent collect) and Roosevelt (prepaid) and messages from other prominent Republicans—John Hay, John D. Long, H. L. Dawes, Tom Platt. It contained editorials by Sid and Stanley, articles by students and professors, my speech from which I have quoted above, and a fatal paragraph in which Sid alluded to the famous economist Charles Jesse Bullock as "a certain bull-headed professor on the faculty," and added: "For some failing, easily credible from present proof, an ancestor of this present subject lost the worthy name and henceforth was obliged to face the world under the name of a younger and weaker representative of the same set."

The next day he was called before a faculty meeting and offered an opportunity to apologize to Professor Bullock. Seeing his teachers sitting in a circle round him with their spectacles and whiskers and solemn glances of disapproval, he suddenly and a little madly repeated what he had said about Bullock, and denounced the rest of them as an assemblage of stuffed bears and beavers not qualified to sit in judgment on anything alive. He was, of course, expelled forthwith, and not too sorrowfully took the train for Carson City, where he really longed to be. Stanley demanded to appear before the faculty and challenged them to fire him also as joint editor of the paper. They excused themselves on the ground that he had not said those insulting things to their faces.

"I do say them now," he snapped out.

But the United States Senate and the Washburn and Crosby Flour Mills of Minneapolis loomed behind him. He was excused with a reprimand.

Sid's departure took a great joy out of the Berkshire Hills for me. He was the sun in the golden morning of my life. "I hardly expect to find anybody else," I wrote in my diary, "who isn't too much of a dope to run just for the pleasure there is in it." But the light did not depart with him, and his influence could hardly have been greater had he stayed. For whether it is a fault or virtue, I appropriate the general trends and essences of things—of books and ideas as well as attitudes and people—very rapidly and without much patient attention to detail. What I was to learn from Sid and with him was already completely mine. It stood clear in my mind, and still stands there, symbolized by his image as health and light were by the image of Apollo. It stands far clearer than any words can tell it, but if I wanted words I think I should seek them in the odes of Pindar, the poet of athletes and famous exploits, the poet of "not being a dope."

"For as much as men must die, wherefore sit vainly in the dark through a dull and nameless age?"

It may seem a little grandiose thus to dignify our college pranks. The automobile has so changed the life, and cement roads the landscape, at Williams, that I fear my whole story will sound quaint to the present generation. We could not whisk away into the great world to find excitement over the weekend. We could not slip into a leather seat and fly from History 1-A to the top of Petersburg Mountain and back in twenty minutes. The trip to that thrilling summit was a half day's walk through wild, leaf-drifted mountain paths. We were *contained* in a small cup of hills for the whole semester; if we wanted excitement we had to make it. We were indeed almost a little "city-state," a copy of the great world rather than a part of it.

Within that city-state, after Sid's banishment, it devolved mainly upon Stanley and me to keep up the tradition of "deeds and famous exploits." One of our exploits did have a day of fame not only in Williamstown, but throughout the country.

"Max, let's get up some honest-to-god excitement," Stanley remarked one morning. "What do you say we kidnap a sophomore?"

"I'm game," I said. "Let's kidnap Rickey Rogers. He's got a good strong constitution."

"What would we do with him? We might find an old barn out in the mountains somewhere."

"That would be a little dangerous, though. You can't tell what his family might do."

"I'll tell you what. You kidnap him, and I'll rescue him!"

Rickey—properly Rochester Hart Rogers—was a fraternity brother of ours, one of those brothers who, notwithstanding a stubborn and serious loyalty and determination, knows how to take a joke. Stanley asked Rickey, in solemn confidence, to come down to his room at nine o'clock one evening prepared if necessary to back him up in a fight.

"I'll be there with both fists, Stanley," Rickey said in a voice quivering with emotion.

"And don't tell anybody," Stanley said, laughing a little in spite of himself. "Come alone—I need a friend," he added earnestly.

When Rickey came nervously but courageously up the little dark alley toward Hi Walden's house, a hack was standing by the horse block, and I was in the driver's seat, concealed behind false whiskers and armed with two revolvers. A saddled riding horse was hitched to a tree behind the house, and three masked figures were crouching in the shadow of the porch. The masked figures were Pat O'Keefe, a wiry Irishman who set up balls in the local poolroom, Tommy Daly, similarly employed, and Eddie Dempsey, the happy clerk with gold teeth who presided at the college soda fountain. They emerged suddenly as Rickey approached the steps and said gruffly:

"Are you Washburn?"

"No, I am not," said Rickey with firm courage.

"Yes, you are!" And they leaped on him with fifty feet of rope and a gag.

Rickey had strong lungs and wiry muscles, and he succeeded in bawling like a branded calf for a good three minutes before they got him tied up and loaded into the hack. A little group of curious townsmen gathered at the corner and began edging up the alley.

But the bawling stopped at last, and the door slammed. I whipped up the horses, shouting and swearing ferociously at them, and the hack rolled and rattled through the little group, around the corner and out into Spring Street at a wild gallop. Stanley rushed from the house as though just roused from a sound sleep, leaped on his horse and started in pursuit, firing his pistol and shouting "Thieves!

Thieves!" I answered with pistol shots from my swaying seat, and Rickey completed the picture by getting a leg loose and kicking the windows out of the hack as we thundered down the main street of the little peaceful town.

In proportion as Rickey's kicking became stronger, the resistance of his captors became weakened by laughter, and before we got far into the country Rickey shook the gag out of his mouth and yelled at the top of his voice:

"I saw your gold teeth, Eddie! I saw you, Max—you needn't go any farther!"

I heard the clattering hoofs of the rescuing hero coming after us, and knowing that we had outdistanced other pursuers, I pulled up for a consultation. When Stanley rode up, Rickey was out of the hack, his hands still bound, but free to express himself, and doing so energetically.

"This is what you needed a friend for, is it?" he shouted. And Stanley laughed outrageously.

"Rickey," he said, "there's only one thing for you to do now—get in on the joke. We've fooled the whole town except you. The sheriff will be after us in twenty minutes. You come back with me and say that you were kidnapped by bandits and I rescued you."

"Get in on the joke, hey?" Rickey said angrily. "Get in on the joke, hey?"

His voice trembled upon these words as though they were enormously significant.

"Look here, Rickey," Stanley said, suppressing his laughter. "You get mad afterwards. At present, if you don't come in on the joke, you're the goat. Can't you see that?"

The logic, or zoology, of this proposition was irrefutable, and after a little grumbling Rickey came in on the joke. He climbed up behind Stanley, that is, and went jiggling back to town in the guise of a man rescued from probable torture and death. I drove a mile up the South Williamstown Road, turned around, and came straight back, trotting calmly through a group of students out in search of the bandits. Going over to Stanley's room I found the sheriff of Berkshire County, among others, busily noting down the details of the crime.

Our kidnapping was taken seriously in a front-page story by the New York *Sun*, and published throughout the country by the Associated Press. "An abortive attempt to kidnap the son of a United States Senator . . ." It was big news.

Stanley was, of course, summoned before the president of the college, but managed, with Rickey's help and that parental senator looming in the background, to persuade him to "leave it at that."

Another exploit initiated by Stanley and me survives in this clipping from a North Adams paper:

"The moving of the big cannon from Soldier's mound in East-lawn cemetery to the campus near the chapel Wednesday night, was a difficult feat, yet it was accomplished with secrecy and dispatch and no one knew about it until Thursday morning, when the big gun was found directly in front of the chapel. The cannon was taken through the lots and around back streets for a distance of three-quarters of a mile. It weighs 2,600 pounds and it was securely fastened to a foundation of cement and stone."

That cannon happened to be a monument to the Grand Army of the Republic, and the Berkshire Post complained to the district attorney. The district attorney put detectives on our trail, and, but for the good offices of a more steady-minded brother in Delta Psi, we were in a fair way to be indicted for desecrating a cemetery and mutilating a federal monument. That steady-minded brother was Gregory Palmer, who lives also in my memory as having read three pages a day of Webster's Unabridged Dictionary throughout his college course. He went to see the local GAR commander and asked him what it would cost to restore the cannon, and what it would further cost to assemble all the old soldiers in Berkshire County for a champagne banquet at the Greylock Inn to celebrate its restoration. It seemed to the commander that seventy-five dollars might perhaps cover these items, and Gregory, a true and loyal brother if there ever was one, promptly drew his cheque and paid it.

The relief to me was immense, for I was in a moral muddle throughout this whole episode, the Pindar motive clashing with an old-wise anxiety about my Thompson scholarship, the pain to my parents, and the blow to my own growth if it should be withdrawn. Prudence must stand guard if one is to live life to the full. And I may have caught a glimpse of this sober truth on realizing that that stubborn cannon, whose donkey-like resistance had given us a night of hilarious laughter, was the sacred property of the United States of America. But I was not sober long; I was more Pindarish than prudent.

"This is the first difference the United States and I have had," I wrote in my diary.

Chapter 21

A Touch of Bacchus

FOR steady excitement, after Sid left and athletics went by the board, I turned to drink and poetry. Alcohol has a useful and fatal charm for shy people, and I am afraid I acquired my first real fame in college as a hard drinker. In this phase my close friend was a brother in Delta Psi named Scott Beacham, a rich man's son from Decatur, Illinois, who had spent much of his time in New York. He was a nattily dressed young hanger-on of theatres, a premature roué with a fine mind which he had used to master every nuance of the life of Broadway. He had also a generous and gentle heart and a rebel-democratic disposition, but he had no purpose, no physique, no morale, no force of character. With remarkably sensible words on his lips, he was sliding straight downhill to dissolution. I knew this, and was far from putting his Broadway sophistication in the place of Sid's high love of Indians and athletics; but still I was eager to absorb it. Moreover, he paid all the costs of our almost nightly trips to the bars and taprooms, dance halls and theatres of North Adams.

In January I moved out of Morgan Hall, where I had roomed with two Elmira boys, and took a small private room with Scottie down on Hoxie Street. We fixed it up in a theatrical style with a poster showing a trim-legged chorus singing:

Tell me, pretty maiden,
Are there any more at home like you?
There are a few, kind sir!

Scott had his breakfast brought to him by a colored maid, and I rang in on this luxury too. Our life together was lazy, irresponsible, unambitious; it was the life of rich boys to whom college is a country club. For me it was sanctioned to some extent by an ideal. I had broken my bonds of shyness, but I was still walled in by the relics of my infantile preoccupation with being good. There was more than a glamor, there was a steady glow for me in the ideal of being bad— of being at ease, at least, in the world of the stage door and the midnight drink.

"We haven't either of us room to turn around up here," I wrote in my diary, "and I am getting so lazy I am perfectly content to get along without bothering to turn around. What's the use? Nothing is easier than holding down furniture, and I sometimes think that the trouble of holding up oneself is not worth while—especially for long stretches."

That, of course, was supposed to be humorous, but my diary is full of serious entries showing a boastful laxity toward studies and a growing habit of sponging on Scottie for drinking parties I could not afford.

"I cut Greek with the intention of studying math all morning, studied math a good hour and a half, loafed and went to Gym in the afternoon, and then took the Math exam. I was very good in it too, and I haven't gotten out a single lesson in the whole course."

"Scottie took me over to see Marie Dressler in 'Miss Print' tonight. She is really the only comedienne there is, and she is great. That makes six days in succession in North Ad. Scottie is thinking of renting a horse and wagon by the week now. He is also thinking of getting a locomobile."

My troubles with the dean were constant, and I was proud of the fact that I was "on probation" throughout the spring term. I find preserved as a kind of trophy a letter from my pathetically kindly German professor: "Before entering my classroom again, you are requested to confer with me." I had been arrogant with him in the class in Faust, but when I saw him in his home, I could not keep it up. I had to apologize to myself in my diary for being "mild" and understanding his point of view. I found it "delightful" to cut my classes, and more delightful the less excuse I had. And I surmised that "there is a great joy in deliberately deciding to do wrong, and let conscience and right go, in every kind of evil . . ."

In one kind of "evil" I had not yet, even with the help of alcohol, learned to attain this joy. And I did not learn it for many years. Although there was a good deal of chippy-chasing in our North Adams nights, and we were sustained by the ever-present possibility of sex adventures, they never got down for me to matter-of-fact. I could daydream of amatory captures and lust-assuaging acts and orgies physiological enough for the wild and sacred bulls of Apis, but I was so shy and squeamish in the actual presence of a girl that I might as well have been a little golden calf.

The only time I ever "passed out" was in a bedroom in the Richmond Hotel after supper with a chorus girl named Gwendolyn Faxon, a slim brown fragrant girl with honest eyes, who was recklessly inviting. I wanted to be as reckless, but I was clamped in a chastity belt woven of the early Christian tabu—what supernatural tensile strength it has!—and sheer bashfulness, whose grip is another of the wonders of the world. Add to these unthinking forces a truly moral concern for consequences and a timid ignorance of procedure, and you have a trap from which even Bacchus can not, in one short midnight, set you free. At least that was my sad experience. I learned, as I suppose many an anxious experimentalist has, that enough alcohol to overcome a psychic impotence is enough to produce a physical one. Gwendolyn's troupe left on a two o'clock train, and I—God forgive me, a virgin—drank myself into a stupor.

Some older boys in the fraternity thought I was "going to hell" and shook their heads in sober disapproval. But I did not actually drink so much as they imagined. I disliked the taste of whisky and gin so heartily that I used to fall frequently back on glassfuls of crème de menthe to keep me "even"—it tasted enough like peppermint candy to go down—and I was also addicted to claret punch. My brother and I and a college mate of his were staying together at a hotel in Poughkeepsie one night, having come to a Vassar dance. When we got back to our room in the small hours, the suggestion was made that we have a drink.

"What will you have?" my brother asked me when the waiter came.

To show my sophistication, I leaned way back in my chair and threw one leg carelessly over the other.

"Well, I think I'll take a claret!" I said.

Throughout my brother's life I never heard the last of that.

I enjoyed being regarded as a hard drinker—and something of a cigarette fiend too. But I never inhaled a puff of smoke, and I used to drink just enough to get an "edge on"—our name for the phase of enhanced self-confidence and spontaneity now called being "lit"—and preserve that "edge" from dulling into drunkenness with much private resolution. You can not, of course, permanently play tricks with a drug that disintegrates the trick-playing organ. But I managed it for a while; I never attained the pleasure that is said to reside in getting "soused."

I did reach a point where the prospect of an evening without a trip to North Adams was morbidly dismal. And that alarmed me and set me thinking. I had wanted to escape my scared-kid limitations and *live*—that had been my justification for drinking. I wanted to live in all directions. Yet now alcohol was confining me to a single enjoyment.

Marcus Aurelius, defending his Stoic faith against the Epicureans, says that the virtue of temperance is "opposed to the love of pleasure." It seems to me, on the contrary, that the Stoic ideal is itself intemperate; it pours the whole life-force into one channel, and that a pathogenic one, the suppression of desire. But pleasures are various; they are like the blossoms in a meadow; if many are to be enjoyed, you can not imprison yourself in any one.

In February I heard the violinist Adamowski with his famous quartet. "His playing was just like a soft beautiful wind," I wrote in my diary. I knew that the pleasure I enjoyed that evening was worth more than my boozy excitements in North Adams. It must have impressed me deeply, for I still remember thinking that in order to receive these delicate delights I must be free of addiction to coarser ones.

In March even my diary begins to show signs of compunction:

"I am living a lazy sort of life these days, and it makes me feel unhappy. Sloppy is the only word that really conveys the feeling I have. If I were rooming alone and attending more to business, I should feel better."

During these lazy and "sloppy" days I was troubled more often than usual by that categorical melancholy which has been as constant a feature of my landscape as though I lived under a cliff.

"There are some states," I wrote on a Sunday in March, "that one can not appreciate unless he has experienced them. But the blackness of a real fit of melancholy one can not conceive in his imagination unless he is right in it. I often wonder, when I am in a black fit, what it is that keeps me doing things that are duties. This evening I went over to Ralph's room to get my Math. I didn't care whether I got it or not. I didn't care whether I should wake up in the morning and be sorry I hadn't gotten it, or not. I didn't care about anything; I went splashing through the mud, and walking across the lawns; and yet I went . . ."

It is a sad picture, and needs to be offset with this from a letter to my sister at about the same time:

"I am spending all my spare time skiing. There is no fun in the world like flying down a long hill for half a mile, standing up, and going so fast that you can't breathe."

And from the same letter:

"I keep a book to put my thoughts and writings in. There is no pleasure in the world like the pleasure of writing things—no matter how poor they are. Just as soon as you begin to write, other ideas begin to come to you . . ."

The discovery described in that last line was as joyful as any I ever made. It was, after my friendship with Sid Wood, the big event of my first year at college, and I want to tell about it in a separate chapter.

Chapter 22

Beginnings of a Poet

MY EARLIEST efforts at writing were mainly in verse. I do not know why, for my verses had little relation to the feelings attending my plunge into life. They were honest, unpretentious, unimitative, unflagging, and incredibly bad attempts to put ideas into rhyme. Here is the very first of them:

> That savages the sun adore,
> Or worship waves and the ocean's roar;
> That Heathen kneel to Gods of clay,
> And worship different Gods each day;
> Always in history's darkest hour,
> That man has felt some unknown power,
> That we today all think we know,
> And bicker and argue to prove it so;
> But shows that some power reigns above,
> To whom, our creator, we owe our love.

In this amusement, too, I found a companion in Delta Psi. It was fra-angelical Ralph Erskine from Tryon, North Carolina. Ralph was a tall, well-moulded, friendly-hearted lad, whose mother, to my unbounded admiration, had written a novel I never read. Ralph had unusual dignity, and only needed darker hair and brows to make him soberly impressive. But his curly blond hair and downy brows and invisible lashes gave him a baby look too, and one of his blue irises was browner than blue, and he was so frankly a dreamer and lover of sweet virtues, and had so unarmed a friendly giggle, that on the whole you were more charmed than impressed. Like most of those brothers, Ralph was a moneyed young gentleman distinguished in my eyes by his finely tailored suits and tweed overcoats. He stood out somewhat because there was taste as well as style in his apparel. In his conversation, I was surprised by casual allusions to the old masters, and to Beethoven, and medieval furniture, and Till Eulenspiegel, and gothic architecture, and other matters that I knew would interest my mother. Ralph first made me feel the need of artistic culture, and first made me want to travel in Europe. He sang and played the cello and loved music with an educated ear, and that also provoked my ambition.

One day, soon after my perpetration about the Creator, Ralph took a place beside me at the dinner table, and drew from his pocket a slip of paper. He said, with a self-deprecating giggle:

"Look here. What do you think of this?"

And then, becoming solemn, he read me a poem in a whisper. I took it and read it over to myself.

"It's fine," I said, "but isn't your rhythm a little off in the fifth and sixth lines? It would be better if it went like this . . ." And I proceeded, as one having authority, to improve his poem. He gazed at me in astonishment.

"How do you know that? Do you write poetry?"

"Well, not to speak of," I said, "but I know how it goes."

"Why don't you try it? I believe you're a poet!"

So I went back with a feeling of companionship to my experience book—the right place to go—and tried seriously to write a poem.

I must remind you that in childhood I had rejected literature *in toto.* There was no *Child's Garden of Verses*, there was not even a Mother Goose, in the depths of me. Poetry had first awakened my delight as a glimpse of nature's beauty through the gloomy walls of family prayers. One morning when I was about twelve, my mother read instead of the Scripture Sidney Lanier's "Song of the Chattahoochee":

> Out of the hills of Habersham,
> Down the valleys of Hall,
> I hurry amain to reach the plain,
> Run the rapid and leap the fall,
> Split at the rock and together again,
> Accept my bed or narrow or wide,
> And flee from folly on every side,
> With a lover's pain to attain the plain,
> > Far from the hills of Habersham,
> > Far from the valleys of Hall . . .

I was ecstatical when she finished, and I begged for that poem every next morning until I knew it by heart. Notwithstanding my

studies of other poets at Mercersburg, "The Song of the Chattahoochee" remained for me almost the meaning of the word poetry.

Thus I naturally turned, as a poet-apprentice, to the guidance of
Sidney Lanier. I bathed my senses in his mellifluous music, and I
gave to his *Science of English Verse* all that zest for real scholarship
which I was arrogantly withholding from my appointed studies. By
an odd chance Ralph was friendly with Lanier's sons and was as
worshipful as I of the southern poet's verse.

So in my own first poem I did what "The Song of the Chattahoochee" does; I attached a human virtue to a feature of the natural
landscape. The feature I chose was Greylock Mountain. I was several
months getting the mountain and the virtue hitched together, and
longer getting up my nerve to offer it to the Williams *Literary
Monthly*. It was, as you already know, an awful poem:

> Alone in majesty thou reignest now,
> And all before thee, monarch mountain, bow.
> But hast thou ever thus unrivaled stood?
> Ah, no! Earth's proudest rulers never could.
> Those scars, that but increase thy grandeur, tell
> Of battles thou hast fought and hast fought well,
> For conquered at thy feet two giants lie,
> Who dared defy, and in defiance die.
> When earth with sea, and earth with earth, and sea
> With sea, all mingled, fought for mastery,
> Then didst thou meet thy foes and triumph then.
> As truly King thou art as Kings of men!

One day I was sitting in Jessup Hall listening to a lecture by
Hamilton W. Mabie, admiring his "diction"— which I had been told
to admire—and thinking in my heart that diction is a pretty dull
diversion. A vivacious, curly-headed senior named Dwight Marvin,[1]
who poured sprightly verses into the *Lit* in untold quantities, poked
his head through the door and beckoned me into the hall. The *Lit*
board, he said, were interested in my poem, and if I would "fix
up the first four lines" they would accept it. He pulled the poem out
of his pocket and read the line:

> "Ah, no! Earth's proudest rulers never could!

"That, you see, is no good," he said, and brushed it off the paper
with his hand.

---

[1] Subsequently editor of the Record Newspapers of Troy, N. Y., and president of the
American Society of Newspaper Editors.

Happy as I was, I flushed with resentment at this insult to my art. I was some hours becoming honest enough to see that he was right. I "fixed up" my poem for the *Lit*, and learned a good deal doing so, but I did not learn to write poetry. I was still running on an induced current. I mean that the words were begetting the emotion, not the emotion the words. This can and must happen at times to all true poets, but it should not form the body of their art. On February 12 I wrote in my diary:

> I questioned God and I detested life;
> The melancholy mood of unformed doubt
> Was on me; faithless, hopeless I went out
> In grief to wander by the sea alone . . .

Immediately under this heartbreaking avowal I wrote: "Nobody that hasn't tried it can imagine the pleasure there is in writing these things!"

By Easter I must have been strongly enamored of this pleasure, verbal though it was, for I resisted an invitation from Scottie to spend the vacation with him in New York, and spent it instead with Ralph and with poetry in the Berkshire Hills. Each morning we would start off with a book of poems and a notebook in our pockets, as hunters start with a gun and a pouch for game. We would part on some hillside and wander in different directions, to meet again in the evening and tell each other what we had seen and felt and read and written.

I learn from my diary that in March I had some resistance to Shelley's lyrics. Not a political resistance, for I was unaware that Shelley had a political opinion, but because they are "so in contrast with the lofty ideals of Holmes"—whatever those may be—and "some of his sentences are so very difficult to see through that I am hardly educated up to him." But on April 6 I took Shelley to be my companion on one of those walks in the hills. I was trying hard to write a poem about sumach:

> These few stark tongues of flame
> Alone are left . . .

Which was all right—but there my moralistic automatisms stepped in and drove both me and the sumach out of the poem. I did not know what was the matter, but I decided that I was no poet and turned to Shelley in humble mood. I sat down against a grey rock in a high sloping pasture, and after reading a little here and there I came upon the "Ode to the West Wind." I have never since read anything which stirred me so deeply. I surprised that grey rock with a bath of hot romantic tears, prostrating myself upon it and sobbing as though my last day had come.

"I read Shelley today," my diary says, "until it made me cry. . . . Lanier says he was an excitable, sensitive boy and would have been merely a boy if he had lived two hundred years. He may be a boy, but so am I, and the longer I may stay so the better, even if I live two hundred years. Shelley is my poet."[2]

After reading the "Ode to the West Wind" I never again composed poetry in the mood of objective experiment in which I had begun. Poetry became for me from that day a sacred, inspirational, exalted thing, a thing somewhat like prayer. My everyday unsabbatical self, with its strong taste for fact, laughter, and logic, seemed hardly to belong to it. Only when lifted out of myself, I thought, by some pure, serious, and very obsessive emotion could I properly turn to verse for expression.

Had my poetry been religious, even in a pantheistic sense, I need not regret this prayerlike sanctification of it. It was quite the opposite, an affirmation of life taking the place of religion. I grew up in a lake country amid hills and waterfalls no less lovely than those which were the prime movers of Wordsworth's song; but mine were never brooded over by Deity. I am not endowed with that "excess in the great social principle of life" which led Wordsworth to transfer his "own enjoyments . . . to unorganic nature." If I love a tree, I love it to be a tree. I have no wish to imagine a dryad, much less the Hebrew God Jehovah, sitting in some position within or around behind it. Aside from belief, it would violate my direct feeling of affection to attribute biped antics to its honest bark and branches.

In describing his poetic development in *The Prelude,* Wordsworth speaks of poetic literature as

> ". . . that interminable building reared
> By observation of affinities
> In objects where no brotherhood exists
> To passive minds."

[2] Those raptures of my literary adolescence cut so deep that they gave rise thirty-odd years after to the only experience I ever had of a dislocated consciousness. From the north side of Mt. Airy in Croton-on-Hudson one looks down into Oscawanna Valley as one does in Williamstown from Stone Hill to the valley of the Green River. One day in 1930, I was wandering on Mt. Airy composing my idyl of unfaithful love, *Swamp Maple*—for ever since that Easter I have remained a peripatetic poet. I came out through the trees to the north side of the hill and looked down suddenly into the valley. I could not find the Green River, and I was bewildered. I stood for more than

He should have said practical as well as passive minds, but otherwise it is a valid characterization of the poet's art. And I too have carried bricks to that interminable building. Not only in finished poems:—all my notebooks contain, together with thoughts and observations, similes and metaphors set down like an artist's sketches with no purpose but their own being.

"The gaslight makes a noise like small black pearls."

"Pursued by a precipice."

"Burning birch bark is indistinguishable in the next room from frying eggs."

"Frogs sound like jew's-harps."

"Redwoods grow like pubic hairs in the clefts of the bare earth."

"The big blackbirds behave like seals; they shine like wet seals."

"Crayfish pass their eyes around like dishes."

Such affinities excite me, but I do not have to reinforce my excitement with beliefs about the universe. Comparison is the life of the mind, and to be alive for me is enough. Therefore, my sanctification of poetry, while perhaps helpful in the task of defining it and teaching its enjoyment, was a bar to my own poetic self-expression. It led me, while so largely classic in my nature, to an excessively romantic conception of my art.

This attitude—of partial suicide, it seems to me now—finds a peculiar expression in my diary. I had written during the winter a series of pasquils against the sophomore class, taunting them with lack of spirit in the animosities supposed to prevail between us preceding the "Shirt Tail Parade" on March 17. Ralph and I had my verses printed on a bill poster, bought a pail of glue, and getting up at two o'clock one morning plastered the town with them.

IN MEMORIAM OF 1903 CLASS SPIRIT

(Being Slick Selections from English Lyrics)

> Grim silence falls on College Halls
> And lofty Morgan's four great stories.
> The Soph awakes, in fear he quakes,
> Because the Freshman o'er him glories.
> Blow, Sophomore, soon you'll hear the Fresh replying;
> Blow, for you'll never do much more than blowing . . .

a minute in dizzy perplexity because I could not find the Green River in Oscawanna Valley! In the trance of creation I had traveled back across thirty years to that Easter week in my college hills.

Toward this quite adequate performance I cherished, after Shelley had romanticized me, a veritable shame complex, alluding to it in my diary as those "far-fetched, fool verses," that I am "too sick of to put in here." And yet my pasquils are very much better than the poems in my diary, and Ralph informs me that they made quite a sensation.

Having plunged through athletics, "exploits," alcohol, and poetry, I wound up my freshman year in a burst of enthusiasm for oratory. Being selected for a toast at the class banquet in Saratoga Springs, I put all I had into making it as humorous as my class prophecy at Mercersburg had been.

"Toast was a great success," my diary says, "and I got a long Williams cheer for it." But it adds, meekly enough: "Do I wish it had been football!"

My oratory gained much from something that happened the day after my speech. The New York Republicans were holding a convention in Saratoga Springs the week of our banquet, and I by chance strolled into the gallery while Theodore Roosevelt was defending the new system of nomination by direct primary. Someone opposing it had remarked that Mr. So-and-so, naming a notoriously corrupt politician, had been elected because of this new system. Roosevelt said:

"Mr. So-and-so was elected not because of the direct primary, but in *spite* of the direct primary"—his voice hitting the falsetto on the word "spite."

The statement was met with an instantaneous and explosive "Boooo!" from the whole hall. He stepped straight into it, tensing his body and clenching his teeth and fists. He looked as though he were about to spring upon the convention. They hushed suddenly, and in a zero silence he said, biting every word off with his teeth:

"In order that there may be no mistake, I will repeat what I just said: Mr. So-and-so was nominated not because of the direct primary, but in *spite* of the direct primary!"

There was not a sound when he finished. He stood tense a second, his square teeth gleaming, then he said:

"There!"

Every man in the hall applauded.

I never forgot that triumph of naked assertion. I never forgot, as an orator, to *step into an attack*.

Chapter 23

A Wise Fool

I TOOK the advice of my diary and lived alone my second year in college. But I studied no harder, and as the advantages of my preparation were receding, got even lower marks. I was still struggling against glooms and earnestly trying all remedies, from violent exercise to a prescription Mrs. Beecher found me in a gospel book:

> When you are feeling a little blue,
> Something for someone else go do.

My oratorical career was brought forward one notch by my election to speak for the class in the March 17 celebration. Joe Ely,[1] who spoke for the seniors, made a disparaging remark about our class of 1904 because as freshmen we had let the sophomores capture our canes.[2] I won some glory among my classmates, I remember, with this peroration: "So I propose a long Williams cheer for the class of 1904, a class that can walk, and walk without canes, and that will be walking without canes when the present senior class have gone tottering into their graves!" It was an occasion of high flight for the ego, and I was generous enough to let my sister share it to the full:

"I was guarded in my room all day by the class president and a committee of football players, so that the Freshmen could not kidnap me. . . . We spoke from the top of a high tally-ho with the whole college to the left by a dying bonfire, and about a thousand people from town and North Adams ranged on a steep hill to the right. O, it was great! I felt as if my voice could reach to the ends of the earth. Afterward, when each class gathered together by the embers

---

[1] Subsequently governor of Massachusetts.

[2] Tradition at Williams demanded that the freshmen order a set of canes and try to bring them into town during a week in March when the sophomores guarded the roads.

155

and gave a cheer for the other three classes, mine carried me on their shoulders. . . . There is nothing in the world that can be compared to making a speech!"

Notwithstanding this dangerous discovery, I kept on writing. The October *Lit* published a story of mine, but fiction did not command my earnest efforts. "I just sat down at my desk," says my diary, "and began a conversation between a girl and boy and before I got through I had a story." In essays I felt a sterner challenge to my ambition: "I tried to write part of an essay on Keats a little while ago and found I couldn't. I believe a good essay to be the hardest thing of all to write—stories, poems, sermons, harangues, dramas and all."

I had a poem in almost every number of the *Lit*, and none of them was quite so bad as "Greylock." But they were still a good deal more homiletic than I was, and still too largely made of word-born emotions. A change came in the spring when my mother brought from a trip to Europe a photograph of the wounded Lion of Lucerne, Thorwaldsen's famous statue commemorating the Swiss Guard whom Louis XVI forbade to fire on the revolutionists raiding up his palace stairs. I did not know who had been forbidden to shoot, nor at whom, nor why, and I did not care enough about "affairs" to look it up. But I loved the lion; I loved him as I had loved my dog Major, or poor Beauty who got killed by a railroad train. I awoke at midnight quivering with pity and admiration for this noble and unjustly treated animal.

> Thou fighting king of that free warrior clan
>   Which roves the tangled jungles of the East,
>   Which makes its prey of every wide-eyed beast,
> And thwarts the force of human craft and plan
> With yellow teeth—feasted on blood that ran
>   Hot from many a large-thewed victim's heart,
>   How fierce and free and mighty grown thou art,
> To weep and bleed unto the gaze of man!
> And we, who publicly and privately
>   Must goad ourselves to fight some frail-armed foe
> Of evil thought, and in each victory
> Replume ourselves, or through some vain belief
>   Pity ourselves—I think we cannot know
> The measure of this fettered warrior's grief.

This sonnet was written in so feverish an excitement and with such minute hallucinations that I began in soberness to think perhaps I had some lyric gift. I had felt, at least, how words can pour unsought-for out of an emotion.

In April I was elected to the *Lit* board—the one presided over by Stuart Pratt Sherman, later a famous literary critic—and I brought a rough copy of my "Lion of Lucerne" to the first meeting. It was not greeted half so warmly as a conventional lyric presented in typewritten form by George Mather Richards, a talented boy who stood at the head of our class. George had his own typewriter at college, and that in itself amounted almost to literary genius, but his poem was not distinguished. I inferred, perhaps rightly, that mine was still less so. It was a heavy blow, the first of many, to my rather frail hopes of myself as a poet.

Writing, however, was still a sideline in my engrossing business of living life, and I can not pretend that I was long depressed by this blow. A letter to my sister at about the same date reveals my state-of-mind:

"I have read a wildly exciting novel—*Graustark*. It's one of the kind where you fall wildly in love with the heroine, and are jealous whenever you hear anybody speak of reading the book. . . . I wish I could get up a little summer love affair. I begin to think it would be a good thing for me to cut loose next summer and get up a romance of my own. How I do long for adventure after I read a novel like that! Life doesn't seem worthwhile without it."

These yearnings for love and for adventure, so conspicuously absent from my preachy poetry, formed the main current of my inward life. I was destined in the year following to have a fair dose of both, and by rare good fortune adventure came first. For love I was still, as Ethel Marble's candy had put it, "too young and too green." This was indeed proven by a little kissing romance I managed to "get up" with one of the factory girls we met at public dances in North Adams. She was a French girl named Angie, slender and dark-eyed, delicate in her tastes. Her father guarded her like a dragon, breathing visible fire at the mention of the abstract concept of a college student, and that contributed a conspiratorial element to our romance that was timely to my yearnings. It was thrilling too, after hammering away at the French language in the dull manner of the American classroom, to have it steal into my understanding as it did when Angie wrote me this little misspelled letter:

"Vous me demander quand et où vous pouvez me voir encore, et bien si vous êtes très bon, vous pouvez me voir Mecredi au soir à sept heures et demies, mais s'il vous plait, voudriez-vous portez votre chapeau, et non le casse que vous avez la coutume de mettre.

Je suis en attendant

Votre petite Angie."

On the said Wednesday evening I sat beside Angie on a dining-room chair while she played French songs on the piano. Her father, lulled by that "chapeau," was supposed to be asleep in the kitchen. My arm had crept no more than half-way around Angie's waist, however, when I heard him snorting in the doorway.

"Alors! C'est assez!"

I turned around flushed and speechless. He stood pointing imperiously to the door.

"Young man, you may leaf my house," he said.

I put out a hand wet with mortification to Angie, and she said in a tone of obedient resignation:

"Au revoir, monsieur!"

It was dawn before I remembered that those words do not mean goodbye!

When I met Angie at the dance again, we took a long drive together in the moonlight. Along the road where a brook came near with its loud gurgle, I pulled up the horse and put both arms around Angie, and we sat listening together while the moon went down. Something happened there much more disastrous to our romance than her father's intrusion. My ghastly moralism raised its head, my infantine egotistical preoccupation with being good. I deemed it necessary to warn Angie against falling in love with me.

The crime was followed by a long silence, and then: "I'm afraid I am in love with you already," Angie said.

I have committed a good many such crimes of conscience—acts of "consideration" which did not spring out of an imaginative regard for others, but a wish to elude in my own heart the feeling of responsibility. This one was especially obtuse because the year was drawing to a close, and I was going away soon for the summer. Time would have taken gentle care of us both.

In the fulfillment of my yearning for what I called adventure I proved not quite so young or so green. The scheme was at first dressed in the garb of a virtuous intention to go out to Nevada and, by working all summer in some silver mines Sid was interested in, pay off the debts that my careless life had piled up. In communications with my family it never laid off that highly moral garb. But when Sid told me that those mines were shut down, I went right on, not baffled of my real intention.

A part was played in these events by the homecoming of Elmira's handsome and legendary adventurer, Fritz Updegraff. Fritz was a wayward son and brother who, after "raising hell" around home until he became a tradition, had packed up and gone off to South America, where he spent seven years in the unexplored jungle at the upper end of the Amazon. To protect his life he had to participate in the warfare of the head-hunters and attend their ceremonial boiling-down of skulls.[3] I felt, when Fritz dropped in at our house one afternoon in the holidays, as though some Thor or Hercules had got home from his illustrious labors. To climax my emotion, Fritz took a great liking to my sister and me, and with the arrogance of the returned hero, declared that we were the only live people in town. He had a jovial humor, and his friendship confirmed my already settled decision to live a life in which something should happen besides birth, death, disease, and marriage.

I must have expressed this feeling in a letter to Sid, for I still have his answer, sent me from Carson City, where he was, for some strange reason, studying law.

"When your letter arrived, announcing your bona fide intention to be a South American barbarian, I felt hope that some day I might have a legitimate excuse to be a barbarian too. . . .

"At some period nearly every man has a craving to get out and live a wild, free life, but with most it soon passes away. I don't believe yours will, for you have a well-grounded poetic instinct. My feeling for such things has perennial youth and novelty, and denial only whets sharper my appetite for it. During the next couple of years I can make sufficient money to keep us going where we can bring the wolf and lion and panther to the door."

In that phrase "make sufficient money to bring the wolf and lion and panther to the door," Sid expressed an ideal of life which had much to do with what I turned out to be. I guessed dimly, even then, that my "wild free life" would lie as much among ideas and opinions as among woods and mountains. But I resolutely determined that it should be such a life, and such especially its relation to economic

---

[3] Twenty years later he published his adventures in a thrilling book, *The Head-Hunters of the Amazon*, with a flattering introduction by Kermit Roosevelt.

security. Money-making, until the wolf actually sat down at the table, should never be the prime object of my endeavors. That decision, taken in early youth, has held firm. It underlies everything I did or became, having a force akin to that possessed in believing minds by the notion of immortality. Harry Emerson Fosdick asserts that without the faith in personal survival, there is no reason for moral aspiration. To me the opposite is true: an understanding that you have brief years to live offers the best argument for living well.

I suppose Fosdick and I would disagree about what it means to live well. To me, in those days, it meant predominantly to have some high reckless individuality and abandon. Each hour should be regarded as a thing created of material that is precious because so limited by oblivion. That is how I might say it now. Although I love Plato, I am at the opposite pole from what is called a Platonist. To me being is concrete and individual, and the generalized, the typical, does not partake in the adventure at all. To be regular, proper, fashionable, correct, is to miss your one chance to exist. And if you have not enough whims springing up in your own heart to enable you to be unaffectedly *not* regular and *not* correct, then you are the mere refuse of the work of nature, a chip that she knocks off in the process of creating a few specimens of real life.

This anti-Platonic evangel took juvenile forms in those days. I remember that Sid once lay down on the sidewalk on Broadway, reclining on his elbow in a meditative attitude. It was both a joke at which we laughed hilariously and a philosophic manifesto.

Sid came home to Bridgeport for a visit in the spring of 1903, and it was during a weekend I spent there that our plans matured for the trip west. He warned me at the station that he had told his friends I was a young Navajo protégé who could not talk English. His well-known passion for the Indians and my sun-browned skin and lean cheek bones made this plausible. We fooled his mother for less than a minute, but we fooled the University Club for a whole evening, Sid expatiating on my fierce and vengeful character, while I crouched glum and sombre in a leather chair. The club provided me with a highball, and gathered around to watch me drink it.

"How about a cigar?" one of the members asked.

"Sure, he smokes," Sid answered. "But don't crowd in too close. He's getting nervous. You can't tell what he might do if he thought you were making fun of him."

The bellboy brought a tray of Havana cigars, and I sprang out of my chair with an ecstatic grunt and stuffed my pockets full of the most expensive brands.

"Don't laugh! Don't laugh!" Sid shouted.

It was in this mood that I set out on a crusade to redeem my soul and pay my debts by working all summer in the Far West.

Chapter 24

Wander-Months

SID and I traveled to Chicago on a regular ticket and in our "bourgeois" clothes. Arriving there we changed to overalls, black cotton shirts, and red bandannas, and had our hair clipped short. The barber took me for a gipsy and asked me whether I walked or traveled in a wagon. Chicago, I thought, was "awful," although "people do more as they please out here and do it in a very business-like way."[1] We went to a cheap hotel, so cheap that the smell of the bed linen kept me awake until I wrapped my head in my shirt. The next morning we crossed the bridge to Canal Street where Mrs. Atwood's Employment Agency was shipping railroad labor to Nevada. We paid our fee and signed up, and the clerk told us he would "ship" that night at nine o'clock.

During the day we amused ourselves by visiting the stockyards, and by diving into Lake Michigan under a NO SWIMMING sign, and getting dressed and away before a policeman visible in the distance could catch us. At half-past eight we presented ourselves to "Mrs. Atwood," where we found two other men waiting in the office. One was redheaded, pug-nosed, Irish, with his left arm in a sling and a happy grin on his face, the other glum, Italian, with head and chin shaven to a blue-black, no forehead, and small hard ears that stuck out like a bat's. The clerk made out a pass for four "laborers" and gave it to the Irishman. He asked us whether he should check our bags, and we declined the offer. The Italian gathered from the floor a small bundle of things wrapped loosely in a newspaper.

"Had I oughta check this? Naw, guess I better not, had I?"

I restrained myself, but Sid burst out laughing.

The clerk said, "Naw, you can't check that," and Sid laughed

[1] The quotations in this narrative are either from letters to my family or from an "Ex Post Facto Journal" that I composed when I got home.

again. "They wouldn't check it for you anyway, eh?" he said merrily as we started for the train.

The man liked Sid already, but felt cool toward me because he did not know my thought, and this impressed me. Out of it came my first essay in praise of laughter:

"Laugh at people or with them or at yourself or at nothing, only so you laugh openly, they will like you."

Our companions—who had no more intention of working on a railroad in Nevada than we had—sat together all the way to Utah and slept propped across the same double seat. The Italian wore a soiled cap, and his dirty trousers and coat matched. His wormy, brown teeth and tobacco-chewing and vile language repelled me, and yet I was distressed to be repelled. I was launched into an adventure whose enjoyment required a certain character, and I was bent on having that character. It made me more unselectively social than I am and less sensitive. It even caused me to sleep well in the seat of a jouncing smoker, a thing I have not been able to do since. To sustain my morale in this Epicurean effort, I fell back on the one thing I can always enjoy—acquiring information. In preparation for my life as a South American barbarian I studied Spanish, and since I also cherished the noble intention to earn money in a mine, I read a small handbook on mining.

We all got off at Ogden, Utah, and waved a goodbye to the train and the job in Nevada. Sid and I still had a little bagful of dollars, and we took a trip to Salt Lake City and a swim, or at least a bobbing around, in the Great Salt Lake.

Walking down the street after our return, we noticed an employment office with the sign: LABORERS FOR LOS ANGELES. FREE FARE.

I said, "Let's go!"

Sid laughingly agreed, and we went in and signed a paper, handing over twelve dollars each, ten to be refunded after a month's work in a tunnel construction at Chatsworth Park twenty miles northwest of the small city of Los Angeles. That night we climbed into another smoking car and went to sleep. When we woke the next day in Nevada we discovered that our pass, which was signed by the superintendent of the Southern Pacific Railroad, contained no allusion to labor. We dug up our bourgeois garments, changed in the toilet, and walked back and took possession of the train!

I was lifted out of all my selves by the climb over the Sierra Nevadas. "Such distance," I wrote, "a great wideness and loftiness that makes you know the sky begins where the earth ends. We are in the sky all the time. One could gladly live his life there and die, and never care to write it down on a stone."

We still had a few silver dollars, and with that pass in our pockets the trip looked sweeter than the destination. We got off at Sacramento, had a bath and sleep in a comfortable hotel, and gave the town and capitol a thorough going-over. We got off again at Lowell where a fellow passenger told us there was plenty of easy work in the fruit, and again at Bakersfield on the same rumor. But all we ever did to the fruit was eat it or sleep under the trees, and the nearest we came to work was to wash our clothes and ourselves in an irrigating canal.

Our bag of dollars was empty when we reached Los Angeles, so we left our suitcases in a rooming house and hopped a freight train out to Chatsworth Park. We found our prospective boss, a burly Scotsman with a stiff-bristled white mustache, at the end of a muddy black hole a half mile deep in a mountain. He was scribbling in a notebook by the light of a sputtering lantern.

"Want a job, hey?" he growled. "Well, ye can have it!"

We asked him what kind of work he could give us, and he scowled and shouted:

"Pick and shovel!"

He wrote something on a leaf of his notebook and told us where to go. We splashed out into the light again and consecrated ourselves to the open air forever. Such a disposition, we agreed, would be the certain outcome of labor in that black hole.

However, we had to earn our living somewhere. So we climbed a near-by hill to a stone quarry where they told us "muckers" were getting two dollars a day and "chain men," two-and-a-quarter. After watching the operation a few minutes, we decided that hitching the chains to the rocks and the pulley block was easier, "if you had the brains," than shoveling the muck that collects as the cliff is blasted. So we hunted up the superintendent and told him we were chain men looking for a job. He told us smilingly that he guessed we could have one. Remembering that the summer was passing and my debts were still unpaid, I asked him, in a moment of moral responsibility, how long the job would last.

"A good deal longer than you will," he said. But to something he saw in my eyes, he added: "The men work all right until they make their stake, but their stake isn't very high. I hope you boys'll stay, though."

We shouldered our baggage, which now consisted of some bread and sardines and a volume of Byron thrown into a sugar bag, and trudged up the hill to the camp. The workers slept in a long wooden structure that reminded me of the back side of the church sheds in West Bloomfield. The long rows of beds stood up on posts as though they differed from the floor, but they were the same rough boards. A trough to wash in ran along the wall, and soiled shirts, pants, and muddy socks were strewn about. We took one smell of the place and went on up the hill. Finding a level spot of sun-baked clay, we spread our blankets, read Byron until dark, and then rolled over to go to sleep. Sid breathed calmly and regularly all night, but I lay staring at the stars. At three in the morning a fog rolled in from the sea and dropped water into my face and soaked my blanket through. I got up when day came, coughing and shivering and well tired out.

Near where we lay a thin stream of water ran down a trough and dripped into a square pond, or cistern, dug in the clay. After combing away the "frog spit" and fishing out a dead mouse, we bathed in that cistern, making a gorgeous lather with a big cake of tar soap. Then we rolled up our blankets, hid them in the brush, and went downhill to the eating shed. There we found "a great abundance of stiff and heavy food, a peculiar thick syrup which I have never seen before except in Mercersburg—'the goo' we used to call it— and those white cups that are heaviest when empty." We sat on benches as at a Sunday school picnic. Everybody ate as fast as he could so that he might rest on a rock a few minutes before the whistle blew, though few achieved it. There was little talk, but a "general rumble of discontent," as it seemed to my wearied spirit. Half of the workers were Mexican, and I noted that discontent is "the same in both languages." I also expressed my squeamishness with the remark that "it was not like a hog pen, because hogs are quiet and contented as soon as they get at the food."

After breakfast we went round the hill and down into the quarry to work. Sid and I found ourselves in a "chain gang" with two Mexicans. From where we stood watching the day before we had not perceived the prodigious weight of the chains or of the pulley-blocks that had to be dragged out from a derrick on the flatcar and hooked onto them. To drape a chain around a rock so that when the chain is pulled taut the rock will not slip out requires no more mechanical sense than we had judged. But when the rock weighs twenty tons and it takes four strong men to carry the chain, when two of the men speak one language and two another, and when this operation is performed all day in a blazing sun with the thermometer at 112 degrees in the shade, it is not child's play. There is mortal danger in it too, if the child is dreamy, for that enormous pulley block is swinging back and forth in giant arcs at the height of his head while he bends to work.

To increase my troubles, Sid's arm gave out after the first day, and they put him to ditch-digging up at the eating shed. His place was taken by another Mexican, and I had to keep up alone and in Spanish the bluff that I was a "chain man." I kept it up for two more days, but ended my career in the quarry as a "mucker."

On the fourth morning, as we came downhill to breakfast, the foreman called us over to his cabin door.

"Say, you boys ain't washing in that cistern up there where you sleep?" he asked.

"We *are*!" Sid answered.

"Why no," he said, "you hadn't oughta do that. That's the water we use in the kitchen."

This did not increase my pleasure in our meals, and it deprived our hard-bottom bedroom of its principal charm. I was easily convinced, when Sid's strained arm gave out completely, that we both needed a change of occupation. Nor did my noble purpose prevent me from agreeing that, to find exactly the right kind of work, we should have to move on to Arizona. From that it seemed an obvious inference that we should spend a couple of preliminary weeks on the shore of the Pacific, training in our bare skins so that we could settle, when we got there, the question whether a white man can beat an Indian in a foot race.

That training took place a little way up the coast from the tiny village of Santa Monica. The whole region is Santa Monica now, but then it was a desert of dunes and dry hills bordering a solitary beach, a wilderness peopled mostly by coyotes and rattlesnakes and terns and pelicans, with giant condors wheeling in the silent winds above them. We unshouldered our packs in a dry gully, unredeemed even by a shade tree, and undertook to go savage twenty-four hours a day. With my brown skin I proved a better savage than Sid, but not much better. A sunburn sent us back to civilization in hilarious agony, and we decided to let the Indians have the foot race by default.

Los Angeles was almost as young as I was then, boasting but two real business streets named Spring and Main. The public library occupied a top floor near one of them, and while we were lurking in a furnished room, hoarding our small earnings and watching the employment agencies for jobs in Arizona, I went over there one Sunday morning thinking I would read a book. The outdoor entrance was locked, but I found a side door open and climbed six flights to the reading room. There a ponderous colored man was down on his knees beside a pail of water, just beginning, with a majesty of reluctance, to scrub the floor. He greeted me as a racial brother—I was in fact several shades darker than he—and asked me if I wanted a job. I said I wouldn't run if I saw one.

"What'll you take," he asked, "to mop this here flo'?"

"The whole library?" I asked.

"Yas, the whole thing. Now looka here, I ain't rich, I'se jus' lazy. I'se offerin' you yo' breakfus'."

I was really hungry, and took his offer. I mopped the Public Library of Los Angeles from Fiction to Philosophy for the munificent sum of twenty-five cents.

To earn our meals pending a free pass to Arizona, I signed up one day for a job driving horses in a suburb called Gardena. When I arrived, the job was gone, and I had to walk all the way back without my dinner. I stopped at a ranch house and begged a meal, a further descent in the social scale of which I was very proud.

I was still deluding myself, if not my mother, that I had come out west to earn money and pay my debts. In fact, I kept this opinion fresh and green in my mind, without doing in all more than ten days' work, right up to the hour I took the train for home. A letter dated at Gardena shows me in the act of self-delusion—also in the act of bragging about my penniless condition in supermanly disregard of my mother's worry.

"We didn't make big money with our pick and shovel, and we decided that a day or two of hunting for a better place would pay. In the meantime, we are living on shredded wheat biscuit which we purchased in the days of prosperity, and 35 cents which is left after our fee to the employment agency . . . Of course we have hundreds of jobs we could get right here, but we have to be on hand to tend to these larger enterprises. A man can't possibly lack work in the West. If something doesn't develop at one o'clock—it's now 12:30—I shall begin washing buggies for a dollar and a half a day."

Those "larger enterprises" consisted, you must remember, not only of bumming our way to Arizona and running foot races with Indians, but also of racing over the plains on broncho ponies earning a cowboy's wages.

That letter ended in a P.S.: "I have a place now. I am supposed to be able to drive 2, 4, or 6 horses and I get $1.50 a day and my board. I hope the horses can understand English. . . ."

And then a postcard: "Dear Folks—This ought to arrive contemporarily with one saying that I am at Gardena. I'm not, I'm at Catalina. The six-horse racket didn't go—I didn't even see the horses. . . ."

Chapter 25

A Try at Determination

I DIDN'T see Catalina either, for the next day a job turned up with free transportation to Flagstaff, Arizona. It was only one job—but this gave me a fine opportunity to say to Sid in an offhand manner:

"You take the pass, your arm is so bad, and I'll come along on a freight."

As Sid was not to be shipped until morning, I decided to board my freight that same night and beat him to his first stop in Barstow the next afternoon. He came down to the railroad yards to see me off, and at about ten-thirty I bade him "goodbye" and "Barstow or bust," swinging my legs from the catwalk along a tank car in the middle of the train. My idea was to stay awake all night and, when I saw a brakeman, dodge him round the tank—a fine idea for Charles Lindbergh, but I fell sound asleep before we reached San Bernardino and woke up with a lantern in my face.

"What the hell are you doin' here—committin' suicide?"

I had my story ready, and thus aroused from dreaming, a firm belief that it was true. I was a forlorn and sickly boy, penniless and desperate about my poor mother on the home ranch up near Flagstaff. In April I had gone down to Los Angeles to try to make my way in the world, found a job in a grocery store, but I wasn't very strong and got awful sick and they had to send me money, and the next thing I knew my father died, and now my mother was all alone on the ranch and got to have me home to help. My words came too fast to be false, and sobs came with them, and tears stood in my hollow eyes. My face does know well how to look sad. The brakeman gave me a rough pat on the shoulder.

"Brace up, son," he said. "An' now lemme tell you something.

169

Don't go to sleep again, you'll roll off o' here. I'll come by next time the train stops and put you in a safer place."

He did come by, and I rode into San Bernardino concealed inside a pile of lumber.

At San Bernardino they made up a new train, and the brakeman came by again, still kindly, but with the sad news that I would have to get off. That lumber wasn't going any farther; dawn was coming; he would risk his own job taking me by daylight.

I climbed down and walked around the train to board my tank car again, but he came after me and put me off once more.

"Now you stay off!" he said.

I disappeared in the shadows, but kept watch on the shifting cars, sneaking out every little while to try a door, or peer into a possible lurk-hole. I climbed an odd-looking car and contemplated jumping down an open chute in its roof, though I was not sure I could get out again. Later I saw it backed into a siding and filled through that shute with ice.

My train left San Bernardino with an engine at each end, and by the time it was ready to go, so many cars, engines, and cabooses had been working back and forth that I was confused. There seemed to be two or three trains, and I could not tell which was mine. I saw a yardman, as I thought, walk out east to open a switch, and I ran after him.

"Say, which of these trains is going east?" I asked. He straightened up and raised his lantern to my face.

"Son," he said, "I told you you can't go any farther on this train and you can't."

I loosed a new flood of heartbreaks: the mortgage, the unmilked cows, the rusting machinery, my mother's lungs—she was coughing blood already when I left—my own shame and failure. We both believed it all implicitly. I had one dollar left to buy food along the way. Would he take that dollar and call it a ticket to Barstow?

"I don't want your money, son," he said. "Go back and talk to the rear-end brakeman. He might take it."

He saw the tears in my eyes.

"I'll tell you something else," he said. "You won't be half so thirsty if you stay off as if you get kicked off in the desert."

The rear-end brakeman was standing by the caboose, thick-chested, surly, rubber-lipped. I offered him my dollar for the ride to Barstow.

"Is that all you got?" he said.

I said it was.

"What's your hurry?"

I launched again into my pathetic story, and he heard me out in silence.

"By the way," he said when I had finished, "who's the sheriff up there in Coconino County?"

I came to earth with a thud. To my surprise, I did not know!

"Will you take my dollar or not?" I said.

He made no answer. He was looking ahead along the train.

"Look here, I'm offering you my last dollar for a ride to Barstow. It doesn't matter why I want to get there. Will you take it or not?"

He caught a signal from ahead and waved his lantern. The engine coughed, the train began to move, and he climbed into the caboose without a word.

"All right, then," I said. "I'll see you in Barstow!"

As the tender of the rear engine passed me I caught hold of its iron ladder and climbed halfway up. I clung there as far as the extra engine went—over a long mountain. When at last we stopped, I climbed down with aching arms and walked past the surly brakeman, who sat smoking in the door of the caboose. Neither of us spoke, and I got on the next car and ran along the top of the train looking for a place to hide. Finding nothing, I jumped down on the other side and ran back toward the rear end, trying all doors. One of them, as though by a special miracle, stood part way open, and I climbed in and pulled it shut.

That car was empty, but its last load had been fertilizer, and the floor was covered with a stinking dust of animal decay. When the train moved, the air filled with that dust and with a racket like the splitting of a million icebergs. I could not see; I could not hear my voice when I yelled. Every few minutes the jouncing of the springs would get into rhythm with the cracks between the rails, and the floor leap up and down so vigorously that I would have to take it standing on my toes. Dawn came as had been promised, and after it an August day in the Mojave Desert. It must have been 130 degrees in the shade outside the car—inside it was a crematory. In early afternoon, when we were still some twenty miles from Barstow, and I half-dead from insubstantial vomiting and unremitting thirst, that surly brakeman rolled back the door of my private car and stuck his head in.

"Young man," he said, "I'll take that dollar now unless you want to walk from here."

When I climbed out at last in Barstow and was staggering across the tracks to a hydrant, he came past me.

"I'll give you some advice," he said. "Next time don't tell the brakeman all you got."

I had enough wit left to answer:

"I didn't!"

But it was not true. I had nothing in my possession but an old white sugar bag full of shredded wheat and bread crumbs. I went up a slope to a little cottonwood grove a hundred yards from the station, and dropped down on the ground and slept. I met Sid's train when it came through, and he jumped out of the smoker full of hard, healthy spirits as always.

"Max, you look like a ghost!" he laughed.

I started to tell him how many times I had been kicked off that train.

"Don't tell me! I know! I know!" he said. "You aren't going to do it again. I've made a discovery. We're both going to ride the rest of the way on one pass!"

Sid's discovery was that a pass is punched differently for each division of the railroad by the conductor who takes the train through that division. His scheme, as it worked out, was this: I took the pass that night and rode to Needles. That covered one division, and the pass was punched accordingly. Meanwhile, Sid walked along the track from Barstow to Daggett, the next station east. At Needles the next morning I put the pass in a sealed envelope, and when the western local came through, asked the conductor if he would mind handing it to a friend of mine who would call for it at Daggett. When Sid got the pass again, he boarded the next train east and came to Needles, explaining to the conductor that his pass was punched for that division because he had stopped off to see a friend in Daggett. From Needles Sid went on to Flagstaff, and I walked fifteen miles along the track to Mellen. There, after a twenty-four hour wait, receiving the pass from a local conductor going west, I took the next train east. My train happened to be full of soldiers coming from the Philippines, and when I saw this I removed my jumper, covered my overalls with a blanket, sprawled myself out in the attitude of a returning hero, and went calmly to sleep. I thus evaded the sole risk in our scheme—that I might be asked to reproduce Sid's signature on the pass.

Mellen was nothing but a shack and a water tank, but I had earned a good meal before leaving Needles by mopping the floor of the station restaurant, so I was not too hungry. I wandered away into the desert and lived my twenty-four hours in companionship with eternity. That burning day and star-cooled night, the slow serene blush of dawn, infinitely far and beyond understanding, dwell in my memory as though I had lived a life in the Arizona desert. It was, in so far as such a thing is possible to an infidel, my mystic ecstasy. I gave a reticent hint of it in a letter I wrote to Crystal sitting in the shade of the water tank.

"I love the desert. It is such perfect solitude to lie in the sand a mile at least from the first lonely Indian shack, and not a sound but the slow hot wind in the sage brush and the coyotes howling near by or barking sometimes within a few rods. I think our sensations go in circles, so that the extreme comes near to the opposite. I was terribly lonesome and unhappy in Elmira after you left, and I'm so happy out here I want to run and sing."

There was, of course, no cowboy work in Flagstaff. It is a timber country primarily, and as we arrived penniless and Sid was too late for his job, there was nothing to do but find work in the timber— or try to. We rode out eighteen miles on a narrow-gauge railroad to a camp that wanted "choppers," and we went on a Saturday, hoping to get our Sunday meals for nothing. They were felling giant pine trees in a solemn forest velvet-paved with brown needles. When a tree fell, the choppers would mount the trunk with axes and clean it of its limbs. The big limbs were young trees themselves in size, and as they stood in all directions round the trunk, the axe had to be swung with mighty force and from every conceivable position. It was work for gymnasts. However, we gaily hunted up the boss, another frosty Scot, whom we found standing in the door of his log hut, and told him we were choppers. He took in Sid's eye-glasses and my physique in one glance.

"You boys can't chop," he said.

Sid laughed, and as usual the frost began to melt.

"Besides, you made a mistake coming up here Saturday. We're working Sundays."

That increased Sid's merriment, and the Scot himself held back a grin.

"I'll give ye your dinner and breakfast, and the loan of an axe, but I'll tell ye right now, ye can't chop."

We slept an azure-lidded sleep on that deep carpet of needles and mounted the trees the next morning like young giants. We dropped off the trees at five-thirty the same afternoon like slabs of dead bark.

I had barely strength to walk. The next morning my palms were so swollen from the blows of the helve that I could not close my hands. Sid's bad arm hung at his side as though paralyzed. There was no question of our going to work. We ate breakfast and went over to the boss's hut to get our wages. He met us again in the door and ran a thoughtful finger along the blade of my axe.

"I told you boys you couldn't chop," he said. "I'll stick to my promise though—I won't charge you for the axes."

Thus ended our career as cowboys! We slept in the woods near Flagstaff for some days, making forays into the town for small jobs that would provide a meal or two. I still cherished the notion that I was looking for steady work and was anxiously concerned to pay my debts, but Sid began to turn his mind to his beloved Indians. A caravan of Moquis had come down from Oraibi ninety miles away and would be starting home in two days. He decided suddenly to go along.

"I'm not coming back," he said with a small laugh and a large grimness. "I'm going up there and live two years at least in the wilds. I like these Indians. I like the way they laugh. They're really happy. They're a lot happier than we are, and more at home on the earth. I like them better than white people."

Notwithstanding my rich brown color, I felt included among the white people in this generalization. There was something almost religious in Sid's hard look of purpose, and religion can be the hardest thing on earth. He asked me to go along, but we both knew I was not going. I wrote home: "The still small voice could barely keep me from taking the trip with Sid to their villages. I never wanted to do anything more in my life." But that was true of only half of me—for it was by splitting myself in two that I had created this recklessly adventuring, freight-train riding, mother-dismaying character. Had my mother been only a mother, my family conventionally respectable or Philistine, my revolution might have been more perfect. But I was revolting against a mother who was herself a rebel, and against a home life that was quite as adventurous in ideal ways as life with Indians. I still had with me the self that loved that life, a self with Cherith Farm spreading down before me to the lake, a small utopia developing round that farm, the romance of education in the distance, writing to be done—"there is no pleasure in the world like writing things"—and the wilds of the mind to conquer. And I had that underlying vein of practical horse sense which I carry with me, sometimes proud, sometimes regretful of it. We were well into August, and those caravans came down to the railroad only once in two or three months. I agreed with Sid about the unwarlike Moquis—they seemed to me "a people standing and smiling as the world goes round, while all the rest of us sit and frown"—but nevertheless I decided to stay with the despised Caucasians.

ENVOI

Sid did live two years with the Indians in the Painted Desert, and he came home then supposedly for a short stay. But he was bewitched by a girl too free and gay to be dismissed as "civilized," and found himself, before Pan could intervene, a husband. I next saw him tethered to a small suburban house in Bridgeport, eating sand for indigestion and desperately struggling to fan up a spark of life in the haggard skin-and-bones and big sad blue eyes of a boy baby. The boy for some mysterious reason could take no nourishment and had lain almost motionless in his cradle since birth. It seemed to me tragic that a son should enter the world with a handicap like that, a son born to this poet of athletics and of healthy life. In a gust of ice-cold rationality I said to Sid:

"Why do you try to keep him alive? Why not let him die and get another?"

Sid was shocked—for he was, in biological matters, far more conventional than I.

"I suppose perhaps you're right," he said, but he did not mean it.

Soon after that he took his family out west to live on the edge of a gold mine in the foothills of the Sierras. I never heard much about the dying baby again until in France one day in 1931 when I picked up a London paper and learned that Sidney B. Wood, Jr., a boy of sixteen, was tennis champion of the world at Wimbledon.

Chapter 26

Ordeal by Battle

SID had to telegraph east for money to buy a horse, and feeling responsible for the default of his Tonopah silver mines, he insisted on providing me with ten dollars and a ticket home. I stipulated that I was only borrowing the money—a stipulation that I now remember for the first time—but accepted the offer. For, while I was ready, underneath my self-delusions, to go home without money, I was not ready to ask my parents to pay the fare. There was a Knights of Pythias convention in San Francisco with round-trip tickets at a reduced price, and we bought from a "scalper" the return half of one appertaining to a Timothy Donahue. It was punched with his description—blue-eyed, grey-haired, short. In the light of our recent modes of travel, this seemed a minor difficulty, but we agreed that if I had trouble with the ticket I should telegraph Sid at Oraibi, and he would have more money sent to me. Timothy had stopped in Flagstaff on his way out, and so my ticket took me first to San Francisco and then home on any road I chose. I did not intend to go straight home, of course; I was still going to work. But work continued to look more abundant as well as pleasanter the farther off it was, and so I left on the western leg of my journey at once.

On the road I learned that I had to take my ticket to a tourist office in San Francisco and get it countersigned for the trip home. That looked bad, and I went there the morning after I arrived. An austere and fidgety dignitary behind the high counter asked me to reproduce the signature of Mr. Donahue, and while I made the attempt compared my aspect with that indicated on the ticket: Eyes . . . blue; Hair . . . grey; Stature . . . short.

It was no use. I had passed for a Mexican, an Indian, a gipsy, a

Negro, I had even passed for a soldier, but I could not pass for a grey-haired, short, and blue-eyed Knight of Pythias. I tried to laugh it off, but the clerk was morally indignant. Didn't I know that forgery is a crime? He smoothed out my ticket with shaking white fingers, placed it under a paperweight on his desk, and with a snap of his lips told me to "get out." I dived up onto the counter, crawled halfway across the desk, and was back down with the ticket in my hand before he could do more than grunt and grab the paperweight. His "Give me back that ticket!" focused a dozen eyes on me, but I scooted out of a side door and disappeared down an alley. This conduct of a shrewd animal on my part was due to the fact that I had just sixty cents left in my pocket.

I sold the ticket to another "scalper" for five dollars—not unaware that I too now deserved that name—and sent a telegram to Sid as agreed. I hardly expected him to get it, and he never did. And since there was no work in San Francisco except for strike-breakers, I succeeded in "living life" for the next two weeks somewhat more vividly than I had bargained for. I slept on the beach by the Cliff House and lived on griddlecakes and free lunches. I would go into a bar when it was crowded, pick up an empty beer glass, and holding it casually in my hand, stroll over to get the lunch that went with it.

"This morning," I wrote Crystal, "I had three big griddlecakes for breakfast, and then started out with the last five cents I had on earth to a place two miles away where I had learned of a job. To show you to what straits I am reduced, it was dishwashing—for $20 a month, board and lodging. Think of it! And they wouldn't have me!

"This afternoon I pawned my knife for 10 cents and got three more big griddlecakes . . .

"The hard part of being broke is not the eating little and sleeping on the ground, etc., but the having no place to go to. It occurred to me when I started back from my dish-washing exploit, why should I start back at all? I belonged out there just as much as in the middle of the city."

My diet was not adequate, and I developed an orticaria which caused both my eyes to swell and turn red. In this condition I went down into Chinatown one evening to spend another "last five cents," or near it, on a smoke of opium. Wandering about after my brief smoke, I started down some steps into a curio shop just as some fashionable tourists were coming out. I flattened myself against the wall to let them pass, but their guide, seeing me there with my red eyes and ragged overalls, said:

"Get out of the way, can't you see these ladies want to pass?"

He gave me a rough push, which I resisted.

"Who do you think you are?" I said.

"I'm a licensed guide, that's who I am," and he showed me a badge under his lapel.

"That doesn't give you the right to push me around."

He called to an idle guide standing near.

"Here, Jim, take this bum to the station. He's hangin' around here insulting women."

Together they dragged me up the steps, and Jim marched me down the street. I soon convinced Jim that I was not insulting women, and he let me go.

"Just the same you better trot along," he said. "There's no use startin' anything around here."

"All right," I said, "but I want that guide's number, and I want to know where I can find him later on."

"He's number 68, and you'll find him up in Halloran's saloon around midnight," he said, and gave me the address.

It was then nine o'clock, and by midnight the wrath had evaporated from my blood. Three hours is an awful stretch for my adrenal glands. Guide number 68 now seemed merely one of a planetary population of snobs and fools, and the fact that he had insulted me instead of somebody else a negligible accident. However, that was not the question. The question was whether I had come out here honestly looking for adventure or not, and whether if I had, I was going to back down because it meant a fight. It meant a fight with a rough guy, in a rough end of the country, with no friends to back me, no name, no money, and the rags of a hobo on my back. The opportunity to exhibit prowess, if I had any—to settle that old nagging question whether I really am a man—was just about perfect.

After some inward debate, I decided to settle it. Feeling that the correct preliminary was to take a drink, I went and bought myself a glass of beer—a very small beer, for steins and schooners were unknown in those days in the West. Thus fortified, I went around at midnight to Halloran's saloon and flung the door open as though I were a high wind. A half dozen of those tough guys in the Chinatown guide business were leaning against the bar. Halloran was behind it, a mountain in a white apron. I must have looked like a caricature of Leslie Howard's Hamlet as I strode in, clad in my old black shirt and overalls. I weighed then only 142 pounds and was a half inch under my present height of six feet.

"I'm looking for guide number 68!" I shouted.

A thick-set chesty thug stepped out, larger by half than I remembered him.

"Here I am! What the hell do you want?"

"I want to know what you meant by saying I was insulting women down there tonight. You know damn well you lied!"

"Well, I'll be damned!" he said, moving as though to rip off his coat.

But the gang came up with questions, and we both began explaining hotly what had happened. Halloran, the white mountain, stepped between us.

"If you're going to start anything, you get out o' here! There's no fightin' in here."

"All right, I'll go," I said, "But just one minute—"

I turned to number 68.

"If you want to continue this conversation, I'll wait for you around the corner."

Assuming a dignity that I thought appropriate to that ferocious remark, I turned and walked through the door. Unimpressed by my dignity, guide number 68 helped me along by planting his fist in the nape of my neck. I went down on my hands on the sidewalk, but recovered quickly, and when he came through the door tackled him like a football player—that being the nearest I had ever come to fighting—threw him, and clambered on him, and got him by the throat. This world is actually so unjust and unknightly that those other guides started hitting and kicking me while I was trying valiantly to pound number 68's head into the flagstones. The issue was still undecided when a firm hand seized me by the collar and yanked me to my feet. I thought it must be Halloran, but it wasn't, it was a policeman, and I was arrested. The policeman marched me down the street with six of those guides crowding after, denouncing me as a drunk, a maniac, a cutthroat, a highway robber, everything a boy's heart could ask except a pirate chief, and demanding that I be locked up.

To make sure of my capture, number 68, my mortal enemy, got hold of my free arm and twisted it behind my back until it hurt.

"Officer," I said, "I'm not trying to escape. What right has this private citizen to twist my arm?"

"You just shut up and come along with me," the officer said.

At the corner he telephoned for a patrol wagon, and after a short wait, amid faint cheers from a group that had gathered, I was loaded in and whisked away to the police station.

My name and crime of disturbing the peace having been entered in a book, I was led away to a tiny iron cell with room for two and already occupied by one, a white-skinned, pimply young man—jailed, he told me, under an unjust charge of indecent exposure.

"I was only brushin' a cigaret ash off my pants!" he argued, and illustrated his argument with a gesture.

What he had done or not done was a matter of supreme indifference to me. I was filled with my own complacence. I lay down on the bare floor of that cell and slept the sleep of the just, of one whose soul is saved—and his body too, by Heaven's grace, still intact.

In the morning the guard handed us through the bars a battered cup of coffee-mud and a chunk of bread. Some hours later my name was called out in the corridor, and the question asked: "Do you or do you not wish to see Attorney Caldwell?" Thinking I would see all there was to see, I said "Sure." The result was that Mr. Caldwell agreed to handle my case in court if I would promise to send him fifteen dollars when I got home. His handling consisted of a few questions bringing out my origin and the motive of my wanderings. The policeman appeared and swore I was drunk. I swore that he was sober and even so was deaf, dumb and blind—couldn't see who was disturbing the peace, couldn't hear a complaint from a respectable citizen, couldn't answer a polite question. A man in that condition who can also be proven by a competent witness to have been sober ought not to be let out at night, to say nothing of walking the streets in a uniform. It was quite an oration, and was incongruous enough with my rags and red swollen eyes to sound funny.

"Now, be honest," His Honor asked with a grin. "Do you mean to tell us this interesting story, and then ask us to believe you spent a whole night in Chinatown without taking a drink?"

"Your Honor," I said, "this is the gospel truth: I had one small beer."

"That's it. I knew it," he said. "It's that small beer habit. That's what got you into trouble. I'd advise you to cut out the small beers."

"I know it's bad, Your Honor," I said, "but out here in the Wild West you can't get a big one!"

Which was so notoriously true that even the policeman laughed.

"Case dismissed!" the judge said. "Get outa here and go back to college!"

Not satisfied with having this adventure, manhood demanded that I report it to my mother in a hard and casual tone as though street fights were a part of my natural way of life.

"I besmirched the family honor by spending last night in jail," was my way of announcing it. "I slept very well in the cell with a horrible looking partner in crime, but this morning I was covered with bedbug bites. I don't see how they fool the bugs into thinking the plank floor of a cell is a bed—there's nothing misleading about it. I got into a little difficulty unavoidably with a fresh guide in Chinatown, and the cop pinched me, and I was taken to jail in the patrol. . . . The cop is the one I'm disgusted with. It didn't show a very good fighting spirit for him to pick me out of a gang of six of these men, every one of them against me and every one of them half drunk, and I alone the only sober man on the street."

Needless to say my mother moved heaven and earth, or at least Glenora and Elmira, to get into communication with me and telegraph the full fare home. By the time her message came, however, I had already received from Scottie Beacham in Decatur a loan of fifteen dollars and was out of trouble. I was indeed never really in trouble. I mean that my hungry destitution at its worst was voluntary and therefore phony. Still it taught me as no verbal teaching could what trouble is. I was as innocent of political thinking that summer as when I wrote my Freshman philippic against William Jennings Bryan. I knew nothing of socialism, and was little impressed in San Francisco by the soap-box orators of the party.

"The socialism they have out here as far as I can make out is 'These are the words which loud shall ring: Down down down with everything!' "

Nevertheless, I arrived at an opinion as extreme as the socialists' about the distribution of wealth, and I took by impulse an attitude of loyalty to the struggle of labor.

"The money is received," I wrote, "and makes me feel like the prodigal son. I have not had to perform any such supernatural feat as eating the husks that the swine did not eat, but I've found out that there are very few husks left in the working world after the swine get through eating. People are waking up out here—I think there is an average of three strikes reported in every paper. I could get rich in a month if I wanted to work when they are striking. I wouldn't blame a regular laborer, but I certainly have no business interfering with them."

On my way home I stopped in Illinois to visit my roué friend Scottie, and that was the last straw in my mother's load of worry.

She sent me a letter there which told me how cruel my sketchy bragging had been:

"Beloved, I am going through the motions of living but it is not life and will not be until I see you and touch you again. At night it seems impossible that I shall ever have you, but the morning gives me hope. I hear the trains when everything else is still, and my heart chokes me when I think that one of them will bring you at last. Can I ever comfort you for all you have suffered? Can I—but alas I know that I can not—so wrap you about with love that you will forget the horrors upon which your young eyes have rested. O my darling! Don't think of anything but getting home. Get the clothes you need and borrow the necessary money—and come."

My mother's anxious glooms were growing upon her in those years. Whatever troubled her would be exaggerated beyond measure. And she was troubled now, I suspect, by other thoughts than of the "horrors" I had seen. She must have perceived the insufferable Pharisaism of my pretense to be perpetually concerned with finding work and earning money. That must have made her clear soul sick. Even my intention to stop off and play with Scottie on my way home had to be rationalized and moralized until I sounded as hollow as a decayed nut.

"Scott has a position for me and I told him I would come in a week. That's the most money in the shortest time, I'm sure."

In a long letter to me in Decatur, Crystal tried to make me feel the extremeness of my mother's plight.

"Don't stay a *minute longer* in Decatur than is *absolutely necessary*. I can't put it too strong. Mamma's happiness not only, but her health and sanity depend on you."

I resented in a mulish mood this interference with my important business of "living life," and stayed on a day or two in spite of it. Now I read the record of that day or two in her loved handwriting in the "Cherith Log":

"Tuesday, Sept. 2—Waiting—listening for trains.

"Wednesday, Sept. 3—Waiting—Crystal, the divine comforter, says nothing but does all.

"Thursday, Sept. 4—Max came—through the path in the woods— at last. Evening about the fire. Rest and peace."

I called this behavior "selfishness" afterward in a repentant letter to my sister, and there was that factor in it. But I was not having so grand a time in Decatur. The parturition of a self would have been a better name for my sin.

Chapter 27

Before a Fall

MY MOTHER begged me before I set off for Junior year at college to promise her I would not drink or smoke. Filled as I was with the great outdoors and myself a stout Cortez adventuring in it, I had no intention of falling back into those effete vices, but I objected to her invasion of my liberty. One morning she came into my room, after an anxious night, and woke me with a devastating question:

"Max, what would you think if you saw Crystal with a cigar in her mouth?"

"Fine!" I said. "If she was enjoying it, why not? I don't see why women should be shut out from anything that men enjoy. I believe absolutely in sex equality!"

It was a deadly answer, for that of all things was what she wanted me to believe in. I remember the harsh way I said it and her mind-baffled, heart-stricken look as she left my room. It was victory enough, and more than enough, for me. When I came down to breakfast, I said that if she would stop talking about "promises," I would tell her the interesting fact that I had decided not to drink or smoke —I cared too much for my health. That was the end of my war for independence. We were very close and full of laughter after that, and every afternoon before her nap I read to her from Robert Louis Stevenson.

I adhered to that decision, but I found other ways to waste my time. Instead of living alone, I joined eight other boys from different fraternities in renting a vacant house to sleep and study in. We laid in a few tons of coal and hired an aged darky with deeply bending knees to tend the fires, make the beds, and even on state occasions sweep the floors. Thus equipped, we went in for economy, freedom, and interfraternity companionship. We were a motley crowd, and 4 Hoxie Street was soon renowned throughout the town and college as "The Sink." The companionship was delightful, the economy so improvident that for several weeks during the coal strike there was no heat at all. And the freedom was so great that all eight of us barely missed being fired from college. For The Sink, at the high point of its flight through the New England heavens— and if you can imagine a sink flying through heaven, that is about right—extended a nocturnal hospitality to some chorus girls who came over from North Adams after the show.

Very little work was done, and most of it by me, for I was the only one who could study while others were talking. Concentration they called it, but I called it being interested in the book. Gordon Grand and I, who roomed together on the top floor, used often to retire early and read Victor Hugo aloud, but that was about the height of The Sink's attainments in the sphere of mental culture. Gordon was a gracious and perfect gentleman, raised above the pedestrian run of mankind by an expert familiarity with horses. He could drive a four-in-hand or an eight-horse tallyho in exquisite style, with exquisite control, in exquisitely correct costume. He has since achieved celebrity as the author of warmhearted stories about hunting and horse racing, but he showed no signs of creative impulse then. He was just a gallant friend to camp with in an attic where frequently the ice in the pitcher would be two inches thick. He reminds me that I once threw my shoe through the window glass to prove that we might just as well be out-of-doors.

My own attitude to the curriculum was a mixture of lazy negligence and scorn. I particularly despised a class in government which might have mellowed some of my subsequent assertions in this field. It was still a topic without interest for me, and I never read the textbook or listened to the teacher except to satirize in my notes his way of using language.

"Why, I won't get a Phi Beta Kappa," I wrote to my sister, "now that I've scorned these last examinations! I got A in Philosophy and Economics, B in Dante and German, and D (the lowest mark that passes) in a Government course. I knew I was going to get that D because I went to sleep in the class and then had a scrap with the little ignorant professor."

The "little ignorant professor" was William Bennett Munro, famous subsequently in Political Science and no doubt brilliantly equipped to teach me then had I but had a humble wish to learn.

Scorn is not quite the name for my state, I think, but arrogance—
a self-indulgent arrogance toward every set and customary task.
Having been elected Editor-in-Chief of *The Gul*,[1] I was supposed to
write for it a series of satires called "Roasts." I postponed this duty
until the scandal, helped on by the evil reputation of The Sink,
spread beyond the editorial board. The whole class was beginning
to wonder whether I would or could do it. I am afraid I enjoyed
this scandal, and I enjoyed sitting down very casually one evening,
taking pains to be even so casual as to leave my cap on, and composing "Roasts" the whole night long. I can not refrain from saying
that my "Roasts" seem pretty good to me—especially *The Munro
Doctrine*, a vicious (but conceivably salutary) burlesque of a lecture by my youthful government professor, who had a habit of
making each statement in plain English and then repeating it in big
Latin words that would frighten the Conscript Fathers. These satires
are better in their kind than many of the serious things I published
in the *Lit*. But since that number of *The Gul* was reviewed by Stuart
Pratt Sherman, and Stuart grew to be a famous critic, I feel obliged
to tell you that he found it "tempting to linger on the pictorial
aspect of the book, because when we come to the literary department it is harder to say anything pleasant."

My arrogance was particularly directed against classes in English,
which I avoided as a fox avoids a trap. Lewis Perry, afterward principal of Phillips Exeter Academy, reminds me that I did register in
my Junior year for his course in "Writing." He was a brilliant
tennis player and a brother of Bliss Perry, famous editor of the
Atlantic Monthly, and this redeemed him somewhat in my eyes from
the general ignominy of English professors. With a little arrogance
of his own, he might perhaps have kept me down. But he only
boosted me into the sky by handing back my first composition with
the remark:

"Eastman, this is written so much better than I can write that
I don't feel as if I could be of help to you!"

I withdrew from Perry's class and registered for advanced physics,
pursuing without moderation an idea which I would subsequently
weigh carefully of the relation between literary art and scientific
knowledge.

"Writers of all kinds," I wrote in my notebook during that year,
"are in need of the scientific spirit: fact or nothing. Writers upon

[1] *Gulielmensian*, the college annual, was brought out each year by the Junior Class.

what must always remain theory forget their responsibility, and are tempted to put down whatever sounds like a good 'thought.' "

This attitude did not, naturally, make a hit with the English Department, and others besides Stuart Sherman attempted to curb my pride. In the *Lit* for January 1903 I had an excitedly imagined speech of "Alexander to his Mutinous Soldiers."[2] That issue was reviewed in the college weekly by an alumnus, an English professor as I remember in Brown University, and he accompanied his review with a letter stating that he had refrained from commenting on Eastman's speech of Alexander, since it was obviously plagiarized from one of the Latin historians. He did not name the historian, and the editor of the weekly showed his letter to Stuart Sherman. Stuart stopped me on the street and asked me rather abruptly one day whether I had had any particular inspiration for my speech of Alexander. I was a little embarrassed to have to say:

"Yes, I did. I got stirred up by the organ music in chapel one Sunday, and got to kind of dreaming I was a great general myself!"

I blushed, and Stuart became a little embarrassed too, for he was not given to intimate psychological inquiries on street corners.

"I didn't mean that," he said. "I meant, had you ever read a speech of Alexander anywhere? It's evident you hadn't."

Then he told me about the alumnus and his unsupported slander.

"Never mind," he said. "It's a compliment. Some of those speeches in the Latin historians are damned good!"

My indifference to Government was mitigated a tiny bit by Crystal's writing that she was thinking of becoming a socialist. "I've often wondered what a socialist is," I answered. "Maybe I'll join you." And a month later: "I read William Morris's *News from Nowhere,* which is a sort of socialism book, I think. If all their textbooks are like that, I'd like to make a study of it; it made me feel very happy."

I did not make a study of it—I was too busy! For one thing I had to go to New York and finish off the course in metropolitan sophistication I had begun with my roommate Scottie Beacham in freshman year. It was bad propaedeutics to know so much about Broadway without ever having seen it. So I skipped school and took a night boat down from Albany to spend a week with Scottie in his apartment opposite the Herald Square Hotel. In order to call those days back I would have to remove Macy's Department Store, for we would be sleeping in the midst of the jewelry on the first floor.

[2] To be found in the Appendix, p. 591.

Except for my disappointment in Lillian Russell as viewed from the front row—she filled her clothes too full for me, and although tractable in the matter, I do not by instinct prefer blondes—I remember surprisingly little of that important phase of my education. As the hero of robust adventures in the Wild West, I am afraid I entered the metropolis and took a whiff of its glamors with a certain condescension. My vividest memory is of waking on the steamboat and peeping out of my cabin window, expecting to see New York but seeing the Palisades, so close and rosy-colored and yet austere in the first rays of the sun. That revived in me the mood of the desert and filled me once more with the elated joy of the romance of travel.

As vividly, though on a different shelf, I keep the memory of my dancing with the prostitutes at the old Haymarket, receiving the shock of their too powdered and too crudely offered flesh. They touched upon, but could not solve, a problem that of course was harrowing my soul day and night. All autobiographies, not excepting Rousseau's, are falsified, so far at least as proportion goes, by good taste. It is not tolerable, outside the clinic, to dwell upon one's erotic preoccupations to an extent comparable to the place they occupy in lusty boyish life. Especially is this true of boys brought up as I was in a state of puritanical repression. The best one can do is to confess in passing that he was a lecherous animal as well as a fastidious man, and that the two coexisted on different levels.

I was animal enough in that period, and goaded enough by my lusts, to cohabit with prostitutes or with any other of the sexual objects so well advertised by denunciation in the Hebrew law. In imagination my lecherousness, when it subdued the ever struggling moral poet in me, was brutishly indiscriminate. And since my imaginings led by a natural path to bodily acts or reactions which I had been solemnly informed would make me insane, and I was wasting my will in a constantly recurring struggle against them, I was ready for brutishly heroic measures of cure. Nevertheless, in the actual presence of those girls-for-sale, a kind of shy, fastidious timor, something not much nobler than modesty mixed with discretion, unfocused my desire.

At that time my reticence in these matters was complete—so complete that Crystal, in a correspondence we had about the dangerous excitements of dancing, surmised that I lacked interest in sex!

Crystal was my dearest friend during that year, and we wrote oftener and more intimately than before or since. Had I but had the power to confide in her completely, it might have spared me shipwreck and made my entire life more sound than it has been. My admiration for her was strong enough, and humble enough.

"You give me a new eagerness," I wrote, "to be perfectly honest, and open and upright with people. . . . You have never built up a mist around yourself . . . you are frank with yourself. You almost make me think there is magic in names—clearness, that is what I would notice first if I had not always known you."

Everyone acquainted with Crystal would acknowledge the truth of that description. Her sincerity was dynamic and absolute—more absolute than it could be in an extremely sensitive person. This very quality perhaps made it difficult for me to come close to her. I was an almost morbidly impressible boy trying on ideal principle to be robust. She was robust by nature and inclined to idealize my more fastidious feelings and perceptions.

"Do you feel afraid," she wrote, "that we will someday grow so far apart in tastes that we can't appreciate each other's thoughts and feelings and fancies? The danger will be with me—because you are the finer, more sensitive one. I shall offend from time to time, no doubt. You should tell me when I do, and try to keep me as near as possible."

I did not keep her as near as possible. I did not keep anyone near. "Sentimental secretiveness is a fool trait of mine—I will get rid of it," I once wrote to my mother. But I did not get rid of it, and that is the failure I most deeply regret. To live well one must have a confidant, and the wiser the better—that is the main ground under the psychoanalysts. But my inmost thoughts were locked in me by an action as irresistible as a muscular spasm. Only in late years have I learned that I can, as though with the same motive, recklessly unlock them. I will do that now and tell you the far from flattering story of my first love.

PART IV

LOVE AND NEUROSIS

Chapter 28

A Berkshire Idyl

IT ALL might be blamed, in a manner of speaking, upon Goethe, for Goethe was my hero during that autumn of 1902. "I'd give my small hopes of heaven to empty his ash barrel," I wrote in a letter. And I was especially entranced with the story of his romance with Frederica Brion as told in *Dichtung und Wahrheit*—his "Idyl of Sesenheim" as our good German professor called those chapters of his autobiography. Indeed I was thinking of Goethe and Frederica a large part of the time. I was identifying myself with Goethe, not as a poet, but as a man who had loved with unconventional abandon. I was filled again with an intense yearning for romance, stronger now than the yearning for adventure, and I was more confident of my power to achieve it. My only need was for a slim, swift-moving, dancing, laughing girl like Frederica.

And there was a girl—a bewitchingly pretty girl—in the very next house but one to our fraternity. She was honest, gentle, kind, and gay and delicate, like Frederica, and like Frederica, she "had read but little altogether." Unlike Frederica she belonged to the aristocracy, or the bourgeois plutocrats, who turn Williams from a college into a *Kurort* every summer. She lived in Trenton but was staying the whole winter, I do not know why unless for the purpose of my destruction, with her dour and dying grandfather—whisked about town by his fine horses and insulated from the public by his wide and manicured and polished lawn. A whole flock of such beauties alight under the elms at Williams every spring and fly away in autumn, and the college boys who have an entrée to their society are both envied and despised. But this single one left over for the winter was quite a princess in her fame and inaccessibility. I followed her with my eyes whenever she was visible, and when she was not visible I followed her with my mind. Her remoteness from me was emphasized by the fact that the most pink and perfect gentle-man in my classy fraternity, a natural man-of-money, called upon her every Saturday night with the regularity with which one draws a handsome salary.

In that respect the terms of Goethe's idyl were reversed. I was the rural pastor's child, she the child of the city rich. But the distribution of real culture in America was also reversed. Pastors were almost the sole repositories of culture in the Gilded Age when our city bourgeoisie got rich. So far as concerns the life of ideas, I was as much her superior as though I had grown up in a state capital and she in a rural parish. It is not untrue, therefore, or unexplanatory of the course of our romance, to call her Frederica, if only you will refrain—and I feel sure you will be so magnanimous—from calling me Goethe.

Another fraternity brother of mine, a High-Church Episcopal rector with a feminine collar, a feminine charm, and a liking for risqué stories, conducted a boys' school in near-by Hoosick, New York. He was a great friend of Ralph Erskine, like him "fraternity conscious," and he decided to give a party to the Lambda Chapter on St. Anthony's Eve in January. I did not like rectors, or rectories, or feminine collars, or risqué stories, and I was shy enough, God knows, at parties that I liked. I thought I would not go, but after a long discussion with Ralph about shyness and the problem of living life in spite of it, I changed my mind: I would go, and I would act the part of a born society man and fluent conversationist. With this firm intention I put on my slightly small and shiny dress suit and took the train to Hoosick with the crowd. I do not know how Frederica came to be at that party or who put her at the table on my right. I only know that I kept my vow religiously, chattering away like a trained monkey, to her immense relief (for she too was breathless in strange company) and to the distress of her pink-cheeked friend, the staid proprietor of her Saturday evenings, who was seated on her other side.

After dinner Frederica and I were victors in a game of guessing great men from their pictures, a game at which I, the hero worshipper, was of course expert. Our prize was a saints calendar, and she divided it and gave me the first half of the year, cutting the ribbon in two and retying mine.

"This will be so that you will remember the occasion," she said, resting her eyes in mine for something above a second.

It seems a very simple statement, but I wrote down after it in my Experience Book:

"I felt then more than I have ever felt before."

Which is a tribute, and not an undeserved one, to the glances of those moistly shining hazel eyes.

After the hero game we danced. My assumed role of confidence had by then become myself, and I danced more embracingly than was customary in those days. Mingled with my audacity and the sudden glory of it was a humble feeling of gratitude to her for being beautiful and for liking me.

I do not know what all my voluble conversation with Frederica was about, but the medium in which it moved was our common love for the hills and woods and pastures surrounding the two houses where we lived. Walking and running and skiing and writing poetry among the Berkshire Hills, sometimes with a companion but oftener alone, had become a central theme of the romance of my being. A similar thing, I now learned to my surprise, was true of Frederica. Whisking about town in that slick and proper coach behind those glossy horses, she was not really proud and far away at all, but shy and romantic like me and filled with the same emotions.

One other sentence survives from our conversation, because she told me later that its tone of assurance pleased her. It was this weighty remark from me:

"I want you to take a walk with me some time in Williamstown."

That night I tossed with joy as with a fever in my ice-cold attic room. We had no coal then in The Sink, but even when we did have coal there was no heat in the tiny cell where Gordon and I had shut our beds. It was no place for tossing, whether in joy or pain. Moreover, on that "walk sometime," which occurred the next Friday, a walk through fields and over fences deep in snow, I wore low shoes. I wore them through false prowess mixed with bashfulness. There is something unmanly about rubbers as everybody knows, but the whole college spent the winter in half-fastened arctics, and there was no reason why I should not have worn mine over to the house where Frederica lived. Notwithstanding my rebel opinions, I did not want to walk up that trim driveway and climb those elegant steps in arctics. And then I did not want to go back either, like a little boy, and get my arctics when we started out. All I now remember of that walk is Frederica's sensible concern about my wet feet and my heroic unconcern.

I was coughing badly the next day, and I was coughing the next many days. There seemed little hope that I would cease to cough while tossing all night in an ice-cold attic. I went to a doctor, and he found my temperature a real one—perceptible, I mean, to a thermometer—and told me to pack my things and move down to the infirmary. There I spent almost three weeks burning with a mysterious fever.

They were happy and exalted weeks. "I am just a thin bundle of sickness," I wrote my sister, "but all is well and I am happy over it." Kindled by Frederica's image and the high heat in my blood, my brain put on a veritable riot of creative speculation. I had "thoughts" on every subject under the sun, even the despised subject of government. I lay on a vast saggy bed on the ground floor, where I could look out across the snow to a small huddle of evergreens surrounding the monument which commemorates the birth in a conversation under a haystack of the idea of Foreign Missions. The trees seemed still to be conversing, still excited, about that rather naïve idea. One Sunday after church time, while I lay gazing toward them, I saw, as though it were a dream, Frederica and her pink-cheeked senior emerge from those evergreens and move along the path that passed my window. They came so near that I could see against the snow the glowing brown-and-crimson color of her skin. The day was shining, and she wore as in springtime a great bouquet of violets at her breast. The two were chatting and laughing with great animation, and I felt for the first time jealousy, the ugliest of human passions, scraping its foul nest under my ribs. As they passed out of my vision I turned away in pain from the window where they had been. In a moment there was a knock on my door, and the pink-cheeked senior entered.

"Young man, consider yourself honored," he said, and laid the violets on my pillow.

It would be pleasant if poetry instead of speculative thinking had burst into bloom in me with the heat of my fever for Frederica. But

I can find no sign that I had an impulse to sing. I wrote a brief
Treatise on Aesthetics, an essay on Gladness, a discourse on Abstract
and Concrete Love, two notebooks full of aphorisms and reflections,
a stream of highly philosophical letters, and I finished an essay entitled *O Mores!*—a declaration of aggressive war on custom and
convention.

"Great men are iconoclasts!" my essay exclaimed. "We may all,
artists or not, hope to create some fresh thing out of ourselves. Upon
this ground it seems well for us to be ourselves and not those who
went before us."

Such was my theme, but I glanced away from it in the conclusion:

"Yet what little matters would the works of 'great men' be, if all
the world did not follow in their footsteps, hand on shoulder—
conforming! These things will go two by two and not one by one—
the conservatives and the radicals, the conformers and the noncon-
formers, the conventionists and the cranks. Two weights in a balance
is the world, and words are many."

My mother wrote: "Your last sentence is a gem. Only the whole
thing is so *old*. It is almost a pity to see through, as you do at twenty.
There are—or seem to be—no blessed illusions for you."

It was indeed a pity, and at that moment a deeper pity than she
knew. For my disposition to "see through" was what dammed dis-
astrously in my nerves the impulse of my first love. I saw that
Frederica could not enter with one genuine breath or tremor into
my fervent rebellion against custom and convention, my religion of
the audacious living of life. And I saw, surrounding and containing
that fact an absence in her, not of mental ability, but of a sustained,
spontaneously fervent interest in the life of ideas.

I knew as well as you do now that a little blind emotion was what
our romance called for. I did not have to analyze her character. All
I had to do was love her utter loveliness and be a poet and be young
and sing. But I am—and was, it seems, from early years—incapable
of this lyric blindness. I saw what Frederica was, and that she was
not the thing my growing self could love, at the same time and all
the time I loved her. And as I loved her with unfeigned natural
passion, my soul seethed up like the rip-tide in a narrow firth where
headstrong waters are trying to run both ways. For a time the vast
generic currents of the sea will conquer, and then once more the
specific forms of the impetuous river will assert themselves. Such
conflicts can not be resolved. . . .

I find this aphorism in my notebook of those days: "Love is our feeling for that which is our kin." It tells how elemental was my love for Frederica. I continued to feel as I had felt when she came into my arms for the dance at Hoosick. It is an experience clearly distinguished from others, a quick and categorical sense of belonging. Whether it really deserves to be called love may be questioned; perhaps love should be the name for a rare fruit or blossom man arrives at, rather than the crude sprout of something nature is intent upon. At any rate, this altogether simple feeling formed the ground of what I refer to when I speak of loving Frederica. Upon that ground, given so unequivocally by the chemism of our bodies, we reared a romance for our minds out of our twin worship of the Berkshire Hills, their woods and ferny glens and sweetbriar-rose-infested meadows. Ours was a landscape love, a pastoral, an idyl. Her hazel eyes and color like dark leaves in autumn were harmonious with the mood of my unmystic love of nature. She seemed born to be the mountain nymph or dryad of a poet who could never find these beings in their spirit form.

That love of nature is so strong and large a part of me that I could, I think, have given myself impetuously to this idyl had it been sound and sweet down to its heart with freedom. It was a manacled and crippled thing, a kind of bourgeois parlor imitation of a woodland romance. Frederica's grandmother watched over her goings and comings with the eye of a hungry hawk—an eye which magnified, I mean, by some fifty diameters any least irregular motion in its field of vision. And beyond that field her faculty of conception was similarly equipped for detecting irregularities in the landscape. Frederica might go on a walk in the hills with a boy friend, but never on a picnic. The walk must start at a decent interval after lunch and must end on the porch before dusk. After that, to be seen Frederica must be called on, and the call must reach its climax before nine fifteen, for at that hour a too gentle voice would announce punctually from the staircase: "Frederica, tell your young friend to go home, your dear grandfather wants to go to bed." Frederica had no choice, being a visitor, but either to acquiesce in this regimentation of her mores or conspire darkly and deceivingly against it. And for conspiring she had no gift whatever, neither instinctive dishonesty nor principled revolt. The geography of our idyl was such that if at twilight she came through the hedge behind her grandfather's stables, and I crossed our tennis court and walked briefly down a curving lane, we would be together in a meadow full of buttercups and daisies, and from there a path would lead us to a grove of pines and birches. But that curving lane, which beckoned when the twilight fell, was only mocking my despair.

Thus while demanding to be conceived as a pastoral poem, our love lacked that breath of natural freedom which would have made such a conception of it true for me. To the best of my knowledge that is why, although I exulted in the kindling of love in my breast, and although the lusts of my body were wholly drawn up like oil into its flame and I was pure and radiant spirit, still I did not sing. I did not glory in Frederica and make a cult of her; I gloried in my own thoughts pouring so miraculously out of me from God knows where.

I see now in my bedside notebooks how little suitable those thoughts were to a boy in a fever of love.

"Whom you fall in love with—that will be the great thing in deciding your character. Your character is pliant enough, it won't decide whom you fall in love with. Chance will do most of it."

"A government can not be better than the people. The *ideal* government must be fitted to the real man."

"The great joys are growth and creation, and the more you create the more you grow."

"The fearful thing about changing in character is that you can not call it a trial and by thinking change back again."

"Not knowing what you mean is meaning nothing."

"If someone has offended you, think whether you would weigh that so heavily against him if it had not been you."

"According to evolution the female developed a beautiful note for attracting the male. But how did appreciation of the beautiful note develop?"

I quote these rather sceptical and factual-tempered aphorisms because I think the conflict between their hold as truth upon my mind and the impulse toward fervent life-abandon in my heart explains much of what I did and failed to do in life. I tried, and I am still trying, to straddle the gulf between classic and romantic. In particular it explains, or begins to explain, a peculiar thing that happened in those days at the infirmary. I experienced a difficulty in getting up out of that saggy bed which kind old Mrs. Brock so artfully smoothed out for me each morning. I never did entirely get up out of that bed. Sitting there against two pillows, writing and meditating in a happy fever, I developed a pain in the small of my back. It is a very ordinary pain that anyone who wants it can acquire by sitting up in any bed too long. But it assumed, for some cause hidden in those organic processes which Freud insists on personifying as The Unconscious, the function of representing, or resolving, the conflict in my breast. The conflict was hardly to be resolved, it seems to me, in other ways. For even had I been as bold as Goethe, and successfully reckless of Frederica's scruples, the fact would have remained that she had no recklessness of her own. She did not like rebellion, or incline in the least degree toward that arrant assertion of self against custom which was then my whole zeal and gospel. I was trapped in the mad love of one whom in this trait so vital to me I could not admire. There was both intelligent force and nobility in Frederica, a true spiritual momentum, but that only made more insoluble the conflict of my emotions. For the orbit of her being was alien in its very shape to the intemperate trajectory I was setting out to travel. It is hard, in the best of conditions, for a mamma's boy to give his heart to a girl. For one whose mother was both gentle and heroic, both intellectual and tenderly maternal, both a haven in the world and a brave sailor against it, it is doubly hard. In the conditions offered by my romance with Frederica it was impossible.

These are thoughts, however, that I read back into the story after forty years. There was no Freudian psychology in America then— no "mother complex" or "complex" at all, no understanding of the role of infantile fixations or conflicts of unconscious motives. The term neurosis was little known. The diagnosis of my pain was therefore very simple: a "cold" had settled in the form of rheumatic stiffness in my lumbar muscles. My cold cleared up with the coming of spring—or the end of the coal strike!—but the "rheumatism" had a deeper hold. I was a semi-invalid for almost five years, forever lying down with a tiny pillow or hot water bottle under my back, or getting up to go in search of cures. And for all the years since, especially now while I am writing this story, that "rheumatism" has been an importunate visitor. I doubt very much whether I have lived through a week since those intense and strangely happy days in the infirmary without some ache, or "jumpiness," or sense of sickly weakness, in my back.

Chapter 29

A Social Success

I MOVED a good way in those days of pain and sickness toward a philosophy of joyful living. In my notebooks at the infirmary I was still building up arguments under the omniscient Deity, but to the best of my memory and judgment, the motive to this was aesthetic rather than religious. I was not genuinely worshipful; prayer played no part in my moral struggles; God was not a fact in my experience but a conclusion in my mind. And the premise from which I drew this conclusion was my very sense of the irrationality of human opinions.

"If we must worship reason alone," I wrote, "let us worship the complete sphere of it. Are there not proofs enough in our every effort to find the absolute beginning and end of a thought that we have but a segment, a limited inconsistent fragment, of the one whole and everlasting reason—inconsistent because it is a fragment? . . .

". . . The whole sphere of reason is the Divine Spirit. We of the earth may not know the infinite round of the sphere."

In this way I drew a belief in God out of my very doubts. But I was not deeply disturbed when I saw the fallacy: that my argument itself was but a human fragment.

"The reason with which I have worked out this theory? Ay, there's the rub!"

That ended my theological speculations. But my thoughts about life's enjoyment were more extended. In an essay of five pages I analyzed the parts played by anticipation, arrival, and continuance of a pleasure, and appraised their relative value as ably as I could now. And in a note on "goodness and gladness" I made a juvenile approach to what I have called the theme of this book:

"One would be good if he never detracted from the world's store of gladness. If a thing will make him happier than it will make some-

197

one else unhappy, then it seems good for him to do it. . . . Maybe conscience is the voice of the keeper of the world's treasure of gladness. Are there not times when we dread the voice of conscience and are surprised not to hear it? It is when our own gladness will be so great as to outweigh the loss and swell the general mint."

Not only in these intellectual ways, but socially too I burst into bloom that spring when love shone upon me. I began to make other acquaintances among those to whom Williamstown was more a mountain resort than a college. Mrs. Elbridge Adams, the wife of one of our Delta Psi alumni, had taken a house near the fraternity, and she was vivaciously interested in literature and the life of ideas. Her house became a kind of little salon for college boys of a literary turn—for Ralph and me, at least.

And through Mrs. Adams I became included in another circle of liberal Christians, a circle warmed and lighted as Elmira was by the memory of a great teacher. Mark Hopkins, who had made Williams famous, was in several ways similar to Thomas K. Beecher. In each the greatness lay in personal magnetism, bold good sense, and a belief in science and human love rather than a thought-out criticism of the old theology. Mark Hopkins' mother, Mary Curtis, though born like him in a town haunted by the specter of Jonathan Edwards, never joined the church and never felt any pangs of conscience about it, even when admonished by two famous sons. Neither did her artist son, Harry, who took the attitude of a scientific critic to the hot wave of revivals which swept the country, and swept Mark and Albert—and my grandfather, too, you remember—in 1831. As far as liberal theology goes, this mother and brother were, I suspect, the chief ingredients in Mark Hopkins' genius. But as a teacher and mover of young men to independent thought and humane reasonable feeling, he has had few peers in American education. Under his influence and that of his brother Albert, Williams became the first college in America to give science a leading place in the curriculum; the first to have an astronomical observatory; the first to build a gymnasium; the first in kindling in the students a living interest in world affairs. It was a generation ahead in regarding education as action on the part of the pupils rather than inculcation by professors. I doubt if, outside Oberlin, any educational principles more advanced than those proclaimed by Mark Hopkins at Williams in 1843 had then found expression in America.

Much of this great man's magnanimity, his respect for independent thinking, and a larger measure of liberality in interpreting the "law of love" than one associates with the idea of a New England theologian survived in the circles into which Mrs. Adams introduced me. They included Mark's own daughter Susan, an elderly and genial spinster who lived alone in a house among lawns and tended meadows with a cat named Smoky. I called her "Miss Suzie," and she became a very dear and generous friend to me.

During this same year of 1903 Mark Hopkins' son Harry, an easygoing Congregational minister, replaced the rather angular Presbyterian Franklin Carter as president of the college. And his family, too, were among my good friends in Williamstown, especially his genial son Hal, who was in college with me. Thus through a series of accidents and the workings of love in my breast, I emerged from the college and became a resident of the town, a member in some degree of its "society"—or by far the most alive and interesting circle in it.

Another light-giving member of that circle was Frederica's friend Jikie, a tall blonde girl, generously big of heart and frame and with a fountain of things to say, a fluent humor, and a gift of impracticality that might have been poetic genius. I was as much charmed by Jikie's handsome golden good looks and witty conversation as I was enamored of Frederica's more bewitching eyes and autumn colors. I could not help reflecting—discourteous though it was to them both—that if God had had the consideration to combine them into one, He would have smoothed my path to the heights of bliss. I was, even as things stood, pretty close to those heights during that April, May, and June. My backache seemed temporary; I thought each morning that it was gone. My verses and essays against custom were widely admired. My satires in the *The Gul* were enjoyed. My professors, although deprecating my desultory attention to the days' lessons, were agreed that I could learn when I wanted to. Thoughts and opinions poured out of me not only in midnight entries in my notebooks, but in conversation with these gay and kindly people. Their affection for me, or mine for them, or both together, eased me of my shyness. I was for the first time in my life a "social success." An outsider would say that I was "taken up" by the elite, and there was a little of that in it. I mean that those genteel New Englanders looked upon my rebel opinions rather as a lively firework varying the monotony of their mode of life than as a serious attack upon its frame and foundation of decorum.

They all did, at least, except Jikie, who has, I think, a genuine strain of the utopian in her. If this were a pleasantly fashioned novel instead of the confused story of a life, Jikie and I would have fallen in love and married and lived happily ever after. Instead, she was a kind of patron goddess to my love, wheat-colored and Demeterlike rather than like Venus, who has more of the rosy apple in her complexion. It was while visiting Jikie at her father's summer home a mile or so down the South Williamstown Road that Frederica did once—and this was the only time—escape from the domestic police regulations which made her such an unrewarding dryad. (Dryads are, of course, supposed to be elusive. It was not against that that my heart complained—not yet, at least. But they are supposed to be elusive among trees, and not because they can not, except at certain discreet hours and for nicely stipulated brief intervals, enter the shadows of the forest.)

Jikie's father was an even more vigilant policeman than Frederica's grandmother. He was a trustee of the college, an elder of the Presbyterian church, a chairman of the New York Board of Education, a New York lawyer and investor, and a personal embodiment of the Divine Law, from whom appeal might conceivably be taken to the Almighty God, but only upon appearing personally at His court in Heaven. For earthly purposes the paternal ukase was supreme. Father, however, was away on the occasion I am describing, and mother was retiring early. We all had dinner together, and after coffee and conversation, when it came a proper time for me to go home, Frederica and I went out to walk together in the pasture by the brookside. I have anticipated this sacred moment in telling about our romance because it seems to me—in the light of subsequent discoveries in psychology—that my fever and my neurotic pain had anticipated it. But it was on that stolen evening, sitting in the starlight where the grass made a bench for us at the edge of the hurrying water, that to my utter and proud wonderment we kissed each other's lips and said something—I can not quite remember what—about love.

It was nearing midnight when Frederica entered the house, and she entered with difficulty or by some super-stealthy system which awakened the housekeeper. Thus the secret of our high crime against chronology slipped out of the keeping of the younger generation where such secrets belong and became known in due course to the omnipotent father. He had done me the honor, I must say—having read one or two of my essays in the *Lit*—to take my declaration of rebellion against custom more seriously than anybody else in town. I was calling on Jikie one evening soon after that and demonstrating my independence as well as easing my back by reclining against a cushion on the floor. It was drawing toward eleven, and I was on the point of getting up to go when this white-bearded Viking, six feet four inches tall, stepped in from the hall and announced in booming tones:

"Young man, the doors close here at 10:30 P.M."

I made some abashed and feeble-minded apology to Jikie—"Why, I had no idea it was so late!"—and, collecting my feet with the dignity of a hen that has lost two large chickens, scrambled to a standing position.

She said, or must have said, "It's all right, it isn't late!"

But I heard nothing. I just backed or sidled out of the place as fast as I could, burning under my collar and in a misery of mortification. The pain of it was so acute that when I got to the road, I leaned my head against the gatepost, searching vainly for some thought that could emit a ray of relief.

A letter from Jikie's tender and impulsive sister came the next day, apologizing as much as a girl dared for her own father. As soon as it was possible, Jikie found an opportunity to meet me at Mrs. Adams' house.

"You mustn't mind," she said. "Father always behaves like that —he doesn't know any better!" And she laughed her gay laugh which always set every small thing right.

Our friendship was conspiratorial after that, for the old man forbade his daughters to associate with a reprobate who had kept a girl out in a pasture until midnight, and crowned that crime by sitting on the floor in the presence of his daughter until 11 P.M. The conspiracy was vigorously promoted, however, by all the other members of the circle, including Miss Suzie Hopkins and the president's family. Instead of the pariah I had expected to be, I found myself the hero of a humorous romance. Whatever may be my fate when I approach the Deity, every mortal who heard about it liked me better for this excommunication by His earthly representative. I had to dodge like Robin Hood behind a tree when the family passed me in their yellow station wagon, so that the question of exchanging a bow with the girls should not arise. And when the old Viking drove by in solitary grandeur I was careful not to be behind a tree, and would pay back his glare of hatred with a glare of scorn. It seems incredible, but only a few years ago when I went up to Williamstown to lecture, as I crossed the street between Hopkins Hall and the gymnasium, that very same erect and implacable figure passed me in the very same yellow station wagon, and gave me, after all these years—at least so I perceived it—the same glare. I should have thought I was dreaming had not the horses been absent and the hood of a Ford V-8 motor in their place.

In the midst of this excited and millennial spring, my day of reckless glory in love and nature and a first treasury of friends, I was abruptly reminded of the economic framework in which such glories are held up by one of Crystal's earnest letters brooding over her beloved "family."

"Max, I feel as if it were up to me to say something about the situation at present in the family. You know there are a whole lot of debts and that Mamma and Dad live on almost nothing and scrimp themselves miserably in their efforts to get even again. . . . Both of them need clothes more than you or I ever needed them, and they need better and richer food and more of it. When we are not at home, they cut down on the food even.

"It's not only plainly selfish, but it's real cruelty to add your debts—any more of them—to the load that is pressing on their minds and spirits. . . . How can Mamma believe in your love and sympathy when you haven't made the slightest effort all this winter to get any work for the summer, and when you have not apparently cut down on your expenses, or made any determined efforts to pay off your debts?

"If you can only realize that your way of procrastinating and not realizing and deliberately putting disagreeable things out of your mind is in this case selfishness and cruelty to the people who are doing the most for you. . . .

"If I were you I would go right off to one of the men who like you and appreciate your ability, and tell him that you are poor and have a lot of debts and have *got* to get some work for the summer."

It was entirely impossible for me to ask anybody in that vernal paradise for a job. I was not close enough down to earth. I was wandering in heavenly pastures, and I knew it. I decided that when I sank, I would sink out of sight. I mean that I decided to go home first and then be as practical and conscientious as the situation demanded. I knew better than Crystal how bad the situation was. I had run up debts amounting to over six hundred dollars. In a family of five, with a total annual income of two thousand dollars, that was little but a crime. My mother had already expressed a doubt about their being able, even with the help of the scholarship, to send me to college another year. She was also insisting that I take my backache seriously and give myself to the task of getting well. Education could afford to wait.

I laid Crystal's letter aside and finished out my three months in paradise with a free mind, clearly aware that on a certain date in June, boarding the Delaware and Hudson train for Elmira, I would climb down on to the practical earth and confront two miserably unpleasant realities—ill-health and the necessity to earn money.

On the afternoon before the day of this descent I walked a long last time with Frederica up through Flora's Glen and over the hill beyond it, and said goodbye to her—before twilight—at the gate in the hedge behind her grandfather's stables. I lay awake long that night with my back aching and my heart full of a sweet sorrow, and I woke in the morning at the note of the first robin in the maple tree outside my window. My sorrow was expanded with a sense of infinitude, of the sorrow of all being and ceasing to be, and particularly of all being that is for its moment beautiful. It was not akin to melancholy, which is abstract and brings no warm tears to the eyes. It was akin to an unbearably sad strain of music. The robins were soon breaking their hearts in a wild morning chorus, each one trying to express the Creation of the Universe by shouting "thirty-three thirty-three thirty-three" with enough rich joy and courage. I laid my pillow on the window sill and listened to the robins with tears welling from my eyes for Frederica and me and for the pathos of the life of man.

Then I got up and packed my things and took my way in a resolute mood to the station.

Chapter 30

A Year of Quiet Growth

MY MOTHER kept a "Log" at our summer home in Glenora, and we all wrote and pasted pictures in it, recording the day's doings, the jokes and endless arguments that enlivened our family, kidding and celebrating each other and the landscape and the weather and our guests (if we liked them)—compelling them too, when possible, to "write in the Log." Those volumes, especially the parts in my mother's handwriting, for her pen was effortless and unselfconscious, convey faithfully the savor of our family life together from 1899 to 1910. I learn from the Log that in this summer of 1903 I initiated a mode of life that I have fairly adhered to ever since. I devoted the mornings to writing or studying, and deferred the more active and more sensuous enjoyments (or duties) until afternoon. On July 8 Crystal made this entry in the Log:

"The student really shows itself in Max. Absolute quiet reigns in his room from 9 o'clock till twelve-thirty. This afternoon he spent among the woods watching birds and a rabbit."

A week later she pasted in these lines which she had found on my desk:

This is the story of a pale blue sweet-pea
Written in pale blue ink;
The pale blue sweet-pea was as pale as pale could be,
Paler than you would think.

"That is all the student has produced so far from his seclusion and meditation," she wrote. "We hope for more."

I can not remember what I was studying those mornings, but the afternoon "watching birds and a rabbit" has left its own record

in the Log. It reminds me how quieted my mood was from that of
the previous summer in the West.

"It seems more than one summer that I have missed, that I am
more than one summer older. I went down hill today for the first
time to sit with my big trees. . . . They have long limbs that reach
out over the lake. When the lake smiles the ripples send up their
murmur to the leaves and the many leaves murmur back. They do
not talk either philosophy or love to each other.

"The ripples just whisper: 'The wind is waking us';

And the simple leaves answer: 'The wind is shaking us' . . .

"A slim brown wild rabbit came hopping down within six feet of
me and looked at me through the leaves, and a red squirrel talked
to me from a branch out over the lake; I counted eight different
bird songs in less than a minute."

This was not exactly the mood of practical resolution in which
I had left Williamstown. But as so often happens to me, my prepara-
tions for a show of virtue proved superfluous. It was easy to decide,
once I faced my ledger, that I would have to stay home and work for
a year. Crystal wanted to study for an M.A. in sociology at Columbia,
and her offer to give it up only made my decision easier. Beyond that
my problems, both ethical and economic, were solved by kind
friends without any more effort on my part than it takes to say Yes.
My mother was feeding her restless mind those years at the Harvard
Summer School, studying with Royce and Palmer and Santayana,
and living with the Brecks (of the famous seed store, Joseph Breck &
Sons) in Newton, Massachusetts. She confided to Mrs. Breck, her
very dear friend, the mixture of debts and ill-health and unconcen-
trated talents in me which was causing her such pain. Mrs. Breck
proposed that her own fifteen-year-old son Charlie stay with me in
Elmira as my pupil. She would pay Charlie's board and lodging
and give me a salary as his tutor. The tutoring would not be too
strenuous for my back; it would leave me time to write and study;
and the salary could be nicely adjusted to enable me to pay, and
expiate, those sinful debts.

The truly millennial factor in this scheme was the beloved and
bewitching character of my pupil. Charlie was born in a state of
revolt against respectability and elegance so instinctive as to deserve the name of genius, or degeneration. As a child he had quietly
deserted the sumptuous mansion of his family and gone out and lived
in the barn with the coachman and stable boy. He still lived essentially in the barn, and lived in old clothes, which he would change

only under physical compulsion. He did not do anything, or learn anything, or play any games in the barn. He just lounged around and tinkered with things and discussed the miseries of under-class life with the hired men, who adored him. He had a poetic taste for being dirty as well as ill-clad that was particularly exasperating to his immaculate father and mother. And he found revolutionary expression in chewing tobacco.

Charlie's thirst for culture was satisfied by five or six poems, which he carried around in his pocket on loose sheets and read over and over until they were as worn and soiled as the clothes he wore. He had inherited the exquisite courtesy of his father, a simple, humble giving of his attention and himself to those addressing him, which stands in my mind as the most engaging of all New England's antiquities. And he had inherited big beanlike blue eyes, a small nub of a nose, and a quaint gnomish humor that played about him like St. Elmo's fire, sometimes illumining and sometimes confusing itself with those antique and perfect manners.

Charlie had already spent three summers with us on Cherith Farm, where we also wore old clothes and lived a life unpestered by elegance. To him those summers had been an escape into life itself, and to us his whimsical presence had become as natural and needful as the flowers and fruit.

Thus my problems were solved within familiar and smooth-flowing patterns, and without any necessity of "showing my mettle," as Dad used occasionally to suggest I might. It did require some tension to make Charlie get up in the morning and go to work, a tension which his whimsical humor made almost impossible to sustain. I threatened one morning, if he didn't get out of bed, to throw him into a tub of cold water, pajamas and all. He looked up out of the bedclothes with the expression of a startled owl and said: "Wherefore?" Aside from these tensions, however, my duties as tutor of a genial companion were far from strenuous.

On the other hand, my own ambition never lets me rest. And this year at home presented itself to me as an opportunity to perform certain wonders, both inside and outside myself, which college leaves no time for. "Piano lessons, stenography, drawing, studying, writing, and mandolin playing, besides tutoring"—so I described my external activities to Crystal. The "stenography," however, was only a two-fingered typing; the mandolin playing a mere climb-down from the violin, which in boyhood I had studied for three years; the drawing, although it began with lessons, soon lapsed into making pencil copies of pictures of great men.

As for my writing of that winter, what I did informally in letters or my Book of Thoughts surprises me quite often by its maturity. What I did with earnest enterprise, an essay on "The Crank" especially and one on "Conversation," surprises me as much by being stodgy and affected. Indeed my writing here lost its spontaneity and passed through a phase of self-conscious effort-to-be-literary, which is the opposite of everything I admire and have in the long run sought to attain.

My plea for the crank, or extremist, was based on the idea that the world progresses like a sailboat by making one crazy tack after another. The truth is in the middle, but those who lead off toward the extremes are necessary if there is to be any advance in the knowledge of truth. It was a way of defending the flaming evangelist in my own bosom against the sceptical wiseacre who lived there too.

Moreover, instead of choosing the art of writing and devoting my undivided force to it, I undertook with all my crazy zeal to learn to play the piano. Those early violin lessons, except for the friendship with a gifted teacher, John Roosa, had been a waste of time. A violinist is either an expert or a public nuisance. The crimes which can be committed on a piano are at least limited by the chromatic scale, and amateurs are not obviously to be shot at sight. Ever since I heard that Adamowski Quartet in my freshman year, I had thought of music with a new and envious affection. "I don't believe I could sink so low that I wouldn't rather get drunk on music than alcohol," I wrote my mother after an evening at the Boston Symphony. And now it occurred to me that on the piano I could make music myself without that lifetime of labor that the violin requires.

I must add that Ralph Erskine's superiority in this field had challenged my ambition. I thus had an urge, both egocentric and egofugal, to do something about music. I also, as usual, had my own opinion as to what should be done. It was an anticipation of a good many things that have been done in education since. I went to a gracious piano teacher, Mrs. Beecher's adopted daughter Julie Farrar, and offered to pay her for lessons provided she would teach me as I told her to and not according to her own system. She agreed to everything in this unflattering proposition except being paid, and with her expert yet flexible assistance I really learned between October and April to play the piano.

"The first thing I want to do," I said, "is to make those big slow chords in Chopin's Prelude No. 20. I'll make them one at a time first. You just show me how to place my fingers in each one, so that afterward I'll be able to combine them."

"First," she said, "you must get your arms and wrists in the right position."

"Yes, that's true," I said. "But let's do that at the same time. I want to be playing something I like from the very first note."

And so we proceeded. I never played a scale or an arpeggio; I never performed an exercise; I never made a sound come out of the instrument that was not part of something I wanted to learn. I think it took me no more than three weeks to play the Prelude slowly. In three months I had several funeral marches in my repertory and was at work on Handel's famous Largo. By June, when I visited Williamstown again, I could play Grieg's "Spring Song" to Ralph Erskine and according to his testimony, play it well.

There were two fatal flaws in my accomplishment. I can not improvise at all; I can no more sit down and play off a few harmonious chords by instinct than a blind pony can; and no effort had been made to overcome this lack. On the other hand, I had not even begun to play from the score. I had learned by heart some eighteen or twenty pieces by examining the score, placing each finger deliberately, and then all too easily remembering its position. I was beginning to read notes and also to study harmony when I went back to college the next autumn, but I had other things to do now and few hours free from pain. I soon tired of playing those twenty pieces; the memory lapsed into my fingers, so that if I went wrong I could correct myself only by starting over; and thus the whole thing ended as a tour de force.

Ralph Erskine maintains that I performed that feat of piano playing solely for the triumph over him. His talents symbolized, I concede, the challenge of a phase of life I could not bear to miss. Of all obvious wisdoms the hardest for me to master is that in order to live largely one must live within limits. I want to do and be everything. I had *been* a poet, now I would *be* a pianist, next year a philosopher, then orator, agitator, reformer . . . and what in the end but a trifler? My piano-playing exploit, notwithstanding the pleasure it gave me, was a sin against the long-time enjoyment of living.

Inwardly I was a good deal preoccupied during that winter at home with the effort to develop a moral character. Four problems especially troubled me. In the old terms I would say four sins beset me, but three of them, Vanity, Melancholy, and Lack of Integration, were on the defensive—I was besetting them!

The sin which beset *me*, of course, was Lust. It beset me in the body of another "Rose," a paler and more fragile and yet equally too-lovely-to-be-suffered Rose, undressing audibly in an attic room next mine. I did not love this pale Rose as I had the darker one, but I mixed with my desire of her a seeing admiration, as these words in a letter to Crystal attest:

"She is dainty and quiet—moves instead of walks. She never actually touches anything, does things with her eyebrows and dimples instead of her hands, and then at the next moment she is crawling right down into the bottom parts of the corners of the cupboard with a big square brush. I think she is a very beautiful and very wonderful person. . . . I don't know why I devoted the whole letter to her . . ."

I did know, of course. And I knew that I was making no head against this Sin of Concupiscence, either to attack and conquer it or to name it one of life's precious treasures and declare it mine.

Against Vanity I made better head. Vanity seemed to me not only unlovely but irrational, being of all faults the most universally disapproved and yet feeding on approval. I had, by a propulsion that seemed absolute to me, perhaps because it was the correction of an inner lack, gone in for being an ego, but I was quite as determined not to be an egotist. If there is such a thing as a natural aristocracy, its first trait after truthfulness, I think, is modesty of spirit. The trait is rare among artists and people in a business of expression, all exhibitionists to some degree, and also among moulders of opinion. The very technique of clear writing, as my humble mother was the first to tell me, demands a papal arrogance. I was determined I would have this necessary arrogance, but I would try to do it without getting in love with myself or making it my preoccupation to "be a big thing."

"There is no quicker or more subtle danger of derailment on the way to truth than a conceited constant desire to be unique."

So I exclaimed in my notebook, and in January I wrote to Crystal:

"I have begun a new life now—which you are to help me with. You are never to tell me that you like me again, or that you heard somebody say that he liked me, or that I am pleasant in even the smallest particular. I don't want to ever hear another word of approval either of me or of anything I do. Will you agree to this? You might think I was much burdened with many years' weight of praise, but I realize myself that it is my vanity which has made it big and heavy. Anyway I know this is necessary."

My battlefield with Melancholy was filled with no such noble monuments as these. It took me years to name this monster Sloth, or clearly realize, whatever his name, that systematic industry is the sole shield against him. You can see me groping weakly toward this knowledge in the fall of 1903:

"Dearest big comforting sister: I am writing to you in the midst of remorse and dissatisfaction with myself. . . . I *must* do something more active, or at least more systematic, than this soon. My moods and my *abstract* thoughts are gaining rule over my real self every day. My inmost soul (in earnest) cries out for a hot game of baseball or tennis. You see, you enjoy painting chairs, and you can't imagine the hopelessness of it when 'the inner life fails' of one who does not enjoy painting chairs. . . . What shall I do about it?"

More unsuccessful still, and to this day unaccomplished, was my effort toward some scheme of Integration. I had adopted as a basic principle that I would be myself, but I found to my dismay that I had as many selves as I had friends and companions. I found further that I could be friends or close companions with almost anybody. I seemed made of malleability and without a core. Henry Adams says in his *Education:* "Life offers perhaps only a score of possible companions . . . One friend in a lifetime is much; two are many; three are hardly possible." What must be the hooks and angles and protuberant square edges and pure mulish recalcitrance of such a character! I could find companions—yes, and friends if I wanted them—in any hamlet of the earth. How can I find my own character? How can I find a self among a million attitudes of tuned accord with every kind of man and woman? That was and is my problem, a problem which I have tried to solve with my mind, since there is no ground to stand on in my feelings.

With Sid Wood I had been an ill-clad tramping rebel against civilization—and quite pointedly against that group of Christian gentlefolk who surrounded Williams College with an envelope of nice manners. With them, the next six months, I had found myself in gay, elated bonds of friendship. I had fallen in love, moreover, with a girl of whom Sid spoke—how sharply I remember that! —with scorn. And yet I could not call this growth. On the contrary, I had come too lightly down, I felt, from mountain fastnesses. I had come in from desert spaces. I was betraying something wild, uncivil, native, nomad, that had been myself.

The problem became poignant in an incident of that winter. One day in my attic room I began a letter to Sid Wood in Oraibi with

the phrase: "Now that I am well settled into this death in life . . ."
I did not finish the letter, but left it lying on my table, and my
mother, dusting the room, saw the phrase and read it. She had been
so happy in having me at home and in my taking it as a year of
quiet growth that words more painful to her heart could hardly
have been written. She came to me directly and with too dry eyes:

"Max, it was lying open and I saw those words before I could
pass by. You know I wouldn't. pry into your secret thoughts. But
now that I know how you feel, let's change our plans. I could not
live if I thought I had stolen a year out of your life just because
I'm worried about money. Money doesn't matter. We can borrow it
somewhere and pay it somehow."

I do not know what I stammered in answer. I was appalled to be
caught in such duplicity. I had spoken to Sid in a certain character
—overplayed the part perhaps, and for that reason not finished the
letter—but it was my own self. I felt that way. I had other selves,
however, who felt other ways, among them none more real than this
morally and intellectually ambitious son of his mother, now pleas-
ingly engaged in reaping the harvest of a year at home. To me this
was all clear and was my own, and I did not feel conscience-stricken
as about a false or furtive act. (There was at no time any deceit or
lying in our family, nor ever the slightest problem about it, so far
as I can remember.) I felt dismayed at what my self had done to my
mother, and what, since this duplicity or multiplicity *was* my self,
it must always do to every one who loved me.

So far as my mother's immediate pain was concerned, the problem
was not insoluble. Few problems are among truth-loving friends.
That night in my room I wrote her an account of this inward fact
and begged her to worry about that, not about my staying at home,
which seemed to me the right thing, and on the whole a happy thing,
to do. I still have her answer:

"It seems to me that a composite personality is to the mind what
flexibility of muscles is to the body. Such capabilities held well in
hand and informed by a high ideal make the leader in the truest
sense. Leadership without this is only bossing—with this the king
is also philosopher and *friend* of men.

"I can not imagine a higher gift than this which makes your
trouble. All it needs is aim and ideal.

"*Don't dream*. Act—act—even if wrongly. Keep on deciding irrevocably and doing!"

I was more alarmed than dazzled by my mother's suggestion that

I might become a leader, but I was relieved that she could look upon my "trouble" as a gift.

The chief event outside my mind in the Elmira winter was an amateur production of Dickens' *Cricket on the Hearth*, in which I played the part of the bewildered husband John. Gretchen Fassett played my wife Dot, and was, to quote the *Elmira Advertiser*, "in face, figure, and bearing irresistibly attractive." I myself, according to the same authority, was "full of suppressed emotion" and my "unselfish expressions of love and faithfulness touched the heart by their realism." Whether they touched Gretchen's heart I do not know, but they touched mine with disturbing force. When she would fling her glowing body into my arms, throbbing and her eyes really wet with the heartbroken lines she had been speaking, and I would clasp her with dramatic joy, I never knew whether I was in the play or out of it, I had waited with so much real joy for that moment.

However, this secret remained locked in my breast. There was, after the play ended, a distance between us. My Elmira self was still something of a church mouse, and Gretchen still a princess. I was shocked, moreover, at my fickleness. So long as I stayed in Elmira, Frederica and the Berkshire Hills and all that idyl which had been my life could, it seemed, be burned away by Gretchen's beauty as though made of fog. And then, if I traveled from Elmira to Williamstown, it would all come back again and Gretchen be a misty image on the far horizon. I saw this clearly, and saw also the total absence in my breast of any hindrance to it, any impulse to be "loyal to loyalty," as Josiah Royce advised. It seemed to me that moral growth demanded I should act as though I had that impulse and be true to Frederica. I did not act—that would sound too noble— but at least I made no effort to transcend my shyness and ask Gretchen to let me see her home.

A friend, remembering those days, exclaimed recently: "You were dreadfully moral!" And it is true. I find in my notebook austere self-commands like these:

"The 'natural' thing is nothing but the thing that is. Do not dread to assume 'unnatural' virtues; assume them and the adjective has no meaning."

"What have I done when I have written a *good* sentence. Nothing, unless action be the result."

There was little religion in my concern with morals, although I still went to church and tried to join my mother in her prayers. She told her congregation one day that if they could find a spiritual uplift elsewhere, there was no reason for coming to church, and that made it easy to come. My "spirituality," however—and hers too, for that matter—was swinging more and more from a concern with moral salvation to the thought of a new society in which life might have moral values for all. At the end of the year I wrote a page in my notebook which reveals the trends that would carry me one day to socialism: a distinctly "agrarian" millennialism, a strong disgust with "bourgeois" life, a disillusionment with Christian preaching.

"O, if I would find twenty or thirty souls—not altogether congenial, but cultured—spiritual—to be a parish (that is a word I love)—a country parish! They would never be polite, urbane. Men had to scrape bare some cities before they could find want of those words 'polite' and 'urbane.' In a pasture there is good-will or else ill-will, but crowded together with brick walls, etc., there is not room for harmonious setting of contraries, so we've devised this paint of politeness that goes over the whole business.

"I suppose if I am dissatisfied I should turn minister or reformer, turn back from my leisurely meadows and be what is called their 'mouthpiece.' But when I think of myself preaching, I am overwhelmed now with a sense of the futility of it—what I call human hopelessness. I wish I believed in the Son of God and his second coming."

It was indeed, as I review it in the Log, a parish-like and millennial summer that followed this year of growth. Our Glenora hillside was made more dreamlike than ever by a visit from my poet-brother, Ralph Erskine, who came with his frail bride Barbara and her mother, Elia W. Peattie. They took the little "Horse Shoe Cottage" down the road from us and dwelt in it for two blissful weeks, Mrs. Peattie making curtains for the windows, cushions for the chairs, and every kind of little ministrant to cozy pleasure as though she planned to spend a lifetime there. She was a distinguished author-critic, conductor of Book Reviews on the Chicago *Tribune*, quite an arbiter of literary opinion in the Middle West, and this made her humble interest in curtains a grateful surprise. Barbara was a dreamy poet too, and Barbara's frail-voiced brother, Don, a sprite-like child of six years with high temples and illumined eyes, was the very unencumbered spirit of poetry as I conceive it. He could not write words on paper, but when something moved him he would quietly rise from his chair and speak out, in a high chanting voice with a psalmlike rhythm, words appropriate to it. The words were

so well chosen, and the child's aspect so sincere and almost supernatural in poise, that we listened with hushed reverence.

"If there is such a thing as genius," I said to myself, "this child has
it. . . . And we shall see!"

Thirty years later Donald Culross Peattie sent me, out of a clear
sky, his *Almanac for Moderns,* which I think contains some of the
finest prose written in our time.

I must add that during this millennial summer and for more than
a year after, I was wearing a steel brace which gripped me by the
hips and shoulders and held my spine immovable. This aid to my
morality had been provided by the famous orthopedist Joel Goldthwaite when I was spending Easter with the Brecks in Boston.
Twice a day I would take it off and strengthen my supposedly inadequate muscles with a series of strenuous exercises. This had no effect
whatever on my pain or on my now alarming disposition to lie down
or lean against the furniture when standing up. It only inflamed my
ethical propensities to a point where, not satisfied with developing
my own character, I had to go to work on Crystal's. I made her
abjure coffee with me that summer of 1904 and had her too confined
in her room all morning long with books.

In August I paid a visit to the Brecks at Loon Lake in the Adirondacks, where I stayed longer than was planned on the theory that the
mountain air was doing me good. In reality I was discovering a new
self capable of fitting successfully, even with a steel backbone, into
the showy-happy, shallow life of a fashionable summer hotel. While
enjoying this discovery, I received from my mother a letter concluding:

"I find that I have nothing to ask for you—to be added to you—
but just that you should *be* more freely what you are."

Her words seemed a kind of diploma after my sober year of
growth, and like other diplomas made me feel embarrassed more
than proud.

Chapter 31

Firm Friendship and Irresolute Love

THANKS to the fraternity, I did not miss my classmates much when I returned for a belated senior year. Except for Ralph, the 1905 boys in Delta Psi were more congenial to me than those of 1904. Two of them, Fritz Judson and Baldwin Mann, remained my friends through life. A third, Charles Whittelsey—"the Count," we called him—a tall, lank, rapid-striding, too grown-up lad with double glasses and a double lip, had as brilliant brains and keen a character as anyone I've known. His position in his class was much what mine had been, except that he was not a poet. He wrote stories and essays, was on the *Lit* Board, and was editor of the *Gul*. In an essay on "Liberal Culture" he objected to Henry Van Dyke's formulation of the aim of a college education: "to learn to judge correctly, think clearly, see and know the truth," and proposed "a finer conception or at least additional: to attain the faculty of pure delight in the beautiful."

As major in command of the famous "Lost Battalion," Count Whittelsey became a great American hero of the First World War. His long legs and eagerness of action led him too fast into the enemy's lines, his communications were cut, and his whole battalion trapped in a ravine by the Germans. For five days, without food or communications, with ammunition running low, shells dropping on them from two hills, wounded uncared for, dead unburied, and the enemy attacking in force five separate times, chewing oak leaves for nourishment, they held their ground and waited for the army to catch up. On the last day, the German commander sent a courteous note begging that they raise a white flag in token of "honorable surrender." A white panel had been spread out on a slope by the battalion's airplane liaison agent to indicate their position to searchers from their own base. Whittelsey did not tell the German commander to "go to hell," as was reported; his only answer was to order the panel taken in lest it be mistaken for a white flag.

When he was decorated with the Congressional Medal and with world-wide fame, I felt as though destiny had outwitted him. For he had seemed more than the rest of us, in the lightning speed and intemperate force of his judgments, designed for fame. And yet he was contemptuous of it. He was contemptuous of all those values that loom so large to the ambitious. He loved speculation and friendship; classic beauty; a jest; an argument; a convivial evening. He was, by contrast with me, sharp-edged, impersonal, and unsentimental, towering like a cliff over a brook. While I wept with Keats and Shelley, his favorite poem was Milton's cool-voiced sonnet:

> Lawrence, of virtuous father virtuous son,
> Now that the fields are dank, and ways are mire,
> Where shall we sometimes meet, and by the fire
> Help waste a sullen day, what may be won
> From the hard season gaining? . . .

One day when the "Count" was visiting us in Glenora, he and I passed a low swampy patch where cattails grew as high as my shoulder. They grew so thick and strong that I thought they would sustain me, or temper my fall, if I did a running swan dive into them. I dared the "Count" to do it, and he laughed at me. But having mentioned it, I had to do it myself. The cattails were grass under my weight, and I fell on the projecting charred stump of a small tree. The point did not catch me in the middle, where it would certainly have ruined, if not ended, my life, but at the outer edge of my chest, where it merely tore my skin and knocked the wind from my lungs. Although I tried to disguise it, I was gasping for breath when I came back to the road, and the "Count" looked curiously at me.

"Why, you really hurt yourself, didn't you?" he said, and gave me a gentle support with his arm.

I felt that he regarded me as a curious specimen and that he was right. I should have felt so more keenly had I known that he contained the hero of a Lost Battalion. . . .

Whether by good luck or because I am sentimental, seven of the boys who became my friends just through belonging to the same fraternity seem to have had as distinctive qualities as though I had chosen them from thousands. I have told of Sid Wood and of Stanley Washburn, the "events man"; now of Colonel Whittelsey; and I have described Ralph Erskine, my companion in poetics. Another friend, Harry Mellen, was also a poet, and was something else not easy to describe. We speak of animals as gentle: Harry was the gentlest human being I have ever known, spirited and strong, a skillful boxer and bold in discussion, but gentle down to the marrow of his bones. He retired after a career in business to cultivate fruit, and a little of his own soul, on a ranch in middle California. All his life long he wrote poems, wrote them for their own sake, and they were often exquisite for several lines and never in any line affected.

Fritz Judson balanced this excess of lyricism in my friends of 1905 with unusual gifts in practical mechanics. He had, after Whittelsey, the highest I.Q. in the 1905 delegation. He would listen with serious interest while I discovered flaws in the textbook explanations of surface tension, capillary attraction, and other such matters, upon which I was quite as glib as upon my System of Aesthetics. And I would spend hours following up his elaborate drawings of a rotary engine that was to revolutionize all industry. Fritz did revolutionize the operation of several large factories in his day, and rose high enough to decline the presidency of a good-sized corporation before he also retired for a time to raise chickens and to invite his soul.

Baldwin Mann was less quick-witted than Fritz, but more stubborn and intense about opinions. He was a stocky youth with iron muscles and an undershot jaw like Sid Wood's. Although born of a businessman's family, Episcopal and modish in their outlook, he discovered in his own mind that God does not exist, or if He does, nobody knows it. When I came back to college after my year at home, still wavering about church and deity, I was surprised to see this well-dressed brother in St. Anthony sitting up in chapel rigid as an oak stump while the rest of the college bowed their heads in prayer. The sight gave me a lighthearted joy and a feeling of affection that never died. I soon joined the stiff-necked brotherhood, and Baldy and I voyaged together into the realms of what used to be called "rationalism." We taunted our fraternity brothers with the primitiveness of secret societies, ridiculed their sacred hocus pocus, attacked college custom in general and the cult of intercollegiate athletics in particular. And we wore unstarched shirts with soft collars attached—at least I did. I was, in fact, so far as I know, the John the Baptist of this revolution in male attire. I abjured starched cuffs and collars in the autumn of 1904 and, except in the exigencies of evening dress, never put them on again. I speak with irony of the revolution, but inwardly, to a person of my timidity and approbativeness, that was no small act of devotion to the life of reason.

There survive as documentary evidence of this two-handed onslaught upon a well-nigh universal irrationality an essay of Baldwin's in the *Lit* entitled "The Evils of the Present Aesthetic System"; an essay of mine on "The Systematic Suppression of Freshmen," in which, still basing myself on individuality as the chief end of man, I assail the most inevitable of youthful institutions; a letter I wrote to the Williams *Record* defending the right of students to stay away from the "Amherst Game" if so disposed; and my poem in the *Lit* entitled "Four Madonnas." I had seen three old-fashioned Madonnas on the walls of our parsonage all my life long and was much moved by a modern one my mother brought from Italy and placed beside them—a girl with full lips, uplifted breasts, and slim strong hips that one could clasp excitedly in dreams. My body was brimful of earthy yearnings in those days, and there was more than philosophy in my choosing her.

> Now mine stands glorying before the morn,
> While just the sky sings out "My child is born!"—
> Lifting him high with her, not God to her,
> But her own self complete! About him stir
> No hallowed angels. Only sunbeams hover.
> I love thee, mother, that wast once a lover!
> Can earth not bear this part in love and truth—
> Earth's heart? Hath wisdom never been a youth?

Baldy was not glib in argument, but he could sit tight and let opinions surge against him. He enjoyed more mulishly than I the clash of battle. I do not know where I should ever have got in that early warfare without him. I am afraid Unreason would have triumphed utterly. He was the fortress, I the light-armed troops. . . .

In love I had no such luck as in friendship. Frederica did not live with her grandfather that winter, but she came frequently to see him, and the course of our romance was determined by a conflict between ethics and geography. We both decided in the fall that it must end: she because I kissed her too fervidly, I because those fervid kisses roused in me a desire I did not know what to do with. I paid Frederica the compliment of focusing upon her exquisite person both an apple-blossom rapture and a carnal passion of consuming force. But she was not brought up in a circle where such compliments are accepted. I do not know whether women really have a stronger monogamous instinct than men. A dexterous mixture of the ideals of purity and prudence formed, in those who attended finishing schools in my day, a hard amalgam very like an instinct.

I was not only baffled but cowed by this adamantine substance. I had come back to college that autumn a dreadfully moral character, as you have seen, a young man valiantly bent upon virtue. It was, to to be sure, an un-Franciscan sort of virtue—sympathetic toward poverty, but not wholly beguiled by chastity or obedience. I was ready to disobey any unreasonable law, and in order to assert my right to the virtue of inchastity, I needed only a warm accomplice. But that does not say that I could make light of the chastities and obediences of others. If Frederica was firmly sure of what she wanted, it became a duty according to my code to help her have it. I had entered into this romance under the spell of Goethe's idyl of Sesenheim, and I had not failed to guess, helped on by a bashful hint from our professor, that Goethe had come closer to his Frederica than he chose to tell. He had, in fact, to put it in the old terms, loved, ravished, and abandoned her. It never occurred to me that she may have conspired with him in this, that to be loved, ravished, and abandoned is better than not to be loved at all. There is no evidence that he deceived her. But I assumed he had, and in my infatuation with morals, turned against my hero of bold love.

" 'I know it is not in beauty that happiness dwells, but in the beauty of goodness.'

(For Aesthetics and Ethics—cf. Goethe)

"In his personal romance one is likely to substitute aesthetics for ethics."

My early obsession with "being good," rooted in baby-imbibed habits of terror and mortification, reinforced by a too-Christian training, and guarded by a morbid reticence about intimate emotions, appears to me now, glancing back, as little but a rotten spot in my nature. This view will become more plausible as the tale of my ineptitudes advances. The net result here was that Frederica and I kept making high resolves against embraces and patching these when broken with still higher resolves not to "see each other any more." It is difficult not to see your next-door neighbor, if your eyes are open, to say nothing of your whole mind and body. I do not know how many times I said a rapturous farewell to Frederica, returning to my lonely room with infinity in the form of sorrow in my heart. It happened so often that we laughed ourselves about it.

My sister wrote in September: "Do you see Frederica? You should be good to yourself emotionally too. That is important in getting well."

"No," I answered, "you may say I don't see her—except vaguely as one that dwelt in poetry or in a dream."

Ethics was firmly in the saddle when the year began; both Frederica and I were convinced that our romance was at an end. Geography's first triumph occurred on Mountain Day, October 5, a holiday given to Williams' boys in recognition of the education, or something better, to be found in wandering among the Berkshire Hills. I had taken a volume of Herbert Spencer, offered for my instruction by Baldwin Mann, and wandered off alone to spend the day in thinking about the problem of Deity. Not altogether by chance I took the Stone Hill Road, the path of my first fatal walk with Frederica and many a walk thereafter. The day, it is needless to say, was not devoted exclusively to thought.

On a Sabbath in the previous January I had written, imitating Emerson: "Heroism is the victory of moral conviction over instinct. Each is a product of evolution, and whose arm is the victor's? In that divine moment is not only proof but presence of God."

Now I wrote: "To the most emotional place, the place of romance, where I can not see a house or a barn, and nothing is there but green and colored leaves and memories, I go with Herbert Spencer, and I become an agnostic, lying flat on top of a big rock."

Having thus dispensed with the God of my fathers, I wandered over to the meadow behind Frederica's grandfather's house. I honestly did not know she was in town. I thought she was in Trenton. But what could I do, arriving there in this godless condition, when I met her wandering too among the goldenrod and asters? Surely the Great Unknown would not expect me to cut her dead!

I can not tell you what I did, for my notebook is always cryptic in a crisis. I only know that ethics did not succumb altogether, and I came out convinced that the moral order does not require support from the Deity.

"O, nobody can read the thoughts that are on this page! And I care little that I am an agnostic—Alas, agnosticism, and romance and poetry together, you could not quite slay my conscience! I shall not be happy when I read this page."

It is true that I am not happy, but only because I can not make out what occurred. Our romance began again—that much is clear from what follows. And it ended again, and began again, five separate times during the following winter and spring. My notebook, at least, contains five epitaphs and five hymns of resurrection.

In February, on the anniversary of our first walk—it was two years now—we took a longer walk, and it was followed, strangely, by the same event. I fell sick with an indefinite malady, lay some days in my upstairs room madly dreaming of her, and she came once more with violets. My notebook reaches here its height of reticence:

> To Remember (violets remember)
>
> Still should we hear our water-voices calling,
> Laughter out of the cataract falling,
> Wild laughter, and wild fancies—forest dim!—
> Thy nymphs and faeries of unfettered limb,
> And mine, that fleeting go,
> Answering the water—a wild echo.

The violets survive, still faintly fragrant although coffee-brown, but they do not remember. I think she brought them again, this time alone and in bold defiance of propriety, to my bedside. I clearly remember only the craving for her that possessed me when I wrote those words "unfettered limb."

The local doctor called this newest illness "neurasthenia," a diagnosis which I smiled at as having "a dignified simplicity and scorn of details which is distinctly philosophic." But I am not sure it could be improved on today.

"The chances were about even," I wrote to Crystal, "whether I could stay in college. I couldn't walk into the next room and back without exhaustion and faintness—and no reason for it. The doctor who said I had neurasthenia told me that a cold might cause the condition, but I had no cold so far as I know."

"Don't be resigned," she answered. "Persist in thinking of yourself as *perfectly well* only a few years ahead. Get back the old childlike big faith in what the future can bring forth just because it is not the present."

In April I answered her:

"I am almost as well now as in the fall—*but* this is while doing no sitting up or studying at all; that was while doing a good deal of hard work.

"I don't feel 'resigned'—very often. I go on dreaming things in the future, but I confess there is a tear in it generally. But my purpose to get well is vigorous enough.

"As for the next year Dr. Nelson suggests that I try doing about two hours editorial writing a day, and *write* the rest of the time. He thinks he could get me the chance, but will make sure. I don't know about that. I think I could get the Oxford scholarship from New York next year—if I want to go on getting educated. Professor Morton keeps suggesting that there may be some way to get a traveling fellowship. None of these things demand immediate action, and Idaho is left if I am not pretty well. . . ."

"Idaho" meant that I might follow my brother to Wieser Academy, which had been founded by friends of my father, and where I could do a little teaching and yet "live an outdoor life"—in plainer terms, become a valetudinarian. I missed, I think, by about the breadth of a frog's hair becoming a professional invalid.

I was well enough, however, on April 13 to be confronting a new problem with my gospel of exuberant life:

> When science poisons wonder in thy heart,
> Drains out the life, the red wine of thy moods,
> To wither up the god that in thee broods—
> Then turn to the still mystery of art.
> Let the day be a drama—night a death!
> Let us not lie while the Creation's sung,
> Like old flutes into an old garden flung,
> Cracked and untuneable to the god's breath!

On Sunday, April 30, another crisis is entered in my notebook in love's secret code—another desperate farewell, no doubt, to Frederica:

"This afternoon in the waking woods over the glen, with all memory and hope! This evening ecstasy and tears!"

The notebook ends with a sudden, frantic and, as I read it now, humiliating cry in very thick black ink:

"Be a vivid individual soul, a live will, capable of acting the imperious part of God in a heroic moment."

It is plain that I was not "being good to myself emotionally," as Crystal advised. I was tearing myself to pieces—or failing recklessly to bind together the pieces of which I am composed. Notwithstanding this sad story of romance and renunciation, nymphs and neurasthenia, backache and steel brace, I did a quite prodigious feat of studying during that year and managed to graduate with a Phi Beta Kappa key after all. I want to describe that intellectual state of growth in a separate chapter.

Chapter 32

My Revival of Learning

IT WAS my year of absence, I suppose, that gave me the odd notion of using Williams College as an institution of learning. Perhaps a little absence from college is a good thing for an American boy. My notebook meditations began now to bear some relation to my courses of study. Indeed I was in danger, and not unaware of the danger, of becoming a "highbrow." But I was determined not to become a prig.

"The chief object of life," I wrote in December, "is to live it, to express yourself for happiness' sake. Therefore I make no distinction of higher or lower between the life of the scholar and philosopher, and that of the athlete and adventurer. If I choose the intellectual life, it is because I have a greater talent and interest that way; the two roads I choose between are level, and I will remember that they are level."

I have remembered that they are level. And I have not altered that formulation of the chief object of life. The more I explore the systems of ratiocination by which men try to make their souls at home in this brute world, the more surely I come back to a categorical assertion of the value of conscious life as the premise of wisdom. It is the only valid meeting place of mind with nature, the only religion which does not play tricks with fact.

Up to that year I can not recall the influence of any teacher. I can behold sitting or standing at their desks, as clearly as I behold my parents at the dining table, teachers whom I have liked, and who gave me their assistance understandingly: Miss Phelps, who taught geometry at the Elmira Free Academy, calm, quiet, sandy-colored with smoothed red hair; tiny and lively Miss Smith, who gave me a

mark of 100 on the regents in American History; Professor Mc-
Laughlin in Mercersburg, a slim wythe with a drab walrus moustache
and three fingers missing from his left hand, who toed in and had a
sideways girlish bend to him and a way of blowing in his fingers
from embarrassment, but who was on the job—as was everybody in
his classroom—all the time; Professor Bracket, trim, straight-up-
standing, with a precise vigor of utterance that made beauty of Greek
grammar. They all stand vivid in my inner mind; and they command
my reverent feelings, for where intelligence replaces superstition,
teachers replace the priests. And yet I never confided my thoughts
to any of them. I behaved in school like a half-wild animal who
comes up to the common trough to get food, but sneaks off with it
to his den where he has gamier morsels of his own and his own ways
of devouring them. Only in this senior year did I begin to realize
that a teacher might become a friend.

My most apparent friend was Henry Loomis Nelson, a former
editor of *Harper's Weekly*, who took the chair of political science in
1902. I elected his course in English Constitutional History because
he was a big thing in the college, having recently arrived from the
"real world"—I beg the pardons of all college professors, but that
was my feeling—because he was a member of my fraternity, and yet
more because he recklessly admired my abilities. He told me in so
many words, breathless as it makes me to this day, that I was a better
writer than Stuart Pratt Sherman.

I had no interest in the English Constitution and no inkling that
I was going to learn about a fight for civil rights. I thought *we* had
done all that fighting in our revolt *against* England! Moreover, I was
still disgruntled that there had to be in this world such things as
politics, business, money, government—obstructions to man's spirit,
all of them. The course was half over before I woke to the fact that I
was reading the story of a glorious struggle. I wrote long papers on
"The Administrative Work of Henry II," "The Tudors from a Constitutional Viewpoint." I read Stubbs and Blackstone and Greene and
Gardiner, read the medieval Latin of the charters themselves, and in
general, for the first time since Mercersburg, conducted myself like
a scholar. Those papers are full of learned allusions to "scutage"
and "firdwyte" and the Curia Regis and the Constitutions of Clar-
endon and other vital matters that have no meaning for me now,
and they are well composed and show some common sense. But I
can not find in them any original thinking. Dr. Nelson had no new
or vital approach to history, and he talked too slowly and loved too

well to talk. But he had humor and worldly sophistication; he led me to E. A. Freeman's *The Growth of the English Constitution from the Earliest Times*, the book which at last made me feel the connection between political and moral idealism. He also introduced me, at occasional dinner parties, to the custom of conversing over a cocktail, helping me forward in my arduous climb from rustic diffidence to urban savoir faire. For these helps and the stimulus of his interest, I owe a more personal debt to him than to most of my teachers, though I can not describe him as an influence.

He had for assistant a young Amherst graduate named Preserved Smith, a thin dark mild shy edge of a man, who seemed to mention what he knew with hesitance as though embarrassed by his knowledge. With that approach he could hardly know, I concluded, very much, and I felt cheated whenever he slid apologetically into the great editor's chair. In 1930 Preserved Smith began the publication of his *History of Modern Culture*, in which it appeared that he knew as much, especially about what is worth knowing, as any person in the world. My regret for this youthful misjudgment is especially keen because in letters to me many years later Preserved Smith expressed a higher estimate of my own thoughts and writings, and backed me more vigorously against my critics, than any other scholar did. I missed a creative friendship.

Besides that diligent excursion into political science, and a course in English history to reinforce it, I did hard work in philosophy (which to my subsequent good luck included three months of logic), in James's psychology, and in a required course in "Theism" taught by the antique, side-whiskered ex-president of the college, Franklin Carter. In these courses, as in biology and physics, I felt more thinkingly alive than in the social and historic fields. This may be due, I suspect, to my strong sense of position, my wish to arrange things in clear patterns. There is plenty of loose detail in the physical, and yet more in the mental sciences, but the general notions are clear. History and sociology consist necessarily of groping with ill-defined ideas in a permanently messy swamp of fact. Wisdom here is largely intuitive; I like wisdom to be logical and highly conscious and succinct. You will find, accordingly, that when I finally do burst out with opinions on society and government, they are not only overloud but oversimplified.

For the present, however, aside from a violent distaste for snobbery and caste, I had few such opinions and little impulse to form them. I was reaching conclusions along such lines as these:

"Theology and 'Theism,' so far as I have observed them, have only succeeded in running out and barking at philosophy whenever it came by."

"Every man must consider the pitiable history of thought, and acknowledge that the logical necessity of any one attitude to reality can not be established."

"This is the perfection of nature as an artist that she never rants. The sea does not expend its power before us, but rolls a glimpse of it, and we listening look out beyond the wave in infinite wonder."

My refutation of Anselm's famous argument for the existence of God—one of the thorns I stuck in the flesh of "Prexy" Carter—still seems to me cogent. Anselm argued that we could not have the idea of God if God did not exist in reality, because it is the idea of "a being than which a higher can not be conceived." To exist in reality is higher than to exist only in thought; therefore "the idea of a highest Being which exists only in thought is the idea of a highest Being which is not the highest even in thought."

It is easy to brush away this argument, I observed, as resting on a misconception of what it means to affirm or deny. But that is not refutation. My refutation consisted of turning the same fallacious argument against the upholders of Anselm thus: "Anselm denies that God does not exist. In order to do this he must conceive of God as nonexistent—that is, he conceives of a 'being than which a higher can not be conceived' as not existing, which is contradictory." Therefore, it must be affirmed that God does *not* exist.

My philosophy professor, John E. Russell, liked my critical attacks upon his teachings, and liked still better, I suspect, the rumors of mutiny in the class in theism. He subsequently achieved philosophic renown when, as a militant opponent of James's pragmatism, he suddenly lowered his colors at the height of battle and confessed himself convinced—an event rare enough in the history of thought to deserve a marble monument. I knew him then only as "Pop" Russell, white-haired but young in step and clean-shaven, patron saint of the athletic field, favorite of the lowbrows, the professor who always gave good marks, and who for fear he might fail to recognize one of his own students, bowed vaguely with lowered eyes to everyone he passed. I wrote a paper for Pop Russell on "Moral Responsibility and Determinism" in which I asserted that both are indispensable postulates and one as well supported by experience as the other.

"Therefore, let Reason conclude that while both are true, neither is complete. 'This is true and that other is true, but our geometry can not span these points.' Emerson said that of Fate and Freedom; it should be said of Determinism and Moral Responsibility. It is a great heart and a humble heart to say that and think it and live it— Affirmative Agnosticism, Pragmatism, Socratic Scepticism, call it by what chill name you will, it is great."

And in a footnote I commented:

"All we know of cause is that certain things have always happened in a certain succession. But why?—we ask. And we assume a 'cause' for that."

All of which I quote not only to show that in these fields I was thinking my own thoughts—or in a pinch Emerson's—but also that my thoughts were sceptical. I am not so naïve as I was then about "moral responsibility." I say now that the concept of valid judgment implies that the judging mind is not determined by causes but swayed by reasons; the very assertion that determinism is universal assumes that one has freedom to decide. We use both these concepts and we must, and if we can not reconcile them, so much the worse for our brains. That is my present thought, and I have not found a better name for the philosophy it rides on than "affirmative scepticism." This philosophy does not say in general what is to be affirmed and what held in doubt. It leaves that for empirical determination as we go along; it is not, thus, strictly speaking, a philosophy. But it is a mental stance, permitting one to acknowledge the hard fate of man without sliding (as Mark Twain did) into moral negation.

That, however, is all this present morning's speculation. I was too much a child of America to have any consciousness of it then. My scepticism of intellectual formulae was as instinctive as my sense of logic. It seemed and seems an axiom to me that any elaborate system of human ideas is invalid. My career as a writer began in my first freshman notebook with a threat to "write something some day about the folly of any man saying that he knows his belief is right, and looking down upon other people as having wrong beliefs." It would require the reckless logic of youth to carry out that threat, but I still think that people who adhere to any complex credo are selling their birthright of good judgment in life's fluxes for a shuck.

On the other hand, my zeal for ideas and their propagation is irrepressible. It was foregone that I would move toward some evangel, and I will now introduce the teacher who gave me help along that way. He is the one with whom I read Dante during Junior year, Asa H. Morton, professor ostensibly of romance languages, but in reality of the life of ideas. He was a man of middle age with a trimmed iron-grey beard—handsome, cultured, cosmopolitan, a past master of intellectual conversation. His wife was a painter, the upper floors of his house a studio, and he brought home from his summers in Europe an atmosphere of Latin Quarter sophistication not elsewhere to be breathed at Williams. Subsequently he persuaded the trustees to give him the chair of religious philosophy and there felt he had found his true function, but his interest in religion was not credulous, and he was an advance on Prexy Carter that amounted almost to a revolution.

Notwithstanding his geniality and his manners of a prince, Morton was a rather lonely man. He frightened people with his brains; he lived too continually among ideas; he was too witty. Once he installed a phonograph in our classroom so that we could go up there and study pronunciation by ourselves. The college librarian undertook to kid him about this when we were all standing around downstairs between classes.

"Morton," he said, "I see you've got a hand organ up there in the Italian Department. Now all you need is a monkey . . ."

"Well, come on up!" Morton said.

You can't stop people that way very often without their feeling about you as they do about lightning. Besides that, Morton was famous among the students for the bad marks he gave—he labored under the impression that they all had cerebral cortexes—and so it came about that a romance language was regarded as a rather audacious adventure. I think that is one reason why I elected Italian, and why I made bold finally to take a walk with Morton and visit him in his house. He loomed as a kind of challenge to the boys who laid a claim to brains. Charles Whittelsey was the only other boy in our crowd who accepted the challenge. Morton told me that Whittelsey came down one evening to ask his advice about becoming a missionary.

"What qualifications have you?" Morton asked. "Have you mastered any heathen language?"

"No, I haven't," Whittelsey said.

"Have you made a special study of the Christian religion?"

"No, I hardly know anything about it."

"Have you looked into the life led by missionaries?"

"No, I haven't."

"Well, do you really want to be a missionary?"

Whittelsey said: "No, but I want to do something that I *don't* want to!"

An interesting sidelight on a military hero, and another instance of what I have called organic puritanism. "I want to do something that I don't want to": Isn't that one of the primary instincts of man?

Morton must have enjoyed Homeric laughter at some of the callow things he drew out of us with his magnetic intellectuality. His wife was deaf, and the first time I dined there I shouted three times as loud as I needed to all through dinner. Mrs. Morton, doubtless for that reason, withdrew after the coffee, and Morton and I spent the evening alone together in the studio. When he came down to the door with me at eleven o'clock and I said goodbye, I realized, perhaps because I was outdoors where the whole town could hear me, that I was still shouting.

It was in his studio that I received my initiation into the idea of schools and movements in art, the Italian primitives, the academicians, the revolt of the impressionists. I first heard on his lips the name of Claude Monet, and I must have taken from him my first lesson in the differences between Italian, Spanish, and Dutch painting. My mother had brought me from Holland a pretty smear in water color of a blue sea with a sail on it—what would be today a hand-painted postcard. This was junior year, mind you, and I brought that down and showed it to my teacher as an example of "Dutch Painting." I saw how fatuous my act was in the constrained graciousness with which he examined my little tourist's souvenir.

When I tell you that I continued to visit him after such exposures, you will realize the combination of charm and challenge in the man. He gave me my first taste of Platonic conversation, as fine and cosmopolitan a taste as one could find in any famed academy of Europe. And by lending me a copy of the French paper *Le Temps* containing a speech by Jaurés, he gave me my first intimation that socialism was something more than literary dream and soap-box gesture, that there existed, in France at least, a powerful political party with an aim like that which had "made me happy" in *News from Nowhere*.

It was a conversation about patriotism which led Morton to give me that paper. And next to that rustic utopianism I have described, a rejection of this limiting ideal was what first brought me toward socialism. "Patriotism is a virtue of the childhood of the race," I wrote in my senior notebook, "as pride itself is a virtue of children."

The statement of Jaurés to which Morton called my attention was this:

"The working class does not reject the idea of the fatherland, but it will not permit itself to be duped by those who use that idea for purposes of repression."

I remember my emotions: pride at being able to read a French newspaper (I had never seen one before); vexation at the moderateness of the statement (Why *not* reject the idea of the fatherland?); curiosity about that expression "working class" (Why drag that in? Aren't people who work as patriotic as anyone else?).

It was a passing query and provoked no investigation. I never asked Morton about it. It was three more years before I learned of the Marxian doctrine of class struggle.

I find it hard to believe, when I glance back at the wealth of thought, growth, and emotion I packed into that last year at college, that I was wearing a brace and lying down with a backache a good part of the day. One half of me, it seems, was really sick, so sick that my mother wrote in February: "If you are able to do work enough to get through and be graduated, that's the wise thing to do." The other half was well enough to enter an extra-curricular competition for a prize of four hundred dollars. Two advanced subjects were to be studied, and the winner determined by examination. As my minor subject I translated Dante's *Vita Nuova* for Professor Morton. As major I read James Mark Baldwin's *Mental Development in the Child and the Race* and wrote a thesis on it for Pop Russell. I won a mark of 100 in both subjects, and since my only serious rival, Roy Hack, told me that he had made mistakes, I thought I had that four hundred dollars in the bag. But Roy had always been a faithful student, the leader of the class of 1905, and neither Morton nor Russell was on the committee that awarded the prize. Out of consideration for the general principles of morality rather than the marks on our papers—at least so Pop Russell told me—they divided the prize between us.

"Those scholastics down there juggled the returns," he said.

I was disappointed, and my bookkeeping badly upset, for I had counted on that prize to ease me of a new crop of debts. But I can not say that I felt indignant. I had sauntered through four years of precious education—so it seemed to the committee—contenting myself with marks from 80 up to 95, and now when there was money in it I had shown what I could do. I saw some justice there. Besides I won other prizes amounting to $125, and by dexterously distributing the total among my creditors, I managed to leave town with my trunk.

My graduation was attended by the President of the United States, Theodore Roosevelt, fresh from his proposal of peace between Japan and Russia. It was further enlivened for me by my "pinch-hitting" for the ivy poet, whose sudden default left me but a few hours in which to compose the poem. And it was made genuinely significant by my resounding victory in the oratorical contest. My subject, suggested with subtle insight by Professor Morton, was Giordano Bruno. Into a eulogy of that stormy and uncertain-hearted martyr I poured all the main currents of thought and feeling upon which I myself was riding forth into a rather tumultuous life.

I praised Bruno as a martyr, not of one church against the other, but of poetry and philosophy against churchly masterdom as such.

"He was for life and truth," I cried, "rather than asceticism and dogma. . . . He tilted through those tents of expression with which the church covers up the frailty of its wonders."

And I took Bruno's casuistries when brought to trial as a text against the casuistries of churchdom in my own day.

"Bruno made a hypocritical distinction in practice between his belief and his creed. He was a Catholic at Rome and a Protestant at Geneva. Yet by both churches he was tried and denounced for heresy, and died finally firm in that heresy, silent in his own defense. . . . His philosophy could fit as well under Protestant as under Catholic forms, since it fitted neither; but he could not spare to be of the church in any land, for he loved it. So in this single soul is epitomized the struggle of ages to follow, the struggle of the love of reason against the love of worship, of philosophy against the church. His scheme for uniting them and its outcome in the conduct of an impulsive man you condemn, but perhaps therewith to some extent you condemn yourselves.

"Is not this the inevitable result of such a dismemberment of truth as Bruno attempted, that the one part should be paramount in its demand upon us, the other secondary and of small moment? With Bruno philosophy was the primary truth, and he let religious creed give way to convenience. This is the stain to which those backhangers point, when we would lift up a statue of our hero in the public square. And yet I count it no more a stain upon him than the modern disloyalty is upon them who make religion the primary truth, and prove turncoat wherever the conclusions of philosophy react to the discomfiture of an elaborate creed. They run after that philosophy which shall support them in church; Bruno sought that church which should let him preach his philosophy. . . ."

I was not going to rest content with Bruno's heresies, you see. I was going to have some heresies of my own—some waverings of my own too when brought to court, though I could hardly have anticipated that.

I did indeed, as though I knew about it, anticipate and defend my political life in my further eulogy of Bruno. For I praised him as "the prophet of an unfulfilled hope," an evangelist whose error, boldly spoken, worked in the service of truth.

"He was the forerunner, the bugler I would rather call him, for he had that war-song nature, of what never appeared—namely, a Universal Art of Knowledge. . . . The lesson to learn from him is courage in individual expression. From one that battled in a cause never vindicated, learn the utility of an enthusiastic error."

I had during that year discovered Emerson's essays on "Self-Reliance" and "Heroism." In them I found those attitudes which I had been expressing with a callow talent and under the stylistic influence of Stevenson expressed with native force and freedom. They became a kind of scripture to me, the only things, I think, that ever stood in my mind beside the image of Sid Wood as endowed with original authority—an authority not supernaturally derived, but derived from the fact that they gave me myself. If I have developed anything approaching a style, those two essays were chief among the influences that determined it. And in my peroration their influence was fresh and raw.

"We count the heads of the past and are dismayed. But a great many men are not God. Believe that they but introduce your vision. . . . Asserting the principle that is within yourself, before men believe it and name it true, to the end that your life shall be, as were the life and death of Bruno, *for* the ultimate truth."

That was my last word at college. That was another solution of the conflict in me between the zealot and the sage, between a belated adolescent's fervor and a prematurely wise man's doubts. In that rather perilous equilibrium I set forth to walk the billows of an age of war and revolution.

Chapter 33

Post-Graduate Interlude

THE previous sentence is an anticipation, for I spent the next year and a half doing little but trying to cure a mysterious pain. Scott Fitzgerald has remarked that "there is no difference in men, in intelligence or race, so profound as the difference between the sick and the well," and I know how true that is. No robust course of action such as might have sprung out of my rationalism, my moral and millennial idealism, my revolt against custom and dedication to a boldly individual experience of life, could be decided upon while I was spending half the hours of the day on my back.

Knowing what I do now of neuroses, I am tempted to say that this avoidance of a decision was a part of what my backache had in view. The affliction did not incapacitate me either for physical play or self-directed mental work. While on my feet I still indulged in agile and breath-exhausting games, and if I had to lie down right after, that only set me free to think and write and study what I pleased. One of the products of those crippled years was an essay entitled "The Folly of Growing Up." It said, whimsically, much of what I still think about life's values: notably that "most people have had too much of their own experience to be wise." Yet I can not help observing that my backache was permitting me to retain longer than a healthy man can the unchanneled experience of the child.

I do not want to oversimplify that neurosis. It is gripping me now, by way of protest against this disparagement, with a sharp and importunate pain. Such pains are as real as any others. Their causation, moreover, is not simple. Some physical weakness is generally mingled with the unconscious motivation which gives rise to them. And unconscious motivations, though the psychical doctors are prone to forget it, can be as complex as conscious ones. The "muscular inadequacy" which Dr. Goldthwaite was so sure of may be real; I do prodigiously hate to stand up or sit in a straight-backed chair. On the other hand, an X-ray doctor recently discovered deposits of calcium in my lower vertebrae which led him to murmur "arthritic." Whichever is true, the conflict of young love with an old-wise rejection of love's involvements was what first turned my physical weakness into pain. And if some dim general sense of the inadequacy of my character-posts to hold up the temple of my aspirations found expression here too, that is not surprising. A backache is a receptive symbol for all kinds of weakness and a convenient mode of escape from active life.

Mine found in this latter role a generous co-conspirator in Miss Suzie Hopkins and in the Reverend John Denison, an invalid theologian who lived next door to her in Williamstown. Dr. Denison had wealth and kindness and a fervent desire to reconcile the philosophy of Socrates with the religion of Jesus. This was to be done by way of essays in the *Atlantic Monthly*. Writing, however, besides being a lonely trade, was a strain on his nervous system and produced both constipation and insomnia. As one sick man to another, he proposed that I become his secretary at fifty dollars a month and let him dictate those essays. I could take the dictation lying on the floor, and besides, the job would consist mostly of talking the whole thing over as we went along. Gentle Miss Suzie backed this up by inviting me to live in her house on the same terms as her cat Smoky. It seemed to me a providential opportunity to get off the family pay roll while struggling, with Dr. Goldthwaite's steel brace and exercises, to regain my health. To my neurosis, if I may so recklessly personify him, it no doubt seemed a wonderful opportunity to go on being sick.

"I am happier than I have been for ages," I wrote to Crystal soon after the work began. "I haven't had a single melancholy time for a week. I don't know how to explain it."

And a month later:

"I am very deeply happy—very, very changed. I know that the only way out of or into anything is self-mastery, complete. My tragicness and insanity are entirely ended. They were because I was not growing. I have an everlasting comfort now in communion with my own ideals and resolutions, and living in imagination the lives of those who in measure embody them."

In this state of high and hero-worshiping morale, I summoned up enough strength to say at last a durable farewell to Frederica. We took a morning walk up into the woods where I had built me a little hut and a bed of balsam branches. Reclining on those branches, with little but hopeless desire in my heart, I told her that I thought our romance had come to an end—a truth of which I found her already fully aware.

In this display of character I was assisted—need I confess to any lover?—by a friendship with another woman. It was a friendship which has endured throughout my life and meant so many things to me that its role just then of a *divergent* seems incidental now. But it was a rare stroke of luck that Marjorie Nott happened to be spending a week at her Aunt Suzie's when I arrived to take my lodging there. Marjorie is the granddaughter of Mark Hopkins and also of Eliphalet Nott, for sixty years president of Union College. Her father was for almost half a century a judge of the Court of Claims, appointed by Lincoln in 1865 and named Chief Justice by Cleveland in 1896, a man of firm and revered character. Marjorie, whose mind is quite as brilliant as this ancestry suggests, had thus every opportunity to achieve a general culture that would take the place of concrete fine perceptions. She impressed me, instead, as the most delicately discriminating person I had met. She still preserves—I do not know quite how—amid the rough shocks of modern life and its more subtly disintegrating smooth polishes, the fine-edged ideality of a simpler and more religious age.

Majorie was a little older than I and not crudely alluring to my boyish passions. She is a woman whom grown men love. She has a gift of sensing one's inmost wish and without effort or obtrusion nestling among his necessities. I was grown then only in my mind, and I loved Marjorie, as Spinoza loved God, with an intellectual love.

Marjorie was a close friend of Henry Adams and "Bay" Lodge, the poet son of the senator from Massachusetts, who were then passing through their phase of philosophic anarchism. She had with her that autumn a volume of Emma Goldman's essays. I read those essays and was amazed that a human mind could manifest such vigor and yet be so obtuse to the terms of a practical problem. I can think of no act of magic that would give me greater pleasure than to wish away all governments, but that anyone with brains enough to write a book should regard that wish as a political program astonished me. Years after, I was similarly surprised at the lack of horse sense in Henry Adams' famous *Education*—an exercise in frustration which I found tiresome both to my practical and poetic sense.

Other authors that I remember high-handedly dismissing in conversations with Marjorie were H. G. Wells, Upton Sinclair, and

Bernard Shaw, who was then just entering the brilliant arc of his career as a dramatist. I never read more than a few pages of Shaw's plays or prefaces; I never read the novels of H. G. Wells (except *Mr. Polly* in 1920), or any of his socialist writings until *The Open Conspiracy* in 1928; I never read Sinclair's *The Jungle*, which made its enormous sensation during that winter of 1906. I laughed at his statement to the press that his best friends had been Jesus, Hamlet, and Shelley, and Marjorie reproached me: "You would not be so intolerant if you had read *The Jungle*." Some obdurate instinct always makes me reject a current best-seller and take down a classic or a textbook in its place. Partly it is a gesture of protection; I want to think things out for myself. Partly it is my old suspicion of the literary mind. Partly it is a wish to escape in meditation from the accidental. *Now,* I keep reminding myself, is no more important than any other time—a speculative attitude not easy to maintain in twentieth century America.

One book which I did take humbly from Marjorie's hands and read with intense absorption, was Sabatier's *Life of St. Francis d'Assisi*. In connection with that I consulted Tolstoy's *The Gospel in Brief* and his violently early-Christian essays in morals. It may have been Majorie, too, who led me to Thorstein Veblen's *Theory of the Leisure Class*, which I read eagerly during that winter, finding in it a justification for my revolt against starched collars and indeed the ground plan for an assault on respectability in general. That book seemed to me scientific—an intensely reasoned generalization of real facts. Together with St. Francis and Tolstoy it brought me several steps toward Marxian socialism, though by a path containing no signs to indicate the goal.

"Grave economists have pointed out how it would have upset the world if the theories of St. Francis had been generally adopted—which is their way of saying it would have upset the science of economics."

"It is a conspicuous fact that if the upper classes cut off expenditure for pecuniary emulation and invidious distinction, there would be enough wealth for all classes to indulge themselves to the same extent. . . . In running a cross-cut through Economics with Ethics, what we strive to do is to turn that emulation at the critical point into the moral, and individualistic, fields—out of the fields of property."

"I might say in this connection that a systematized study of biography will be, if I can make it, the thing to take the place of decadent and devitalized Christianity in school and college . . . My personal dream is hidden here."

There was to be no dogma in my dream; it was all still based on "affirmative scepticism." Indeed, side by side with this revolution of ethics against economics, I projected a book to be called *The Agnostic's God*, in which I would substitute an attitude for a creed as the substance of religion.

"Whether we name this attitude mysticism, with reference to the emotions aroused by our baffled imaginations, or agnosticism with reference to the agency of our reason in arriving there, matters not. Indeed the conclusion of the whole work might be summed up in the statement that we shall ultimately call it religion—the conclusion, the emotion, and the acts resulting."

As a critical biographer, I must point out that this proposed revolution of ethics against economics is only my old life ideal, or Sid Wood's, becoming earnest and evangelical. I was still determined to burst the bonds of generality and the commonplace, to "live a wild life," a life that would "bring the wolf and lion and panther to the door." I could not do it in the upper reaches of the Amazon any more, I was too burdened with intellect and a backache. I had to stay home and be good. But it wasn't to be a tame, conventional, thrifty kind of goodness. I was going to be wildly good, so good that it would overthrow the very principles of science—especially a science that assumes all mankind to be only trying to keep the wolf *away* from the door!

With Marjorie I plunged into these adventurous thoughts, as with Sid I had plunged into active adventure. I had the joy of defending them against a mind that cared vitally and was keen-bladed and relentless in debate. I found in Marjorie too, as strong as in Frederica, that love of natural beauty that makes it a poem to walk across the fields. And I found in her a taste for poetry so tuned and minutely demanding that it became a major influence in my life. I was still filling notebooks with my verses, and still in the same humble spirit. "I am not a poet, but I know what it would be like to be one," I wrote under a quite adequate sonnet to my mother. Marjorie lifted me some way out of this damping diffidence, which, notwithstanding a compensatory arrogance, is one of my chief failings. I could not, for the life of me, have said with Sidney Lanier: "I *know* . . . that

I am in soul and shall be in utterance a great poet." This, or words of similar import, Marjorie said for me in the course of our friendship. And for five years she made it one of her life-tasks to read and criticize my manuscripts, both poetry and prose, demanding with an authority I gladly gave that in every page to its last dot and comma I should keep burning the flame of perfection. She would have confirmed, had her influence prevailed, a tendency to creative self-esteem and self-consecration not sustained by my own nature or the environment into which I fell.

I saw an example of such consecration that winter in the sculptor, Augustus St. Gaudens, who came up to examine the placement of a medallion he had made of F. F. Thompson, the founder of our fraternity chapter. I was the head of a committee to entertain him and stood at the foot of the stone steps when his cab drove up. He rushed past my polished greeting, a shy, abstracted man with a slim auburn beard and a strong handsome nose, took one glance at the medallion, one at the windows, and hastened back toward the door. I managed to get in front of him and ask him if he wouldn't join us in a cup of tea.

"No, thank you, I'm suffering," he said. "I want to be alone."

I was told afterward that he was mortally sick with cancer, and it moved me deeply that he should have traveled so far for that one reassuring glance at a minor piece of work.

Besides helping Dr. Denison, I wrote two "essays for the *Atlantic*" of my own during that post-graduate winter: one in aesthetics called "Poetry as Nature," and one in ethics called "Patriotism, A Primitive Ideal." Having decided that all values are to be found in the mere living of life, I proceeded quite systematically to an examination of life's values. So it would seem—and it is true, I guess, that exploring these unmystic values has been my most systematic preoccupation as a writer. But I was unaware of any such neat sequence then. Ever since Sophomore year I had been writing little disquisitions on poetry, trying to define and explain the subtle thrill sent running through my nerves by certain juxtapositions of mere words. "Poetry as Nature" was the sixth of these efforts. For a longer time, I had been pondering my distaste for flags and flag waving, for club and party loyalty, sentimental partisanship, indeed collectivized emotion in general. In Tolstoy's denunciation of patriotism I found support, but he based his denunciation on a religion of love; I wanted it based on good logic and loyalty to truth. "To shout for one's country in the face of others that stand equal is to sell for sentiment one's birthright to the universal judgment," I wrote. And I backed up my position with fourteen pages of purely dialectic, but not wholly amateurish argument.

I sent my essays in due course to the *Atlantic* and was rewarded in each case with a personal letter from its noted editor, Bliss Perry.

"Dear Mr. Eastman, If you will put the same amount of literary skill which you have shown in this essay into the discussion of some more distinctly 'magazinable' topic, I think that the Atlantic will open a hospitable door to you. We have nothing but praise for the essay itself . . ." So he encouraged me about "Poetry."

And about "Patriotism": "We are sorry to be obliged to return any of your essays . . . Yours is such an essay as belongs, really, I think, in a book rather than a magazine. For my own pleasure in reading your treatment of a theme in which I have a strong personal interest I am sincerely indebted to you."

"Patriotism, A Primitive Ideal" appeared in the *International Journal of Ethics* the following summer—my first burst into public print. "Poetry as Nature," renamed "The Poet's Mind" appeared in the *North American Review* two years later. But for the time being Bliss Perry's kind letters marked the end of my career in both Ethics and Aesthetics. Within two weeks of the receipt of his second letter I was up to my ears in the study of Abnormal Psychology.

The cause, as usual, was a mere drift of circumstance.

Chapter 34

A New Thought Sanitarium

B Y MIDWINTER Jesus and Socrates, with the help of insomnia and constipation, had pretty well got the best of Dr. Denison. His nicely adjusted theological pinfold stood ready, but the gods refused to go in. I would lie down on the floor with expectant paper and pencil, and he would pace the room in a brown study for an hour or two and then say with his engaging yet pathetic smile:

"Well, Max, I guess the Greeks have outmaneuvered us for the moment. My brain seems to be all clogged up."

He took flight finally to Dr. Gehring's neurological sanitarium in Bethel, Maine, and I to Dr. Sahler's New Thought sanitarium at Kingston on the Hudson. I do not remember how I first heard of that unique institution. The New Thought movement was a kind of practical-minded first cousin to Christian Science, a mixture of suggestive therapeutics, psychic phenomena, non-church religion, and a business of conquering the world through sheer sentiments of optimism. It leaned heavily, and perhaps not unfairly, on Emerson and Walt Whitman. Edwin Markham stood within its influence, and John Burroughs' poem "Waiting" with the refrain "What is my own shall come to me," was part of its Holy Writ.

My mother had a weakness for health regimes and quack nostrums and panaceas. She was never so happy as when she could get me to join her in some newly concocted scheme for keeping well and happy. We would stop eating breakfast, or go in for raw food, or abjure salt, or walk barefoot in the dew, or take up Fletcherism, or deep breathing, or absent treatments by Miss Isaphine Granger—it didn't much matter what, so somebody had written persuasively about it. She especially liked those schemes which went at the body through the mind—and moreover in this field she had much intuitive wisdom.

"I am pretty sure," she wrote, "that your trouble is nervous—and more temperamental than local—it has simply settled in the weakest spot."

And in another letter:

"I feel sure something is troubling you. Perhaps you don't acknowledge to yourself what it is, but I wish you'd think it out and dare it to hurt you."

Thus it was all but foreordained that I should arrive at that millennial and mystical and funny and fantastically kindhearted institution, the C. O. Sahler Sanitarium at Kingston, New York. I arrived, my notebook tells me, at 8:00 P.M. of a January evening on top of an express wagon with my trunk. I entered a high narrow hallway which was given the appearance of being cluttered by one hat-and-coat rack, one "pale-colored imbecile" sitting in it with her back to its mirror, and one spoon-faced, tall, skinny gentleman, who stalked through from time to time on legs that seemed petrified.

Dr. Sahler did not welcome me, but sent instead an expert in that craft, whom I described as a "white-dressed, blue-eyed angel." Her method of welcoming, I noted, was not to smile all the time, a smile that lies to you, but to speak solemnly and then deliver the smile all of a sudden when you had given up hope. I was to have supper as soon as she could get it ready, and meanwhile I could entertain myself either in the "men's lounge" or the "women's parlor."

(I am paraphrasing here a record I kept at the time.)

The men's lounge was a narrow chamber, a tight squeeze for a pool table, but containing also three players, several onlookers, a thick fog of tobacco smoke, and two guinea pigs in a dry goods box. Its red walls had been practiced upon by a painter of pale-green trees with stiff-necked deer browsing among them. Charles Darwin and Thomas Henry Huxley in gilt frames peered from a clearing in the trees. The space at the ends of the table was so small that it was necessary to stand the cue on its head and strike downward, by which process the table had been lacerated through the ages and was patched with court plaster in great stars and crosses. Of the three men playing, one was irritably bossy, the other chestless and obliging, the third big and oracular, a sort of ward politician, rotund at the front (but hollowing in at the back to correspond, as he afterward showed me), and wound up to say every three minutes: "Oh, I get sick o' this damn game!" Other pale ones stood around obstructing the game by looking on. It was plain from the attitude of the big man, whose name was F. J. Hornbeam, that all but him lacked common sense, of which he had a plethora. The guinea pigs looked healthy and happy, and what they were doing in a sanitarium I could not imagine. Upon everyone else it was written plain.

After a taste of the heavy smoke in the men's lounge, I tried the ladies parlor, but found the ladies distributed over chairs and sofas in a variety of debilitated attitudes that left no room for one of mine. The spoon-faced gentleman stalked through from the front hall, dodging the prostrate and clearing his throat thunderously. "He won't hurt you!" a nervous voice laughed. I murmured that I wasn't afraid, but slank back into the hall where the sandy-haired imbecile still sat motionless against the mirror. Here my blue-eyed angel found me and led me to supper down a flight of stairs at the back.

I had stewed prunes and a fried egg for supper, and the vision of the girl disappearing up those stairs. When I came up after eating I had another vision of her through the open door of an "electric room." She was earnestly lowering a serrated gold crown over the head of a small cringing citizen in underwear, who received it more reluctantly than any Julius Caesar—for it contained a lively current, as I subsequently learned. The vision of that scared little plebeian dodging the weight of empire and the girl's delicate and serious concern as she urged him to accept it made me laugh aloud. In the background a bulky old lady was lying on an operating table rocking like a cradle, first her heels and then her head being jerked upward by some mysterious force I could not locate. She poured out an incessant stream of slangy and ungrammatical protestations in a high nasal whine that could be heard throughout the building—for all doors were open, it seemed to me, at the Sahler Sanitarium. I was relieved when a boy led me away to my room in a rented house across the street—a first floor room with big windows and a private entrance from the porch. It was clean and peaceful, and I slept well.

I wanted to believe in this institution. I wanted to believe in mental healing. Indeed I was convinced that no other healing would ever touch my trouble. But I came to breakfast, I must say, prodding my enthusiasm and wondering whether I was a snob after all. My first surprise was the cheerful, almost amused, greeting I received from a lot of brown and blue eyes in the region of my table. I felt like a new toy arriving in a happy nursery. The lady nearest me, I learned, was going home that day.

"All well?" I asked.

"Not perfectly well," she said, "but *perfectly able to get well.*"

Her emphasis was evangelical, and there ensued a conversation about psychic power, self-culture, the road to poise, the therapy of love, the accessibility of the universal life-force, and other such large yet intimate matters, that abashed me, though I come of a race of preaching heretics. Religion, ethics, and therapeutics were never more naïvely—and yet I could not say unwisely—mixed together. I decided to wait and see.

My first diagnosis occurred at the hands of the rotund Mr. Hornbeam, before mentioned, on the front porch after breakfast.

"Trouble with your back, hey? Do you take baths?"

"Why yes, occasionally."

"Cold baths, hey? That shocks the spine. Most people that take cold baths in winter have trouble with their back or somewheres else. A cold bath in winter's as bad as a warm bath in summer. Ye've got to git hot baths and ale in winter, and cold baths and lager beer in summer. Now I myself can't drink an ale in summer.—Insomnia, hey?" Here he threw out his chest as if about to take on a medal. "I've had insomnia for twenty years at a stretch, and there's just one thing'll cure it. Many's the night I've got up at twelve or one and slipped around the corner for a swig of whisky. I don't take no drugs, but give me seven or eight whiskies and I'll sleep like a lamb. It's Christian Science, that's what I believe in—Christian Science and pure will power backed up by whisky!"

Following this diagnosis and prescription, Mr. Hornbeam and I played pool on that wounded table. The game was not very satisfactory. We agreed that the facilities were better for cockfighting. The balls when they got tired would sit down with a little circular motion like a dog. We had not played long when the doctor stepped up and invited me into his office—into the Holy of Holies, that is to say, of the New Thought movement.

It was a dim and fragrant chamber, lighted by a single gas jet which the doctor turned up higher while he examined me, and then turned down again. It contained many beautiful roses, many of the best books and some of the worst. Ralph Waldo Emerson rubbed elbows with Ralph Waldo Trine. There was exquisite Greek sculpture in the room, and there were painted plaster casts of American Indians. There was a real skeleton, and an imitation skull to receive burnt matches. There was a case for surgical instruments, and in the far corner a draped and canopied couch suggestive of mystic slumber in the deep Orient. The doctor had a round head with brown hair neatly plastered to it boyish-fashion, round brown eyes, a round chin, and gushing grey side whiskers flowing to his waist and smelling of bay rum. He was reputed to be, besides a master hypnotist, the best surgeon in the town and a graduate of "both schools of medicine." He went over me no less carefully than Dr. Goldthwaite had. When he had finished, and had turned down the gas so that his whiskers blended with the atmosphere like those of a wizard in his cave, he seated himself with a most unwizardly thump and said:

"Wal, you think this thing's 'n yer back, but 'taint, it's in yer belly!"

Having discharged the atmosphere with this shock, he led me over in the corner, stood me with my back to the couch, and placed a warm magnetic hand at the nape of my neck.

"If you feel an inclination to fall backwards," he said, "don't resist it."

I did of course fall back, and he lowered me gently to the couch. He then placed that same warm hand upon my brow and stood beside me in silence. He stood for five minutes, and then went away and let me rest for fifteen. When he came back, he enlarged somewhat upon his diagnosis. My trouble was a lack of vital force in the nerve centers, especially those of the abdomen, which prevented my making any considerable exertion without weariness. Any weariness is likely to hit you in the back. He would not give me drugs; he would give me electricity to arouse the physical apparatus; but for the rest, temperance in work and play with psychic treatments morning and afternoon would make me well.

After that first interview I rarely spoke with the doctor. He turned me over to a colleague supposed to be equally endowed with psychic power, a grey-haired, gracious-mannered, stately woman of about fifty named Miss Page. I would retire into a little cubicle containing a couch and pillow, and Miss Page would come and stand beside me with her hand on my brow for about five minutes; then she would go away and let me rest for half an hour. During that five minutes she was supposed to be rectifying my condition by a concentration of her will—letting the psychic force, of which there is a great plenty in the universe, pour into me through her as a focusing glass or funnel.

It was a shrewd and simple way to employ suggestion in therapeutics. It cost but little in time or effort, and at the very least gave the sick man a good rest twice a day. But in order to make it effective, the doctor and Miss Page had to keep up among the patients a sense of their special magnetic power. This they did by means of Sunday night lectures, at which, besides talking a lot of good medical common sense and early Christian morals, they would hypnotize two boys and stick needles into them or tell them cayenne pepper was candy and let the patients see them lick it gladly up. That proved, you see—and indeed it really does—the power of an opinion firmly held. It proved enough to "carry me through the worst phases of my incredulity," as I put it in a letter to Miss Suzie, and I would try hard to have faith while reposing in the little cubicle with health-in-the-abstract pouring into me.

Even more than by the treatments, I was impressed by the moral and social atmosphere in which they were given. "The spirit of the place is 'towards democracy,'" I wrote. "That's what you are to imagine—people united in a higher commonalty than recognizes distinction of clothes, and grammar, and 'my kind' and 'your kind.' They know Edward Carpenter here, and I am reading him again, and drinking the thoughts that make me drunk. . . . I am more optimistic about the world than ever in my life before."

This optimism was undoubtedly tinged, as my optimisms usually are, with an amative joy. I have said that I could soon find a friend in any hamlet of the earth. I could also, if a life's experience proves anything, find a girl to love. In Kingston I found two, both in white uniforms. The one I have described as my welcoming angel was named Rosanna. She was quaint-lipped, curvy-shaped, with ruddy cheeks, brown hair, and a girlish mischief rather than a grown-up yearning in her eyes. Her sister Charlotte, whom I met in the hall the next morning, was paler; her hair was golden, her body slender, her face in its bony structure, no matter how gaily or lovingly she smiled, wistfully beautiful. She was, officially, the house matron, and Rosanna was the supervisor of the dining-room. But they were both, in a less explicit way than Miss Page and the doctor, sources of the loving-kindly radiance that filled the place. I described the patients to Miss Suzie as "a various family united in helpfulness by their love of Miss Page and Doctor Sahler and Rosanna and Charlotte." And to her inquiry about Charlotte, of whom I said less because I loved her more, I answered:

"Is she a little less beautiful than Rosanna?—and not quite so nice?—Who but the gods can decide? I think it is not known on earth. I will say this, though—after reflection—the most beautiful vision my eyes have *ever* beheld is Charlotte's head at certain moments. And perhaps the simplest and purest-white soul that was ever entangled in the wreckage of this world . . . but enough. She is for contemplation."

From Charlotte I learned to "kiss with the inside lip," to borrow a mild expression from Shakespeare, and our embraces were avowedly amorous, but never more than that. I lacked the art to seduce with adoration. I never put my hand on Charlotte's tempting breast. She was tireless and conscientious to the point of sainthood about her tasks, which were unending, and that helped her to elude my invitations to walk in the near-by woods. With Rosanna there were many walks in those woods and no embraces. I never even kissed her cheek. But I came closer to her in another way than I did to Charlotte.

As a part of her dining-room duties Rosanna adopted a custom of leaving a note at my plate each morning containing a favorable thought about my health or a droll comment on my neighbors. She had no critical intelligence—there was none of that at Dr. Sahler's —but she seasoned the New Thought sweetness with a grain of sly humor that made her very dear to me. We became close enough friends to take a long day's walk together to the lonely farmhouse in a clearing high up in the Catskills where her parents lived, wading in a mountain stream and murdering a copperhead along the way. I described her home to my mother as "a little paradise of natural beauty and human goodness and genuineness," and said that I had come back after a night's sleep there "very much strengthened in my ideals."

And we made another trip down the Hudson to Highland to visit her grandfather-like friend John Burroughs, whom my journal reminds me I "loved for his simplicity."

"There is no striving after uniqueness about him, or about his cabin Slabsides. He is not a crank, and doesn't want to be, but he does love to wear his old clothes and be earthy and sit rocking gently in the sun. He loves Walt Whitman and Emerson. It did me good to hear *somebody* say they were the two greatest, they deal with the elements.

"Whitman had been there at Slabsides. His exercise would be to carry a big stone, toss it in the air and catch it, or to bend down a sapling and then spring up and down with it, gently—and he would look like a great grey man of the woods. Mysterious he was, and gentle, not boisterously athletic. He had much of the mother in him, although primally masculine like the mountains. Burroughs said that Whitman's skin was very soft and delicate, that his body was like a baby's—smooth and pink."

As we walked through the woods, Burroughs picked out an appropriate sapling and showed me how Walt would bend it to the ground and work it up and down very slowly with his arms. So large and leisurely a form of exercise! So little akin to any play of mine! I felt as though he were telling me about life in the kingdom of Saturn before the revolt of the lesser gods. He too seemed slow-moving and serene, also a little flameless and impersonal, as if only partially surviving from those more spacious times.

Although swept so far in by the idea of mental healing, and by the millennial good will attending it at Kingston, I was sceptical of much that I heard about psychic powers and entities. I was sceptical of the magnetic force supposed to be wielded by the doctor at those Sunday night exhibitions in hypnotism. I suspected that anyone bold enough to speak the same words could accomplish the same results. There was a very simple way to decide this—especially simple because of the outdoor entrance to my room. I invited his two boys to slip over privately one evening, and I hypnotized them myself. My room had once been a dining room, and only a thin partition separated it from the room occupied by a very gossipy housekeeper and her daughter—not an ideal location for an Institute of Psychic Research, but that is what it became. The boys, one of them a stutterer of good upbringing, the other a delinquent from New York's East Side, enjoyed the conspiracy and would come any time I asked them. One of my first suggestions to the New York boy was that a lion had jumped in the window. I realized my recklessness when, instead of crawling under the bed, he pulled a loaded revolver out of his pocket. No lion ever made a quicker exit.

The doctor's library was an indiscriminate mixture of mystical and scientific books on psychic phenomena, and I plunged in there and soon forgot my regime of moderation in a fit of hard study reminiscent of Mercersburg. In the space of three months I covered a master's course in abnormal psychology, trying out everything I read in the books, so far as I could, with an experiment in my bedroom laboratory.

This was in the pre-Freudian days. To be exact, it was just a few months after Freud made at Clark University his first unsuccessful attempt to get scientific attention in this country. Liebault and Charcot and Bernheim were still the great names, and "suggestive therapeutics" the advanced and rather disreputable mode of treatment. Even these names and this treatment were little known in America. Hypnotism had no scientific standing; it belonged to mountebanks. One of my Elmira doctors, Frank W. Ross, informed me solemnly that there was no such thing as hypnotism—it was all a trick. Dr. Quackenbos, author of Quackenbos' *Rhetoric*, was using it in his practice, however, and defending it in brilliant if unreliable language. In general, the science of mental healing stood about where alchemy did in the seventeenth century when Robert Boyle laid the foundations of chemistry, and mixed a good deal of magic into the cement he used. Dr. Sahler's mind, his library, his half-surgical, half-thaumaturgical inner chamber, his wizardly whiskers and matter-of-fact twang represented the state of things at its best.

Among those bold enough to believe in mental healing without delusions was Beatrice Hinkle, an attractive, not over-credulous, and intelligent young physician, who came to look into Dr. Sahler's Sanitarium while I was there. We got to talking in the dining room, and discovering a common taste for the experimental suspense of judgment on "psychic" questions, became friendly. She was interested in my clandestine experiments, and when I expressed a wish to have the experience, she kindly offered to try to hypnotize me. I went down to New York one weekend for the purpose, and she did try several times, but unsuccessfully.

There was an inner mystery about Dr. Sahler and his sanitarium. He had, the patients would whisper, some occult source of information, some contact with the spirit world, not mentioned in his lectures. Something "went on" in that dim inner chamber when no patients were present. I took this at first for a revival of the Faustian myth, natural enough in the circumstances, and gave it no thought. But it was singularly persistent and became finally a challenge to me in my enterprise of psychic research. By the end of February I would have given all my dwindling hopes of Dr. Sahler's therapy to plumb the secret of his relations with the unseen world. He was, however, underneath his casual and genial twang, a man of austere reserve, and I saw no way-in to the heart of his mystery.

That way-in was revealed to me by sheer accident, or rather through the impish connivance of the god of love. Being in honor bound to keep that god's confidence, I never revealed even to my own family the secret I am now going to tell. It is forty years old, and only I am left to tell it.

Quite casually one morning, though in a whisper, I told Rosanna about the Institute for Psychic Research in my bedroom. She accepted the news with surprising calm.

"I wonder if you could hypnotize me?" she said.

"Have you ever been hypnotized?" I asked.

She glanced round the dining room, and then leaned close to my ear.

"The doctor hypnotizes me every day!"

"What!" I exclaimed, turning around in my chair.

"It's a dead secret. Don't you ever tell a soul, but I'm his medium. I diagnose the patients and everything—at least my astral body does."

She was gone before I could answer, and kept out of my sight for two days. I met her finally in the front hall.

"Will you come over to the institute and be hypnotized?"

"Yes, I will," she said firmly.

"When?"

"Sunday night while everybody is at the doctor's lecture."

In order that you may admire her nerve as I did, you must know that next to the doctor's relations with the unseen world, the main topic of speculation at the Sahler Sanitarium was the imagined amours of these two adorable nurses. I doubt if any Sunday night was ever more pregnant with scandal. Suppose I should put Rosanna in a trance and be unable to get her out? Suppose the gossipy housekeeper should hear me trying to make Rosanna go to sleep in my bed? Suppose Rosanna's astral body should flit across the street and tell the doctor in the middle of his lecture what was going on!

The housekeeper, of course, did not attend the lectures, and as the moment of our rendezvous approached, I could hear her talking with her skinny daughter in the next room. I met Rosanna with my finger to my lips, and we conducted the approaches to our experiment in whispers. She lay down on my bed like a mischievous lamb, submissive but with laughter in her eyes. I held a glass marble a little above them, and she fastened her attention on it.

"You're only going to sleep," I said, with a note of apology hardly appropriate to the hypnotic art. But she was an adept and passed into a trance of her own free will. Her face turned a little paler; her lips purpled like fading rose leaves; a blue shadow crept under her eyes; absolute stillness possessed her as though she were carven **on** a tomb. I saw the change many times thereafter and was always subdued by it, for she would seem both dead and more delicately alive. But that first night I was frightened so that I could hardly draw my breath. They would be expecting her at the main building in an hour, and she looked as though she had gone to sleep for a century. I made a record of our seance, which was, as you may guess, exceedingly brief.

"My room, February 28 (1906)

"After about three minutes Rosanna fell asleep with a sudden exhalation of breath. I waited a moment and then said:

" 'Can you see anything?'

"There was no answer. My voice was trembling and scarcely audible, so I waited some two minutes for control.

"Then I said again: 'Can you see or feel anything?'

"In a moment the answer came in a low natural voice: 'Doctor, everything seems dim to me tonight. I can't see anything plainly.'

" 'Can't you distinguish anything?' I asked.

"The answer in a plaintive voice: 'Doctor, you seem very far away. There is another present. He is very near me. He must be thinking about me.'

" 'Can you see who it is?'

" 'Somebody taller than you'—perplexed voice.

" 'Is it Max Eastman?'

" 'O yes. I thought that face seemed familiar'—with relief as if smiling.

" 'Can you see anybody else?'

" 'Doctor, I can't see anything. I am very tired tonight. I am going to sleep.'

" 'You are going to *wake up* when I have counted eight!'

" 'No, I am going to sleep!'

" 'You are *not* going to sleep! I am going to count eight, and when I say eight, you will wake up. One-two-three-four-five-six-seven-eight. Wake up, Rosanna!'

"She woke up, stretched, and with a smile said: 'I went to sleep!'

"At first she had wanted to laugh, she told me, and then had resolved to put that out of her mind, and let herself go as usual. Soon after making this decision, she felt as if she left half her body lying on the bed and the rest was taken up into me, and after that she remembered nothing."

Rosanna had so badly frightened me with that "No, I am going to sleep!" that I never invited her to my room again. We conducted our further experiments under the pine trees deep in a neighboring woods. I filled two notebooks with my records of these seances, the earlier ones largely occupied with suggesting to the trance-Rosanna that she would never tell the doctor about our acquaintance.

The everyday-Rosanna had no memory of what the trance-Rosanna said, and we would talk over my notes and plan new experiments as though discussing a third person. One of our plans was that her astral body, or "Rosanna 2" as I more dryly called her, should visit my bedside on a certain midnight at the stroke of twelve. I hoped fervently for some relevant experience on that midnight. I thought at least I might see her in a dream, and for that purpose tried with all my might to go to sleep. I tried so hard that as midnight approached, I was lying stark awake and tense as one is toward the climax of a ghost story. About two minutes before midnight, an explosion took place on the floor not three feet from my pillow. My body leaped in the air as though shot upward by that explosion, and then lay rigid with terror. When I found courage to switch on a light, I perceived that a large volume of Plato's *Republic,* which I had stood edgewise on the mantel, had chosen that moment to fall flat-side-down to the floor. I tried hard to believe that Rosanna 2 had pushed it off, but it seemed rather heavy work for an astral body. Moreover, when I asked her at our next seance about her visit, she merely said that she had stood by my bed and placed her hand on my forehead.

That was the nearest I ever came to getting a "psychic experience" out of Rosanna, although I tested loyally every power she was supposed to possess, pestering my family and Miss Suzie and my fraternity friends with inquiries as to where they were and how occupied at such and such an hour and minute. I convinced myself—reluctantly indeed—that Rosanna 2, although more acute in her perceptions, more imaginative, and able to learn faster than Rosanna 1, was not possessed of any supernormal powers. I had to content myself with improving the first Rosanna's grammar by post-hypnotic suggestion and with telling the second Rosanna what mysterious wisdoms—especially as to the conduct of my case—she was going to impart to the doctor. She obeyed my suggestions implicitly, and by the time I left Kingston I had in my hands the authority of the celestial powers whom Dr. Sahler thought he was consulting.

This did not make me feel toplofty or cynical, however, for it was not superior knowledge but a sounder approach to the problem which had put me in this position. I had taken an attitude of inquiry toward psychic phenomena, Dr. Sahler an attitude of faith. We neither of us knew anything about them. In spite of the failure of my experiments with Rosanna, I was still hospitable—and am today—to evidences of supersensory communication, or even of premonition. Of the latter I am incredulous, but not more so than I am of the actuality implied by the "space-time units" of modern physics. The behavior of mathematical symbols upon which this concept is erected will someday, I suspect, be explained in a manner more akin to common sense and sense perception. In neither case, however, have I the inclination to close my mind. Wisdom aside, it is much more fun to keep it open.

Notwithstanding this mental detachment, there was an element of flight in my departure from Kingston. What with one Charlotte and two Rosannas, my heartstrings were getting more exercise than was good for my health. I was resolutely inattentive to Rosanna's earthly body as it would lie unpossessed beside me, or possessed rather by a sacred stillness, under the pine boughs. Chivalry, I felt, demanded this of a man communing with a girl's astral body. But that astral Rosanna was growing dear and very exciting to me, and was growing daily more tender in describing her rapturous sensations when she would arrive from nowhere at my bidding and find me near. I could not quite see the end of this adventure. I was exploring with high emotion a region where cool science had hardly begun to grope. Morton Prince's startling book, *The Dissociation of a Personality,* was published during that very year of my friendship with the two Rosannas, but not in time to give me any guidance. I was troubled, and not unwisely I think, about the effect upon the earthly Rosanna's mental health if these emotions of the heavenly one should grow too strong.

And then the adoring hunger in my heart for Charlotte seemed only to reproduce in pastel colors my renounced romance with Frederica. Charlotte was more free and natural than Frederica, and although ungrammatical and unschooled, she seemed to my rebel mind a more commanding character because she had a work to do. But she was not commanding enough to solve the conflict in me between life and love. It began to trouble me seriously that there should be so many beautiful girls in the world, that I must "fall in love" in this absorbed yet uncommitted way wherever I go. Others fall in love as casually, of course, and through mere accident of propinquity, but they have enough weight or viscosity so that when once in love they stay in love. They stay in love, most wonderful of all, with the same girl!

These things troubled my conscience a little. And moreover a night-and-day diet of books on psychic phenomena, varied only by experiments in hynotism, telepathy, clairvoyance, astral somnabulation and ghost culture by post-hypnotic suggestion, was beginning to make me feel spooky. The mountainous Mr. Hornbeam who believed in whisky and pure will power began screaming one midnight in the room above me, and I had to go up with the housekeeper and hold his quaking flesh in bed through an attack of delirium tremens. Another patient in our annex peered in my window in the small hours of a dark night, all dressed in flannels and a sport shirt, proposing a game of tennis. The Sahler Sanitarium did not in principle admit insane patients, but at the high point of its faith in the New Thought it cherished a somewhat liberal definition of insane. I learned much from the New Thought movement, though mostly what its prophets did not teach, and what between love and learning I was serenely happy during my sojourn in its holy place. But after three months amid so much queerness and sickness, with no improvement of my backache, I wanted to get away. I wanted to stop thinking about the occult.

ENVOI

I find among my treasures two letters surviving from those times. One from Rosanna, left at my breakfast plate, says:

"Max, I am going to speak frankly. I do love you (I am not going to use the word *like*, it isn't the right one)—not passionately, tragically or unhappily, but with the sweet happy love that one can give to a true friend."

The other from Charlotte, sent to me after I had gone back to Williamstown, reads: "I love your letters, Max. I have nothing to send. You have all."

I find also a letter I wrote to my mother about Charlotte and Rosanna: "There are few much deeper lodged in my heart than those two girls."

We exchanged a few letters; they came for a four-day visit the summer of 1907 to Glenora; and once during the next winter I spent a weekend at the sanitarium. I always thought of them, when the thought came, as my dear friends. But though I lived the better part of my life within sixty miles of Kingston—this is a bitter and terrible confession—I never saw either of them again until the writing of this book brought me back vividly into that phase or section of my divided being. Then suddenly one morning I got in my car and drove to Kingston at high speed with hurried feelings like a man who has forgotten a treasure. I knew that Charlotte and the doctor had died, but I thought I might still see Rosanna. I did not know how to ask for her when I stood in the office of the sanitarium. I mumbled like an astral body.

"I guess you want to see Miss Charlotte," an attendant said.

My heart jumped but sank again.

"Yes, that must be what I want," I murmured.

While I sat waiting in the parlor, I heard a plaintive cracked voice, and a little invalid old lady tottered from the electric room, clinging to the wrist of an attendant. She moved on into the hall where I had first encountered the pallid imbecile, the spoon-faced relic, and my welcoming angel, and they labored together up the stairs. I knew it was Rosanna, although I could not perceive an item of similarity. I sat frozen, as though confronted for the first time in my life by reality.

A Charlotte came—beautiful in a polished way, and of the same rare pale color. She was the niece of my Charlotte, an adored niece to whom she had left her place and her share in the sanitarium, and said with her last breath: "You have all."

This new Charlotte led me upstairs to Rosanna in her bedroom, a tiny room and a little withered blue-eyed old lady bravely dying of cancer. Rosanna had strength enough to speak wanly of our walks in the woods and how much she had loved to lie down on the pine needles and fall dreamlessly asleep beside me. I had strength enough to answer without bursting into tears. When I kissed her goodbye she murmured:

"Why did you never come to see us?"

I said: "I don't know. I think I have, like you, more than one person in me. The one who loved you and Charlotte seems to have been here with you all these years. I have only come back to him."

She closed her eyes. She was too tired to think it out. The simple fact was clearer that I had not come.

Chapter 35

A Pre-Freudian Mind Cure

ALTHOUGH I rejected the occult and spiritistic hokum with which Dr. Sahler surrounded his practice, I did not reject mental healing. I seized upon its least occult feature, auto-suggestion, and decided to withdraw from the world and cure myself with that. To withdraw from the world was, of course, pure folly, but I had to make a romance of my doings in those days. "I know I can get well now," I wrote my mother, "and I'm coming to Glenora to do it. I am going to sleep and live outdoors and work in the soil little by little until I am well. I shall get my own meals and read Walt Whitman."

Dr. Nelson offered me Preserved Smith's job as instructor in political science at $750 a year, with assurance of a $500 essay prize besides—another nice berth for my neurosis. But I was determined to get well, and I was determined not to live my life in books.

"I learn from biography, which is my bible," I replied to Dr. Nelson, "that the highest good is a right union of the active and the contemplative life. But I should destroy the balance if I chose to stay here and take up that course now. I need and want activity and practical experience . . . A successful ward boss would be a better instructor in politics than I."

To my mother, who reminded me of my debts and the joys of a scholarly life, I wrote:

"My idea of a scholar is a man who has merged out of experience into contemplation; and my ideal of a man is one who has lived the life of his time and knows what he is talking about . . . I don't want money. I don't want a wife. I don't want dignity. Is two hundred dollars' debt a reason for compromising my ideals?"

This fell in with her own mood, for she was in the midst of a battle against stodginess in all its forms. My father had come out for

255

Sunday baseball, and surrounding Christendom was in arms once more against the Park Church. "I'm *sick* of ministers!" she exclaimed in that connection. And as to my refusal to become a scholar: "I take a proud joy in your determination to stick by yourself."

When I came home I found her launched on a raw food diet conducted by correspondence with a famous balloonist, Dr. Julian P. Thomas of New York. Dr. Thomas supplied diagnosis, prognosis, and three months' weekly prescriptions, also consultations by special delivery if a crisis arose (and he didn't happen to be up in a balloon), for a cash payment of eighteen dollars. It seemed to fit in admirably with my program of autosuggestion, getting my own meals, and reading Walt Whitman. So I signed up too and departed for Glenora in the mood of an anchorite, with a raw food bill-of-fare in my pocket. It began largely with lemon juice and hot water, but in three weeks I was drinking five quarts of milk a day, eating six raw eggs, three bananas, four oranges, two handfuls of nuts and raisins, a handful of raw oatmeal, and six cakes of raw pressed wheat specially prepared (and charged for) by Dr. Thomas. I find in the Cherith Log a hymn composed by me with the refrain:

> O Julian P. Thomas, have mercy upon us!
> The hens are aweary, the cows are azew!
> Have mercy upon us, unmerciful Thomas,
> And may these kind creatures have mercy on you!

That word "azew" means *dry* in the Dorsetshire dialect and reminds me that I had read Thomas Hardy's *Tess of the D'Urbervilles* that spring and been rapt away by it into another world. The cry against God's indifference with which his tragic story concludes echoed in my heart like a bugle call. I became an implacable infidel and never felt again the temptation to pray. I did not, however, become rabid or choked with a metallic negation, as so often happens when people renounce worship. On a still Sunday morning when I would hear the church bells ringing in the little hill town of Hector two miles away over the lake, my feelings would be mellow rather than rebellious. In the serenity of those June days of lonely resolve, I wrote the first poem I do not want to correct when I see it today.

> Borne on the low lake wind there floats to me
> Out of the distant hill a sigh of church bells,
> Mystic, worshipful, almost unheard,
> As though the past should answer me,
> And I in pagan solitude bow down my head.

My serenity was very real as long as it lasted, and my determination prodigious. I would not let my mother get off the train as she went by on the way to Geneva, though I consented to present myself at the car window. She was to hand me Stevenson's *Travels with a Donkey* and *The Black Arrow*.

"This doesn't mean that I am reading. I just want to have them here—I get awfully lonesome sometimes. . . . I don't want any pencil or paper. I'm not going to do anything. It comes to me more and more that this absolute cessation is what I need. . . . I am unspeakably happy, like a rising flood exulting at the dam."

My unspeakable happiness and my prodigious determination lasted less than two weeks. Autosuggestion ran a losing race with its cousin hypochondria, and my backache grew steadily worse. My mother wrote later in the Log: "M. E. proposed to try the benefits of solitude for a month—he got them all in ten days, and departed leaving a bachelor kitchen behind him. He gained a certain humility which only a good dose of solitude can give, and was grateful for the society of his parents."

I was indeed grateful, and to prove it I yielded to my mother's long-rejected pleadings to "try Dr. Grebus." Dr. Grebus was an expansive-hearted quack who lived in a little drizzly-white house out Water Street and came to town on the trolley. He was as big in the belly as two men and as dirty in the collar and coatfront as two hogs. He wheezed when he walked and kept trying to poke his stringy grey hair back under his sweat-stained felt hat, an enterprise for which he seemed to lack both force of character and clarity of conception. He had found out, in some anatomical preliminary to a course in medicine, exactly where the principal nerves in the body are exposed to a probing finger, and his racket was to stick a finger into these loopholes, or if possible two fingers, and cause the patient an astounding pain. It took an hour to distribute these pains and screw them in at every undefended corner, and by the end of the hour the patient was convinced that he was either killed or cured. A surviving ability to gasp a whispered farewell to the doctor was proof that he had not been killed, and there remained only the alternative that he had been cured. In this way Dr. Grebus made his living, relying on that organic puritanism, that instinct for doing or undergoing what you don't want to, which is woven into the tissues of man's life. He was a charlatan, and he used the crudest tricks of the trade. Did I have wet dreams and emissions? Did I see sharp colors when suddenly shutting my eyes in the sunlight? Did it hurt when he pressed this nerve? and that one? Yes? Then there was no question, I had locomotor ataxia. But it was in an early stage, and he could cure it by nerve massage if I could stand the treatments as often as once a day. Well, I stood them—for a few days. But that is not the point of this story. The point is that because of his belief in my mother and her religious teaching he brought this whole battery of unmitigated fraud, this cheap shameless ritual of predatory imposture, into play upon me for nothing! He announced in advance that, cure or no cure, he would not accept a penny, and when we sent him a small check, he returned it. From which I learned that a well-rounded scoundrel is as hard to come by as a perfectly honest man.

My mother soon gave up the raw food diet, pleading the fear that she might be too long dying: "If I should live two hundred years I'd have to make a new set of friends in each generation, and I'd get to be a joke." But I stuck to it for the whole three months, gained fifteen pounds, and acquired a contemptuous distaste for everything cooked, greased, buttered or remotely associated with the smell of a kitchen. It took me another three months to get back to the habits of the degenerate race to which I belong. But it did nothing for the ache in my back.

Having got no benefit from "absolute cessation," I went to the opposite extreme. I bought a riding horse—"a good hard nerveless beast-colored bronco named Besom"—and tried to cure my backache by what may best be described as a cavalry attack. I would race around Yates County for two or three hours every morning, defying the universe to hurt me, and then spend the rest of the day on the floor with a hot-water bag or my little red pillow, "the divine comforter," under my back. There was no sense in all this, but there was a lot of reliably violent determination, which only needed scientific guidance.

It was the good Dr. Denison in Williamstown who opened the path to such guidance. He wrote to say that he had told Dr. Gehring in Bethel, Maine, about my case, that the doctor had agreed to treat me gratis as an out-patient, and that he himself would like to pay my expenses in a Bethel boarding house until I got well. Thanks thus to a rare mixture of wealth with the religion of Jesus and the philosophy of Socrates, I arrived on October 1, 1906, in a cool, forest-hemmed village and in the hands of a great physician.

A large ward in the Neurological Institute of New York is dedicated to Dr. Gehring, and a shrine in many grateful hearts. He practiced the mind cure, or rather the mind-and-body cure, at its early best.

He began by making me write my life story and that of my parents and grandparents, and then conversing with me about the whole family. He would spend two weeks getting acquainted with a patient in this way before venturing a diagnosis. His diagnosis in my case was that I had imperfect nerve tissue, to begin with—"All the Brahmins have," he added—and that I would probably never get well. Nevertheless, if I would co-operate with him, he thought he could teach me how to live a useful life. Having let me down deep in that way, he let me deeper with doses of strontium bromide three times a day for ten days. During those days he would come to my drowsy bedside once in a while and in a gruff, gentle voice "suggest" tranquillity and fortitude rather than health.

I have wondered since whether he really thought I would never get well, or deemed it a useful sedative to say so. It did key me down remarkably and almost reconcile me to the idea of a literary life. "I guess I shall have to give up being an adventurer," I wrote to my mother. "The amount of musing I can do is beyond belief. One day I spent six or eight hours lying on my bed, unable to see outdoors, not reading or writing, and quite happy the whole time . . . I am an impregnable calm."

When he had got me into this earthlike state, Dr. Gehring told me one morning that he was going to put me on a schedule that I would find very difficult, especially the easy part of it. I was to get up and go outdoors and be active, whether with rake, axe, saw, sled, skis, snowshoes, or my own legs, for the first five minutes out of each daylight hour, *no matter how I felt.* For the rest of each hour, *no matter how I felt,* I was to go indoors and lie down. Approximately every week thereafter for eleven weeks he added five minutes to my active period and subtracted five from my repose. It left me with no responsibility, no worry, no ever-recurring question: "Does my back ache?" "Is it going to ache today?" "When is it going to begin?" I was on a timetable, and he put it up to me to adhere to it, no matter what I thought or felt.

I adhered to it with the exactitude of a fanatic and throve so well that by the end of November the doctor was convinced that my trouble was "an idea stuck in the subliminal, an obsession, and nothing else." What the idea was, having probably never heard of Freud, it did not occur to him to ask. He merely told me: "You can be well if you have the force of character to act on the assumption that this is nothing but an idea."

I suppose that my mother's formula: "I wish you would think it out and dare it to hurt you!" was closer to the modern therapy than Dr. Gehring's. He treated the symptom only, and I sometimes think that if he had been a psychoanalyst I might have been more completely cured than I am. Other times I think that if he had been a psychoanalyst I might not have been cured at all. I was caught fast in a habit of pain, and he liberated me by a simple and sound device. His taking upon himself the mental problem "what to do?" with which my untethered mind was running wild, and putting up a naked moral problem to my will, was subtly adapted to my character and condition.

He always used to compliment me on my morale, and it is visible in my letters. I spent three amazingly happy months in Bethel in a square little room with a wood stove to heat it and no bathroom and no view from the window. But I must confess that the principal reasons for this were neither the doctor's therapy nor my response. The reasons were Anna Carlson and the Swedish language. (Several times I have retired into some bay or bypath where fate has combined for me a romance with an orgy of learning, and those have always been the happiest times of my life.) Anna was tall, strong, lithe, straight-limbed, gay, honest, rosy-blonde, full of ideals and enthusiasms—"a peach of a girl," as I wrote to Crystal. And I added:

"Great Heaven, how I do *love* a girl that I admire! There's no denying the delicious fact that I don't live long happily without getting the other things *focused* around my enjoyment of that."

Fourteen years earlier Mrs. Gehring had hired a Swedish cook, newly arrived with a little daughter from the old country. The daughter had been so bewitching that Mrs. Gehring fell in love with her, and with admirable freedom from class prejudice, brought her up almost as her own child. Now that she was grown, however, and was not only bewitching but in a hundred ways useful, Mrs. Gehring's love proved something less than maternal, and her freedom from class prejudice not quite complete. Anna worked all day in a very dubious position—nurse, house matron, servant, stepchild, adored daughter, she never knew quite which—and was taught to regard her wish to get away and live her own life as treachery to a benefactor. She was baffled and bewildered, as many have been, to find herself clutched in iron shackles by a very tender love. She had need of a liberator. But she was such a good girl, so valiantly conscientious, that her liberator had to have high ideals—he had to present her escape as a moral duty.

Thus I came in the nick of time with my gospel of "living greatly." Anna was intensely magnetic to me physically, and as her goodness precluded so much as a kiss before marriage, all the thirsts raging in my body were sublimated into the task of her spiritual liberation. I preached freedom to Anna with a fervor that would have swept Gibraltar into the sea. I even preached it to her in her native language. Although I can not read a word of them now, I find letters exchanged between us in Swedish, and my poem, "Til Aftonschernan" expresses, as well as anything I had then written, the ideal by which I was living. I spare you the original, but in translation my poem says this:

To the Evening Star

Star out on the heaven blue,
Why do you go lonely,
    You are so great?

Call your wide gleaming host
To be comrades for you there,
    You who are great.

No—often shall you be alone,
And mournful be your beauteous light,
    Because you are great.

With these accessories, and the doctor's strict regime, I flourished in snowy Bethel like a bay tree in the tropics. My room was across the street from my boarding house, and up at the street-end three hundred yards away was the doctor's house—the house, I mean, which sheltered Anna. I used to test my strength of will by trying when I crossed the street not to turn my eyes as though they were attached by a taut string to the door of that house. In this I had less success than in carrying out the doctor's most exacting orders.

By November 23 he had me active forty minutes out of each hour in a six-hour day. By mid-December I was on my feet from nine to twelve, from two to five, and for an hour in the evening. I still suffered a good deal of pain, but was learning to disregard it. The doctor was sure now that I could ultimately get well, and I began to think of myself as leaving the sanitarium in the spring, and after a quiet summer at Glenora beginning my career in "activity and experience" the following autumn. With this leisurely program in view I suggested to my mother that she visit me at the sanitarium on a trip to Boston she was planning in February. This comfortable letter was dated December 14, and on December 15 Dr. Gehring called me to his office.

"I have been wondering," he said, "if it isn't about time for you to get out into the world and start your life work. What would you think of leaving here the first of the year? That would give you two weeks in which to decide what you want to do and where."

I learned afterward that the doctor expected a violent remonstrance from me, and banking on his usual experience, was allowing a month or two for persuading me to go. I did, as a matter of fact, turn pale at that sudden sentence of doom. I went back to my room frightened and bewildered. My backache returned full force, and I lay suffering two-thirds of the night. In the small hours it seemed not only cruel but mad and fantastic to throw me out just when I was *beginning* to get well.

In the morning, after I had washed my face, I realized that the violent recurrence of my pain as a result of the doctor's suggestion was a confirmation of his hypothesis: the pain was not physically caused, it was "an idea, an obsession, and nothing else." I could be well if I conquered that obsession.

I doubt if any saint wrestling with the devil ever had a livelier bout than I did that December day with my infantile emotions and my pain. I stood at a crossroads and I fully knew it. One way led to health and the bold enjoyment of living, the other to disease and weakness and a fussy, fugitive, bedridden, self-protective, wholly negative half-existence. And the choice rested with me. There was no help ultimately anywhere in the universe but in my will. Either I could act upon my mind's knowledge and be free, or I could succumb to my body's feeling and be chained.

I made two momentous decisions before the day was past. I decided that I would open my career, whatever it was to be, in New York City. That was the stiffest purgatory I could put myself through, for I hated all cities and mortally dreaded their noise, tensity, and cold commotion. At the same time it was a practical thing to do, for my sister was in New York, and her many friends would help me find a job. I decided, further, that from the date of my arrival in New York, I would never lie down after getting up in the morning until I went to bed at night—not if I cracked in the middle and dropped dead. Subsequently, at the doctor's suggestion, I modified that decision: I would lie down three times a day for a short rest, but always at the same hour and without regard to the feelings in my back.

In that state of mind, which only neurotic invalids will wholly comprehend, I lifted myself out of Bethel on December 31 and arrived in New York with the New Year of 1907.

PART V

PHILOSOPHY, FEMINISM,
AND POETRY

Chapter 36

Conquering New York

I HAD no idea what I was going to do in New York. Although entering my twenty-fourth year, I had no more definite ambition than not to be a professional writer. In asking Crystal to be on the lookout for a job, I cautioned: "I don't want the work to be *writing* at all. I don't care what it is otherwise. In order to enjoy either making my living or writing, I've got to keep them separate."

A purpose was, of course, implied in that remark. I was going to write, and my writing, however little there might be of it, was going to be performed to my own sovereign taste. There was to be no influence of the market, no editorial blue pencil, no pressure of necessity on science or mixing of business with art. No compromise with commercialism! This became a fixed law to me and one of the few clear contributions of my will to my destiny.

In my wrestling match with New York City it was a considerable handicap. New York was not quite the quintessence of cityhood that it is now. Indeed Greenwich Village, where my sister lived, was still almost rural, for Seventh Avenue had not yet crashed down through it, biting the very houses in two. That roaring north-and-southbound monster was still confined above Eleventh Street, and below there was quietness and quaintness, there were neighbors who knew each other, there was sauntering in the streets. The saunterers were not artists as yet, but reformers and social workers rather, people engaged in various schemes for doing good. As Arthur Bullard used to say, New York had an ethical, where Paris had an aesthetic, Bohemia. Crystal, during her year in sociology at Columbia had come in touch with this Bohemia. And now, while studying law at New York University, earning her living running a recreation center five nights a week, and frequently dining at Greenwich House Settlement, she was in the very middle of it.

She had tried before I came to instill in my rustic bosom a sense of the glamor of life in the metropolis.

"I am sorry you don't like New York at all," she wrote. "I love it for the people there and the thousands of things they think and do . . . especially the radicals, the reformers, the students—who really live to help, and yet get so much fun out of it."

My answer was: "I have appreciated that feeling about living in the city and meeting humanity. It is just the same as my desire to live in the country and meet the universe. I think it's the same poetic life-zeal with us both."

For a year she had been sapping in this way my stubborn ruralism, and I now deliberately undertook to feel the romance of life among the Bohemian reformers. She lived at 12 Charles Street with a social worker named Madeleine Doty, and I hired a near-by bedroom at twelve dollars a month and took my meals with them. One of Madeleine's good friends was David Graham Phillips, the muck-raking novelist. He was the first celebrity I met in New York, but I did not read any of his writings either then or afterward—so strong was my distaste for the cheap sensational magazines in which they were published. He stepped out of the Gramercy Square Hotel one day and was shot dead in the street, nobody ever knew why. It shocked our little household and put a gruesome pause in my developing romance with the metropolis.

Another of Madeleine's friends was Ida Rauh, a sadly beautiful and mysterious young woman who would move in for weeks at a time and share her room. Ida was a truant from a family of rich Jews who lived uptown behind a brownstone front, and she had renounced so hotly all the frills and luxuries of bourgeois life that she lived almost like a pauper. She would bring one informal garment, a simple, self-made, unobtrusively becoming garment, and lie in

Madeleine's room reading or sleeping all day long. She had the voice of a great actress and would come to life sometimes at table and converse with brilliant intelligence and rebel emotion about everything under the sun. For the rest she seemed remote, indolent, impersonal, and wilfully unalive—as alien to me as a beautiful ground hog, if there could be one. I was told afterward that she was in love, or hate, with a famous personage, and that a private grief, or grievance, combined with her revolt against bourgeois society to make her into such a decorative negation. At the time I merely felt that she was too adult, that she was hostile to my childish love of life.

Crystal was exceedingly beautiful, dark yet richly colored—more of an Eastman than I, with browner eyes and brighter highlights in them. Claude McKay, the Negro poet, describes her in his autobiography as "the most beautiful white woman I ever knew." "She was of the heavy and solid type," he adds, "and her beauty was not so much of her features, fine as they were, but in her magnificent presence. Her form was something after the pattern of a splendid draft horse, and she had a way of holding her head like a large bird poised in a listening attitude." I quote this because I find it as hard to describe my sister's looks as though they were my own. She was not the kind of girl around whom men gather like flies around a honey pot, but she had a joy in life and a genius for friendship that equaled her beauty, and there was always a devoted male or two within call.

The news that her younger brother was coming to New York and needed a job produced action on several fronts. The day after my arrival I declined—disdainfully, for I was still out for "activity and experience"—an offer of a fellowship at Columbia for the following year. And within a week I received, through her good friend Paul Kellogg, editor of *Charities and the Commons*, an appointment as tuberculosis impresario for the Charity Organization Society. My task was to arrange illustrated lectures on the prevention of tuberculosis in union halls and chapels throughout the East Side. I was provided with a rolled-up white curtain and a stereopticon machine, and had to go and hang the curtain and set up the machine in advance, then come back and operate it while the doctor talked. As I had no taxi fare and did not know my way around New York on streetcars, and that curtain and magic lantern were a stevedore's load, my thirst for activity and experience was soon satisfied. I suffered terribly with my back and had a desperate fight to keep from lying down out of hours. Many a night I would decide to go back to

Bethel, but in the morning pick my purpose up again. Of course I was a complete flop as an impresario—it takes iron nerves. I was saved from the disgrace of losing my job before receiving a pay check by the timely death of an instructor at Columbia University who was teaching "The Principles of Science."

Another good friend of Crystal's, Vladimir Simkhovitch, then bibliographer at the university, had the audacity to propose to John Dewey that I be appointed in the dead instructor's place. I am sure no other philosophy professor in the world would have entertained the proposal, especially as a Ph.D. who had studied in Oxford and Heidelberg was angling for the job. I knew little of philosophy and had only a three-months' acquaintance with logic, but good old Pop Russell came through with a statement that I had a "distinctly philosophical mind, keenly, clearly analytical, etc." Dewey was aware that I knew nothing about the principles of science; he satisfied himself that I would like to know something about them, and as he has said, "There is one kind of coeducation everybody believes in, and that is the coeducation of teachers and pupils."

On that theory he lifted me out of my hall bedroom in Greenwich Village and set me down in an office next door to his in the Department of Philosophy and Psychology at Columbia University. The news reached me on a Friday afternoon that a week from next Wednesday at ten I would meet a class of thirty sophomores—who had presumably just killed my predecessor—that the textbook was Jevons' larger volume of 769 pages, and that the class were now on page 374! It was a stiff test for my bluffing capacity, and I entered it rather in that spirit. I soon moved up, however, to a tiny room in Hartley Hall and through mere drift of circumstance became a student again.

I must have taught some highly original logic, for I wrote my mother that Jevons was "useless for such a class, erudite and full of hot air"—a crude slander against an admirable book. And I bragged of "lecturing for one hour last Monday, with only a note or two on my desk, on the History of the Observation of Nature," and "reading Walt Whitman to them as the culmination and ideal attitude to nature and natural science." I justified Dewey's recklessness, however, by turning in once more and working like a scholar, "going over to the library and really studying—forgetting things—just enjoying the *power*." I did not take any formal courses, but I delved seriously in logic and scientific method during that year and with Dewey's private assistance learned a mindful. Somewhat to my alarm, for I still had more adventurous ambitions, I found out that I have a natural gift for teaching. I established myself in the hearts of my students one morning when Joseph O'Mahoney, the bright boy of my class, and now senator from Wyoming, stuck up his hand while I was expounding the mysteries of the syllogism, and said:

"Teacher, what's the use of all this?"

I answered: "I'm ashamed to say it nets me only five hundred a year!"

Subsequently Joe and I used to tour the East Side attending meetings of socialists, trade unionists, single taxers, anybody who aspired to make the social system better. Notwithstanding the syllogism, we managed to contribute to each other's education.

Another of my bright boys was Bill Langer, a vast good-natured square hulk of a lad, who, after a stormy career in and out of the governorship of North Dakota, has also found refuge in the United States Senate.

That five hundred a year was pieced out by another of those bonanza jobs that so frequently fell my way. Dickenson S. Miller was in the Philosophy Department then, a brilliantly erudite young friend of William James, who had passed through Spencerian agnosticism on his way to the Anglican Church. He was an odd-looking philosopher, with rather babylike features, a fine forehead, and the manners, diction, habits, and haircut of an Episcopal prelate. He vastly admired Cardinal Newman and had the elegantly discriminating taste in style and ideas that such an admiration implies. His health was poor, and the doctor had prescribed fresh air and mild exercise. He had decided to take these strange medicines in a canoe on the Hudson River, and to make them palatable, he conceived the idea of having me in the business end of the canoe and mixing them with intellectual conversation. As nothing could have better fitted my own hygienic requirements, and as those conversations amounted to a complete course in the history of human thought, he might well have charged me a good round fee as my tutor. Instead he paid me thirty dollars a month as his gondolier.

We would meet at a precise hour and walk briskly down to the foot of 110th Street, where the canoe lived in an old wave-slapped, slubbered wooden boathouse, impossible to conceive there now. Miller, impeccably clad for the sport, would climb into the boat with exquisite care and sit down facing me, bolt upright, balancing himself dexterously, yet as out of his element as a pope on a roller coaster. Miller could not loll; he could not loaf; he could not drift with his instincts. He lived by volition. His well-thought-out decision to take canoe rides on the Hudson seemed never to be absent from the boat. I used to wonder what would happen if it went overboard and left him there. But all these irreverences would vanish when he started talking about ideas: about the idea of romantic-versus-classic, for instance. Thanks to my scorn of English courses and my fitful reading, I had never happened to hear of it.

"These two concepts," he would say, "have no exact differentium, and nature does not adhere, in distributing the attributes either of men or of art works, to the groupings implied by them. We can only say that the temper we call classic tends to place a high value on the friendly and familiar, whereas the romantic seeks the strange and unexpected. The classic enjoys clarity, the romantic yearns over mystery. The classic loves order, the romantic freedom. The classic mind is objective, the romantic subjective. The classic temperament finds rest in the lovely, the romantic finds glory in the sublime. Perhaps it might all be summed up by saying that the romantic loves excitement and the classic seeks refuge from too much excitement in a regulated experience. . . . Wouldn't you consider that a fair outline of the connotation of these terms?"

"I think that's acceptable, at least as an approach to the subject," I would say, making a mental note: Don't forget, you ignoramus, to fill up this hole in your cerebrum before we come out again!

In such ways, without costing so much as an intention, education continued to descend upon me. Dewey hired me to study the principles of science, and Miller gave me a canoe ride through the history of ideas and paid me to paddle the canoe. For me the big and important thing in those days was freedom from pain. I did not want the responsibility of an ambition. I wanted to revel awhile in the flux of experience.

"I am gloriously healthy," I wrote home, "and, but for my very scattered character, might be well content. I even have gleams of interest in the old city. They had a brace of monomaniacs at Greenwich House the other night—Socialists, Russian revolutionaries, one-eyed folk, harmless as a Cyclop if you can put out their eye. . . . I went to dinner with the Adlers this noon, had a good simple jolly time, liked them all, felt mellow and unaffected. Felix (founder of the Ethical Culture Society) is a funny-looking cuss—couldn't be my spiritual guide, I'm afraid. . . . I went all day without lying down yesterday for the first time in four years, and feel like a king today . . . I had a chance to teach philosophy at Ann Arbor—

$900! . . . Saw Sid Wood today. We are going to investigate spiritism. . . . I have a chance to be headmaster of a prep school at Grand Rapids—whoop-la! . . . Rosanna sent me a box of beautiful arbutus. I have been to Princeton two days to see Marjorie. Tomorrow Crystal and I are going to some socialist speeches at the Rand School. Tuesday I am going up the Hudson to Croton with a nice girl named Nancy. And so it goes. Events, events, 'charging like ceaseless clouds across the sky!' I am thirsty for them these days as of old, and I am letting it go. But I shall do work when I come home for the summer."

"Rosanna," "Marjorie," "Nancy": these were the tunes in my heart strings—and I must not forget that Anna was still echoing there too. As Crystal wrote to mother: "Max has so many girls on his hands in some way or other—it's hard to keep track of them." Anna sent me, in both anxiety and affection, a stream of buoyant, warm, faith-giving, and extravagantly admiring letters that make me sick at heart now to read and remember, for I pushed her friendship deliberately away. She did make the break from her love prison four months after I left Bethel, spurning a suitor Mrs. Gehring had picked for her and moving to Boston with her mother. She was exuberantly happy, and moreover gave me the credit for her liberation. "Oh, Max, my friend, how grateful I am to you for your dear help you'll never know. You are in reality my prophet . . . I couldn't do it without you." But I, by that time, was appalled at the small trace left in my daily thoughts of those two months' total immersion in Anna. Lovely as her letters were, and platonic too, they pained me because I could not keep up with the emotion in them. In one of my fits of sanctimonious virtue, or dread of responsibility parading as such, I told her piously that I had "finished my task" and must "slip away out of her world." She took it like a princess: "I hope we will meet sometime, and if we should not, you will remember that I am always deeply grateful, and my faith in my best and greatest friends is *great*." But what she thought of me in her deep heart— whether she thought as poorly as I do now—I shall never know.

Nancy was a nurse, a slim, strong-bodied, brown-skinned, southern girl, free as the wind in all ways but the biological—I only mean she would not let me kiss her!—and we romped the meadowy hills around Croton like a boy and girl just out of school. Her patient was a mildly afflicted woman who lived on the dark north slope of Mount Airy which looks away to the Catskills, and I slept the night there in an upper room opening on a roof. I dragged my mattress out on the roof and watched the dawn creep down into lush, wild-wooded Oscawanna Valley—wilder-wooded than you would expect within forty miles of the metropolis. It occurred to me as I lay there under the fading stars that if I had a little house among those hills, I could combine living with humanity in the city and living with the universe in the country, and make my sojourn in existence richer and more varicolored than if I perfectly settled one way or the other.

Of all the events that charged that spring across my sky, the two days' visit to Marjorie Nott in Princeton was the most momentous. Marjorie, with her characteristic subtlety, sent me for a long lonely walk in the country the morning after I came. "You must want solitude more than anything else after all those months in the city." So I wandered along the banks of Stony Brook, happy in health and freedom, and fell into what I call the trance of realization. I was filled and brimming, not with any truth or godhead, not with any mystic principle inside of or behind the life I was living, but with a joyous consciousness of life itself. It is a state more clearly defined in me, I imagine, than in most poetic people, for I am impatiently onward-going in my everyday nature. Starting with my infant thought about castile soap, I have been haunted throughout life by the feeling that I can't quite get hold of any experience.

> Life fled before me. Every spear of grain
> Would beckon and I run, but it was gone,
> To the next pasture placidly withdrawn.
> I could not drink the wet and pelting rain
> That I would run in dancing down the lane.
> Though I have slept all night upon the lawn,
> I never rose in time to clasp the dawn. . . .

Thus I complained in an unfinished sonnet, and on this day in Princeton, sitting against a corn shock in a meadow within sound of the brook, I escaped from this prison of practicality. I escaped into pure poetry—for whatever the logical objections might be, I knew that this trance of realization is what the technique of metaphor and versification is fashioned to achieve. This is the defining element of poetry. If it would take a book to prove it, why not write a book? And why not anyway? Marjorie had put some slips of paper in my pocket. Sitting there in the May sunshine, I wrote the outline of my first book, which I thought perhaps I would call "The Realization of Being."

Chapter 37

A Lakeside Utopia

I FULFILLED my promise to do work when I came home that summer. Indeed I imposed on Mother and Crystal and several of the neighbors a "system" of hard study from 9 to 12 A.M., punctuated with ship's bells which I sounded on a triangle fashioned by a near-by blacksmith. I never could endure to be alone with virtue.

My work was not on the proposed book—that could wait—but mainly on gathering into an essay the harvest of my experience of "mental healing." This was a new and much agitated subject then, and I wanted to explain that the philosophic problem of mind-over-matter is not involved; the question is to what degree brain states attending an idea can influence other parts of the body. I also wanted to break down the dogma that these states can not influence "organic" disorders, for the distinction between organic and functional is not basic: all disorders, I surmised, involve organic changes, if our instruments were fine enough to detect them.

My essay prophesied that the whole movement exemplified in Christian Science and the mystic cults of the New Thought would "resolve itself into a momentous reform in the practice of medicine." I called it "The New Art of Healing," and actually sold it—at last —to the *Atlantic Monthly*. Their check for seventy-five dollars I sent to Dr. Gehring, who sent it back with a gracious and warm letter. The essay was published in May 1908 and traveled far enough to be quoted by the famous French psychologist, Pierre Janet, in his *Medications Psychologiques*. It brought me many letters from invalids, too, and I conducted quite a correspondence course in what is now called "psychosomatic medicine." But that was a year later; this summer I was still only trying in the mood of a novice to get the essay written. Moreover, on the stroke of twelve, I was ready to drop all essays and race downhill through the woods to the "swimming party."

Glenora hillside had by then become a millennial little community of outdoor idealists with our cottage as its temple: I must go back a few years and tell you how this happened. After graduating from Princeton in 1901, my brother went off to the Philippine Islands as one of three hundred teachers sent by the government. My father, with only a daughter and a thought-happy son to help him, found thirty acres of land a burden. On the northern ten acres he built a Cherith Cottage for us to live in. The remaining twenty he sold to a "club" consisting of our own and three other Park Church families—the Beardsleys, MacDowells, and Pickerings. The MacDowells took the original farmhouse; the Beardsleys and Pickerings built cottages of their own; and the club erected a common dining hall and hired a cook and a serving girl. Sixteen people ate in that dining hall; each paid five cents a meal; and each adult took his or her weekly turn at housekeeping. Housekeeping meant collecting the dues, planning the meals, buying provisions in near-by Dundee, gathering fruit and vegetables from the farm, and toting ice from the ice house. My father, just for love of it, took care of the garden and orchard, but otherwise it was a strictly business scheme —invented of course by my mother—and was a notable success. At least I recall but one insurmountable objection in my breast: namely, that I was not in a position to compel all the children of those three families to chew with their mouths shut.

The club sold off other pieces of the farm to friendly Elmira people. Still other friends built cottages beyond the farm on the road that slants down to the lake. One or two, indeed, had been summering there before we came. But they all blended, by some magic of open-minded aspiration and good will, to form something definite enough to be known in that region as the "Glenora community."

In the economic aspect it was an ordinary bourgeois community. Mr. Pickering was unusual because he was so poor, having inherited a one-horse dye works with a debt of $250,000, which, being a Quaker, he felt obliged to pay. He brought up his three supple daughters and sent them through college on pure will power, so far as an interested observer—and I was more than interested—could see. Mr. MacDowell was a lawyer, and Mr. Beardsley secretary of the Elmira Water Light and Power Company. Florence Wyckoff, who bought a little piece of the farm, was the daughter of a lumber merchant; Kate Dean Andrew, who bought another piece, was

Elmira's public librarian. Dr. Jennings, a physician who spent his declining years painting landscapes, and Seymour Lowman, a Republican state politician of some prominence, took the rest.

Farther down the road was Mr. Bowles, a traveling salesman, and his son Claude, a dentist.[1] They had been there before us, and so had Miss Anna Fraser of Brooklyn and her aged but militant feminist mother (she died in 1940 at 103). On a point a half mile down the lake lived old white-whiskered Dr. Willis, a retired Rochester physician, who had known Emerson, and who cherished a pale halo of fame as the original of Laurie in *Little Women*. His wife, an admired friend of my mother, was an artist, and his daughter, Edith Willis Lynn, wrote poems. But they were all three lifted higher into glory by a noble and solemn cathedral that a great stream falling from the cliffs through the ages had built in the forest behind their house. It is one of those spots where nature sings a hymn to infinity.

Besides these, to whom Glenora was a summer home, there were native citizens who enriched the life of our hillside utopia. Wise old Charlie Gay, who ran the village store, was loved and laughed with by every customer. Will Gardner mixed poetry with plumbing. Gene Henderson, who supplied us with milk, provided I came up before breakfast to get it, also supplied fiddle music for the dances in the Town Hall on Glenora Point. Those dances belonged to the farmers, and we had to sandwich in our ultramodern two-steps, barn dances, and cakewalks between the lancers, the quadrille, and the immemorial Virginia reel. The Old Dan Tucker, in which your partner falls to you by chance, would give the countryside a thorough social mixing. To an unusual extent the Negro servants in our dining hall, Annie of blessed memory, and Mercy Virginia and "Eleanor Elnora," shared in the pleasures of our social life.

John Roosa, my old violin teacher, and his young wife Herberta, who had three jolly sisters, bought a bit of shoreland and put up a tent north of where Cherith brook came down. Just south of it my father, felling the trees above the wet cliff, built a dock and tiny harbor for the whole neighborhood to use. Jack Roosa and I adorned this dock with a diving tower and a technically perfect springboard. In a moment of pure heroism I decided (at the age of twenty-five) that it was all nonsense about having to hold my nose when I went under water. I took a clean dive from Dad's new dock, and thereafter, with Jack providing agile competition, went in for learning "diving stunts" in the same crazy-zealous way I had once

---

[1] Claude's son is the well-known composer Paul Frederic Bowles.

gone in for piano playing, once for poetry, once for adventure— once indeed for scholarship.

As the years passed, a small army of children sprang up miraculously along the hillside, and Jack and I became the leaders of a veritable diving academy. We taught everything up to and including the One-and-a-Half-Dive and the Flying Dutchman, which Jack "invented" and named the Dream Dive, the idea of jumping off forward and turning a back somersault having come to him, he firmly insisted, in a dream. Our dives were amateurish, but that may have been in some of them a merit. For the "proper form" in natatory matters is at times established rather from the standpoint of gymnastic prowess than artistic grace. At any rate, we became thoroughly amphibian. Our springboard stood three feet above water, our tower fourteen, and we spanked and hammered ourselves to a degree unimaginable by a land animal. For water, when you arrive upon it *in extenso* from a height, is practically indistinguishable from a cement walk.

I have never been anywhere in summer where "kids" have more fun than they had in the "Glenora Diving Academy," or the swimming parties up in the glen when the lake was cold, or on the canoe and sailing picnics, the boy-and-girl baseball games, the banquets in the orchard or the berry patch, the riotous dances in the Town Hall. I have never myself enjoyed life quite so constantly since. I am sure there are many grown-up boys and girls who would say the same thing. And a principal reason is that our sensuous pleasures were suspended in a stream of thoughtful and idealistic emotion.

The downstairs part of our cottage consisted mainly of one big room with a fireplace and an antique square piano. There on Sunday mornings the whole hillside would gather for an informal service—a hymn, a violin solo by Jack Roosa, a reading of poetic literature and a word of prayer by my mother. They would gather again on Sunday evenings just to play and sing. On Mondays and Thursdays the adult members of the community would come together at four in the afternoon for a "Supposium." Somebody who knew something, and no matter what, would explain it, and the others question him. My mother had a gift for overcoming the skittishness Americans feel about being intellectual. It was natural to her to care about ideas in the same humble and humorous way she cared about things, and she made it natural to others. There is no real lack of brains in America, nor any real contempt for them— merely an inferiority complex dressing up now one way and now the other. In either phase this malady would clear up in my mother's maturely childlike presence, and an afternoon of Platonic conversation would become as offhand as a swim in the lake.

I call the community millennial because of this complete absence of pose in its interest in ideas, and because a more than normal good fellowship, emanating largely from those services in our cottage, pervaded the hillside. To me it seemed pagan as well as millennial, and increasingly so as the years passed. By this summer of 1907 there was indeed little of the churchly part of Christianity left in my mother's ever-evolving aspiration. She had, during the preceding winter, changed the Park Church—to put it very succinctly—from Congregational to Unitarian. Acting through my father, "because they would never take it from a woman," she had persuaded her congregation to abandon the old creed of Trinity and Virgin Mary, and say only that they believed in God and the life-example of Jesus. God meant a great deal at certain times to my mother, more, I think, in spite of her doubts, than to my father. But her doubts increased as she grew older—or grew young again with her children. She came into my bedroom early one morning, her face flushed and her eyes sparkling as they would when she had got hold of a brand new, and at last a *right* way of living life.

"Max, I'm going to make a new resolution today, and I want you to make one too. I'm going to resolve that I will never again doubt the existence of God, and I want you to make up your mind from this day forth"—speaking now much more emphatically—"to *chew your food!*"

She never put up any such resistance to her doubt about churches, or whether "preaching is not the most useless of human labors." Indeed, privately during the last year of her life she was seeking a place outside the church, and was delighted when a movement was set on foot to make her dean of Barnard College. All this restiveness expressed itself with complete freedom in those Sunday services in our cottage. They were "sacred" only as life itself is sacred to those whose religion is to live it. She would read secular literature for the most part, and Jack would play whatever struck his fancy. The children, sitting on the floor, would make a noisy scramble when they got up to sing. We sang songs as well as hymns, and never any of the "bloody" hymns. Nobody in our house was ever, except with loud laughter, "washed in the blood of the lamb."

One Sunday when my mother was to be away, she persuaded me to conduct the service in her place. My scripture reading was from

Emerson's "Essay on Heroism," and when I had finished, I bowed my head and spoke a prayer like this:

"We receive out of the dark hands of mystery the gift of sunny days. We pledge ourselves to take them with a hearty will, and live them out to the full measure and expanse of joy—yet never with a loose or temporary mind. In the moments we will not forget the hours, nor in the hours the years, nor in the years the complete stature of our lives, framed in eternal silence."

Several times each summer after that I would conduct the service, reading and commenting on some poem or prose meditation, and making what I called a Pagan Prayer. Here is another example:

"We pause upon the swift moment to remember our ideals. In autumn we remember liberty. It is the season of the running winds and the leaves that die gaily. It is the time for change and ungovernable motion—time for us to make sure that we are free—we are whimsical, and ruled by no passion and no habit but by our own wild wills. To which end we joyfully lay aside the bonds of customary opinion, and our timidity and baby thoughts, and undertake with all our hearts the adventure of being."

I am not sure anyone ever noticed the absence of God from these prayers; I did not advertise it. But in my own mind I was demonstrating that a sceptical philosophy, which affirms only the values of temporal life, can retain what is beautiful and essential in a system of mystical belief. I was asserting that it is possible to combine mental courage with moral aspiration. A Stevensonian literariness still mars my style in these prayers. I had not yet learned to subdue the garment of words, no matter how many colored, to the lines of the meaning. But they do, I think, reveal how unessential a creed is to the reverent pursuit of life's values.

Underneath these moral and social exaltations, and to an extent which troubled me sustaining them, lay always a romantic excitement about some girl in the community. In this summer of 1907 I was still riding my "beast-colored bronco," Besom, and Florence Wyckoff had a riding mare named Merrilegs. I fenced off a pasture for them both to live in, and Florence and I rode them up together from Elmira. On our way a small black dog followed us with mysterious persistence. When I leaned down from the saddle and said, "Go home, little dog," he put back his curly ears and opened his red mouth and laughed at me. I could find no answer but to laugh back.

"All right, come along then!" I said. He came all the way, and stuck by me as though he had never known another master. I named him from a line of Whitman, "The Black with his Woolly head," and wrote about him in the Log:

"Woolly is of the Comraderie of the Open Road. He fell in with us along Pine Valley way, liked us, and voted to stick by us. We left him at the station at Montour Falls yesterday, and found him waiting for us today at the hotel where we left our horses. We lost him again in Watkins when we went sailing, and found him waiting as we rode out of town. He is ours—he can spatter up the porches—he can come or go—or stick by us as long as he lives. 'Here the profound lesson of reception!' "

Woolly stuck by us for two months, and then trotted away as casually as he came.

"Tears are in my heart for him; I dream of him vividly. I think he was an earth-demon or wandering sprite—the genius of real freedom, perhaps, who was here because for a short season we had truly caught his spirit."

Florence and I had caught a goodly measure of his spirit. Florence was an apostate from elegance—a handsome blonde daughter of the "big bourgeoisie," bold and square in character, a little square in build, but with a celestial rebel's eyes and a skin of satin. She subsequently stepped down far enough from her leisured origins to study agriculture at Cornell, buy fifty acres up the lake a way, and become a farmer. We were in love together with Walt Whitman and with his English disciple, Edward Carpenter, whose "Love's Coming of Age" taught us a good many things. It was a vagabondish summer. I wore nothing but a shirt and pants and, if the wind blew cold, a ragged orange sweater. Florence dressed as simply, and her Veery cabin was little more than a roof and a room to sleep in. We would read in the evening "The Song of the Open Road," and the next day explore on horseback the ravishing homeland of the Iroquois with its long slim fingers of lakes. We never actually rode as far as an Iroquois would run—for that I am sorry—and our shy love never quite came of age either, but we were full of the spirit of far riding and free love. . . .

That summer ended with a moonlight steamboat ride for all the children of the Glenora hillside, and some who were not quite children went along. May Elmore was not a child—at least she ought not to have been, for she was a graduate of Bryn Mawr and a teacher of English in one of our best-behaved girls' boarding schools. In the very middle of the lake four miles from home she suddenly screamed: "Man overboard! Stop the boat! Stop the boat!" The panic this caused among the children was indescribable and in a strictly ethical view, I am afraid, inexcusable. For while emitting these sincerely hysterical cries, she was concealing my sneakers under her coat, and I was drifting serenely down the moonlit wake of the little steamer waiting to be picked up. I waited long, for the captain had heard something of our diving exploits at Glenora. When he did reach a grudging arm down over the railing and grasp my hand, he came near to pitching in himself, for it was my role to arrive in a sinking condition. My gasps and shudders were so realistic that he took me to the engine room and placed a blanket round me with his own hand. The Elmira *Gazette* explained next day that the Park Church pastors' son was affected with a nervous malady which impelled him irresistibly to fling himself from high places. The day after, George B. Carter, insuppressible organist of the Park Church, explained in the same paper that "All our pastors' son needs is a broad shingle well laid on."

Chapter 38

Philosophy in Passing

CRYSTAL, having graduated from law school and been admitted to the bar, went to Pittsburgh in the fall of 1907 to investigate work accidents for the Russell Sage Foundation—a part of the famous Pittsburgh Survey. I drifted back to my five hundred dollar job at Columbia and my little room in Hartley Hall, still with no more concrete purpose than non-commercial writing and "growing." "I am afraid if I don't form the habit of writing now, it will be all over with, for I am not ambitious," I wrote to my mother. And in a little notebook that now rode in my pocket:

"The greatest thing in this world is an honest, avowed effort to grow."

My growing was given some direction by the sense of a problem to be solved. "The Poet's Mind" was still unpublished, and Miller, my canoe-sitting friend, took the proofs up in the Adirondacks with him and wrote me a painstaking twelve-page criticism of it—the act of a most generous teacher. His objections made me realize that I had got hold of an idea about conscious life, and not just literature, and that I had work to do in philosophy and psychology, and even biology, before I could write my book.

So here was an added reason for staying on at Columbia. While lecturing on the principles of science, I could ponder with some real cogency their application to the definition of poetry. It wouldn't hurt my writing either, or stop my growth, if I attended John Dewey's advanced course in Logical Theory. As an assistant teaching logic I could hardly do less.

Dewey looked like a young man then, a man just starting his career. He reminded me of the portraits of Robert Louis Stevenson —a Stevenson without vivacity but with the same luminous eyes.

281

Dewey's eyes are wells of dark, almost black, tenderly intelligent light, such as would shine more appropriately out of a St. Francis than a professor of logic. The rest of him is pleasant but not quite so impressive.

He used quite often to come into class with his necktie out of contact with his collar, a sock down around his ankle, or a pants' leg caught up into his garter. He came once for two weeks with a large rent in his coat sleeve which caused a flap of cloth to stick out near the shoulder like a cherub's wing. His hair always looked as though he had combed it with a towel, and being parted if at all in the middle, gave his face a rather ewelike contour which emphasized the gentleness more than the penetration in those wondrous eyes. He would come in through a side door—very promptly and with a brisk step. The briskness would last until he reached his chair, and then he would sag. With an elbow on the desk, he would rub his hand over his face, push back some parts of his hair, and begin to purse his mouth and look vaguely off above the windows, as though he thought he might find an idea up there along the crack between the wall and the ceiling. He always would find one, and then he would begin to talk—very slowly and with little emphasis and long pauses, and frequent glances up there to see if he was gettting it right.

He was thinking rather than lecturing, evolving a system of philosophy before our eyes, and taking his time about it. The process was impersonal and unrelated to his students—until one of them asked a question. Then those glowing eyes would come down and shine into that student, and draw out of him and his innocent question intellectual wonders such as he never imagined had their seeds in his brain or bosom.

Education does not, according to the Dewey System, mean "drawing out." But drawing out was never better done than it was in his classrooms. John Dewey's instinctive and active deference and unqualified giving-of-attention to whatever anybody, no matter how dumb and humble, may have to say, is one of the rarest gifts or accomplishments of genius. He seemed to me to embody in his social attitude, as Walt Whitman did in his poetry, the very essence of democracy.

Another trait of John Dewey's, very impressive in the classroom—and very little conveyed, I am afraid, in the above paragraph—is his personal dignity. Careless as his dress used to be, he never seemed, as so many eccentric professors do, inwardly sloppy. You felt his moral force. You felt the rigorous self-discipline beneath his sagging manner.

To find such a man in high place, and have him for a friend and boss, was a rich experience. There was, in reality, nothing of the boss about it. Neither Dewey, nor my other superior, F. J. E. Woodbridge, nor anyone at Columbia ever made a suggestion to me as to how or what I should teach. I poured into the moulds of logic all the ideas I believed in or found interesting, from anti-patriotism to the poetic values of obscenity. You have to think about something when you are learning to think, and it might as well be something exciting. Not only was I permitted to be as cocky as I wanted to in the classroom, but in the office I was lifted above my position by having Dewey consult me as an English teacher!

"You know how to write," he said one day with his calm smile. "I wish you'd show me how it's done."

Thereafter he would come into my office and sit beside me in a straight chair while I leaned back and explained in a teacherly way my blue pencilings on some manuscript he had in preparation. He brought me the proofs of Dewey and Tufts' *Ethics*, and asked me to revise his chapters without regard to printer's costs. If he should do that now, I would be swift and conscientious in the task. Then I loitered so long over it that he finally took a few unfinished galleys from my desk and sent them to the printer as they were—a thing we never spoke of but which I remember with acute remorse.

It was a puzzle to me, and remains so, how a man with the thinking ability of John Dewey could be so obtuse as he is to the logic of grammar. While he was teaching me in the classroom the most subtle concepts of logical theory, I seemed in the office to be teaching him the meaning of simple grammatical relations, or of word-order in the English language. He says in a personal statement contributed to *Contemporary American Philosophy* that he had a "native inclination toward the schematic and formally logical" which he regarded as a weakness and that he had to compel himself to take account of the actual material of experience.

"During the time when the schematic interest predominated, writing was comparatively easy; there were even compliments on the clearness of my style. Since then, thinking and writing have been hard work. . . . I have been acutely aware, too much so doubtless, of a tendency of other thinkers and writers to achieve a specious lucidity and simplicity by the mere process of ignoring considerations which a greater respect for the concrete materials of experience would have forced upon them."

When I read that, I realized that while I was teaching Dewey English composition at Columbia, he was probably thinking things which he did not say about his teacher. I was pretty good those days at achieving lucidity by ignoring considerations. But I am the more puzzled, if he had that native flair for logical relations, to understand the obviously unseeing manner in which his style at times plods over them.

I leave this puzzle about my pupil's mental faculties unresolved. Thanks to his low syntactical I.Q. I was led to read with meticulous attention a number of profound philosophical essays which I would not otherwise have read at all. And thus—again by a process of purely accidental absorption—I kept getting better and better educated.

Every Sunday during my first two years at Columbia I would take dinner with the Deweys, and sometimes supper too. I would just move in and become a member of the family one day out of the week. After the dishes were cleared away, Dewey and I would sit and talk together, or, when talk ran out, just sit and think—sometimes for a whole afternoon or evening. We must have talked or thought about pretty nearly every subject that ever engaged the attention of a philosopher. No young man could ask a better chance at education. I did not make the most if it because I did not read enough; I let talk take the place of reading. I have inherited both my mother's rapid way of sensing the implications of an idea, a gift not always easy to distinguish from bluffing, and my father's taste for painstaking logical exposition. (That, I see, is a large boast, but I can't help it.) In my golden opportunity as friend and assistant in philosophy to John Dewey I banked too much on my mother's gift. I swallowed down Dewey's total mind and attitude in great gulps just as I had that of Sid Wood. I used to "know the answer" when he would be fishing for something in the classroom, not because I had read the lesson, but because I knew him. I had taken into my self the ways and habits of his thought.

A native like-mindedness underlay this, I suppose, and rays of his influence may have helped to mould me long before I heard of him. I find this in a letter to my sister written during my year at home from college:

"There is a certain age—that at which we begin to hesitate about asking questions—at which we begin to let all the views and attitudes which are our very own go by unexpressed. Then they acquire a transient habit, or even cease to appear at all, and in older age, when everything is more or less jelled, it is impossible to catch in words one whit more of that fleeting self than has been our habit to put forth. We have lived in front of it, and now it is not ours. Children are always interesting, and if it were not for this tendency which is fostered by most education, they would become more and more interesting the more they learned. . . . There is an incipient system of education somewhere which leads children to sing their own tunes. That is all I know about it, but I dare say they speak their own thoughts and make their own gestures. . . ."

That had been my reaction to a distant rumor of the Dewey school; and my essay on "The Folly of Growing Up" amplified these ideas. When I showed Dewey that essay, however, I did not know it was a reverberation of his theories. I did not know for some time after I came to Columbia that he had educational theories. I knew that he was an instinctive democrat, and I soon learned that he was an ardent feminist. There too he filled out so simply the patterns in which I grew up that I can not now say how much he was an influence and how much an enhancing companion.

Even in philosophy I had, in an amateurish way, approached his point of view. "Affirmative Agnosticism, Pragmatism, Socratic Scepticism," I had shouted in my thesis for Pop Russell, "call it by what chill name you will, it is great!" That was in the fall of 1904, three years before James's *Pragmatism* was published. It does not imply that I knew anything about the subject. I was making one of my advance grabs at a whole universe of discourse. It did, however, accurately anticipate my attitude to pragmatism when I came to study it. I liked the new philosophy because it gave a biological foundation to my instinctive scepticism. If the brain, and the mind with it, is primarily an instrument of survival in the life struggle, then no absolute or universal truth is attainable, but this need not stop us from using specific and relative truths in improving life. That was the way I got the "feel" of pragmatism, and for a time I confused Dewey's instrumental definition of truth with my attitude of affirmative scepticism. Dewey and I were alike in our early preoccupation with morals, and that made it easy for me to learn his language. But when I understood, I could not follow him in his effort, by redefining truth, to give moral judgments the same kind of validity possessed by judgments of fact. His instrumental philosophy seems to me, like the philosophies it so keenly criticizes, to be in its root a rationalization of his prevailing interest.

William James visited Columbia while I was there, and my friends the Goldmarks invited me to dine and spend an evening with him. I was reading his psychology then and had heard him deliver the famous lectures on pragmatism—that had been the first "event" after I came to New York in 1907—and I felt a reverential love for him. My heart was beating high when I went over to the Faculty Club to meet the great psychologist and walk down to 94th Street where the Goldmarks lived. I remember only one thing that was said in the course of those twenty-two blocks. James warned me against the habit of dictation, asserting that since books are written to be read with the eyes, the author must have them before his eyes as he composes. And the following remark remains in my memory, I think, almost verbatim:

"I have a brother who writes novels, and he used to be a very good writer too, but since he got lazy and began dictating, his style has become groping and repetitious. I for one am no longer able to read a word he writes."

I often think what a lot of high-flown verbiage about the art of Henry James might be replaced by that well-informed remark.

Aside from that, my sole recollection is the eager warmth and energy with which James talked to me of technical problems in psychology, treating me as a colleague and an equal, and how I wished I could be with him long enough to get back into my own brain cells and function as myself. For I am apt to stop like a run down clock when I particularly want to seem bright and original; with all my faculties alert and my face in good order, I am unable to put forth so much as a tick or a tock.

The simplest remedy for such a paralyzed condition is a few stiff drinks, but I can sometimes fortify myself against it by a purely mental process. I can, with a strong motive, decide in advance to mount the upper side of my inferiority complex (or go back to the "sturdy" and "spunky" baby I began as), and instead of being mute be overconfident. I did that on a later evening when we gave James a dinner at the Faculty Club—"we" meaning the departments of philosophy and psychology. After dinner he stood up at his place, and we each in turn asked him a question. When it came my turn,

I did not ask one question, but four or five connected ones in the manner of Socrates.

"You said, didn't you, that it was possible to perceive a certain constellation in the heavens either as a Wain or a Big Dipper?"

"Yes, I did."

"And you used that as an example of the way the mind can organize experience into truths?"

"Yes."

"Experience is such that it can be organized in different ways, you said, according to the practical needs of the mind?"

"Yes, yes."—He was getting a little impatient.

"That is a true statement?"

"Of course."

"Well, if it is *true* that experience can be organized in different ways, then isn't truth something else besides these different ways in which experience can be organized?"

There was an embarrassing pause—partly filled, no doubt, with a feeling that, for an assistant in philosophy, I had been a bit pompous. James grabbed his head in his two hands and shook it in mock desperation.

"Oh, I never did have a head for logic!" he said.

Another nervy act of mine that winter was to preach a sermon in the Park Church, and offer from that Christian pulpit one of my most pagan prayers: "We bow our heads in humility and aspiration. We do not ask to be fashioned on any other pattern, but only to know from this hour forth that we are free . . ." To distinguish nervyness from self-conceit I took "Blessed Are The Meek" for a text and continued my old battle against "thinking you are big," which is certainly the pettiest of human vices.

There was plenty of nerve too in another show I put on that winter. We had organized a Philosophic Society among the graduate students, and I was scheduled for a speech at the first meeting. "Is Ethics the Ultimate Basis of Metaphysics?" was the subject of discussion.

"Don't be afraid of that library title," I began. "I was at first. I told the committee I was a plain man and couldn't understand it. But Mr. Green took me aside and whispered to me that it was nothing, I could find the whole thing on his bottom shelf in a book by Lotze. That sounded more like my own methods of scholarship, so I decided to sail in, if not about that subject, then about something else, and here's what I think . . ."

With that rather jaunty beginning, I proceeded to point out that philosophic reasoning always has to start somewhere; its point-of-departure, though usually not "painted on the stern," is the crucial point about it; and this point is not determined by reason, but by the interests and accidental experiences of the philosopher. My own philosophy, I said, would frankly take off from the assumption of the validity of biological science and therefore the primacy of choice or motive. Then if you objected that this assumption was arbitrary, it could answer: "Sure, I told you choice came first!" That way it would get you both coming and going.

It would distinguish three different kinds of thinking:

"I. Thought arises as a means of attaining ends, and is perpetuated as such. Thinking in this category is determined by the motive and the accidental environment.

"II. Thinking in which the motive is to think gives rise to systems of metaphysics and has no validity outside the brain.

"III. Thinking in which the motive is to cultivate or educate the will is a third kind and is superior to metaphysics."

Those, I said, would be the "categories" of my philosophy. And I concluded:

"As many as are not practical philosophers, or futile philosophers, will go straight to the education of the will—the cherishing of such moral ideals as are consonant with reality and the individual temper, matters strictly relevant to the business of having a good time. A gesture in this direction is my ultimate metaphysics."

Arthur O. Lovejoy, then a visiting lecturer from Johns Hopkins, a fervent scholar and a thinking mind, took an expert swipe at my too facile scepticism. In answering him I said that scepticism, even if a little facile, is apt to be more fruitful than the tight dogmatic egotism of the professional philosophers.

The next day I received a letter from my Anglican friend, Dickenson S. Miller, asking me to come to his room. When I got there he showed me a letter he had written to President Butler stating that I had insulted the visiting lecturer, Dr. Lovejoy, by applying to him in a public meeting the epithet "tight dogmatic egotist," etc. Miller also told me that my speech had been amateurish and ridiculous, and that I apparently did not know what a category was. I set him back a little by giving him the correct definition of a category, but I was faint with mortification and assured him with an appalled respectfulness that I had not meant my words to apply to Dr. Lovejoy at all.

When I got back to my room I saw that my face was pallid and haunted with shame as though I had been exposed in the stocks. I began gradually to wonder whether such emotion was not a little extreme in the circumstances. Miller had been wrong about my intention—could he have been wrong also about the way my words sounded? Could there have been one or two present who did not think I had insulted Dr. Lovejoy? He had been wrong about "category" too. Might he conceivably be wrong about my having made a fool of myself intellectually? And then, anyway, didn't I believe in boldly being myself, and aren't philosophical opinions a part of what one is? Isn't it better to make a fool of oneself by being alive than avoid it by being a stodgy philosophical prelate? By such reasonings I finally worked my way back to the spunky baby again, and the next morning I wrote Miller a note approximately in these terms:

"Dear Miller:
I wish hereafter you would send your letters to those to whom they are addressed, as I do not want to read any more of them.
Yours sincerely,"

Notwithstanding these bold words, I stuffed the notes of that speech away in a deep envelope marked DISASTROUS DISCOURSE ON METAPHYSICS, and I never opened that envelope until this morning —thirty-one years later. It would be edifying if I now found my speech "amateurish and ridiculous," but I don't. It has a breezy stride, I must say, and tosses the austere concepts of ethics and metaphysics in the air as though they were made to play with, but it does not fumble them. Indeed, one paragraph I find still expressive of my basic equilibrium:

"I must say at the outset that I have a temperamental abhorrence of the word Ethics. Ethics means, I suppose, the classification and evaluation of human motives and conduct in the light of some general standard. I don't believe there is any general standard. I see such variety of persons and predicaments in this world that I believe no rule to be ultimate but the rule imposed by the given man in the given situation. Only for the most cursory and inaccurate uses can we say at large that truthfulness, humility, chastity, self-sacrifice are good. Ethics sweeps on in gestures of lofty generality and abstraction while the man himself sits tangled in a mess of concrete particular trouble. . . . Furthermore, we do not like a man who classifies his motives and ours, counting ten before every act; we like a man who comes down into the world with rough strokes of spontaneous action. So I am logically and temperamentally repelled by the idea of Ethics, and must ask to redefine the problem: Is the fundamental and determining factor in philosophies the will or the intellect? Are we not totally balked and ultimately brought to rest by the personal factor in every map of the universe which is not checked by the facts in a practical application or a sensuous comparison? Not 'Ethics is the Basis of Metaphysics' but 'Morals is all the Metaphysics there is.' "

I turned yellow in April 1908 and spent three weeks in St. Lukes Hospital with jaundice, and then three more at home in Elmira getting well. The combination of spring and convalescence made me happy and creative. I wrote, among other things, a poem, "Ice Is Marching Down the River," a humorous essay, "Mastication and Morality," and a story, "The Outlaw Destroyer," featuring my handsome but hard-eyed nurse as the daughter of a rich man who tried to get a fortune out of her father by kidnaping herself. And I filled a small drawer full of "thoughts" and projected essays jotted on scraps of paper—among them these four which illustrate their general tone and drift:

"The thing we laugh at in a joke is not satisfaction but disappointment."

"Some of the worst of us are pretty virtuous when it comes to conduct."

"Change is the only permanent thing science has discovered, but one is enough if you like it."

"If the meaning of an idea is its result in action, then the meaning of Pragmatism is to resign your chair of philosophy."

Such were my preoccupations at the age of twenty-five while living in the metropolis at the height of what is called "the Muckrake Era." To the best of my recollection I did not read an article or book by Lincoln Steffens, Ray Stannard Baker, David Graham Phillips, Charles Edward Russell, Ida M. Tarbell, Frank Norris, George Kibbe Turner, or any other of the vigorous evangelists who dominated the political journalism of the moment. I was not interested in journalism; I was not interested in politics; I was not adequately interested in "the moment." I remember seeing a magazine cover advertising in big letters an article entitled "Treason in the Senate," and reflecting that there was probably a little treason in the Senate and a lot of exaggeration in the article.

To me the whole aspect of popular magazines, that messy conglomeration of illustrations, advertisements, and exaggerated headlines that the masses are supposed to admire, is nauseous, and I passed this one by without a notion that I was in the midst of a "movement." When Teddy Roosevelt called some too ardent reformers "muckrakers," I was *for* the reformers; I guessed that Teddy, being a practical politician, was holding out against progress. But that was the extent of my interest. If anybody had told me I was living in an "era," I would have thought he referred to the growth and influence of biological psychology—to such men as James and Bergson.

This was partly due to Crystal's absence in Pittsburgh. When we lived together she pulled me toward the social problem; she pulled me downtown. I rarely left Morningside Heights now except to dine with the Deweys on Sunday. I added three hundred dollars to my income by tutoring graduate students; I also added a slab of opera tickets about five feet long, for one of my pupils was the son of the manager of the Metropolitan Opera House. But these earnings did not enable me to go in much for "seeing New York." Instead of nubile girls to be in spirit-doubt and body-anguish over, I had a married woman friend, Constance Herreshoff, who played me great music on the piano and introduced me to the fine and somewhat austere art of listening. She was a trained and gifted musician, and lived with a girl baby and a handsome husband across the street from Hartley Hall—another accident by which fate contrived to keep right on filling me with education.

To me these accidents were so enjoyable that I decided to co-operate to the extent of registering for a Ph.D. It did not mean that I was going to become a professor. I had not renounced my career in "activity and experience" or departed in the depth of me from Sid Wood's formula of earning enough money to "bring the wolf and lion and panther to the door." I merely saw that the universe, or reality-at-large, belongs among those wild beasts and that it might be a proper part of life's adventure to have a tussle with it. Plato in one of his sublimest moments calls philosophy a study of death; I took it in the mood of a toboggan slide through life. It would mean only three years more at Columbia and when I had fulfilled all the requirements, I could express my scorn of scholastic trinkets by not taking the degree!

Chapter 39

Too Many Interests

HAVING thus condescended to take the universe in my stride, I went home to Glenora and focused my fickle attention on song birds:

"Florence and I have counted 51 different kinds of wild birds in Glenora," I wrote in the Log. "Birds are on my brain. I dreamed I discovered a new variety, the 'yellow-crested Auk'—asked Louis Agassiz Fuertes to blow one of their eggs for me. He tried, and it exploded in his face . . ."

"The 52nd bird—lightest and joyousest of all—the linnet, hundreds of them along the hillside hover and warble, falling through the air, beautiful with crimson feathers . . ."

I continued, however, to work with my manuscripts from nine to twelve every morning. I do not know how otherwise—except for an occasional outburst of poetry—I should have become a writer. For my natural disposition is to throw my whole energy of interest into any activity, poetic or practical, that happens along. I plod straight ahead like a mule with blinders on in whatever direction I am going. To hustle myself from the breakfast table to the desk each morning has therefore been a necessity to me as an author. Even for less dispersed and more indubitable geniuses, I think a creative routine is a good thing. The "inspiration" will come oftener, and the faculties be more in exercise to serve it, if you keep plugging away.

My father was still raising crops on his ten acres of the little farm, toiling away all summer with the joy of a playing child. One afternoon as I was scooting out to go swimming, he stopped me: "Max, I want you to help me get the weeds out of those catawbas in the lower vineyard this afternoon." It was a frequent affliction that I had learned to bear, but this time a miracle happened. My mother leaned over the rail of the upstairs porch where she was adjusting her hammock for a nap.

"Sam," she said in her mildest tone of persuasion, "you know, I think when Max works all morning with his books and writings of his own accord, we ought not to ask him to do physical work in the afternoons. Don't you think we'd better just give him up as hopelessly intellectual?"

My father laughed and patted me on the shoulder.

"All right, my boy, go your way," he said.

And from that day he never asked me so much as to pull a burdock or take a hoe in my hand.

I was working that summer of 1908 on a popularization of Veblen's *Theory of the Leisure Class*, imagining that by explaining the standards of "conspicuous leisure" and "conspicuous consumption" more simply, I could persuade people to abandon them. I was also finishing two world-shaking essays on Walt Whitman, one on his art, the other on his morals. I believe I spent the best of my morning hours for almost two years laboring over those essays—and the labor, alas, is apparent in their style. I was maturing, in an absorbed study of Whitman, my own theory of poetry and my attitude to life. I particularly matured my attitude to physical sexuality, learning to blend my dream of its most abandoned expressions with the mood of exalted and fastidious idealism. "I know that amativeness is just as divine as spirituality," Walt Whitman said. And that, I think, was his chief contribution to human culture —or to those humans who can raise themselves to it.

I made much in those writings of my hero's statement: "This is no book—who touches this touches a man." But in the unwriting part of me I did not fail to reflect that Walt Whitman put less of his concrete self in a book, or even a notebook, than any other modern writer. We do not even know whether he had eight children or none at all! I wondered whether anybody would ever really break through the film called literature and put himself in a book.

With less ambition and more success I wrote during that summer a piece called "Liquefied Baseball," describing the antics of our hillside on a Sunday morning in the lake, and a more thoughtful essay: "Why English Does Not Simplify Her Spelling," which was published in the *North American Review*.

There were gigantic forest fires in the Adirondacks which cast a baleful haze over all New York state, and gave the Seneca moon a brassy lumor. Sleeping outdoors one night under that moon, I expressed the sorrowing mood of it in a poem called "Earth's Night," which I believed until morning would make me immortal. In a happier mood one afternoon while mending our path down the brook to the lake, I composed a hymn to the veery, or tawny thrush, which did at least find its way into print.

> Pine spirit!
> Breath and voice of a wild glade!
> In the wild forest near it,
> In the cool hemlock or the leafy limb,
> Whereunder
> Thou didst run and wander
> Through the sun and shade,
> An elvish echo and a shadow dim,
> There in the twilight thou dost pour thy song,
> And give the stilly woods a silver tongue.
> Out of what liquid is thy language made?
> A sister of the water thou dost seem,
> The quivering cataract thou singest near,
> Whose glistening stream,
> Unto the listening ear,
> Thou dost outrun with thy cascade
> Of music beautiful and swift and clear—
> A joy unto the mournful forest given!
> As when afar
> A traveling star
> Across our midnight races,
> A moving gleam that quickly ceases,
> Lost in the blue black abyss of heaven,
> So doth thy light and silver singing
> Start and thrill
> The silence round thy piny hill,
> Unto the sober hour a jewel bringing—
> A mystery—a strain of rhythm fleeing—
> A vagrant echo winging
> Back to the unuttered theme of being.

I felt great power in me that summer both for poetry and life. I traded my horse Besom for a sailboat, a genuine little wave-walking keeled sloop, and left a standing challenge with nature to heave up a wind I couldn't cross the lake in. That summer too I fell into a state of everlasting passionate friendship with Ruth Pickering. It wasn't a long or sudden fall, for I had been bewitched by Ruth's slim sullen little lazy and yet agile figure ever since she first showed up in Glenora eight years old. I never could keep my eyes off her in the glen when she would dive with the other children into the curling pool and beat them, boys and all, across to the hiding place under the falls. She seemed always to have some brief black silky rag on that clung to her actively and made her shine like a wet otter.

When Ruth was eight, I was eighteen, and it did not occur to me that within calculable time she might cease to be a child. Even as I watched her grow and measured from summer to summer the increasing candor of her breasts, as my father might watch the ripening of two perfect peaches on his "White Mixim" tree in our orchard, I was not waiting for her. I was, on the contrary, with a feeling of irremediable guilt, fighting against my thoughts and glances, trying to bring them round to something it was not a dreadful sin to rest upon. Ruth was fourteen now, and one day she was alone at the dock when I went down to launch my boat into a cold gale blowing out of the north. She helped me push off, and I said:

"Come on along—jump!"

We sailed all that afternoon in the tossing white caps and frosty-colored sunshine—sailed far out of sight of home and into a deep and beautiful danger of love.

By virtue of my special combination of pagan prayers with athletic instruction, I had become a kind of moral counselor to all the kids along our hillside. And I was supposed to have a fraternal-fatherly love for the whole bunch. The hidden armature that held that overlarge emotion up was my secret yearning to be near this little supple-bodied water nymph, whom I could, and did successfully in almost every contest, champion against them all.

The heroic trend of my love pattern—or as Freud would say, the homosexual component in my libido—was further demonstrated that summer by my setting out to compose a dramatic epic about rebellious women, a subject no poet had chosen before, an immortal poem to be called "Child of the Amazons." That was the summer, too, when my radical friend Baldy Mann and I undertook, by way of dissertations at the Supposiums and disquisitions in the Cherith Log, to introduce Glenora to what was then the new frankness about sex and to denude all Glenora girls of stockings when they went swimming. Baldy had fallen in love with my cousin Adra, and his public or generalized zeal for plain talk and dress reform was kept at fever heat by a more specific concern with Adra's personal emancipation. The picture of him with his gentle brown eyes and stubborn jaw, discoursing in a quiet voice about "sexual inter-course," "methods of contraception," etc., to a circle of elderly and refined Elmira churchwomen, is one that I cherish with abounding love. In those matters, as in the rejection of theism, Baldy was, if not intellectually, at least socially bolder than I. We called our-selves the "Apostles of Nakedness"—it seems an extreme term now for legs bare up to the knee—and with the help of Crystal, who drew up a sixteen-point brief on the subject for presentation to our male parent, we managed to carry the day. Indeed we carried it so far, and so tyrannically, that one or two dissident females gave up swimming at our dock because they were *afraid* to appear in stockings!

"Grand fight in the afternoon on going back to nature," says the Log for August 4. "Dad, after a polite conversation with Crystal and Adra in their bathing suits, suddenly decided they were too bare to sit in the parlor. The Apostles of Nakedness came forward with time-honored and obvious truths, and many scattering dialogues followed the main skirmish. Mother, returning from Elmira, be-draggled but brilliant in the midst of an evening thunderstorm, was informed by her husband that the family had been 'scrapping all afternoon.'

" 'You can't talk,' Max said. 'You started it.'

" 'I made just one solitary remark,' said Dad.

"And Mother: 'Sam, that's all the Lord made at the beginning of creation.' "

With such preoccupations in my real or summer self, I returned to New York for the winter of 1908-09 to register for a Ph.D. in philosophy and psychology. As the subject of my thesis I put down "The Sense of Humor," and that marked the birth of a large ambi-tion. I was dead sure that a fascinating body of facts and under-standings lay behind my observation that disappointment rather than satisfaction is what we laugh at in a joke. In a premonitory way I felt that I had the explanation of humor, so to speak, by the tail. I had only to drag the rest of it out of the facts, develop its implica-tions, and make it sure, in order to add a page to science. At the same time I was laying claim to a gift for humorous writing, and the notion arose to combine these two things: to explain comic emotion and have it present during the explanation, to write the science of laughter laughingly. It was the same thing I was attempting with poetry, only far more difficult—indeed the most difficult feat, I thought, that a writer could set himself. Though I soon dropped it as a subject for my doctor's thesis, I never ceased to feel the challenge of that feat. It became, in the intermittent way of all purposes in a blend of character like mine, a life ambition.[1]

Crystal and I took a fourth-floor apartment on 11th Street just where it turns south and against all geometrical propriety runs head on into 4th. This was soon to be a part of the notoriously colorful locale, or state-of-mind called Greenwich Village. But even that name was rarely spoken then. I described it to my mother as a "mixed, respectable, quiet, peaceable, home-going, house-cleaning neighborhood of general Americans." I spoke sarcastically of "Bohemian café dinners," and avowed that the best thing about New York was the nearness of Bogota, New Jersey, where I fled away weekends and paddled up the Hackensack with Jack Roosa's wife's laughter-loving family, the Bowmans. Muriel Bowman had been the only one of Glenora's kids to swim across the lake, and there were moments, with Ruth so far away, when I thought maybe Muriel was after all the little Amazon I loved the most. In further defiance of the metropolis and pursuit of rural vigor, I bought a bicycle and set out to ride up to Columbia three days a week. I rode two days, up "Death Avenue" and through the Broadway traffic, then took my bicycle to a store and sold it.

Crystal and I were ideal housemates because we lived such different lives. She was writing her book *Work Accidents and the Law*, publishing chunks of it in *Charities and the Commons*, and rapidly becoming an authority on workmen's compensation. This, together with her zeal for feminism, swept her into the main stream of social action, on the banks of which I, at Columbia, sat reading or fishing now and then for an idea. As the year passed, our little apartment saw many intriguing parallelograms of social and personal forces. Annette Kellerman, the Australian diver, made her great splash on

[1] The history of that ambition is itself something of an ironical joke. In my first attempt, *The Sense of Humor*, published in 1922, the miracle did not come off. The main reason was that I had not completely developed my theory, and lacked the freedom of mind to handle it playfully. I was still troubled, and I was still *at work*. In *Enjoyment of Laughter*, published after another twelve years, the theory is complete; a multitude of loose problems are solved; and the book is as mature scientifically as I can make it. It supersedes the earlier work on every point. But for that very reason I was able to write it gaily enough so that it sold almost as a joke book. And this has misled the pundits of the subject into imagining that *The Sense of Humor* is a deeply-pondered contribution to psychology and *Enjoyment of Laughter* a "pot boiler" or a "tour de force."

Broadway that winter, bringing a full-size tank and springboard on the stage and showing off her seal-like shape, declared by Dr. Sargent, director of the Harvard Gymnasium, to be the most perfect ever to swim into his ken, in a single-piece black bathing suit—also then a prodigy of daring. Crystal got Annette down to a Sunday breakfast (at noon) to talk over some scheme for the regeneration of the female sex. Nothing happened—I am just trying to suggest the social fun we had. No amount of shape could make up to me for a girl's letting her legs flop when she dives.

A different sensation of that season was Walter Hampden playing the part of Jesus in *The Servant in the House*. One day, after meeting a well-known photographer named Alice Boughton, I received a note asking me if I would consent to pose with Mr. Hampden in pictures of the miracles of Christ for the magazine, *Good Housekeeping*. My mother happened to be visiting us at the time, and I said to her:

"You see what it is to be a beauty—I just knock them cold at first sight."

She said: "You'd better wait till you see what she wants you to pose for."

When I came back from the studio, she asked me what it was.

"The corpse of Lazarus," I said meekly.

Just the same I was proud of my performance in those pictures, and when they led to my having a part in a miracle play put on in the Berkeley Theater by Ben Greet, I dreamed that I might, among other things, become an actor.

Another sensation that Crystal brought into our home was Inez Milholland, a radical-minded Amazon just graduating from Vassar College and already famous for her beauty. It was a brilliant, large-featured beauty, causing audiences to gasp when she got up to speak, but at close range I found it disappointing. I wrote after she came to tea with us:

"Inez was nice, but rather lacking in humor—though she laughs well—and even more immature and really not *onto* things than I expected. The nicest thing about her is the way her hat sits on her hair."

Inez showed that she had real force of character at one of the "Collectivist Dinners" we used to attend in Kalil's Restaurant down on Park Place where now the Woolworth Building stands. She had come from Vassar to speak on "The Social Problem and the College Girl," and had learned her speech by heart. She remembered it up to the point where the college girl needs "integration," and on that word her memory went blank. She repeated the word three or four times until it became a piece of perfunctory nonsense, and the audience began to giggle.

She said: "Wait a minute, I have forgotten what I was talking about."

The audience waited a minute, and she stood there, struggling inwardly. It waited two minutes. Then one by one it began to laugh again. Then it began to make suggestions. She said nothing, paid no attention to anything said, just stood there, flushed and harshly scowling, beautiful as a goddess and forgetful of her beauty, forgetful of everything in the world but her determination to remember that speech. She stood in that mute solemn stubborn state of determination for three whole minutes by the clock, while the audience, what between fits of laughter and sobs of sympathetic anguish, became literally hysterical. Then finally she said: "Well, I can't take any more of your time," and sat down amid storms of applause. She was, within a year or two, a poised and admired speaker for suffrage and socialism and acquired a reputation for brains as well as beauty.

My mother was not well that winter, and to cheer her I wrote long letters about my doings and feelings. A few quotes from that bundle of letters will convey—with some exaggeration of its buoyancy—the mood in which I pursued my scholarly labors.

"We have two bedrooms, two living rooms, and kitchen, with laundry and refrigerator and gas stove—all for $33.00. It is four stories up, but good legs on the both of us . . . I bought a desk, with any quantity of cubby- and pigeon- and worm-holes for $2.50—fine old piece—and a new couch bed of most hospitable consistency (price $15.00 including a fine hair mattress!) . . . My hours at Columbia leave me mornings, and all day Tuesday, Thursday and Saturday to work down here . . . I'm *so* glad to be away from the knowledge foundry. It is more real and human down here . . . I write in the mornings. Afternoons I read or go to a class—but always play tennis and swim . . . I am going out to Bogota to a dance tonight and canoe-trip tomorrow!—O I'm wild for the country. But I tell you it's fun in New York if you're really in it, and yet have a good nest to fly home to . . . I do want to do the poem I told you of ["Child of the Amazons"]. I spent all Sunday on a beach with it—after a cool and glorious swim in the green surf. O I had a great day! . . . I'm correcting the proof of the Thrush today . . . I'll get the history of philosophy behind me this year, and I'll praise God always that I did it. Next year I'm going to study economics and politics and American history . . . Well, it's great fun having an intellect—and then wisdom is somewhat different . . .

"Tuesday I read Leibnitz all morning, and didn't think his 'system' was any better than any of the others, or my own, although I believe he is the only philosopher of modern times who has had the grace to permit the universe to have all the *diversity* it wants to. I believe he is somewhat looked down on for this laxity of discipline. I suppose he must have let his mind be wheedled by facts. He said the world was made out of monads, you know, every one different from every other. You remember that poem of Sill's about the monads? They were spiritual beings and—as near as I can make out—they give the characteristics of matter because they have a will, and are somewhat mulish, so that if you go to lay hands on them you feel a resistance.

"You know there is an ancient feud between the world and philosophers, the world having a pugnacious and wholly unjustifiable intention of being several, and philosophers being decorously and with ample authority resolved that it shall be only one. Just as soon as a philosopher has succeeded in roping it in—and this is accomplished with the utmost dignity—the universe will kick and explode . . . Now I suppose the reason Leibnitz is not admired is that he didn't stand by the colors. You might say he deserted to the universe. He thought he could anticipate the explosion by dividing it into any quantity of little bits of universes to begin with. Of course this was mere pandering to diversity, and even God himself, brought in for protection, couldn't wholly save Leibnitz from the obloquy which justly falls upon the betrayer of a great principle. That principle is that the universe is only one. Let us stand by that great truth whatever befalls us!

". . . I am setting sail on Emanuel Kant today. He doesn't frighten me a bit either. There's nothing like scorning these fellers. There's nothing like scorn anyway as a general method for a kid that was born scared the way I was . . .

"I had the happiest ten minutes of my life last Saturday evening, walking through Morningside Park . . ."

Life was not straight-along so gay as that, nor mind so cocky. There were darksome problems. I was sad that nobody wanted to publish the things I wrote. My mother sent them around; I couldn't. My story "The Outlaw Destroyer" never drew a personal answer. "Liquefied Baseball" rang the bell with *The Christian Register,* a small religious weekly that published my mother's sermons. *The Christian Register* also accepted "The Folly of Growing Up" and another piece called "Mastication and Morality," which I thought proper for a comic paper. My hymn "To a Tawny Thrush" was published in *The Forum,* a stately mausoleum among magazines, a burial ground for poems. "Earth's Night" was ignored. "Child of the Amazons," which I finished during the Christmas holidays, was too long to think of sending to a magazine. An essay called "The Pragmatic Meaning of Pragmatism" was rejected by Woodbridge's *Journal of Philosophy, Psychology, and Scientific Methods,* I still can't see why, for he later published less timely things of mine. "Healing at the Shrine," a historical study that had been ordered for a popular series on mental healing by a person wearing the memorable name of Stark Young, was found too highbrow.[2] A poem I wrote on the St. Gaudens Memorial Exhibition at the Metropolitan was accepted by the *American Magazine*—the triumphant day of my youth—and then sent back with the "subsequent decision" that they couldn't find room to print it.

While drunk on their first communication, I took my two Whitman essays to the office of the *Century Magazine* and sent my name in to the editor, Richard Watson Gilder. Gilder was himself a poet who had known and liked Walt Whitman; and I had another reason for thinking he might take my essays. An aged friend of mine in Elmira, an artist named George Waters, had painted two portraits of Whitman in Camden. Waters had the gift of eidetic imagery, and when he got home to Elmira, he painted another portrait from the clear-edged vision in his mind. He offered this unknown portrait to me for publication with my essays.

To my surprise Gilder himself came out immediately in response to my name, a slim and gracious person, and gave me a very cordial handshake. Perhaps he had read "The Poet's Mind," for he reached both hands for the manuscripts as I held them toward him. But when he read the title on the top one, "Morals of *Leaves of Grass,*" he placed the manuscripts back in my hands with a rapid deftness as though I had handed him a turtle. "Oh, you must realize this is a family magazine," he said. "We can't do that!"

I tried to explain that I was not overthrowing the family and

[2] He published it long after in *The Texas Review* (September 1915).

urged him at least to read my essays, but he firmly declined. Whitman was quite out of the question in a "family magazine."

Though I had some success behind me, I lost its savor in these failures, and took a fair dose of the disheartening process of "getting started" as a writer.

A heavier sorrow was the difficulty I had getting started as a lover. I was romantic about two free-hearted girls in the course of that winter and lustful of their shapely bodies. Every night or two I would undress and ravish one of them with bold yet tender admiration in my thoughts. But in the reality I could not bring this to pass. It was not they who stopped me, for although captive to virginity they were not unwilling to be set free. The trouble was in the interplay of my own instincts. My fastidious reticence made true intimacy impossible, and without intimacy I could not feel or behave with the ponderable girl as I had with her diaphanous image. Either I would be overexcited and tremble beyond the ecstasy before she was unclothed, or I would be chilled by a fit of shyness when the image was stripped of its glamor of unreality. I could not be matter-of-fact enough, it seemed, to function as a man. And the longer it remained so, the more so it became. Fear is a heavier-freighted instinct than lust; it has the right of way. The fear of impotence is the chief cause of it. And this fear, as time passes without an experience to refute it, piles up to the size of a panic. I have mentioned this before, but it was now becoming an anxious sorrow, a sombre undertone in me which my mother sensed but no one knew the cause of.

How bountiful and yet baffled is a mother's love! How seeing and yet how deeply in the dark! And what precious gift else in this world is so little valued by the receiver! I read my mother's letters today with surprise as though I had never quite happened to notice how much she loved me.

"Have I ever told you that of all the good and blessed things of my life the best is knowing you—and being loved by you? I have often told it to myself . . .

"I go over our walk at Glenora as the devout Catholic makes the stations of the cross—I mean with the same kind of fervor—stopping where we stopped—seeing certain trees—and glimpses of the lake and cove and the grassy lane . . .

"But with all my joy in you I do not lose the feeling of sadness about you, and when that persists I'm pretty sure there is a reason. You seemed to lack buoyancy, and your face was sad. Are you at

Morgan Lewis Eastman, a Congregational minister in St. Lawrence County, N. Y., married Evelina Thorpe, daughter of a blacksmith in Ogdensburg.

Sarah King Stehley, member of the Dutch Reform Church in Harrisburg, Pa., had a daughter, Catherine, who married George Ford, a gunsmith in Peoria, Ill.

Morgan Eastman's son Samuel, enlisting at eighteen, fought in the Civil War, then went to Oberlin to study for the ministry.

Catherine Ford's daughter, Annis, won local fame at eighteen by her witty and eloquent introduction of Susan B. Anthony. She too went to Oberlin, and she and Samuel fell in love and were married in 1875.

Four children were born to them: Morgan, Anstice, Crystal, and Max.

Max was a beautiful child but soon got over it. Crystal was beautiful right straight along. Max's first love was Crystal's little friend on the right in the picture. His greatest love was the Irish setter Ajax.

When her husband's health failed, Annis Ford Eastman entered the ministry, and subsequently they became joint pastors of Thomas K. Beecher's Park Church in Elmira, N. Y. The principal influence in Elmira besides Mr. Beecher (top left) was Mark Twain, who is shown in his study on Quarry Farm. Lower right, Rodney Day and Max Eastman, pigeon fanciers.

Cherith farm and cottage at Glenora on Seneca Lake was home in the happy and complete sense to the Eastman family.

The girl I liked best in Elmira was Gretchen, daughter of the wealthy political leader, J. Sloat Fassett. My great friend at Williams College was Sid Wood. Other friends in the fraternity were Fritz Judson, "Baldy" Mann, Harry Mellen, and "Bing" Myers (top row, left to right). Lower row, left to right: "Rickey" Rogers, Max Eastman, and Ralph Erskine.

My loves at the Sahler Sanitarium in Kingston, N. Y., were Charlotte and Rosanna Atkins. Rosanna took me to see her friend, the famous naturalist, John Burroughs.

The man who saved me from a life of invalidism was Dr. John George Gehring of Bethel, Maine.

As assistant in philosophy at Columbia University I learned from John Dewey, argued with William James, was backed up in my revolution in poetics by J. McKeen Cattell.

As a feminist I admired Susan B. Anthony's gifted friend Nanny Miller, of Geneva, N. Y. I thought Emmeline Pankhurst "one of the greatest persons I shall ever see." I respected Mrs. O. H. P. Belmont's will-power. I fell in love with Inez Milholland.

As an agitator I stood with the militants against the moderate, or "yellow," socialists. Top left: I address an Ettor and Giovannitti protest meeting on Union Square. Top right: Mother Jones at the Colorado coal strike. Below: Carlo Tresca, Elizabeth Gurley Flynn, and Bill Haywood at the Paterson silk strike.

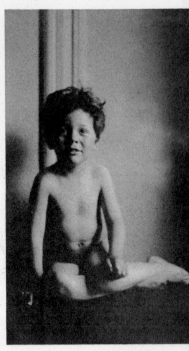

My wife was Ida Rauh, actress, sculptor, lawyer, agitator. Our baby was named Daniel, after Daniel Webster, Daniel in the Lion's Den, and Daniel Boone.

At a dinner for Jack London (lower left) I met the humorous artist Art Young, and he condemned me to the editorial chair.

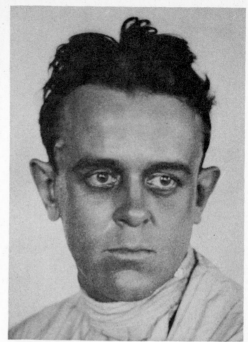

As editor of *The Masses* I tried to load the steady work off on John Sloan (top left), who was too wise, John Reed (top right), who was too rambunctious—succeeded finally in placing it in the competent hands of Floyd Dell.

Two of the famous artists on *The Masses* staff were Boardman Robinson and George Bellows (top left and right). Two of its eminent angels were E. W. Scripps and Amos Pinchot (lower left and right).

In 1916 I moved into an apartment with Eugen Boissevain, and my sister sent Rosalinde Fuller to invite me to dinner.

I fell whole-heartedly in love with Florence Deshon.

peace with yourself about Florence? Is there any way of being—if you are not?"

No, I was not at peace about Florence, or about any other girl, nor was there any way of being so until I could escape from my prison of romantic reticence.

In other matters, physical as well as mental, I had aggressive self-confidence enough. I pieced out my five hundred dollar salary that winter by revising manuscripts for *Charities and the Commons* and running a club in a tough section of the lower East Side known as "The Gap." The club was sponsored by Hamilton House Settlement, and the idea was to save the offspring of the underworld by giving them the rudiments of social good fellowship and maybe a little parliamentary law. It was the only job I ever tackled harder than teaching logic to sophomores. One of my "boys," nineteen years old, had already earned money in the prize ring. Any one of six of them could have knocked me cold with a hand behind his back. But they never found that out. I happened to have a skill in "Russian wrestling," and I spent the first night on that, throwing them all off their feet one after the other. The next night I devoted to boxing, but now I just refereed in a particularly case-hardened manner, or stood at the ringside urging them with a ripe appetite for bloodshed to sail in and wallop each other. The ease with which I got the psychological drop on those boys—a trick I learned, you may remember, watching pigeons in the Park Church barn—was astounding. Although I believe they were as tough a gang as you could find in New York, I never had a second's trouble telling them how they were going to spend the evening or making them do it. Every one of them, from the prize fighter down, confused my moral authority with prowess.

We ended the year with a parade around the gymnasium, and for months the great question was, who should march at the head of the parade. Jimmy Connolly, a pale and handsome Irish boy, was entitled to the honor as president of the club, but that prize fighter, as the outstanding athlete, asserted that he was going to do it. I heard them arguing the question:

"You can't take the place of the president of the club," Jimmy said.

"Just who's going to stop me?" said his rival, putting a fist under Jimmy's chin.

"I'll tell Mr. Eastman," Jimmy said, "and he'll throw you out on your ear. Won't you, Mr. Eastman?"

"Sure," I said. "You're the president of the club. We'll let Tony, as the strongest man, march next."

I had no plan of action in the event that Tony put his fist under my chin.

It was good for my character running that club, and I tried to believe it was good for my style. "I have half the time the feeling that I don't want to do it," I told my mother, "because I want to write poetry and humor. But I dare say the poetry and humor will be better if there is less of it and more human experience under it."

Whatever may be the truth of that, teaching logic, studying for a Ph.D., writing poetry and humor, and running a boys' gymnasium club proved too much for my resistances. I came down with a gruesome whitish-yellow sore throat one day in February, and my brother, who was spending that year as an intern at City Hospital, came over and told me it was diphtheria. To see that monstrous creature growing in my throat, avid to strangle me, and see it stop growing and back down and fade into nonexistence under shots of antitoxin, was a miracle like life itself. I always recall it when I hear light-headed people say they "don't believe in doctors." I had to spend four weeks in the pest house on East River and then go home once more to convalesce.

As usual when I go to bed, I put on a riot of "thoughts," and one of them I will quote because it expressed an ideal that helped to mould my life.

"I'm reading *Anna Karenina,* and I don't know that I ever read a book with a less gratifying flavor. There seems to be no zest for anything in Tolstoy. He fails to make it appear even for a moment that anything is worth while. This makes him about as good for nothing a prophet as could appear at the present time. He fills a page of the Sunday *Times* today with denunciations and prophecies containing not a ray of poetry or joy. The first office of a reformer is to convey in his personality an impression that life is worth reforming. Isn't it?"

In reporting my recovery to Crystal on April 2, my mother summed up what I have told you in this chapter:

"Max is doing well. . . . If he could get some of his 'works' accepted it would do him more good than anything else.

"He goes to see girls now and manages to keep outdoors a good deal. He looks well—eats well—sleeps well—but he hasn't much energy. He lies down a good deal. My, but I wish he had some *real* work like speaking.

"His poem has been worked over a lot and seems to me perfect. But a person has to have a bit of public recognition once in a while to keep him going."

Chapter 40

"Like a Big River"

BESIDES my other too-many activities, I undertook during the spring of 1909 to organize a Men's League for Woman Suffrage. Just how this came to pass is not easy to explain. The movement was going into its militant phase then; in London Emmeline Pankhurst and her hard-headed followers were turning it into a stand-up tussle with the government. To me it seemed the big fight for freedom in my time. All my immediate influences, as well as the general mood of America, backed up the reformer rather than the poet in me. "I wish you had a life of doing things," my mother wrote. Crystal was always and incorrigibly a reformer. Even Marjorie Nott was now putting half her soul into social work; it was she, indeed, who got me the job with the boys' club. And John Dewey, supposedly my guide in exploring the universe, abetted me in this further diversion of energy.

You must not exaggerate the extent of it, however. For a long time, as I said later in writing its history, the Men's League for Woman Suffrage consisted of myself and a newspaper notice. The newspaper notice, I added, deserved more of the credit for its formation than I did. It was a notice in the New York *Herald* to the effect that I had stated, at some suffrage rally, that I was going to form such a league. That statement followed me around and nagged and bullied me until I had to make good. When you have a painful thing to do, just make a public announcement that you are going to do it— pride will carry you through.

Like most innovations in history, the Men's League had a disputed origin. For while I thought my indiscretion before that *Herald* reporter was the authentic fountain source, I learned later that Oswald Garrison Villard of the *Evening Post* had on his desk a letter from Anna Howard Shaw suggesting that he organize such a league.

He had consulted Rabbi Wise, and they had agreed to share the ignominy, provided someone turned up who would do the work. From their point of view, therefore, I merely turned up. From mine, coming with that newspaper notice on my conscience, I was a Men's League for Woman Suffrage before I ever saw them.

I called on Rabbi Wise first for some reason, and he discouraged me. He was too enthusiastic. I saw at a glance that I couldn't hold his pace as a reformer. So I went down to Mr. Villard. He dwelt more upon the ease than the glory of the task, and I felt better. He gave me cards of introduction to twelve men in New York—men of "civic importance" as I afterward informed the public, though the only one I had heard of was William Dean Howells. He also gave me two dollars as dues to the league. This was far from the only contribution he made, but it was the most effective. That two dollars nailed me down. I was the organizer now; I held the funds. There was nothing to do but go ahead and organize.

The first man I called on was a lawyer named Hector S. Tyndale. He received me volubly, said he believed in woman suffrage, but he didn't want to join a men's league. The truth was he believed in suffrage so much, so profoundly—with him it was a kind of religion —that he'd be damned if he'd see it made ridiculous! That was a severe blow. I didn't go to see another of these civic wonders for about two weeks.

When I did, I had better luck. I was informed by my next victim that his wife was an antisuffragist, and that his reason for being a suffragist was that he thought women ought, if only for the sake of their husbands, to try to be more intelligent than they are. I expressed my sympathy, told him that although not yet a husband my motive was substantially the same, and he joined the League. All the rest of the twelve joined it—Charles C. Burlingham with a humorous amusement that put the thing forward as far as Hector S. Tyndale's religious fervor had put it back.

After those men of prominence were corralled, my task was comparatively easy. I wrote a letter naming them as members and appealing to other men to join. The argument with which I appealed was brief. It consisted of two assurances. One was that no public announcement would be made until we had a hundred prominent names on our list. The other was that no member would be called upon to do anything—the essential activity of the league would be to exist.

Even so it took me eighteen months and about five thousand

stamps to capture a hundred members. By good fortune, however, and with the help of Mr. Villard, I captured the banker-philanthropist George Foster Peabody among the first, and his generosity made the rest possible. The league owed its pecuniary life to him and a great part of its early standing before the public.

Our plan to lie low until we had a hundred members was more foxy than practical. One May morning a New York *Times* reporter called me up to say that he had a copy of my letter and wanted a few more details. After consultation with my backers, I decided to give him all the names we had—twenty-five at the time. So we went off under a small charge of power after all, though there was enough force in those names to give us a headline on the front page and a very delicate handling by the reporter. He satisfied his sense of humor by making public the fact that the existence of the league would not be made public until it had a hundred members, and that it now had twenty-five, and adding: "There is one peculiar thing about the league as stated in its prospectus, and that is that it is not going to do anything!"

The afternoon of the day this appeared, one of the most "civic" of my twenty-five, Dr. John Brannan, the city physician, sent in a brief and caustic resignation. It was a sickening experience to me: my first taste of public ridicule reinforced with a private rebuff. I wrote to my mother:

"Has my enviable fame as a suffragette reached Elmira? Judging from the feeling in my stomach I guess it has. . . . Dr. John Brannan resigned from my league when it came out in the *Times*—poor cuss —I wish I could!"

Mr. Peabody wrote me a kindly letter saying that neither the leakage nor Dr. Brannan's excitement need disturb me; the advance publicity was excellent, and we would get more when we organized. That braced me; and I soon forgot my mortification, anyway, in a joyous adventure. It started with a trip to Williamstown, including a pause at Vassar to see Inez Milholland and give a lecture on pragmatism to a class in philosophy she was attending. I paused again at Vassar on my way back, and Inez, who was through college and had her father's touring car and chauffeur there, drove me down to New York. At least she drove me as far as the Nikko Inn at Harmon-on-Hudson. There, while we had a sandwich, she got to telling me about her wonderful friend, Mary Borden, who lived in Hartford, Connecticut. Mary, although a genius in her own right, was marrying a missionary—foolishly, Inez thought—and leaving for

India. I must meet Mary before she left. Why not drive over to Hartford right now? "Pater" and "Mater" would miss their car—and their daughter—but they would probably get them back before morning.

Cars were not common in those days, and an impromptu trip to Hartford for an evening call was like jumping over the moon. It appealed to me as my adventures with Sid Wood used to; and in much the same way I was excited by Inez. I remember Mary Borden vividly, a slim, far-away-looking, entrancingly lazy-voiced girl, amused but unperturbed by Inez' unannounced arrival with a man. Had we not been introduced as two geniuses, Mary and I might have had something to say to each other.

She would soon, in any case, have been forgotten in the excitement of the swift drive home with Inez through the June midnight. We wrapped ourselves in warm coats and sat with a fierce wind blowing in our faces, talking of our emancipation from the hours on the face of the clock and our freedom to act and think when, where, and how we pleased. I had not been so thrilled with the mere adventure of being since I fell sick at college. Inez suggested a life of the same venturesome audacity among ideas and social forces that Sid had among barbarians and mountains. She had the same obstreperous candor, the daring to be real. I never knew anyone more immoderate about telling the truth. It never occurred to me that I might sit warmly close to her in the June midnight, that I might even put my arm around her. She was bigger than any girl I had put my arm around, more self-active, more momentous. I had not yet got sex thoroughly diffused through my being, and the part which it occupied was not the part to which her overstartling beauty and fervent brains appealed.

I went home to Glenora for the summer happy in her friendship but heart-whole and eager to renew my moral and natatory leadership of a gang of kids, with its core of insatiable desire for Ruth Pickering. Again my mother reported to Crystal: "Max is steadily gaining in vigor and health . . . I feel very happy about him—he seems so sane and contented." Her letter is dated June 6, and on the same day I find this entry in my notebook:

"I herewith resolve that I will renounce self-consciousness, and egotistic excitement, and drinking praise for the rest of my life. I will listen in devout forgetfulness of myself to anybody that will talk to me of his interests. I give up subtle bragging forever, fully convinced that anyone who has his head turned in this sharp world is skin-hardened and blind."

My mother was to speak at the Monroe County suffrage convention at Ontario, New York, on June 14, and just for the fun of it suggested that I go in her place. The speech was to last forty-five minutes, and the fee was fifteen dollars, but I prepared a speech that any audience would have paid fifteen hundred to get away from. Here is a glimpse of the outline I drew up in preparation:

I. Arguments from authority.
  A. B. C. D.
II. Deductive Arguments.
  A. A_2 B. B_2 B_3 C. C_2 1. 2. 3.
III. Inductive (scientific or experimental) arguments.
  A. B. C. 1. 2. 3. 4. 5.
IV. Arguments from accepted sentiments.
  A. 1. 2. A_2 a. b. A_3 B. 1. 2. B_2 B_3
V. Miscellaneous.
  A. B.

My speech contained citations from Theodore Roosevelt, William Howard Taft, Martin Luther, John Knox, Bishop Doane, St. Paul, Adam, Governor Hughes, William Hard, W. I. Thomas, Abraham Lincoln, John Stuart Mill, Plato, an American anthropologist, a British anthropologist, Governor Brady of Idaho, and Marie Corelli. It occupied, in mere geometric outline, five large pages each containing two columns of script. It might, if I talked fast and left no time for rhetorical pauses, have been compressed to the size of a small college education. Of course I didn't expect to go through it all: my idea was to be thoroughly prepared and trust the inspiration of the moment. The moment brought panic instead of inspiration, and I plunged and floundered around in that thorough preparation like a man trying to find his way out of a swamp. I never did find my way out. I just kept talking slower and slower until finally I stopped through sheer lack of momentum.

My mother went to Harvard again that summer. ("I wish you could see Professor Santayana," she wrote. "He is dangerously fascinating. Only once before have I seen such eyes. He looks like Milton's Satan or like a Mephistopheles I saw in Dresden.") Crystal was away in July too, and my father and I were alone in the cottage together. His exquisite gentleness and tranquil nobility of character came home to me more clearly than they could with a tempest of more stressful natures around him. We both slept on the porch, and I would sometimes waken before dawn to hear him steal softly past my bed. I wrote him a sonnet which I want to put in this book for his sake and mine.

> The eastern hill hath scarce unveiled his head,
> And the deliberate sky hath but begun
> To meditate upon a future sun,
> When thou dost rise from thy impatient bed.
> Thy morning prayer unto the stars is said.
> And not unlike a child, the penance done
> Of sleep, thou goest to thy serious fun,
> Exuberant—yet with a whisper tread.
> And when that Lord doth to the world appear,
> The jovial sun, he leans on his old hill,
> And levels forth to thee a golden smile—
> Thee in his garden, where each warming year
> Thou toilest in all joy with him, to fill
> And flood the soil with summer for a while.

I learned to do the Flying Dutchman that year, both the dive and the flip, and a back dive from our fifteen-foot tower; and I taught Ruth to do that back dive too. I preached a sermon on magnanimity, with readings from Emerson and Epictetus. If everyone should obey the Emersonian dictum, "Be yourself," the world would become something of a madhouse unless everyone also learned from Epictetus to accept with magnanimity the selves of others. And I "prayed" as follows:

"This is our prayer: That we will not be devoured by our own passions and opinions, but hold them to be only portions of the wish of the world. And we will greet as equals the passionate opinions of others, which are portions also of the well-loved world. We will not sniff and grin at those who have not the aptitude or sophistication that we think we have, but will remember that in the eye of universal wisdom they are likely to be our superiors. We will be of the great hearts who in all ages have risen into the atmosphere of universality, and like the sky enclosed all men and things in their determined sympathy."

One moonlight night when all the kids were in our cottage singing and Jack Roosa playing the violin, and I sat on the porch looking out over the lake, I found myself sobbing with that insatiable hunger which beauty begets in me. It was no new experience—my first "thought" on the Old Farm, you may remember, had been of the unfairness of the same defect in castile soap! But this time the feeling became so painful that I got up and went into the house to escape it. The next morning, sitting down in the grass, I wrote all in a rush, as though it had been gathering through the night, my poem "To the Ascending Moon."

> . . . Like rapturous thought,
> Which can the rigorous concrete obscure
> Unto annihilation, and create
> Upon the dark a universal vision,
> Thou, even on this bold and local earth,
> The site of the obtruding actual—
> Thou dost erect in awful purity
> The filmy architecture of all dreams.
> And they are perfect. Thou dost shed like light
> Perfection. . . .
> Shine in the children's eyes. They drink thy light,
> And laugh in innocence of sorcery,
> And love thy silver. I laugh not, nor gaze
> With half-closed eyes upon the awakened night.
> Nay, oft when thou art hailed above the hill,
> I lean not forth, I hide myself in tasks,
> Even to the blunt comfort of routine
> I cling, to drowse my soul against thy charm,
> Yearning for thee, ethereal miracle!

It was a more important event to me than any other that year, because I was so proud of the unbidden way the words poured out. I do not know any good reason why we should value the work done by our unconscious brains above that in which our minds participate. It is not better work uniformly. But for one who romanticized the whole realm of poetry as I did, it seemed a certificate of citizenship there. Marjorie, besides, called it "great"—the word every artist yearns to hear—and when I read it in the fall to Inez, she took it to her friend, Mitchell Kennerley, and generously offered him the opportunity to introduce the coming American poet. He agreed to publish a volume as soon as I should write or collect it, and I felt for a time a certain confidence in myself as a poet.

I was not confident enough, however, or not united enough, or had too wayward an ideal—too much of "the wolf and lion and panther" left in my heart—to dedicate myself to poetry or even to writing. The first requirement, I thought, is to be a man, and a man has to earn his living. The next is to be a good man, and a good man doesn't live entirely to himself—he puts forth some effort for his neighbors, or progress, or the commonweal. After that, if he has time, he can express himself, and then the expression will be both pure and hard. Since my artistic conscience forbade me to earn my living as a writer or bind my writings to serve any cause—to that I clung as my grandfather clung to Jesus—these large moral conceptions split me up instead of integrating me. Like the monk Copernicus, who gave one-third of his time to his cathedral job, one-third to acts of charity, and one-third to his play-work with astronomy, I shunted myself back and forth between earning a living, serving some cause I believed in, and my own true function of thinking-studying-writing. This conception of my life scheme as threefold became habitual with me and still largely prevails. It helps to explain why, after producing lines that I felt were not unworthy of a major poet, I became within six months a professional "suffrage lecturer."

I had hardly got back to Columbia in the autumn of 1909 when I was invited by Anna Howard Shaw to address the New York State suffrage convention to be held in Troy in October. My highly wound-up speech at Ontario had apparently been bearable enough, or had run down soon enough, so that they wanted to give me another try. And I, in the misery of it, had learned something about speechmaking. A speech has only one dimension; it starts at the beginning and flows to the end. You can not spread it out, or carry it back and forth, or take it here and there. You can not dig around under it. A speech should be rapid, clear and energetic, and make but one main point. It should run like a river between high banks, the floods of emotion adding to its force, but never widening the territory it covers. This can not be accomplished extemporaneously except once or twice in a lifetime; it can not be accomplished by taking successive starts from a series of penciled notes. The more impassioned the language, the more it will in these circumstances tend to expatiate and meander. All great orators have known this, and all great orators, from Deuteronomy and Demosthenes to Daniel Webster and Mark Twain, have written their speeches and learned them by heart whenever they could. A great orator is both a dramatist and an actor; he can write as though he were speaking, and he can speak as though he had not written; he can act the part of himself. This is obvious in history, for otherwise the great speeches would not have come down to us. And it is stated by all who have spoken with deep knowledge of this art.

"For the poet it sufficeth," said Thomas Hobbes in condensing Aristotle, "with what words he can set out his poem; but an orator must not only do that, but also seem not to do it: for else he will be thought to speak unnaturally and not as he thinks."

"Careful and assiduous composition," Cicero said, ". . . is the true source of the admiration and applause bestowed upon eminent speakers."

Daniel Webster learned his speeches by heart. So did Wendell Phillips. So did Abraham Lincoln. And Mark Twain, who was, if humor can be great, a great orator, said: "A person who is to make a speech at any time or anywhere upon any topic whatever owes it to himself and to his audience to write the speech out and memorize it . . . A speech that is well memorized can, by trick and art, be made to deceive the hearer completely and make him reverently marvel at the talent that can enable a man to stand up unprepared and pour out perfectly phrased felicities as easily and as comfortably and as confidently as less gifted people talk lustreless commonplaces. I am not talking morals now, I am merely talking sense."[1]

This obvious, yet for some strange reason esoteric piece of good sense is what I learned in that purgatory at Ontario. I learned it all at once, in a lump, without instruction and without hesitance or self-persuasion.

"My God!" I cried inwardly in my extremest misery. "What couldn't I *do* here if I had a speech to do it with!"

So when I went to Troy the following October I had a speech. I had it in my head and on my tongue to the last dot and letter. And so far as the money-earning side of my three-cornered life-scheme went, it settled my fate.

"I was introduced," I wrote my mother, "with the halo of your fame around me. I will tell you what the man who spoke after me, Rev. John Wesley of the Metropolitan Temple in New York, said to me when I see you. I would blush to write it down. But he wants me to speak in the Temple—whatever and wherever that may be. I've had two other invitations already—one from Mrs. Ivins to speak in New York; and one from Buffalo to speak with Mrs. Snowden!"

Mrs. William M. Ivins, wife of a leader of the Republican Party, was the most eminent asset the movement then had in New York City. And Mrs. Snowden, beautiful and femininely eloquent blue-

[1] *Mark Twain in Eruption*, p. 301.

eyed wife of the British MP, subsequently Chancellor of the Exchequer and Viscount Snowden, was the sensation of the year in lecture circles. We spoke in Buffalo to an audience of five thousand. Leonora O'Reilly spoke there too, representing the woman worker. We were all young and all gaily rather than somberly idealistic. It was a big event in the liveliest social movement of the time, and I was off to a flying start on another rather accidental career. I should certainly not have chosen to get my first taste of fame as a suffrage orator. But so it fell out. And since the movement was then becoming fashionable as well as popular, I tasted a measure of affluence too. In February 1910 I earned $225 over and above my salary of $40 a month at Columbia and was, to the considerable amazement of all, the richest member of our family.

I was particularly successful in addressing men's clubs on this ticklish question, and I attribute that to a psychological strategy I adopted. It grew, perhaps, out of the reflection quoted in the previous chapter about Tolstoy and about reformers. It was not hard, in those days, to raise a laugh at the expense of a man who was going around urging votes for women. My strategy was to get the audience laughing *with me* before they had a chance to laugh at me. Humor is one of the short roads to friendship, and I have used that road constantly in making friends with audiences. Another factor in my success was that I dismissed at the start the mollycoddle arguments —the miracles motherhood was going to accomplish with the state— and went straight to the real question, what kind of people you want women and their children to be. A clipping surviving from those days begins:

" 'Women are no better than men, no purer—their enfranchisement would not cleanse politics.'—Thus did Max Eastman, ardent male suffragette, shatter a favorite fallacy of the sentimental upon his arrival in Minneapolis this noon."

I am so often asked how I came to be that "ardent male suffragette" that I want to make sure I have explained the process. Underlying it all was my unqualified liking for women with brains, character, and independence, a taste I share with Plato and Shakespeare and owe, as I suppose they did, to my mother's nature. I wrote her after attending the suffrage convention in Troy: "I bet it was the jolliest bunch of reformers that ever got together." And a few weeks later, after hearing Emmeline Pankhurst in Cooper Union:

"I think Mrs. Pankhurst is one of the greatest persons I shall ever see . . . a great political leader . . . a complete and triumphant soul."

Again, after one of my speaking tours:

"The women who want to vote are the finest in the land. There's more real humor in a little anteroom before a suffrage meeting than anywhere else I've ever been where a lot of women get together. They're different from mere reformers—they're the people that want to live."

Next came my basic need to suffer a little in the cause of an ideal, that "wanting to do something that you don't want to," which so agitated my hero-friend Count Whittelsey of the Lost Battalion.

"I go to Albany to the legislative committee this morning," I wrote, "to sit in sultanic grandeur among fourteen suffragettes. To a believer in the cause, I suppose it is not—and must not be—ignominious. But to the part of me that is as it used to be, hypersensitive to the view-from-the-road—well, that part would rather stay home."

How *much* I would rather have stayed home I never admitted even to myself. There was nothing harder for a man with my mamma's-boy complex to do than stand up and be counted as a "male suffragette." It meant not only that I had asserted my manhood, but that I had passed beyond the need of asserting it. "I am not such a sissy that I dare not champion the rights of women": that extreme demand upon myself was, I think, a part of my motive in accepting the role of a suffrage orator.

Once I got started, however, it solved magically my second chief problem: how to earn a living with a part-time job that did not consist of writing. I have twenty-six different suffrage speeches in my files, but they intersect and inter-ramify in various complicated ways, one biting a slice out of another to save labor in writing and memorizing, so that on the whole the job was one of repetition. I would choose my ramifications and refresh my memory in about twenty minutes as soon as I got on a train, and the rest of the way to a lecture I would read philosophy, or write poetry, or dream of things as remote as possible from this evangel job, which so happily united martyrdom with money earning!

A letter to my mother in February shows how secondary to my real purposes I felt this oratorical career to be.

"I want to live without froth and sentimentality, like a big river. I could do it better if I didn't have so many thoughts. But I am nearer to it than I ever hoped I would be. I am going to Baltimore tomorrow to 'make a speech' (decidedly not apropos of what I said above). But perhaps I shall spend a day or two in the warm south—somewhere where I can forget the disgrace of speechmaking . . ."

To return, then, to that better third of me, the thinker, student, writer: he worked his brain during the season of 1909-10 as he rarely has since. Dewey, to relieve me of the grind of teaching logic, had given me a five-hundred dollar job as his assistant. It was really a scheme to provide me a fellowship when none happened to be available, and I decided, with that help, to come up for my degree the following spring instead of hanging around another year.

"O but I went to work Tuesday morning!" I wrote my mother September 23. "I sit with my feet and knees irrevocably *under* the desk, and I *read* a dictionary of technical terms in Philosophy, all German—500 pages of it. My reading accelerates at about the rate of falling bodies—and its rate of acceleration is therefore incalculable to people with lit'ry brains like yours and mine.

"I think I'll take an examination after I finish the *a*'s—that'll be about twenty pages—and then if I don't pass I'll take another after the *b*'s. I don't see any use corrupting a perfectly good mind with any more German sentences than is necessary . . ."

I passed the examination after finishing the *a*'s, and I wrote again answering her amused reply:

"I wish you'd try reading all the *a*'s, in an English dictionary, and see if you don't get most of the important words in the language before you get through . . . I found out that if I get a degree in June I have to pass all those exams by the first of October. It is that today, and I passed the Latin yesterday and the French the day before. I read a page of Cicero's *De Natura Deorum*, which is *hard*, and a page of French about Epicurus, which is dead easy.

"I can avoid the embarrassment you suggest (about the books beginning with *a*) by not getting any German books, or any philosophy books, at all. All I want is the Ph.D.—and that I don't want, only the getting of it . . .

"If you want to read the most perfect lyric in this world, read Burns's 'To a Mountain Daisy.' That's the way to write poetry! It makes me afraid of 'learning.'"

There was little time for the Men's League in my schedule, but its activity still consisted only of sending out letters, and for that I myself employed an assistant—no less devoted a one than my mother! She had come down in November to see what the new science of psychoanalysis could do in the person of Dr. A. A. Brill for a mysterious pain in her foot. I put her to work with envelopes and addresses right in the same room with me while I was reading philosophy and revising a long essay I had written on Plato. We never had more fun together.

That essay on Plato was my chief creative adventure of the autumn. I conceived Plato as divided into two contrary characters, one intensely moral or practical, the other intensely aesthetic. All the main differences of opinion in him and about him I reduced to examples of this deepest of differences. To dramatize my thesis I identified the dialogue called *Protagoras* with the moral Plato and *Parmenides* with the aesthetic, and introduced a chapter in which these two dialogues converse together in a language imitative of the style of Jowett's translation. Dewey found this exploit entertaining, and Woodbridge took it down to W. C. Brownell at Scribner's with the suggestion that they publish it as a book. A letter from that eminent critic expressing his regret that he could not find it practical to publish "so distinguished and novel a production" was added to my collection of encouraging disappointments, and the essay put away in a drawer. But that was not the end of it.

While playing in a holiday mood with Plato's style and character, I had been making notes toward a more laborious study of the relations between Plato and Aristotle. It occurred to me that if I mastered that topic, I would really know philosophy. So I went into Dewey's office one day in January and asked him if I might call back *The Sense of Humor* and adopt this more technical subject for my doctor's thesis. It was an impulse of self-discipline on my part, and a wholesome one, for like many pupils of the Dewey schools I had taken full advantage of his tolerance of individual variation. To my astonishment, Dewey said:

"Why, you've already written your thesis!"

"What?" I said. "Do you mean that Plato thing? Is that a thesis?"

"Of course. What do you think a thesis is?"

"Gee, I don't know," I said. "I thought it was something terrible!"

ENVOI

I reminded Dewey of that incident while writing these pages, and told him he had deprived me of a real philosophic education.

He said: "Well, what could I do? It *was* a thesis in a very technical sense." And he proceeded—after thirty-five years—to tell me with precision what the thesis was!

Chapter 41

My Amazon Comes True

CRYSTAL was living like a big river too during that winter of 1909-10. Governor Hughes had appointed her a member of the Employer's Liability Commission, and they had elected her secretary-on-salary, and practically turned over to her the drafting of a workmen's compensation law for New York state. It was high office for a woman in those days; the papers were full of Crystal's beauty and intelligence, and our apartment was full of her friends. We had moved our secondhand furniture over to one-eighteen Waverly Place just off Washington Square, and made a home in which, with accommodation, two big rivers could joyfully flow. One-eighteen Waverly Place! What a freight of emotion those words, mere syllables or digits to my reader, carry into my heart! And what a lame and limited thing this art of writing is!

Inez Milholland, a Vassar graduate now, full of integration and also of "socialism," lived with her family at 9 East 9th Street. That too is just off Washington Square, and just off the Square in a third direction was the center of the famous shirtwaist-makers strike. Inez was backing that strike with all her intense, immoderate zeal—raising money for the union, joining the girls on the picket line, going into court to get them out of jail. Although rather spasmodic in what she actually did, her feeling about that strike was fervent to the point of fanaticism. I was attending Henry R. Seager's course on labor problems at Columbia and feeling mutinous against his benign academic judicialism. Although I did not call myself a socialist, I was as deeply a rebel as Inez, and we were both bent on feeling life to the quick. We were twin rising stars on the feminist horizon, too, her female beauty and my masculine oratory providing just the combination that the movement wanted. There was almost, you might say, a public demand that we fall in love.

Inez wrote me a note in October and said she wanted to come over and consult me about the strike. The papers were making such a sensation of her participation in the strike, and were so lavishly spreading her fame as a great beauty, that her remembering our friendship was exciting. But when she came, I was disappointed in the same way that I had been when I first saw her. The lights and colors that she brought in the door were dazzling. Her eyes were a deep hue of the jewel called aquamarine, bright mischievous lakes of eyes, her skin's crimson and ivory was as vivid as though it had just been rubbed with snow, and her hair was a deep lustrous brown like Juno's. But I did not like her walk. I did not like what happened to her face when she became intense. Its bony structure was not exquisite; you could never see her beauty in a picture. Moreover, my earlier feeling that she lacked humor grew now into the more subtle notion that she was like my father—lacking a quick sense of what things mean to others. Her wilfulness about that speech she could not remember had seemed admirable to me, but also—I now recalled—a little insensitive.

Our conversation was impersonal, and except for my agreeing to come over and join the picket line, had no special direction. I was surprised, therefore, when after a day or two she came again. One-eighteen Waverly was just halfway on a rectangular walk between the striking factories and the Jefferson Market Court where the girls were tried and where Inez herself was twice thrown in jail. Thus it was just a matter of geometry, or so I thought, for her to drop in of an afternoon and tell me about the progress of the strike. I did join her on the picket line, and once or twice went into court with her. It gave me a sense of participation in the labor struggle, not well earned, but all I could afford while writing a book on Plato, studying for a Ph.D., and traveling all over the eastern states to suffrage meetings.

At one of the jolliest of those meetings Inez and I spoke together. It was in Cleveland, Ohio, and our hostess, a classmate of hers at Vassar, reminding us that orators need plenty of air, put us in two beds on the sleeping porch together. I could hardly have thought this a geometrical accident, but whatever my thoughts, I took it as a joke and went quietly to sleep—or to yearnings for Ruth—in my own bed. Inez was a "hunting leopard," as she used to tell me afterward, and my cool behavior, not only there but on the ride to Hartford in June, acted upon her like a love potion. I suppose my disposition to educate her with sympathetic admiration instead of pounding her down with harangues about Satan, as her father did, also contributed to this effect. She was filled with youthful aspiration; she wanted to be a great person; she recognized in the ideals I loved the thing she wanted to be. For these reasons, and I think no others except a fully ripened, adventurous, and overwhelming thirst for love, she decided that I was her natural mate.

I was both slow to realize this, and slow to be convinced that it was true. It may seem ungallant to tell this story, but no one who knew Inez would dream of being gallant to her at the expense of truth. It would cost him a half-day's struggle to extricate himself from her contempt. The truth is, then, that the more I saw of Inez, the more I admired the elevation of her mind. It was a no-compro-mise mind such as I was accustomed to look up to as more swordlike than mine in my sister and mother. I began also slowly to feel what I thought at first had no existence—her immense, although to me somehow coarse-grained and alien, physical magnetism. Swept into its field by her sheer will to have me there, I could not help gradually believing—or shall I say knowing—that she *was* the Child of the Amazons I had been writing about. Her faults of harshness and slow sympathy, or headstrong selfhood—even the swamp-flower coarseness of her beauty—were just what would trouble a poet in a gorgeous female warrior if she came to life. And then, when at last I kissed her, ever so gently, one evening at the door of 9 East 9th— just a friendly kiss, I thought—I found it burning on my lips when I came home. Her adoring passion and the tender personal un-Amazonlike thing she suddenly became when I did finally take her in my arms as a woman was an overwhelming surprise to me. She had never loved before, and more than half that blundering abstract intensity that had seemed to me a little wooden and bluestocking was but ignorance of what her own emotions meant. To have such a palpitating transformation happen in my arms was thrilling to my pride—more thrilling than the facts warranted, for it was bound to happen in someone's arms, and that right soon. I was stubborn for two weeks even then about saying at her demand: "I love you." And to her merry plea that we "run away and get married," I re-plied with a sobriety that would have rejoiced the agonizing hearts of her parents had they but known of it. To me the notion was both practically and poetically distasteful. Nevertheless I declared myself in a brief enough span—on December 3, to be exact—unreservedly in love with Inez.

Instead of getting married, we decided to visit my mother during the Christmas holidays. I went home first and spent one week in an absolute and stainless rapture of love, a state of being associated quite often with the absence of the beloved. The heart of my emotion was neither sensual desire nor friendly delight, but hero worship. I made out of the famous and strong beauty of my love, her unconventional force and noble devotion to truth, and now also her boldly impassioned letters, an object of adoration that raised me up out of all trivial thirsts and diversions. Doubt, my twin brother, was shut out completely from my heart. I walked about in a perpetual joyful surprise at the constancy of my emotion and the sureness of my mind's assent to it. Love is, after all, I avowed, a unique and prepotent force, and I am capable of containing it. My reluctance toward Inez had been the reluctance of a child, of one who had not yet learned to link reality with his dreams, one who loved greatness but had not conceived that it might now and actually exist. I said this in a sonnet to her during that exalted week in Elmira.

> The passions of a child attend his dreams.
> He lives, loves, hopes, remembers, is forlorn
> For legendary creatures, whom he deems
> Not too unreal—until one golden morn
> The gracious, all-awaking sun shines in
> Upon his tranquil pillow, and his eyes
> Are touched, and opened greatly, and begin
> To drink reality with rich surprise.
> I loved the impetuous souls of ancient story,
> Heroic characters, kings, queens, whose wills
> Like empires rose, achieved, and fell, in glory.
> I was a child, until the radiant dawn,
> Your beauty, woke me. O your spirit fills
> The stature of those heroes, they are gone!

I could endure her absence while I was wrapped up in the sonnet. But when I sent it to her I said that she must be ready to walk over mountains to me if she loved me. She said she would come. She said it more than once. But only letters came, and finally I sneaked out of the house one early morning, leaving a note for my mother: "Excuse me, I've gone to New York to get my girl."

When I reached 9 East 9th, Inez sneaked out too, leaving a note for her so different mother, and we took the night train to Elmira. Those two or three days that she spent in my home lifted me high in one way and let me down low in another. My mother adored her and felt so joyful in our love that her own dark long-wandering baffled life-stem of yearning seemed to have found its bloom. My father adored Inez too. Indeed, now that love had clasped her in his subduing hands, everybody where she would alight and glitter for a few hours or days adored Inez. That she was only alighting there would not appear immediately, for she gave herself utterly to each new experience as it came.

Inez admired and loved my mother, too, and so much needed that kind of a parent that she became quiet and childlike by our fireside and more than ever eager to marry into the family. We went to church together and heard mother preach one of her famous "children's sermons." Seeing Inez' eyes dance at my mother's humorous wisdom, and being myself melted by her eloquence, I whispered:

"After all, don't you think this does some good?"

Inez shook her head ruthlessly, not even bothering to say no, and that was characteristic of her. The shock helped me along in my journey toward a clear-angled radicalism; it does not hurt my feelings now.

Another and more significant shake of her head still hurts. We were skating together on the Chemung River, and while she stood resting I did a few mighty circles around her—not showing off exactly, for I am not a good skater, but rejoicing in my speed, the brisk morning, and her presence there. She watched me, and as I glided back in a happy glow, made that same brusque statement of "No" with her goddesslike head. It was the first intimation I had of what became clear in the sequel, that I was no more attractive to Inez physically than she was to me. She did not like *my* walk. She did not like my lazy-bashful drawl or my languid way of slumping into a chair. She liked vigorously athletic, upstanding men with good tone in their muscles. She adored somewhat pathetically the one thing of that kind I have about me, symbol of my triumph over complete spinelessness, a haughty way of carrying my head. Her decision to make me her lover was based quite as much on ideological considerations—to intrude with a too modern term—as was my tardy ascension into the raptures of love.

With that information, if the reader has already grasped what I have tried, somewhat diffidently, to tell him about my sexual constitution, he will know that Inez and I remained virginal in this love adventure of ours. We went sleigh riding one day up the Chemung Valley, and to show our independence of convention, not to mention the law, broke into a long-abandoned farm house and built a fire in its fireplace. We were going to find out what it would be like to be married. We found out what it would be like for two people without physical affinity to be married. My key memory is of Inez informing me in the midst of a caress—an aspect of that truthfulness which I most loved in her—that I was feeling more passion than she was. I denied it with some vehemence, for I had sensed the hollowness of my own gestures. She misunderstood my vehemence, thinking I was attributing more feeling to her, not less to myself, and I let the misunderstanding pass. We never came any closer than that. We were naïve and celestial enough, however, to go on believing we were lovers. At least I was, and if Inez had a different opinion, her candor must for once have broken down.

As I reread now, in the daylight of mature reflection, her recklessly passionate letters to me, I see that I made no answer to what they asked. I failed her completely as a lover. But in the bewildered half-light of my sexual experience then I managed to conceal this from myself. The lack of "body" in the wine of my love was not what troubled me when I came back to New York in January. It was the spiritual loneliness in which I drank it. I found in her no companionship for my moods, no spontaneous sense of their existence even. My cool knowledge that I did not want to marry her turned gradually, in spite of my will to the contrary, into a knowledge that I did not really care very often, especially in her own home, to be with her. "I would go mad in two months in that house," I wrote to my mother.

We were no better playmates, in downright truth, than we were bodily lovers. I was poor and rural and studious, or if not too studious, at least creatively dreamy. Inez, for all her radical opinions, lived a high-geared metropolitan, function-attending, opera-going, rich girl's life. Her time was full of meaningless appointments, and her house always full of male guests—a kaleidoscopic succession of men about town, millionaires, bounders, authors, opera singers, labor fakers, with now and then an earnest socialist or a real celebrity. Most attractive among them in my memory is Signor Marconi, whom I found homely and simple and unassuming, and who found me, as Inez told me afterward, "delightfully haughty, and I hope he can get away with it for a lifetime." I also met young and brilliant Joe Medill Patterson and heard him avow his belief in the principles of the IWW. He was going to hold this revolutionary belief in suspense while he piled up enough money to bring with him a real power—it would take about seven years—and then "go back to the Haywood woods." Another character that Inez introduced me to was Ernst Franz Hanfstaengl, a big-featured, hollow-faced, genial, superficial, piano-pounding, idea-gushing German, who ran an art store on Fifth Avenue at 43rd Street. I can not imagine where this man discovered in his amiable anatomy the force of character to join Herr Hitler in his beer-hall putsch, but that he became a kind of official musical and jocular entertainer and purveyor of rationalizations for that lunatic idealist was not wholly surprising. He was too fluent not to be phony.

There is a species of people whose conversation, while radically democratic, always, as though by some gravitational magic, takes place among the rich, swanky, or distinguished. Inez did not belong to this species, but she did not recoil from it either. By profession during that winter she was an aristocratic publicity getter for the shirtwaist strike—a dubious aristocrat, so far as derivation goes, but making up for it by being elegant and assured—and this made her a natural magnet for creatures of this species. I found myself being dragged along endlessly into such companies, where she would shine and I would feel embarrassed. The joy of being a young and beautiful woman is about as heady a joy as this life holds, and I could not resent her intoxication with it. Even when I felt that she was exchanging animal electricity as well as ideas with some of these tea-and-cocktail radicals whom I despised, I could not openly object. I find a quaint notation among my papers, which tells of my struggle to hang on to love:

"January 23, 1910

"Never brood—get up and read.

"When you want something and don't get it—think you are giving it. Never condemn her as being inconsiderate of your wants until you've tried condemning yourself.

"Never complain until after you've done one day's work, and had one night's sleep.

"Never go where you *don't want to* (in that peculiar way) and when you go, make up your mind to demand *nothing*—go for her sake.

"Remember that you have never determined that point at which jealousy is justified—either aesthetically or morally. Doubt yourself on this point.

"Now do your damnedest, it's your last hope."

I must add that Inez tried hard too, and suffered acutely in this rapid fading of our love. She was sick with appendicitis as well as with a dying dream, and instead of a surgeon, her father and mother kept calling in faith healers and clairvoyants, who concentrated their batteries largely on the task of exorcising me. Her father believed in a personal devil and detected, according to Inez, unmistakable signs of his presence in my visage. And her mother herself acknowledged years after, in a beautiful and regretful letter, that she disliked me "just as much as it was possible for that very proper lady to dislike anyone." Except for an inexhaustible flow of Irish wit and laughter in which all wounds would be frequently washed, Inez' home seemed more like a battlefield to me than a place to dwell. Inez was really sick and in personal misery, and the shirtwaist strike on which she had concentrated a degree of impersonal passion phenomenal in one so young was losing its hold. The girls were going back, and all her gifts of money, beauty, and publicity could not stop them.

One midnight after I had left her with an innocuous lounge-lizard whom I scorned to consider a rival, she called me up in dreadful agitation and asked me to come over to her house.

"Something tragic and terrible has happened," she said.

I dressed and went over to 9 East 9th with my heart in my mouth. "Billy," she told me, had suddenly grabbed her and kissed her madly all over the lips and eyes, and she had allowed it. She had not wanted to, she had been thinking of me all the time, but she had been just weak and languid and unable to resist.

That must have been while our rapture was at its height, for she spoke as though those kisses were the sin against the Holy Ghost, and I on my part was stricken with hardly bearable pangs of jealousy. I behaved with a magnanimity that must have been sickening to behold, remembering my ideal of personal liberty and sticking to it with a drawn and saintly face. I "forgave" her—whatever exactly that word means—and we parted tearful in the small hours of night. In the morning she was deadly pale and told me she had turned on the gas and tried to commit suicide—but not until her father was out of bed and near enough to smell the gas and turn it off.

The tide of our love was running out, and we made these frantic efforts to dam the little streams where it trickled too fast. I continued longer than she did to make these efforts. Though I had been the coy one at the beginning, I was the one to suffer at the end.

She disappeared once for four days without leaving me any word, and finally called up from a country club on the Hudson to tell me she was having a grand time resting and playing squash with a young publisher of wealth and athletic reputation. On another occasion when I had not seen her for several days, I was greeted in the newspaper by a front-page picture of her in the company of a well-set-up young lieutenant in the United States Army with whom she had been arrested on the picket line. It is not a treat under any circumstances to have your sweetheart's beauties spread before the public in the company of another man, and when the man is a soldier, and a certain unsoldierly limpness of constitution has been expounded to you by that same supercandid sweetheart as your chief defect, the pleasure to be had from it is minute indeed. However more complicated the facts may have been, I endured all the pains—the carnal jealousy, the spirit's envy, the inferiority, the task of propping up a crumpled ego—that are proper to an aggressive lover flouted for a better man. And these pains found no brighter thing to replace them in moods of composure than the realization that I had not been really in love at all. This "heroic character" notion which I had taken for a final and sublime answer to all the doubts and ferments in my heart was juvenile nonsense. My noble sonnet about "reality" had been a hoax I played upon myself.

"December gave me," I wrote to Inez in a letter never sent, "the highest moments that complete life offers, moments for which twelve years I had yearned. January is as I look back over it, morning to evening, and hour to hour of controlled sorrow, the darkest month of my life."

My love-fever was intermittent and did not subside finally until the end of March. Its chart is best preserved in letters to my mother, for she was so closely concerned in my attempt to be in love with Inez that I confided in her as I never had before. On January 21, apologizing for not having written, I said:

"How to combine being in love, and earning my living, and taking a Ph.D., and running a reform society, with the fulfillment of the desires of filial love is quite a problem—especially when your lady love is spending part of the time in jail."

On January 27: "I haven't been able to write a word lately—all of the life of me going into the joys and sorrows of youth in love."

On January 31: "Crystal and I are over here at 9 East 9th to supper—amid a noise-making bunch of youths—and I take a minute out of it to send you my love. If you knew how I long to see you—and sort of put myself in your arms—it would make you happy."

On February 14 from Geneva, New York, where I had gone to stay with her friend, Nanny Miller, and make a speech, and had asked her not to come:

"I don't know *exactly* why I wanted to come alone. Strength was what I had to feel, and I had it in myself. I needed to taste the flavor of liberty and the adventure of life, as one needs religion I suppose. I hope you understand—I don't!

"I am deeply sorry not to be a person of abiding faith. All the motions of her mind are noble . . ."

On February 21: "Inez is resting three days in the country and Wednesday she has her operation . . . O my mother, how I love you —and how I long to put my head in your lap and have you touch my hair with your hands while I pray God for her."

On March 26: "It's a soft spring day, and I have a new tablet, and I guess I'll come back to you. I come with what will be sad news . . . I hardly know what to say, but any way I say it you will know. Inez and I are not trying to love each other any more.

"I won't try to tell you the reasons in a letter. I just decided one afternoon that all we lacked was the will to renounce what we couldn't have, and with much momentary resolution I went over and told her so. And she realized it, and so the resolution was strengthened, and then Time came to my help, and with awful glooms and weakenings and tears for all the world, and with dread of my pillow, he still managed to bring me through. And here I am, back on your hands again!

"As for Inez she came through more easily, both because she has so much less stability of motive than I (to think that anyone could have!), and because she found a man to help her through. . . . She does baffle language with the sure nobility of her mind—and I hope you will know it has been a great adventure, and believe that I have grown in grace."

Chapter 42

Halfway to Ruth

I WAS saddened by the failure of my attempt at a great love. I became convinced that in a person of my too various nature the union of romantic exaltation with real companionship was impossible. I was not, however, seriously retarded in my work, which has always been, for one so much preoccupied with girls, singularly independent of their propulsions. In the midst of my heaviest gloom about Inez I made one of the few steep and real decisions of my professional life. Early in February I spoke on Woman Suffrage at a luncheon of the City Club, then a vital center of reform movements. Oswald Garrison Villard was there, and after I spoke, I saw him write something on his place card and hand it to the waiter. The waiter brought it to me, and I still have it:

"I think your speech the ablest, most original and stimulating I have heard in years. I congratulate you most heartily."

A few days later Mr. Villard invited me to come down to his office on the top floor of 20 Vesey Street. He presented me to the editorial staff of the New York *Evening Post,* showed me around their comfortable rooms—which he described, I remember, as having a "pleasantly bookish atmosphere"—introduced me to that breathtaking view of the Hudson River and the harbor which would make downtown New York a kind of Valhalla were it only populated by heroes, and offered me a job as editorial writer on the *Post* at $50 a week. It was a stiff test for my devotion to free writing, and I was some days declining the offer. My mother thought I was making a mistake. "It would be fine training, and a great lever for moving things and a steady and sure living. What are your reasons?"

"To me it's all a question of how well I can write," I answered. And I pleaded with her to believe that I could write better than one does for hire in a daily editorial: "*Please* back me up. It's awfully hard to throw down a chance to be respectable."

To Mr. Villard I wrote March 29, 1910: "I take a brave spring morning upon which to decline the fine opportunity you offer. Editorial writing is not what I ultimately desire to do, and my creative energy is so limited that I could never do the two things at once—hence I should only postpone myself if I came to you next year. By earning a small living at noncreative work, with time free for writing, I shall foster my real purposes . . ."

Although so decisive about the terms of my writing, I was still vague as to its purport. I was drifting with my generation, more reluctantly than many, from a bright clear joy in moral character and great ways of living toward the muddy turmoil—so it seemed to me—of social, political, and economic reform and theories of reform. I sensed this drift sharply when Mark Twain died in April of that year. His death was a very personal grief to me, intensified by the fact that my mother, then just recovering from a futile operation, was unable to conduct the services at his funeral. It would have been, I felt, not only a kind of self-expression for me, but an event in history, if she had.

"I was broken-hearted," I wrote to her, "that you couldn't say the words at Mark Twain's funeral. I prayed you would get well. It makes me happier to know you wrote them—but O, I wanted you to do it! Nobody on earth could express how the world was full of his death for me that morning, but you could say the best things . . ."

In the same letter I revealed the change that would have to take place in me before I could become a socialist.

"I think of him as the last of those four great Americans—Emerson, Lincoln, Whitman, Mark Twain, and I don't believe I will always be so much alone in thinking so as maybe I am now. I feel as if we were coming to a time when there aren't going to be any great individuals because everybody that's good has got to spend all his time having 'social consciousness.' I'm glad Mark Twain belonged to the 'old regime.' I'd stay there gladly if I could be with him. And I hope to God some day this world will get sick of 'society' again, or get the thing settled, so we can go back to the days of heroes and friends and strength, liberty and hospitality."

My mother answered: "O Max, nobody can talk about individuals as long as society is so bad a machine—blundering away, tearing people to pieces—women and girls glad to get a chance to work from

6 to 6 for five dollars a week! And a few of us talking about Faith, Hope and Charity."

I replied: "No—I know we can't talk (or overtalk) about individuals. We've got to mend the whole machine. Still we needn't forget."

Georges Clemenceau's remark, "Not to be a socialist at twenty shows lack of heart; to be one at thirty shows lack of head," has no application to me at all. I was almost thirty before I became a socialist, and I was over fifty when I abandoned the socialist idea as disproven by an experiment. In this letter you see me resisting its allurements at twenty-seven. It was not, however, the class-struggle socialism of Karl Marx that I was resisting. Although my final examination for the Ph.D. was due in a month, and I was to be questioned in political science as well as philosophy and psychology, I was still ignorant of that now commonplace notion. In the climate of opinion then prevailing in America it had not happened to drift my way.

The *viva voce* examination is a survival of the initiation ceremonies which diversified the lives of savage tribes, and to my overcivilized nature it loomed as a minor variation on the tortures the Lord put Daniel through. What made it especially terrible was the easy and equal terms on which I lived with those who were, on some sudden day, to become my inquisitors. They knew me too well, and they also knew too well my attitude of scorn toward that Ph.D. I expressed it on one occasion which sticks in my mind because it had a result that made me happy. Professor Woodbridge had taken me downtown to a meeting of the American Philosophical Society. Dr. Felix Adler was about to sail for Berlin as exchange professor, and he had prepared a paper which he wanted the society to comment on. Speaking of the differences between European and American culture, Dr. Adler remarked that no American could possibly feel that it embellished a man like Emerson to call him "Sir Ralph Waldo Emerson." When it came my turn to comment, I said that I agreed with Dr. Adler about Sir Ralph Waldo Emerson, but I hoped that, in talking to the Germans, he would not exaggerate the difference this implied between America and Europe.

"Perhaps the question is suggested by my own loneliness in the present company, but I think we all might in honesty ask ourselves whether it would be an embellishment to say Ralph Waldo Emerson, Ph.D."

Professor Titchener of Cornell, the last-ditch defender of introspective psychology, happened to be at the meeting—a man who might have renown as a brilliant scientist if brain physiology ever grew expert enough to discover physical states corresponding to his definitions of the elements of consciousness. At any rate, far from being the Narcissus you might expect in one who made a lifework of introspection, Titchener was the lustiest, most exuberant great radiator of extrovert energy I ever met in the shape of a professor. He sought me out that evening in Hartley Hall just to grasp my hand and exclaim: "You're excellently right about these piddling baubles of doctor's degrees and all the academic poppycock that goes along with it!"

This was very fine when I was on the upper side of my inferiority complex, but when I was down under, as I surely would be on the day of that examination, it made things very much worse. The day finally set was May 17, and the place a sumptuous chamber opposite what was then the president's office as you enter the Low Memorial Library. I had a suffrage lecture in Boston that same night, and I brought along a packed suitcase and left it against one of the big pillars in the hall. It emphasized my thought that this academic ordeal was a side issue in the real business of living, and my thought needed emphasizing, for my feelings were of the opposite kind. I was weak with fright.

Professors Cattell and Woodworth were there representing psychology, Dewey, Woodbridge, and Montague for philosophy, Seager and James Harvey Robinson for the social and historical side of what I fantastically pretended to know. They were all sitting in a dreadful circle around a twenty-ton mahogany table when I slunk in. Cattell questioned me first, a teacher with a notorious gift for seeming ferocious.

"What is your special line in psychology?"

"Aesthetics, I guess," I said.

"Do you know anything about Theodor Fechner?"

"Why, yes," I said. "He was the founder of experimental aesthetics, wasn't he?"

"Please let me ask you the questions. What great artist did Fechner have working with him in his laboratory?"

It was a purposely easy question. Any well-regulated brain that ever dipped into the subject would know that Fechner performed some experiments in collaboration with Weber, the composer-pianist. But I rarely know anything I am supposed to. I just blushed and stuttered. Cattell turned to Dewey and said:

"Well, I told you so, didn't I? What's the sense of all this fakery?"

I had had some argument with Cattell as to whether I should take one of his courses, and decided not to, and I assumed this meant I was done for. Dewey came to the rescue of my feelings with another easy question.

"Was there any weakness in the sceptical position taken by Sextus Empiricus at the end of the Hellenic period in philosophy?"

Dewey knew I could be glib about scepticism, the terms and circumscription of which seem to me the only entirely serious philosophical problem—the only one on which, if conclusions were urgent, philosophers would spend their time. Sextus's own answer to Dewey popped into my mind: "Scepticism is like a purge—it carries itself off with everything else." I remember *not* quoting this, and in my confusion wondering why I did not, but I made an adequate answer of my own.

One thing more I remember from that miserable half-hour (for my inquisitors were merciful so far as the time factor went). It was Dewey's last question: "What did John Locke mean when he said that all knowledge is derived from sense experience and reflection?" I did not know what Locke meant, but I knew Dewey's thoughts, and gave without hesitation the answer he wanted.

"Locke meant that knowledge has two independent sources—the reflection is not merely of or about sense experience, but is a source in itself."

Dewey looked around at the others and said: "That's the first time any pupil of mine ever answered that question correctly."

He then added: "Well, I guess that will do," and murmured as I slid for the door: "Will you please wait a moment outside?"

I heard this distinctly, but I was sunk beyond comfort in the shame of Cattell's disapproval. I grabbed my suitcase and fled as though seven devils were after me. Nor did I appear in those sacred halls again for almost a week. When finally I stole into the office, Dewey looked up with a whimsical smile.

"Congratulations," he said. "What did you run away for?"

"Congratulations! What on?" I exclaimed.

"On getting your Ph.D.!"

"Do you mean to say that I passed that examination in psychology? I thought Cattell said I was just faking?"

Dewey laughed.

"That isn't what he said at all. He said: 'I told you these examinations are all fakery.' What he meant was that he knew you had an adequate knowledge of psychology, and there was no sense in trying to catch you on specific questions."

I had been scornful enough of that degree, but a most unscornful balm spread through me when Dewey spoke those words. And though I never went up and got a gown hung on me, I find carefully preserved among my papers a communication from the University Council dated June 6, 1910.

"You have fulfilled all the requirements for the degree of Doctor of Philosophy, with the exception of filing the printed dissertation with the Registrar of the University."

I now felt qualified to tackle for the seventh time, and in mature earnest, my task of defining poetry scientifically and showing the natural path to its enjoyment. I should say the eighth time, for my thesis on Plato had dealt with this same theme. My attitude to the scholarly information I had acquired is revealed in the Cherith Log for that summer of 1910.

"Monday, June 13. I am launched into the first chapter of a book about enjoying poetry, the first sentences not very promising, but I am still afloat."

"Tuesday, June 14. Some rather more promising sentences—had to pick my way among the reefs and tugboats of psychological theory. Once I am out to sea, to hell with them!"

"Wednesday, June 15. Edging toward the open channel this morning. Got by Pleasure-and-Pain without damage to my steering gear, and now rounding the Emotions."

"Thursday, June 16. Clear out to sea! Overhauled and ran down the Artistic Temperament about one o'clock. Hard work stopping for dinner."

My mother records that I worked five hours every morning that summer, and played baseball or built docks in the afternoon. Under the heading "Encouragement from the Family," I made this entry on July 26:

"Mother: 'Max, don't you think you ought to take a vacation these hot days? You might as well be a clerk in a store as sit there in the study all the time.'

"Crystal: 'Might *better*—you'd get paid for it!' "

It was one of the most balanced and happiest summers of my life. Although my mother suffered almost continually with the pain in her foot, and I could never, while living in the house with her, escape from the sense of her suffering, she was not too sick in her body to "swim seven strokes" on July 24—the first time in her life. Her mind, too, when not worrying insanely about the family finances, was full of new ideas and ambitions.

She had decided in the spring—helped on, I suspect, by a conversation with ruthlessly truth-telling Inez—to leave the ministry and take up some sectarian work of education or reform. And she had made up her mind, perhaps with this in view, to learn to speak without a manuscript. Her first attempt at a free-spoken sermon— a bold venture at fifty-eight, or indeed at any time—had been successful, and she was full of eagerness for learning this new art. "Max, the world is so clean-washed and bright with hope," she had written me in April, "Wouldn't it be wonderful if *we* could come forth all new every spring?" And at times, especially in the mornings when we would go up the hill together to breakfast in the dining hall, or in the late afternoon when she would stroll down the road to carry some little garden flower or other friendly token to a well-loved neighbor, it seemed as though she had accomplished that miracle. She never for one second surrendered to advancing age. Her thirst of wider experience and fresher wisdom, her zeal for new light on life and new living of life, were as durable as she was and filled the community with the joy of great ambition.

In my memory, that summer has two highlights. One is the hour by the fireside when, after reading Aristotle's *Rhetoric* and noting his trivial treatment of metaphor, it dawned on me that metaphor is nothing less than the essence of consciousness cultivated for itself. The other is Ruth. My first glance when I arrived on our porch was across the brook and along the rows of grapes to her neighboring cottage to see if she had come. And all summer long I was polarized by that cottage where she lived; I lived in relation to it; wherever I went and however I turned, an axis within me swerved perfectly to point in that direction. New York and my great joy and sorrow in Inez were a million miles away. Instead of crying to four narrow walls about the loss of my love, I was breathing thanks into an open sky for my escape from it. I was free, I was out of a trap set for me in my hibernal migration. I was at home. I was myself. Never again would I fall in love in winter or in New York City!

We converted my father's alfalfa field into a baseball diamond and used to play big games out there every afternoon, Jack Roosa and I "choosing up" among the Glenora kids. When I won the toss,

I invariably and unblushingly chose Ruth first—an act which looked practical, for she played as well as most of the boys. But the truth was that it spoiled the game for me if she was on the other side. I was, by the end of the summer, fanatically absorbed in the problem how to be near her for some minutes of each day, and my nights were clean of all but the desire of her. Every atom and electron of me was involved in this dangerous and divine madness.

Ruth was a lithe, strong, beautifully proportioned girl, ash blonde, with a petulant mouth, most lovingly tender and far-seeing blue eyes. Of Quaker origin she was belligerently pacifist, not revolutionary, in her temper; and she was a poet—a girl who concealed under a great deal of silence a rare and individual gift of speech. She was seventeen that summer and I but twenty-seven; there was no cogent reason why I should not say, at least to her, how much I loved her. But it was a kind of parish that we lived in, my father's and my mother's parish, and I had made myself a kind of first-assistant pagan pastor of it. The less I cared for God, the more I had to toe the line of morals. Besides, I feared that Ruth would tell her parents if I said I loved her, and I would be to all intents and purposes "engaged." It did not come into my mind that Ruth and I might, if I spoke, become closer friends than she was with her parents. I had never been close friends—I had never really confided in anybody.

We did have a free and intimate meeting that summer. We paddled three miles up the shore to Shannon's Point together with no clock calling us back. Ruth, who was entering Vassar, did not have to return to Elmira when the schools opened, and Crystal invited her to stay a few days in our cottage after all the four parents had left. Those days were less athletic than usual because I had a scalp wound three inches long, and my head was wrapped in white folds like an injured soldier's or a sultan's.

I acquired that wound in a way that will puzzle those who think it is important to grow up. I had been fretting about a certain muscular reluctance which marred my execution of the Flying Dutchman dive, and I decided to cure myself of this mortal imperfection by doing it twelve times in succession. I did it eleven times. The twelfth time my legs failed of their leap, and the back of my head struck the edge of the springboard. I dropped into the water like a green oak log. I was dragged out by the hair, loaded into a canoe, and paddled down to the Roosa's lakeside cabin, where I bled profusely while Ruth ran up the hill to call a doctor from Dundee.

The doctor took five stitches in my scalp; Jack's wife fed me five resuscitory pancakes; and with Ruth's strong arm supporting me I climbed the hill.

It was that doctor's bandage that I had on my head when Ruth and I paddled together in a late afternoon three miles down the lake to Shannon's Point. My wound and her solicitude had brought us perilously near to an embrace. We climbed a gnarled old willow south of Shannon's, and sat on a limb that hung out over the water. The little waves lapped among the flat stones under us; the sun went down; our silence grew enormous in the twilight. Ruth said:

"This is kind of hard on me, you know. You just play around with me in summer and then go and live your own life in New York."

"I don't just play around with you, Ruth," I said. "I care more than I dare tell you about our friendship."

I wanted to say more, but I could not. I was too "moral" and too intellectual. My mind would not let go even for a minute of its habit of itemizing the relevant facts. To wit: six months before, in a different environment, I had been a different person; I had been in love with a girl as little like Ruth as fancy could manufacture. Six months hence—what reasoning mind could deny it?—I would be another person, in love with another girl. Only a willingness to pledge himself, I thought, could entitle such a many-colored shift of sands to say "I love you" to a girl as alarmingly young as seventeen. But far from the will to pledge myself, I had the clear and perfect knowledge that we would never live together. What then could I say?

The answer is simple: all that I am saying now. Then Ruth and I would have been friends, and friends so utterly that I think my further course would have been widely swerved, and much disaster avoided—I do not know quite how—by her deft mind.

But I had not that free power. Secretiveness and shyness, two forces rarely mentioned in biographies, were determning my life that day. I could not tell these vital truths to Ruth whom they concerned, and to no one else in the world could I even mention my love for her.

We came down from the gnarled tree and strolled over to the north side of the point and lay on the sun-warmed pebbles of shale while the moon came up. Shannon's is a little piece of primeval forest running out into the lake; nothing lived there but crows and screech owls and a racoon. The dream of buying it and dwelling there forever had been one of my private possessions. I shared it now with Ruth. I invited her into the dream, and she came. I reached out, for the first time without a pretext in all the nine years of our friendship, and touched her. I touched her shoulder. She was lying face down on the pebbles, her blouse open at the collar. I could see the beginning of the sweet outward curve of her still growing breast. There, before my hands and eyes the single thing of all things that existed, or ever have existed, which moved me most and was to me most beautiful. Might not my hand flow down around her breast? The little lapping waves were still audible. There was no other sound. There was no house, no human being, within a mile of where we lay. Nor within any stretch of hours or years was there any but us two who need *know* this moment. It was ours. The night was ours, its whispered admonition in our ears, "Live now!"— its complete gift of privacy.

Ruth was drenched with emotion as I was and as aware of the tense weight of the moment. She had a store of subtle things to say and often surprised me with her maturity. But she did not know me and could not. I had not spoken my heart when the time came on the old gnarled limb. I had only said how constantly I thought of her. Some demon—or some guardian angel, as you choose to name it—prompted her to say the one thing that could rouse my sickly sense of guilt and make me weak with infantile compunction. She said—and the words were as though all our four parents emerged from the woods:

"Is it forever, Max?"

I am sorry, for I think perhaps that with Ruth in my arms where she belonged, the trivial difference in our ages swept aside, I might have learned right then to speak the truth. I said, instead, a little and evasive thing:

"My heart is full of foreverness."

And I took my hand away and became again, with fantastic resolution, her moral captain, her swimming master, sailing teacher, elder brother—anything but what in simple truth I was, her lover.

Chapter 43

My Gravitation Loses Its Earth

CRYSTAL and I renewed our lease at 118 Waverly for the winter of 1910-11, and our claim on dark old kindly-quaint unforgettable "Sadie," who fed us and made our beds. I stayed on at Columbia for the purpose of starting a revolution. My revolution consisted of overthrowing the humanities, or little less than that—making the study of literature a branch of psychological science. I warned the class in my first lecture that I had a natural taste for revolutions of all kinds, but begged them not to be alarmed:

"This revolution I'm going to advocate today I have selected with some care. It is a bloodless revolution and will probably not upset the family. It is a revolution in our methods of teaching, or trying to teach, the appreciation of literature. I advocate that the methods be turned exactly upside-down and back-end-foremost, and to the support of this revolution I bring, and I think I need to bring, nothing but a little smattery knowledge of genetic psychology . . ."

That is all that survives of my lecture, but its extreme drift can be inferred from the early preface to my *Enjoyment of Poetry*: "The separation of the study of literature from that of the subjects it deals with suggests the barren and formal character of it. As usually taught for three years to post-graduates in our universities, it is not worth spending three weeks upon. The best lovers of literature know this, and the academic world will some day know it and will cast about for a real science which they may teach to those who are going to read literature to the young. That science will be psychology in its widest sense."

Such being the nature of my revolution, it was a satisfaction that my ferocious inquisitor, J. McKeen Cattell, joined me, so to speak, on the barricades, giving credits in psychology to students who attended my lectures on poetry.

Except for prestige and the title "Associate in Philosophy," I drew no pay for this job. But that did not matter; I was getting fifty dollars for suffrage lectures now, and more lectures than I wanted. The course in poetics was a part of my preparation for a book which, besides defining poetry, must teach its values. The book must be scientific, yet not obtrusively so. I must live my way so deeply into the concepts of psychology that I could express them in the language of life. That was my ideal, and I was mature enough to know that a little actual teaching of the subject would help me achieve it.[1]

In matters of love I was still juvenile. My failure with the beauteous Amazon, and the barrier of Ruth's youngness—she was only a few miles away, but how many years as a Freshman at Vassar —kept up a nocturnal sadness in my heart. I loved my mother in this period, I think, more than ever before—"more freely, and, as it were, overtly," as I said to her in a letter. Our intimacy about Inez had made a breach in my reserve. Indeed I had come near, once in the spring when she was ill, to actually saying what she meant to me:

"It makes my soul give out to think of you lying there mournful —all that brilliant, beautiful, humorous life stopped. O how I loved you this time! . . . I kind of feel as if you were my child, and I must go home to you—but all the same I know you are not, and that I depend on you as much as I did at first for the very power and spirit of life. Be as peaceful as you can for my sake, and be well in your mind. I need you and love you forever."

Crystal was still drafting a workman's compensation law for New

---

[1] Fourteen years later this revolution was started all over again at Cambridge University by I. A. Richards. It was started with the highbrow terminology which I had been headstrong to avoid, but with a conception of the thought process which is remote, in my opinion, from psychological science. According to this conception thought has, and need have, nothing to do with action. And on the basis of it, Mr. Richards arrives at the fantastic proposition that while the scientists confine themselves to "pure" knowledge, the poets should take over *without knowledge* the task of determining our actions. "It is not necessary to know what things are in order to take up fitting attitudes to them," Mr. Richards asserts. And he expects the poets, by selecting "attitudes" in total ignorance of facts, to save us all from "chaos." This doctrine of sentimentalism in art and obscurantism in morals, being put forward in the guise of psychology, has made critical minds impatient of the very idea of a scientific approach to poetics. All this seems very unfortunate to me, but it does not prevent Mr. Richards from being a wonderfully devoted teacher and evangelist of poetry. (Mr. Richard's theory will be found abundantly quoted as well as criticized in *The Literary Mind: Its Place in an Age of Science*, pp. 297-317, and in the enlarged edition of *Enjoyment of Poetry*, pp. 247-264. His own chief books are: *Principles of Literary Criticism, Practical Criticism*, and *Science and Poetry*.)

York state, but was also preoccupied with a robust young insurance agent from Milwaukee named Wallace Benedict. A common interest in work accidents had brought them together, hers having its focus in the workers, his in the insurance fees. He was quick and open-minded, genial, witty, and ready to embrace anything from socialism to Shinto, if you could prove to his honestly logical brain that the stream of daily pleasure would be increased by it. Although philo-sophically I stood near him, Bennie's concentration on pleasure was a little abhorrent to me—it was so brash, and pleasure for him had so little to do with attaining ideals. He was temperate and ruled by his intelligence, and yet he always seemed to me more epicure than Epicurean. From the world of devotional humanitarianism in which Crystal had grown up he was so far removed that their close friend-ship was a pain to my mother and a topic of curious speculation to us all. His sturdy boyish masculinity, contrasting with something milk-blooded in the cerebral and social-worker types around her, aroused Crystal for the first time physically. And he was one of those rare males—why rare, only nature's perversity can explain—who like to have the woman they love amount to something. His admiring passion gave her poise and confidence.

I had no such source of poise but only the wish for it. Marjorie was still my good friend, but ours was a specialized intellectual and literary relation. She did not live in my world of athletic fun and informal adventure. And apart from her, it seemed to me I had never found pleasure in a girl without romantic or amorous emotion. I knew that a life friendship could not be built on these emotions. I wanted to experience with a girl companion the same simple realistic enjoyment that I did with a friend like Sid Wood or Baldy Mann or my mother. It seemed to me that the girls who attracted me romantically were not fertile enough in ideas to keep a conversation interesting. "If only I could get rid of these cumber-some and inconsequent brains of mine, you know," I wrote to my mother, "I believe I could get along with some heavenly female form. But I get impatient if people don't start a new idea every day or so. I'll never stick to anybody else the way I do to you."

I did know a girl who could give me this realistic enjoyment, though I had not thought so. It was Ida Rauh, whom I had rejected as a "decorative negation" in Crystal's apartment when I first came to New York. I ran into her one day on the diagonal sidewalk crossing Washington Square, and she asked me to come home with her and have a cup of tea.

"Home?" I said. "Do you live anywhere?"

"I live right up there," she said, pointing to one of the big corner windows of the apartment house at 4th Street and MacDougal. "It's a wonderful place to see New York from—and hear it too, if you like noise."

She smiled vividly, and I discovered adorable crinkles at her eye corners that I had never noticed before. I turned back with her, and she actually ran up the little outside steps to the door. She behaved like a child—like a living and growing thing. I could hardly believe my eyes.

It seemed that the long sulk about her eminent friend had spent itself, and Ida had decided after all, and even at the risk of being "bourgeois," to spend her tidy little income living a life. She had a maid, and not only gave me tea, but a very good dinner and therewith much vivacious debate.

"Brownstone front" was our word for bourgeois then, and I laughed at Ida because her apartment house did have such a front. But there was no truth under the gibe. She was a fervent rebel still—half-Nietzschean, half-Marxian, half-anarchist, believing in free love and a freed proletariat, and as various in conversation as anyone I ever knew. Besides having read omnivorously and critically, she had studied law and been admitted to the bar. And all this wealth of knowledge seemed to have come suddenly to life. Just as the dark, city-bred, tragic quality in her nature had once repelled me, it now charmed me, and for the same reason—because it was alien. I wrote to my mother:

"Ida Rauh has a motto on her wall—'Honesty, Simplicity, Intolerance.' I didn't like it at first, but I do now. It suggests an untrammeled and dynamic character. I want to be one."

Ida had a very admiring friend named Elsa, who was as bright to my spirit's eyes as Ida was sombre. Plump and pearly toothed and wild-rose cheeked, and free, impulsive, courageous, a born Bohemian girl, taking all things with a laugh, Elsa as contrast and complement made dining at Ida's an Elysian pleasure. Others came for this pleasure and enhanced it: Jo Davidson, jocular black-bearded young East Side Jew with a genius for sculpture; Arthur Bullard, slim, calm, and sallow, erudite and kindly, who was beginning to write socialist novels; Hutchins Hapgood, philosophical anarchist with a deep voice and a groping mind, both swayed completely by his emotions; Mary Field, another anarchist, but witty and mischievous about it instead of philosophical; Genevieve Onslow, the banker's daughter from Chicago, who roamed the earth searching for the ultimate wisdom, but could not put the simplest thought into intelligible speech. These were some of the friends who came to Ida's table or dropped in for tea and sat by the big window looking across the square. I found myself often among them, and often returning to finish the argument with Ida after they had gone. The miracle had happened: I really loved to talk with a beautiful woman!

For however they might argue about it, Ida was beautiful. Elsa and I agreed about that, and I quoted Bacon's aphorism: "There is no excellent beauty that hath not some strangeness in the proportion." Besides the irregular charm of her features, Ida possessed the grace of a black panther and a voice like a viola. These traits gave pleasure to me without making me desirous of anything beyond her presence and our conversation. And in my state of dismay with myself as a lover, my sense of failure with Inez, my sure knowledge that with Ruth I could never come down from passion to daily companionship, this fact was reassuring. I am afraid I had lost my nerve about the folly of growing up and was worried lest I be a boy all my life. My friendship with Ida persuaded me that I was a man. I did not have to exhibit myself in swimming and diving and sailing and baseball and pagan sermons and prayers in order to be happy. In Ida's company, especially with Elsa's mirthfulness forming the background, I could even flourish in winter and in the city. I could be, or seem to be, notwithstanding my unslakable madness for Ruth, a normal person. Ida's friendship thus became to me a kind of refuge from the problem of love.

Such was my emotional equilibrium when one night as Crystal and I were going to bed the telephone rang. It was long distance—it was Elmira—it was my father's thin but firm voice:

"Max, your mother has had a stroke and is very sick. You and Crystal must pack your things and take the first train home."

"Is she dead?"

"No, but she is very sick."

"Is she unconscious?"

"Yes."

"All right, Daddy. Be brave. We will take the midnight train."

My mother's body was lying on her bed fighting desperately for breath when I came in. The evening before she had gone into her bedroom to undress. My father, in his room across the hall and up a little stairway, had heard her call "Sam!" in a muffled voice as though someone were strangling her. He had found her clinging to the bedpost, trying to hold herself from falling, and had lifted her onto the bed. She had not spoken since. Her whole body was inert, her face drawn all out of shape, her mind apparently extinguished, and the paralysis was rapidly encroaching on her power to breathe.

The struggle of her life-force, or what was left of it, to keep up that breathing was astounding as well as horrible to me. It continued for forty-eight hours, loud and raucous and resistless as the detonations of an airplane motor. I never had realized what an engine a living body is, what a literal and real explosive force is denoted by that abstract phrase: the will to live. Once, subsequently, when I held a captured swallow in my hand and felt the lightning speed of its heart-beats, I realized this truth again. Most of us take life for granted as a languid-flowing thing, not much more tense or miraculous than the winds and rivers. But we are high-power, internal-combustion engines, all of us.

It may be that few bodies would have fought so hard for breath as my mother's did. Her mind's everlasting thirst of experience must have reflected a highly dynamic conjunction of physical forces. In the last year of her life, as I have related, she had learned to swim, had begun to speak without a manuscript, had gone to Dr. Brill, the first psychoanalyst to open an office in America, and had decided to leave the church. "Dad wants to die here, but I say I'm not going to get 'stuck' anywhere," she wrote. Dr. Brill remembers my mother with a wondering admiration. Her coming to him at all at that time when "even to people who were not ministers, psychoanalysis was regarded as obscene," astonished him, and still more the bold and determined way in which she told him of her intimate sexual life —or lack of it.

"She had so sound a view of things and so much melancholy," he tells me, "that I did not think I could help her. To go into it deeply would have disturbed more than relieved her."

That melancholy was mine, too, and in its shadows I had grown so familiar with the thought of my mother's death that its coming was not an overwhelming event. The violence I have spoken of, the violence of her body's effort to breathe, was the sole new thing in the experience. As we tiptoed around the house waiting for her to die, I was conscious of a disturbance of my skin and circulation such as might attend extreme emotion, but I could not find the emotion. I was blank and matter-of-fact and very intellectual in naming over to myself the things that still made my own life interesting—chief among them my volume of poems and my growing book, *Enjoyment of Poetry*. In these I had a sense of her companionship, for she had written to me in one of her last letters:

"You have the gift of the word fitly spoken. It is yours in full flower, and if only I can somehow feel this, in all the various places to which the various parts of me go when I die, it will be immortality enough for me."

Second after that came my love for Ruth, and a decision I deduced from the presence of death to take her wholly into my arms at the next opportunity and pour out the truth of my passion while it was still young. And third my free life in New York, with its developing romance of political ideas and beliefs, so companionably shared with Crystal and finding so friendly a focus in Ida's dinner table and the big couch by her window on Washington Square. These interests sound sane and collected, but they contained enough conflicting charges of electricity to split me in two once the binding gravitation toward my mother was removed.

Our family did not believe in funerals. My mother particularly, though she had officiated with a specialized talent at hundreds of these mundane ceremonies, regarded them and yet more the doctoring of corpses that preceded them as barbaric. She had written an essay on this subject which no religious journal found the courage to print, and had many times expressed a wish that her dead body be burned and disposed of as useless, and no fuss made about it. We all agreed with her and we obeyed her wish. The day was Saturday on which she died; the church was closed the next day, and on the following Sunday a memorial service was held with selected music and words of appreciation by a few fellow citizens. The most eminent, Z. R. Brockway, after testifying that of all his religious teachers she had been closest to him, said:

"Annis Ford Eastman was brave—possessed in full measure the courage of her convictions—but her bravery was so mingled with gentleness, delicate considerateness, and was so unpretentious that this characteristic did not always appear upon the surface. She was hotly intolerant of sham and consoling sophistries. At the same time, she was most tolerant of honest difference. . . . Withal she was extraordinarily tactful, far beyond mere adroitness and finesse."

And these words were spoken by the Baptist minister from across the Park:

"I may say here what I said in my own pulpit last Sunday morning, that she was the only woman I ever knew who took up public speaking that did not, by so doing, lose something of that fine flavor of womanliness which is so attractive to us all. . . . I do not mean simply that in everything that she said and did she was natural, sincere, and unaffected. I mean something more than that. I mean that in herself she was natural according to God and according to the harmonies of the universe. As I understand her theological views I do not agree with them, but I do believe that Mrs. Eastman was one of the choicest saints of God. . . ."

As I sat there, bereft and yet proud of my heart's possession of her, it seemed to me that her rarest trait was that one which she preached with the most eloquence—unceasing growth. It seemed to me as though almost every morning of my youth I had been lifted and launched anew by some vividly conceived scheme she would propose for making life a great thing.

I had looked at my mother's shrunken and bluish face just before her body was taken to the crematory, impelled to experience the real and complete fact of death, and I looked at the ashes of her bones when they came back in a small can with a hinged cover too much like the one she kept cookies in. Even in this way I could achieve no adequate emotion. I was shocked, but I was not deeply moved. Only when I left it all behind and went up to Glenora and wandered in the yellowing woods beside the lake—wandered along the path where she had met me with tears of joy when I came back from my western adventure and my harsh rebellion against her love —only then did this demon of numbness let go of me. There at last I lay down among the falling leaves, moved rather by the sentiment of her death than the fact, and cried until I was tired out. And for relief, for companionship, for the poet's indispensable weakness, the need to *make something* out of his emotion, I wrote down the thoughts that attended my grief in a letter to Ruth. Young as she was, Ruth would have to share my sorrow, because she was the one—at least while I was in Glenora and among those leaves of the dying summer, she was the one I loved.

It never entered my mind that my mother might still be living in another world. The idea of immortality for the innumerable billions of human beings going back to the Stone Age, and then the absurdly exact line to be drawn between human and animal, make the conception almost inaccessible to a factual mind. My grandfather believed in it, but with a struggle that made him cry out: "O, that I could hold the tho't and reality vividly and constantly before my mind during the brief period of my stay here!" My father said: "Max, I hope for it." My mother: "I do not feel that there is anything in me worthy of eternal life." And in me the notion of immortality faded so early that I can not remember ever dwelling upon it. I think this may be true of many good church members. To "be a believer" as a mode of social adjustment in this world is so different from *believing* in another.

My heart was overfilled with that yearning which, mixed with sentiments of infinity, pronounces impossible the ceasing to be of one so justly loved as my mother. But my mind was too firmly committed to fact and logic to hear the voice of this yearning. I knew well that if I believed in immortality only after my mother died, that would be evidence against the belief—just as the slogan, "There are no atheists in foxholes," argues against God's existence, though few pause to perceive it. I at least had no choice; I was a born bondsman to reason; I had to take my sorrow straight. Not only my mother had ceased, but the loves in her heart—this for me is the supreme pang in the pathos of death—had ceased to be. Her love for my lost child-brother Morgan, never once flickering or dying down in her breast, never for a day forgotten, had been to me sacred and sublime. It lay beyond the outmost boundaries of any noble trait or achievement I might aspire to for my shallow and fluid self. And now that divine thing too was gone. No one loved Morgan any more. No one would ever say again so long as time stretched out: "Oh, how I love you *all*, but nothing can cure the ache and longing in my heart for Morgan. Eternity can not be long enough to make up for these years without him . . ."

PART VI

EDITOR AND REVOLUTIONIST

Chapter 44

Marxism and Marriage

W HEN I returned to New York I found in my mail a letter from my mother: "I'll be *very* glad of a speech opportunity in New York. I'm so well! Wonderful weather, and I've had two automobile rides—long ones—this fall." It was dated October 20, the day that she was stricken down. For twelve years now, ever since I went away to Mercersburg, these letters had been pouring a stream of zest and vitality into my languid nerves. I sensed dimly when I held this last one in my hand the magnitude of my loss. I have her omnivorous interest in life and growth, but lack the energy to fulfill it. I get tired when I am not excited and want to lean on something or lie down. My mother never lay down except to take a nap. Even her melancholy was an active task, a painting of the whole world black. I say that I sensed dimly how I had been sustained by this vital force in her, but that is hardly true. Only as I look back now, after years of blind wandering and blundering among loves, do I realize that this was the essential thing my mother gave me. This was the quality I most needed in a woman friend.

It was, by a sad chance, the quality most notably lacking in both Ruth and Ida. Notwithstanding feats of brilliant vigor when her shapely body was at play, Ruth sagged as I did when the game was over. She was a moody girl—at times you would be tempted to say glum—and like me inclined to let the rest of the family do the work. And Ida, though her sparkling verve at conversation time concealed it, was a prodigy of indolence. She was not only too lazy to work but too lazy to play. I used to tell her that she would rather do nothing than do what she wanted to.

Ida would answer that her "race" had lived too many thousands of years to have an energetic interest in life. "We Jews are all filled with a cosmic ennui," she would say. And I would unsheathe against her the fact that there is no such thing biologically as a Jew and that I have had ancestors in the world as long as she. She would retire before my logic, only to come back after a while and say the same thing again. And then I would not answer, but inwardly I would turn sharply away as from death itself.

My first task in the new solitude was the practical, and now that Mother and I could no longer laugh over it together, rather forlorn one of "organizing" the Men's League for Woman Suffrage. With all the letters we had folded and stamps we had licked, only fifty of those "men of civic importance" had signed up as prospective members. Their civicness was of such high quality, however, that we decided to go ahead. At Mr. Villard's direction I prepared a press-release, describing the nature and prospects of the league, its membership, the principal events of the meeting, the officers elected and what they had to say. We met at the City Club on a late afternoon in November. The press was not invited; it was told about the meeting afterward. And it was not told how many of the officers elected, to say nothing of the electing members, were present at the meeting. To the best of my recollection there were five in all. However, it is a matter of history that some fifty of the biggest and best of New York's citizenry assembled at the City Club on a late afternoon in November 1910, and formed themselves into a League for Woman Suffrage. The newspapers of the whole country were full of their pictures, of interviews with them, of statements by them that they meant business and that many thousands of dollars were behind the movement.

I was amused at the large press blossom born by our slim stemlike gathering at the City Club. It taught me something that one has, alas, to learn. Later in the season when we gave a public dinner at the Aldine Club, and six hundred people paid three dollars and stayed until midnight to hear why woman suffrage is important, it was really exciting. When we filled Cooper Union to the doors, with Governor Brady of Idaho speaking, a row of political big shots behind him on the platform, and an audience largely composed of men cheering votes for women far into the night, it was still more exciting. But the newspapers could not see it. Even when the Men's League occupied five blocks, four abreast, marching solid in the suffrage parade up Fifth Avenue the following May, the press could see only a grudging thousand of them.

Although my heroic appearance as I marched at the head of that parade has been eloquently described to me, I was not there. I was miles away on the Atlantic when it took place. I do not like parades, and moreover the suffrage movement was getting too fashionable to appeal to that in me which desires to suffer a little in some high cause. Marching with a thousand men, after what I had been through as their lonely organizer, did not strike me as heroic enough to demand my presence. However, the particular cause of my absence was personal, and to explain it I must go back to the story of my heart's driftings after my mother died. . . .

Seeing how important a happy love is, it is strange we so rarely go in search of it. The idea that the world contains all kinds of girls, and that among them must be one shaped aptly to my needs, seems never to have occurred to me. At least I never thought of enlarging my acquaintance in order to find that girl. A romantic young person rarely does. He leaves it to chance, to an accidental environment, to circumscribe him on this momentous question.

I was especially passive, because so firmly convinced of my inability to combine the romance of love with the fact of companionship. That I should be in love with Ruth and in friendship with Ida, and not mated or completed by either of them, seemed a part of my inevitable lot in life. It now seemed inevitable too that romantic love should belong to my outdoor, rural, summer self, and real companionship to the indoor winters in the city. The summer self, although he worked as well and probably wrote better, lived only three months as against nine for his more sombre companion; and this suggested that he was not only rural, but incidental, a creature not of serious life but of vacations from it.

> Warm-limbed and lively-eyed and full of youth,
> Quick-laughing youth, with all things swift and gay
> Hovering round you on your wilful way
> Into my passionate heart, I love you, Ruth . . .

So I began a sonnet of annunciation, but I did not finish it. I could not take the helm and sail in any direction. Between city and country—realism and romance—exotic and familiar—oriental and occidental—dark and blue-eyed—I drifted back and forth.

I did write a complete sonnet to the Ruth of my dreams, the one I possessed so perfectly. I had gone down to Tryon, North Carolina, after my mother's death to visit my poet-brother, Ralph Erskine. The real Ruth wrote to me there, but I dared not answer with my sonnet. I was still resolved to put my arms around her and try to explain my whole feeling when we should meet, but until then I could hardly burst upon her with a poem of our consummated love. So my timidity told me. In truth I do not know what better way to avow a secret passion I could have devised.

> As the crag eagle to the zenith's height
> Wings his pursuit in his exalted hour
> Of her the tempest-reared, whose airy power
> Of plume and passion challenges his flight
> To that wild altitude, where they unite,
> In mutual tumultuous victory
> And the swift sting of nature's ecstasy,
> Their shuddering pinions and their skyward might—
> As they, the strong, to the full height of heaven
> Bear up that joy which to the strong is given,
> Thus, thus do we, whose stormy spirits quiver
> In the bold air of utter liberty,
> Clash equal at our highest, I and thee,
> Unconquered and unconquering forever.

I stuck firmly by my resolution to come close to Ruth at the next opportunity. Indeed I solved with Napoleonic strategy, when I went up to Elmira that winter, the problem of getting off alone with her —difficult because we belonged to separate groups and generations. Fortunately the river froze, and the whole town went skating. It was natural to skate with Ruth, and I guided her way up the river into the hills, where we took off our skates and disappeared in one of those pine-enfolded, stony glens that none but lovers have a use for. I brushed away the snow from a plot of pine-needles and made a fire to keep us warm. We sat close but very much wrapped up in bunchy winter clothing, very woolly, and thereby not only insulated but a little estranged from each other, for ours had been a summer friendship.

Ruth was a sufficiently physical and lustful little girl. At the age of twelve she caused a sensation in Sunday school when a handsome male Sunday school teacher asked her "What is love?" by answering, "Love is a funny feeling in your stomach." But through some kink or cantankerousness in her instincts, she reserved these feelings for such lowly beings as Sunday school teachers and felt for me a perfectly celestial adoration. Whether it is a matter of the basic chemisms, or what I had to pay for disguising my love as diving instructions and pagan prayers throughout her girlhood, I could never tell. But that celestial adoration has stood between us for a lifetime, as darkening at times to me as it has been a kind of eternal dawn to Ruth. On this occasion it was disastrous. For I had only a little more than put my arms around her when she managed again to speak words that made me feel guilty and frightened because she was so young.

"I love to be close to you, but I wish you wouldn't be quite so physical."

Knowing in my private mind that I needed nothing so much as to "be physical" freely and completely, those words caused in me a mood of despair. Eight years had passed now since I had taken Goethe for my hero, and I was still, to my strong shame and very real anxiety, a demi-virgin. It was not narcissistic preoccupation that caused this, not any genuine habit of pleasure in myself; my erotic preoccupation with girls whether in image or reality was complete. The cause was only that mixture of sheer bashfulness and reticence with the relics of my baby mania for "being good." To a sophisticated lover Ruth's innocent remark might have been a challenge. To me it was an insurmountable barrier. It meant that my rural and wilfully youthful self could not solve the central problem of his life. It pushed me back into the drift toward the city and toward the folly —as I still in many respects regard it—of growing up. My friendship with Ida, although not built on passion, was developing in an atmosphere of mature belief in freedom which made a complete passionate experience at least possible.

Another factor swaying me in this direction was a crystallization of my political views, which occurred during that same winter in New York. I owe this rather to Karl Marx than Ida Rauh, but still it was Ida who taught me the pith of the Marxian doctrine. I had arrived by other roads, as I have related, at an agnostic, antipatriotic, and extreme rationalism. I hated class distinctions, and I had yearned toward a kind of pastoral utopia where people would be more free and equal, more friendly, more given to dwelling in truth and reality, than they are in this money-getting world. I had felt a duty to do something in the cause of this utopia, "to turn minister or reformer," as I put it, but had been "overwhelmed with a sense of the futility of it—what I call human hopelessness." People are what they are, and you can't preach or argue them into being something else: that is what I had learned by living so close to a church. And so in spite of my belief in joy and unconventionality, my revolt against God and the national flag, I was in political matters far from a "wild radical." In those conversations with Ida which were becoming so dear to me I played in general the sceptic's role. Ida was the flaming rebel, dramatic and exciting to my admiration, I the cool and relatively scientific critic, sharing her emotion, but checking her results with my sense of the sad brute facts of man and nature.

The story used to be told later that I was kicked out of Columbia for my socialist opinions, but nothing of that kind happened. Indeed the historian Charles Beard recalls that he was especially requested by President Butler to persuade me to stay. I had never intended to teach, however, except for the purpose of learning, and when I finished my course in poetics in February, I felt that on that subject I had learned enough. I left Columbia because I wanted to concentrate on writing my book and writing poetry.

During the same winter, however, and very soon after leaving Columbia, I took the final step to socialism. Ida and I attended together one of those Collectivist Dinners at Kalil's Restaurant, and as we were riding home on the elevated, I remarked that the speeches had been pretty good, Morris Hillquit's especially.

"It seems fine to work for an ideal like that," I said, "even though you may never achieve it. I wouldn't mind calling myself a socialist if I could be permitted to have doubts. Only I can't understand the rant about class struggle and class war. Classes, it seems to me, and all that prejudice and hate and bitterness, are just what we want to get rid of."

"Why, Max, that's the heart of the whole Marxian doctrine," Ida said in surprise. "Didn't you ever read anything by Marx or Engels?"

"What do you mean?" I said a little belligerently.

"You don't think the people who own the earth are going to let go of it voluntarily, do you—that you can educate them into it? That's utopian socialism. Marx's idea is that the working class, acting in its own economic interest, will take over the industries and socialize them. After that you'll have a society without classes, a real society, and real reform and education can begin."

She summarized it as clearly and forcefully as that, and I gazed at her in amazement.

"Ida, that's a perfectly wonderful idea!" I exclaimed.

"Of course! And it's an international idea too. The class division cuts across all national boundaries and puts an end to patriotic wars. Marx would have been a great statesman if he had never thought of anything but the one phrase: 'Workers of the world, unite!' "

I remember that conversation so distinctly because it was a turning point in my intellectual life. My impulse toward an extreme social ideal and my obstructing sense of the hard facts of human nature were reconciled in a flash by this Marxian idea of enlightened class struggle toward socialism. Here was a method of attaining the ideal based upon the very facts that made it seem unattainable. I need no longer extinguish my dreams with my knowledge. I need never again cry out: "I wish I believed in the Son of God and his second coming!"

I began the next day to read the books Ida told me to, including an old Aveling translation of the first volume of *Das Kapital* that she lugged out. I found them disappointingly alien in idiom and mental attitude; it seemed to me that Marx and Engels did not know how to formulate their method of progress in a scientific manner. They had an involved, abstractly pretentious way of presenting ideas which were in essence simple and clear. But I was not energetically curious about this; my real subject, after all, was poetics. When I finished *Enjoyment of Poetry*, I could write another book expounding in my own terms this doctrine of "hard-headed idealism," as I called it—of the *way to go* from the real toward the ideal. Meanwhile, taking the good with the bad, I would call myself a revolutionary socialist.

This, of course, was a very act of separation from our Cherith utopia with its pagan prayers and Emersonian moralism. Whatever role Marxism may have played in history, it played a critical role in my personal life. It gave New York and Ida such an advantage over Ruth and the sun-warm vineyards that I drifted steadily now —I can not pretend I steered—into the delicately offered haven of Ida's love.

A great favoring force was my escape in her arms from that prison of bashfulness and overexcitement in which as a romantic lover I had been confined. My love for Ida was classic. It was factual, familiar, everyday, indubitable reality, giving the mind as well as the senses vital pleasure. If I missed some sort of transport in this experience, I learned in the course of it, perhaps for that very reason, to be a lover.

Even with such factors pulling the same way as her charms, I would not have chosen Ida for a life companion had the choice presented itself in those antique terms. We were emancipated from all that. We were radicals, revolutionaries, unposing pioneers of what was soon to become a conscious pose called "Greenwich Village." Marriage had always seemed utterly unromantic to me, and "husband" and "wife" among the most distasteful words in the language. I do not know how rare this form of idealism really is. In poetry it is solely expressed, so far as I know, by Thomas Carew in his erotic verse "The Rapture":

> . . . the hated name
> Of husband, wife, lust, modest, chaste or shame,
> Are vain and empty words, whose very sound
> Was never heard in the Elysian ground.

In me, at any rate, it was native and surefooted like my sense of beauty, or my recoil from patriotism. And although I think Ida had, under the surface of her consciousness, more primitive and self-protective instincts, she was of like opinion. All we ever decided upon was that we would take a trip to Europe together. To that end, however, considering my prominence in the suffrage movement and my father's position in Elmira—he was still head pastor of the Park Church—a legal marriage seemed obligatory. It was, after all, if no property was involved and no children contemplated, a negligible formality. So I told myself in moments of painful hesitation, and Ida agreed.

Crystal and I had not been drawn closer by our mother's death. It seemed rather to increase my strong resistance to intimacy with her. Though we lived together, we did not talk often about our sorrow. We did not talk in complete frankness about her interest in Bennie or mine in Ida. Only long after her death I learned from Dr. Brill that she went to him for help in bringing her "libido" down, as he put it, *von oben nach unten*. And she never knew anything about the anxious problem that sex presented to me throughout the years that we were together. It is astonishing what good and constant friends people can be without coming close to each other at all. I wonder how it really was between Dorothy and William Wordsworth!

Crystal had decided by midwinter to marry Bennie in the spring and move to Milwaukee. She was sick in February—perhaps the decision made her sick—and went home to Elmira to rest.

"I've been feeling very scared about getting married all through this sickness," she wrote. "Getting back to New York and living with you was the hope I fed my drooping spirits on—not Milwaukee and the married state. Your suggestion that if I can't stand it, you'll know it's not for you, gives me a humorous courage. Perhaps after we've both experimented around a few years, we may end up living together again."

That was the mood in which we both approached this fatal step —though Crystal, I must say, really decided to take it, whereas I tried with all my skill both to marry and not to marry. A lecture trip took me to Milwaukee in April, and I spent three pleasant days with Bennie and liked him in his home as well as I had in ours. Crystal wrote me there:

"I somehow feel my whole life trembling in the balance while you are in Milwaukee with Bennie. And yet I believe, in this choosing of a man or woman, your relatives and former companions and dear intimate friends, your whole past associations in fact, don't play much part. It's a thing you've got to do bravely all by yourself— without looking back."

She added in a postscript: "I'm thinking much about Ida and Ruth."

But I did not respond to that. I never could speak to Crystal about my feeling for Ruth—there was too much naked lust in it. And now especially, since that dismaying afternoon in the woods, it had lost somewhat its quality of ideal dream. In protecting her own exaltation Ruth had injured mine. She had made my ineffable yearning to share with her life's purest ecstasy seem like mere prurient exploration—an effort to "make" a girl, as men say who have no gift either for the mutuality or the beauty of sex relations. I did not take this view of it, but I was less than ever inclined to discuss my complicated feelings with Crystal. I knew, of course, that if I went back to Glenora for the summer, I should be madly in love with Ruth again, and that Ida, together with the whole of New York City, would fade to a shadow. But I also knew, or thought I did, that this love was only the spiritual ebullience of unsatisfied desire. Ruth was too young, I told myself, and not intellectual enough for me. Once the romance of yearning, once that delicious drink, the thirst of the unattained, was removed from between us, we would have little to talk about. I felt falsely sure of that. With my mother gone, and my sister about to be married, a friend with grown-up wit and a mind full of ideas was what I wanted. I wanted someone with whom I was moved, miraculously, to conversation. That was what I had in Ida. And I had it, or so I thought, without any prison taint from the word "forever." Who that believed in the poem of life would renounce, out of mere childish attachment to a summer landscape and a neighbor's ungrown daughter, an invitation to see Europe with a strange, dark, beautiful, and brilliant woman whose companionship he loved? What did a little thing like a marriage ceremony matter?

The choice seemed merely intelligent. Ida was going to Europe anyway and had already taken her passage. She had enough money to pay my fare, and I had a few hundred dollars to take along for expenses. In this casual way it came about that on May 4, 1911, Ida Rauh and I went over to Paterson, New Jersey, and were married in the City Hall by a round-bellied justice of the peace. He took a cigar out of his mouth for the ceremony, and said to me, when I confessed I had not brought a ring:

"Well, just step up here and clasp her hand—kick that spittoon out o' yer way, if it bothers you."

Although pleased by his way of looking at it, I was not deeply reassured. I came back from Paterson feeling that I had betrayed my ideals; I came back feeling homesick. I did not want to get married. I did not want to go to Europe either—not until next fall anyway. I wanted to spend the summer in Glenora.

"But you can't be a romantic baby all your life," I said to myself. "You believe in Marxism, not utopianism. You would be even less downright ready to marry Ruth than Ida. In mere fairness to her, you ought to stop dabbling in that irresponsible romance. It is not the realness, but the unrealness of Glenora, not your ambition but your exhibitionism, that beckons you. Aren't there lakes in Europe, and doesn't the sun shine on the hills there as in America? You can write your book wherever you are, and that is the real job. At twenty-eight, isn't it time that you started living in the real world?"

There was enough truth in these reflections to suppress a bewildered child. And therefore it was a wholly mature and resolute adult who walked up the gangplank of the *Königen Louise* on May 6, 1911, and set sail with a dear companion for Gibraltar.

Chapter 45

I Lose My Religion

IN THE morning when I awoke to find myself on a boat with
Ida, and the boat in midsea, I was seized with a craving to escape as sharp and shocking as a cramp in the muscles. Its grip
was alien to me and outside my scheme of volition. It was not the
result of thinking and would pay no heed to a thought process. I
had no self-knowledge against it. All my self-knowledge could do was
make me sure that, even though I conquered this spasm, I would
never feel pure love for Ida again. I would never be joyous in our adventure.

Shamed and horrified at this morbid growth which seemed over-
night to have converted me into a monster, I made elaborate movements to conceal it. I went through all the forms of that affirmative
excitement which, though shadowed with doubts, had been actual
before and accessible to my will. It was no longer accessible. I was
sorry I had come. I was sorry I had been married. It was no fun to
go to Europe with a hopelessly grown-up person, a stranger to my
childish delight in experience. It was no solution of the problem of
my divided self to wed the more congenial of two that were half-
loved. To say, moreover, that we did not believe in marriage, or
that we had made this little concession only to placate public opinion,
was flagrant self-deception. In order to placate public opinion we
would have to announce our marriage, and we would have to *not*
announce our mental reservations. Since announcement is all that
marriage consists of, the reservations are nothing. . . . Such truths
fled racing through my undermind while I performed the motions,
and the speech, and even gradually the surface thoughts, of a happy
lover.

I found that I could hide my malady, not perhaps from Ida's
subtler feelings, but from the mind of her that talked with me. I

could, at times, be extra tender because of the vile trick my character had played upon her. I could even, in moments which I cultivated assiduously, hide from myself, or forget, or forswear into annihilation, the fact that I was captive to an absolute, implacable, and all-pervading sense of loss. This feeling would lurk octopus-like, sometimes for hours, in a deep crevice of my being, and only when the impulse came to taste a joy, or speak a word of abandoned love, his ruthless tentacle would creep forth and strangle it.

This process of suppression was accompanied by physical symptoms without which, as I look back, I think it might have been impossible: an overpowering day-and-night-long sleepiness while I was on the boat and, after we landed, an attack of hives that placed me among the untouchables for more than a month. I described that sleepiness to my father laughingly, for I was concerned to keep his spirits up, but it did not amuse me as much as I pretended.

"Somewhere between the Azores and Gibraltar I take my pencil in hand, and myself too, for the first time, to pass you a remark . . . I haven't had a thought or made a voluntary motion since we started. This letter is an act of heroism. I've slept all the time, in my bunk and out of it. I'm asleep now. I dream about little short-legged energetic people—clergymen and cripples mostly (you know these earnest cripples) steaming around the deck as though they were bent on the enterprise of the century. It's a bad dream. I roll over in my chair—and behold the band is assembling on my left. Another nightmare—a German band. It brausts ein Ruf wie Donnerhall. There's one good thing about the band, though. It drives away the people. They do their energizing on the other side of the ship, and I pass into a deeper coma.

"I did do one other act of heroism yesterday. I did it out of respect for my heredity, and if I do say so myself, I did it like a man. I went over the ship from stem to stern, asking questions in all languages of everybody who had anything to do with anything, and creating the impression that I was both alive and conscious. I kept thinking how proud you would be of me . . ."

The ultimate source of humor, as Mark Twain said, is sorrow. I do not mean to boast of the humor here, but only to underline the sorrow.

This was my honeymoon!

I had lost, in marrying Ida, my irrational joy in life. I had lost my religion. I had committed—irrevocably, it seemed to me—the

Folly of Growing Up. How poignantly I remember the effort it required to lift my will, against the drag of her indifference, to a state
of normal interest in examining that ship! How tired I was! I had
written two years before a Pindaresque poem to Leif Ericson, celebrating him above Columbus because he sailed into the unknown
without purpose except to sail and without practical result.[1]

> Not they that safe in a haven of certainty steer
> From mooring to mooring with faith and with fear,
> And pray for a map of the universe, pointer, and plan,
> When all the blue waves of the ocean the courage of man
> Challenge to venture, not they are the praisers of thee!
> Nor they who sail for the cargo, and dream that the sea,
> In its wanton wild infinite wonder of motion and sound,
> Is bound by a purpose, as their little breathing is bound.
> The profit of thy great sailing to thee was small,
> And unto the world it was nothing—a man, that was all,
> And his deed like a star, to flame in the dull old sky
> Of the story of apathy, age after decorous age going by!

It was the hymn of my religion of earthly living, and I remember
standing in the prow of the vessel in a storm, saying its long lines into
the sea as the great waves tossed me, trying in vain to think that I
was fulfilling them. No—I was a renegade. I was a miserable sinner.
I was lost.

To understand this you must know how charming Ida was—how
gentle and humorous and vivid-tongued and comprehending. In
her company at mealtimes, or times of rest or of ease-taking, I was
at home to a degree that captured and tied me completely. With
strangers she took the burden of conversation and lifted my shyness
so that I enjoyed social exploration as I never had before. She fed
my love of laughter and poetry, too, with little quick-spoken phrases
that recalled Sid Wood and that furnished examples for my coming
books. "That old white horse looks as though he had been used to
scratch matches on." "You find these tall big-toothed English women
all over Europe. They increase the population—I mean they increase
it just by being there." "You look so grouchy, pansies, and yet you
are so bright!"

I have never greatly enjoyed anyone with a cultivated reputation as
a wit; the task of constant appreciation irks my vanity. But this quiet

---

[1] I have been told, since, that Leif Ericson was a Christian missionary, but that only
makes the hero of my poem more divinely lonely.

liveliness of mind and language is mother-dear to me. I copied Ida's little colorful sayings down with my own thoughts in my notebook. And in our daily intercourse I poured her a stream of admiration —that gift or weakness I inherited from my grandfather—which must have compensated in some degree for what she surely felt in her heart I withheld. Otherwise, I do not know how she could have continued to be so kind.

On the other hand, Ida gave me, so far as could be detected, no admiration at all. She was as stingy with praise as she was generous with possessions. She treated me, from the beginning to the end of our relation, as though I were a conceited and overconfident person who needed to be damped down. As I was still engaged, when we came together, in my campaign of self-discipline against egotism, I first thought of this as a trait in her favor. But when we were alone together it made the world very bleak. The Eastman family were strong on mutual appreciation, and I, the youngest and most diffident, had fed on this like a lamb in lush pastures. Now I had to forage for esteem in a stony landscape.

Since we had come out to see the world, and I remembered at Gibraltar that Africa, only eight miles away, is a part of the world, we took the boat over to Tangier. There we found a room at the top of a three-storied hotel that overlooked the Moorish market, a scene which I described to my father as "the strangest, vividest, and almost the most beautiful I ever saw." I was delighted by my first look at Arab life. "It's as though we had crossed right into the Bible. Moses holds the stirrup for you, and Elijah beats your mule from behind. I would almost say Christ himself brought us off in a punt. As beautiful men as I ever saw."

More vividly than these men, I now see Ida walking through that market. The lines of her body are exquisite, her movements as lithe as those of the Arabs, but without buoyancy, without eagerness, without the friendly delight in people, the participation, the merry laughter that would have made Sid Wood or my mother or Crystal so wonderful a companion on this journey. I did not feel revulsion, or even, alas, rebellion, but only despair—a purely painful emotion which I extinguished by catching up to her quickly and beginning to talk. It does not matter, I thought, what woman I am tied to—I don't want to be tied. Only with a sister, a mother, with another boy, only with irresponsible freedom, can I have the full taste of any adventure.

For this reason, with that reverse logic which organic puritanism and a too churchly upbringing perhaps explain, I plunged deeper into my bondage and locked an easy exit. I sat down the next morning in our hotel room, and with donkeys braying the chorus, announced in sixteen letters to my friends that I was married. I wrote a letter to each friend that I thought might be seriously hurt to learn it from another source. When it was done, I felt debased by this unnatural letter writing, unnatural because to me the ceremony meant nothing, and tore up all but six of the letters. I did not send one to Marjorie or Miss Suzie Hopkins. To them I took the liberty of being rude, and to Ruth I wrote merely a friendly statement of the fact.

Aside from my distaste for it, marriage always seemed to me a gauche intrusion on the part of the state and society into the intimacies of a private romance. I had submitted perforce to the state's intrusion, but I still cherished the notion of keeping society from making a fuss over the fact that Ida and I were living together. I wrote to my father:

"You will not be surprised now that Ida and I are married. I've written Crystal and Peter and Baldy and Adra and Aunt Mary. The rest can find out. I don't want them to think of it as 'settling down' and all the rest of the ideas I don't like, so I'm not formally telling them . . . Don't think of it as much of an event. Don't write to Ida or anything like that. Just let it be what it turns out to be."

My father was somewhat bewildered by my attitude, but he was accustomed to that and tried his best to live up to it. His way of being casual was not to mention the subject at all until somebody asked him, and then announce it through the papers. By that time Ida and I were in Italy, and he had another letter in his pocket from Sorrento. In his embarrassment when asked where and when I was married, a contingency I had not been considerate enough to foresee, he allowed the reporters to infer that it was in Sorrento. So instead of a cool statutory function in Paterson, New Jersey, I was credited with a union of throbbing hearts amid the beauties of the Bay of Naples.

"Your friends are happy," my father wrote, "and one would think you the most popular man in the city. All the high-ups and every Tom, Dick and Harry, Susan, Jane and Mary, stop me and want to know about it. 'Married in Sorrento, Italy—very romantic,' is the expression. I've had lots of fun over it."

Dad was a good sport about his rebel children and never failed to back them to the limit before the public. Privately, however, it was anything but fun he had over a blow like this—especially coming, as it did, a few months after Crystal's equally unceremonious marriage in the New York City Hall. She wrote me in Sorrento:

". . . My wedding certainly hit Dad awful hard, but he bore up bravely, and I think his sensibilities were so dulled by the shock that he took your news calmly. It's hard for him to understand your insistence on not being married even though you're married—but he's resigned to not understanding."

Her letter disturbed me, and when I answered my father, I tried to explain myself:

"All right—we were married in Sorrento! Anywhere so it's done, over with and forgotten. Dad, maybe you'll understand me better if I say that I straight out disbelieve in marriage, the whole idea, significance, consequence, and specific result of it. It has done a little good some times, but a lot of harm always. Having this opinion, and also this so strong distaste, you can imagine how restive I would be —having only submitted to it under compulsion of an equally distasteful prudence—to have all my friends 'make much' of it as not only an acceptable but a signal event. No law or ceremony had anything to do with the natural growth and culmination of our friendship, and they won't have anything to do with its ceasing if it ever ceases. So I am glad you got us married at Sorrento and laughed about it . . ."

Ida and I stayed a week and a day in Tangier. Except for a mule ride out into the flowery plains and the usual drive down the coast to the Sultan's palace, we saw little of Africa that was not visible from our hotel room. A plan to journey with a caravan to Fez or Marrakesh arose in my mind, but languished for want of reverberation. I tried conscientiously to have a little adventure of my own. I got up at 2 A.M. one night, hearing weird cries and sounds of running feet and of music echoing up from the city. Taking with me a revolver I had bought in contemplation of that trip to the interior, I crept out just as the moon rose and lost myself in a deep, intricate maze of narrow streets—so narrow they seemed to me like passageways in a beehive. They continued to resound with wailing tunes and drums, and mysterious cowled figures hastened through them, giving me a stare of resentment as they passed. The Moors were holding some kind of a jamboree, and Jews and foreigners were not wanted. It scared me a little without real danger, a pleasant sensation.

My steps led me up finally to a high garden over the city, luxurious and fragrant, and there, as the pale dawn mingled with the moonlight, I heard for the first time a nightingale singing. I heard also the solemnly hollow voices of the muezzins chanting their greeting to the Eternal from the four slim delicate minarets that stood in the sky above the sleeping city. Across the Straits of Gibraltar, as the dawn advanced, I watched the dwindling of a spark of light in some window on the hills of Spain.

That much I achieved in Tangier. But I turned from this my first venture into foreign lands with words of mockery that covered a feeling of defeat:

"It's a climate that puts up a sort of pretense at being hot and then stays cold. I wore thick winter underwear all the time. As I came over here mainly for the purpose of lying in the sun in a white shirt and pants, you can imagine my exasperation. When I think of the town I hear an everlasting hum and chatter of Moors buying and selling and bickering, a continual braying of donkeys, and wailing of oriental horns and chants. This mixes up with a large quantity of dirty smells and scenes of utter poverty—in the midst of which general reminiscence I catch the anticipatory tickle of a flea bite, and I repeat that Tangier is not for us."

Gibraltar I described as "a bleak bare old rock full of foolish little soldiers who think the British Empire is something besides an abstract idea."

I do not know whether I really had hives, or only a violent allergy to flea bites. Or was I perhaps expressing with my whole skin the simple truth which I lacked the courage to state in words, that in taking this trip to Europe with Ida I had made a mistake? Whatever the cause, I was throughout our travels in the Mediterranean about as companionable as a Jersey cow in fly time. I was rubbing myself with ice, or alcohol, or bathing in oatmeal water, from morn to dewy eve, and often several times in the night. It hurts to think what a disheartening soul-mate I must have been from Ida's viewpoint. She did not fail, however, of that long-suffering maternal tenderness which captures both the judicious adult and the bewildered child that dwell in the breast of the elusive male.

When we arrived back in Gibraltar on our way to Italy, I was seized with a dizzy nausea and a veritable paroxysm of itching, my whole hide seeming to be in purple flames and my interior surfaces about to be consumed. I went in desperation to a British physician, who examined me carefully and informed me that I was not dying.

"In fact," he said, "it is a parasite."

"What do you mean, a bedbug?" I exclaimed.

He replied firmly: "A parasite." My first taste of England.

Ida's conduct in this hysterical seizure was so wonderfully tolerant and kind that I praised her extravagantly in a letter to Crystal, and Crystal sealed my doom with: "I can't ever forget that Ida was so good to you when you were sick with all those diseases. That's a big test, isn't it?"

O yes, I was married all right—I wasn't just taking a trip to Europe!

From Gibraltar we sailed for Naples on May 29, and in Naples Ida surprised me with a mutiny. When we arrived late at night in a hot, windowless, inside-opening, cheap hotel room with one lumpy bed instead of two, I proposed as a matter of course that we gather up our bags and go on a hunt for a better place to sleep. But she said very calmly:

"You ought to learn to take things as they come."

Therewith she lay down on that bed, gracefully acquiescing in its undulations, and refused to budge.

It was a crisis in our friendship, the first time anger arose between us. To me the act epitomized that in her which I found horrible: a heaviness of spirit, a lack of resilient interest even in so simple an aspect of life's enjoyment as having comfort. And yet now, as I reflect upon it, I see that she, unaware of this larger fact, was not without justification. It was necessary, even from a therapeutic standpoint, to call a halt somewhere to my fast-galloping hypochondria. I would soon be flat on the floor again with my little pillow, the "divine comforter," under my back.

At any rate we stayed where we were. And after a sleepless night in that unfriendly bed and hot unventilated room, I had little interest in examining Naples except to find the quickest way out. We "did" the museum from 10:30 to 12:00 in the morning, and took the afternoon boat around the bay to Sorrento.

A quartet sang "O Sole Mio" as we danced like a rocking-horse over the waves. I tried to feel excited about being in Italy, but succeeded only in feeling resolute about going to work—on my book, on the Italian language, on the history of revolutions. "Ida is really an angel, and if I study something, I'll be all right." That was my inmost thought as we approached Sorrento, the scene of our supposed romantic marriage.

Our month of June at the Hotel Cocumella was indeed lived in a surf-beat of orange blossoms, and with songs from wedding-bell-like voices, voices of the old life-loving Italy, chiming at happy intervals with their fragrance. We had two rooms with a private terrace that floated in sunshine on the tops of orange trees, and we looked across their dark green billows to the jewely azure of the Mediterranean and beyond to the calm ironic silence of Vesuvius. In this most classic and romantic scene, I tried heroically to find, without the sense of self in liberty, the sense of joy in life.

For the classic element, the day-to-day unthrilling interest, I relied, as I always can, upon learning. I bought all sorts of grammars and dictionaries, applying every known "method" of acquiring foreign languages—except, of course, the best, the love-conducted one—and gradually shook down and melted into a slow-moving fluid the vocabulary I had stowed away when reading Dante in college. For romance I read books about revolution, cherishing the sole aspect of my urban and Ida-marrying self which seemed to possess that flavor, the Marxian revolutionist revolting even against Marx. And in an effort to restore some continuity to my broken-off life, I bought a huge hemlock plank, the only sizeable piece of lumber in the town, and rigged a springboard on a great brown rock that jutted out under the cliff into the bay. There I took a few miserably lonely dives from time to time. Hemlock has no spring in it, and neither had my dives. There was nobody to play with, nothing to do but grow up and be an unmitigated intellectual, and that I tried with my best energy to do. I tried to write; and failing that I tried to think out the basic answers to the two problems I had chosen to write about: the nature of poetry and the causes of humorous laughter. I did jot down one thought which forms the ground of my *Enjoyment of Poetry* and all my writings on aesthetics: "The perfect perception in sympathetic abandonment of a real thing is the highest poetic art." It is a good thought and one that has been exploited since, but I could not proceed with it then. I could not feel, as a writer must, that my thoughts were important.

I found one day lying on our terrace floor in its pale grey envelope the letter that Elsa had written to Ida on receiving the news of our marriage, a letter we had read together. I picked it up and saw that on the reverse side, in and around the postmarks, Ida had been writing with a soft pencil one of her forever unfinished poems.

Sweet breath of night, drawn from each leaf and flower,
Filling the empty places of the soul,
Soothing the pain and aches the heart held hidden,
While the bright glare of day . . .

I opened the envelope and read for a second time the words that our exuberant friend had written:

"Idi—Ido—Ida!!! Dear little Jesus child—you lovely, beautiful creature, you! I cried with joy, big tears rolling over my cheeks, and danced up and down for about half an hour, until S—— reminded me that the underneighbors might not enjoy the wedding as much as I did . . . Oh, my beautiful lovely dream come true—of the sun and the flowers and the birds and the mountains and the little golden fishes in the clear water—and last not least the two beautiful children, laughing for love, Max and Ida. . . ."

I put the letter back, put our love back, it seemed, into the envelope, and read its epitaph once more with tears in my eyes. I never told Ida that I had found this twofold poem. Knowing that she was careless enough of such things not to miss it, I put it away among my own writings. But I took her sorrow more deliberately into my heart after that. To my very self, or to that only clear part of it, my reasoning mind, Elsa's letter had conveyed a new piece of bad news. It had told me, since Elsa was Ida's close friend, that our formal marriage had meant a great deal more to Ida than to me. My foolishly cherished opinion that we were merely protecting by this public act the private enjoyment of a trip to Europe, or at the most an experiment in living together, had not been her opinion at all. I do not mean that I felt she had deceived me, merely that her mind—the feminine mind in general perhaps, while entertaining these excessively intellectual notions, reserves to itself an inside sense of the situation in its practical terms. My feeling was that I had deceived myself, acting as usual with confused motives, that the contingency was unthinkable in which I would act as a lover with clear motives, and that therefore the best thing I could do now would be to make good as a married man. Thus the net effect of the discovery of this epitaph was not to make me bury our love, as would have been wise, but try to conceive it more unselfishly and make it live.

Hypocrisy, like most accomplishments, consists largely of accurate timing. You learn to express an emotion at the precise instant when it exists, and at other times remain silent. In trying to be something too noble for your instincts, you fall through mere force of character into these chronological maneuvers. For of course you succeed at times, and to generalize these times is the very business upon which you are engaged. Your faithfulness thus becomes your falsity. You seize the advanced point of an imagined progress in order to make solemn avowals. You lie in wait for a favorable emotion in order to write a confiding letter. You are forever committing yourself, with the utmost sincerity yet at dexterously chosen moments, to a pattern of feeling that is not yours. With my heritage of infantile moralism, my disposition to act by ideals instead of by impulse, I was a fertile field for this insidious growth. I became a past master at choosing the inwardly appropriate moment.

Thus Ida and I hired a horse and carriage one day and drove round the peninsula and down the coast to Amalfi and Ravello, one of the loveliest drives in the world. More sharply than its beauty, I remember the sinkings of heart that its beauty caused me. I remember the weariness that assailed my body and spirit at a certain point in the long slow climb, 1100 feet straight up from the sea, to Ravello. Yet when I reached the height, these all dropped away in the sublime grandeur of the scene. I was raised fully up to the noble role I had chosen, and was able from the hotel on the summit to write to my father about the "gloriously happy times" we were having—a phrase I had long felt the urgent necessity to write.

I have a similarly twofold memory of our visit to Capri, where we called on Maxim Gorky and his wife, Madame Pyeshkov, whom Ida had known on a previous sojourn in Europe. I was thrilled by the theatrical beauty of the little island, so like a castle in the sea. I was thrilled at the meeting with a great revolutionist, an exiled enemy of the czar. But I remember as vividly my wishing to visit the famous Blue Grotto and not finding enough force in the wish to overcome Ida's indifference to grottoes green or blue. I also remember Madame Pyeshkov's going to the stairs and calling "Maxim Gregorivich!" and Gorky's deep growling musical answer in the unknown tongue.

She turned to us and said: "The voice!"

I sensed the adoration in her tone, and my heart whispered to me: "That is what a writer needs!"

Gorky came down and sat at table with us, but as he knew no French or English, said next to nothing. He was supposed at the time to be stricken with tuberculosis and rapidly dying, but he impressed me as a hearty Slavic giant who, if he could only learn to laugh, would live many years. After lunch he went away to visit a poor Russian family he was helping through a crisis, and Madame Pyeshkov told us with reverence that he spent almost all his leisure hours in such deeds of neighborly mercy. It made me feel humble and unworthy, and so helped me in my effort to be a loving friend to Ida. It helped me to regard as unimportant the fact that in a month at Sorrento I had not found the verve to climb to the summit of Vesuvius!

"Just a word to you this rare morning before we start—for where do you think?" I exclaimed to my father. "For the top of Vesuvius!" And in the next letter: "I discovered I couldn't make it very well from Sorrento and we went to the ruins of Pompeii instead."

Human life is intrinsically so tragic, the need of sympathy so great, that when people have lived a sorrow together, even the sorrow of their own lost love, they are often drawn closer by it. I began, after we moved northward from Sorrento, to feel at times an impetuous tenderness toward Ida, an urgent wish to cherish and multiply her smiles. I learned the trick of regarding her as a child, and in that role I found new charms in her vivacious mind and flexuous body. I often confer upon a woman friend that parental affection so rarely evoked in me by children, and this impulse was a further aid to me in my too moral effort to grow up.

What an inward death this effort involved is revealed in the letters I wrote to my father, letters filled with ill-considered objections to everything in Europe.

"We were glad to leave Naples after one night, and I gave Vesuvius a reluctant farewell without climbing it . . ."

"The valley toward Rome from Naples is beautiful . . . but yet it leaves your eyes thirsty. There's no water visible, no brook, pond, not so much as a watering trough, no not even a cow. It's a thirsty land . . . And then the fertility doesn't run up the mountains. The mountains are rocks bleak as death ('smorto'). They are the kind of mountains that don't invite you, because you know they'll be just exactly the same thing when you get there as they are in prospect (which is the annihilation of romance *per definitionem*) . . ."

"We 'did' the Vatican and St. Peters and a few parks, monuments and ruins yesterday morning, slept yesterday afternoon and most of this morning, and are now planning our departure. . . . Rome is no place for me. . . . There are great works of Greek sculpture there, but all crowded into a cold stone gallery, giving a pallid

and life-exhausted impression that pure beauty of form is unable
to cope with . . . Add to that the disgusting gas of popery, priest-
craft and sanctimonious hypocrisy into the very midst of whose
foul font and origin they have, by the irony of time, got themselves
incorporated, and you can imagine my adoration of the Greek more
exasperated than fulfilled . . .

"St. Peters is about the most inconceivably hideous inside of a big
church I ever saw—and I'm glad of it."

"The cathedral was very poor at Milan—the poorest we've seen.
I should say that the cathedral *outside* is, with the exception of the
inside of St. Peter's at Rome, the rottenest output on a large scale
that the impulse of decoration ever fell to. (By strange contrast the
inside is magnificent—vast dim simple grandeur of a house for
God.)"

"The Appenines are not richly beautiful, neither was the valley
of the Arno, nor any Italian country that I saw. A sort of dry short-
ness of vegetation, want of meadows, want of great shadows and
glades and amiable trees. I didn't want to stop and stay anywhere—
least of all perhaps at those famous lakes, Como, Lugarno, Maggiore.
Scene-painting—that is all it is . . ."

"Alpine scenery is magnificent and exquisite, but it's an awful
drain on the attention, and it's not open. . . . You go there and see
it and you get a great emotion. It makes you want to do something,
as all emotions do and should. But what is there to do? Just about
three things. You can go outdoors and turn upside down so as to
see it again, climb 5000 feet up a cliff so as to see something else,
or buy souvenirs. If you are rich, there's one other thing you can
do—pay your hotel bill. I left the latter things for Ida to do, and
climbed up the cliff to the Gornergrat. It was hard, hot, steady, uphill
work, so hard that I took a train. Even with that help it took me
an hour and a half to make it."

What a fall from the mood of my wander-months in the West
with Sid Wood! What a mocker and rejecter of life I had become!
In our *pensione* at Rome, I met my admired teacher of Greek from
Mercersburg, Professor Brackett, and instead of delighting in the
incident, felt a wistful pain as though I had died early and defeated
the promise of my youth. I had another implacable attack of sickness
there, and my most vivid memory from the Eternal City is of a tiny
inside bathroom where I tried to vomit quietly enough not to wake
up all the guests.

Of course I was engaged in being a "Marxist." The social revolution was my "romance *per definitionem*," my mountain that wouldn't be the same thing when I got there (*crede experto!*) that it was in prospect. And this romance, this adventure in belief, was vital to my enterprise of loving Ida. Although not due primarily, I think, to her influence, it was a kind of armature for the shape of life I was trying to build with her. It led me to greet three things in Rome with affirmative emotion: "the statues of Garibaldi and Giordano Bruno, and the grave of Shelley."

Keats' grave I gazed on with pure despair.

By the time we reached the Alps I was all through seeing Europe. I said to Ida:

"Can't we find some simple lake among quiet hills where there won't be any tourists, and I can just write all morning and go swimming in the afternoon?"

"I suppose there must *be* one somewhere," she said, in a voice, I thought, of more than usual dismay, "but I don't know how you'd find it. The only thing they advertise is scenery."

"Well, I'm going to find a simple lake," I said.

It seems pitiful now and perhaps a little manic—and may have seemed so to Ida then—but I gathered up all the maps and guide books to be found in the village of Zermatt and went on a hunt for a place in Europe as similar to my Glenora home as I could find. My unspoken thought was not insane. What with hives and flea bites and sleeping sickness and indigestion and my ghastly disappointment at the bottom of them, I had not yet been able to write a line. I would sit down to a blank sheet of paper and remain as blank as the paper. My hope was that in familiar surroundings and with a regime I was accustomed to, I could make the old habit of "having thoughts" come back. I settled on the Lac du Joux in eastern France, and on July 15, a short two months after setting out together to see the world, we fled to that most insignificant spot.

It *was* like Glenora, surprisingly so, and I did put into operation a "system" similar to that I had organized on our utopian hillside. To my father I made it sound like an idyl:

"I'm writing, swimming (not much and no diving), playing tennis (in French), reading the history of social revolution, and drinking Swiss milk.

"Every morning at 6 and every evening at 7 the cows are driven down from the hill pastures, 25 or 30 big fawn-colored cattle, each dangling a bell. They march along the town street in dignified procession, departing by twos and threes up little alleys and into doorways where their owners wait to milk them. Then in about an hour the procession starts back, the cowherd blowing a horn as he comes to the houses where they live, and they saunter out again by the same twos and threes. The bells of the procession wake us in the morning. I go down with a pail to get my milk, cream, and fresh unsalted butter, and we breakfast between seven and eight."

But I stayed in this idyl only eleven days. I could not really write. How could I create a book about the realization of life when I was flying from it into the refuge of routine? And moreover, in exchange for fleas, heaven sent me a plague of flies—innumerable and enormous flies, as broad in the beam as locusts and as insolent as those Jehovah commissioned to drive the Egyptians out of their skins. Ideas would not come. Whoever had managed to convince me that I was a writer? I was nothing at all. When we fled from Le Pont on the Lac du Joux, my faith in myself was at its lowest. . . . And yet the lower it fell, the less was my courage to break free from this anchorage, this guarantee of daily generous and tender companionship.

Fear is the main force that holds unhappy couples together, fear of the solitary battle. But reticence also had to do with my pusillanimous condition. It never occurred to me that I might burst out and tell Ida all I felt. Bashfulness too was a factor: I wanted to go back to my younger, gayer, more admiring friends in Glenora, in Williamstown, to my creative relation with Marjorie in Princeton, but I did not want to go back blushing at a foolishness. To be seen backing out of marriage in a sudden crablike spasm before I had got well in! It sometimes seems to me that I would rather drown than cry "Help! Help!" at an embarrassing moment, and here I well-nigh proved it. A more creditable cause of my condition was that I had no alternative plan or prospect except, after playing this mean trick on Ida, to go and play the same trick on Ruth. It was my character, not Ida's, which had undermined our adventure. She was the same generous and vivid-minded companion after we got on the boat as before. It was in me the sickness lay. In me it must be cured. I must settle down, as any toothless wiseacre would advise me, and "accept the duties and responsibilities of matrimony."

In that inward condition I arrived in Paris—the capital of the world's gay pleasure. I remember nothing of that first visit to Paris except Ida's bringing me to call on her spinster friend, Helen Marot, in some rented room and my sitting down after an embarrassed "How-do-you-do" on a chair that collapsed and landed me on my head in the corner. I learn from a letter, however, that "we finished up Paris in pretty hot speed—especially the last of the three days when I believe it was 85 in our room"; also that "I read a French History through and a History of the Revolution besides, and that contributed depth to my enjoyment of being there."

From Paris we fled again, to Benerville, a small place on the coast of Normandy between the famous resorts of Trouville and Deauville. Here, in the pension of Madame Rideaux, I passed some of the most desolate hours of my life. There was a little sort of office room in which Madame Rideaux permitted me to write during the mornings, but I needed permission from a higher source. I persistently told myself, and told my father, that I was writing, but it was only mechanically true. I was staring at the pages with unfocused mind. I did this staring every morning, faithfully, until the lunch bell rang at twelve. At twelve-thirty lunch was over, and I faced an afternoon eight-and-one-half hours long—for dinner would be served at nine— with nothing before me but a broad flat beach and a shallow ocean.

In my own person I could have gone to Deauville or Trouville in search of sports or amorous adventures, or with someone excited about life I could, even as a husband, have gone there and gambled or danced a little or at least looked on at France's famous gaiety. I could have hired a boat and sailed for the first time in the salt sea. I could as a last resort have gone fishing. None of these things existed in Ida's world. She was not intolerant, but only so adult, or in her spirit so blasé, that such diversions seemed unnecessary to her. It seemed enough to lie around and read, and perhaps have a cup of tea afterward, or take a drive and admire in twilight the lush green fields and orchards and the steep sweet mossy roofs of Normandy.

And I, on my side, was too weighed down by her lethargy to do any of those things by myself. I often say that I can not be bored, and in complete freedom to dispose of myself I think it would be true. But what I experienced in those interminable afternoons at Benerville was, I suppose, what people mean when they say "excruciating boredom." The thought that I had voluntarily exchanged my gay, playful, passion-laden, admiration-filled, romantically altruistic, and hard-workingly egotistical summer in Glenora for such a blanket of hours hanging round me in a hole between two pleasure resorts was unbearable. My mind hid from thinking it.

Ida had been wise enough to suggest that we go back to Glenora for September, and invite Crystal and Bennie to come there. It was not an unmitigated relief to me, for I could not imagine Ida in

Glenora. I could not without inward shriveling imagine my arriving there with her attached to me. Both Ida and Ida's husband belonged in New York; they belonged in winter; they belonged where there was no Ruth. However the suggestion let in some dubious light from an end of this tunnel-under-a-summer that my trip to Europe had turned out to be. In that light lay at least the hope that in my own study and among my youthful friends I might again begin to write.

We sailed from Liverpool August 19 on a small steamer jammed with extra passengers because of a dock strike. Five snoring men breathed the stagnant air in the tiny stateroom allotted to me in the hold. I sneaked out every night and slept on a wall bench in the dining-room. Rather I lay on that bench a few hours and then roamed the deck in the insomniac's frenzy, asking myself how it could be that a poet and a young man dedicated to the enjoyment of living had found it impossible to spend three interested months in Europe.

Chapter 46

Truth Sinks Wanly Down . . .

IDA accomplished the feat of arriving in Glenora as my wife with astonishing ease and grace. In one respect she was already in the Cherith tradition—she wore as few clothes as possible. We had traveled through Europe dressed about as one dresses for a tennis game, and we got off the train at Glenora in the same casual attire. A guest from Elmira remarked: "Wasn't it thoughtful of Max and Ida to put on their *outing clothes* for the arrival in Glenora!" But the "bunch" knew better, and they took us into their hearts, and into the lake, within an hour after we got off the train. The fact that Ida swam as a mere matter of course in a one-piece bathing suit, a deed up to then achieved only by Ruth, helped delicately in this process of adjustment. The Log records on September 9 the final triumph of the revolution Baldy and I had started three years before in the mild proposal that women swim without stockings. On that date the "Apostles of Nakedness" announced: "We will no longer call them *boys'* bathing suits."

I think Ida really experienced a kind of rebirth in Glenora. She cast off the pall of ennui that had hung like a fog around her, permeating her mind and spirit. She joined us childishly and without reserve in our cultivation of the amiable, clear, undelved-for joys of rural life. She won my father's heart by taking a genuine interest in his tiny pine trees and even helping him to mulch them with big armfuls of dead grass. She won mine by buying some clay and a modeling stand and turning a little shanty we called "Barneycastle" into a studio in which to develop her unusual talent for sculpture. She learned to enjoy going up to the station with a wheelbarrow and bringing down boxes of groceries; and she was there for the suitcases when Crystal and Bennie arrived. Although she made no friends outside the house, she was so genially alive and gay and humorous within its walls that to us intimate with her it seemed as though she had always been a member, an indispensable member, of our family. She not only largely reconciled me to herself, but by taking them together into her friendship, went far toward reconciling Crystal to Bennie—a feat also not fully accomplished. Crystal wrote me from Milwaukee after this visit:

"I think those two weeks with you and Ida at Glenora were as completely happy a time as I ever had. It's almost unbelievable that we all four like each other. I don't see how we ever got along without Ida, do you? She is the most charming grown-up person I've ever known, I believe."

In this miracle I found emotional repose. I found a solid point of support for that romanticizing of the future without which human life is too pathetic to be lived. I felt sure that Ida was entering upon a great career as a sculptor, a life of her own that would at the same time withdraw her a little from me and feed my admiration. And as a partner in this creative companionship I saw myself again as a poet. I began fluently to write my book.

Still striving for continuity, and slightly in defiance of Ida's sophistication, I conducted the Sunday service in our cottage on September 3. There is pathos in my entry in the Log: "I do some more preaching at the old stand. It gets harder and harder to preach. . . . But Jack is still playing faithfully and the kids still stand up behind the piano and join in." And there is pathos in my "pagan prayer" of that Sunday—the last of those milestones on my march from Christian evangelism to proletarian revolution:

"Our hearts demanding the realization of life, our eyes fixed on the prize of individual glory or achievement, we can not but go joyfully forward. Yet we will not forget that the world holds millions who have no hope of glory and no taste of life. And we will know that the highest prize and the supreme individual achievement is his who fights a great fight for the liberty of others."

Thus I managed to combine prayer with revolution. But they were not happy together, and I never prayed even in this godless fashion again.

Ruth was eighteen now, full-curved and complete, and every movement of that lovely body whose growth I had watched and hovered over, every cool glance from those once warmly shining eyes, called me back into the past. Continuity was not to be thought of here. I had lost Ruth, I had thrown her into the discard just when she was ready to be mine. In the same obsessed way that I had once plotted all summer long to find myself alone with Ruth, I now plotted against coming upon her accidentally in the glen, or between the grape rows, or on some leaf-secreted pathway through the woods. We did meet once at Carpenter's spring, and I quickly filled her pail for her, and we both hastened away.

There was nothing for us to say—nothing until I learned the art, so strangely withheld from me who have a native gift for it, of telling the intimate truth to a friend. I do not know what power enabled me to stay away from Ruth, unless perhaps, as the reader may already be thinking, it was Ida's force of character. She knew nothing, then, of this magnetic center upon which the rays of my attachment to Glenora converged. But I was aware, without its ever having been mentioned, that her conception of our relation precluded my taking a lonely walk with an eighteen-year-old girl. Like many another prophet of antimarriage, she was violently monogamous—unaware even of what the words "free love" sound like to a lusty man. However, I also was trying to be monogamous, and I was helped surprisingly by the undiscovered riches in her nature. I was, in and of my own will, caught in by the sustained whimsical gaiety and abounding warm good humor with which she filled the empty space so present to us all in Cherith Cottage. What with her charms and my own creative revival, my absorption in writing about poetry and life, I managed—except for midnight meetings with the face of truth—to believe myself liberated from Ruth's increasing lure and settled in a faithful companionship with Ida.

I wrote during this period a sombre poem, which is perhaps rather a symptom of schizophrenia than a criticism of life:

> Midnight is come,
> And thinly in the deepness of the gloom
> Truth rises startle-eyed out of a tomb,
> And we are dumb.
>
> A death bell tolls
> And we still shudder round the too smooth bed,
> For truth makes pallid watch above the dead,
> Freezing our souls.
>
> But day returns,
> Light and the garish life, and we are brave,
> For truth sinks wanly down into her grave . . .
> Yet the heart yearns.

The garishness of life was emphasized for me when we got back to New York by the torrent of noise in Ida's apartment. A second-floor triangle, with windows on Fourth Street running down one side and windows on MacDougal down the other, it contained no square-inch of quietness, no room or closet where I could shut the door and rest. Living in that noise was like having no place to sit down. As *her* home I had loved this apartment with its big window facing across the square. As mine it would not let me sleep.

Looking for a home together ought to be fun for two young people, but for Ida such things were a bore. She was well settled and at peace in this hideous uproar, and I dreaded to press the needs of my more sensitive nerve-endings. I played the stoic for three weeks, and then, Bruce Barton having conveniently vacated the floor above, we moved up there. The relief was infinitesimal, but I played the stoic for two weeks more. Then I found, over on Charles Street, a cramped but quiet place up six flights of stairs, and I dragged poor Ida and all her furniture up those stairs. She was gracious, sympathetic, humorous—all that could be asked—but that is not like having fun.

I jot down in my notebooks from time to time traits in my make-up so odd and yet so irreducible that I have entitled them: "Reasons why I don't belong to the Human Race." One of them is this violent allergy to noise. To most travelers it seems natural to find the principal hotel of a city located at its busiest intersection; to me it is absolutely incomprehensible. In the crowded low-ceilinged cafés where most of the world's intelligentsia congregate, I can not converse for an hour without exhaustion.

Another of these irreducible traits—and I am not forgetting where we are in our story—is a repugnance to the notion of calling the girl I have chosen "Mrs. Eastman." This pinning of your own name on the object of your love displays an egotism and lack of outgoing loyal devotion that I find comparable to the similar defacement of shrines and monuments by small boys. That a "Lucy Stone League" should have to be established to advocate so obvious a point in romance or classical common sense as calling your love *by her own name*, or at least not—in God's mercy!—by *yours*, seems to me outlandish, freakish, a tale which could not believingly be related of the species, whatever it may be, to which I belong.

Naturally then, when we moved over to Charles Street, where there was a row of mail boxes at the door, I put both IDA RAUH and MAX EASTMAN on our box. And just to make it emphatic I put IDA RAUH first. That, I judge, had not been done in New York before.

It brought as one of our first visitors a reporter from the New York *World*.

Would we mind expounding our views on the marriage relation?

Yellow journalism was young in those days, and the gulf wider than it is now between public and private life. Ruthless reporters on a hunt for scandal were dreaded as though they had fangs. In our fright Ida and I made the mistake of most innocents when threatened with publicity—we appealed to the good will of the reporter. Finding him apparently sympathetic to our views, we confided in him completely, and with his eager help worked out a plan for presenting them in a mild and persuasive form to the public. What appeared in the paper, of course, was not our plan but our confidings. And they appeared with photographs and startling headlines on the second page:

No "Mrs." Badge of Slavery Worn by This Miss Wife

"Our attitude toward the marriage service," Miss-Mrs. Rauh-Eastman said, "is that we went through with it; then we can say afterward we don't believe in it. It was with us a placating of convention, because if we had gone counter to convention, it would have been too much of a bother for the gain . . . There may be some who still feel that marriage is a sacrament, but the idea is passing away."

"I do not want to absorb my wife's identity in mine," explained Mr. Eastman. "I want her to be entirely independent of me in every way—to be as free as she was before we were married. I wish you would say, if you are going to say anything, that my wife works just as regularly at the Women's Trade Union League for the things she is interested in as she did before marriage. She has her regular hours of work, and devotes herself as zealously as she ever did."

So it went on for three columns. Besides making us both sick with a blushing sickness, it worried me acutely, because, although I had an assistant to tend the files, I was still nominally secretary of the Men's League for Woman Suffrage. The interview was, indeed, reprinted and circulated anonymously by some enemy of the cause, but to my surprise I never heard an echo from any of the dignitaries on my letterhead.

In Elmira, however, where the papers reproduced our interview, the effect was cataclysmic. A very important Colonel D. C. Robinson celebrated his Thanksgiving Day by writing a letter to the *Star-Gazette*:

"May I use your columns to voice the thought of many nauseated citizens . . .

"Our sons and daughters read this stuff spread before them in journals claiming to be reputable, and next day they see common perjurers sent to prison for taking an oath whose sanctions they defy precisely as 'Professor' Eastman and Miss Rauh defy the bonds of the sacred marriage service which they swore to reverence while at the very hour of its taking they knew their oath was false. If they are married and entitled to live together in the state of New York, their names are Mr. and Mrs. Max Eastman under its laws. If their names are Mr. Max Eastman and Miss Rauh, they would be classed in the police courts under titles which politeness forbids me to put upon this page . . ."

Colonel Robinson was backed up by the pastor of the First Methodist Church: ". . . Against the entrance of this serpent of lust and falsehood let every man's hand be raised, and let every sword of manly and fatherly honor flash death to the intruder who would mar the tree of life."

The pastor was backed up by a columnist in the Elmira *Advertiser:* "We can't say we agree with brother Eastman's rabbit system . . . Take away the home and the obligation man and wife owe it, turn her loose to become the tool of fortune, the dual-role individual that man has become, and you tear the very heart out of the American republic. . . ."

The pastor of the Southside Baptist Church chipped in with a sermon on The Marriage Tie: "He who strikes at the sacredness of marriage or its permanence is an enemy of the home and of the nation. . . ."

And for climax Elmira's own yellow journal, the *Sunday Telegram,* under the heading "Maybe We'll All Go Dippy Soon," combined some choice quotations from the *World* story with a comment from my father, whom they had called up in Florida, and whose only thought was to be loyal to himself and us:

"Some people think my children have strange ideas," he said. "Perhaps they inherited them from their father . . . Yes, I think the time will come when it will be legal for a couple that can not live compatibly to separate without the formality of going through the courts at a large expense for lawyers, etc."

On a separate page, under the headline EASTMAN DISCLOSURES SHOCKING, the editor himself had this to say:

"In another column appears an interview with Rev. Samuel E.

Eastman, the father of Max Eastman and Crystal Eastman. It should be read by every person in Elmira. Doubtless it will greatly astound our people. Recent disclosures apparently made by Max Eastman put him in the list of the no-longer-to-be-noticed in this community.

"Upon the authority of her father it is given out that Crystal Eastman has on the marriage problem about the same ideas as her brother. If that be the fact it will add another to the list . . ."

I tried to calm the waters with a letter to the *Star-Gazette* stating "our views, or inquiries" as mildly as I could:

"I say inquiries, because for my part, I have no final conviction upon this problem, except the conviction that it is a problem . . .

"Aside from adjustable matters of legal convention as to property, I can find only two genuine values in the marriage contract. First, it is a contract upon the part of the man to support his wife. Second, it is a contract upon the part of both to support and rear their children.

"Now the first of these values disappears when the woman is economically independent, as some women are and I believe the majority will be. But the second—the contract of joint responsibility for the rearing of the children—will, so far as I can see, never disappear. That seems to be permanently necessary.

"But to construe the necessity of responsibility for their children into a necessity of holding two people together, although they discover that their union was a mistake, and their companionship is misery, and their home is filled with a grief that has no end and no value, is, in my opinion, stupid.

"I do wish my wife to be free to leave me and accept the love of another, if and when she decides that she wants to. I should think everyone who loves would feel that way.

"I do not regard my public contract as a sacrament. A sacrament is a thing that makes sacred, and no ceremony can make anything sacred . . ."

The night after this appeared I was awakened at 2 A.M. by an urgent wire from John Moore, editor of the Elmira *Telegram*:

"Do you know that marriage of yourself and wife contracted in Sorrento Italy is not valid in this country, that your living relation is adulterous under the law and punishable in this state, and that any child born to you would be illegitimate. That being true have you any statement to make supplementary to your letter tonight's *Star-Gazette*. Please wire answer."

I called up my friend, Boyd MacDowell, a lawyer, a deacon in the

Park Church, a member of our Glenora club, and a man who loved a fight. Between us we composed a telegram which I sent to John Moore at 3 A.M.:

"I warn you that you are on the verge of publishing matter that is punishable by law in this state and that both the money and the lawyer are on hand to see that you get your punishment."

That ended the public scandal.

Privately I received three letters which I preserved with those clippings.

The first was anonymous, but well provided with teeth: "Dear Max: . . . We have enjoyed you so much it is hard for us to give you up. It DOES seem that the DEVIL has taken complete possession of your soul. I must ask that you and your wife never again enter our home, and it is our advice and desire that you never show your faces again in this City or at your summer home . . ."

The second, from D. C. Bliss, the Superintendent of Elmira's Public Schools: ". . . Nothing that I can say will take away the sting, but I want to assure you of my entire respect and confidence."

The third, from my father in Florida: "Yes, I have seen all the abominable stuff, but I am having the time of my life, perhaps because I have such confidence in you and Ida. The people have 'wagged their heads and said ah! ah!' at me more than once . . . It is soft balmy summertime here. With great love to you both, my children . . ."

When my father got home he preached an eloquent sermon on "The Home and Its Defenses," repeating his old plea for "Purity Essential to the Highest Culture," but also advocating complete equality of men and women, the right of married women to retain their own names, frank sexual instruction in the schools, plain talk and public action against syphilis, laws which would make divorce easily accessible when seriously needed, and accessible to rich and poor alike. He made no allusion to the other ministers, but remarked incidentally that "there is no escape from polygamy as a Divine Institution if we take the Bible literally." His sermon was published in full in the *Advertiser* and circulated subsequently as a pamphlet. Efforts of the *Telegram* to find a whisper against him in the Park Church congregation were unsuccessful.

Had I been wholehearted in the concrete venture, that battle over my abstract beliefs about "Mr. and Mrs." would not have deeply troubled me. My argument required that I be happy in love; and in my midnight meetings with truth I was not happy. I could not ignore at such moments the bitter irony in this episode. It struck home deeply when I saw in print the words: "My wife works at the Women's Trade Union League as she did before marriage. She has regular hours of work . . ."

Ida did not know what regular hours of work meant. And her sudden rejecting of the great career in sculpture so eagerly begun at Glenora, her dropping back, without finishing one figure in the clay she had bought, into this pretense at a profession, this spasmodic, irresponsible, idealistic fooling with the labor movement, had been a painful disappointment to me. It took a vital prop from under my plan for feeling romantic about our future. I never said so, however. I let the truth sink wanly down and put my shoulder under the brave pretense that Ida was going in for a real career as an agitator.

My own morale had become in some degree independent of her. I was "having thoughts" again; I was working successfully on my book; I was even writing poetry. I had a besetting wish to appear in the world as a poet before I appeared as a writer about poetry. Therefore I worked hard to assemble enough poems during that winter to make a volume that Mitchell Kennerley could publish. I even perpetrated a poem or two—I mean went to the work of creation deliberately instead of driven by an exigent emotion. "The Thought of Protagoras" was an expression of my scepticism about philosophy; "In a Dungeon of Russia," an attempt to blend the poet in me with the reformer. This might have been accomplished had some accident sustained me and forced me along, but nothing in my environment encouraged me to believe in my lyric gifts. When Mitchell Kennerley did accept *Child of the Amazons and Other Poems* in April 1912, and contract to publish it "in the fall," he took pains to assure me he would never sell the first five hundred copies on which he was paying no royalty. It was a correct prediction, but not just the encouragement I needed as a poet.

Chapter 47

I Choose Revolution

AS A political orator I needed to be held back rather than encouraged, for I was getting swept into a life-career on the lecture platform. My name was beginning to lose its narrow association with the woman's movement. Even as a suffragist I always felt more at home with male than female audiences, and it was my special task to address men's clubs and professional associations. John Dewey and I spoke together to the Republican Club in New York City, I remember, and I told those politicians how I thought life could be most richly enjoyed. But I was also moving on from woman suffrage to the larger aspects of democracy. My essay on "The Unlimited Franchise," published in the *Atlantic* in July 1911, said some things about "the social importance of a political system" which I often find myself repeating today: The benefits of a democratic system are not to be found in the government but in the people. The judgment of a majority is not better than that of a few— it is not judgment, primarily, but interest, that is expressed on election day. "Democracy will meet the problems it has produced, if we will but keep our pride in it, and if we will remember that things human are never to be condemned by comparison with perfection, but by comparison with other things human that we might put in their place."

After a speech to the Chamber of Commerce in Syracuse the chairman of the entertainment committee, J. R. Clancy, seized my hand and said: "Look here. You're not a propagandist. You're a humorist. I'm going to invite you up to our annual banquet this spring, and I want you to forget all about your principles and ideals, and just make 'em laugh, will you?"

It crowned my boyhood ambition to be called a humorist; it out-valued fifty college degrees. It pleased me still more when I learned

that Woodrow Wilson, then campaigning for the presidential nomination, would be the other speaker. I do not know whether my
reputation had really risen so high, or whether Mr. Clancy had
taken a fatherly liking to me and decided to give me an extravagant
boost. But the menu cards were elaborately got out in Princeton's
orange and black, with a full-page portrait of the candidate on one
side and a full-page portrait of the humorist on the other. And when
the throng entered the banquet hall and Wilson was planted by the
door to shake each man's hand as he came in, I was planted alongside and, like it or not, they had to shake my hand too!

There was a suaveness about Woodrow Wilson, a scholarly poise
and fluency of diction, that made those small-town businessmen
acutely ill at ease. He would help the conversation along with quotations from Edmund Burke or Lord Acton that paralyzed it altogether. With a Ph.D. under my feet and Plato at the tip of my
tongue, I refused to be daunted by this alarming phenomenon. As a
result we were placed together at the banquet and conversed almost
without interruption for two or three hours. His first remark to me
at the table was:

"They tell me you are interested in woman suffrage. I am badly in
need of instruction about that. I have a feeling that these women
are avoiding their duties rather than demanding their rights, but it
is only a feeling. I really should be grateful if you would teach me
what I ought to know about the whole question."

As Woodrow Wilson was the first president to come out for a constitutional amendment and make woman suffrage an issue in national
politics, I like to think I did some important teaching during those
hours. I never taught with a more subtly stimulated personal elation.
For although Wilson was no great orator, his manner too smooth and
his thought not concrete enough, he inspired in private conversation
a heady mixture of self-esteem and admiration. He was scrupulously
attentive to your thought and meticulously candid in stating his
own. I wondered in after years how a man in high office could be so
candid without giving anything away. The topic of sex relations
leads into many an intimate speculation, and by the time we rose for
our speeches, Wilson and I were in a smilingly friendly mood.

I have related in my *Enjoyment of Laughter* how Mr. Clancy
drew me aside and said he would pay me a dollar a minute in addi-
tion to my fee as long as I would keep Wilson laughing. When I got
up to speak, I saw Mr. Clancy pull out his watch and set it down
significantly on the table. I began my speech by telling Wilson about

this little arrangement and saying that if he didn't enjoy hearing me talk, I was sure he would enjoy watching Mr. Clancy lose money. It made a grand beginning, and throughout the speech, whenever Wilson chuckled, I had only to glance toward Mr. Clancy in order to turn the chuckle into a laugh in which everybody joined. I earned $40 that night in addition to my fee, but when I look over my manuscript now, I can hardly see why. Humor is very strictly confined to the time and place.

Of course Wilson's friendliness was a strong factor in my success, and he crowned it by saying, when he got up for his own speech, that mine had been the most delightful combination of thought and humor he ever listened to. It made a wonderful quote for my lecture manager and yielded me income in future years as though he had handed me a jewel.

Had I not been afflicted with those "principles and ideals" that Mr. Clancy wished away, I might, starting with the oratorical successes of that winter, have acquired a little "civic importance" of my own. But I was engaged now in being a revolutionist. Three months before—on February 14, to be exact—I had joined the Socialist Party. And during the same month that I reached that small pinnacle of respectable glory at Syracuse, I published a letter in the party organ, the New York *Call*, denouncing respectability, defending violence, and declaring my scorn of "the good or bad opinion of everybody in the world but the whole fighting proletariat."

The occasion of that letter, my first public utterance as a socialist, was this: The Socialist Party, which was in the hands of the "reformists" led by Morris Hillquit and Victor Berger, had recently adopted an amendment to its constitution (the notorious Article VI), prohibiting members from advocating sabotage or violence. This article had been passed with the special purpose of expelling Bill Haywood, the chief of the Industrial Workers of the World, America's first and greatest revolutionary union. A stubborn minority was excitedly opposing this rightward movement of the party when the working class was moving left. The Structural Iron Workers were fighting the steel trust with dynamite. One of their dynamiters had exploded a bomb alongside the Los Angeles *Times* building. The IWW was conducting a giant textile strike in Lawrence, Massachusetts, and its two brilliant agitators, Ettor and Giovannitti, were in jail on a framed-up murder charge. To spurn the IWW and denounce violence at such a time was to abandon the theory of class struggle and betray the workers just when the fight was getting hot.

So it seemed both to the rigid Marxists and the temperamental rebels in the party. The question whether a socialist was "yellow" or "red," "reformist" or "revolutionary," was as sharp as it ever became until the two wings lined up in Russia six years later and started shooting it out.

Since the idea of class struggle was the pith of my hope in socialism, I took as a mere matter of logic the revolutionary position. I took it with a verve and arrogance that had little to do, I'm afraid, with logic. There was an "overcorrection" here, it now seems, of my naturally mild, and by training Christian, approach to life. But I combined with my revolutionism a revolt against dogma which put me in a rather unique position. Indeed what I said about opportunism versus dogmatism was as little to the taste of the "reds" as the "yellows":

"I gather that this bull was issued by a majority which calls itself 'opportunist.' And I guess it is the first time a piece of pure dogmatism ever got called by that name. For a party who recognizes that the world is not a thing but a process, opportunism in its true sense is the only attitude intelligently possible. But the opportunism of this majority apparently means freedom from absolute principles when it comes to conciliating the powers that be, but absolutism of the worst kind when it comes to conciliating the extremists on their own side of the fight . . .

"I am a member of the Socialist Party because I endorse its positive program and policy. But I also advocate sabotage and violence as having been, and as likely to be in the future upon many occasions, excellent tactics in the fight of an oppressed class against its oppressors. Is there not liberality or room enough in the Socialist Party for this opinion?"

While flaunting such views in the socialist press, I could not long continue on good terms with chambers of commerce. That seemed obvious, and it raised a problem as to how I should earn my living. Ida had an income that, with an occasional check for an essay, would have been ample for us both. She was, moreover, so generous by instinct that, had I been single in my devotion to writing, it would not have mattered whether I got paid for it or not. But I had that fixed heroic notion that I must earn my bread and do something for my fellow man before I could devote myself to the sacred play of writing. As Plato said, when abandoning his dialogues to set sail for the great revolutionary enterprise in Syracuse, "I feared to see myself at last altogether nothing but words."

For such reasons I began to feel around for a service to socialism that might combine, as my work for suffrage had, a small income with a participation in the struggle. A part-time editorial job on some socialist paper, a column of labor news or comments—these were the projects I had in mind. I thought of them as teaching rather than writing. The whole labor and radical movement needed to learn how to think experimentally, to think without anarchist impetuosity or Marxian dogma: that was my modest opinion. And I was also modest enough to believe I could teach them this wisdom *on the side*, or that we could learn it together while I was devoting my morning hours to creative writing on other subjects.

As I look back, this state of mind, especially in one so easily and so often tired, seems complex and foolish in the extreme. But I must remember that in looking back I am more ambitious for myself than I was in looking forward. In autumn we judge all by the harvest. A long shelf of the aspiring works in prose and poetry that I have conceived and begun and postponed because of some practical enterprise would add much to my pleasure in life today. Its absence often makes me sad. But in those years my satisfaction was in the living rather than the fruit of it.

Chapter 48

A Book and a Baby

MY NOTION of a paid part-time job in the service of socialism was not fantastic in 1912. The socialist idea flourished to its highest bloom in America in that exciting year. Eugene V. Debs of Terre Haute, Indiana, got a million votes for President, and *The Appeal to Reason*, a socialist paper published in Girard, Kansas, attained a circulation of 761,000. In New York a group of artists and writers, rounded up by a Dutch organizer of co-operatives named Piet Vlag, and subsidized by a vice-president of the Metropolitan Life Insurance Company, started an illustrated socialist monthly called *The Masses*. Harry Payne Whitney, the polo-playing millionaire, rather took the wind out of its sails by buying up the already popular *Metropolitan Magazine* and installing as editor a British Fabian socialist named H. J. Wigham.

When Fabian socialism invades the Sixty Families, revolutionary socialism invades the labor movement and the intelligentsia. Jack London, a fair barometer of these changes, was in New York that winter in his most iron-heelish mood. I remember his sparkling yet rather too meaty vigor as he stood on a chair at a crowded Greenwich Village tea and answered questions.

"Don't you think the influence of the emancipated woman is going to mitigate the severity of the class struggle?"

Jack turned with bright laughing eyes, raising his fist with the thumb downward.

"It was always the women who turned their thumbs down when a gladiator cried for mercy."

Graceful, swift, imaginative! I agreed with him and liked him, and remembered for my own use that trick of letting the gesture precede the words. A dinner was given for their literary hero by the radicals, and I attended in the hope to hear him speak. For some reason Jack would not speak—perhaps he had been drinking too much—but fate met me at that dinner in the genial figure of Art Young.

I have portrayed Art Young's benign, dreamy, slow-moving, humorous genius in my book *Heroes I Have Known*, and tried to suggest his place in America's comic art. To me it was quite an event to meet him, for I could remember as a boy in Elmira going through the funny papers looking for his cartoons. To learn he was a socialist had been a happy surprise, and it occurred to me to consult him now about that part-time job I had in mind. Art was a fabulously impractical person, and his helping me to a remunerative job in the socialist movement was as likely as the millennium itself. He was warmly enthusiastic, and laid away in his memory the idea that I was yearning to serve the cause. How far that idea would lead me from the neat three-track scheme of living I had mapped out for myself, I will relate in a little while.

For the present I let the whole problem slide, for I had still five months of creative work to do on *Enjoyment of Poetry*. And Ida—I have neglected to tell you—had the same to do on a baby she was rather unexpectedly producing. We rented a little farmhouse on a salt-water inlet near Waterford, Connecticut, and moved out there in early May to spend the summer.

It was a wistful summer to me, a summer in which I wrote fervently of the pure joy of living but searched for it in vain. I would stand by the tupelo trees gazing out across the bay and *wish* for the sense of life's adventure as of old it had flooded me, but only an aching sense of loss would come. As once I had fled from the moon's rising because it was too beautiful, now I fled from all poignant realization because it was grievous. I would cling to the "dull comfort of routine"; I would "hide my eyes in tasks." And the principal task—most bitter irony!—was a book celebrating that very realization from which I was turning away.

I had two feelings about the baby Ida was producing, neither of them auspicious of devoted parenthood. One was that by its arrival I was permanently trapped and shackled: with the duties of a parent added to those of a husband, escape from a lifetime of conscientiousness was not to be thought of. The other was that by providing Ida with a second object of attachment, this unexpected guest might at least mitigate the rigors of my captivity. I dreamed fitfully, as many a fondly expectant father has, that a fine bouncing baby, by diverting a portion of its mother's libido, might make me less precisely a husband.

Ida's interest in her own life had declined still more, it seemed to me, with the prospect of a baby. Even her intellectualism had become reminiscent. She read nothing but the advertisements in the magazines—a matter of laughter between us because it seemed obviously not her real character. Yet it was what she did. When we first settled in New York, I had got out my essay on Plato and asked her to give me her criticisms of it. It had lain on the table all winter long in its blue cover; it lay on another table all summer long; it lay on a third table a good part of another winter before I put it away, preferring chagrin to the strain of keeping up a forlorn hope.

Had I been a wholehearted mate for Ida she might not have sunk so deep in her sin of lassitude. My dividedness of motive and her weariness of life augmented each other in a vicious circle from which there was no outlet short of separation. They also, in different ways, made separation impossible to each of us: I lacked the integration for such an act; Ida lacked the interest in being happy.

Again that summer I bought lumber and, driving piles out in the deep water, erected a diving tower and mounted a springboard on it. But again I had no one to play with—except for one week, when Ida's slim, firm-breasted friend, Esther Andrews, came to see her. Esther's lithe and pliant figure in a silken bathing suit made my program of conjugal fidelity feel as shaky as the diving platform, and I was relieved as well as saddened when she left. I further eased my nostalgia for lost childish joys by installing three pairs of fancy pigeons in a little tool shed in the garden. One of my nuns, whom Ida named "The Lady Imogen," was seized by a rapacious chicken hawk and carried away into the skies. I ran out shouting, and he dropped The Lady Imogen, who dipped and fluttered down like a falling kite into the garden. She sat quiet after that and died in two days from the red wounds made by his talons. The event stands sharp in my memory, as though death and not birth had been the business of the summer.

The house we lived in belonged to an old maid whose main interest was in the Society for the Prevention of Cruelty to Animals. She had a box in the barn for chloroforming homeless cats and dogs, and I made up a quite ghastly story by imagining that her real zest was for killing. When published, it was noted with two stars by Edward J. O'Brien in his *Best Short Stories of the Year*, and I added the idea of becoming a novelist to my quite adequate burden of ambitions. I did write a novel many years later, but with a peculiar impediment. To write in prose things which are not true does not, apparently, seem serious to my instincts, for I had to make a continual effort to keep from turning the story into burlesque. Even that gruesome tale, "Lover of Animals," had to be weeded— under Marjorie Nott's blue pencil—of drolleries not inherent in the plot.

Ida's sister Florence came to spend two weeks with us at Waterford—a gentle, sweet, dark, bloodless spinster-girl, who looked enough like Ida and carried Ida's inaction to a sufficient extreme to seem a travesty. She had the same income Ida had and gave almost all of it away, because besides being similarly generous she lacked, it often seemed to me, the energy to spend it. I felt sometimes, living inside four walls with these two languid and inactive creatures —my family!—absolutely incredulous. I could not believe that it was I. And yet how warm and kind they were! How undemanding and considerate! There was really no sense in rebelling against it. Just get to work!

I must here remark—in justice to the truth and not to Ida, for I am trying to be no more influenced by her pride than mine— that memoirs of a period in which one's will is divided are subject to a special correction. They are the memoirs of two persons really, and two persons who rarely occupied the field of consciousness simultaneously. First one and then the other had possession. He who looks back, however, is one person; he is the one who triumphed and survived. He will inevitably tend to read himself back into the whole picture. The other, the rejected one, will fight a losing battle even to be remembered.

Thus when I say, in recalling those years with Ida, that "I" felt thus or so, the remark may well be only one-half true. The "I" who accepted her as intimate friend and child and mother, resolutely adapting himself to her rich if unsuitable nature and achieving happy hours innumerable, is dead and gone. The rebel against that kind of happiness, which in truth could never rise to joy, took full possession finally and lived to tell the tale. Had the battle gone the other way, or could we with some psychical engine dredge up the recollections of a defeated self, the tale would wear a different color.

I am reminded of this by a thoroughly worn-out sheet of paper which survives from that summer, bearing the legend: *Ida Rauh's poem to me Aug. 8, 1912.* It was her first word, I think, of loverlike exaggeration. And I carried it in my breast pocket for over twenty years, cherishing the fancy that it might act as a kind of amulet against diffidence.

> Young as the dawn, yet old as the first thought of man,
> Thou hast taken into thy deep cavern mind
> All aspirations, fears, all loves, all hates,
> All ponderings that groping we have bound into a
> soul—
> Straight and erect over the road, straight on into the
> spacious future,
> Sending swift smiles into the hearts of those who have a
> waiting eye to catch the beams of light,
> A heart that ceaseless searches for the vibrant truth,
> Look toward me twice so I may be assured
> That you and I are more than passers-by.

One day in Waterford in late August I received a letter scrawled with a brush on a torn-off scrap of drawing paper, and signed by the artists John Sloan, Art Young, Charles A. Winter, Alice Beach Winter, Maurice Becker, and the writers Louis Untermeyer, Mary Heaton Vorse, Ellis O. Jones, Horatio Winslow, and Inez Haynes Gillmore. It read as follows:

"You are elected editor of The Masses. No pay."

I had seen a copy of *The Masses* and remained indifferent to it because of its dull make-up and very "yellow" brand of socialism. Its brotherly evangel of humanitarianism and zeal for consumer's co-operatives I then regarded with scorn. But I had no other information about it. I did not know that it was itself an experiment in co-operation, being owned by artists and writers, and run without thought of profits. Nor did I know that after a year of hand-to-mouth existence, it had expired with the issue of August 1912 and been left in the hands of the "co-operative" by its volatile creator, Piet Vlag, who had moved to the warmer climate of Tampa, Florida. Therefore this abrupt communication in rough black letters from John Sloan's paint brush had little significance for me. It meant only that Art Young had misconstrued the subtle thing I told him. He had turned my design for living exactly upside down, making my service to socialism the unpaid factor and assuming that I intended to earn my living with my pen.

I was intrigued, of course, and thought it would be fun to look up this whimsical bunch when I got back to New York. But I was not seriously interested. My writing was a job with no pay; I did not want another.

We came back early and took an apartment at the top of 27 West 11th Street, a quiet dwelling with a roof on which a baby could sleep. The birth of my son took place on September 6, 1912, in a private hospital on 46th Street. It was a dark and confused rather than a joyful event to me. It wears the same quality in memory as my youthful attempts to pray, a disturbed and earnest but unsuccessful striving after the appropriate emotion. My real emotions, so far as I remember them, were an anxious and rather desperate sympathy with Ida, she being my child and the baby an alien and slightly pathological intrusion; an impatient aversion to the whole experience as distasteful and unwanted; a shame of this feeling as unpoetic in a deep sense; and a happy surprise when I examined the baby and found that he was not the shapeless white slug I had expected, but a well-formed, rather golden-yellow individual toward whom one could without total hypocrisy adopt a social attitude. Even the news that he was slightly jaundiced did not destroy my pleasure in this unexpected color effect. I can not say that I took him into my heart, or felt reconciled to his hold on me by any upsurge of paternal emotion—I had no such experience—but I decided that if he was going to be good looking, I could stand it.

I had drifted with a divided motive into this state of monogamous wedlock and responsible fatherhood. I was soon to drift with a like indecisiveness into an unchosen profession. Only among ideas did I show any positive force. There, I must say, I was laying about me those days like a conqueror. From Aristotle to Otto Jespersen, all philosophers, aestheticians, grammarians, heroes of rhetoric or philology, had to give ground before my psychological explanation of figures of speech. I knew what the truth was, and I had no doubts or double thoughts about it.

"The treatment in rhetorical theory of figures of speech appears to be one of the greatest blunders that an overspectacled scholarship ever obtruded on the world . . .

"Metonymy, synecdoche and other long-tailed monsters are what bar the entrance of a simple human into the realm of poetry. The reason for mentioning only two at this point is that we have now arrived at a suitable place to forget these two."

So I was proclaiming in *Enjoyment of Poetry*.

And in my notebook I was equally cocksure (though not so right!) about programs of social reform.

"The joy of struggle, repressed by civilization, lies sleeping in the veins of everyone. Awaken that and make of it your god. Make clear that it puts Christ in the class of those who celebrated the *aim*, and negates him for the knowledge of fact and method. Don't scorn utopians, show their place."

"The sudden insurrection or the long little-by-little—no matter, it is revolutionary power and not reform emotion that does it."

Intellectually I was so full of these clear decisions, and I was so belligerent in their defense, that I seemed to some people not only forceful but arrantly complacent of my force. "I felt an overpowering ego," Hutchins Hapgood wrote of me in his autobiography, "and a charm certain of itself, both of which qualities I think sadly interfered in later life with his public activity. . . . I felt . . . that the only thing in which he was really interested was himself and the attainment of his personal ambition."[1] My own opinion is that I lacked miserably exactly that headstrong and defined ambition by which he thought I was totally possessed. In practical life, when confronted with one of its diverging grand highways, I was incapable of any decision whatever. I wanted to go both ways; I wanted to go all ways. I never could find the reason for a choice, and I rarely made one.

If you will bear these two facts in mind, you will understand, at least as well as I do, the tale which follows. It tells how a poet and philosophic moralist, with a special distaste for economics, politics, and journalism, became known to the public as a journalist campaigning for a political idea based primarily on economics.

[1] *A Victorian in the Modern World*, pp. 312-14.

Chapter 49

I Drift into a Crusade

THE winter of 1912-13 began with a joy and a disappointment. The joy was a letter from W. C. Brownell, the noted editor-critic at Scribner's:

"October 2, 1912

"My dear sir,

We shall be glad to undertake the publication of your manuscript, 'Enjoyment of Poetry.' . . . We have been much impressed with the quality of the essay. I myself, if I may venture to say so, have enjoyed a very unusual degree and kind of pleasure in reading it . . ."

The disappointment was Mitchell Kennerley's exasperating behavior about my poems. He would not publish them; he would not answer my letters requesting, begging, beseeching, demanding that he publish them; he would not receive me when I went around to his bookshop-office to explain the intimate reason why it was important to publish them at once. Scribner's had set a date in April for *Enjoyment of Poetry*, and my chance to appear as a poet *first* was dwindling away. The emphasis my egotism gave to this fine point in chronology was of course absurd, and I always remember it when I hear young authors, flushed with the dream of fame, denouncing the callousness of some publisher who is merely trying to run a business without loss. In my case, however, Kennerley must take some blame. He published *Child of the Amazons* a year later than he contracted to and without deigning to utter or transmit a word of explanation, or even a perfunctory answer to my repeated appeals to his conscience and kindness. By the time the book came out I was avoiding the vicinity of his office and had almost ceased, because of the pain involved, to think of myself as the author of poems.

Has the history of publishers in their relation to literature ever been studied? It is not a question of sales only but of sympathy.

As soon as the birth of my baby was over, I looked up Art Young in order to tell him I did not want a job without pay and did not want to be an editor. He explained the "co-operative" nature of *The Masses* and assured me the job was merely nominal, they all edited the magazine together. He also assured me, in hearty *non sequitur*, that they would gladly pay me a salary when the thing got on its feet. Art was a master of practical-sounding phrases like "when the thing gets on its feet."

"Come on up and meet the bunch, anyway," he said. "I read them your history of the Men's League in *The Woman Voter*—that's how you got elected—and they want to see you."

The meeting was in Charles Winter's dimly lighted studio on 59th Street east of Park Avenue. Winter was a dreamy-hearted utopian with large blue eyes, a rounded belly, and a pointed beard. His studio seemed full of goldfish bowls and enormous academic drawings of draped symbolic figures illustrating poems for the popular magazines. He was well paid by those magazines, and so was his wife, Alice Beach Winter, who drew equally academic and more sentimental pictures of little children with their stockings coming down. "Academic" means the deliberate perpetration of something you have learned how to do; it means a minimum of that free and fluid movement in which the artist himself, as well as his subject, lives. John Sloan was all for that free and fluid movement—all for realism too, and realism in its foulest and most urban aspects. As an artist of the Robert Henri persuasion, he was in violent revolt against everything the Winters exemplified. Only a taste for bold thinking and the dream of socialism held them together. Sloan and his young protégé, Maurice Becker, a curly-headed Jewish boy, richly talented, at once effervescent and inarticulate like a bottle of pop, were sitting around a long table with Art Young and the Winters when Ida and I came in.

Some other artists and the literary contingent drifted in later. I remember Eugene Wood, the Socialist Party's official humorist, father of the Peggy who is now a famous actress. Eugene was handsome behind his nice brown whiskers, genuinely funny too, but not happy unless the crowd was laughing at his jokes. Louis Untermeyer, also a joke maker, was a thorn in Eugene's flesh because he had a quicker tongue. Ellis O. Jones of the comic weekly *Life* was there, a slim, prim, stiff little person, so stiff that he curved backward, but he had a smiling eye. Horatio Winslow, another gifted humorist, who was on the staff of *Puck*, was big and friendly hulking and looked as solemn as a hound dog. Mary Heaton Vorse, the popular story writer, was pale and fragile, and although abounding in energy had a permanently weary look. Inez Haynes Gillmore, also a well-known story writer, was dark by contrast, youthful and full blooded.

Those were the editors who really cared about the magazine. They were warm and charming people, and to me impressive. They were men and women who had made a name for themselves. Moreover, their conversation, led in the main by Louis Untermeyer and John Sloan, who has an Elizabethan flow of metaphor, was intellectually exciting. The whole scene and situation lent itself to my effort and my then very great need to romanticize New York life and romanticize the revolution.

The dummy of an inchoate next number lay at the end of the table with an empty chair before it. I had never even heard the word "dummy" before, and had no idea how a magazine came into being. But I soon found myself in that chair with Charles Winter above me smilingly explaining how to "paste up the dummy." No more fascinating sport has ever been invented. You have your text in a long continuous ribbon called galley proofs and your pictures on a big sheet reproduced in various sizes that have been calculated beforehand, and you take a previous issue of the magazine and, with a mighty pair of shears and a brimming pot of mucilage, insert, in whatever pattern pleases you, the new material in the old forms.

I don't want to be boastful in this book, but in order to explain what fate did to me, I am compelled to admit that I have a natural genius for pasting up a dummy. This art combines the infantine delight of cutting out paper dolls or keeping a scrapbook with the adult satisfaction of fooling yourself into thinking you are moulding public opinion. I felt my fitness for both these tasks as soon as I got those scissors into my hands. Inside of twenty minutes I was telling Winter how it should be done. All the joys, and none of the pains, of the divine act of creation were filling my soul. Moreover, nobody interfered. Nobody else in the room had any desire to do anything but talk and drink beer. The talk was radical; it was free-thought talk and not just socialism. There was a sense of universal revolt and regeneration, of the just-before-dawn of a new day in American art and literature and living-of-life as well as in politics. I never more warmly enjoyed liking people and being liked by them.

I still had no intention of becoming editor of the magazine. Indeed, throughout the evening, I stood my ground with much apparent character against a charming stream of persuasion on that subject—charming because so irrational. The magazine did not really exist. It had no single asset—only a few thousand unfilled subscriptions and a tiny office down on Nassau Street with the rent some months in arrears. The editorship was not only unpaid, but would cost the incumbent, I figured, in the neighborhood of six hundred dollars a month. Evidently it was not only as author of a history of the Men's League that I had been selected for this honor, but as *organizer* of the league. What this enterprise needed was neither a writer nor, primarily, an editor, but a business executive, a promoter and entrepreneur.

Though I saw this clearly, I did not make a clear decision. I was having too much fun. I agreed before we parted to get out one number, dated December 1912, and insert in it an appeal for funds. I would write some editorials indicating the policy that I thought the magazine ought to pursue, and if we got the funds, I would join the co-operative on equal terms with the rest and contribute a monthly page of such editorials. Meanwhile we all promised to canvass our rich friends and see if we could raise a little money privately.

Life is relatively simple for an artist who is completely impractical, but I am afflicted with the ability to organize a job and stick at it until it is finished. This inconsequential talent has got in the way of my career as a writer and caused a constant leakage of energy from what I ought to be doing. None of those creative geniuses who owned *The Masses* ever paid the slightest attention to the business end of it. The "office" was in charge of John Sloan's Irish wife, Dolly, a tiny, vital, scrappy, devoted, emotional secretary of socialist locals, organizer of socialist picnics, collector of funds for strikers. Dolly, with Piet Vlag in Florida, had the whole thing on her hands, including a rosy-cheeked, unpaid stenographer named Rose Greenburg. And she was pretty nearly distracted with it. There was no one in that bunch of utopians with whom she could even discuss such a question, for instance, as paying the rent or, in case that proved impossible, closing up the office. I could at least talk about such things with a sense of what they meant, and Dolly took refuge in my practicality of mind. Before we had that experimental number out, I was to all intents and purposes president and general manager of The Masses Publishing Company as well as editor of the magazine. Dolly and I alone raised the money to get it out, she in small sums, I in fairly large.

Our experimental number, chiefly because of Art Young's double-page cartoon portraying the "capitalist press" as a whorehouse, made quite a splurge. There was a recognizable portrait of Arthur Brisbane, famous editor of Hearst's New York *Journal*, in the vestibule. And there were other not-too-subtle features in the picture. We put a good deal of spit in our derision, and I received letters of shocked remonstrance from some of my refined friends, notably Oswald Garrison Villard and George Foster Peabody. Mr. Villard wrote:

"I feel that in sorrow and in friendship I must add my protest against the extremes to which you are going, particularly in *The Masses*. Your cartoon on the press I thought vulgar beyond anything I have ever seen in an American magazine, and very unfair to the press."

Mr. Peabody confided: "I think it is distinctly injurious to your great powers given for Man's inspiration to so deliberately throw away that refinement which is true power, and make appeal, as it seems to me the paper does, both in illustration and reading-matter, to prejudice and distrust, and I fear it also invites to careless living both as to care of body and mind."

These fatherly admonishments did not bother me greatly, for I had committed myself now to revolution and was glad to break the ties still binding me to what I called reform. It did bother me that our appeal for funds brought in only twenty dollars through the mail, and that when we foregathered for a second meeting not one of the other editors had raised a cent. Not one of them had made a motion in that direction, or felt apologetic for his broken promise. This cured me once for all of the illusion that *The Masses* was, or ever would be, in a true sense co-operative. Piet Vlag had evidently been a shepherding parent to these creative children and I, if I stayed with them, would have to take his place.

That should have been enough, in view of my scheme of life, to make me abandon the project. Running a pseudo-cooperative enterprise which had no funds was as far as the North Pole from the part-time paid job I had set out to get. And indeed for several weeks I did regard the venture as canceled out. But I had made too energetic a beginning. I had, for one thing, changed the policy of the magazine from extreme right to extreme left socialism—this without a protest from any one of its editor-owners. Militant class struggle was more to the taste of those times than co-operative stores, more to the taste of artists and poets, I suppose, in all times. I called my double page of editorials "Knowledge and Revolution," and in my first paragraphs took sides not only with revolution against reform, but also (although I doubt if anybody noticed it) with experimental science against Marx's mystical determinism.

"By Knowledge we do not mean a set of intellectual dogmas which can not change and to which every new fact must conform whether it wants to or not. . . . We mean experimental knowledge —a free investigation of the developing facts and continuous retesting of the theories which pertain to the end we have in view.

"The end we have in view is an economic and social revolution, and by revolution we do not mean the journey of the earth around the sun, or any other thing that is bound to happen whether we direct our wills to it or not. We mean a radical democratization of industry and society, made possible by the growth of capitalism, but to be accomplished only when and if the spirit of liberty and rebellion is sufficiently awakened in the classes which are now oppressed. A revolution is a sweeping change accomplished through the conquest of power by a subjected class . . .

"Between revolutionist and reformer there is . . . a flat contradiction of wish, belief, and action. The reformer wishes to procure for the workers their share of the blessings of civilization; he believes in himself and his altruistic oratory; he tries to multiply his kind. The revolutionist wishes the workers to take the blessings of civilization; he believes in them and their organized power; he tries to increase in them the knowledge of their situation and the spirit of class-conscious aggression . . ."

With that for an opening I backed up the rebels in every industrial or legal battle then in progress: the IWW in Lawrence; the anarchists in San Diego; the Structural Iron Workers in Indianapolis; the Timber Workers in Louisiana; the miners waging a "civil war" in West Virginia; and I declared that "every vote cast for Eugene V. Debs is a vote for revolutionary socialism and the class struggle." No one would suspect that those editorials were contributed to a defunct literary and artistic magazine just to see whether funds would pour in to revive it. They sounded like a political locomotive under full steam ahead. Although I do nothing, I always talk politics like a man of action, and that makes it necessary at least to go on talking.

Moreover, I had picked from my then unpublished *Child of the Amazons* the poem I thought most appropriate to *The Masses*. "At the Aquarium," which still usually represents me in school books and anthologies, appeared on page two of that first issue side by side with a "Poetry of Earth" by Louis Untermeyer which I had found in the galleys. It gave notice that I was an artist as well as an editor and did much, I think, to make it difficult for me to back out. A letter from John Sloan made me feel that I had arrived in a companionship which might go far to indemnify me for my lost rural soul:

"It was well worth while to raise *The Masses* from the tomb to put these lines into print," he wrote. "They hit me all of a heap."

On Louis Untermeyer, whose "Poetry of Earth" was far from his best, the effect was less happy. At least I date from that moment a smiling disagreement between us as to whose poems are the least immortal. As a good friend Louis has not failed to enwrap my prose works in encomiums far exceeding their merit, but he can prove with the logic of Euclid and the disinterestedness of John Calvin that I was predestined not to be a poet.

The lack of funds might have stopped me, in spite of my editorial and poetic momentum, had not fate led me, at a certain hour and minute of that month of December 1912, into the lobby of the old Manhattan Hotel. My gorgeously radiant once-love, Inez Milholland, was passing at the same instant in the opposite direction. She greeted me with dancing eyes. She had read our first number and was as delighted as Mr. Villard was shocked.

"You're going on with it, aren't you?" she said.

"I'm afraid not. There was no response to our appeal for funds."

"Have you tried Mrs. Belmont?"

"Why Mrs. Belmont?" I said. "She isn't a socialist."

"What of it? You're a militant—that's all that matters."

Militants were the followers of Emmeline Pankhurst, the hards as against the softs in the feminist movement.

"Let's get Mrs. Belmont to put up some money. I'll help you. She doesn't know anything about socialism. Just let her know it's a fight, and she'll like it."

Mrs. O. H. P. Belmont was the belligerent bride from Alabama who made social history in 1895 by divorcing W. K. Vanderbilt. Dixon Wecter, in his *Saga of American Society*, calls her "the indefatigable duchess of the Gilded Age," and credits her with finding the structure of American society brick and leaving it marble. She also found woman suffrage feeble and left it fashionable. She was always backing some young Amazon as companion-in-arms and half-adopted daughter, and Inez just then occupied this hard-working but luxurious post.

I found myself three days later in a palatial dwelling on upper

Madison Avenue, dining at the right hand of a henna-haired, pug-nosed and pink-painted old lady who, but for the genuineness of her jewelry and the imperiousness of her will, might have been the very caricature of an aristocrat. Inez had roped in the novelist John Fox, Jr., to lend a savor of literary success to the occasion. Mrs. Belmont liked to conceive herself in the role of noble-born patron to people whom some talent had raised, not up to her height to be sure, but above the common level. She had a taste for the real thing in success, and in that no American writer surpassed John Fox. His charming southern romance, *The Trail of the Lonesome Pine,* out-selling Jack London's *Call of the Wild,* had made him the national literary champion. Thus John's interest in *The Masses,* although imparted to him by Inez only a few hours before, was reassuring to Mrs. Belmont, and he brought a promise from his friend Finley Peter Dunne to contribute a Mr. Dooley dialogue to the next number. It was a jovial evening, and not more insincere than such evenings have to be. Mrs. Belmont said she would put up two thousand dollars toward getting the magazine started, and John Fox, having lifted her to that peak with a brilliant flow of enthusiasm, could do nothing in the rather hollow pause which followed, being a gallant and good sport, but say that he would add another thousand to it.

Thus our super-revolutionary magazine owed its send-off to a leader of New York's 400—to the fortune of old Public-be-Damned Vanderbilt, in fact—and to a southern gentleman with as much interest in proletarian revolution as I had in polo ponies.

I had estimated, God knows on what data, that three thousand dollars would enable us to extend our experiment for another six months. At the end of that time the thing would surely be on its feet—or if it wasn't, I would quit. That was the mood in which I kept on with this job that I did not want. In calling myself practical, I meant merely that I am able to conceive things in their practical relations, not that I have what is called "acumen." I believed the fable left behind by Piet Vlag that the magazine had been self-supporting and that only some injudicious advertising had put it on the rocks. I thought it momentous that writers and artists well paid by other magazines were putting their best work into *The Masses* for nothing. I never thought of examining the books, or investigating the ratio between payment for contributions and other costs of magazine production. The notion of a paper's advocating the abolition of profits, and flourishing because its contributor-owners took no profits, seemed to me as businesslike as it was consistent. That such a magazine could not depend upon advertisements did not matter much—good-will would make up for that.

At the end of my six months' experiment the magazine was costing more than at the beginning, and no sustaining funds were pouring in. Nothing was pouring in—not even subscriptions on a scale that promised success. From a practical standpoint our co-operative magazine was a flat failure. But something else had happened. *The Masses* had gathered to itself a character. It had crystallized a cultural event that hung ready in the historic moment. It had acquired in the public mind, or that part of it which is alive to new developments, a meaning and a momentum which made quitting a more heroic task than raising money.

Finley Peter Dunne was the first to make me feel the eventfulness of such a magazine as *The Masses*. I found him, when I went up to discuss the promised contribution, beaming with delight in its audacity and animal spirits. He cared as little as John Fox, I suppose, about the division between revolutionist and reformer, the split in the Socialist Party over the IWW. The words in my editorials which to the initiated placed me on the side of working-class revolution were probably put down by Mr. Dooley, if remarked at all, to literary exuberance. *The Masses* was to him primarily a revolt against commercial journalism. The idea of writers owning a magazine where they could say what they really thought was the focus of his delight.

"There's a lot o' things I've never been able to say," he exclaimed, "and if you don't mind this horrendous dialect in which I write, I'll hand them in gladly."

Humor is a passion, and those feebly endowed with it will not understand the weight these words from Mark Twain's successor carried. (Indeed that stiff-ribbed species will not understand *The Masses* at all.) A magazine where Mr. Dooley could laugh the laughs that a commercial press had pushed back into his throat was a big thing. . . .

He never fulfilled his promise. He renewed it more than once, but each time those wide, genially-dimpled cheeks would seem more florid, the red veins more pronounced, the eyes more momentary in their brilliance. I do not mean that he changed, but I gradually perceived that Mr. Dooley would never say the things his market had prevented him from saying.

"I'm too old to start over again," he said at last. "I'm with you boys, but I'm played out. I can't write any more."

Mr. Dooley was old, but others were young, and they flocked to the standard we raised as though history herself had announced a new era. Sloan brought to our second meeting a drawing by Robert Henri, leader of the "realist" painters. I received through the mail a ballad from Arturo Giovannitti, whose poem "The Walker" had just made a national sensation in the *Atlantic Monthly*. And while I was yearning for a piece of prose to match these acquisitions, my home telephone rang one morning and a strange voice said:

"I am a person named John Reed. I work on the *American Magazine*, and I've got a story they won't print. I'd like to offer it to *The Masses*."

"Fine!" I said. "Send it along."

"No, I'm right here on 11th Street, and I'll bring it over. I want to see you."

I agreed reluctantly, for my idea was to forget *The Masses* every day until after lunch. I was also not much impressed by John Reed when he arrived. He had a knobby and too filled-out face that reminded me, both in form and color, of a potato. He was dressed up in a smooth brown suit with round pants' legs and a turned-over starched collar, and seemed rather small and rather distracted. He stood up or moved about the room all through his visit and kept looking in every direction except that in which he was addressing his words. It is difficult for me to get the sense of togetherness with a stranger, even if he looks at me. And when he looks at the walls, or the house fronts on the other side of the street, and talks into the air, and walks around in this excessively steamed-up manner, I am hopelessly embarrassed and want to lie down and rest after it is over. I was heartily sorry I had ever let myself in for *The Masses* after John Reed went away. I decided to bring out one more number and quit.

And then I read his story, "Where the Heart Is." It was the simple story of a New York prostitute who took a trip to Europe and South America and greatly enjoyed it, but enjoyed most of all getting back home to the Haymarket. I still suspected that a magazine which set out to publish what could not be sold in the market would probably be filled for the most part with claptrap. I always have with me that strain of sceptical common sense. But here was a man writing about a significant phase of American life that no other magazine would dare to mention unless sanctimoniously, and writing with unlabored grace—a style both vivid and restrained.

The idea that *The Masses* might be *good*, that there really was a creative literature stifled by commercial journalism took a firm grip on me after I read John Reed's story.

Another phenomenon that helped convince me was Howard Brubaker. I had met him at the home of Frances Perkins, who dwelt then somewhere along the edge of socialism, and it was her husband who suggested that I write to Howard for a contribution. Howard responded with a grotesque paragraph about J. P. Morgan's testimony before the Pujol Committee and a promise that if I would tell him the deadline, he would send a few paragraphs every month. He did not care how I used them, he said, or how much of them I used, or whether I signed his name to them or not. Howard Brubaker never came more than once or twice to a *Masses* meeting, but he sent me a column of those inimitable paragraphs, now so highly prized by *The New Yorker*, every month exactly on the deadline, without a miss, without a procrastination, throughout the ten years' life of *The Masses* and *The Liberator*. He has been kind enough to say in a recent letter: "I know better than anyone else how much I owe to you and *The Masses* for this little specialty of mine." But it is not true that he owed anything to me. He sprang, full-armed with paragraphs, from the head of Jove—full-armed and, what is most unusual in humorists, reliable.

In the first few months I had to write a "filler" or two, which I signed with a pseudonym, but soon contributions began to pour in —and contributing editors too. For the March number Ida got us a drawing from Jo Davidson, then already growing a great reputation. Stuart Davis, John Sloan's wry and skim-milk colored protégé, brought us a picture as harsh and lusty as he looked sick. Glenn O. Coleman, a shy, mild, soft-spoken genius, pale as though starving, unrolled three drawings that had the depth and richness of paintings. Cornelia Barns, an elf-eyed girl with smoothed brown hair, turned up with a picture that was brilliantly comic and not like anything else in the world. James Hopper, chief candidate those days for the mantle of O. Henry, sent us a story too exquisitely horrible to be sold, about a man whose job was eating live rats in public. George Bellows, America's great outdoor-athlete painter, drew us a double-page cartoon for the April number, and joined the staff in May. A baby-eyed pigwigeon named Robert Carlton Brown sauntered in from Cliffside, New Jersey, and began tapping out elsewhere unprintable stories with the ease, at least, of genius. Gelett Burgess, famous humorist of the *Purple Cow*, sent us a deadly earnest "Hymn to the Anthropomorphic God." Oliver Herford, of similar fame, sent us an equally earnest drawing. Horace Traubel mailed us a paragraph that seemed a benediction from Walt Whitman. Upton Sinclair endorsed our politics with a contri-

Drawn by Cornelia Barns

VOTERS

bution opposing our views about sex. Witter Bynner, William Rose Benet, Carl Sandburg, Harry Kemp offered their best, and not their second-best, poems. Ernest Poole, Leroy Scott, Wilbur Daniel Steele, Susan Glaspell, popular story writers, had each a "better" story for

The Masses. Even Franklin P. Adams found something to say that he could not print in his celebrated column.[1]

I have gone forward somewhat in listing these names in order to convey the size and brightness of the creative constellation which formed around *The Masses.* But the process was in full swing within the first six months. At the same time the militant leaders of the working class without a single exception took the magazine into their hearts. Bill Haywood, Carlo Tresca, and Elizabeth Gurley Flynn, leading a great strike in Paterson, New Jersey; Ettor and Giovannitti in jail at Lawrence, Massachusetts; Schmidt and Kaplan in jail in California; Mother Jones and John Lawson battling the mine owners in West Virginia; Frank Tannenbaum marshaling the unemployed; William Z. Foster, starting a little syndicalist movement in Chicago; every agitator who really intended to overthrow capitalism and inaugurate a working-class millennium in the United States felt that he had a body of friends and colleagues in the writers and artists of *The Masses.*

Our magazine provided, for the first time in America, a meeting ground for revolutionary labor and the radical intelligentsia. It acquired, in spite of its gay laughter, the character of a crusade. And although I continued to push it from me and struggle toward its fringes like a fly in a gluey web, I was hopelessly caught in with this glamorous march of events. Having set out to find a paid part-

[1] Others not then so well known published some of their earliest work in *The Masses*: among them, Sherwood Anderson, James Oppenheim, Djuna Barnes, Helen R. Hull, Arthur Bullard, Mabel Dodge, Vachel Lindsay, Alice Duer Miller, Sara N. Cleghorn, Leslie Nelson Jennings, Phillips Russell, Amy Lowell, Norman Matson, William Carlos Williams, Konrad Bercovici, Randolph Bourne, Babette Deutsch, Elizabeth Coatsworth, Philip Littell, and George Creel. We received contributions from Romain Rolland, Bertrand Russell, Maxim Gorky, and letters from our enthusiastic reader, Bernard Shaw. The painters Maurice Sterne, Arthur B. Davies, Randall Davey, Morris Kantor, Mahonri Young, John Barber, Eugene Higgins, Abraham Walkowitz gave us drawings. The cartoonists Robert Minor and Boardman Robinson came in and made *The Masses* their own. We published a drawing by André Ruellan at the age of eight.

The Liberator, which succeeded *The Masses* after its suppression by the government in 1917, attracted some new bright stars to this constellation. The woodcuts of J. J. Lankes and the humorous drawings of William Gropper got early attention in its pages, as did the plays of Elmer Rice and the writings of John Dos Passos. Clive Weed contributed slashing cartoons. S. N. Behrman, Claude McKay, James Weldon Johnson, Evelyn Scott, Ruth Suckow, Frances Winwar, Genevieve Taggard, William Ellery Leonard, Edmund Wilson, Stuart Chase, Joseph Freeman, David Morton, Carlton Beals, Marya Zaturenska, William Troy, Hellen Keller, Alexander Berkman, Maxwell Bodenheim, Siegfried Sassoon, Olive Tilford Dargan, Freda Kirchwey, Lewis Gannett, Arthur Ransome, Roger Baldwin and Francis Biddle (both these last in the role of poets) contributed to its lustre.

time job in the service of socialism which would free my too moral mind for creative writing, I had become the unpaid editor, promoter, money raiser, and general manager of a revolutionary magazine— a full-time job if there ever was one.

Chapter 50

The Policy of The Masses

A GOOD deal has been written from time to time in critical judgment of *The Masses*, and I should like to have my say on that. For me the magazine had one plainly evident superiority, a clean and clear make-up. My contempt for the crazy clutter of type and pictures that is considered "popular" by American magazine editors was enthusiastically shared by *The Masses* artists. We all liked plenty of space. We wanted each object, whether art or literature, presented as a unit, in adequate isolation, unpecked at by editorial sales talk. We wanted the text to read consecutively as a work of art should, not be chopped up and employed as a lure to jump the reader over into advertising pages at the back. The only clash between me and those artists, and that a brief one, concerned the importance of size in reproducing pictures. The generous dimensions of the drawings in *The Masses*, a notable innovation in American magazinedom, were due entirely to them. I merely yielded to their arguments—and raised the extra money required.

Another feature I can not take credit for was the dominantly realist note in text and pictures. *The Masses* marked, I have been told, the first appearance of "realism" in an American magazine. But I was ignorant of, and indifferent to, schools of literature, and of the new movement in art represented by Sloan, Bellows, and the other pupils of Robert Henri, I had never heard. My theories of poetry did, to be sure, assert the kinship of its defining values with those of real experience, but rather as a scientific fact than a contemporary enthusiasm. They fitted me to preside with sympathy over an outburst of dirt and dreariness in realms before consecrated to sweetness and light. But I can not say that I had any tendency of my own to disparage reality as a means of demonstrating my interest in it. Indeed, I think I exercised a moderating influence upon this not wholly rational factor in the realist enthusiasm. I tried to qualify with an occasional happy color that triumphal flaunting of the sordid for which *The Masses* became rapidly and quite justly famous.

Another innovation that gave character to *The Masses* was our abandonment of the old "he-and-she" joke and the elaborate two, three- and four-line dialogue under a picture.

"My dear, I'll be economically independent if I have to borrow every cent!"

"Oh, papa, that poor little birdie hasn't got any cage!"

"Your Honor, this woman gave birth to a naked child!"

"Why a fella says to me only yistiddy, he says, 'This ain't war, it's murder!' "

In the prevalence of these one-line captions we departed sharply from the tradition set by *Life* and *Puck* and *Judge,* although none of us was conscious of this change. It just came natural, in pitting creative art against commercial journalism, to title pictures in this more energetic fashion.

The long-time result of our pictorial revolt, it seems to me, was to introduce into commercial journalism some of the subtler values of creative art. This change, at least, has taken place, and *The Masses* led the way. Norman Hapgood saw it coming, and when he took over the editorship of *Harper's Weekly* deliberately set out to imitate our pictures, employing our artists to produce them. The public was not ready, and he himself lacked experience or the instinct for it. We used to smile at him because he would pay big fees for photographs of paintings which the artists were only too eager to give away. America was then still provincial in these matters. But in 1925 *The New Yorker* found it natural to do what Norman Hapgood had awkwardly strained after, and the pictorial revolution for which *The Masses* artists worked without pay turned out to be one of the most profitable innovations in the history of journalism. At least that is my view, and I take no credit for this innovation except as a willing pupil. The central force in putting it through was John Sloan, and I consider my aesthetic development under his guidance one of the lucky turns in my very accidental education.

I can see Sloan at a *Masses* meeting, holding up a drawing by Stuart Davis of two sad, homely girls from the slums of Hoboken, and proposing the title:

"Gee, Mag, think of us bein' on a magazine cover!"

That formed our June cover, which was much commented on.
It was realism; it was also revolt.

Inside that number—to take it as an example—the revolt was
defined in a manner unmistakably left socialist. We endorsed the
general strike in Belgium, supported the "War in Paterson," backed
Karl Liebknecht's fight against the Social Democratic majority in

JUNE. 1913   10 CENTS

The MASSES

STUART DAVIS 1913

Drawn by Stuart Davis

"Gee, Mag, Think of Us Bein' on a Magazine Cover!"

the German Reichstag, affirmed that the so-called "bandits of Mexico" were the real patriots of the country, satirized the "fifty-seven varieties of national religion," ridiculed an Old Testament story, and featured a lyric by a striking Paint Creek miner longing, in anything but pure poetry, for the coming of the spring:

> I will not watch the floating clouds that hover
> Above the birds that warble on the wing;
> I want to use this GUN from under cover—
> Oh Buddy, how I'm longing for the spring.

An editorial reads: "You don't believe in class struggle? Go out to Paterson and try to make a noise like a free citizen. That's all John Reed did, and he got twenty days in jail. It's getting so you can't collect your thoughts without being arrested for unlawful assemblage."

At the same time, in the brief fourteen pages of that number, there were five jokes without social significance, two merely humorous drawings, a piece of fanciful fiction, a lithograph by George Bellows of happy children playing in Central Park, and an unsigned lyric by the editor entitled "June Morning":

> De sun am shinin' bright,
> Am fillin' me full ob light;
> Ah done git up ea'ly,
> An' wash mahse'f mo' thor'ly.

It is this catholicity of *The Masses*, its freedom from the one-track mental habit of the rabid devotee of a cause, for which I as editor was most responsible. I never could see why people with a zeal for improving life should be indifferent to the living of it. Why can not one be younghearted, gay, laughing, audacious, full of animal spirits, and yet also use his brains? The everlasting cerebral attitude of such papers as *The Nation* and *The New Republic*, the steady, unbillowy, unjoy-disturbed throbbing of grey matter in their pages, makes me, after some months, a little dogsick. And yet on the other hand I hate and always did hate smart-alecky and irresponsible left-ism. This posture of mind was, I think, my chief contribution to *The Masses*.

My theory that art is in general essence, whatever practical functions it may take on, a technique for arresting the onward stream of action and damming up a deeper pool of consciousness, was already made clear in *Enjoyment of Poetry*. I was reading the proofs of that book while we were starting *The Masses.* Naturally then, as editor, I did not harp incessantly on propaganda. I tried to have plenty of things in every number which had nothing to do with socialism, and some whose values were wholly comprised in themselves—some items, if you will, of art for art's sake.

Aside from enhancing life, that seems to me the wisest way to conduct propaganda. The cherished idea is there, and it is there in clear and honest form. But it is not so drummed upon that only those already interested will listen. Loyalty to principle takes the place of zealotry, and enlightenment that of indoctrination.

This distinguishing quality of *The Masses* was understood, I think, by most of the editors and by a large circle of readers. It was, in my mind, the central and spirit-giving trait of the whole enterprise. But as the struggle tightened, and the bloody years ensued of actual revolution and counter-revolution, the very concept of it seems to have got lost.[1] In a recent thoughtful book on *The Little*

---

[1] A misapprehension of this policy by those who look back is no doubt partly due to the work of historical rewrite men associated with the Communist Party. The communists found it advantageous at one time to represent their cultural organ, *The New Masses*, as an adult proletarian-revolutionary magazine which had grown up out of a semi-Bohemian embryo called *The Masses*. They even went so far as to celebrate in 1936 a "twenty-fifth anniversary" of *The New Masses*, which was then in its tenth year.

If the world goes communist, this myth may well become authentic history. But meantime the reader of this book may want to enjoy a little knowledge of the facts: *The Masses* was nine years dead, and even its successor, *The Liberator*, three years in its grave, when *The New Masses* was founded by an entirely different group of artists and writers. The old editor-owners were not consulted; nothing but the name was borrowed, and that after some dispute. At its birth in May 1926, *The New Masses* had six editors and sixteen members of the executive board. Of these twenty-two people only two had ever been contributing editors of the old *Masses*, and they had resigned (because the magazine had a policy!) a year and a half before it was suppressed in 1917. Only two of the twenty-two had ever been contributing editors of *The Liberator*, a secondary position in any case, since *The Liberator* was not a co-operative magazine but was owned and controlled by my sister and me.

During the year or two in which *The New Masses* tried sincerely to be a "free magazine," it had some similarity, though no historic identity, with the magazine whose name it borrowed. After it submitted to the authority of the communists, the last trace of this similarity vanished.

It would be hard to invent two vehicles of expression more radically contrasted. Not only my experimental philosophy, antipractical theory of art, and constant militance against dogma, but the zest for obstreperous truth-telling which actuated all the leaders of the old crowd distinguish the two ventures completely. Dissimulation was tabu in our gang; jesuitism an arch-enemy; loyalty to an organization treason to the truth; to put over a "party line" unthinkable. For us the end and the means were at one: we were a free magazine devoted to setting "the working class and therewith all society" free.

(I went into this question more elaborately in two articles called "Bunk about Bohemia" and "New Masses for Old," in the *Modern Monthly*, May and June 1934.)

Magazine[2] the authors say of *The Masses* and *The Liberator*: "The struggle between comic playboyism and serious reportage went on in the pages of these two magazines almost from the beginning." Nothing describable in these terms ever occurred in either magazine. Indeed to anyone who remembers a *Masses* meeting, the idea of a "struggle" between hilarious laughter and serious work for socialism is fantastic. The derogation of humor implied in the word "playboyism" is alien to our whole state of mind. Humor holds a higher place in America than in other national cultures, and *The Masses*, notwithstanding its internationalism, was in that respect constitutionally and very fervently American. We would give anything for a good laugh except our principles. And we had the same attitude toward a good story, a good poem, a good picture.

There were a few members of the staff, to be sure, who did not care much about, or bother to understand, this policy. There were a few who wanted the magazine as a whole to have no policy. They were not the most playful members, however, but those most serious about self-expressive art. I got along with them because of my taste for variety. I wanted everybody to express his own individuality to the limit, so long as he did not transgress the principles of socialism. And I could always see to it in the process of make-up, and if driven to the wall by an ultimatum as the holder of the purse strings, that nothing antisocialist or counter-revolutionary should appear in the paper.

Thus just as it differed from most propaganda magazines in being full of irrelevant song and laughter, *The Masses* differed from most song and laughter magazines, especially those giving voice to an aesthetic revolt, in defending a political program. To make the program unmistakable I opened a department called "The International Battle Line," in which William English Walling gave our readers a monthly education in the problems of world socialism. Walling was the one left-wing socialist in America who, like Lenin and Trotsky in Russia, Rosa Luxemburg in Germany, Jules Guesde in France, was doing some real and rapid thinking about the revolutionary movement. By carrying his column, *The Masses* declared its position in the world socialist movement with a trumpet blast. And the position taken in my editorials was even more extreme— exactly, perhaps, because born of reflection and not of the natural love of battle.

The birth of *The Masses* coincided with the birth of "Greenwich

[2] By Frederick J. Hoffman, Charles Allen, and Carolyn F. Ulrich.

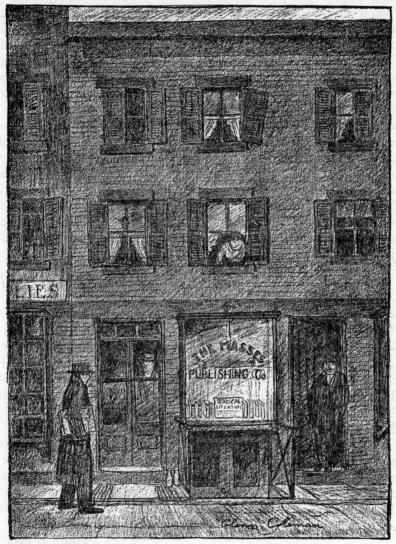

Drawn by Glenn O. Coleman

The Masses Office at 91 Greenwich Avenue

Village" as a self-conscious entity, an American Bohemia or gipsy-minded Latin Quarter, but its relations with that entity were not simple. I lived in Greenwich Village, and believed in the life that flowed there so brimmingly, and I moved *The Masses* office up there from Nassau Street as soon as I could. But I disliked the developing self-consciousness. I took tacit exception when people first began to say "the Village," and fastidiously refrained from using the term myself. To me it all only meant being alive, and this complacent self-labeling was the beginning of a new death.

This attitude of mine, together with my zeal for the Marxian concept of revolution, and the serious dedication to socialism of a majority of the editor-owners, gave *The Masses* a distinctly anti-Bohemian tenor. A letter written to me long after by Robert Minor illustrates our way of talking and thinking about Greenwich Village. He had taken my place[3] for a month or two while I went to California to work on a book, and I, knowing him as an anarchistic rebel, had sent him a telegram of warning on this subject.

"April 8, 1921

"My Dear Max,

What the devil—'surrendering to Greenwich Village studio art!!' . . . The only thing in the paper that could even with the slightest of reason be questioned on that score is the small picture by Morris Kantor. And I think that mature deliberation will convince you that that picture, as well, is worthy of publication and is not of morbid, mad or dilettante origin; that is, that it is of serious intent and fairly good execution . . .

"Now that number was definitely a labor movement number of the most realistic sort. Nothing could be more timely or important or more serious than the Haywood article on one hand and the comparison of Foster and Haywood's labor philosophy on the other. . . .

"I am going to make the double cartoon this month, so I suppose the coming issue will be vulgar-realistic enough to suit you.

Yours as ever,
Bob."

Another thing that gave *The Masses* a special flavor was my steady objection to dogma and insistence on experimental thinking. In

[3] As editor of *The Liberator*, which had then succeeded *The Masses*.

our second number John Sloan and I took a stand (in editorial and cartoon) on the chief issue then agitating the socialist movement, that between "political action" and "direct action."

"Now one and now the other is more important," I insisted. "All these questions of method are to be answered differently at different times, at different places, in different circumstances. . . . The one thing continually important is that we keep our judgment free. Tie up to no dogma whatever."

Later Art Young drew a picture of a complacent cherub carrying a tiny pail of water dipped from the "Ocean of Truth." The pail was marked "Dogma," and my editorial read:

"I publish this little picture in answer to numberless correspondents who 'want to know just what this magazine is trying to do.' It is trying *not* to try to empty the ocean, for one thing. And in a propaganda paper that alone is a task."

This freedom from dogma enabled us to join independently in the struggle for racial equality and woman's rights, for intelligent sex relations, above all (and beneath all) for birth and population control. Socialist dogma declared that all these problems would be solved when the economy of capitalism was replaced by a co-operative commonwealth. I was convinced to the contrary. Indeed, I was not at any point millennial in my thoughts about that commonwealth.

"Some future age looking back will be horrified at our unconscious subjection to a money power, and those looking back will be unconscious under the tyranny of some other power," I wrote in my notebook.

Another distinctive trait of *The Masses* was its emphasis on liberty as the goal of the class struggle. The socialist doctrine appeals to three major motives: the love of liberty, the yearning for brother-

hood or human solidarity, and the wish to plan and organize things in a rational manner. There is also the religious motive, the desire of God's orphans to believe in something beyond reality. Socialists differ profoundly according as one or the other of these passions stands in the center of their motive-pattern, and all four were doubtless represented in the old "*Masses* crowd." But I think most of the contributing editors shared my dominant interest in human freedom. So far, at any rate, as I shaped its policy, the guiding ideal of the magazine was that every individual should be made free to live and grow in his own chosen way. That was what I hoped might be achieved with all this distasteful palaver about politics and economics. Even if it can not be achieved, I would say to myself, the good life consists in striving towards it. As my notebook of those days declares: "I can bear the prospect that the world may never be free, but I can not bear the prospect of my living in it and not taking part in the fight for freedom."

Together with our support of the IWW, this emphasis on the goal of freedom attracted people who had no taste for the socialist notion of scientific procedure toward a goal. George Bellows, for instance, who threatened sometimes to leave us for Emma Goldman's paper, *Mother Earth,* could never quite carry out his threat. John Reed, too, was originally attracted by this aspect of our policy. He knew little of socialism, but was much under the influence of Lincoln Steffens' Christian anarchism when he took up with *The Masses.* He came round to see me a second time before our January number went to press, dressed now in a soft collar and a loose tweed suit that made him seem as big as he was, and as kindly and sagacious. He had a "Statement" in his hand that he proposed—hesitantly, since he was not a member of the staff—might be run every month at the masthead of the magazine:

"We refuse to commit ourselves to any course of action except this: to do with *The Masses* exactly what we please. . . . We don't even intend to conciliate our readers. . . . The broad purpose of *The Masses* is a social one: to everlastingly attack old systems, old morals, old prejudices. . . . Standing on the common sidewalk, we intend to lunge at spectres—with a rapier rather than a broad-axe, with frankness rather than innuendo. We intend to be arrogant, impertinent, in bad taste, but not vulgar. We will be bound by no one creed or theory of social reform, but will express them all, providing they be radical. . . ."[4]

[4] Fully quoted in *John Reed, The Making of a Revolutionary,* by Granville Hicks.

To me Reed's statement presented a diplomatic problem of some delicacy. It prickled with notions I could not endure. To a pupil of John Dewey, making an intellectual fuss *without* committing yourself to a course of action was anathema. To a revolutionary experimentalist (if I may give that grandiose name to my position) the word *radical* was interdicted as strictly as the word *reform*. "Creeds" also were interdicted. A phrase like "all creeds and theories of social reform providing they be radical" was either a joke or a carefully embroidered red rag to a bull. I knew from his preparing the statement that Reed expected to join the staff, and I wanted him to. But I thought it strange that he had read my editorial page with so little reflection, or not read it at all. I called his attention to what I had said there about reform and revolution, and tried without being professorial to explain that this was not just rebellious talk but a carefully thought-out program of class struggle which put us in relation to a world movement.

Borrowing his "arrogant, impertinent," and his phrases about doing as we please and not conciliating our readers, I composed a statement of my own which I inserted in an appeal for subscribers on the inside cover of the January number. At the next meeting I read it to the bunch, and they voted that we run it permanently at the masthead as Reed had suggested.[5]

THIS MAGAZINE IS OWNED AND PUBLISHED COOPERATIVELY BY ITS EDITORS. IT HAS NO DIVIDENDS TO PAY, AND NOBODY IS TRYING TO MAKE MONEY OUT OF IT. A REVOLUTIONARY AND NOT A REFORM MAGAZINE; A MAGAZINE WITH A SENSE OF HUMOR AND NO RESPECT FOR THE RE-SPECTABLE; FRANK, ARROGANT, IMPERTINENT, SEARCHING FOR THE TRUE CAUSES; A MAGAZINE DIRECTED AGAINST RIGIDITY AND DOGMA WHEREVER IT IS FOUND; PRINTING WHAT IS TOO NAKED OR TRUE FOR A MONEY-MAKING PRESS; A MAGAZINE WHOSE FINAL POLICY IS TO DO AS IT PLEASES AND CONCILIATE NOBODY, NOT EVEN ITS READERS—THERE IS A FIELD FOR THIS PUBLICATION IN AMERICA.

[5] These facts gave rise to an erroneous recollection on Art Young's part that Reed wrote the statement (*Art Young, His Life and Times*, p. 276). Reed could not have written such a statement at that time, for as a disciple of Lincoln Steffens he was innocent of its most serious ideas: non-capitalist ownership and absence of the profit motive; revolutionary socialism as a scientific search for causes; and my own particular idea of teaching socialism how to be resolute without being dogmatic. Art Young's error was a natural one, since the proposal to run such a statement was Reed's. It had appeared, however, in two numbers of the magazine before Reed was elected to the board.

Drawn by John Sloan

THE EXTREME LEFT

"Why don't those strikers *do* something—let a few of them get shot, and it'll look as if they meant business."

Chapter 51

The Sentimental Rebels

IN THE period I am discussing, which might be called the Adolescence of the Twentieth Century, anarchism was still an active belief among left radicals. I was more than once described as an anarchist and my name coupled in the press with that of Emma Goldman, but I waged a war on anarchism, and I never liked Emma Goldman very well. Her force and eloquence impressed me less than her impermeability to humor and logic. She was a square little solid block of blue-eyed belligerent energy, and had, besides a fiery hate, a warmly human kindness in her. Knowing that she was slandered as a criminal hoyden by all respectable editors, I instinctively defended her. She had a certain regard for me, too, because my war on socialist bigotry sounded a little like the opposing bigotry of the anarchists. But she could not understand purposive thinking. The idea of method or procedure had no lodging in her head. Her whole life-wisdom consisted of comparing reality with an absolute ideal, and breaking her neck, and if need be all necks, in some obviously desperate leap for the ideal.

I find this in my notebook of those days:

"Lincoln Steffens asked me today: 'Why aren't you an anarchist?' I am not an anarchist because I have no need of an intellectual infatuation. I have no interest in creeds or isms, or any form of theory which is not a working hypothesis, containing fact, aim, idea, all alive and passing along the orbit of current time in a state of constant mutual correction. I call that intelligence. I am afraid of faith."

I once agreed to preside at a Carnegie Hall meeting called to welcome Emma Goldman out of jail. She had been locked up for distributing information about birth control in defiance of the uncivilized law against it, one of the most sensible of her extremisms.

423

In the last two days before the meeting I learned that Ben Reitman was to speak. Reitman was a white-fleshed, waxy-looking doctor, who thought it radical to shock people with crude allusions to their sexual physiology. I did not want to associate my feminism with this juvenile diversion, and I told the committee I would not preside. I explained that this was a practical judgment and that the principle of free speech was not involved; I had as good a right not to speak as Reitman had to speak. I knew how futile, so far as concerned Emma Goldman, my logic was.

"The incident once more proved," she says in *Living My Life*, "how poorly some alleged radicals in America have grasped the true meaning of freedom. The 'cultural' leader of socialism in the United States . . . permitted personal dislikes to stand in the way of what he claimed to be his 'high ideal.' "

This put me in bad with the anarchists, and I made it worse by pointing out in *The Masses* that they were trying to save the world with a negation, and by calling anarchy "the raw material of despotism," and a "dying scream of the eighteenth century attempt at human freedom." Notwithstanding these sins the anarchists sensed my genuine love of liberty and dislike for bureaucrats, and thought of me as a soul less hopelessly lost than most socialists. I thought of them as kindergartners in the school of revolutionary thinking.

Toward the Sentimental Rebels I was more diplomatic. I use this term to designate a mental type of whom the outstanding representatives were Lincoln Steffens, Hutchins Hapgood, Fremont Older, and Clarence Darrow. They had no historical tradition and they had no international connections. They were as purely American a phenomenon as the red Indians. They sometimes called themselves, or were called, "philosophical anarchists," but that means little besides an irresponsible distaste for politics. Their defining trait was that they came into sympathy with the labor struggle, not by the road of theory or plan of action, but by the road of Christian sentiment bereft of Deity yet carried to a bellicose extreme. Our American democratic faith grew, or degenerated, out of the extreme left wing of the Protestant Reformation in Europe, the zealots of universal brotherhood among the children of God and of arrant individualism in dealings with the Father. These amorphous American radicals whom I call Sentimental Rebels tried to recapture that early extremism without the belief in God upon which it rested. They were all characterized by a distrust of intellect such as one finds among men of religious faith. And they were characterized by a Christlike fondness for the society of publicans and sinners. Indeed almost a cult arose among them of making friends with criminals.

In Hutch Hapgood both the revolt against dispassionate thinking and the idealization of sinners were conditioned by traits of his own character. He could not think dispassionately, and he had a natural impulse toward sin. He tells in his beautifully candid book, *A Victorian in the Modern World,* of his uncouth backwardness in everything but what he calls "the temperamental side of knowledge." And he tells of his gravitation toward depravity:

"There has been much in my life which I am the first to recognize as definitely vicious. I have often drunk to excess and for long periods of time. I have had indiscriminate sexual relations with all types of women, including the depraved. In fact, in depravity, in viciousness itself, there has been something that seemed to me a release of the spirit. I have often been impelled to go as far as I could in extravagant gestures of what is called immorality; and in social victims I have almost habitually found something that appealed to my imagination, more than people of ordered life, unless these latter were highly endowed with the grace of the human spirit."

Naturally, then, Hutch developed the idea of a "revolution" which did not care much for scientific thinking and in which criminals occupied a front-line position.

"I would suggest that, if we must have a method, it should be the aesthetic method . . . We must love before we can make laws that are valid . . . [We must] see the criminal, the outcast and the disinherited with a new and wondering sympathy; . . . a mental and imaginative sympathy which sees in revolution the hope of a more vital art and literature, a deeper justice and a richer human existence; a sympathy which is in its character aesthetic—the sympathy of the social artist, not of the mere reformer nor of the narrow agitator . . ."

Hutch's book, like the man it describes, lacks vigor and dispatch. He seems to have puttered endlessly, like a grandmother over some tangled knitting, with a thing called "life," and never taken enough actual stitches to give it shape. Nevertheless, I admire the book, and I admired him more than any of his colleagues on the sentimental left. Amid a good deal of clumsy reasoning that seemed almost perverse, as though he found "release of the spirit" in fallacy as well as depravity, Hutch always managed to get something fruitful said. His courageous sensualism and dogged candor and sweet yet grim determination in the pursuit of honest values seem to me, as I look back, one of the noblest things in that small sphere of time and men through which we moved together.

In those old *Masses* days, however, I was too full of the arrogance of what I called revolutionary science to perceive this. I could not contemplate with composure, even as a curiosity, the philosophy of muddle-headed loving-kindness with which these belated Christians proposed to redeem the world. It appeared at its worst, I thought, or most vexatious, in Hapgood, because he had a philosophical vocabulary, a deep bass voice, and the manners of a man profound in argument. I remember shouting at him—in a tiny room containing John Reed, Mabel Dodge, the poet Ridgeley Torrance, and one or two others:

"Well, if words don't mean the same thing to you twice in the same sentence, what's the use of our talking?"

The shout would not have been so bad, but I also turned away and stopped talking. Hutch says in his book that he does not understand why we constantly crossed swords in this manner, but it seems clear to me. I was not egotistical, as he paints me, but I was youthfully intolerant of the one thing dearest to his heart, "the temperamental side of knowledge" — whatever in real fact that may mean.

In Darrow this same distrust of intellect was boldly pessimistic. Darrow was intellectual enough so that his falling back from logic upon unillumined love was consciously a gesture of despair. He was a magnificent figure with his slow-swinging shoulders and heavy sorrowing head, a symbolic figure, too. He seemed almost physically to be hanging on a cross, an orphaned son of God, a Man of Sorrows without the resurrection hope. Only his undying humor made the scene endurable.

I first met Darrow in Chicago on a lecture tour, and after dining with him and his little circle who met monthly to discuss, more in pity than anger, the cruelty of the universe, I wrote this poem, which I called "A Modern Messiah":

> Scarred with sensuality and pain
> And weary labor in a mind not hard
> Enough to think, a heart too always tender,
> Sits the Christ of failure with his lovers.
> They are wiser than his parables,
> But he more potent, for he has the gift
> Of hopelessness, and want of faith, and love.

Steffens' obscurantism was, by contrast with Hapgood's and Darrow's, pertly optimistic. Steffens learned to be happy without hard thinking by developing a kittenish delight in paradox. If he could find a pause in which to remark that "the good men are worse than the bad," or that "enough organization will disorganize anything," or some such sly jab at rationality, he would feel that he had arrived at the end and summit of the life of reason. He would sit back and watch it "sink in" with a complacence which I, with my damnable paternal inheritance of soft-soap, always played up to instead of saying as my soul wanted to: "Steff, let's lay aside our cleverness for once and try to think things through!"

I first saw Steffens at a small dinner in a restaurant where we both made speeches on some social problem. He had not then learned to speak loud enough so that he could be heard beyond the first row; he was years learning this simple trick, hindered, I think, by the conception he had of himself as a sort of confidential philosopher. I found his sententious muttering about good people being bad and bad people good, a sort of inverse romantic moralism which he never transcended, embarrassingly immature. He was perhaps equally disaffected—at least he was vastly surprised—by my breezy explanation of the dependence of all ultimate freedoms upon the taking over of the means of production by the working class.

A year or two after making that poor impression on me as a lecturing muckraker, Steffens swam into a still more distasteful notoriety in connection with the aborted McNamara trial. As that trial, and the trials which flowed from it, formed the spearpoint of the labor struggle in the years when we were starting *The Masses*, I want to recall it briefly.

The Structural Iron Workers, in order to protect themselves against the assault of the National Erectors Association, an organization supposedly formed with the backing of the Steel Trust to destroy their union, had resorted to dynamiting nonunion constructions. As a by-incident to this violent warfare, one of the dynamiters, J. B. McNamara, exploded a small charge of dynamite in an alley alongside the Los Angeles *Times* building. The Los Angeles *Times*, edited by Harrison Gray Otis, was then the most violent anti-union paper in the country, and McNamara's purpose in planting this "pineapple" was to throw a scare into the enemy's camp. Owing to the proximity of some kegs of ink, the explosion started a fire which spread like a whirlwind through the building, and twenty-one workmen, trapped by a locked door, were suffocated. J. B. McNamara and his brother, J. J., secretary of the union, were arrested and brought to Los Angeles for trial. There were twenty-one separate indictments against them, and since they had been trailed for the preceding two years by a detective, and hostile opinion was concentrated on the court like a blow torch, there was very small chance indeed of an acquittal.

Clarence Darrow, who had reluctantly undertaken their defense, decided before the jury had been selected that the best thing he could do for his clients would be to secure from the state's attorney, and those behind him, a guarantee that their lives would be spared if they changed their plea to "guilty." Such a settlement had obvious advantages to the other side: it would save the state what promised to be an enormous expense; it would kill the campaign to elect the socialist Job Harriman mayor of Los Angeles, a campaign that had the bosses of the town in jitters; it would quench a mounting public indignation against the Erectors Association and the Steel Trust. Having established the guilt of its secretary from his own lips, they could easily indict the other key men and carry to swift success their campaign to smash the union.

It is evident from Darrow's account of the matter that the prosecution welcomed his suggestion. It is noteworthy also that the actual dynamiter, J. B. McNamara, was reluctant to enter the agreement. His trial was part of a fight, and he did not want to let his comrades down. He preferred to risk his life. His soldierly instinct had to be overborne, and in this not only Darrow and his assistants, but also Lincoln Steffens, who had come down there to try out "Christianity as a working principle," played a part.

The whole labor and radical world was shocked by the change of plea, and the militants—particularly those of Los Angeles, who were fighting in their shirt sleeves for Job Harriman—were so outraged that Darrow, when he left the court room, felt in danger of being mobbed.

There is no reason to doubt Darrow's statement that he acted solely in the interest of his clients, nor his judgment that the terms they got, life imprisonment for J.B. and fifteen years for J.J., were the best to be hoped for. Whether he was right in overbearing the impulse of his client to act from larger motives is a more searching question. It would be answered one way by a revolutionist with a social program based on working-class struggle, another by a Sentimental Rebel. It was, in fact, three of these Sentimental Rebels who made the decision, for Fremont Older came down from San Francisco to join in the work of persuasion.

One thing Darrow leaves beyond question: that the state's attorney acted upon motives that had little to do with Steffens' evangel or with the Christian gospel of forgiveness. Darrow's words are: "He received the suggestion quite favorably, but could not act without consulting with some of the others interested, and that would require word from the Erectors Association of Indianapolis." The negotiations dragged on for a number of days, and then the state's attorney reported that the head of the Erectors Association "was willing to accept the proposition, and it looked favorable so far as the others were concerned. We urged haste, for we feared that publicity would be ruinous. Finally . . . the agreement was made subject to the action of the judge, who was likewise reported in favor of the plan." (*The Story of My Life* by Clarence Darrow, p. 183)

In short it was on all sides a practical bargain. And since the Erectors Association held the trump cards, it naturally got the best of the bargain. Its object was not to hang a murderer. As Darrow says, no one ever claimed that J.B. had intended to take human life. Its object was to smash the Structural Iron Workers Union, and to that end a plea of guilty from its secretary was more useful than a conviction.

Notwithstanding this glaringly obvious fact, Lincoln Steffens managed to convince himself, and almost to convince Darrow, that he had secured this settlement by persuading the "big, bad men" of Los Angeles in personal interviews that "the doctrine of forgiveness instead of punishment for the sinner is sound."

All that Steffens actually secured with his talk was a "promise" of immunity for the other members of the Structural Iron Workers Union, a promise without which J.B. refused to enter the bargain. It was a promise which these "big bad men," even if they had been small and good, were not in a position to carry out. And it was, of course, merrily ignored by those really concerned in the matter, the National Erectors Association and the law officers of the United States. Thirty-eight of J.B.'s colleagues were convicted at Indianapolis during the following winter; Mattie Schmidt and Dave Kaplan were sent up for life in Los Angeles soon after; Darrow himself had to stay on two years in Los Angeles defending himself twice over against a framed-up charge of attempting to bribe a juror—attempting to bribe a juror *after* the agreement to a change of plea had been reached.

"Christianity will not work with Christians," Steffens tells us, in introducing his account of these events. "But, as Jesus learned by hard experience and taught so clearly, Christianity does work with sinners. I proved that for myself. Political bosses and business bosses, out-and-out crooks, hard-boiled editors, rough-neck rascals—they never failed to respond to the (unnamed) Christian appeal, especially for mercy. . . .

"Having proved this to my own satisfaction by many small private experiments—with sinners—I had long been looking for a chance to try it more openly in a more spectacular situation which all men could see. This long-looked-for emergency seemed to have arrived with Darrow's wish to settle the McNamara case out of court."

Although he entered the business in this mood of experiment, there is no evidence that Steffens learned a thing from its disastrous result. His only mistake, he thought, was not to go to Indianapolis and "see" the heads of the Erectors Association. Since these men were the only ones who could with a shadow of plausibility "promise immunity" to dynamiters scattered all over the country, this certainly was a mistake. It was so fabulous a mistake as to suggest that he was acting out a story in his own head, a story which had no vital connection with the real world at all.[1]

It would be difficult to find a parallel in naïveté to the forty pages which Lincoln Steffens devotes to this episode. If read in connection with the four brief pages in which Darrow describes how and why he reached a settlement with the state's attorney, and the attorney with the Erectors Association, they acquire the virtue of an object lesson in sentimental self-deception.

Steffens' autobiography, like Steffens himself, impressed many of his fellow citizens as filled with wondrous wisdom. It is a delightful tale warmly told, and gives a picture of certain phases of American life that only a very brilliant and boldly inquiring reporter could give. To me, however, its contribution to wisdom lies in the unconsciousness with which it portrays a sprightly and rather self-pleased

[1] Not only did Steffens continue to preach his doctrine that "bad" men, if properly approached, are better than "good." In setting on foot the Bullitt Mission to Soviet Russia nine years later, he tried to prove it with a similarly pseudo-Christlike intervention. He went along with Bullitt and explained to Lenin and Trotsky that Wilson and Lloyd George, although good men, were not hopelessly good, and that they could be trusted in their proposal of an amicable meeting with the bolsheviks on Prinkipo Island. They could be trusted to act as "Christian sinners." Again he was double-crossed by his principles, and again he felt "defeated and disgraced." At least he felt deeply wounded when he visited Moscow again in 1923 and found that none of the big bolsheviks would see him.

cork bobbing about on currents of which it had no understanding and upon which it had no effect. Steff's kindness was genuine and was much wiser than his mind. He was truthful, too, and filled with honest curiosity about truth. His habit of prodding people with the sharp corners of odd points of view would have made him an excellent teacher had he had some serious thing to teach. It was these personal qualities in him that led me, and many besides me, to hold back our sense of the triviality of his performance, and join him in the conspiracy to coddle his frail and rather childlike vanity.

Steffens relates that he, too, on leaving the courtroom after the McNamara trial, "got definitely the sense of an angry mob," which seemed to move toward his hotel. "My part in it was known enough to keep my name sounding, a most unpleasant, almost frightening experience." And he adds: "When I got back to New York, I felt defeated, disgraced somehow, and helpless . . . Jack Reed, 'my own boy,' wrote a fierce poem, 'Sangar,' denouncing me . . . At a gathering of writers, artists, radicals, they all hated me. . . ."

Steffens exaggerates about the poem. Reed did not "denounce" him; he only killed him and sent him to heaven, where Jesus and he could have a grand laugh together over their common folly. But Steffens does not exaggerate the contempt in which he was held by the intelligentsia for "butting in" and betraying the class struggle with a sanctimonious imitation of Christ. We talked of him as an old-maidish fuss-budget who ought to be teaching a Sunday-school class.

Although I no longer think that our position in those days was wise, I recall with satisfaction that it had some relation to the actual forces in play. While Steffens was securing from the "big bad men" of Los Angeles a promise of "mercy" that they were powerless to keep, I was asking in *The Masses* a serious question:

"If the Steel Trust is determined to fight the emancipation of its workers by every means that money, and fraud, and the control of government provide, how do you expect its workers to fight the Steel Trust? For my part I expect them to fight in two general ways: The first is *class*-conscious as opposed to *trade*-conscious, or even *industry*-conscious, agitation, leading to an organization of workers on the same vast lines on which capital is organized . . . The other is *united class-conscious voting*. . . . Combine these and you have the power that will yet free the workers of the world . . . If you will stand *with* the dynamiters and *for* them as your brothers—whether you think they went wrong or not—you can make of this event not the end of a secret conspiracy, but the beginning of an open revolutionary agitation that will strike into the very heart of capitalism in this country."

It was more than a contrast of political opinions; it was a contrast of method against mumbo-jumbo, of factual thinking against cerebralized sentiment as the ground to build a hope on. Steffens moved a good way from his dawdling with Christianity-among-sinners; he moved so far that for a time I thought of him as an objective and penetrating as well as a brilliant reporter. But he never transcended that kittenish and evil trick of calling good bad and bad good, of exalting his own self-pleased cleverness above reasoned reflection, above standards of judgment, above "old, exploded ideals like right and wrong, liberty, democracy, justice."[2]

I have dwelt on these "philosophical anarchists" because in opposing their sentimental leftism with a program that I thought practical, I clarified my own private thoughts. That attitude of "hard-headed idealism" by which I set myself apart from liberals and yellow socialists came into sharp relief against these rebels who stood closer to me. It was not a wish to be hard in the sense of condoning brutality, or imagining that in a social movement the means can be vile and the end healthy and good. I was not that kind of a fool. By hard I meant objective; I meant ruthless in confronting the facts, whether they be tough or tender, and clear in conceiving the ideal, whether it prove easy or arduous to attain. I meant employing thoughts in order to better the real world, the world of all men, not in order to attain a comfortable equilibrium in your own mind. The vice of soft-headedness, now better called wishful thinking, is what has caused liberals and liberalism the world over to fall for the organized deceit and principled lying of the totalitarians. I have done my full share of it, but I still deem it the chief enemy of human progress.

[2] *The Letters of Lincoln Steffens*, II, 851.

Chapter 52

Towards Liberty *Is My Theme*

MY *ENJOYMENT OF POETRY* was published in April of that first year of *The Masses*, and it was received in a manner that, had my egotism been finite, might have turned my head. "A masterpiece . . . alive to its last letter," said *Life* magazine. "One of the most original and gallantly indited books we have ever had the luck to find in the daily bundle," said the London *Morning Post*. "The best definition of the writer's art ever given," said Jack London. "I want to shout it from the house-tops," said Edwin Markham. "The best of modern feeling is in this book," said Walter Lippmann. And my teacher John Dewey: "Good sense, wise philosophy and correct psychology." English teachers ordered it in lots mounting to a hundred for their classes; Scribner's got out a special leaflet containing professorial endorsements and a "school edition" which sold in astonishing numbers. In short, my revolution in poetics was a success, and if I had been single in ambition, less avid in my thirst of experience, I would probably be writing this book, as my mother predicted "in a rambling old house on some beautiful college campus with elm trees full of birds right outside the window."

To be sure, nobody noticed that I had overthrown the humanities and introduced science into the study of literature. It was not remarked that I had explained metaphor, a task that had lain unaccomplished since Aristotle declined the challenge of it! But these points might have been driven home, if I had moved onto that campus, accepted the despised Ph.D., and pursued the career so triumphantly begun. So at least I told myself in confident moments in those thrilling days, and I still think there is a grain of truth in the opinion. I still believe—God help me!—that I explained metaphor. As there is small recognition among rhetoricians or psychologists even of the fact that I tried to, I must admit that the probabilities are against it. But I can not portray my state-of-being in that year of beginnings

433

1913 without reminding you that there existed in my breast, along with some redeeming humilities, this obdurate block of egregious self-esteem.[1]

The humilities were helped along a few weeks later when Mitchell Kennerley brought out my thin volume of poems, *Child of the Amazons*. It was received with the enthusiasm that attends a corpse on its way to private burial. My sister's friend Paul Kellogg persuaded Vida D. Scudder, socialist teacher of English at Wellesley, to write an article in praise of it for *The Survey*, and she did so with generous words, launching my "Aquarium" poem in particular on its rather lonely career. "Considering the range and quality of the verse," she concluded, "one certainly begs Mr. Eastman to work harder and not to abandon the Muse for Causes, however sacred." Encouraging advice—but, secured by sisterly intercession and published in a social workers' magazine, it could not raise me from the dead.

Miss Scudder's advice to "work harder," I must pause to say, was not due to any laziness in my verse, but to an innovation which I did not explain, or explained somewhat secretly in a Note to *Enjoyment of Poetry*.

"One so-called 'law of prosody,'" I said in that note, "has entirely dominated English poets, and often, I think, to their misfortune. It is the law about leftover syllables at the end, or beginning, of a line in blank verse. Suppose the division between two lines properly falls in the middle of a word, or of an indivisible phrase, as in this example:

'To hím the wáll
That súnders ghósts and shádow-cásting mén
Becáme a crýstal, ánd he sáw them thróugh it.'

[1] My explanation is fully developed in the essays "What Poetry Is" and "Art and Biology," to be found in *The Literary Mind* and the enlarged edition of *Enjoyment of Poetry* (1939). It rests upon the assumption that the defining purpose of poetry, as of all art, is to heighten consciousness. "It seems that consciousness is, arises out of, or depends upon, two things—a blockage of action and an identification of one experience with another so that action may be resumed. That being the case, what could a person do who desired to heighten consciousness, or intensify, or preserve, or prolong, or in any other way cultivate it for its own sake—what could he do that would be more fundamental than to suggest *impractical identifications*? Poetic metaphor is the employment of words to suggest impractical identifications. You may choose this or that identification for any one of a thousand reasons, all of them very interesting but none general enough to enter into the definition of poetry. *Any* impractical identification that you can induce somebody to listen to is poetic, because it is the essence of an attentive consciousness. It is mind suspended on the brink of action."

Prosodists diagnose that contrarious syllable *it*, which properly belongs to the next line, as a sort of abnormal excrescence upon the
old line, call this by the terrifying name of acatalectic (or catalectic,
or hypercatalectic—one never remembers which) and require that
the next line shall begin all fresh with another unaccented syllable.
Thus:

> 'Becáme a crýstal ánd he sáw them thróúgh it
> And heárd their voíces tálk behínd the wáll.'

That is, they require that we sacrifice the flow of the accent rhythm,
in order to preserve the integrity of the lines upon the page. It is,
perhaps, foolish for them to 'require' anything, but I think it would
be less foolish to require that we cut off the real excrescence, which
is the syllable *and*, allowing the syllable *it*, which is the first syllable
of the new line, to remain, if it must, upon the end of the old.
Thus:

> 'To hím the wáll
> That súnders ghósts and shádow-cásting mén
> Becáme a crýstal ánd he sáw them thróúgh it
> Heárd their voíces tálk behínd the wáll.'

I think so, because the visible rhythm, although more obvious, is
not so important as the audible rhythm. I believe that one who
composed blank verse in natural freedom from the idea of a printed
page—while he might anywhere introduce extra syllables for his
pleasure or convenience—would usually overcome this technical
difficulty by sacrificing the regularity of both lines rather than by
sacrificing the regular recurrence of his accent."

My innovation was identical with that which Gerard Manley
Hopkins called "rove over" lines, and which, since the publication of
his poems in 1918, has won a certain recognition.[2] And he too based
it on the idea that rhythms should be heard, rather than seen.
Rhythms *are* seen, however, in our modern way of life. Moreover,
it is not necessary that the frame upon which one weaves a pattern
of beauty should be rational: it can be set up as well by custom as
understanding. For these reasons I surrendered my "rove over" lines
finally, feeling that English poetry as it has existed for five hundred

---

[2] "Remark also that it is natural in Sprung Rhythm for the lines to be *rove over*,
that is for the scanning of each line immediately to take up that of the one before,
so that if the first has one or more syllables at its end the other must have so many
the less at its beginning; and in fact the scanning runs on without break from the
beginning, say, of a stanza to the end and all the stanza is one long strain, though
written in lines asunder." (From the Author's Preface, *Poems of Gerard Manley
Hopkins*, edited by Robert Bridges, Oxford University Press, 1930.)

years has a say in the matter more weighty than any theory about rhythm.

I do not know how I expected readers of my poems to find the key to their prosody in the back of another book. It was a part of my sacrosanctimonious attitude toward poetry to feel that there must be no prose comment within the same covers. Nobody ever found the key, of course, and this, I believe, is the first time I ever mentioned the subject. My innovation made "Child of the Amazons," "To the Ascending Moon," "The Thought of Protagoras"—most of my best things in that early volume—seem amateurish where they were most expert.

It all poured together, my foolish reticence, my publisher's obstinacy, my very success in prose—and the inadequacy, I had to assume, of my poetic gift—to dig a well of humbleness in me just at the moment of my proud success. I said nothing even to Crystal or Ida—even to myself I said nothing—of my disappointment. I pretended that an article by Vida D. Scudder in *The Survey* was a great send-off. But I was heavily influenced by this failure. It deterred me from cultivating myself as a poet. It confirmed me in the habit of writing poetry only when an emotion took such romantic hold of me that I had to.

My next big undertaking, I decided, must be prose. And it must be on a subject remote from the one I had just distinguished myself in. I must have a brand new creative adventure; that seemed obvious to my thirst of experience. Why not, then, while the secular member of me was waging a political struggle in *The Masses*, put the sacred member to work on a theoretical book about politics, a book that would build up under and fortify my editorials? It would be a sort of Bible of Revolution, a reconstruction of Marxism in the terms of experimental science. I might call it "Marxism as Method," —though that, on reflection, would be too Marxian, not my own enough, and not specific enough about the *goal* of the revolution. Marx mentioned the goal once or twice, but I never felt sure he cared as much about it as I did. For me, at any rate, the goal was liberty, and "Towards Liberty" must be my title—"Towards Liberty, the Method of Progress." To that I decided to devote the energy of my mornings, exception to be made only for irrepressible songs, for the next five years if need be, or even six. And I sat down with fluent conviction and a big soft pencil, and wrote a "preface." It was never published, never even finished, but it is the one exact statement of the shape of my mind during those years on *The Masses*. It shows how I was reconciling, in a new way, the old-wise sceptic in me with the ardent evangelist.

"All through the ages we have lived and labored and met together in the same excitement, we young and revolutionary and impatient minds, believing our 'radical spirit' to be the new force of history, believing the day of liberty was just beyond tomorrow. And all through the ages we have died, and the day has not come. We have been the toys of evolution. For there was nothing new in our force, nothing in our rationality, our generosity, our willingness to give leisure and even life to the hope. Nature had always produced a few like us, whose food and love was human liberty. She always will. It is one of her sportive ways of varying the type she breeds. . . . Perhaps if we could choose the children who love liberty instead of wealth and honor, breed from them alone, we could engender in posterity a world spontaneously free. But not by preaching, and still less by merely dying for our aim, can we escape the isolation and the end that time allots to ineffective sports of nature. That is what we are, and that is what we usually have been through all time.

"But though the dream, the love, the sacrifice, the rational ideal, are old, and give no better promise now than in the days of Christ, there is a thing among us that is new. That is the spirit and the method of experimental science. If we can master and possess, towards our extraordinary ends, a method of procedure that at every point accords with current science, and renew it with each fresh conclusion or discovery, and hold it more important than our dream, then it is not impossible that, though we are so few, we shall profoundly touch the course of evolution.

"Those who now for sixty and more years have labored in the cause of 'scientific socialism' will perhaps dismiss these words as dealing with a theme long since exhausted. Marx and Engels turned from the utopians, and took the road of science. Yes, they did; but science is a wholly different thing today from what it was to Marx and Engels. And though they took the first and creative step in building a technique of revolutionary progress, they took this step in ignorance of its true nature, and they took it inaccurately or with erroneous definition. For in the first place, their concept of what it is to be scientific was wrong. And in the second place, they had no suspicion of the limitations which the discipline of genetic and experimental psychology must impose upon their economics, for such a discipline did not exist in their day. If you are unwilling then to see recast and revalued the whole of 'scientific socialism,' in the light of a true conception of the nature of science, and in the light of modern psychology, you may well dismiss these words, for that is all that one who writes upon the method of progress towards liberty at this day can wisely do."

It was naïve to think that I could, by merely transforming the class-struggle doctrine from prophecy into plan of action, give the character of experimental science to a movement involving all mankind throughout an age of history. A scientific experiment requires a scientist—I am sure this flitted across my mind—and I was dodging the perfectly obvious question who he was to be. My real program was a dictatorship of "the few," "the sports of nature." I was blind not to perceive this. We are all blind when arranging ideas in such a way that our juvenile drives into life can function.

I spent hundreds of mornings in the next three years arranging those ideas—as many mornings as I could rescue from the melee that my life became as editor, agitator, poet, money-raiser, lecturer, president of a publishing company. As I describe the more dramatic excitement of those years, 1913 to 1916, I hope you will remember that this great work, *Towards Liberty, The Method of Progress*, was what my axial self was supposed to be engaged upon.

Drawn by John Barber

YOURS FOR THE REVOLUTION

Chapter 53

Floyd Dell Seals My Doom

BESIDES holding *The Masses* to a policy, my chief task as editor
was diplomatic. I had to make contributing editors contribute, a hard job even when they get paid. And I had to preserve amiability if not order at the meetings of those editors. These
famous meetings occurred monthly, at night, usually in some author's
apartment or artist's studio. A few manuscripts were read, a few
pictures exhibited, and they were voted on. We had a custom of
inviting our friends to these meetings—a good part of New York's
intelligentsia turned up one time or another—and we always urged
them to join the voting. Art Young tells how, at one of the meetings,
after a vote on a poem, a man from the corner of the studio shouted
contemptuously:

"Bourgeois! Voting! Voting on poetry! Poetry is something from
the soul. You can't vote on poetry!"[1]

The voice was that of Hippolyte Havel, a small round-faced mis-
chievous-eyed intellectual, with glasses bigger than the moon and
hair flung down on his shoulders in token of his faith in anarchism.
His protest was long remembered because it contained so much good
sense.

To me, however, this question of principle was unimportant, for
I regarded the whole "co-operative" venture with the scepticism of
one who takes the responsibility for a result. The material accepted
at these meetings was not sufficient in quantity, or good enough, or
timely enough, to make a magazine. Between meetings I would go
round to the more flexible and congenial editors, and provoke,
evoke, suggest, select, or talk up, or talk over, or otherwise get put
into my hands, a vital and timely contribution. The cartoons especially were often a product of such consultations. "Some of these

[1] *On My Way*, p. 281.

439

pictures are yours as well as mine," Art Young wrote in sending me a volume of his drawings. It was fun, and a rare privilege, to work out pictorial ideas with great cartoonists—and the greatest of that period were certainly on *The Masses*—but it was also a responsibility, a diversion from my own creative life. . . .

Art Young, in describing *The Masses* meetings, speaks of me as "not always looking happy," and that corresponds to my remembered feelings. There was an equivocation about it all. I did not feel bound to publish everything that was voted in by the general public at those meetings. I did feel bound *not* to publish anything that was voted out, and for the general illumination they provided I was modest enough to be grateful. Especially in the realm of art I was guided, and indeed from the ground up educated, by the hour-long arguments that an offered drawing would sometimes evoke. But I could not join in the illusion that these once-a-month meetings had much to do with the job of editing a magazine. I longed to be *one* of the *"Masses* crowd," and attend those warm, witty, colorful and brilliantly lively gatherings in the same mood of carefree idealism that the others enjoyed. But I never reconciled myself to being the anxious parent who made this mood possible to the rest. The reward of having my name on the masthead as editor was not adequate, for I had never wished or chosen to be an editor. I had other and larger ambitions.

The extreme irony of my position was that this "part-time job" which had swollen to such proportions paid me no salary at all. For two years after I took charge of *The Masses* the "no pay" part of the contract was faithfully fulfilled. During that time I continued to earn my living with lectures and to kid myself that I was merely "putting the magazine on its feet." As soon as it got on its feet, I would turn it over to a real executive and become a contributing editor with the rest. One of the things I have learned from life is that magazines do not have feet.

"I'm going to find money to pay me the beginnings of a salary on *The Masses* or quit it," I wrote in desperation to my brother. "I never intended to be an editor at all. I've not written a word on my book. I have five jobs:

1. Editing *The Masses*
2. Directing the company
3. Raising a subsidy
   a. Worrying about raising it
   b. Recovering from raising it

4. Earning my own living
5. Writing my editorials

"It just simply doesn't leave enough strength (or rather enough vigorous idleness) for real creative thought or imagination."

As a result of this mere confusion of character, I acquired a reputation for self-sacrifice in those days that I was far from deserving. It seemed natural to suppose that so cocksure and belligerent an editor was capable of making a choice; and that granted, it was plain that I had chosen to renounce literature for a life of unrewarded service to socialism.

"My God, suppose I have!" I would say when these rumors reached me. And then I would think up some great new scheme for loading off the work on someone else.

First it was John Sloan who came to my rescue. Sloan has real executive ability—that is, good judgment, confidence in his judgment, and the faculty of directed action. He knows all about make-up, all about printing and engraving, and he understands socialist politics. He is indeed, as Art Young remarked, "a man of universal vision and understanding." Moreover, once he got me educated a little in matters of art, our ideals for the magazine were identical. He took the whole job off my hands while I went up to Glenora for July and August 1913 to slake my thirst of creation in "Towards Liberty." He only consulted me once or twice by mail, sending for my approval a tiny model of the magazine with each drawing parodied in miniature—a precious memento today. Sloan loved *The Masses* and would waste time on it in the same childish way I would. We were potentially, I always felt, a perfect team. But he had sense enough to know that his real work lay elsewhere.

Another man on whom I tried to shuffle off a part of my burden was Harry Kemp, the "Hobo Poet." Harry joined his voice very early to those singing in *The Masses*, and he sang a strong tune of his own. Indeed Harry was in two respects a kind of John the Baptist of modern literary trends. He raised the banner of neo-classicism and bore it up, lonely and neglected, a voice crying in the wilderness, while T. S. Eliot and his confrères were still in short pants. And he anticipated Ernest Hemingway in his cult of red-blooded he-male bellicosity and death-in-the-afternoonism by about two decades. Harry used to come round to *The Masses* office and spout his rather delicate poetry and brag of his achievements in the prize ring, thumping his mighty chest like a gorilla and offering to take on Masefield and Jack Johnson, Kipling and Jess Willard, with his typewriter in hock and one hand behind his back. Underneath this mighty swagger he had good taste and a very honest mind. Moreover, he needed food and clothes and a chance to sing without anxiety. *The Masses* was a hobo among magazines, and it seemed as though this tramper on life would make an appropriate assistant to the editor. I hired him one afternoon at ten dollars a week and gave him a bunch of manuscripts to take home and read. I found them in a basket beside my mail the next morning and a note pinned on the handle:

"Dear Max, I don't want to be editor any more. I must live and die a poet. Please don't get mad. I leave this note because I hate to come up and tell you. Harry."

Jack Reed was a third victim of my frantic effort to divide those five jobs. I did so much grumbling and threatening at our editorial

Drawn by John Sloan

RACE SUPERIORITY

meeting when I returned from Glenora in the fall that Reed came round the next morning and offered himself as managing editor. He had worked on magazines at college, he said, and would gladly give half his time to keep *The Masses* from going under. I accepted his offer joyfully, but my joy did not last long. Jack had too many wayward ideas, too rich a flow of impulses; he lacked judgment; and he had too much else to do. We agreed almost before he started that his help would be temporary, that what I needed was a paid associate who would sit up to a desk in the office—once in a while at least—and actually be there.

Jack's too spirited help, somewhat like that of a wild colt eager to enjoy the harness, came near driving me out of the office for good. For I was desperate about my book, a sense of my awful ignorance of the subject matter having dismayed me when I got down to work on it. I was, in fact, for some months in the autumn of 1913 on the verge of taking my life into my hands and making a decision about it. You may think it was a simple decision to make—I had only to resign. But where could I resign? What could I resign? To whom could I resign it? I was, from an operational point-of-view—I say it with anything but pride—the whole thing. With all its fame and its gorgeous accumulation of talent, its distinctly orchestral if not co-operative character, there was no way in sight for the magazine to survive if I handed it back to "the bunch" and walked out. The decision was no more simple than I was strong. Even so there was a critical moment that autumn when I came near to making a wise decision about the employment of my powers.

Fate forestalled me by bundling into an upper berth on the Empire State Express in Chicago, at just that moment, the most perfect example of an associate editor that nature's evolution has produced. Floyd Dell may have some faults as a human being, and I have even thought at times that I detected one or two, but as a friend in need to a man who has dragged down upon himself through sheer foolhardy zest for life the job of running a co-operative magazine, he is without a flaw. I never knew a more reasonable or dependable person, more variously intelligent, more agile in combining sociability with industry, and I never knew a writer who had his talents in such complete command. When we would be down at the printer's correcting page proofs and revising our make-up at the last moment, as we always did, and would find some unfilled space staring at us, all I had to do was give Floyd its dimensions. He would sit down in the midst of all the ear-and-cortex-splitting roar and riot of a press room, where I could barely retain the faculty to measure a space, and write a shapely verse or paragraph, timely, witty, true, acute, and perfectly designed to fit it.

Besides these virtues so specifically adapted to set me free of editorial detail, Floyd brought to *The Masses* a gift of literary criticism as fine as we had in the country. I thought, and still think, that he wrote the most charming and judicious book reviews of the whole period. They had already made a name for him in the Friday Literary Supplement of the Chicago *Evening Post,* a paper which, thanks to him and Francis Hackett, flared up for a year or two as a beacon of American letters visible both from New York and San Francisco. He had been in New York only a week when one day as we sat at lunch in a café on Greenwich Avenue, Jack Reed and Berkeley Tobey, Horatio Winslow and I, Tobey said:

"There goes your associate editor—that's Floyd Dell."

"I hope you're right—I'd like to meet him," I said.

Horatio rushed out and surrounded Floyd with his big frame, herding him into the restaurant. I don't think more than a half hour passed before I had offered Floyd twenty-five dollars a week to become associate editor of *The Masses.*

"You'll be the only one getting paid," I said, "and you know what that means. It means that you'll do the work."

"That's all right," he said, "I like work. But I have one stipulation. I want to really get paid. I've heard about *The Masses,* and I understand the stenographer and business manager receive their salary or not, according to whether there's any money in the till. That's all very charming and Bohemian and everything, but I'm not that kind of a person. I expect to be paid whether there's any money or not. The first week when my check doesn't come, I won't say anything. The second week I won't say anything either, but I won't be there."

That conversation occurred in late December 1913, just a year after I had drifted into this job of editor. From that date my doom was sealed. With Floyd Dell in the office, I could devote my mornings to writing and guide *The Masses* almost as a recreation in the afternoons. So I told myself in my folly, and my intemperate zeal for being and doing.

Chapter 54

My Soul and the Proletariat

AS LENIN pointed out, most of the leaders of the workers' revolution came from the bourgeois classes. I aimed to be at most a teacher rather than a leader, but I did come from the bourgeois classes. I identified myself with the workers' struggle by an act of volition based on speculative thinking. I believe I was more aware of it than most of these idealistic intruders are. Although bold intellectually, I still had in me the mamma's boy overcoming his chronic mortification, the church mouse worshiping his heroes, the rustic trying to romanticize the metropolis. My feeling toward the intrepid agitators whom I backed in *The Masses*, the disreputable and real heroes of the class struggle, was one of admiring inferiority. Gods on Olympus could hardly have brimmed me with the elation I felt when Arturo Giovannitti sent from his prison cell in Lawrence that ballad for our January number; when a few months later Mother Jones addressed with me a meeting in Carnegie Hall to raise money under the auspices of *The Masses* for the West Virginia miners; when in August great Bill Haywood himself, the arch rebel, the one-eyed gigantic satan who scorned even to answer except with an oath the Socialist Party's excommunication of him, asked me to publish a statement over his signature. It was like being admitted to the inner circle of some heroic order.

Notwithstanding this attitude of an acolyte, I did not commit my soul to the proletarian religion. I did not experience that sense of soul-and-body consecration to the working class which filled these agitators and which is hallowed by the Marxian metaphysics. I *like* plain, simple, and unprivileged people better on the average than people who have some place or position. The flower of character blooms best, to my taste, in a lowly soil. But I could not deceive myself that in the mass, and still less in idea, the industrial workers

445

were my comrades or brothers, or the special repositories of my love. I had renounced national patriotism before I ever heard of Karl Marx, and I had not renounced it for class patriotism but for the right to be an individual in the universe. I held to that right, no matter what method of progress I might espouse.

I did, however, feel the obligation to have personal and real contact with the struggle I was advocating. With that in view I attended the 1912 convention of the American Federation of Labor and described it in the second number of *The Masses*. I also attended—and little more than that—the great silk strike led by the IWW in Paterson, New Jersey, in 1913. I followed Frank Tannenbaum through his trial and conviction as militant leader of the unemployed in 1914. When civil war broke out in the coal fields of Colorado, I went out to Trinidad and made a two-sided study of the state of opinion and passion in that region. My participation in such conflicts consisted only of making speeches to the strikers, but one learns more sometimes by making a speech than listening to one.

I knew already, from my wander-months in the West, that wage-workers are not radically different from other people. At the AF of L convention I learned that their leaders, too, are of the same mould. "Raisin' Hell in School" was the title of my article describing that first attempt to unseat Sam Gompers and go in for industrial union-ism. When one of his henchmen intimated that Johnnie Walker, a leader of the revolt, was "advocating free love and Fletcherism," and Johnnie got up and started for him, Gompers screamed out: "Return to your seat at once!" shaking his gavel at the culprit, for all the world like an irate schoolma'am with a ruler. He had a schoolma'am's manner too, when the delegates finished reciting their lessons, of telling them whether they were right or wrong. He had the same disposition to sacrifice the true aims of the institution— so I then thought—to the necessity of maintaining discipline.

I met Gompers afterward in the lobby of the hotel and was impressed by his short stature, the solidity of his stance, and the dirtiness of his teeth. He was not only a cigar maker but a cigar chewer, a special breed of animal to one with my queasy sensorium. I buried him a little prematurely in the article I wrote for *The Masses*: "An old carcass of rotten politics and officialdom will be all there is left of the American Federation of Labor in about three years if it sticks to its present policies."

The strike throngs of the IWW in Paterson were more exhilarat-ing, but they also were composed of familiar people. Forbidden to

assemble in the city, they would troop out every Sunday, fifteen to twenty thousand of them, to the near-by village of Haledon where a socialist mayor guaranteed free speech and assemblage, and a petty-bourgeois sympathizer offered them his house and lot. The house was in a meadow, and had an upstairs balcony from which the leaders made their speeches to a crowd that brightened with sharp colors several acres of the grassy slopes around it. Many brought their babies, and their bread and wine, and gave the meetings to my eyes somewhat the aspect of a Sunday school picnic. On my first visit I stood in the crowd alone and listened while Bill Haywood and Carlo Tresca and Elizabeth Gurley Flynn addressed the strikers. It was the first time I had ever seen an "agitator" on the job, and I saw three of the most able and courageous in the country.

Of Tresca's speech, which took possession of all outdoors as an organ does of a church, I understood only nine words: "Occhio per occhio, dente per dente, sangue per sangue!" They did not, I must say, chime with the idea of a Sunday school picnic. But when Elizabeth Gurley Flynn came out and began giving earnest and sensible advice to the strikers, I felt again and strongly the likeness of all human beings and their problems. I felt at home, and knew that I would always feel at home, not with the proletariat especially, but with simple men and women anywhere. Strong and sturdy, perhaps a little too sturdy, a little four-cornered, but with handsome, warm, motherly-honest grey eyes, this girl seemed, instead of agitating the crowd, to take charge of it.

She talked, of course, an angry language—you can't lead a fight without anger—but the way to fight right now, she said, was to be calm and stand firm and not let anybody provoke you to acts of violence. She gave explicit and detailed directions as to the conduct of the strike: the "soup-kitchens," the distribution of literature, the sending of their children to New York where sympathizers would take charge of them. Her speech was anything but a harangue. Only the very careful practicalness of it conveyed the sense of a determined will and a purpose worth fighting for. "Stand firm and come to me with your problems, you can trust me," she seemed to be saying. . . .

It is a sorrow in my life that Elizabeth Flynn has accepted the Russian mock-socialist state, and gone over to the party of totalitarian communism. No regime in history, I suppose, is less like the dream of the IWW than the new industrial serfdom under police rule to which she now gives allegiance. In writers and artists such defections do not pain me so deeply. Their business is expression, and it is not entirely vital to them whether the thing they express is a fact or a fancy. But her business was to achieve the goal, to win liberty and life for the workers. Her thoughts, and her whole voluntary nature, on that spring day in Haledon, were bent on reality and directed action. I feel the same sorrow about William Z. Foster, another early star on my horizon. They lived brave lives fighting one enemy, but lacked the pluck to tackle another who arose in their own ranks at the moment of victory. The tragedy was too sad for them to take, the needed shift in strategy too nimble, the way of self-deception, the short walk over to the tyrant, too carefully made easy for them. . . .

Bill Haywood was a natural wonder in those days that one would travel miles to see. It is hard for today's reader to imagine what an infernal and awful, underprowling, hate-filled, satanic beast he was in the public mind. One really expected him to smell of sooty smoke and brimstone. He impressed me mainly on that first visit to Haledon by his simplicity. He had a Gibraltarlike bearing; he really had majesty as he moved slowly along, planting his feet deliberately, and surrounded by smaller and more jumpy beings. The big coal-black felt hat of the revolutionary agitator—where, I wonder, did that custom come from?—increased his vast size and enhanced his dignity. He had a voice like velvet, nearer the tenor than the bass, and his address to the workers was more poetic than I expected. He roused their hatred against the bosses, and left no loophole for those who thought to get rid of bosses without bloodshed. He was a thorough-going revolutionist, prepared to storm the fortress of capitalism with a proletarian army as soon as he could get one together. But he spoke to those hard-bitten workingmen about the beauties of a society in which there would be no bosses with a certain tenderness. "The IWW," he said, 'is socialism with its working clothes on." And although he scorned socialism in a business suit almost as much as he scorned the bosses, he did love socialism.

Notwithstanding his mountain mien and infernal courage, Bill Haywood's mind was feminine and childlike. He sensed things better than he understood them, and was more at home in figurative than analytic language. His famous pamphlet on Industrial Socialism, which laid the foundation for the IWW, was thought out and written, with the guidance of Bill's practical intuitions, by Dr. Frank Bohn, a wide-cheeked and bubbling professor of economic history, who had earned his Ph.D at Columbia, Wisconsin, and Michigan universities. If the new society had "ripened within the shell of the old," as scheduled by these authors, Frank Bohn would be a supreme figure in its history, the author of its Magna Carta. As it is, he is a lecturer and contributor on high politics to the New York *Times*, and his biographical notice in *Who's Who* only remarks that he was "engaged in the western labor movement 1904-06." I mention it to remind the reader how high-reaching our dreams were in those days, and how far down to earth we have come. The new society Frank and Bill Haywood saw looming so clearly on the near horizon has vanished without a trace, and their charting of the way to it is hardly worth remembering.

It was with Frank Bohn that I went out to Colorado to the coal strike. On the train he entertained me with an account of American history from the standpoint of the subsoils that I remember as a delightful chapter in my education. We arrived in the coal fields the day after the "Ludlow Massacre," the most depraved act of savagery committed against union labor in my lifetime. The mines are in little canyons running up into the hills, and the strikers and their families were living in a tent colony on the plain below. It stood just north of the junction where branch lines of the Colorado & Southern ran up the canyons to the mines, a strategic position for warning strikebreakers on incoming trains. Governor Ammons of Colorado had sent the state militia into the field, and after a little experimentation with neutrality, they had openly taken the side of the mine owners. Their commander was riding around in company cars, and they were ganging up with the mine guards. The miners were armed with rifles, the militia with machine guns, and the militia provoked a battle.

To safeguard their women and children, the miners left the tent colony in a body, carrying their rifles and entrenching themselves in a railroad cut some distance away. Seeing this, the militia opened fire, not on the miners, but on their families in the tent colony. Women and children fled from the tents in a hail of bullets, seeking shelter in a creek bed, climbing down a well, racing across the plain to a ranch house. Others lay flat in the tents or crawled into the earth holes they had dug under them. When night came the soldiers crept into the camp with cans of coal oil and set torches to the tents. The verdict of the coroner's jury stated the result:

"We find that (here follow twelves names of women and children) came to their death by asphyxiation, or fire, or both, caused by the burning of the tents of the Ludlow Tent Colony, and that the fire on the tents was started by militia-men, under Major Hamrock and Lieutenant Linderfelt, or mine guards, or both."

When Louis Tikas, the strike leader, saw the tents burning, he ran to rescue the women and children from the flames. He was caught by the soldiers, dragged across the railroad track, and shot.

This happened while Frank and I were on the train. The tent colony was still smoking when we arrived, and a civil war was in progress. Unions all over the state voted rifles and ammunition; National Guardsmen mutinied; trainmen refused to move reinforcements; armed miners flocked into Trinidad and took over the government. With the city hall as a base, they issued into the hills destroying. As I wrote in *The Masses*: "For once in this country, middle ground was abolished. Philanthropy burned up in rage. Charity could wipe up the blood. Mediation, legislation, social-consciousness expired like memories of a foolish age. Once again as in Paris in '71, an army of the working class fought the military to a standstill and let them beg for truce." And my comment was:

"It would have been a sad world had that not happened. After viewing the flattened ruins of that little colony of make-shift homes, the open death hole, the shattered bedsteads, the stove pipes still standing, the dishes and toilet trinkets broken and black—the larks singing so incongruously over them in the sun—it was a joy to travel up the canyons and feed one's eyesight upon those gigantic tangled piles of machinery and ashes that had been the operating capital of the mines. It was no remedy—it solved nothing—it was not even adequate retribution—but it was good for the eyes."

Posing as reporters for a proper Christian magazine, we invited to tea at the Hotel Coronado a dozen ladies representing the town's most correct and churchly elegance, all the way from the governor's sister to the Presbyterian minister's wife. For an hour and a half I took down verbatim what they had to say about the strike.

"The miners are nothing but cattle, and the only way is to kill them off."

"They ought to have shot Tikas to start with." (This from the minister's wife.)

"You know, there's a general belief around here that those women and children were put in that hole and sealed up on purpose because they were a drain on the union."

"Yes, those low people, they'll stoop to anything."

"They're brutal, you know. They simply don't regard human life. And they're ignorant. They can't read or write. They don't know anything. They don't even know the Christmas story!"

Fifteen minutes after this conversation ended, I was talking with the wife of a miner, a delicate French woman who had lain all day in a pit under her tent until the tent was "just like lace from the bullets." At dark she heard a noise "something like paper was blowing around."

"I looked out then, and the whole back of my tent was blazing, with me under it, and my children. I run to a Mexican tent next door, screaming like a woman that has gone insane. I was fainting, and Tikas caught me and threw water in my face. I was so thrubled up, I says, 'My God, I forgot one, I forgot one!' and I was going back. And Mrs. Jolly told me, 'It's all right. They're all here.' And I heard the children crying in that other hole, the ones that died, and Mrs. Costa crying, 'Santa Maria, have mercy,' and I heard the soldier say, 'We've got orders to kill you and we're going to do it!'

" 'We've got plenty of ammunition, just turn her loose, boys,' they said.

"Oh, I tell you, that was one of the saddest things was ever went through! When I was lying in my tent there, Mr. Snyder come running in to me with his two hands out just like this. 'Oh, my God, Mis' Toner,' he said, 'my boy's head's blown off. My God, if your children won't lay down, just knock 'em down rather'n see 'em die.' He was just like wild.

"I didn't like to say it before the children—but I was going to have this baby in a day or two, and when I got to that tent I was having awful pains and everything. And there I had to run a mile across the prairie with my five children in that condition. You talk about the Virgin Mary, she had a time to save her baby from all the trouble, and I thought to myself I was havin' a time too . . ."

I never came nearer to a sense of identity with the working class than I did there in Colorado. Frank Bohn and I addressed a mass meeting of the miners, and Jack Reed and I traveled the whole region in search, you might almost say, of a battle. I truly wanted to fight for Mrs. Toner and her babies against the bosses, and if necessary against all bourgeois society. And to the extent that I could do so in *The Masses* I did. Our May and June numbers, with their flame and blood-colored covers by John Sloan, cartoons by Art Young and Charles Winter, a decorated testimonial to "120 soldiers of the National Guard of Colorado for distinguished and heroic service in refusing to obey the command of their superior officers to entrain for Trinidad . . . ," and my two articles, "Class War in Colorado," and "The Nice Ladies of Trinidad," were as proletarian-revolutionary as anything that had appeared in the United States. They did much to make *The Masses* known to militant socialists and syndicalists throughout the world.

Nevertheless I spent a long afternoon of that week in Colorado in a state of mind remote from that of a class-struggle fighter. It was that rather of the spectator at a Greek drama, where inexorable conflict is the theme, and the fatality with which each side acts out its will and opinion is the only truth. A cliff towers up out of the very edge of Trinidad, a steep-sided, meadow-tufted butte, from whose summit the whole region can be viewed as from the high seats of an amphitheatre. Frank and I climbed up there one Sunday, and I lay for hours in the grass in meditation. I thought not only about Greek drama, but about my poems, and specifically—unless fancy is painting on memory—about my song "To A Bobolink":

> If I could warble on a wing so strong
> Filling five acres full of song,
>
> I'd never sit on the grey rail fence,
> I'd never utter a word of sense,
>
> I'd float forever in a light blue sky,
> Uttering joy to the passers-by.

How incongruous! And to these concentrated class-fighter and fighting-thinker friends of mine—"All history is a history of class struggle, isn't it?"—how mollycoddle and contemptible! Well, I didn't agree with them. I could be practical when necessary; I could postpone realization for the struggle to a higher end. But I would not discard realization, expunge it from the record, declare the struggle to be all there is. To find one's life in losing it is a prospect that never appealed either to my logic or my sense of fact. The notion that moral problems can be solved by this sleight-of-hand trick I regard as a hoax.

Another unMarxian thing I did during that insurrection in Colorado was to take a rough census of the attitude of various types and institutions toward the rebelling workers. I wanted to test out, in however amateur a way, the assumptions of my revolutionary science. In an earlier issue of *The Masses* I had faced up to the chief difficulty in Marx's dynamics: his erroneous prediction of the decline of the middle class and the catastrophic increase of the proletariat and its misery. This prediction, I said, is not coming true, but from the standpoint of method it does not have to.

"If the 'pure proletarians' stood unitedly for the Social Revolution, millions of people whose economic interest is indifferent, or not strongly, or not in the long run, opposed to the revolution, would stand with them. . . . Every battle line passes through the center of the souls of thousands of people, but when the battle rages these people have to take their stand upon one side or the other. In this fact lies the promise of social revolution."

It was this promise that I sought roughly to test out in Colorado. I went around like a visiting pastor sounding the attitudes of all men and institutions: the schools, the coroner, the state and municipal government, the Jesuits, the Protestant churches, the uplift workers, the Jews, newspapers, reporters, tradesmen, prostitutes, sisters of charity, railroad men, farmers in the surrounding country. My report, "Class Lines in Colorado," was published in *The New Review*, a theoretical journal of American Marxism that a group of us had set going in the same exciting winter that saw the rebirth of *The Masses*. I offered it only as a suggestion of what might be done if *The New Review* would send a real census taker to a scene like Trinidad. "A little more verification, a little less assertion, would be so much to the health of the socialist hypothesis." But I felt that, sketchy as it was, my report proved that "when the class line is once fittingly drawn, all other divisions of society sink into obscurity, and every man, woman and child is compelled to take a militant stand."

Thus I returned from Colorado strengthened in my belief that to back up and enlighten the workers' struggle was the way to freedom for all. My "hard-headed idealism" had grown harder, my "method of progress" more assured. Even the bitterest, least militant, the shameful part of my task, to wangle a subsidy for revolutionary journalism out of the bourgeois class, became a binding obligation, a disciplinary affliction that I must, in duty to what I believed in, continue to undergo.

Drawn by Mahonri Young

FRIENDS

Chapter 55

My Career in High Finance

THE MASSES was a luxurious magazine, in all but opinion aristocratic rather than proletarian. Dolly Sloan and I used to tell each other it would take seven thousand a year to run it. Before we got through any year the amount raised would be twelve thousand and sometimes fifteen. A little of this would be gathered in from labor and radical circles by letters, meetings, personal holdups, and the annual *Masses* Ball. Berkeley Tobey, who succeeded Dolly as business manager, inherited a fortune of $2,060, which he turned over intact to the magazine—a symbol of the state of mind that kept it going. One winter I toured the country for its benefit, offering lectures on "Revolutionary Progress," "What Is Humor and Why," "Feminism and Happiness," "Poetry Outside of Books." This yielded quite a harvest of dollars, one thousand handed to me in Denver in a solid roll as I stepped off the platform.

In general, however, this revolutionary magazine lived as it was born, on gifts solicited by me from individual members of the bourgeoisie. Proletarian revolution was still a diversion then; the idea had not acquired a content of violent fact. And moreover, the art and humor in the magazine, its variety and absence of rant, made it seem less extreme than it was. It could be regarded—and usually was, I suppose, when I was soliciting funds—as mainly a co-operative experiment, a magazine in which artists and writers could have an independent say.

Our subsidy from Mrs. Belmont and John Fox was just running out, when one morning Amos Pinchot telephoned:

"I called up to tell you fellows you're getting out a swell paper."

John Reed and I were in his office on Wall Street before the day passed, and we came away charmed with his sagacious humor, and richer by two thousand dollars.

Amos Pinchot was a prince—a subtle thing to be in America, and not easily defined. It requires hereditary wealth, but many who have that do not attain the princely bearing or prerogatives. Amos never had a political appointment, and ran only once for Congress in a district where his Progressive ticket was sure to lose; his chief job throughout life was to manage a relatively small estate. And yet if he wanted to make a statement on some public question, he had only to call up *The New York Times,* and they would give him a top headline and a double column. As his statements usually supported labor and attacked the industrial and financial hierarchy, there can be no explanation of this except hereditary nobility; he assumed the prerogatives and they were accorded to him. He became a kind of royal patron of *The Masses* crowd, defending and helping us in private as well as public ways. In particular he became my silent partner in the task of raising funds, a crucifixion which his amused and friendly-humorous counsel made it easier to bear. He also shared with me the responsibility of handling those funds.

One night Amos invited to dinner, together with his distinguished brother Gifford, Archer Huntington, the son of California's famous railroad "buccaneer." Gifford is much more conservative than Amos was, and lacks his suavity and virile humor; he abhors alcohol in an old-maidish way and leans too heavily upon virtue to seem strong. We did not dream of Gifford's giving money to *The Masses,* but thought he might act as a catalyst in whose presence a little of the Southern Pacific's surplus value could be precipitated.

Archer Huntington has a vein of poetry in him, and he and I took a liking to each other. After the dinner he drove me up to visit his beloved Hispanic Museum, rousing the caretaker at midnight with a great banging on the windows. After burrowing some hours among its more recondite treasures, we came back at dawn to his house on Fifth Avenue, where he showed me a sheaf of sonnets he had written in his youth. We had a farewell glass of wine together in broad daylight. He impressed me memorably as a robust and real man, and I endowed him with daring intelligence and used him years after— or the image I had treasured of him—as the model for George Forbes, the imaginative financier, in my novel *Venture.* But I did not get any money from him. I got, on the contrary, a feeling of remorse that throughout that whole delightful twelve hours of friendship, instead of giving myself to it for its own sake, I had kept wondering what I would get out of it for *The Masses.* That is what I mean by calling the money-raiser's task a shameful one. His motive may be noble, but his state of mind is shabby. Huntington told Amos afterward that I was a charming fellow, but seemed to have no force—a judgment which chimed perfectly with my feelings of self-contempt.

I would spend weeks working up my courage to go into these money-raising campaigns, and weeks unruffling my spirit after they were over. Nothing, I am sure, but that *wanting to do what you don't want to,* which diverted my grandfather's lustihood from laughing affirmation on this earth to tears and agonizings over heaven, can explain my putting myself through these semi-annual spells of torture. They were penitential disciplines.

One lavish giver to *The Masses,* who became too much my friend for any of these feelings to persist, was Betty Hare. She was Betty Goodwin when I met her, and her real and right name is Elizabeth Sage—for I do not know any person upon whom it seems more absurd to pin the label of an incidental male. Betty is the granddaughter of the genial philanthropist who founded Sage College for Women at Cornell, and put a mattress of white horsehair in each of the rooms for the young ladies to sleep on. Our first meeting was the result of a deliberate conspiracy against her bank account. Alice Duer Miller, who liked *The Masses* for combining witty writing with militant feminism as she was doing, said to me:

"Betty Goodwin would give you lots of money for the magazine if she happened to like you."

So she invited us both to dinner, and I came resolved to make Betty Goodwin like me for that lofty purpose. I found myself absorbed in liking her. In the warm, magnetic, simple and unaffected, joyous and yet serious flow of her thinking interest over all of life—the very fluid of poetry pouring out of those large and slyly sparkling blue-grey eyes—I lost all remembrance of my ulterior purpose. More exactly, I called it up once into my mind and dismissed it as a blasphemy. I went home rejoicing that I had not destroyed with any tricks of ingratiation this encounter with a truly beautiful person. I still possessed my soul.

The next day I received a note from Betty containing her check for three thousand dollars—an "unexpected dividend," she said, which had come in providentially just after I told her about *The Masses.* Subsequently I often and openly conspired against Betty's bank account—more often, I think, and more fruitfully than against any other, and with less pumping up of courage. For she is one of the few people I have known with an authentic instinct of generosity. Asking her for something is like asking your mother, for if she can not give it she suffers more than you do, and feels obliged to explain the situation very clearly and meticulously as though her honor were involved.

In contrast with Amos Pinchot and Betty Hare, who came inside my problem and shared the hazard and the humor of it, there were other philanthropists like Samuel Untermyer and Adolph Lewisohn, who, having been approached through the proper channels, would pass me out a small sum, or one which seemed small to them, as though paying their annual taxes. Fred Howe, I remember, commended *The Masses*, to Adolph Lewisohn as worthy of a donation.

"Perhaps you'd like to see the magazine," I said to Mr. Lewisohn, after pocketing his check for one thousand dollars, and I offered him a carefully selected issue of *The Masses*.

"Oh no, that's all right, I have no time to bother with it," he said, and brushed me out of his office with a two-handed friendly push as though he had given me a stick of candy to keep me quiet. He was a lovable little unwrinkled apple of an old man, full of quaint and kindly impulse, and I was sorry that, when the time came, I felt compelled to attack his views all the more implacably because of that thousand dollars.

A man whose giving more flattered my pride was the aging monarch of small-city journalism, E. W. Scripps, founder and owner of the Scripps-McRae (now Scripps-Howard) newspapers. "E.W." had just bought a vast ranch sloping up from the sea near San Diego, California, and retired there to think his own thoughts, boss his family, and let the world—except for an occasional peremptory command over the long-distance telephone—go its natural way to hell. He had a mind like Montaigne's, fertile, discursive, full of extremely rational and therefore revolutionary doubts and speculations about everything. And like Montaigne he produced essays, fifty or sixty a year, I should say, smoking an unbroken procession of mild but excellent cigars while dictating them to his secretary. These essays went into an iron box and were locked up. If any of the opinions enshrined in them had an influence upon the policy of his papers, it was indirect. For to him writing down your deep beliefs was one thing and conducting a newspaper another, and the less they got mixed the better.

This was close kin to my own credo, except that to me writing was the main thing and economic enterprise incidental. To Scripps enterprise was the main thing: he wanted property and power, and did not even ask a public for his writings. He did, however, hungrily enjoy reading them to me, and I had a standing invitation to visit him in his ranch-house castle.

Scripps was a mighty tyrant in his own domain. His castle was all on one story in a vast square, and as you passed from room to room, you would find tacked up beside each doorway in his handwriting:

SHUT THE DOOR. *E. W. Scripps.*

At breakfast just before we rose from the table, he would issue an order-of-the-day:

"Bob, I want to confer with you immediately, and I will see you again at 2:30 P.M. Emma, I will drive with you at four. Ida, your time is your own—make yourself at home. Max, we will talk in my office at ten."

Notwithstanding these imperial habits, and a feeling that it is still lese majesty to say it, there was at times a wistfulness in Scripps' attitude to me as though he were intruding upon a more serious person's time. He knew that I had chosen the better part. After having his fill of mature and recklessly intellectual conversation about things that really matter, four to five hours of it sometimes, as I would stagger from the room groggy with nicotine and sheer exhaustion of the brain cells, he would thank me almost apologetically for the refreshment.

When it came to giving money, however, E. W. was himself again.

"If I put anything into a publication, it is because I think it can succeed as a business. I do think *The Masses* can, but I am not sure whether I think so because I like you and enjoy reading it myself or because my journalistic experience leads me to believe it has a public. I'm going to give you two thousand dollars by way of experiment. You come out here next year and show me your financial reports, and I'll know whether I acted from sentimentalism or good sense."

Tobey made a wonderful report the next year, one from which the inference was unescapable that Scripps ought to increase his contribution from two to four thousand dollars. I explained this to him while he glanced the paper through.

"Max, you make a good speech," he said, "but I knew that already. I heard you down in San Diego. The figures on this paper, on the other hand, convince me that your magazine is a failure. It's a delight to me personally, but it isn't good business. You'll have to find a philanthropist. I'm a businessman."

Like most people addicted to property Scripps had a strong sense of identity with his family. Thanks to his lifelong guidance, his sister Elizabeth had become almost as rich as he was. She lived down by the sea at La Jolla, and he asked me before leaving that afternoon to stop in with him and meet her. Elizabeth Scripps was thin and scrawny, and so old that her skin was yellow and caked in large squares like a crocodile's. I never saw another walking thing that looked so old. Her mind, however, was not dimmed except by the impulses of her heart, which were more pious than his and more benevolent. She believed in church and Sunday school, and gave large subsidies to religious as well as educational ventures. She believed still more in her brother, however, and received me with great warmth because of our friendship. I said goodbye to E.W. at her door and drove away—but I did not drive very far. I was lurking behind a bush in her lawn when E.W. took his leave, and a few moments later I rang her bell. I had come back—just on an impulse —to ask her if she wouldn't help me with my magazine. I showed her the figures that had been so convincing when prepared for E. W., and they became again miraculously logical and clear.

"How much does your magazine need?" she asked. "I've pledged almost all I planned to give this year to a little paper that our church is publishing."

"I only need six thousand dollars right now," I said.

"I'm really very sorry," she said, "I couldn't give you that much right now. I wonder if it wouldn't be possible for you to get along if I sent it in three annual installments?"

Many years later, when Jo Davidson made his bust of E.W., the old man related with gusto how, when he refused to give *The Masses* four thousand dollars and told me to find a philanthropist, I went down and lifted six from his benevolent sister. It added, I think, to his respect for me.

Scripps had modesty as well as empire in him. When I asked him why he had no paper in New York, he said:

"I'm not big enough. I'm a small town man. I know my limitations. I leave the metropolis to Hearst."

I admired E.W. greatly and enjoyed him in the same way I had once enjoyed the meditative old pagan, Z. R. Brockway of the Elmira Reformatory. I believe that from savage times there have been in all communities these doubting thinkers, men who love fact and valid reason too well to join the gullible fuss that goes down in history as the mental culture of the time or tribe they live in.

Scripps, I am proud to say, had also a high opinion of me—indeed the rather exceptional opinion that I am not lazy. I treasure a letter he wrote in 1916 to another financial backer of *The Masses*, a flattering, and yet also to me now a saddening letter.

"Business is not Eastman's line by any means. However, he is a beautiful and effective writer. . . . He has few equals in literature in America today.

"It is all well enough for him to have a few months or even a year of practical business affairs. Such experience couldn't help being valuable to him on account of the general mind-broadening effect.

"However, Mr. Eastman is not robust physically, and his nervous system is such that it should not and can not be safely submitted to the strains inevitably attendant on such a business as the publication of *The Masses*. . . . Even many of the hardiest and toughest of men younger than myself, who have been my lieutenants, have broken down completely under lighter burdens than that Eastman is attempting to carry now. . . .

"I am not a socialist, as you know, and I do not agree with many of the details of *The Masses'* propaganda. But most of the art work and the larger part of the text of *The Masses* is great art and the finest literature. Mr. Eastman himself is an extraordinary and beautiful character. Why even I, tough and coarse-fibered as I am—thirty years past my days of romance and poetry—read with extreme pleasure, from cover to cover, his book on poetry.

"But every one of Eastman's excellencies and his fine qualities are just those which unfit him for the task he has imposed upon himself."

It was the wisest and kindliest advice I ever came by, but I had not the clarity of character to act upon it. After *The Masses* began paying me a salary, it seemed a guarantee of creative freedom, as well as a service to my ideals, and when one of these motives did not compel me, the other did.

I used sometimes, when our subsidy was running low, to consult Lincoln Steffens, and we would go over together the possible sources of help. Once he conceived the colossal idea of getting a whole year's subsidy, no less than twelve thousand dollars, out of the Chicago millionaire Charles R. Crane. Crane was a much-traveled liberal, a connoisseur of Russia and the Orient, who had achieved the honor of being appointed ambassador to China by President Taft. As the appointment was revoked without explanation before the ambassador got as far as San Francisco, he was esteemed by us on the left to have a little piece of revolution hidden in him somewhere.

Crane had a vast square head, a pudgy and impassive body, and round fat hands which rested without life or motion in his lap. Asking him for money was like praying to a statue of Buddha. He never let fall a word. After my prayer was over he began, still without moving, to tell me irrelevant but interesting stories about mandarins and Russian czars and muzhiks. He told these stories all through lunch, and I listened with that sincere and carefully not-too-exaggerated appreciation which money raisers have to cultivate. It seemed to me that something must be gestating behind it all. He certainly had been listening when I presented my request. He had not shuddered at the mention of twelve thousand dollars. Moreover, Steff had explained to him what I came for. I waited after lunch until my cigar burned out. I waited until three o'clock, and when still nothing happened, I shifted in my chair and remarked:

"Well, Mr. Crane, I have enjoyed this talk and thank you. I think I must be going."

He lifted up one of those expressionless hands.

"Wait just one moment," he said. "I want to give you something before you go."

He tiptoed into his study with surprisingly lively steps, and I sank back into my chair in relief. The tension at least was over. *Something* was going to happen. He came back too quickly with a little square package held carefully in both hands.

"Now this," he said, releasing one hand to pat the package, "is Russian tea, and I want you to see if you do not find it superior in flavor to the very best of China tea."

Charles R. Crane had a sister, also a little Buddha-like although very handsome, Mrs. Kate Crane Gartz, of Altadena, California. Mrs. Gartz really does have a little revolution in her. She has at least a childlike way of actually believing in the ideals we all profess and an untrammeled logic in drawing conclusions from them. Combined with restless pity and a fluent pen, this has made her into a sort of epistolary gadfly of the state almost as nobly exasperating in a small way as Socrates. I dare not guess how many thousands of letters she has written to public personages, asking them in embarrassingly plain language why they do not live up to their professions, and incidentally to the obvious demands of decency and sound reason. Upton Sinclair's wife, Mary Craig, has collected ten little square volumes of these "Letters of Protest." They would make admirable object lessons if one were teaching people how to think; their assumptions are so obvious, and yet almost always, if you are practical minded, your sympathy goes out to the recipient. It is not quite fair, when one's task is merely writing letters, to be so all-fired noble and logical about the far more complicated task of getting something done.

Mrs. Gartz has qualities dearer to me than this rather facile didacticism that has been so praised by other radicals. A bold forthright rejection of religious consolations is one. A wish to range all over the earth and see everything is another. A mischievous delight in the clash of fierce opinions is a third. If she could get Stalin and Pope Pius XI into her drawing room for "tea and a brief discussion of the social problem," she would ask nothing better of life. She got Charlie Chaplin there once and suddenly, while he was peacefully sipping a cup of tea, tapped on the table and announced to her guests:

"If you will take your places, I am sure we shall be glad to hear a few remarks on current conditions from Mr. Chaplin."

Charlie, in complete consternation and also extreme inward recoil, stammered:

"Oh no! Thank you very much, but I— I—"

"What's the matter? Haven't you got an opinion?" she said.

The Masses never let her down that way. *The Masses* always had an opinion and was always ready to entertain her with a fight. For that, and not only for its devotion to social justice, Mrs. Gartz cherished our magazine and gave it money like an indulgent parent. I did not even have to go to see her. She would write and ask us if we didn't need some money!

Such was the economic character of *The Masses*, a luxurious gift to the working-class movement from the most imaginative artists, the most imaginative writers, and the most imaginative millionaires in the Adolescence of the Twentieth Century.

Our fortunes reached their peak in 1916 when Aline Barnsdall, heiress of the Barnsdall Oil Company, sent me out of the blue a check for five thousand dollars and the single line: "Congratulations on your stand against the war." And they reached their low point in 1917, when the war came, and the high-cost-of-agitation, and we had to abandon our fine paper and expansive format, and bring out a little squarish mud-colored sheet that made our eyes very sad. By that time, however, so many troubles had gathered round us that we were glad to be able to bring out anything at all.

Chapter 56

Educating the Associated Press

NEXT to the Paterson silk strike, the great labor war of 1913 was in the coal fields of West Virginia. There the white-haired proletarian Valkyrie, Mother Jones, divinely gifted with love and profanity, "wove the web of battle" for the Paint Creek miners. It was a violent battle, so violent that for the first time in our history the civil courts were superseded by a military tribunal. And yet it was a mysteriously hushed-up battle. Our Carnegie Hall meeting at which I introduced Mother Jones to her first New York audience was an effort to break this mysterious hush. I learned from her lips what seemed to me, in connection with it, an outrageous fact: that the local representative of the Associated Press was an officer of that military tribunal. It made me mad, and it made Art Young mad, and we decided to hand the AP a sock on the jaw that they would be a long time forgetting.

Art drew a picture of the head of the AP pouring "lies" out of a bottle marked POISON into a reservoir which supplied "News" to a city with the American flag flying over it. I wrote an editorial to accompany his picture:

"Up to the day of Senator Kern's speech in the Senate, how many people knew that a military despotism had prevailed for months in West Virginia? How many people knew that men were shooting each other a dozen at a time only seven hours from the metropolis? For some secret reason West Virginia has hardly leaked a drop of news in the last fourteen months.

"And that secret reason is the Associated Press.

". . . So long as the substance of current history continues to be held in cold storage, adulterated, colored with poisonous intentions, and sold to the highest bidder to suit his private purposes, there is small hope that even the free and the intelligent will take the side of justice in the struggle that is before us."

That insult was published in our July 1913 issue, and, so far as we went, forgotten in the general rush of business: business of defending sabotage, the right to suicide, the General Strike, the Birth Strike in Germany, mutiny in the French army, the indicted IWW, the impeached governor Sulzer, Philippine independence, the suffragettes; business of attacking Organized Charity, the Manufacturers' Association, the Stock Exchange, Woodrow Wilson, Frank A. Munsey, Rudyard Kipling, Welfare Work, sermons, hymns, Jane Addams, Theodore Roosevelt, Adolph Lewisohn, philanthropy, Fabianism, preachers, poets laureate, Louis D. Brandeis, Hugo Munsterberg, Sidney Webb, Bernard Shaw . . . everything and everybody not ready to mount the barricades with the embattled workers. In the autumn of 1913 we got together and planned a "Special Christmas Number," in which with one accord, artists and writers all, we ganged up on the Christian church. I doubt if anything comparable to that issue of *The Masses* in combining idealism with impiety has ever been seen in America.

The cover, drawn by Art Young, was a billboard announcing a speech by "Jesus Christ, the Workingman of Nazareth" on "The Rights of Labor," with "He stirreth up the people" for a slogan. The frontispiece entitled "Their Last Supper" was a vicious drawing by Maurice Becker of a gang of gluttonous prelates dining extravagantly with Christ hanging on a cross above them. For the double-page, John Sloan got into the pulpit behind a fashionable preacher and ridiculed his back and the faces of his congregation.

"Thus, friends, we see the masses, filled with a vague, unChristian spirit of discontent. They cry out upon work, bewailing their divinely appointed lot, forgetful, my brethren, of the heavenly law which ordains that only through toil and tribulation, by the narrow path of self-denial, may we enter into the higher values of spiritual blessedness . . . Let us pray!"

Glenn Coleman showed a young pauper girl gruesomely kneeling to kiss—"Forever and Ever, Amen!"—the fat hand of a flabby-mouthed, greasy priest. Chamberlain drew the Rock of Ages as a dollar sign. Stuart Davis's picture was titled: "That's right, girls— on Sunday the cross, on weekdays the double cross." Art Young contributed three blasphemies besides his cover. I filled three pages with a sermon entitled "The Church is Judas."

"No mind that reads the synoptic gospels with faith, and the subsequent history of Europe with reason, can escape knowing that the

Drawn by Maurice Becker

THEIR LAST SUPPER

The crowning ceremony of the Episcopal convention was a banquet tendered to the clerical deputies by a church club. It cost $10,680—about $20 a plate.

Christian Church has been, and is, the betrayer of Christ. To what extent the Carpenter of Judea was an agitator, a militant champion of the oppressed in this world, and to what extent purely a moral and religious genius, a prophet of God and the next world, is indeed a problem. A vexed problem in this time, and I think for all time. But whether that Jesus of Nazareth, the Friend of Man who had not where to lay his head, the informal well-doer, the poet of nature and candid life, comrade of the rejected, loving and enclosing all sufferers in his sympathy as the air loves them and encloses them, as generous toward truth as toward humanity, as intelligent as he was supremely exalted—whether that Jesus of Nazareth has had any real part in this institutionalized, aristocratic, sentimentally hypocritical hierarchy of the powers of conservatism that has arrogated to itself his sacred name—this is no problem! . . .

"I know that a few ministers are doing their best to break loose from the bonds of respectability and stand where Jesus stood, with the oppressed. But as class issues are drawn with increasing firmness by the development of business, these ministers will find their task not lighter but more and more difficult. They will find themselves held fast in the old grip of capitalistic interest. They will find that as they could not serve God and Mammon, so they can not serve Christ and the church . . ."

I always felt that this Christmas number had something to do with what happened on December 14. It was on that date, anyway—six months after our attack on the AP—that I learned from an evening paper which I bought on 8th Street and Broadway that Art Young and I had been indicted for criminal libel on complaint of the Associated Press. The police, I further learned, were hunting for us. I happened to know that Art had left his studio to spend the holidays in his little farmhouse at Bethel, Connecticut. I myself on reading this news thought pleasantly of Connecticut, and after calling up my sister and asking her to raise some bail and try to find a lawyer, I took the train for Bethel. When Art and I came to town the next day, everything had been arranged. Gilbert Roe, an ex-partner of Senator La Follette, an aging deacon of the Single Tax church, had agreed to defend us without charge. Amos Pinchot had put up two thousand dollars bail with his congratulations. We were arraigned and released—a little to my poetic regret—in a very respectful manner. For the drama's sake we should have been locked up in jail.

We had not much more than got settled to work after this ceremony when Mr. Roe called up and told us we had been indicted all over again—this time for libeling the president of the AP personally. We had better demur, he thought, to this second indictment, but he was too busy to handle the matter just then. Remembering that Ida had been admitted to the bar, he suggested that she go into court with us and enter a plea of *not guilty* "with leave to withdraw the same in ten days and make such motions as may be deemed necessary." This gave us a good press story—PRISONER REPRESENTED IN COURT BY HIS OWN WIFE—in which Ida was played up as "a sculptor, an actress, a suffrage orator and a writer, as well as a lawyer."

Another good press story was Roe's argument of the demurrer, which occupied the front page of the New York *Law Journal*. In general our clash with the AP was big news, and good for the health and circulation of *The Masses*. The New York *Evening Post* published a long article glorifying the AP, and quoting one of its high officials as saying that the case "was not being prosecuted in a spirit of revenge"—the AP, in fact, was only taking this opportunity to clear itself of charges frequently made in other publications, in the houses of Congress, and even within the corporation by its own members.

To this we answered in the February *Masses*:

"Just why this particular 'opportunity' was chosen for the clarification is not made perfectly plain.

"Nor is it made plain just why the people's taxes should be used to pay for an investigation of the Associated Press in the criminal courts, when every precedent points to a civil action for damages as the natural procedure.

"Nor is it made clear just why 'in no vengeful spirit' it was found necessary to have two people indicted, to say nothing of having two people indicted twice for the same alleged offense.

"Nor is it made clear just why, in order to secure a judicial investigation of the Associated Press, it should seem necessary in the second indictment to shift the issue to the personality of its president.

"These are simply some questions that remain unanswered after one reads the evidently official announcement in the *Post*. Undoubtedly all will be made clear before the general 'clarification' is over. Meanwhile watch this page for indictments."

We learned subsequently that Gibert Roe had subpoenaed the records of the AP's Pittsburgh office to find out how they really did handle the news from West Virginia. To block this move, Arthur Train, assistant district attorney conducting the case, proposed to withdraw the original indictment and prosecute only on the charge of personal libel. To this charge he hoped the Pittsburgh records would be judged irrelevant, but they weren't. Roe got access to them, and, moreover, when the Trinidad strike came on he had investigators in the field—myself among them—making further damaging discoveries about the AP's labor news. I believe the simple truth is that it had never occurred to those running the AP to present as news the workers' side of a strike. It had never even occurred to them to make a pretense of doing this. Our libel case set going a

ART YOUNG. MAX EASTMAN

process of self-scrutiny which has had very beneficial results. A candid account of this process might have relieved the monotony of the encomiastic volume this organization subsequently dedicated to itself.

People gathered around to help us as though we had accidentally bumped into a bees' nest that everybody had been intending to go after. A mass meeting in our behalf at Cooper Union was packed full, with hundreds in the aisles and hundreds turned away. Inez Milholland presided, and the meeting was addressed by Amos Pinchot, Lincoln Steffens, Charlotte Perkins Gilman (brilliant poet-feminist), William English Walling, Norman Hapgood (then editor of *Harper's Weekly*), and Joseph Cannon of the Western Federation of Miners. I can not describe the meeting, for Art Young and I, dining together at Polly's restaurant, decided that martyrs ought not to attend their own canonization.

"We ought to be either dead or in prison," Art said. "The least we can do is keep out of sight."

The climax of the meeting was Amos Pinchot's bold act of participation in our guilt.

"I am perfectly willing," he said, "to stand behind the charge made by Eastman and Young that [the Associated Press] does color and distort the news, that it is not impartial, and that it is a monopolistic corporation, not only in constraint of trade but in constraint of truth."

Amos was rebuked by the *New York Times*:

"Mr. Pinchot should understand that this is not an Associated Press suit; it is a government suit, an action brought by the people to punish the lawless."

He was also visited by the AP's Washington attorney, who came up to demand a retraction under threat of a libel suit for $150,000. Amos's answer to the attorney—whom he happened to have known in college—was: "They can go to hell, and let's have dinner at the Century Club and talk it over." At dinner he opened the attorney's eyes to the fact that the labor struggle was conducted by human beings, and that other people besides fanatics are interested in hearing the union's side of a strike. He explained to him that the AP automatically suppressed that side—"you know it as well as I do"—and that if they went into a fight on that issue they would be licked. The suit against Amos Pinchot was never brought, and our prosecution also seemed for some unannounced reason to hang fire.

I judge that the AP, having got *The Masses* between its teeth and got all set to eat us up, began to feel some regurgitory movements of a purely instinctive character in the deeps of its being. I can not trace the movements, for I am not familiar with those deeps. But the upshot was that a brilliant young man on Wall Street, then just springing into fame as a banker who knew something about banking, Eugene Meyer, Jr., wrote me a note suggesting that we have a drink together. The drink proved warming; he showed a liberal and really cultured appreciation of *The Masses*; and we struck up what might be called an intellectual friendship. In the course of it he told me what a nice fellow was Melville Stone, his very good friend, the world-famous manager of the Associated Press. They had been talking the other night about the libel action against *The Masses*; he had praised the magazine and provoked the old man's curiosity.

"In fact, I think Melville would be glad of an opportunity to see you and talk the whole thing over," he said.

"Well, I'm perfectly willing to discuss it, if he wants to," I answered.

"Would you mind coming down to his office if I make the appointment? He's an elderly man, you know, and pretty busy. I'll be there to introduce you."

"Why, naturally," I said. "Of course I'll come down any time you like."

In a few days I received word at what hour Eugene Meyer, Jr., would meet me in the AP offices and introduce me to Melville Stone. He was there when I arrived, and did his part manfully and with grace. But Melville Stone, without getting up from his desk or even, as I remember it, extending a hand, glared at me through a pair of opaque eyeglasses under his short bangs, and said:

"Well, young man, what did you wish to say to me?"

For once in my life I got mad when it was the right thing to do.

"Not a damned word!" I said. "I was informed by Mr. Meyer that you wished to say something to me."

"I gave Mr. Meyer no such information. I understood that you had something to say."

"All right, that ends the interview," I replied, and after an elaborate handshake with Eugene Meyer, I stalked out of the room.

Perhaps I was wrong, but I began to get a feeling that this fight was going to be too rough for Gilbert Roe. He was a slow, sweet, grandmotherlike lawyer-friend, a man you could easily knock out physically, at least, because his head was too large for his body. Moreover, he was not publicly known and had no access to the "inside dope" on the AP. At the risk of hurting his feelings, I went for advice to Ida's friend, Arthur Brisbane, editor of the New York *Evening Journal*.

Brisbane invited me to lunch—a skew-gee sort of a lunch, it turned out to be, for I could not climb aboard his rapid train of thought at any point. Arguments by analogy poured out of him so fast as to leave no time, had there been an inclination, to consider logic. A genius of speed, energy, safety and picturesqueness of opinion, he seemed also to me a kindly-sentimental man. He told me one thing that I have never heard reported. His father, Albert Brisbane, had been a quite famous or notorious radical, the leading apostle of

Fourier in this country. Arthur, on reaching years of discretion, bought up all surviving copies of Albert's mildly shocking autobiography and withdrew it from circulation. This I knew beforehand, but he told me that out of respect for the memory of his father he never attacked a radical. That, he said, was an absolute law of his life, and I think, if one examined his editorials, it would be found that he lived up to it. He had deserted the lonely camp of the radicals because he loved wealth, power, and glory, but he would never fire a shot in that direction. His father was still there.

On the question of our libel case, his answer was crisp and instantaneous:

"Go and see Sam Untermyer. I'll call him up this afternoon."

Samuel Untermyer was a little man without warmth and with a convulsive eye-wink which robbed him of personal dignity, but so astute and hard fibred that he had risen to the height of his profession. Having put away millions as attorney for the "robber barons," he had taken up public-spiritedness, somewhat as one takes up golf in advancing years, and made himself both feared and hated by those barons. I found him in a sumptuous office, seated at a desk that measured twice his length, with fountains of red roses spraying out of vases on either side of him. He greeted me without emotion, took from my hand a copy of *The Masses* containing our crime, read it carefully, and said:

"This is libelous beyond a doubt. I'll tell you what to do. Don't let anybody know that you have seen me, or that I am interested in the case. If they find that out, they'll drop it. Just let Mr. Roe go ahead and prepare for trial, and when you get into court I'll come in and we'll subpoena the whole gang from J. P. Morgan down. We might as well have this thing out now as later."

I must have chuckled in my surprise, for he gave me at last a human smile and said:

"I guess you didn't know how true those words were about putting the news in cold storage."

"You can prove it, can you?" I said.

"Young man, I don't want to be indiscreet, but I will go so far as to say I have been present when it was done."

He put some significance into those eye-winks, I thought, as we shook hands. I never did tell anybody about his promise, except Art Young and Gilbert Roe and no doubt Ida, and I don't know whether it leaked out or not. All I know is that after hanging over our heads for more than two years, this "government suit," this "action by the people to punish the lawless," mysteriously disappeared into the air, and our bail was returned without explanation by the district attorney. Gilbert Roe turned over the material assembled for the defense to Upton Sinclair, who continued the slow task of educating the AP in his brochure, *The Brass Check*. Art Young drew a picture for *The Masses* of February 1916, which suitably concludes the story:

"Madame, you dropped something."

Chapter 57

Kicked Out of Various Places

SO MUCH war and revolution have shaken the world since those days it is hard to realize what an outrage against peaceful opinions *The Masses* was. That AP indictment was only the high point in a hurricane of abuse. We were kicked off the subway stands in New York, suppressed by the Magazine Distributing Company in Boston, ejected by the United News Company of Philadelphia, expelled from the Columbia University library and bookstore, stopped at the border by Canada, and swept out of colleges and reading rooms from Harvard to San Diego. I toured the country in 1916 with a lecture "What Socialism Really Is," an oratorical preview of *Towards Liberty* designed to bring in dollars and subscribers, and President Van Hise helped vastly by debarring me from the campus at the University of Wisconsin. The students rented a hall, and I addressed a quadrupled mob a little way down the street. The story was in all newspapers, and a similar mob greeted me at Ann Arbor, Chicago, Minneapolis, Denver, Butte, Seattle, Los Angeles— wherever my lecture was booked.

While so violently stormed at, we were also vigorously defended— defended by people who believed less in our opinions than the athletic honesty with which we expressed them. Our eviction from the subway stands happened to coincide with a legislative investigation of the Interborough Rapid Transit Company, and one day when the banker, August Belmont, was on the stand, I went down there with permission to question him. I took with me a distinguished cloud of witnesses, among them Charles Scribner, the publisher, Professor John Dewey, Mr. and Mrs. Amos Pinchot, Walter Lippmann, Herbert Croly, editor of *The New Republic*, Mrs. O. H. P. Belmont, J. G. Phelps Stokes, the socialist millionaire, his beautiful bride from a sweatshop, Rose Pastor Stokes, Emily Polini, the

actress, Franklin P. Adams, Inez Milholland, Oscar Cesare and
Boardman Robinson, cartoonists of the *Times* and *Tribune* re-
spectively, the Reverend Charles Sanderson of Brooklyn, the Reverend Percy Stickney Grant of the Church of the Ascension on
Fifth Avenue, and the Reverend Charles P. Fagnani of Union
Theological Seminary. It was a gala day for the opposition, and I
greatly enjoyed baiting the unhappy banker. All I remember of it is
the look of surprise on his face when I got up, in the midst of a
sufficiently painful grilling on the subject of stocks and bonds, and
began to quiz him on the right of American citizens to choose their
own reading matter. A clipping from the *Evening Post* remembers
this much more:

" 'Is not the subway public property?' Mr. Eastman asked.

" 'I cannot give an opinion,' Mr. Belmont said. 'I do not believe
anyone has a right to reject magazines. I can not give an opinion,
but I should think if there is any legal method of preventing an
objectionable magazine from the newsstands, it should be done.' "

What made us so "objectionable" was not primarily our attack on
capitalism—that question was still a trifle academic in America. But
we voiced our attack in a manner that outraged patriotic, religious,
and matrimonial, to say nothing of ethical and aesthetic tastes and
conventions. The state, the church, the press, marriage, organized
charity, the liberals, the philanthropists, the Progressive Party—they
were all game for our guns and always in season. And when the
war started in Europe, that too was something to shoot at—and so
was patriotism, "preparedness," and the rising cult of the army over
here. "The country is rapidly being scared into an 'heroic mood,' "
said John Reed in a slashing attack on military appropriations. It is
easy to denounce the whole existing world when you believe that a
millennium lies just over the hill or behind the sky—or on the
other side of the planet. And there was a good deal of that too-easy
denunciation in our magazine. We had no sense of history; we were
pretty juvenile.

Even more "objectionable" than our juvenility was our determination to say the same things in public that we said in private. Out-
spoken truth-telling was what got us into the worst trouble, and out-
spoken truth-telling was the best thing we did. In that respect,
indeed, *The Masses* might perhaps appear a kind of landmark in
American culture if one had the wish to see it so. In 1908, only four
years before we started our magazine, Mark Twain confided some
thoughts on this subject to his diary. In a private conversation with

Elinor Glyn, he had expressed approval of the unconventional behavior of the lovers in her notorious novel *Three Weeks*. She had asked him to publish this opinion, and he had replied that such a thing was unthinkable.

"I said I had been revealing to her my private sentiments, *not* my public ones. . . . I said I was in the common habit, in private conversation with friends, of revealing every private opinion I possessed relating to religion, politics, and men, but that I should never dream of *printing* one of them, because they are individually and collectively at war with almost everybody's public opinion, while at the same time they are in happy agreement with almost everybody's private opinion. As an instance, I asked her if she had ever encountered an intelligent person who privately believed in the Immaculate Conception—which of course she hadn't; and I also asked her if she had ever seen an intelligent person who was daring enough to publicly deny his belief in that fable and print the denial. Of course she hadn't encountered any such person."[1]

We were in conscious revolt against this blight on American expression. As I phrased it in the masthead, we were for "printing what is too naked or true for a money-making press." If we linked this blight with the capitalist system, and believed that truth-telling would become general on the adoption of complete collectivization (instead of taking that moment to depart permanently from one-sixth of the earth), you will pardon, I hope, the slight mistake. Our revolt was no less significant for that. And we carried it, as though we had read Mark Twain's diary and taken his dare, to the very extreme he cited as unthinkable. Our issue of January 1916 contained a "Ballad" in which Joseph was praised above all others in the birth legend of Jesus for his large-heartedness toward a wife who presented him with a baby that was not his own. It would be hard to find a more real and recurrent life-problem, or a more simple and musical and genuinely idealistic treatment of it, than is contained in this ballad. But because it *published* a point of view deemed suitable for private communication only, it became a kind of high crime on my part, and the main point of attack whenever anybody went forth against *The Masses*.[2]

In Detroit, where I was scheduled to lecture on socialism at the Church of Our Father (Universalist), a Presbyterian minister got

---

[1] From *Mark Twain in Eruption*.
[2] The poem will be found in the Appendix, page 592.

hold of this poem and gave me and the pastor of that church such a lambasting in his pulpit and in the papers that the town was in an uproar when I arrived. My audience occupied almost the whole block both ways from the little church where I spoke. The incident brought me an oratorical celebrity in Detroit that I have been thirty years reaping the fruits of. I believe I have given twice as many lectures in that town as anywhere else, and charged twice as much, and I owe it all, at bottom, to the Reverend Doctor H. Wray Boyle, pastor of the Woodward Avenue Presbyterian Church. I still have his excommunication as featured under a front-page headline in the Detroit *Journal* for March 13, 1916:

"Showing a depth of feeling remarkable even in a man of his intense earnestness, Dr. Boyle used these words:

" 'I protest against a Christian Church being polluted by a man like Max Eastman, whose blasphemy, published in poem form in *The Masses*, his publication, is a desecration of the most sacred ideals of the Christian people.'

"Dr. Boyle had been handed a copy of *The Masses*, and his attention called to a poem in which the writer vilified Joseph and burlesqued the divinity of Christ and the Virgin motherhood of Mary.

"He began to read the verses to his congregation, but stopped, exclaiming:

" 'I cannot go on. It is too horrible!' "

Dr. Willis A. Moore, the Universalist pastor, replied to this with an interview stating that I was lecturing on socialism, not religion, and that the hall in which I was lecturing, while in the church building, was not exactly the church. "I can't lay down any moral code for which I have a right to demand the obedience of other people," he said. But he was plainly worried. My friend and hostess, Kathleen Hendrie, described as "the wife of a millionaire who has an estate near Pontiac," defended me with a little more verve and some "throaty melodious laughter." And the reporter himself put in a word at the end of his story:

"Eastman is acclaimed by his admirers in Bohemian Greenwich Village, New York City, as the American George Bernard Shaw, and he has as many admirers in Europe as he has in the United States. His own poetry is of the gentle sort, and his beautiful style is in striking contrast with the militancy of *The Masses*, which he edits and which is excluded from the reading room of Columbia University, as well as from many newsstands."

On my arrival I was, of course, interviewed by all the papers, and another series of front page stories advertised my lecture.

" 'Christianity is one thing, the religion of Jesus Christ is another,' said Max Eastman, mild-mannered, gentle-voiced, soft-spoken socialist, who arrived in Detroit during the morning . . .

" 'The more you reverence Jesus Christ, the less you reverence the modern church and its ministry, "the right reverend successors of Him who had not where to lay His head," as Oliver Wendell Holmes called them. . . . When the masses have a genuine grievance against plutocracy, the church is always against the masses.'

"Mr. Eastman cited the Colorado miners' strike as an instance of this.

" 'Every one of the eight churches in Trinidad was against the miners,' said Mr. Eastman.

" 'The dividing line between this Detroit minister and myself is that I have a reverence for reality and he is trying to get reverence for a myth,' continued Mr. Eastman."

After my lecture the row started all over again. Dr. Boyle, speaking now through the Detroit *Times*, was more violent than ever.

" 'Hobbes was a saint and Ingersoll a Christian gentleman compared to a man who edits such a paper. It encourages blasphemy, sows the seeds of anarchy, and puts the stamp of approval on that which would crucify the Son of God and put him to an open shame. "

Dr. Moore, on the other hand, had now taken arms in my behalf:

" 'In my judgment of men I know of few who express more finely the spirit of Christ. In his gentleness, fearlessness and sincerity and desire to make a contribution to the common good he exemplifies this. As to his address we have never had a better lecturer in our hall than Mr. Eastman . . .

" 'The language of "A Ballad" is the language of men at their work, uncouth and rude. The teaching of the poem in regard to the immaculate conception is believed by many with whom I have talked. At any rate our church holds the matter of the immaculate conception non-essential. We accept the philosophy of Christ revealed in his life.' "

Thanks largely to such publicity, and still more to the backing of the genius-rebels on *The Masses* staff, I forged ahead—just as though

I were a born fighter!—to a point where the press could describe me, plausibly though not correctly, as "the most influential radical in the country."[3] In an editorial in *Life* magazine, Edward S. Martin did me the honor to link my name with that of Frank Tannenbaum and Pancho Villa under the rubric of "professional hoboes." I thought it would be amusing to voice my protest in a meticulously correct sonnet on the Petrarchian model and call it: "To Edward S. Martin from a Professional Hobo." Mr. Martin rather took the edge off my joke by sending me fifteen dollars and printing the poem in his magazine. But it was a serious poem and will suggest—I wish a little better in the sestet—the mixture of proletarian revolt with revolt against the genteel tradition which gave much of its character to *The Masses*.

> How old, my friend, is that fine-pointed pen
> Wherewith in smiling quietude you trace
> The maiden maxims of your writing-place,
> And on this gripped and mortal-sweating den
> And battle-pit of hunger now and then
> Dip out with nice and intellectual grace,
> The faultless wisdoms of a nurtured race
> Of pale-eyed, pink and perfect gentlemen!
> How long have art and wit and poetry
> With all their power, been content, like you,
> To gild the smiling fineness of the few,
> To filmy-curtain what they dare not see,
> In multitudinous reality,
> The rough and bloody soul of what is true!

In this war on the genteel tradition, I played a special role for two reasons. First, I was excessively squeamish about risqué or ribald jokes. I still think they are not funny unless they are, which seems to be a minority opinion. But in those days I was something of a prude. Thus while bold in its serious views on sex, the magazine I directed was delicately modest in its laughter. It did not add "obscenity" to "blasphemy," and might have come to a quick end, I suspect, if it had.

In the second place, I am in style and personal manners—shameful though it is!—genteel. Worse than that, I am meek. I am lamblike.

---

[3] I am refreshing my memory with an old batch of clippings, and I find that phrase in a feature story in the New York *World*.

That "spunky" baby who so enjoyed "striking" lives somewhere down inside me—he loves to get a pen in his hand—but in ordinary converse he hasn't a word to say. I remember writing to Arthur Brisbane one day when the New York *Journal* called me "a notorious anarchist, frequently arrested in connection with bomb outrages," asking him if he didn't think that was going a little too far even for an evening paper. It never occurred to me that I might have made Hearst support my magazine for several years by starting a libel suit. Brisbane wrote back apologizing, assuring me that the reporter had been fired, and adding: "I must say I think you are the best-natured man in the United States."

That irremediable good-nature of mine—not meaning that I can't get mad, but I don't like to—was appropriate to the position of class-struggle socialism in this country at the time. Marx himself said, when first introducing his ideas to European workingmen: "*Fortiter in re, suaviter in modo* is the thing." The phrase perfectly describes that lecture, "What Socialism Really Is," with which I raised money for *The Masses.* I had not the approach of the proletarian fighter; I argued the battle rather than fought it, a weakness of which I was privately conscious. But in the America of those days, so through-and-through bourgeois except for a little band of genuine rebels in the IWW, my weakness was a temporary strength. It got a hearing for the ideas.

Drawn by Art Young

The Latest

Only a few days after explaining the proletarian seizure of power
and confiscation of capital to the striking miners of Butte, Montana,
I was invited to address the Colony Club in New York on the same
subject. I did not alter my manner or tone down what I said. Indeed
I did little but shift my account of the matter from the second to the
third person. After describing the struggle of the English commoners
for political freedom, I placed under the same banner the struggle
of the workers in our own day for economic freedom. Here is the
peroration of that lecture as I gave it before New York's exclusive
woman's club:

"Those heroes, the social criminals of old, are the subject of our
songs. And so is that class struggle in which they fought—because the
victory in that struggle is already won.

"But of the class struggle of our own times—the struggle of the
working class against those privileged by the possession of hereditary
capital, of that struggle we sing no praises in our public schools, and
its heroes, the social criminals of today, are still to the respectable
exactly what John Elliott was to the King's Court, 'outlawed men,
desperate in mind and fortune.'

"I ask you to pause and realize how those men of old fought
against all refined society and the power of established law, not
blindly, but with an ideal that was approximately our ideal of political liberty.

"And then also realize that these men, the agitators of today, the
same men and women, are fighting against all refined society and the
power of law, not blindly, but with an ideal, the ideal of industrial
liberty, the abolition of class rule forever. And they are saying to the
workingmen among whom they go as strike leaders exactly the things
that John Hampden said to the Burghers in the House of Commons:

" 'To have printed liberties and not to have liberty in truth and
realities is but to mock the kingdom.

" 'Shall it be treason to debase the king's coin though but a piece
of sixpence and not treason to debase the spirits of his subjects, to
set a stamp and character of servitude upon them?'

"That is what they are saying. It is the same sacred struggle, the
struggle of the common people against the powers that exploit them.
And it is conducted in the faith that those powers can one day, by
the gradual confiscation of rent, and profit, and interest upon which
they live, be absorbed into the body of a working and producing
society in which men are free and opportunity is equal."

The attendance at my Colony Club lecture, I was told by the chairman, equaled anything the club had ever seen. But that was due to an irate old lady who issued a circular inviting the members to boycott the lecture. For this purpose would they please meet her in the rooms upstairs *before the lecture* and hear some readings from *The Masses?* This brought to the club house those who did not want to hear me as well as those who did, and after the readings—which of course included our famous "Ballad"—they all came downstairs to see how far I would go. I was introduced with delightful humor by the eminent jurist, Judge Learned Hand of the United States District Court, and my lecture was listened to with respect and applauded, it seemed to me, by almost every person in the room.

I glance through the manuscript today with mixed emotions, for although it is as eloquent as I know how to be, I no longer think it correct. On that ground I ought, I suppose, to be glad it was never published. But I keep thinking what an excellent pamphlet it would have made, backing up our fireworks in *The Masses* with a carefully thought-out point of view—and how essentially it belongs in the record of my opinions.

Some lassitude in my ambition, some rift in my evangelistic ardor too, led me to lay away this glowing gospel and let the world stumble along as best it could without knowing what socialism really is.

Drawn by Art Young

President Wilson: "I summon all forward-looking men to my side."

PART VII

RETURN TO MYSELF

Chapter 58

Half-Given Love

THE MASSES was such a gay and boisterous magazine, and
put so much laughter into revolution that I seemed to be
at the peak of life's enjoyment during its five years of life.
My book on poetry went through many triumphant reprintings too.
It corrupted the austerity of I don't know how many potential saints
and Sunday school teachers with its frankly epicurean evangel. "The
purpose of this book is to increase enjoyment," it began—a new and
jocund note in criticism. But I was not truly lighthearted during
those years.

At first, in the winter and spring of 1913, it seemed as though Ida
and I were becoming well-adjusted friends and lovers. Both the
baby and the magazine drew us close. The thought never quite left
me that the smoother our adjustment, the more hopelessly my real
self was lost. But I confided that to no one, and was for those
months so good a companion and father that even Ida, I think, got
a small grip on joy. We took the baby to Glenora for the summer of
1913, and she entered with genial resolution into the life of the
community there. She became rural. She became sociable, utopian—
almost a Park Church Christian. It was good for her to have a baby,
and I think she was growing to be an affirmative source of life for

those around her. Her letters to me, when I went back to New York to bring out *The Masses*, were love letters—the only ones I ever received from her. In one of them she even gave me words of praise.

"Yes, *The Masses* is a great adventure, and you have done wonders. It is because you are so sweet and just and patient and tolerant that it is succeeding."

I have to quote those words, for I had just read them—they were warm in my heart—when I committed the crime that checked her genial growth and turned our loving friendship into a nightmare.

I had been faithful to Ida until then, not because I was so moved, but because I wanted a truth-telling relation between us. Hatred of deception is often the chief motive to marital fidelity, and in my case it was the only compelling one. I was faithful because I sensed the jealous passion in Ida's proud nature and knew that I could not confide in her if I was not.

She on her part was blind enough to my emotions to hire a ravishingly pretty "Carol" to tend the baby and blithely send me off swimming with her in the glen on her free afternoons. I managed to hold off from Carol's lush, wet, slim, eagerly inviting beauty, because Ida was so near as to be almost in our presence. But another blind impulse of hers was to let her merry and buxom young friend, Elsa, sleep in our New York apartment during the summer, on condition that she "take care of me" when I came down every month to bring out *The Masses*.

Well—it was a good long apartment, and I slept in my end for the better part of two weeks. But one night I was in Elsa's end conversing before going to bed. I was certainly thinking wishfully about her cozy bed, but I was sitting in a chair on the far side of it when she began very deliberately to take her clothes off.

"I hope you don't mind if I strip," she said.

I am a romantic soul, and this abrupt speech and procedure was chilling to me in its direct effect. Elsa, besides, was the plump apple shape that appeals more to Turkish sultans than American poets. Still, she was an extremely rosy apple—fresh and with firm muscles and bright red lips that uncovered a dazzling row of teeth. When I had undressed, I got into that cozy bed with her—what could an angel less?—and took her in my arms.

It was nice there for my body, but my brain was busy about Ida. It was at its old work of thinking up compunctions. The compunctions were rather belated, however, and time was pressing. Something had to be done.

"If you cling to the letter of fidelity"—that was the best my brain could do in a hurry—"if nothing quite happens, you won't have to mention this adventure to Ida."

And so I was duteously disloyal both to the adventure and to Ida. I mean that I made a demi-virgin love to Elsa, assuaging with caresses the motive that had made her "strip," but not actually partaking of the communion. Elsa understood it all—she knew Ida intimately—and spoke only two words before she went to sleep.

"Poor Max!"

My brain's stratagem was pitiful, and moreover it was unsuccessful. When Ida inquired casually about Elsa on my return, I did not find it true that I could answer casually and be honest. I found that I should be deceiving my closest friend; I should be entering a life of deception. I had still too absolute an ideal of my friendship with Ida to do it. Devout people may sympathize if I say that living in the truth is my religion. I have no other god but Conscious Life, and a feeling that I have lost the reality of life is insupportable.

So I burbled some carefully offhand remark about Elsa's excellent food and caresses. . . . I don't know what I said. Few women understand the tribute contained in a man's desire to tell them the truth. Even if her own possession of me had been whole and final, Ida would not have understood it. As it was, she was ravaged. She was transformed into a vengeful animal. Not immediately—her first expression was humble. It was an expression of excruciating pain, scorched into my memory beyond forgetting.

"Max, I can't bear it, I can't bear it!" she gasped, as though I had put her body on the rack.

I was appalled at what I had done. I lost all poise, all pride, all self-identity, all simple common sense, in an overwhelming Conviction of Sin.

To cure her torture, Ida had to hear every detail of my movements in Elsa's bed. She had to "know it all." But this turned out to be torture for me, too, the torture of indelicate exposure and abject humiliation. And that also was medicine to Ida. It helped her grief transform itself into a more bearable anger. So then she had to hear every detail of every little pass I had made toward any girl during those two years of cerebrally motivated fidelity. I must "tell the whole truth," since that was my religion. She behaved as my mother had when, ruler in hand, she compelled Anstice to repeat every smutty word he knew.

And I behaved like a more cringing Anstice, an infant shamed and appalled at his flagrant sinfulness. I had been a morbidly "moral" infant, and Ida threw me back into that state and dominated me completely. My core of mother-loving timidness, my almost hereditary mortification, responded to her need for righteous indignation as though shaped for the purpose.

Her vengeful rage was clear to me at times, but I could not continually see it. I could not steady myself against it. I had no drive in me like hers, no heavy and relentless force, no singleness of character, no character at all as I have said, only the ability to imagine and assume one. I have the fatal gift, once recklessly prayed for, to see myself as others see me. And I saw my sins, whenever Ida willed, exactly as she saw them. I had vowed a thousand times that I would never live in a house inhabited by anger, but here I was, and I lacked the power to walk out. She had me down. She had the drop on me. She had the authority of an irate parent, the pity-claim of a fatally wounded one—the appeal, too, when she wished to use it, of a hurt child. I could revolt and rave against her and denounce her, but I could not stick to it. . . . I could not leave her. I was afraid. How could I go out alone into the world, at an emotional age of eight years, with nothing in me but a sense of withering guilt?

All my bold theories about "enjoyment of living," "progress towards liberty," "bringing the wolf and lion and panther to the door" —everything I stood for and stand for, I hope, ultimately—were swamped and whelmed over by what I had been as a child. There is a lesson in this. To some it will be sufficient to say that a grown man ought not to be a weakling, and that I admit is true. But there are so many weaklings, especially among men in their relations with women, that I am disposed to draw a less obvious lesson. What made it impossible for me to escape from that trap was reticence. If I could have talked it over with someone else, with anyone else—if I could instantly have thought of a person with whom I might talk it over—I need not have suffered this harrowing as I did. But my secretive shyness, that spastic defense-reaction against mortification that got planted in me in babyhood, made this impossible. I was locked tight. I could not speak a word of my spiritual agony to anyone—to sister, brother, father, teacher, intimate or loving friend. I fooled them all into thinking I was serenely happy. It never occurred to me to do otherwise. Thus there was no let-up in my absolute intimacy with Ida. She was my counselor and confessor as well as my lover and destroyer. That, I think, was my chief mistake. And notwithstanding my very special and indeed slightly psychopathic make-up, I am inclined to generalize this lesson. I think everyone needs an intimate friend who is not a lover. The inmost citadel of selfhood ought not to be surrendered in love, much less in marriage, and few can hold it alone.

Although so much the stronger, Ida too, in a sense, was trapped. She could not escape from her love for me; turning it into anger was no escape. She could stand like an ice Maenad, throwing darts of inflexible illogic into me, until I wept and raged and threw myself around the room like a bull in a ring—a babe in a tantrum rather. She could torture me, yes, and had to, because goaded beyond endurance by my dividedness. But she could not walk out. She had no interest, or activity, no wish even, to walk to. "I don't see how anybody can study astronomy and have ambition enough to get up in the morning," she had once said. That was the absolute bleakness of her universe, and she had found in it an equally absolute passion. No matter what color the passion—love or hate—it was a fortress against bleakness, it was a refuge against the stars.

Thus Ida was held by her strength as I by my weakness in the grip of this intimacy which tortured her clear and hard-cored nature even more, I suppose, than my vague and divided one. At least I can imagine nothing more maddening to a proud and wilful woman than to live with a man who can not make up his mind whether he loves her or not.

Ida never spoke to Elsa again, her close friend and devoted admirer. And I—this is the worst of the crimes I remember with shame—was so dominated by Ida's alien standards that I never looked her up either until years had passed.

We left Glenora that autumn forever, and down in the New York apartment I found myself imprisoned. That hand of gloom which had reached out and snatched me back from any feeling of joy began now to hold steadily on. I had never ceased yearning for Ruth's body, and now the yearning grew into an obsession. My sense of loss became fixed and sickly. I would go through the day sanely enough, but at night I could not hold my legs still in bed. As I drowsed I would jump awake with a full-length spasm like that of a dying fish in a boat bottom. A feeling of unrest as big as the universe, a feeling more unbearable than pain, would occupy the place of my old backache. For relief I would get up from my bed beside Ida's and go into the front room where my sorrow was pure. There I could fall asleep on the hard high couch by the window.

One night Ida awoke and came looking for me. I opened the blanket and invited her with excessive tenderness to lie down beside me. As I turned over to go to sleep, my hand snatched the pillow rudely from under her head. She was astonished and hurt, but I was a little alarmed. It was as though my hand without my knowledge had done this rude deed. Other things of a similar kind happened. Accidentally strolling home with another girl from a party I had gone to with Ida was the most unforgivable of them. We called these lapses absent-mindedness, but they suggested, more accurately, the presence of another mind.

On one restless night I had a dream in which that other mind seemed to express himself almost in automatic writing. I dreamed that I saw all lovers walking back and forth under the trees where Inez and I had once strolled on the campus at Vassar. I took a pencil that lay on the window sill, and while still in my dream, or but half out of it, wrote these lines:

Death is more tranquil than the life of love,
More calm, more sure, and more unanguished.
O the path among the trees is far more tranquil to the dead
Than to these anxious hearts, uptroubled from their beds,
Who pace in pallid darkness on the leaves,
For no good reason—for no reason
But because their limbs will not lie still upon the sheet.
Their limbs will not lie still. O how I pity them.
Sad hearts—their marrow is a-quiver,
And they can not lie them down in tranquil sadness like
the dead.

It was myself that I was pitying, and self-pity, I knew, is a quicksand into which those who sink are forever lost. To live at all a man must be something of a soldier. Knowing this in my mind, I tried to build up my will against Ida's self-assurance. I tried making a declaration of temperamental independence, asserting my right to be the volatile and inconstant poet that I am. It was the beginning of a war that the scattered, ragged, and ill-armed guerilla forces-of-character in the command of such a poet could never possibly win. With traditional morality and my ancestral load of virtue to back her, Ida plowed through my fitful volitions and frail theoretical defenses like a battle tank. I fled away somewhere to "think it over," taking her point of view right along with me as a runaway horse takes the harness, and wrote her, while in the frame of it, a solemn and almost holy letter, promising eternal and absolute fidelity as a mere matter of sound reason.

"I recognize the insanity of my saying I love you and not immediately proceeding to make of myself the demand that I be true to you. My happiest days were days when I thought after all the sorrow of the trip to Europe, still we were going to be true lovers. I thought we were growing to be. . . . So I will simply say that I love you, I want to live with you, and I will be true to you. And if I should ever fail you again, if I should touch or fondle any woman but you, it will signify and seal my unworthiness to love you, and I will tell you and go away alone. You shall at least have a clear spirit, for it is your clear spirit that I love."

To balance this vow I asked Ida to make three changes in herself which would help me to fulfill it. I begged her to stop assuming a mortally stricken look every time a remark or an incident recalled any of the feeble passes I had made at girls.

"I surely have been tender," I said, "when other things have made you sad, but when I see you wilt because you see, or hear the name of one of these girls—I hate it, and that hate swallows everything. It seems to me we have got to make this very tragedy sacred. . . ."

The two other things I spoke of as inimical to our romance were her indolence, her "not finding activity, creation, the use of· her powers *worth while*," and her "uncanny lack of appreciation both of my work and my play—the play of my mind in conversation." "I feel shut in instead of overflowing in your presence. But to be in love is to have lustre added to every idea, fancy, or feeling that goes through your mind because it is precious to your lover."

I also asked her not to expect me to talk about my sexual nature any more. "I am humble, dear. I am penitent. I am lower than those I despise. I will not cover it up. But it is mine, and I can't talk to you about it any more."

Having thus surrendered my independence—and alas my self-esteem—I tried by altering the environment to get back a sense of being, or possessing, myself. I deployed my defeated forces of rebellion against something that I associated with surrender to Ida —city life. If I couldn't be free, I would at least be rural. So I went off on the Erie railroad as far as Tenafly, New Jersey, conceiving that the urban influences extend rankly only to the northern outskirts of Englewood. There I found a house a short walk from the station, but not a long walk from woods and meadows, and I compelled Ida for a second time to gather up her household in mid-autumn and move it to a new place.

It did no good, of course—no more than the three stipulations in my letter had. We spent a miserable period of time—it must have been eight months—in Tenafly. Even my woods and meadows turned against me, for on returning from a long walk in which I had failed to compose a poem, I asked of them some brilliant autumn leaves to take home as an offering to Ida, and they gave me poison ivy. By the time I reached the house I was smeared with oily sap. For five weeks I was as sick and wretched, and as disgusting to con-template, as a dying leper. To me, with my mad horror of itching, those weeks were a crucifixion, and to Ida, injured by the recent discovery of my trespasses, a test her love could hardly stand. She gave none of the tenderness that had been so persuasive during my similar, and yet so much milder, affliction in Gibraltar. I do not mean that she failed of ordinary human kindness, but just that she was not interested. I lay like an outcast in my room, reading, read-ing, and drenching my arms and eyes and innumerable swollen parts with lead and opium until the opium put me to sleep—and only by good luck (a doctor told me afterward) the lead did not put me to death. Those weeks stayed in my mind, and I used them long after in a poem, as a symbol of poisoned love—

> The love that brought in with its blossoms of autumn the blight
> Of the leaves of the ivy that glitter with vitreous light.

I wanted to use my brains about my problem; I wanted to talk objectively about it. Such talk was impossible with Ida because she could not assume, even for the sake of argument, that her instinct might conceivably be wrong. I never in my life knew anyone so sure of herself. It was not egotism; her reason simply would not operate on such an assumption. I could not discuss this with Crystal either, for between us the subject of my sexuality was tabu.

Once more bashfulness determined my conduct. Instead of going to a friend, I went to an almost total stranger, Dr. Beatrice Hinkle, whom I had not seen since Kingston days. She had been in Europe subsequently, and after studying with Dr. Jung in Zurich had come home an enthusiastic psychoanalyst. I knew that much, and I re-membered her venturesome yet critical mind. She had tried to hypnotize me once; maybe she would psychoanalyze me. I called her up one day and went over and poured out in a deliberate burst of candor, hardly pausing to say hello, the tangled mass of thoughts and feelings I had been hoarding in my breast. She recalled my neurotic history and thought I ought to be psychoanalyzed, but advised me—I never knew why—to go to a male analyst. She gave me a note to Smith Ely Jelliffe, a famous psychiatrist, and next to Dr. Brill the leading exponent of Freud's ideas in America.

Instead of a social diversion stemming in a truth, wrapped up in a mystification, and surrounded by a racket, psychoanalysis was in those days a disreputable therapy struggling desperately for recognition. Dr. Jelliffe may have thought of me as potential help in the struggle; he may merely have found my case interesting. At any rate he agreed to psychoanalyze me for a fee that would be a song today, and I went to him four times a week for several months during the winter and spring of 1914.

Jelliffe was a round-bodied, hearty, friendly, energetic doctor, prodigious in memory, bursting at the seams with knowledge, credulous of unverified ideas (as Freudians must be), but held in poise by Roman Catholic emotions and a religious love for Bergson's philosophy. He was a Niagara talker, and as I am a Lake Ontario listener, our sessions were more like a lecture course than a clinic. I read Freud and every book on Freud then available in English, rehearsing the doctrine point by point with its agile-minded apostle, and becoming once more a kind of amateur specialist in mental healing.

My problems, needless to say, were not solved by this feat of learning. I turned up no new memories of childhood and never appropriated emotionally any of the unconscious drives that seemed to appear in my dreams. They all were plausible to me—homosexuality, mother fixation, Oedipus, Electra and inferiority complexes, narcissism, exhibitionism, autoeroticism, the "masculine protest." I never heard of an infantile fixation of which I could not find traces in my make-up, and which I was not quite willing to accept as basic if the proof appeared. Whether because curiosity outweighs my other passions or because my extreme reticence, once abandoned, turned into extreme candor, no strenuous "resistance" ever developed in my sessions with Jelliffe. I suffered none of the healing pain at confronting my true nature that those liberated by psychoanalysis like to boast about.

I felt the peculiar affection toward Jelliffe which Freud calls "transference." Indeed I do not see how anyone could lay bare his most intimate personal preoccupations day after day to a sympathetic friend without coming to love or hate that friend. Freud regarded this excited attachment of neurotics to their doctor-confidants as "the most unshakable proof" that all neuroses have their origin in sex, a jump to conclusions which I regard as lacking in simple common sense. Jelliffe himself was full of these wild Freudian jumps, and my affection for him could not carry me along. I wish I had hit upon a more sceptical neurologist, one who employed with free judgment the indubitable truths to be found in what is so well called "Freud's" psychology. I believe that I might have learned something about my neurotic constitution. As it was, I merely learned about Freud's psychology.

Jelliffe mislaid the notes he made of our analysis, but he gave me years after his surviving impression of the problem I presented:

"You weren't quite aware of the Oedipus situation, the hostility to the father working itself out in prejudiced radicalism. You were tied up also in a complex situation with your sister which made relations with your wife uncomfortable. There was a sister-identification, and through that identification a fundamental narcissistic cathexis or investment."

Jelliffe was too glib with ideas to be of sure help among facts. His dismissing class-struggle socialism as "prejudiced radicalism" was, in part at least, mere ignorance. Far from being a cause, I doubt if my attitude to my father and mother was even a condition of my embracing this seemingly practical way out of the dilemma in which tender ideals and a tough sense of fact had placed me.[1] I doubt also whether the element of narcissism in my make-up, or a suppressed love-interest in my sister (probable enough on general grounds), had anything to do with my being "uncomfortable" with Ida. By way of experiment, I have asked another famous Freudian whom I later consulted, A. A. Brill, for his impression of the ground of my emotional troubles. I quote his words also verbatim:

"People are always repeating some pattern from their childhood. You and I have not talked much, but from what I know of your history and your family, I think you have a strong mother-fixation. Your pattern is that you want to get away from your mother and yet be with her."

Brill is no more convincing theoretically to me than Jelliffe was, but he has an intuitive sensitivity toward people that makes him a master in the clinic. They both had, I must add, a breadth and

---

[1] To distinguish effective cause from indispensable condition exceeds the patience of Freudians as of Marxians, both being more greedy of belief than understanding.

sweetness of character that did much to launch Freud's doctrines on a high plane in America.

Even this Delphic intuition of Brill's, however, would not have helped me out of my troubles in 1914. Indeed it would have plunged me deeper in. I myself was aware of something holding me back from surrender not only to Ida but to any woman. My preoccupation with Ruth's image was mad and beautiful enough to make me fly to her from the misery of a half-given love, had I not known that the same misery would arise with her. I craved Ruth and Glenora's sunny fields surrounding her with the last degree of physical and romantic desire, but I did not want to be hers. I did not want her to be mine. Those words, "Is it forever, Max?" still rang like a bell of doom in my ears.

The sole object of perfect and eternal desire in me is life in the universe, a life that has to be free and be my own. At the same time I have an inclination to put my arms around some loving girl and be close friends, and cherish and take care of her and be taken care of. I think it questionable whether anything useful is added to the knowledge of these traits by calling them "mother fixation" or "narcissistic cathexis." Even supposing such terms justly described their origin, that would not determine their nature or decide what wisely to do about them. As for inducing by conversation a state of consciousness in which they become identified with, or converted back into, these infantile tropisms and get lost, that would seem to me—from the standpoint of a robust wish to enjoy life—a misfortune.

If man had some celestial pattern handed him by gods, it might be wise to shatter for its sake the pattern flowing from his birth and his experience. But to replace that special self which nature and history combined to create in him with the general dictates of tradition, or with something that some accidental doctor considers "normal," strikes me as a downward procedure not to be confused with growth.

Psychoanalysis, to express it otherwise, is for people who are sick. Where the fragile thing called individuality breaks down to such an extent that healthy life becomes impossible, it may be necessary to clear out the debris and go back to mere animal and traditional commonplace. I was not in that condition. I was not sick. I was merely bewildered. What I needed was not a scientific picking down of my pattern, but a little common sense about handling it. The technique of psychoanalysis stood in the way of my getting that common sense, or at least postponed it beyond the stretch of my patience. The summer came—the fateful summer of 1914—and Ida and I joined in the trek of New York's intelligentsia to Provincetown. My conversations with Jelliffe were abandoned without result—or rather they were replaced by a soliloquy in the loft of a boat-house next door to the cottage in which we lived.

Drawn by Pablo Picasso

A PORTRAIT

Chapter 59

A Search for My Wish

ONE day Ida remarked: "What makes it so difficult for me is that you don't know what you want."

"You are perfectly right, Ida," I said, "but it is partly because what *you* want overwhelms me. While I am with you I can't feel my own self clearly, much less express it."

"Suppose I go away for a few weeks and you write it down."

The idea seemed good to me, for I had been thinking of trying to psychoanalyze myself.

"I will have to write only for myself, though," I said. "If I think I'm going to show it to you, it won't be me."

"I'll never ask to see it," she promised.

And so on July 27, 1914, Ida took the train to New York to visit some friends, and I bought a schoolboy's composition book and went back to my boat-house loft to undertake a self-analysis. Thus during the approach and outbreak of the First World War, this international revolutionist, "cultural leader of socialism in the United States," was engaged in a search within the tiny corridors of his own brain for his own wish. I filled three notebooks with intimate findings. I have been urged to use them as material for a novel, but that again would be literature and not life. Omitting some accounts of dreams and their associations, which would interest only a psychoanalyst, I will present my self-avowal as it stands.

July 27, 1914

Truth, be more precious to me than the eyes
Of happy love; burn hotter in my throat
Than passion; and possess me like my pride;
More sweet than freedom; more desired than joy;
More sacred than the serving of a friend.

She is gone, and with her going all her little properties and the clothes she wore, especially the older ones with a bare thread here and there, have acquired so dear and poignant a charm that my throat aches to look at them. The house, wide-eyed and silent, the chamber with its nightly beds disheveled, the baby, happy and tousle headed and pausing only a minute to have it explained that Mamma is "all gone"—they each speak sadly to my eyes. And yet there is a certain pleasure of romantic interest in that sadness, interest in the change. There is more than that—there is a real up-springing in solitude of the old enthusiasm for the free realization of all life, which was my religion. It is as though something were lifted off, my share of a double harness perhaps, and I were turned loose alone into a familiar pasture where I was wont to graze and wander among the grasses in the light and shade.

That is to express it very extremely, however, for I would not shake off that harness, that sweet one-side companionship, for good, if I could possibly help it. I would return often and with voluntary delight from whatsoever scenes more perfectly united my nature to this strange friendship with one so different from myself, which has nobly expanded and yet also fatefully inhibited my joy of life.

Strange friendship, I call it, and yet not strange in the way of romance or moonlight waverings. In those overtones of imaginative feeling our souls never chimed. Though Ida would have had it so, it could never be so, for the tonal quality of our emotion is as different as two colors. She with the ever burning, deep, flamelike, realistic passion of an Oriental; I with the shallower, shifty, exhibitionistic romanticism of a western poet. So, for me at least, it was distinctly a daylight friendship, though full of tender and almost aching childlike affection. It was indeed the most real, the most unsentimentalized, unhistrionic attachment of my life. And I am almost ready to forego that image of the pasture and the grasses, and say that what is being lifted from me is the burden of an excellence that demands everywhere realistic truth. I am being loosed into an emotionalized limbo, half fantasy and half boasted fact, where I used to live and grow, luxuriant with moods.

I am reminded that four years ago, when I was undecided about our marrying, I wrote, or half-wrote, this sonnet to her. It is the only poem I ever quite spontaneously attempted in her honor, for poetry, the lyric exhibition, belongs rather to the part of my nature she inhibited than that she caused to flourish. Here, then, is a significantly unfinished sonnet of loving rejection:

> Go, go, my love, on thy too poignant way—
> Dark, merciful, mysterious and true!
> Truth like a sword hath pierced thy bosom through;
> Truth like a tear in thy low voice doth say:
> The world is full of sorrow all the day.
> I am too like thee in thy gift of rue!
> And like thee in thy naked vision too—

And to this now I must add a few lines I wrote in the hot anguish after one of our last despairing, angry efforts to straighten and understand our unhappy relation:

> The living summer has no voice for me.
> The water-laden winds of the old sea,
> The wild-heart wailing of the lonely gulls,
> The busy rhythm of the dipping sculls,
> That sang of life and purpose, sing no more.
> I am a drying weed upon the shore.
> Too hot and secretless the sun, too clear
> And avid through the sapless atmosphere
> His vision burns abroad, too stark
> Of mystery and moisture and the dark
> Of that dim ocean region green and cool,
> Where I grew dank and lush and beautiful . . .

These two unfinished, and somehow unfinishable poems, and two others—one deliberately composed for her pleasure, and the other, painfully made after I had hurt her, as one should fashion a jewel to present in token of repentance—these are all the lines of poetry I have ever written that have reference to her. And yet she has been the heart and essence of my world for more than three years, and only this morning has gone away in a sort of tentative sorrow, or perhaps a more final sorrow and seeking for new wishes than I know, to let me be alone and write down here the nature of my being if I can.

Later

Yesterday, or the day before, in our final quiet heart-searching, she asked me if I was sure that my melancholy was general and not merely the longing for some special person. We both knew the person; and remembering that, deeply as I want that person's body, I do not want to live continually with her, remembering also how much of my yearning is indefinite and not even overtly sexual, I said, "No, it is not a special person." As I reflect upon it, however, I do not know that there is anything I wish more than that I might have that girl at my pleasure, an adventurous and heart-whole pleasure, and yet not lose the recourse to my dearer daily companion. Two things I should have then that I seem starved of, besides the bliss of satisfying a lust so long possessing my private imagination. I should have romance, intense, flagrant, and mutually exhibitionistic. And I should have active adventurous athletic play and ambition under-running the hours of that companionship. What I shall try to write here tomorrow is a delineation in general outlines of my psycho-sexual character—my instinctive infantile selfishness, my neurotic pains, deficiencies, indolence, which are all doubtless in their root, if I could uncover that, an unconscious fixation of life-interest upon the early image of my mother. (I doubt this, however.)

July 29

This morning I lay looking at her untroubled pillow, and as that sad gust of loneliness for a missing heart wafted across my spirit, followed immediately by the inhibition, "No, that is impossible now," which obvious imperfection has laid upon the poetry of our relation, I thought something like this: Truly, is it possible for two separate beings to live so closely together as we have sought to in happiness? And is it altogether true that I am the source of the unsatisfaction? Has not every wedding of vivid people in all history ended, after three or four years, either in a working acceptance, a matter-of-fact companionship, or in trouble? I find no instinct for marriage in the fundamental nature of man, and I wonder if the too close union of men and women in our culture is not an accommodation of life to the abnormal which can never be achieved except at a sacrifice of interest and force. *Is* our problem individual or general?

Well—whichever it is—as I stepped into the road this morning, and the sun spilled over the edge of a wet cloud, and the leaves glistened, and a fragrance of wild roses came over the fence of the meadow, I felt the old surge of poetry, the romantic love of being, that has not risen unalloyed in my breast for three years. It was as though I and the morning—the morning fresh from her bath—stood hand to hand and heart to heart, "the long brown path before us." I felt as though I could do and be and behold great things, and I would immediately go about it. And even now as I have come in here to my desk and among my papers, the same zeal persists. I feel powerful, free, and all-important among them, as a creator must.

And how long, how long it is since I have had this full-hearted rebirth of being with the coming of a new day! It is as though nothing had brimmed over my edges for years. There was always a paucity, a derogation, a defined limit for any enthusiasm as soon as it rose in my breast.

I do not know what this is. I had thought perhaps in etiology it was only the lust of new sex experiences; the limitation that I felt in so high a region of idealism was in basic reality the limitation imposed by the ideal of faithfulness to one. But strange to tell, all day yesterday and this morning too, I had been thinking of faithfulness to her in the physical relation, and friendship—an unpretentious friendship such as might be possible after she should read this book or parts of it—as perhaps the thing my spirit needs and truly wants. And the reflection that my promise of faithfulness is still holding *did not* seem to taint or alloy my joy in the morning. My spirit seems to have been set free by our broaching the possibility that I do not find our love a satisfying thing, that I am not quite myself in it, and by her going away begging me to find my self, no matter what it turns out to be.

July 30

I dreamed last night that, being in some new place with Ida, I complained that she would not speak to (or introduce me to) anybody or that she alienated them. I set about introducing myself with elaborate cordiality to a vast crowd of people one by one. Later a pretty girl, composite of the two that are sweetly attractive to me in this neighborhood, came onto the porch and said "Hello" in a very friendly way as if she were coming to see me. I was delighted.

The dream seems to mean that I miss, in living with Ida, the many real friends, the loved and loving neighbors, that used to surround my life at home. Ida is impersonal and does not care about many people. She does not enter into relations of friendly interest with them as my mother and sister did. And I am so suggestible, so pliant to her influence, that I do not either. It does not seem "worth while." And this, whether the rationalization of a desire to reject her upon other grounds or not, is one of the conscious factors in my melancholy, my feeling that I am starving for something.

I am compelled to state that I am still happier, though alone and with no special events or excitement in view, than I was while she was here. Though sad too with the weight of this experience, I am unafflicted with that starving melancholy that drew down my features and was a muscular struggle to overcome.

The morning's fragrance reminded me, by some chemistry of imagination, of North Carolina, and I thought I would go wander there, carefree and heart-whole and in love with the earth. The repression of such romantic impulses was "off"—that is how I must express it—and I inhaled the fancy and the fragrance with joy.

North Carolina is where I went in that mood of indecision I spoke of, before we decided to marry and go to Europe together, and where I received letters from her and from Ruth too. But I did not think of this until now. What I thought of this morning was how Plato celebrates the love that does not beget children, except such children as the *Iliad* and the *Odyssey*, and of my writing somewhere that "Homer so loved the world" that he begot these children. And I felt that perhaps the true sublimation of the animal hunger for me is a modern Platonic one—not especially, or only, a love of ideas, but a love of the whole world. I felt that Ida might be (if she would!) a dearest friend in that world, but the world would be my love.

But now for the general analysis, so far as observation and knowledge have made it possible.

I think that with a very pronounced maturity of intellect and objective thinking, I retain an infantile attitude subjectively, and the foremost quality of this attitude is a supreme selfishness. In a life-crisis like this, or indeed any real crisis, I can not act, or think for any length of time, in terms of surrendering my happiness to any large degree *in* the happiness of another even though beloved. I can't face a life of unfulfilled craving. I can be wonderfully generous on occasions, especially upon showy occasions, but in a large way, and in many small ways that do not show, it is the instinctive assumption of my thinking that I should have what I want.

And the quality that has most mitigated this foremost trait of selfishness in me, giving me in the eyes of many friends a character of instinctive generosity, is exhibitionism. Now exhibitionism, combined as it not often is with a sensitiveness to the real thoughts of others and a high taste in human nature, is no poor promoter of character and morality. And I have no hesitation in saying that in me it is, and always has been, the essential one. My frequent dreams of bodily exposure, as well as the exposure of various forms of nobility and heroism in my soul, confirm this knowledge.

July 31

This morning the truth shone in on me with my waking clearer than dawn. I had dreamed—though I'm not sure the dream was essential—a symbolic dream. Daniel [our baby] was in reality whimpering in the next room, and I in my dream was standing on the dock where I had been putting up a springboard the day before. I said: "I think you'll find that he simply wants to be freed, and that accounts for all the noise he is making." I so evidently meant myself and my strange behaviors toward Ida by "the noise he is making," and the springboard is so clear a symbol of the interests that separate me from her, that upon waking I took the real thought for granted and immediately began to pass over in memory the whole period of our relation. And I knew, as straight as though God had told me, that the desire to give it up, to cease being her lover because I knew I could not be happy with her, long ago repressed into unconsciousness, has been the motor source of all my strange actions. I remember now when that wish was first palpable and present to my mind—in Gibraltar on our return from an unhappy two weeks in Tangier. And then I remember the gradual and dreadful fighting suppression of it all that summer, a thing never quite accomplished until after we came home and I found that my friends loved her, and that she made me happy and at ease with other people. I remember how my soul seized on that fact and declared it was true that I loved her. From then on, even in the stress of my unfaithfulness and agonies of repentance, I've never entertained for one second the idea that I did not. And yet in my soul I seem to have known all along that my wishes toward her were not true love, nor was there anything I desired more than to be free of the effort to be her lover.

I know now that all my uncanny acts in "absent-mindedness" that so hurt her were expressions of that unconscious wish.

I need not enlarge upon this. It is what this writing was coming to—surely. It sheds light into all the crumpled corners of our trouble. Not the light of joy, for that is a dream, and the pathos of this story is now almost overwhelming to me; I have to shut my heart to the thought of her in order to write these sentences at all. But still it is light; it is truth. And somehow I feel it will relieve her as it relieves me. For the joy of love was surely long ago a dream to her too, and yet she holds me dear as I hold her and will be glad to know there is *some* explanation, *some* integrity (even if not goodness or generosity) in me.

I remember now that the one thing I always insisted on and elaborately explained to Dr. Jelliffe was that I did love her, and that I had chosen wisely and ideally—to which, of course, I made him agree. But when he suggested that I write down for him "any little ways in which my wife seemed unsatisfying to me," I managed to postpone and let him forget it.

We learn about repression and the unconscious, and then we look around for some conventionally "horrible" thing that we may have repressed. It turns out not to be horrible at all, and of course what we have repressed is, by definition, something we are *not* looking around for!

I think the motives of my repression were three.

First, I am so sensitive through imaginative sympathy to the sufferings of a person I am near, I am so much of a "Sentimental Tommy," that I cannot deal such a person a clean blow. I never was long, or definitely enough, absent from Ida before so that I could say these things even to myself.

Second, my excessive shyness, social consciousness, exhibitionism, or as the phrenologists used to say, "approbativeness," made it seem that I could not face the return home "separated" after that rather spectacular trip to Europe. We thought we were making it easy to separate by not announcing our marriage; instead, we were making it ridiculously hard. For ridiculous is what we should have been, as well as pitiable, if we had come back on different ships.

Third, and perhaps really an intelligent foundation for the others, I wanted to be *somebody's* lover. I never had been, and I terribly feared that I never would or could be, if I lost this chance with one who was surely and really a friend and lovely companion. So I fought my own soul in a way that I fear a simple and instinctive nature like hers will never understand.

August 1

Yesterday afternoon came a sad letter from Crystal telling of her melancholy, which is a good description of mine, and concluding: "Tell Ida I love her—I don't dare tell her but really I was crazy about her this summer."

And that gave me a kind of fright, and made me sad and sick. For I love Ida too, just as Crystal does, and I love her most of all when we are having good times with Crystal and Bennie, or Baldy and Adra, or some other of my friends with whom she is at home and happy and so utterly charming. And then they have taken for granted our happy love so long that when I put myself with them I take it for granted too. For I know as they do that Ida is the most radiantly lovely person we have any of us ever known. She is to me almost continually beautiful—beautiful motions of her mind and body, beautiful color, figure, speech, features. That such a body of charms should be the dwelling of that mind and spirit, the most original and quick and spontaneously creative I have known, is a perpetual miracle to me. No one who knows her could wonder that I am frightened and sick at what I have written here.

And yet in all this sadness there is not the blankness, the "nothing is worth while," that afflicts me when she is here. I am excited about the sadness. It is important. I "care." And also, though I go to bed very lonely in our room, I am able to say that what I have written here is true nonetheless, and I will face out the whole world alone if it locks her heart against me.

For that, I fear, is what it will do. Ida has no love, properly so called, except for her mate. So at least it seems to me. Her affectionate admiration for a few friends is for their qualities, not their selves. With selves she has little to do. It is things, qualities, ideas, or else a lover, that her life-hunger fastens upon. That is why Crystal is "afraid to tell her" that she loves her. That is why Ida's comment on Crystal was not "I love her," but "she is a lovely girl." And that is one of the reasons why I feel such a stranger to myself in living with her. Yes, I know that reading this book will lock her heart against me in a way that mine never will be locked against her. She is my dearest friend; she is the one to whom I show the book. To me that means everything.

(Just at this point Fred Boyd called up to my window and told me the final news of a general European war—one of the great determining events of all history, if it is confirmed. And I felt how little are all these personal matters! And I thought how much bigger and higher and more divine an attitude to the world Ida has than I, even if she won't *do* anything! But after all that is not a reason for revising the decision I have made, for the only way to realize my own self is to make it flourish to its height in its own direction.)

Later

I believe I can find in my dreams *all* the "polymorphous perverse" components of infantile sexuality, and I doubt if any single one predominates. When I said, a while ago, that I thought a fixation of the mother-image was the heart of it, I was under influence, not of dream analysis, but of the memory of what a mamma's boy I was, and of my unsatisfaction with Ida's indolence, which seemed to find explanation in its contrast with my mother's energy.

As a matter of fact, the more I seek to analyze myself, the less do I find indications of any "fixation," unless it be the desire to see through the clothing of women, beginning especially with their breasts, and that after all is only preliminary. What torments me, so far as consciousness goes at least, and many of my dreams too, is an unsublimated heterosexual lust. And this has tormented me more instead of less, as I had hoped it would, since my relations of assumed fidelity to Ida began.

August 2

After a night of life on an organic level, the day was sad. It was Sunday, and I wrote letters for an hour or two after a walk with Daniel, and then took a walk alone. The air was misty and the sunshine dimmed down to a hush as though all nature were a church. Sad and solemn indeed, and though I was excessively conscious of every woman I passed, had to see her points with more than usual care and examine whether she attracted me and I her, still that fact made me all the more discouraged in my heart. I felt that maybe all I have written here of the repression of my disappointment in living with Ida, how I wanted to be a lover of the earth, and all that seemed so beautiful and relieving, was perhaps in reality only a rationalization of my desire for a promiscuous, lecherous sentimentality.

I was vividly aware that solving the problem of our relation, however we do it, will not solve the problem of sublimation that is mine for life. I wished to God I were a simple, right-minded person to whom the things of the day are by a natural order and inevitability the interests of the day.

And yet I did feel then, and do still, that my problem of sublimation would be easier if I felt free.

August 3

Sometimes it seems as though my whole nature waits for the appreciative eyes of a woman. Yesterday a little luminous beauty, the daughter of one of the players, came to watch our tennis game— lifted that game out of the flat atmosphere of routine recreation, and created there, by the mere moving over it of two lovely eyes, a glamorous adventure amid scenery, and with glory to be gained through skill, humor, and enthusiasm.

Always unsatisfied, though, always restive, eager for the unattained, and ending in disillusionment if one cannot return to some place and custom of routine content!

Yesterday and today I've felt profoundly homesick and lonely for my dear companion. I just achingly wanted to see her beside me at the table, and do some little thoughtful act for her pleasure.

I suppose I wish that Ida could love me as I love her, almost as much as she wishes I could love her as she loves me. So I've wanted to go over and revise all that I've said here, *after analyzing the word love,* so that everything should be expressed in more specific terms.

To her love means (and I use the terms of the only science that ever approached the question) a fixation of the libido, full and undivided (except what may serve one's impersonal work in the world) upon a person of the opposite sex. And that fixation, but for times of unsatisfied romantic passion, I've never experienced. There is no question that my libido is all split up and runs a thousand ways. And there is no question, absolutely none, that my relation with Ida has contained a vast amount of deliberately controlled pretense. I've acted the part, the best I could, of the kind of lover she regarded as alone worthy of the name. And this acting, this moulding of my emotions to a foreign pattern, is what has grown intolerable and what I feel so buoyantly relieved of in her absence. It is what perhaps she feels buoyantly relieved of in mine.

Let us say then, if that is the definition, that I am not "in love" with Ida. Then I can go farther, and say that I think I never would or could be, except for short times when tantalized, in love with any girl. *I am in love with the unattained.* That is where the word "love" belongs, and I am willing to leave it there now.

But does not that make the word affection, the word friendship, more important and more sacred for me? I love Ida as a friend whom I would wish to serve always, and join with in doing and seeing the things we both like, and to whom I would turn in a thousand joys or troubles. My picture of what happiness in life I can see now is that I should live a little way round the corner from her, either alone or with a male friend if I could ever find him, and come to her house often and always (as I used to) and find her heart open and free toward me and yet not asking what I have not to give.

It was so in that fall and winter before we sailed to Europe, and then I was happy. Nor was it my urging, but hers, that broke the mystery of that perfect companionship. It was her wish, and my devotion to her, together with some feeling of moral necessity, of my inferiority to her wish, and also a strained hope that this might *be* the unattainable—that with loving access to her beautiful body all my vagrant striving might cease—it was these motives, not any impetuous instinct, that led me to commit myself to the word love even knowing what it meant to her. I say this in retrospect, forgetting that the time was packed with ecstasies and all shades of mood. But yet I think it is essentially true. And I reflect that in a manner she has often told this truth to me and I have often denied it. It was indeed the knowledge of this truth, the realization of my mistake, rather than any statement about love or non-love, words which always seemed foreign to my life, that I repressed after the miserable awakening at Gibraltar.

What I want now is what I had before I made that mistake and subsequent repression, a beautiful friendship with Ida, which should find me free of pretentious emotions and alone with my own problems of love and sublimation. Just such a friendship as our happiest hour was to me, only with the inestimable added blessing of our common love for Daniel.

I know that I cannot have this, for Ida can open her heart only to a lover. But I believe that this is what I want, and my duty is to face clearly the reality, not only of life but of my own wishes.

I dreamed that Joe O'Carroll was telling me endless, endless dreams, and finally, after being perplexed and bothered for a long time, I insisted that the interpretation was "sexual and single." Did this dream disguise from me the fact that the cause of my trouble with Ida is sexual and single? Am I afraid to say that to myself?

I am not happy with Ida because I want to be free to satisfy other sexual desires.

There! I have said it. Now the question remains: is it the essential truth?

August 5

And the answer:—no, it is not.

The reason I say this with such certainty is that if asked to make a *second* choice of what I truly wish, I would make the same choice only with that element of physical freedom removed. I can see no other way to save any of the precious and sacred friendship between us but for me to abandon the entire system of pretense, live apart where I can find and become again my true self, and for Ida to learn to be happy and herself without what *she* can call my love.

I talked all yesterday afternoon with a westerner, a person of the type I call a real man. Such an encounter always brings me a poise and reinforcement of my intellectual and adventurous interests, as though there were in truth a homosexual factor in my nature ever unsatisfied because of my overcorrection of it. I went to rest with a quiet and happy equilibrium, as I imagine those lucky souls do for whom, because of spontaneous objective interests that are absorbing, no problems of sublimation exist.

I woke in the small hours of morning, stepped in for a look at the baby to see if he was all right, and returning propped my pillows and lay awake thinking and judging in that same happy poise for more than an hour. Though I was quite poignantly lonely for Ida, full of sweet images of her coming, and tenderest thoughts about our happy hours together, our happy sacrifices for each other which seemed the sacredest things in the world—still I was quietly sure of the truth that my daily relation with her as a lover is so full of faithful and pathetic pretense as to be impossible. It has been impossible ever since the day we arrived in Gibraltar. I could not acknowledge it then, because she was so dear to me that I wanted to love her, and because I was afraid of life without her. And I *could* attempt the manufacture of a lover-self because to a degree my self has always seemed to be a made-up thing. My instincts seem a formless and universal material, so many and so lightly changed, out of which my volition can with nearly unlimited freedom create a character.

I remember how in this respect my attitude in youth disturbed my sister. She used to say, "I would hate that way of talking in anybody but you." But when it comes to founding a daily companionship, an intimate love, upon this act of volition, in the face of such a disparity of instinctive and day-level emotions as exists between Ida and me, I discover that poetic drama has its limits. I have used all my dramatic power only to make three years of sorrow and bewilderment for her. That, I guess, is all that I have done.

I have thought all along that, before she comes back, I would itemize here, as Dr. Jelliffe once suggested, the points of disharmony between us. Such a list would be a complaint rather of myself than of her, and even so, of what value? The general truth is so clear that the details ask to be forgotten:

Our feelings are of so different a quality, tempo, intensity, and duration, and her personality has so much more poise and momentum, so much less sympathetic suggestibility than mine, and yet is so sensitive to a hurt, that I must inevitably and continually accommodate my personality to hers. And though such an accommodation is a pleasure at many times and intervals to one with a facile instinct for it, as a basis of life-union it can only result in sorrow and depression. For me it has resulted in the feeling that I have lost myself altogether. And the gradual finding and recovering of myself in solitude, and in this book, in spite of the sorrow of life that is now mine forever, has been attended with a kind of parturition joy.

August 6

Perhaps she is coming today. I've been imagining it, I've been longing to watch her with Daniel, and tell her about him, and have her blessed spirit in the house, so much that I can only wonder at the truth of what I've written here. Surely there was every reason for my wanting to live with her, even if there were so many reasons why it failed. . . .

Yes, she did come. She read this whole book, and we strained and suffered through the night. Never do we seem more different than in sorrow. And still this morning I am so heartsick and lorn of her and her old tenderness, so aching for what we had—once at least— that I want to cancel all I've said here and say this instead:

If she could expect less of love, if she could put her life energy as I do into some objective matter so that I would become incidental or taken-for-granted in her mind, we might weather all the differences (even my wandering sexuality if I repressed it) and call it love at the last. But she can neither do this nor acknowledge that she does not do it.

Well, perhaps even though we learn to call it love at the last, we shall learn best by not calling it love now. At least she is going to try to be a "dear friend"—though it means little to her, I think. And I am going to try to show that friendship includes "tenderness." I will remember that word at all times, if I can.

I am not going to say that I will be true to her physically. She does not want me to say it to her, and I do not want to say it to myself, lest it erect the old barrier. I hope I shall be true to her, and I shall take all steps to keep my life-energy occupied, but I shall make no vow or declaration, for I think there is a greater chance of our finding true love in friendship if I do not.

In living partly in her house, partly in an outside study of my own, I intend to be a man of work and action. I shall not waste my energies or dissolve my self-esteem in trivial fooling around with pretty girls.

One thing I noticed, and noticed painfully, so that it seemed almost the essence of my starved feeling in her companionship: she gives nothing to my self-love. I know this book is the revelation of a sorry character. It can be perceived that way. But has not its uncompromising truth in one so gifted with hypocrisy, has not its vain striving for something good and great in life, a grain of merit for one who should wish to "love" the author?

Two things I saw so clearly in yesterday's tearful argument: first, that my whole instinct seeks at such a time nothing but self-justification before her; second, that she on her part never drops an instinctive word of admiration or appreciation of my qualities. They starve for praise. They starve and dwindle away, and in their place sits a feeling of ignominy, deficiency, and self-contempt which is somehow *her* contempt for my self.

(New York) August 11

In our last discussion before I came away, it had seemed to us both that self-love was a canker at the very heart of my character, that self is what intrudes in my poetry between the words and their object, that self is the fantasy that flits between me and my life, and that the failure to gratify that vampire with appreciation is her failure to fulfill my dreams of love.

In brief, of all that I had written in these notebooks in her absence, that statement of the central self-motive in all my conduct was, when expanded to its true proportions, the nub and essence.

In her presence this conclusion seemed to me altogether true, and I came away thinking to examine whether there is anything at all in me whereon I could found a new character in which that passion should have smaller place. And as I watched myself and my occupations during the hours, I came to the conclusion that both I and she had exaggerated the predominance of that motive in me. Though it is there, and though it is a danger, there is much else there, a great love of the world, work, play, and ideas, interest in the perfection of things not my own, and energy for them.

I know it is my deepest flaw and danger. And I know too it is a great part of our intimate disharmony. But as soon as I escape from the unreasonable dominance of her thoughts over me, which leads me even to overbear her own doubts of them, I know it is not the nub and essence of that disharmony—nor yet, in the supreme way I had pictured it, of my character.

But I have had little else in me either of thought or feeling since my leaving, except an overwhelming bodily sense of the sorrow I have caused her. She told me she did not care now whether she lives or dies, and that holds fast in my breast. I can not return, even in busy solitude, to the actual joy of life that came at first with the relief of this truth-telling. I am not obsessed as before with melancholy; even in aching loneliness I put up my hands and say, "I am glad I have faced the truth." But deep in me all the time resides this quailing pain and actual fear of her sorrow.

August 12

Her letters say, too, that perhaps we exaggerated a little the dominance of the "Narcissus complex," that perhaps her very dread of it, and withholding food from it, *made* it emerge excessively in my consciousness.

I think the truth is, our companionship of ideals has greatly subdued that complex. I am far more objective and outflowing in my enthusiasms through the influence of our friendship, and through my love and admiration of her inner attitude to life. But in consciousness, it is true, her unappreciativeness has brought sharply forward that complex and its unsatisfied hunger.

Her letters also suggest that the essential cause of our failure is the fact that I *have* romantic love for another, and that but for a pain of jealousy she might long ago have insisted this was true. This suggestion stirs a great commotion in my breast and out along my arms and legs, and I think with a dry mouth of going to Ruth now I am free to do so. But I cannot say these thoughts or feelings are very romantic. They are what I would call pure poison of desire, beautiful—beautiful as water in the lake—but not beautiful with dreams or visual reflections, beautiful only to plunge muscularly in and drink. It is what I want. But whether I want it because it is a fantasy or because it is a fact, whether there would come a true exaltation or a rank disillusionment of mind, only the experiment could tell.

And from that—what withholds me? A sense of Ida's jealous pain, a sense of the indecency of taking quite all that life offers? Is there in fact anything that withholds me except the certainty that I must say fairly and clearly to her, whose love and wishes are so dear, what I am doing at this time and why?

Provincetown, August 17

I did say fairly and clearly in a long letter to her just how I felt, and what I wanted. I said there was only one thing to hold me from going to Ruth, and that was the fear of interposing an insurmountable barrier between our hearts. "Our friendship," I said in substance, "is the one thing more desired than that passionate experience."

But in the meantime she had written me a letter, enclosing statements of her true feelings—feelings of hate against me for what I have done to her.

Just as I was penning, in my mind, a letter to her which should say: "I have tried with all my power for three years to love you as you wish to be loved, because you are so dear to me; now that I've failed I ask you to try for a year to love me as I wish to be loved, because I cannot bear to lose you"—just as I was ready to put that in written words, came the letter of hate. She sent it, as she said, because she wanted me to know her as she truly is—but it cut my heart open. I lay sick and dry-hearted for a while, and then got up and lost consciousness in a debauch of work. I worked, after having worked all day, from eight in the evening until four in the morning.

After four hours sleep I got up, staggered broken-heartedly through dressing and breakfast, and over to the office to find the one message in the world that had power to make me radiantly happy. It seemed as though the revulsion of feeling would drown me in my own joy, it was piled so high in the rush.

I quote the letter, for it tells what I would have her be and feel more purely than I could tell it.

"Friday, 2 A.M.

"Somehow I feel as if you can be free to have your loves whenever and wherever you want them and we can be friends, the dearest friends the world has known—for we have seen one another face to face—we know—and your dear presence is so precious to me that I feel there is something tremendous and unique between us. I don't know what it is—but it is there to enjoy and treasure and to cherish—not to destroy. Your very failings, your struggle, and your victories have made you real to me. I am awake with a sudden sense of preserving some jewel from a deep burial in oblivion. No more restraints, no more fear. We will have something fine from this yet. Fine and free. I wish I could talk to you now. I am aloft on the wings of the dawn. I love you strangely now. Let the dead bury the dead.

"That sounds like poetry, doesn't it!

"Another thing I have thought of is this. I don't suppose any boy or man with your sexual make-up has ever really gone through his whole youth as you did before you met me without actual sexual and complete experience. There are two things that may happen now. It may relieve you from the insistence of these overwhelming impulses if you do have love affairs, or it can make you the victim of them so that you become a professional Don Juan. But I think, Max, that perhaps you can find your way out—"

The sweet joy of friendship, of wanting the same thing at last, and the sweet adoration of her nature that followed the reading of this letter, need no painting. Only I must say it was not the "other loves" that possessed my imagination then, but the golden possibility of that platonic love of our own—the thing I know so surely now I have always wanted of her, had I not fooled myself with the mirage of our uniting and "living happily ever after."

It was that possibility of friendship that possessed my soul to race for the train and go to her.

In which rapid exuberance I was checked within fifteen minutes by having handed me a telegram of the night before which had come to my sister's house.

"Please see Jelliffe for me will you. Can't sleep. All in. Tell him to send directions telegram and letters."

This message had been sent the afternoon after her precious letter was written. So after all that letter, which had come so naturally and inevitably into my own thinking, had been in her the expression of a momentary exaltation. It could not be sustained. Simultaneously with this bitter knowledge, my heart sank to pallor at the thought of her having still no answer to her cry for help. I spent an agonized and crazy two hours getting hold of her by long-distance telephone, begged her to take the train to Boston, so that we might meet before the next morning, wound up matters at the office, and took the noon train.

I found her in despair—sobbing, and running round and round the subject of my kind of feelings for her and for other girls. There was no ray of light, no ray of interest in anything, even intellectual comprehension. I can not remember anything we said, nor can she, nor was it of any avail, until a packet of veronal brought sleep. In the morning we spoke a little more objectively, and after discussing a return to Dr. Jelliffe in New York, decided to take the boat to Provincetown and make a try of living along as friends.

No words can express the agony of sympathy and regret that possesses me at these times. But I want to express here some other phases of my feeling.

First, she is terrible and unapproachable in her grief. There is no mitigation, no handle, no standing ground, nothing that can bring me beside her for a second. I could not endure ten minutes of such grief myself, and as my imaginative sympathy is capable almost of making her my self, I can not endure it in her. I become frantic. I want to yell, I want to seize chairs, tables, and throw them about. I want to grab her and shake her fiercely, cruelly. The effort of self-control is almost insupportable. And so I alternate between tearful sympathy, which is really designed to win her out of herself by making her pity me, and transports of crazy intolerance, almost antipathy—a feeling that is simply and perhaps adequately expressed in these words: I simply can not stand this so long without some mitigation, some let-up.

The truth is, her feelings are deep and absorbing and last long; my feelings are shallow and easily objectified and shift with my thoughts. They have to shift, for they are so keen-cutting I can not endure them. And yet she dominates me utterly, so that I *have* to endure as long as she does. Thus a kind of impotent anger, as though I were chained down and being bitten, is inevitable. It makes me seem hard and alien, and as she has no idea what torture I am suffering, for nothing but loud screams would express it, that makes her grief only the more intense.

Also in the long run there results from these scenes a complete abjection and sense of guilt in me. All the poise, the certainty that I have told the truth, and that we have chosen, not the best but the only way except separation that remains, deserts me. I feel contemptible for not having "made good" in the regimen of love, all the laws and customs of nature and man telling me I "ought" to have done so, and I impute this judgment to her and feel that she is expressing contempt for me. This feeling, combined with my aching desire to make her happy, is so strong that I begin to "hedge" again. I begin to experiment how near I can come to saying what she wants me to say.

So yesterday and last night the whole matter was clouded over with remorseful doubt. In that state the clear and simple confessions of this book seemed altogether alien. It was not until I came over here to the boat-house, and sat in solitude with my own desk, and the book itself, that I recovered a true vision. I can see now that this is not a question whether I shall try to be her lover again or only her friend, but a question whether I shall be her friend or we shall separate altogether.

In particular I was tormented yesterday with the thought that I ought to tell her, whether she will or no, that I will never have any sex relations with another woman. Having protested that the essential fact is not that I *am* in love with another, but that I am not in love with her, I ought to "make good" by sacrificing to friendship with her all quest of love experiences elsewhere. I was thinking of this all the hours of yesterday. But I observed that, even in my approaches to the resolve, I would always make a tacit reservation that it would turn out to be temporary. It rarely enough happens that celibacy is preserved even with God helping, to say nothing of a human friend. And yet somehow it seemed my duty, and my conscience was harassed, and all my clear apprehension of my life-problem as I had set it down here and she had set it down in her letter, was lost. I was full of guilt and the conviction of sin. And when I woke this morning it seemed as though I'd been dreaming all night of somebody's handing me an official document declaring that I could not possibly enlist and go to war with my sex desires unsatisfied.

How easy it is in the unconscious!

Can my ideals pass me such a document?

August 18

Last night I lay awake for hours in a languid trance of tranquil happiness. She had let me comfort her, and gone to sleep quietly after a few tears, and there had been laughter and real understanding, I thought, during the day. My hopes were high. I thought with joy of the world and myself free in it. I thought with joy and in a persistently spiritual manner of my visiting Ruth and discovering in a way that seemed altogether right and natural what she is and what she is not to me. I thought with joy of the future of my relation of dear friendship with Ida, and when she woke I was able to comfort her and see her fall asleep again. It was a time of pure and quiet joy.

But this morning I am sick again with the old feeling of guilt. I think what a heroic thing, and worthy of my thought and training, it would be to say to Ida: "Come what come may, I will deny myself this wish, and all these wishes that I know pain you. And though I know for certain we cannot flourish as intimate lovers, at least I can do this to make you happier as my friend."

I know that some people—saints and great hearts of the past and present—would do this. I suspect my father or mother would have done it. And would that be only because they had a less free and naturalistic view of life or because they were intrinsically nobler in their souls? This thought torments me especially this morning because of a letter from my brother discussing life and death in his bold, generous, and loyal way. His letter recalls the exaggerated moralism of my youth.

Perhaps I am so tormented because all this "confession" about not "loving" her is but a rationalization of the desire to have other physical and semi-romantic gratifications without losing her love. At this moment, in a stupendous way, even the whole of our intercourse presents itself to my remorseful heart as a long-headed cunning eternal ruse of my Machiavellian intellect to attain that end without moral reprobation!

But now I think also of the inharmonies of our feeling, the unhappy pretenses that were forced upon me by our differences and her touchiness, the years of oppression, sweetened with dear affection though they were, in which I seem to have been living under a weight, not myself. I remember the sane and outflowing equanimity of so many hours since I wrote this book. I reflect upon these things, and I know that the substance of the book is true. It is not a rationalization.

Yet even so—the sense of guilt comes back—why not renounce for her sake a thing that pains her? I can only answer, though it makes me desperately sad and sick with scruples: I know that I *will* not do it. I am not unselfish enough.

So then I will have the other virtue. I will at least strongly and candidly, like a man grown up in the daylight, go and have my way.

Rowayton, Conn., August 20

After two days of feeling alternately exalted, and sad, and strange, there came an hour of tender understanding and a night of love. In the morning with two sobbing hearts we parted. As I stood upon the deck of my waiting steamer, and watched her adored and quiet figure, quiet in heroic sorrow, dwindle down the long dock and flicker out at its end, such pain possessed me as I have never known. All this busy book of intellectual reflections whirled into oblivion because I loved her.

I love her and I shall always love her, and I shall never betray love in order to vindicate my character again. For that is what I have done—to vindicate my character according to *her* standards of what love entails.

We were so near together in last night's tender-passioned darkness, because she made it known to me that even after all I'd told of my desires and restiveness, and even though these desires were free to be fulfilled, she still could *let* me call it love. In the instant of that knowledge, like a dam let down, the waters of my soul went over and encompassed her. For though the dominance of her mind upon me is so great that I could not even think it, what I *yearned* to think and say through all these weeks was this: I love you, Ida, as I shall never love another. But love, like life and poetry itself, for me is a surge of inspiration; I am the creature of successive alarms of passion. And though the knowledge of my love persists in all the valleys of my feeling, I can not say the love persists. My mind and body too much become absorbed in other things, in other passions less complete, less deep of trend, less sacred, yet in their time entrancing. There is in me no instinctive sense, either of the priority or the exclusiveness of the one grand passion. Unless it can in very truth underlie, and not overlie, my experience of life, this passion will bring only cruel fret and melancholy to my heart. I neither offer nor ask monogamy. And only because of my accursed diffident suggestibility have I accepted this hitherto impregnable assumption of all your thinking about love. Only because of this have I betrayed that deepest passion of my own heart, my love for you.

We have parted "for a few months" (and O that is a long time!) in order to find each our own self in the world, and in order that in drawing together upon the new terms, whatever they shall be, we may come no nearer than we wish.

As a first step toward my self-finding, I came to visit Richard Le Gallienne, who carries forward the tradition of Grant Allen's idealism. Richard speaks of love with free and beautiful praise, and yet of the monogamic temper as only one, and that often a tragic one, of love's varieties. In this air my heart is at home. I am most happy and am filled full of the old ideal love of life and high endeavor. Yes, but for the dread that invests the thought of her feelings at this hour, my joy is pure and energetic, which is the sign and seal of virtue. My mental rectitude seems at last, after these contemptible and ravaging attempts and pretenses and soft-hearted falsifications, completely restored. I would to God I could believe that she also is happy.

Cherith, August 26

The night I took the train for Glenora I was so possessed with loving homesickness for Ida that it seemed almost impossible to do it. Much as a crude part of my nature desired it, I came here *against* many other impulses, often reassuring myself with the knowledge that for Ida as well as for me it is best that I face this reality.

As I came across the lake in the early sun, I sighed with joy to be returning to the loved scene alone, a gipsy again. I love this place.

It is the essence of "nature" in my life. When I think of nature I see Glenora. And as I looked along the shore, it was that pagan love of nature that made me happy. I thought of my boyhood, my mother —and of Keats. So—the longing to come to Glenora in freedom was not all physical passion. Ida never loved this life, nor entered into it. Perhaps that is the reason, perhaps other reasons, why only in the freedom of separation from her can I revive the old love and happiness here.

Perhaps other reasons, for my sane and wide-spreading delight gave way to a more concentrated excitement when I saw Ruth and realized that toward her too I am free. Yet this excitement did not take hold so deeply of me as of old. It is a light rampant thing, and naturally less intense when unconstrained. It has to do chiefly with her motions and her body, which affect me like a flame. But it gives way now very quickly, or gave way several times yesterday—the times when I was alone—to that tenderest loving homesickness again. Last night I noticed especially that the cottage and its furnishings remind me more poignantly and with a sweeter sorrow of Ida—our tragedy and our baby here—than of any other thing. I wanted to find something she had used, to have with me by my bed as I slept. And I was sad to think of this other excitement possessing me during the day. Sad, not because I seemed to myself to violate my love for Ida. Either that is not my nature, or it is not that kind of love. Sad only because what I am doing and feeling would hurt her. I had to reassure myself once more with the memory of our dilemma, the certainty that even for her this act is best.

It was folly to try to build happy love upon the denial of so intense a passion. I see that it was utter folly to do that.

Honesty compels me to say, though, that sometimes the love of Ida was so strong in my heart that I did not even want this other passion. It was so as I went to bed last night.

New York, September 2, 1914

Ida dear, suppose that when we first came to love each other I had been what with your tender and heroic help I have become, a grown-up person able to face the truth. Suppose that I had said:

Ida, I love you, and tonight I want your body and soul. But first I must tell you what love is to me. Love is an inspiration that enters my heart and fills it to brimming with divine emotion, and soon is gone. Nothing is more fleeting, nothing more unreliable, and yet nothing is more full, palpable, precious to me than love. I can not catch or confine it. I can not change it into a less divine but more constant thing. I can not accept any responsibility for its presence. Even its own aching wish to be eternal—that everlastingness which bursts my heart—even that I must deny. For love will vanish like the wind and never come back to its place again if I decide to confine it there.

I think I will never love any other in so high and passionate a way, body and soul, as I love you tonight. And I will love you so, often and long, if you will let me. But perhaps and probably I shall love others. I do not want to be so near to you that I cannot love others. I am a lonely wanderer. Even in the very depth of my spirit I violate nothing when I say this. If you ask either a constant or a faithful love from me, you will have nothing in your hand but my enduring friendship, tinctured with sadness for the lost fire. And yet I love you, and I ask you to give yourself to me and your love, tonight, and be happy with me.

I wonder how you would have answered . . .

I *can* not be any but a gipsy lover, Ida. I can not get my heart, still throbbing and alive, into a pattern of constancy, even though the pattern be molded by your most natural instinct and reinforced by every assumption of society and language. It is foreign to my life, and it kills me.

I am no patient of a doctor. I am filled with the joy of life and labor. I love everything in this room, and seek its perfection. I love my material responsibilities and the responsibilities of friendship. I greet them with abundant gladness, and I could go singing around this house all day if I could forget your sorrow and that I am the bitter cause of it. I am only a vacancy in your heart. I long to be something that in a high and special way you love—as I think I might have once, if I had known myself and the world.

All this is so surely written because by going back to myself, by not writing to you or even wondering about you (except as I could not help it), carrying with me all that you and loving you have given to enrich my mind and heart, I learned it and I know. I've been in Glenora, been all the way back to my childhood, and seen that everything is sweet and sacred but my pretenses. And yet I'm joyful to be here in New York again, fixing the house for you and Daniel, dedicating my strength to poetry and truth and liberty.

It is all I ask—that and your happiness: to be myself, and to have some love out of your heart that I can sometimes feel.

Chapter 60

Towards a New Harmony

IDA was generous toward my wish, now that I seemed to have found it. She agreed to my having an independent life with a room not far off where I could stay when I wanted to. As a result we lived together more closely, and far more happily, than before. Our house was a tiny, quiet one "in back" on 13th Street west of Seventh Avenue. You went three steps down from the sidewalk, ducked through a narrow tunnel, and crossed a court to reach its quietness.

Ida wrote to Dr. Jelliffe: "Max is wonderful and harmonious now . . ."

I wrote: "You will be glad to know I'm well and happy, and my family no less, and functioning more creatively as I should. I raised nine thousand dollars for *The Masses* in six days this fall, and out of that I get a salary, which leaves a little more time for art. Isn't this better?"

My room, in which I spent that "little more time for art," was on Waverly Place next door to 118, where I had last lived with Crystal. If I were a dog, it would seem pathetic that I crept in there so close to my old self to dream. When Crystal and I first took that apartment in 1909, I was so enamored of freedom that I hated to bind myself by signing the lease.

"Fifty-five a month for twelve months by contract," I exclaimed in a letter, "and me the only person in America who would sell all properties, talents, hopes, ambitions, friends and relatives for personal liberty!"

Now after four years of bondage I was free again—in principle

519

at least—and I celebrated the fact by writing a perfectly truthful
love poem to Ida.

> Hours when I love you are like tranquil pools,
> The liquid jewels of the forest, where
> The hunter runner dips his hand and cools
> His fevered ankles, and the ferny air
> Comes blowing softly on his heaving breast,
> Hinting the sacred mystery of rest.

I doubt if this rang any bells in Ida's proud spirit, but it was all
I could say. In letters I had learned to repress the inner voice that
objected whenever I put down a phrase of sustained or unqualified
love. I repressed it because I thought it was a faulty incapacity in
me, an emotional stutter begot of too much thinking. In poetry I
could not do this. Poetry is a test of sincerity. Poetry has to pour
out, and not a line will pour—for me at least—except with my total
self consenting. Maybe Keats meant something like that when he
said "Beauty is truth, truth beauty"—a sentimental notion otherwise, so little native to his brave clear mind.

I must add that my freedom in this new pattern of living was
largely formal. Once it was established that I did not have to be
faithful to Ida, and did not have to confide to her whether I was or
not, desire was no longer a torment. If I kissed any other girl full in
the lips during that entire winter, I can not remember it. The reality
of Ruth, of our coming together at last, had been dismaying to me.
Her wish that I "wouldn't be so physical" had not been maidenly
reserve toward man in general, it turned out, but a stubbornly spiritual attitude toward me in particular, which was, and remains, one of
life's empty spots and sorrows. Thus I had come back from Glenora
rather chastened in my desire to be unchaste. I was still pursued in
day and night dreams by naked visions of the girls I had yearned over
and never clasped. They all came back at times, each alone and commanding all my love, to my troubled pillow. (They do still for that
matter.) But I reasoned that dreamhood was the essence of our bliss
—that the reality of each would have cooled me as did that of Ruth,
who had been the queen among them. I was, in short, once again
convinced of my ineptitude as an adventurous lover, and inclined
by diffidence as well as duty to center my affections upon Ida and
our baby, and "dedicate my strength to poetry and truth and liberty."

One reason I succeeded so well was that Ida found something of
her own to do. She had long talked of founding a theatre to be

sustained by subscriptions instead of ticket sales, one which could ignore the box office and adhere to pure standards of art. It was a protest against commercialism akin to that we were making in *The Masses*, and I suppose it had various origins. From my point of view, however, the conception of the Washington Square Players was Ida's, and the organization was born at a meeting in our house attended by Lawrence Langner, Eddie Goodman, and others who subsequently put it across. Ida was absorbed in its beginnings and had the lead in one of the three plays put on at its first performance in the Bandbox Theatre. The easement of spirit produced in me by this outward flow of her interest was enormous. Love in me is so largely composed of admiration that, if we are to be happy, the woman I live with *must* go somewhere and do something in which I am not involved.

Another factor in the new harmony was my gradual recovery of self-esteem. It is plain that a man pinned down in the "ignominy, deficiency and self-contempt" which I described on August 6 and 11 was in no state to enjoy life, to say nothing of love. I had to surmount Ida's conviction that our whole trouble was my "egotism" before I could get going at all. In this, chance gave me a timely lift —chance acting once more through my beautiful, truth-telling Amazon, Inez Milholland. She had happened, returning from a holiday in Europe, to board the same boat with a man who possessed as Sid Wood did, and no other I have known, the genius, the audacity, and the uncompromising determination to enjoy the adventure of life. He was a Dutchman with an Irish mother, Eugen Boissevain by name, the wandering prodigal of a famous family—his cousins rich bankers, his father the editor of Holland's greatest newspaper. He had himself been recently psychoanalyzed by Dr. Jung in Zurich, and surpassed Inez herself, if such a thing could be, in the art of casually blurting out, as the sole thing worth mentioning, the intimate truth. They got married when they came to port, and they were living together that winter of 1914-15 in a sumptuous "bungalow" built by the opera singer Nordica on a secluded hill above Harmon-on-Hudson. I met Inez one day in the street on her way to the station, and she said: "Come on along and meet Eugen, you'll love him!"

I did love him—as much as any man I have known since college days. He is handsome and muscular and bold, boisterous in conversation, noisy in laughter, yet redeemed by a strain of something feminine that most men except the creative geniuses lack. We talked all that evening and far into the night, the three of us, reclining in soft chairs in the high-vaulted chamber that Nordica built for her voice. We talked about love, and I truly think that, had the record been made, our conversation might rival in poignancy of interest the most famous discussions of this subject. Inez and Eugen, to insure each to the other the whole wealth of experience, had taken a vow of unpossessive love. Not a vow, either, for it was the natural motion of love in the heart of each to wish thus to protect the freedom of the other. I suppose only two very young people, full blooded and confident of their charms, could have undertaken this, much less achieved it. But that is what they had done, and they were as happy together, and as totally in love, as any boy and girl I have seen.

In me this boldly idealistic talk was like an Act of Emancipation. It released me from the clutch of a force that was stronger even than Ida's will, my sense of guilt. I knew now, and could remember forever, that I am *not* an abject, abnormal, morbid, immoral, or irredeemable sinner—there is a beauty and a potentiality in my sexual constitution and a possibility of companionship for it.

The next day, when Inez and Eugen had gone to town, I took a walk through Croton a mile away, and up on Mt. Airy, where seven years ago I had come to see Nancy and dreamed of a little house and a life lived half in the city, half in the country. I found the little house too, vacant and for sale, just where the road turned at the top of the hill. It stood very close to the road so that its front steps were almost a horse block, but you could go round to the back porch and look down through a tangle of wild trees to the river. If I owned this, I said to myself, I would pick it up and turn it around. And yet maybe I wouldn't either. Maybe if I lived alone, I would like to have my door open on the public highway.

"He was a friend to man, and he lived in a house beside the road."

The line from Homer ran through my mind, and I walked along musing about solitude and hospitality, and dreaming my way through a whole life lived in that house. When I passed it again on the way back, I had reached a compromise with reality. I would live there part of the time only. I would do my work there, commuting in reverse, and be a friend, if not to man, at least to myself.

Another slight factor in the recovery of my self-esteem was Mabel Dodge's peyote party. Mabel was then in her salon days. She had taken an apartment at 23 Fifth Avenue in a house that belonged to General Sickles of Civil War fame. The general, with all his heroic memories, was still sitting in a straight-backed rocker on the first floor, while Mabel collected the Bohemian intellectuals upstairs. I must pause to tell you what a powerful and peculiar collector of intellectuals Mabel is. She has neither wit nor beauty, nor is she vivacious or lively minded or entertaining. She is comely and good-natured, and when she says something, it is sincere and sagacious, but for the most part she sits like a lump and says nothing. She seems never to have learned the art of social intercourse—a rather dumb and stumpy little girl, you would say, and move on to someone who at least knew how to make conversation. You would move on just to escape embarrassment, but before long you would be around there trying to talk to this little girl again. For there is something going on, or going round, in Mabel's head or bosom, something that creates a magnetic field in which people become polarized and pulled in and made to behave very queerly. Their passions become exacerbated; they grow argumentative; they have quarrels, difficulties, entanglements, abrupt and violent detachments. And they like it—they come back for more. Many famous salons have been established by women of wit or beauty; Mabel's was the only one ever established by pure will power. And it was no second-rate salon; everybody in the ferment of ideas could be found there, from Walter Lippmann, representing the drift toward respectability, to Alexander Berkman, representing revolt *in excelsis.*

Salons exaggerate three things that I don't like: literariness posing as wisdom, opinions passed around like confections, organization of what ought to be spontaneous. I attended Mabel's only once, I think, and that was when she induced Bill Haywood—her crowning achievement—to give a talk on proletarian art. I have described the event with some flourishes in my novel, *Venture,* and I described Mabel there too—without flourishes—as "Mary Kittredge." Moreover, Mabel has described herself with both art and honesty in her own memoirs. So I will resist now, as I always did, her witchlike fascination, and return to the story of my inferiority complex and how her peyote party helped me out of it.

It is a winding story, and begins with a friend of Ida's named Genevieve Onslow, a brown, slender, frog-eyed girl with a rich father in Chicago. Genevieve traveled alone round the world on a tense pursuit of what she called "philosophy," and Ida regarded her as a very superior being, a truly disinterested intellect. Therefore, when Ida confided to me—at a time when her own affection was not running very strong—that Genevieve thought I was "too personal," it had a quite overwhelming effect. It transfixed me in an attitude of

shame, not only for myself but for my rustic and pastoral beginnings. I got to thinking that all the Eastmans were too personal,
that there was something meanly provincial in our frankly excited
pride in each other's talents or achievements. This feeling of family
ignominy extended to the Cherith Log, in which Ida had not deigned
to write when she came to stay there—except to say, "Glenora, I
was pleased to meet you." For years I blushed a little over that
simple and charming chronicle of a home, and thought of it as
naïvely self-cultivating and self-conscious.

This was assuredly morbid and not to be blamed on Ida, but it
was a heavy and real shadow. And Genevieve Onslow, with her
highly adult, urban and impersonal absorption in the life of the
mind, may be said to have cast the shadow. She had just got back,
this winter of 1915, from gathering quite a new and important lot
of philosophy in China. And she imparted this cargo in a line of talk
so involved and abstract and recondite as to convince Ida that she
had grown almost superhumanly profound. It convinced me that she
was insane. I decided that her lucubrations had more to do with her
father than with philosophy, and that in all her wanderings over
the globe, she was merely wheeling around Chicago. By joking with
Ida about this, I began to climb up, on a rather long slope, out of
the state of humility in which the mere mention of her name had
always sunk me. I don't know how Mabel felt about this Chinese
philosophy; I suspect she exercised the Will to Believe in regard
to it, and she had, as I have implied, a mighty will. At any rate,
Genevieve was visiting Mabel at the time of the peyote party, and as
a fellow seeker after the central mystery of life, she was naturally one
of those present.

Peyote, technically called mescal, is the fruit of a cactus eaten
by certain cults among the red Indians to induce a state of trance in
which they commune with occult powers. A friend of Mabel's named
Raymond Harrington, doing ethnological work in Oklahoma, had
fallen for the peyote cult and himself got the habit of communing
with these powers. Mabel was carried away by the tales he told, and
asked him to put on a ceremony in her apartment. As a rare tribute
to our openness of mind, she invited among five others Ida and me.

To describe our arrival I must tell you that on the second floor
of Number 23, between Mabel and General Sickles, lived William
Sulzer, ex-governor of New York, a tall, gaunt Andrew Jackson of
a man with a ten-gallon black hat and a madly glittering eye. He
had been impeached and flung out of the governorship for kicking

down the ladder by which he had climbed into it, a ladder named Tammany Hall. Whether he did this in an acute fit of virtue, or out of chronic lunacy, nobody was quite prepared to say. But I can testify that while Ida and I stood shivering at Mabel's door—for her party occurred on an icy winter night—this sombre giant swung in from the sidewalk and strode toward us with a gait and a look which said "lunatic" to me so distinctly that I stepped in front of Ida to protect her from attack. I did not know who he was; I did not know then that Sulzer lived there. Whatever this testimony may be worth, it made an appropriate introduction to Mabel's peyote party.

Bobby Jones was there, the still-to-be-famous stage designer, with his red beard and thin lit-up face of Jesus starving in the desert; Hutch Hapgood, broad and bearlike, uttering Bohemian anarchisms with a gruff, church-organ voice that made them sound devout; Andrew Dasburg, the handsome, limping painter, mighty-chested too and with blue eyes like a cornflower; Hutch's wife, Neith Boyce, a slim, pale, silent woman whom we used to describe as an "early Italian stenographer."

Harrington arranged an electric bulb with red tissue paper to represent a campfire, made a tom-tom out of one of Mabel's big vases, unrolled a strip of cheesecloth to indicate the "peyote path," and we all sat down at about ten in the evening and began to chew these nauseatingly bitter buttons. Hutch, Dasburg, Genevieve, and Harrington were intensely serious. Mabel, to whose audacity the adventure was due, became prudent when it got started and slipped the buttons under her big skirt instead of eating them. The ceremony was supposed to last all night and the transfiguration to come with the dawn. In my own character I would have gone through this experience with excited interest, not looking for occult powers but for the effects of mescal. In my character of Ida's companion, I lacked the zest. I spat out the bitter dose at midnight, and we went home in zero air through snow-piled streets to our little house a third of a mile away.

I was awakened out of a sleep containing rather kaleidoscopic dreams by a pounding on our door and a shrill voice screaming "Ida! Ida!" I opened the window and down there at our entrance in the bitter cold, clad in a nightgown and a fur coat, was the great philosopher Genevieve. She was raving mad, as well as chilled to the bone and shaking like a harp string. We got her in, piled blankets on her, and tucked her forcibly in bed, trying vainly to call her gibbering mind back to reality. She must see her father—she must see her father, and pour this manic chatter into his ears. I called up Herman Lorber, physician and friend to all of Greenwich Village and half of the East Side, and asked him what to do. He gave me the name of a sedative which I should buy and administer immediately, and told me to bring her back to Mabel's in the morning.

When we arrived with her at Mabel's, the place was like a den of wild animals. Hutch was pacing back and forth among the relics of the campfire, a caged bear absolutely unable to hold himself still.

"I have learned tonight something wonderful," he said to Mabel. "I can not put it into words exactly, but I have found the short cut to the Soul."

Bobby Jones and Harrington were asleep or lying in a stupor. Dasburg was hiking on his cane from one end of the apartment to the other with a look in his eyes as mad as Genevieve's. Mabel, though calm and still able to laugh, was inwardly frightened. When Genevieve's absence was discovered, Hutch had said something about a possible police investigation. Genevieve sat mum now, but showed no signs of returning reason. She had to spend some years— I never knew how many—in an insane asylum. I refrained for quite a while, though not forever, from saying to Ida: "I told you so." But in my own thoughts I decided that it was better to be "personal" and even "egotistical" than achieve a sublime indifference to self at that high a cost.

With such episodes helping, and Ida herself finding me "wonderful and harmonious," I managed to pull up a good way out of my "ignominy, deficiency and self-contempt" during that winter of 1915. Our new harmony was helped on when Crystal and Bennie abandoned Milwaukee and came to live in the apartment on the street in front of us. Crystal knew nothing of the earthquakes I had been through, and she still thought Ida a charming and very perfect companion for me. I admired Bennie's good health and merriment, and kept myself in condition by playing handball with him in the little court between our homes. A process of engraftment was taking place between Ida and me, alien as we were, through the mere fact of a house holding us together. It seemed only to require that she go forward with normal enthusiasm on her own career, that she be to that extent at least a member of my species. But that is just what could not happen.

I was not dismayed when she was eased out of the management of the Washington Square Players, for Ida could not manage or administer anything—she was too hard, too rigidly herself in dealing with people. She lacked the yielding and surrounding instinct so notably possessed by water and other liquids. I knew this, and had no firm hopes in that direction. But I did believe, and do still, that she might have been a great actress. She had everything that goes to make one—voice, frame, gesture, expressive fervor, grace, intelligence—the presence, as Mabel Dodge says, of a "noble lioness." She had everything but steady will to do the work and take the training, everything but purpose.[1]

It was black by our fireside when she came home one night after some unpleasantness at the Bandbox, flopped down on the couch, and announced that she had given up acting. She was going to be a sculptor, or write chants for labor, or agitate for birth control, or work at the Women's Trade Union League, whatever the next weightless gesture was to be. My feeling was one of absolute despair. I did not express it—no one could preach to Ida—but it struck down once more the central pillar of our temple, my romantic pride in her talents.

Witter Bynner has a sonnet in his *Guest Book* written years after, which smiles from the outside at what to me was the cause of such despair.

TRAGEDIENNE*

She chose to be an actress long ago
And so continues to the bitter end,
Not knowing now, nor will she ever know
The role that she intended to intend.
She picks the book up, as she used to do
When it was stage, and sees herself appear
Before an audience, herself and you,
And weighs the ultimatum of a tear.
But whether this play or the other play
Or still a third contain the better part
She can not answer any more today
Than when the question first troubled her heart.
She puts the volume back upon the shelf
And has no part to play except herself.

* Reprinted by permission of Alfred A. Knopf from *Guest Book* by Witter Bynner. Copyright, 1935, by Alfred A. Knopf, Inc.

One need not invoke the "mother image" to explain how a boy grown up in the atmosphere of sustained endeavor that prevailed in the Park Church parsonage would fret against such lassitude.

[1] For a brief period long after this story, Ida did achieve distinction as an actress with the Provincetown Players.

My father and mother woke up every morning full of excitement about doing things. If I differed from them, it was only in dispensing with supernatural props for this excitement. For their worship of God I substituted a vow to myself to live life in this world flagrantly and to the full. I still have the little program of "Morning Worship" on which, while my mother administered the Holy Communion, I scribbled the creed of my own pagan religion.

"Existence was not perpetrated in malice or benevolence, but simply is, and the end of our thinking is that here we are, and what can we make of it. We have a planet to act upon, a sense of the drama. We will not squat and argue, nor balk and try to justify God, but will make with high hearts of abandon our entrance and our exit before the congregation of the stars."

That was my act of consecration, my taking of the sacrament. It was against that, and not only my parents' example, that Ida's spirit of negation sinned. To her the stars were a symbol of man's nothingness, to me the audience of his dramatic life. And she dragged me down into her sin with her, for she was impervious to my influence, and I could not lift her weight. That, I think is the deep ground under the new sad story which follows.

Chapter 61

How I Went to War

THE war in Europe had less effect on American thought and feeling during that first year than one would think looking back. It gave us a new subject to lampoon in *The Masses*— and Teddy Roosevelt's "preparedness campaign" gave us another. Our socialism became violently antimilitary, so much so that many regarded *The Masses* as a pacifist organ. I was not pacifist, but I did add to my theoretical heresies against Marxism a practical one which set me apart more completely from orthodox socialists. I decided that war is not a result of "capitalism," nor is it of peculiar interest to the business class; it is a result of group psychology in a pugnacious animal. The only way to end war is to form larger and larger groups until you have a federation of the world. And moreover, the chief force in accomplishing this will not be the workers but the capitalists. War in modern times is "bad business," I said, and those interested in business will get rid of it before the socialists come to power. Since military patriotism destroys their struggle for power, the workers should join the capitalists in a movement to eliminate war by world federation. "Anti-militarism and Federation of the Bourgeois states should be the rally call of the new International."

These heresies were of no public importance, but they served a vital purpose in my mind. I hated organized fighting. I hated drills, guns, stripes, bars, flags, drums, fifes, bugles, salutes, uniforms, the whole theme-with-variations of militarism. I could not bear to see this corruption begin to swell in the United States. My sister had come to New York to organize an "American Union against Militarism," and I supported her enthusiastically. On the other hand, I was a revolutionary socialist, prepared at least in principle for a forcible confiscation of capital by the workers' state. With however sketchy a realization of what it meant, I was advocating a "Dictatorship of the Proletariat." The incompatibility of these attitudes was not immediately clear to all as it is now; Lenin had not yet split the heavens with his denunciation of "the disarmament cry" and his slogan: "Turn the imperialist war into a civil war." But it was clear to me that Crystal's organization was "bourgeois," and that any attempt to keep America out of war, and militarism out of America, had to be bourgeois. It belonged with "reform," not "revolution," and yet its appeal to my heart and mind was too strong to be denied for theory's sake.

It may be, too, that I was beginning even then to lose a little of my zest for revolution. My self-analysis at Provincetown contained a rather startling passage, omitted from the previous chapter because it had no direct connection with my personal problem.

"No, no, I make velly bad Clistian, I no can shoot"

"I dreamed that Joe O'Carroll at the word 'Revolution,' said 'Wait till I go downstairs and get my coat,' as though the coat were what made him revolutionary. This and some other dreams make me suspect that unconsciously I want to get free of the attitude to which I'm committed by that word 'revolution,' that it suppresses an instinct of universal love and sympathy which was once very strong in me. I ought to get more love into my revolutionism, I guess."

I imagine a great many revolutionists have these secret qualms, though rarely so strong a motive as I had to put their secrets on paper. But the revolution being to them an article of dogmatic faith, they have no choice except to shut their eyes and harden their gullets and swallow the whole thing down. To me, the doctrine being hypothetical and subject in any case to experimental verification, it was possible to be a little more attentive to facts and to my feelings. War was more abhorrent to me than capitalist exploitation, and I cared more about putting an end to it. I felt surer of the possibility of putting an end to it. I could not, perhaps, bring love into the revolution, but I could push off the revolution a little, and make room for a movement more closely related to love.

I don't suppose a hundred people noticed the formula by which I accomplished it, but *The Masses* attained a great vogue because it thus managed to reconcile "bourgeois" anti-militarism with a doctrine of proletarian class war. For that was the mood of the American radicals: they wanted to be Marxian more or less, but they also wanted to be kind of Christian. They liked pictures of a giant workingman rolling up his sleeves in preparation for a knock-out battle with capitalist society, and they liked pictures of Christ being dragged into the barracks by a "Christian" recruiting sergeant.

While the political member of me was occupied with these practical adjustments, the poet was urging upon me the duty to "experience" the European war. I can not simply say that I *wanted* to go to Europe; I felt that in loyalty to my religion I ought to want to go to Europe. The mightiest event in all history was happening while I was young, and I was not even seeing it. I was breaking the first and great commandment: Thou shalt live thy life with all thy heart, and with all thy soul, and with all thy mind. The pressure of this precept grew so strong that, in order to obey it, I transgressed a lesser law that I had set above myself. I wrote for money; I hired myself out to a commercial magazine editor. The magazine was *Everybody's*; the fee was one thousand dollars; the articles were about Freud's psychology. By good luck, my editor was William Hard, one of the kindliest and most subtle minded of these alien monsters. Bill and I sat down at a table in the Brevoort Café and went over my articles together three separate times. After each going over I rewrote them from beginning to end. For me it was purgatory, a reverse purgatory in which I worked my way down through torture from the paradise of free expression to the inferno of paid writing. With a less understanding guide, I should have bolted back to my heavenly home long before the torture was over. As it was I pulled through, pocketed my wages of shame, and took the boat to Paris in obedience to a higher law.

There is no blanker passage in my life than the two months I spent in Europe trying to experience a war. I could not get near the trenches because I was not an accredited correspondent; I could not get into the ambulance service without pledging myself for a long period. I could not get free of my commitments to Ida and the baby and *The Masses.* I was homesick and yet not happy in my thoughts of home. I was seeking experience, yet feeling that in such a holocaust I had no right to seek it. In the face of this wholesale dying, a religion of abundant living, though it be the last and only honest cosmic justification for any human thing, is an impertinence. My creed seemed puerile and my living of it pusillanimous. Such was the depth to which my nerve pressure sank in the days of that abortive and light-weighted trip to Europe in 1915. I was getting ready to be sick. . . .

As usual when all else fails, I found solace in the pleasure of learning. A French teacher of middle age fell in love with me on the boat going over, and I devoted myself to her with an ardor which only stopped short—she never could understand why—at the door of her cabin. I can not understand now myself why I was so stingy. From Bordeaux to Paris I composed verses in French to a younger and more alluring teacher, but nothing came of that either except knowledge. I stayed with Ida's novelist friend, Arthur Bullard, somewhere on the Left Bank, and read assiduously about the French Revolution and the Napoleonic Wars. I combined this reading with visits to museums and conversations with cocottes who would teach me a little French for a drink. I wrote nothing, and I had no ideas. I ceased almost to think of myself as a writer. Arthur Bullard took me out one Sunday to Versailles, and recited as we went along the whole story of the French Revolution—a feat which filled me with a too humble admiration. I met Albert Boni, a small, bright, swarthy, curly-headed cherub, who afterward published two of my books. He was dangling in Paris as loosely as I, and we played catch in the court of an apartment house—to the disgust of the occupants, who thought that two sound young men of whatever nationality ought to be fighting for France. We went together to the Red Cross to inquire about the ambulance service, neither of us, I fear, seriously intending to serve. In the waiting room I saw some photographs of operations that had been performed on mangled soldiers. I pretended that I had seen the soldiers and wrote a gruesome poem, the only creative act of this whole excursion.

> Today I saw a face—it was a beak,
> That peered, with pale round yellow vapid eyes,
> Above the bloody muck that had been lips
> And teeth and chin. A plodding doctor poured
> Some water through a rubber down a hole
> He made in that black bag of horny blood.
> The beak revived. It smiled—as chickens smile.
> The doctor hopes he'll find the man a tongue
> To tell with what he used to be.

One can not experience an effort without making it, and war is the supreme human effort. Nothing else will ever so engage men's energies. My philosophy of living was reduced to absurdity in this attempt to pry in at the edges of a war and get some taste of it. But I had the worst of luck also: I did not find a friend. In all that two months of travel I never happened upon a single person, man or woman, into whose orbit I felt magnetically drawn. It seemed as though without Ida I was flat and sterile and lacking in gravitation. In truth I was not without Ida; I had brought her along. I had failed of the courage to leave her. My tendrils were not extended either in her direction or any other; they were curled up around nothing. One does not find friends in that condition.

My state of negation led me to see only a dreariness of horror in the First World War. I dubbed it "The Uninteresting War," and convinced myself that, with modern equipment, war in general is not only bad business, but dull business as well. It has lost for all and forever its dramatic allure.

"They shoot and kill five thousand Frenchmen every day. They shoot more Germans, and still more Russians. All those men die in **bom**bardments, battles, assaults, reconnoitres, charges, that old-fashioned historians would leer over and detail with expert delight. But when there is an absolute continuum of such things all over a continent for a year, and substantially nothing lost or gained on either side, how can you find anything to call interesting, and when you do find it how can you tell it from the rest? . . .

"There are deeper reasons why this war is dull. One is that, although it may have mighty consequences for the world, they have no connection with its causes or the conscious purposes of those who fight. A greater or a less degree of freedom and democracy for Europe will be the result of victory for the Allies or for Germany. There is no doubt of that. But that is in a manner accidental, a by-product. It is not what the war is about. . . . It is a war of national invasion and defense—nationalism, the most banal of stupid human idol-worships. And the fact that liberty is more or less at stake is adventitious."

I wanted a more methodical and scientific progress "towards liberty." And so I turned from the war—and from history—to my half-finished manuscript on that subject. I had brought it along as an alternative in case "experience" failed, and I lugged it out now and tried duteously, while Bullard was working on "the great American novel," to make it move again. But I came up against what would soon stop me altogether, my ignorance of Marxian philosophy. I needed to browse among the sources, and it occurred to me that Jean Longuet, Marx's grandson, a leader of the French socialists, would surely have them. So I sent Longuet a letter asking if I might have the privilege of consulting his Marxian library. He gave me an appointment at 7 P.M. in a remote suburb, apologizing for the difficulty of getting there at that hour. It required three trips on a trolley, one on a train, and then a taxi ride, and I would have to start from Paris at five o'clock. This surprised me, but it seemed a small price for the pleasure of dining with a grandson who had grown up in personal contact with Karl Marx.

When I finally knocked on the door, I was admitted into a tiny square front parlor with a small bookcase in it, and asked to wait. I waited long enough, I thought afterward, for a man to finish his dinner. Longuet was affable, however, when he came in, and he pointed generously to a shelf in the little bookcase where he had separated off about three feet of books.

"Those are the volumes dealing with Marxism," he said.

I saw at a glance that they contained nothing I could not find on the table of my socialist local on 19th Street. After a few minutes of perfunctory conversation, I felt obliged to inquire about trains, trolleys, and taxis back to Paris. Longuet told me the journey was a little more complicated in the reverse direction, but with good luck I could be there by 9:30. I thanked him and made my hungry way back to Paris with reflections on the laws of heredity that are not fit to print.

In London, where I stopped for a week on my way home, a quite opposite thing happened. I was so forlorn by that time, and so preoccupied with nervous indigestion, that I made no further attempt to "live life." I took a cheap room in a garish hotel called the Strand Palace and spent a very large part of the time lying on the bed, sick both at heart and stomach. I had failed in what I came for, and I was a failure in what I was going back to. I was at the bottom of the ditch.

One day when this inferiority gloom was at its thickest, a maid rapped on my door and said:

"Mr. Shaw is on the telephone."

"Mr. Shaw?" I said. "It can't be for me—I don't know anybody in London."

"It's a call for you just the same, and his name is Shaw."

I had to go down a flight of stairs and walk to the end of a corridor to reach the telephone, and I was halfway there before it dawned on me that George Bernard Shaw's last name is "Shaw." I had dropped him a letter of introduction on arriving, just because I had it with me, and without the slightest hope of an answer.

He was actually *on* the telephone when I got there, and greeted me with a delight and excitement that seemed absolutely incredible. I never shot up so fast from the depths to the heights. I was not a disciple of Shaw, but he was the most famous living writer of English, if not of any language, and I have always in my breast the boyish hero-worshiper. I was still in a tension between shyness and sudden glory when I went over to 10 Adelphi Terrace and waited for him in the front room, studying his bust on the mantel. In about two minutes he came on a dead run down a long corridor, bursting into the room like a magnetic storm, white-haired, pink-skinned, excessively clean, and seized my hands as though I were a long lost brother. It was really true—he knew me, he admired our magazine, he had even read some of my editorials!

I was tongue-tied, but that made no difference. I couldn't have said anything anyway. I sat looking, listening, and laughing through the most richly hilarious and astutely sparkling and seemingly inexhaustible line of conversation I have ever encountered in this world.

Perhaps Oscar Wilde could have surpassed it, or stopped it, or done something else about it. I could do nothing. I was in the presence of a master, and I was content to admire.

I am sure Shaw expected me to write about him in *The Masses* when I got home. There must have been some of the famous egotism behind the brilliant show he put on. It is a measure of the gloomy lethargy into which I was sunk that I made nothing out of this bright and startling experience, which would have shone like a hill-top beacon in my magazine. I was not, in my lethargy, the editor of a magazine; I was not a poet; I was not a propagandist. I was a melancholy adolescent walking the streets in search of the romance that never comes when you seek it. I wanted something to happen to me—something that would certify my freedom and my ability to live a sanguine life on my own.

There is always, of course, a romance to be bought, and I even tried buying the loveliest one in the market on Leicester Square. She was exquisitely shaped and well mannered, and nice-minded enough to point rather shyly to the bruises on her body as a way of convey-ing what she expected of me. But I could not meet her expectations. I could not do anything, alas, but praise her shapeliness and pay for her wasted time. It was hard enough for me to be intimate on a basis of love; to be intimate on a money basis was beyond my powers. It was harder even than writing for a fee.

So I came home from Europe defeated—as was just, perhaps, for one who had "gone to war" in so unheroic a fashion. On the boat I succeeded for the length of a short poem in believing that my homesickness was a very final kind of love for Ida, a love too real to clothe itself in words.

> Someday I'll bring you back a song,
> But now—no sound or meaning of the mind
> Can pace the motion of my spirit to its home . . .

I wrote a truer thing, and a very different one, in prose in another notebook:

"I walk the deck like a sailor, and my thought is that men's desire for marriage, or a God, or a philosophy, is but the little child in them running home to mother. It is the assumption of all academic, sacerdotal, and even scientific thinking that the sole purpose of mind is to seek unity in the apparent variety of the world. To create variety where the world's unity appalls the soul is the original out-ward impulse of all life. The rest are seeking a return to the womb."

Chapter 62

Towards Liberty *Gets Lost*

IDA and I moved again in the autumn of 1915, I cannot imagine why. We moved into a narrow apartment on the corner of Washington Square and West Broadway, another sounding-board for city noises like the one I first had fled from. We were both glad when Mabel Dodge invited us to spend a week in the little white house she had rented on Mt. Airy at Croton-on-Hudson. Mabel was just lifting herself out of a tumultuous love affair with John Reed. I remember his stamping out of her bedroom in the small hours of the night, slamming the door and plunging away in a heavy rainstorm, none of us knew where. I felt that Mabel was on the hunt again, and that I was in a dangerously convenient position. She seemed to be sending out waves of more than the usual potency in my direction, but I may be wrong about that. All she ever said was:

"Max, why don't you arrange your life?"

I was not yet confiding in anyone, least of all in Mabel, whose sudden short bursts of sagacity embarrassed me as much as her long dumb-animal silences. I dodged her remark, but it stayed in my mind as the most compact piece of good advice I ever ignored. Hardly a page of this book gets through the typewriter without my saying: "Max, why didn't you arrange your life?"

I did take one step in that direction. I walked down the road from Mabel's and bought the little house I had dreamed about, paying down twenty dollars—all I had left after Paris—on a selling price of $1500. The heirs were scattered, the agent told me; it would take some time to prepare the deed, and meanwhile I could move in. So I assembled a bed and a chair and a table, and began from that day, October 6, 1915, to live in a house beside the road and be a friend to man—part of the time! Indeed only a very small part, for I would

537

bring Ida to Croton with me, and the baby too, indulging in domestic-sentimental emotions while holding in reserve the happy thought that the house belonged to me and not to them.

It was a miserable year for Ida, not only because of this exasperating doubleness of me, but also because I got sick. I suppose it was inevitable, with these conflicting currents in my breast, that I should get sick. I came home from the Uninteresting War with indigestion, and I kept getting worse all winter. I was thin, green-shadowed, tired, always either refusing to eat or eating too much. Endocrine glands were just coming into fashion as causes, and on the advice of Dr. Harlowe Brooks, I took bi-weekly shots of pituitrin for several months. This mysterious substance enables you to observe your own death in a mirror, for it drives the blood in from the periphery to the vital organs. Your face turns from its natural color to an ashen white, from that to greenish blue, from blue to purple, and what looks out at you in the end is to all intents and purposes a corpse. It is the farthest you can go from mental healing. I was, as usual, deeply interested, read all I could find about endocrine glands, and never failed to have a mirror with me when I took the shots. But that was all I got out of it.

Notwithstanding this sag in my body and the battle in my soul, I accomplished many things during that year 1916. I published a book on the war and the socialist policy, another called *Journalism versus Art*, a short story, and one of my most original poems. I took, with Ida, a two-months' lecture and money-raising tour across the country to San Diego. We stopped at the Grand Canyon, and I compelled myself to mount a mule and ride down the Bright Angel Trail to the bottom of it. As I am afflicted with the horror of high places in its panic form, that twelve hours' ride along the edge of eternity was probably the severest discipline of manhood I ever put my baby constitution through. Another overambitious venture of that year was an attempt to bind in with *The Masses* a highbrow scientific review and create what I called a "universal magazine." Another was a promise to publish there my still unwritten book, *Towards Liberty, The Method of Progress*, a promise I fulfilled to the extent of three installments. I also, in that enterprising year, went down to the White House and lectured the President on the folly of enlarging the national army!

Of all these accomplishments, only one gives me a firm satisfaction today: that is my poem, "Coming to Port." In that I shaped a new vessel of emotion out of these "rove-over" lines which had been instinctive to me in writing blank verse. Steaming into Newport one midnight on the Fall River boat, I saw a frail girl standing on the deck gazing over the star-silvered ripples toward some warships riding in the harbor. There were tears in her eyes, and I attributed to her the thought of sorrow in my own heart: I had established my freedom; I could have my wishes now and seek their fulfillment; but what had I gained after all but the seeking? No wish of mine, not even the strong wish for Ruth, could be fulfilled. The only thing I had ever loved, or ever could love, was the unattained. That was my thought, or my state of being. It asked for an unarriving rhythm, and I achieved it by alternating "feminine" with "masculine" verse-endings, and following the one with a trochaic, the other with an iambic line.

> Our motion on the soft still misty river
> Is like rest; and like the hours of doom
> That rise and follow one another ever,
> Ghosts of sleeping battle cruisers loom
> And languish quickly in the liquid gloom.
>
> From watching them your eyes in tears are gleaming,
> And your heart is still; and like a sound
> In silence is your stillness in the streaming
> Of light-whispered laughter all around,
> Where happy passengers are homeward bound.
>
> Their sunny journey is in safety ending,
> But for you no journey has an end.
> The tears that to your eyes their light are lending
> Shine in softness to no waiting friend;
> Beyond the search of any eye they tend.
>
> There is no nest for the unresting fever
> Of your passion, yearning, hungry-veined;
> There is no rest nor blessedness forever
> That can clasp you, quivering and pained,
> Whose eyes burn ever to the Unattained.
>
> Like time, and like the river's fateful flowing,
> Flowing though the ship has come to rest,
> Your love is passing through the mist and going,

Going infinitely from your breast,
Surpassing time on its immortal quest.

The ship draws softly to the place of waiting,
All flush forward with a joyful aim,
And while their hands with happy hands are mating,
Lips are laughing out a happy name,
You pause, and pass among them like a flame.

How shall I, without a humility that is bad manners, explain why of all the other achievements of that year, not one is good to look back upon?

I have described how running *The Masses* was in my thoughts a moral service, a task I had to get out of the way before I could abandon myself to creative writing. After two years of doing this service for nothing, I was now making it pay me a small weekly wage —enough to relieve me of the nag of lectures. Thus in the hours I could save from money raising, managing, and editing, I was free of every pressure, even that of duty to mankind. I could in a complete sense write as I pleased. But since the "I" in question was editor of *The Masses* and so known to the public, a good deal of what he pleased to write was "copy" for his magazine. It was not commercial journalism, to be sure, but it was journalism just the same: ephemeral, unstudious, not highly wrought, not intense, not cut and chiseled to perfection. With only a few exceptions I find my editorials and articles in *The Masses* inferior in style to my other writings. And the reason is that they belong to my secular and moralistic, not to my sacredly creative self.

If this can be understood, then I can make plain why the achievements of that year 1916 are unpleasing to my pride. The taint of the secular, the secondary, the supplemental, pervades them all. The books are not books, but collections of magazine articles, each suggested by a publisher. Norman Hapgood, as I mentioned, wanted to make *Harper's Weekly* over into an up-to-date paper with drawings like those in *The Masses*; he asked me to write him an article "explaining that kind of art." I told him the contrast was not between one kind of art and another, but between journalism and art. He did not agree; he thought the drawings in *The Masses* were "crude" or "offhand" or "sketchy" or something like that—but he promised to pay seventy-five dollars for the article whether he used it or not. He did not use it, and I published it in the February *Masses* under the title: "What is the Matter with Magazine Art?" It eased my feelings about popular magazinedom, and it made a great hit with *The Masses* artists, one and all.

To balance it off, I wrote another piece called: "What is the Matter with Magazine Writing?" And just at that moment I got my first request from a publisher for a manuscript—a new and adventurous publisher named Alfred Knopf. I suggested these two articles and the title: *Journalism versus Art*. He agreed to publish them if I would add enough to fill a little square book. So I dug up my juvenile essay (not so juvenile since it has proven true): "Why English Does Not Simplify Her Spelling." I threw in some illustrations by *The Masses* artists (and by Rembrandt and Daumier), and added a more recent essay appraising the current free-verse epidemic as "Lazy Verse." Alfred did his part with daring good taste, and the little book was quite a success. But what is the weight of it after all?

There is a fertile field and good seed in those essays contrasting journalism with art. But the field is vast and has never been cultivated; it spreads to all history; it touches the problem of timeliness, of truth, of art and propaganda. If I had prepared the soil, and nourished the seed, and given it time to grow, as I did my thoughts on poetry, I could be proud of a harvest. I was too busy with journalism to write adequately of "Journalism versus Art." I was running a magazine—that was my trade, no matter what contrary motive dragged me to it—and the habits of the job corrupted me both as artist and thinker. You can not do one thing and be another.

This is more crudely evident in the other collection of magazine articles I dressed out for a publisher that year. The war was closing in on us, and everyone was having his say about the coming enemy. I had mine in a brief piece called "Understanding Germany," which *Harper's Weekly* published. It did not say much more than that Germany had something to teach us, and England also. But the title was timely, and it appealed to the publisher of my still-born *Child of the Amazons*, Mitchell Kennerley, a man I had tried diligently to forget. He wrote proposing that I expand the article into a book. I answered that I did not know enough to write a book about Germany, but that I would like to put together all my essays on war and world federation, and call the book "The Only Way to End War." He said he would be glad to publish a collection of those essays, if I would make "Understanding Germany" the title, and write one good long chapter opposing our entrance into the war. He would advance me something on such a book—how much did I need? Remembering unpaid bills, and summoning my last ounce of courage, I murmured "six hundred dollars." He wrote me a check without batting an eye, and I wished bitterly I had said a thousand.

So I wrote a long, learned-sounding but not learned, essay, discrediting "the anti-German hate" and advocating peace without victory:

"The forces that bring liberty are at work in Germany as elsewhere in the world, and her imperial despotism will rot within its own heart and fall. We can only lend our aid to those slow forces. And the best aid we can lend is to take out of their way this obstacle, whose power is new to our knowledge—exalted nationalism."

There is good sense in the essay, and the book as a whole, being a plea to subdue nationalism through world federation, is not outdated. I would make today no basic correction in that plea. But I would really write the book! I would not throw a lot of magazine articles into a bag and name it, at a publisher's suggestion, after the least informed or informing of them all. *Understanding Germany*! —by a man who had never been in Germany, never studied its institutions, never read its history—and moreover wasn't writing about it!

And then those three chapters prematurely published in *The*

Drawn by Cornelia Barns

THE FLIGHT OF THE INNOCENTS

An alarmed patriotess has appealed to the ladies of the Boston Auxiliary of the National Security League to "register their automobiles for the purpose of carrying virgins inland in case of an invasion."

Masses of my magnum opus: *Towards Liberty, The Method of Progress.*

"In a series of connected articles under this general title, I am going to present the scientific basis of the policy of my editorials in *The Masses.*"

A gorgeous boast! But what folly to imagine that a treatise on such a subject could be thrown together in monthly fragments and have depth, wisdom, or validity as a whole.

Here I must discriminate a little, however, as to the grounds of my humility. In the first place, I doubt whether any amount of work at that time would have brought me to the knowledge I have now: that an equilibrium of opposing social forces, not the victory of any one force or class, is the basis of freedom. I had to live the history of the Russian Revolution to receive that knowledge into my mind.

In the second place, I did do the work—in Moscow ten years later. *Marx and Lenin, The Science of Revolution* is *Towards Liberty* grown up and somewhat instructed by history. And twelve years after that, when history had taught me a deeper lesson, I did the work all over again. About *Marxism Is It Science* I have no humility whatever, but a pride as stubborn as it was long postponed.

And in the third place—I can't stay humble very long, it seems— the three chapters I published in 1916 are not *entirely* amateurish. I think they stated correctly and for the first time what is the matter with Marxism from the standpoint of scientific method. That this statement was published before the Bolshevik Revolution is again a matter of pride. I think they also described correctly the method of hypothesis as applied in a social effort. They rejected the immoralism of the Marxian metaphysics. And they defined in terms I would not modify today the purpose toward which my political efforts have always been directed: "to make all men as free to live and realize the world as it is possible to make them."

Contrasting the agitator with the evangelist, I wrote:

"The purpose of life is that it should be lived. It can be lived only by concrete individuals; and all concrete individuals are unique, and they have unique problems of conduct to solve. And though a million solutions must be generally proposed and praised in order that each may choose the true and wise one for himself, they are all futile, these solutions, and the whole proposal to live life in wisdom or virtue is hypocritical and absurd, if men and women are not free to choose. That we should give to all people on the earth a little liberty to be themselves before we lay out such elaborate efforts to make them 'better,' seems to be a point of common courtesy that the entire idealistic trend of culture has ignored. Yet around that simple friendly purpose, dropped by the wayside in the grand procession, the revolutionary storms of history have always gathered."

So I wrote as an unconscious herald of the Russian Revolution, and so I would write now in condemning the moral, political, economic, and cultural strait-jacket into which it has led.

But that is about all I can say for my loudly proclaimed "series of articles under the general title *Towards Liberty, The Method of Progress.*" The folly of this method of progress towards a book must have come home to me by the end of the year. "The title of the next chapter," I announced in November, "will be 'The Basis of Caste.' " (That was my new name for capitalist production, about which I knew, in a scholarly way, next to nothing at all.) But there never was a next chapter; and that is, perhaps, the most indubitably scientific feature of *Towards Liberty, The Method of Progress.* I had not settled my accounts with either pragmatism or dialectic materialism; I had not read history with a sense of its reality; I had not read the life story or examined the mental development of Karl Marx, or mastered his system. I had a bear by the tail the size of the universe, and I was sensible enough to let go. I can not remember the exact date of our parting, but during the next year I was in the library, hard and modestly at work on my once-contemplated doctor's thesis, my second real book: *The Sense of Humor.*

Together with my *magnum opus*, my "universal magazine" crawled ignominiously out of existence. It had been, in less grandiose terms, an attempt to save our expiring Marxian journal, *The New Review*, by binding it in with *The Masses* as a supplement called *The Masses Review.* The lowbrows, I thought, could read the first, the highbrows the second; the super-elite, the true man of the future, would enjoy them both. The experiment began in July with a great trumpet blowing on the front page and ended with a subdued editorial murmur in December. The best objection to it was written by an earnest young contributor named Irwin Granich (now Michael Gold).

"I hate the new *Masses*! . . . It has lost its youth and has become pedantic and verbose. It is fit only for incurable Marxians and college instructors to read . . .

"Yours for liberty, fight and *joie de vivre*."

Our unfailing humorist, Howard Brubaker took the opposite view:

"*The Review* is neither too large nor too heavy. There is no law compelling the flippant to read it. I think the paper in its present form is bully."

The editorial decision was a compromise, a rather apologetic one, as inept as the experiment itself had been. We would merge the two magazines completely; *The Masses* would be there as before, but its "inconsiderate spirit of revolution" would be "a little explained and backed up by facts in these editorial paragraphs."

I must again discriminate, however. Life was becoming serious as the war approached; Europe was drawing nearer; it was natural and right that *The Masses* should grow more thoughtful. And another change was taking place in Floyd and me and Jack Reed, and all the political-minded editors. As the bloody events in Europe sobered us and made real the kind of fact implied by our ideas, we moved steadily away from the "catastrophic" view of the coming of socialism. We lost a little of our naïve faith in the permanence of the liberties already achieved. We sensed, however dimly, that history might conceivably go backward, that political democracy might get lost, that the existing Rights of Man, no matter how uneconomic, are worth defending. Together with the American Socialist Party and a good part of the IWW, we became more interested in staying out of war than in overthrowing capitalism. Jack Reed wrote a eulogy of Bertrand Russell, who went to jail for opposing the war: "An Heroic Pacifist." Boardman Robinson gave his genius almost wholly to the cause of peace. I, besides promising to back up with facts our "inconsiderate spirit of revolution," replaced my old battle-flag title "Knowledge and Revolution" with a milder one: "Revolutionary Progress." By this phrase I meant any event or measure which narrows the gulf between the owning and laboring classes. In stressing the difference between such changes and a general improvement in social conditions, I thought to distinguish my program from "yellow" socialism without necessarily implying an insurrectionary seizure of power by the workers. This maturing of my natural judgment was checked a year later by the astounding fact of the Bolshevik Revolution and by Lenin's colossally practical brain. I became again a rather indiscriminate advocate of "Knowledge and Revolution," differing from the bolsheviks, I thought, only in my more scientific conception of what knowledge is. For the present, however, I favored the adjective over the noun, and rejoiced in the permission it gave me to be hard-headed without being violent.

This change of syntax, together with my unorthodox attitude on the war question, made me care more than socialists were supposed to about Woodrow Wilson's campaign.

"It is the hour and the day," I had written in February 1915, "for President Wilson to take the first step towards international federation. He has it in his hands to make his administration a momentous event in planetary history—a thing not for historians, indeed, but for biologists to tell of, because the elimination of war will profoundly affect the character of evolution.

"Will he do this, or will he rest satisfied with that ludicrous incantation, the national petition to God? Is he capable of a man's prayer, a great act of resolution?"

I received my answer in May 1916 when Crystal, as secretary of the American Union Against Militarism, arranged a delegation to the White House to protest against increased military appropriations. James Maurer, the socialist president of the Pennsylvania Federation of Labor, was scheduled to represent the workers, and when he fell sick at the last moment, my sister put me, somewhat incongruously, in his place. It was not a bad move, for Wilson remembered our long talk at the banquet in Syracuse and greeted me very warmly.

We sat in a circle around his desk—several distinguished citizens, including Oswald Villard, I think, and Amos Pinchot. Each made a little lecture, to which Wilson replied with that facile gift of abstract diction which floated him so securely above the flux of fact. He did, however, very concretely declare for world federation after the war as the central aim of his policy. Indeed he talked so glibly about the establishment of permanent peace by a "family of nations," who would say "we shall not have any war," and back that "shall" up with force, that I felt like cautioning him about the practical difficulties of the task! I still think he lacked a hard knowledge of the forces in play in European diplomacy, and I find it impossible to think of Woodrow Wilson as a great man. Jefferson said: "It is a maxim with us, and I think it is a wise one, not to entangle ourselves with the affairs of Europe. Still I think we should know them." That a president should entangle us in the affairs of Europe without knowing them is something Jefferson could hardly have imagined. But that is what Wilson did, and Franklin D. Roosevelt after him. That is to me the tragedy of this whole epoch, the lack of a great American statesman.

However, those are subsequent reflections. At the time I was charmed by the President's skill in conversation, and delightedly surprised that he had answered my question in the affirmative. I felt that he was thinking straight on the main issue, and I was irregular enough to say so during his campaign for re-election.

This brought me one of my periodic denunciations from the socialist press, and I replied with one of my sermons against dogma:

"What the party has to do now is to get rid of all this sectarian dogmatism, this doctrinaire, *index expurgatorius* mode of thinking, and this infatuation with an organization as an end in itself. Let us try to use our brains freely, love progress more than a party, allow ourselves the natural emotions of our species, and see if we can get ready to play a human part in the actual complex flow of events."

This must have been exasperating to anybody who was trying to run a party, and I made it more so by stating that, notwithstanding this public endorsement of Wilson, I had voted socialist!

On that too it is impossible to look back with satisfaction. Under the cloak of an intellectual virtue, I was concealing the fact that I could not make up my mind.

Drawn by Art Young

SUGGESTIVE THERAPEUTICS

Doc Wilson: "You're all right! You're all right! There's absolutely nothing the matter with you!"

Chapter 63

Greenwich Village Revolts

ICAME very near escaping from *The Masses* in the spring of
1916. Up to that time the free-for-all fight in which producers
co-operatives normally come to an end had been miraculously
postponed. Like Daniel in the lion's den, I had walked unscathed
for three and half years in a pack of artists and poets to whom an
editor, even though chosen by themselves, is a natural and mortal
enemy. This abnormal state of things could not go on forever. Hell
had to break loose. It broke loose in March 1916. Even then the attack
was not against me or against my policy, but against policy as such.
It was a quarrel, essentially, between art and propaganda, poetry and
practical effort—between the very two interests whose satisfaction
within the same covers had made the magazine unique. In more
personal terms, it was a war of the Bohemian art-rebels against the
socialists who loved art.

As I have said, my labor to keep *The Masses* poetically alive
and yet not "Greenwich Villagey" had been continual. Hardly a
month passed that I did not take some action designed to hold the
propaganda of revolutionary class struggle clear of the mere rebel
moods of those who mistake the delights of a venturesome life, or of
creative art itself, for the effort toward world transformation. I expounded this at the time in a letter to Norman Thomas:

". . . I do think you might feel a little differently about *The
Masses* if you got a deeper taste of its mood. I think there is an
Elizabethan gusto and candor in the strong taste for life which must
be won back over the last relics of Puritanism. But nothing is less
like what I mean when I say that than the puny, artificial, sex-
conscious simmering in perpetual puberty of the grey-haired Bac-
chantes of Greenwich Village. I have fought off the encroachment
of Greenwich Village's provincialism on *The Masses* from the
beginning."

548

What raised this fight to a pitched battle in March 1916, I do not exactly know. Maybe the mounting war fever and my extreme anti-war policy had something to do with it. The magazine was headed for trouble, and was subject already to various pressures. Nothing was said about this, however. Policy as such was the object of attack, although it was, of course, personified in Floyd Dell and me, and epitomized in our crowning sin of inventing captions to put under the artist's pictures.

"Max, there's a strike on, did you know it?" Floyd said one afternoon when I came into the office.

"A strike? Against what?"

"Against you!"

"What do you mean? Who's striking?"

"You're a dictator and you've got to be overthrown. You're going to be overthrown in the name of Art with a capital A, which means pictures without captions and publicity without policy. The strike leaders are Stuart Davis, Glenn Coleman, and Robert Carlton Brown."

"Brown isn't exactly an artist."

"No, but he likes to raise hell."

"I must say I sympathize with them about the captions. If I put my feelings into a picture, I'd hate to have some editor come along and stick an idea under it."

"So would I, but what can you do if the artist hasn't got ideas? We're running a magazine, not an art gallery."

We agreed that there is a difference between these two institutions. (We agreed, with very few exceptions, about everything.) I remarked that it didn't sound like a very interesting rebellion to me, but Floyd said:

"It is, because they've got Sloan on their side."

That surprised me. Sloan was a Socialist Party member, one of the original founders of Piet Vlag's *Masses,* an ardent propagandist and a natural-born editor. But Sloan has a touch of the "unrecognized genius" complex. Stuart Davis, moreover, one of the least recognized, was his protégé. In loyalty to some fixed whim in his disposition, he took sides with a rebellion against what he himself really liked and stood for. So it seemed to me, and I note that Floyd Dell, in his autobiography, says the same thing.

Though puzzled, I was not deeply disturbed even by this surprising news. In such a crisis my dividedness made me strong. A good half of me, and the better half, hoped it would end in my getting out.

I called a meeting of the editor stockholders and prepared a serene statement tendering my resignation.

This being a business meeting, it was held in the office instead of a studio. The chairs were uncomfortable, there was no beer, parliamentary rules were observed, and minutes were kept. Thus I can give a fairly accurate account of it. As soon as the minutes of some remote previous meeting were read, Sloan asked for the floor, and with a good-natured jest by way of introduction, offered the following resolution:

"*The Masses* is no longer the resultant of the ideas and art of a number of personalities.

"*The Masses* seems to have developed a 'policy.'

"We propose to get back to the idea of producing a magazine which will be of more interest to the contributors than to anyone else. To this end we propose the following plan:

"The editorial work of *The Masses* to be done by three meetings a month.

"1st—The literary meeting of the contributing editors.

"2nd—The art meeting of contributing editors.

"3rd—A make-up committee meeting.

"The position of 'Editor' and 'Managing Editor' to be abolished.

"The final decision on acceptance and rejection of contributions to rest with the meetings of contributing editors . . .

"All correspondence to be opened by the business office and there answered whenever possible. Letters which cannot be thus satisfactorily answered are to be referred to the meetings . . .

"We must go to our money contributors for just as *little* as possible—form committees or ask for volunteers to do this unpleasant work.

"Let us lift *The Masses* out of the Organized Charity class of drains on the purses of the rich."

Sloan's program was, of course, fantastically impractical; it was the elaboration of a millennial wish. The proposal to "form committees and ask for volunteers" to raise the subsidy was to me— and to John's wife Dolly too—an especially hilarious joke. But the idea of letters, to say nothing of manuscripts and pictures, being systematically and really passed upon by those desultory and delightfully irresponsible "*Masses* meetings" was also hilarious. Sloan was well able to know this. I have a letter from him, written during the summer when he took my place as editor, that I could appropriately have read at that moment. It showed him doing with the pictures, and with things in general, just what any sensible editor is bound to do.

"Dear Max:—

I think the use you suggest for the Coleman drawing is a *good one* —very.

I have the suffragette street meeting drawing ready. It would make a good cover (in my opinion) and would be very *different* . . .

I think the *bunch* should be allowed to smell the viands before they are cooked—this don't mean too many cooks.

In haste with love
John Sloan."

That being Sloan's real nature, I did not have to hide my grin at his blue print for the millennium. He grinned, too, and we argued in good humor the question whether there is such a thing as an "editorial art." We could easily have reached an agreement because we liked and respected each other. But Sloan was, so to speak, retained as a leader by his younger and less successful colleagues, and their grouch against an unappreciative universe was largely concentrated on Floyd and me.

I learned years later that, beyond my hearing, there was a muttering against that "salary" of which I had so proudly boasted to Dr. Jelliffe. It was a hundred and fifty dollars a month, or thirty-five a week—not a munificent reward for raising a subsidy, running a publishing company, and editing a magazine. But after performing these services two years for nothing, I seemed to these hard-up artists to be plunging into a career of robbery and graft at their expense. At least it satisfied their emotions to say so in hushed whispers and, had I been a little wiser, I should have known it would. Generosity retracted is worse than stinginess; it violates the vested rights of the beneficiary. Even Floyd's salary was superfluous in the millennium contemplated by Sloan's program.

However, nothing of this was said at the meeting. After a little amiable discussion of the inherently criminal character of editors, and the indispensability of their crimes, I read my prepared statement as follows:

"With every year since *The Masses* started I have grown more sceptical of the principle of co-operative editing, and at the present time

I am completely disillusioned. I do not believe in it any longer, and I do not want to take part in it any longer.

"I do believe in the principle of co-operative ownership and ultimate control.

"But the editing of a magazine is too complex and continuous to be carried on by a large group meeting occasionally, even if the occasional meetings were attended by the group. In the case of *The Masses,* many of the editors who have given most to the molding of its character are rarely or never present at a meeting. And so all the more in our case the co-operation scheme is a failure.

"Even if I were not convinced by those reasons, however, I would be by this third one, which is that there is not a single point in the public or private policy of this magazine about which its present editors are agreed. Under such circumstances co-operation is a pretense. And the strain of the situation would be too difficult for me, even if I believed in the principle.

"The inevitable consequence of this is that I should offer you my resignation, which I do.

"There is no use pretending, however, that my relation to *The Masses* is as simple as that of a mere employee. You have done us the honor to call your protest against our editorial methods a strike, and while as a point of fact we are the only ones that can strike, because we are the employees, still there is a certain amount of sense in recognizing that I, at least, am in the position of a boss. I am, because you have left it to me to raise the money for your magazine. In doing that you have given me the power to suspend your magazine whenever I want to and whether you want to or not.

"Therefore I want to add to my offer of resignation a statement that if you can find an editor who is willing and able to throw a magazine together without editing it at all, I am willing to try to raise money for him on commission, so long as I can believe in his magazine. I will not do this for nothing.

"If it proves impossible to find such a person, I can think of only three things that you might do.

"1st—You might employ us to edit your magazine for one year, making a contract which enables you to recall us at any time.

"2nd—You might sell *The Masses* to somebody who would invest the money in it, and run it on a basis which would include payment for contributions.

"3rd—You might call *The Masses* a good thing well done and quit.

"I hope there are other alternatives but these are all that I can think of."

This calling to mind of the actual situation in its practical terms had little effect. A suggestion was made, I think by Stuart Davis, that Sloan's plan be adopted in regard to the pictures, but that the literary side be run as before. I said that my statement applied to the text and pictures equally, I would not edit half a magazine.

That being settled, the argument proceeded as before. My three alternatives were not discussed, nor was the problem of running the magazine without me touched upon. The argument continued on the high plane of irrelevance to fact and action. Should we have a policy? Should we have three meetings a month? Would anybody come? Is there an editorial art? Is there in the ideal realm such a thing as an editor or even a managing editor? Should all the eighteen editors answer the mail? Should we depend on subsidies from the rich, or ought such a magazine to be supported by the proletariat? . . .

Never before did the difference between practical and impractical come home to me so strongly. There was no vital difference here except that Floyd and I were confronting the actual job of getting out a magazine. The rest were enjoying ideas in happy detachment from facts. As though my statement had been the intrusion of a child among the serious preoccupations of adults, they ended the meeting by taking a vote on the question whether Sloan's plan should be put into operation or not.

The vote was a tie. In favor: John Sloan, Stuart Davis, Glenn Coleman, Maurice Becker, and Henry J. Glintenkamp. Opposed: Art Young, Floyd Dell, Max Eastman, Mary Heaton Vorse, and Kenneth Chamberlain. Someone remarked that the meeting was too small for a decision in any case. There was not a quorum present —there was not even Bob Brown, whose right to enjoy this ruction would be conceded by all. So we decided to mail Sloan's proposal and my statement to all the members, and call a more urgent meeting.[1]

[1] The contributing editors at that time were: in literature, John Reed, Louis Untermeyer, Howard Brubaker, Mary Heaton Vorse, Robert Carlton Brown, Max Eastman, Arthur Bullard, Floyd Dell, Frank Bohn, William English Walling; in art, John Sloan, Art Young, K. R. Chamberlain, Maurice Becker, Cornelia Barns, Alice Beach Winter, Charles A. Winter, George Bellows, H. J. Glintenkamp, Glenn O. Coleman, Stuart Davis.

Others who were on the staff at one time or another, were: Eugene Wood, Ellis O. Jones, Inez Haynes Gillmore, Horatio Winslow, H. J. Turner, William Washburn

Politics is a habit-forming drug: you can abstain entirely, but if you partake, you are swept along irresistibly to your doom. In my calmer moments I wanted to see *The Masses* go under in this crisis; I wanted to be free. But that tie vote and that fantastically impractical discussion put me in the mood of a race horse. It had the same effect on Floyd. It was sense against nonsense, and sense, by heck, must win. With the help of Art Young, we rounded up fourteen editors for the meeting of April 6, and had proxies in our hands for four more. Sloan's proposal was voted down 11 to 6, and on a motion by Floyd Dell seconded by Dolly Sloan I was re-elected editor by the same vote. It was a meaningless election, for nobody else had offered to take either the responsibility or the job. But it appeased my political passion—the passion was for victory, not power —and it enabled Sloan also, or so I thought, to calm down.

However, Floyd jumped up the moment I announced the vote and moved that Sloan, Davis, Coleman, Brown, and Glintenkamp be dropped from the magazine. The motion was seconded, to everyone's astonishment, by Art Young—the most genial and easy-going, most tolerant-hearted, and also most loved of all the contributing editors. That really was a bombshell, and the whole maneuver a total surprise to me. Maurice Becker leapt from his seat, as though exploded out of a gun, and demanded that his name be added to those to be dropped.

"I accept the amendment," Floyd said sharply.

"I also accept it," Art stated, his face set and his mild eyes burning as no one there had seen them burn before. "To me this magazine exists for socialism. That's why I give my drawings to it, and anybody who doesn't believe in a socialist policy, so far as I go, can get out!"

The silence which followed this Olympian bolt was broken by John Sloan, who produced laughter, if not logic, with a discourse on the relations between a no-policy policy and a socialist policy. I put the question quickly, for I knew it would be lost. It was lost by a vote of 11 to 5. Young's position in the magazine was unique: he was the most ardent propagandist of socialism, and yet his artistic genius and incomparable gift of humor were respected even by the most "arty" of the Bohemians. He was the most faithful contributor,

---

Nutting, Charles W. Wood, Edmond McKenna, G. S. Sparks, John Barber, Robert Minor, Boardman Robinson, Helen Marot, Arturo Giovannitti.

For a month or two after I became editor the following were listed as contributing editors, but they never appeared at a meeting: Hayden Carruth, Thomas Seltzer, Joseph O'Brien, Leroy Scott, Alexander Popini, and B. Russell Hertz.

and he was the oldest. His burst of indignation produced, in consequence, the opposite action from that which he proposed. A contrite feeling, a feeling that "things had gone far enough," took possession of the whole crowd. Instead of throwing out the rebels, we elected them to office: Sloan, vice-president of the company; Coleman, treasurer; Becker to the Board of Directors. Everyone became amiable again, and even, I thought, sensible. We parted like a happy family.

In the next day's mail, however, I received the following letter from somewhere in the deeps of John Sloan's complex nature:

"Dear Max:

'If thy right hand offend thee, cut it off.' This afternoon I played the part of one of the five fingers in the above suggested tragedy, and foolishly resisted amputation. Now, alone at night, I have decided to submit to the operation. I hereby tender my resignation as Contributing Editor of The Masses, as Art Editor of The Masses, and as Vice President of The Masses Publishing Company.

"May The Masses live long and prosper is the rather sincere wish of yours truly,

John Sloan."

Sloan was followed by the artists, Stuart Davis, Glenn Coleman, and Maurice Becker, and the writer Robert Carlton Brown. It looked like quite a crash, and the New York papers, of course, had a grand time over it. One or two of them even tried to understand it. *The Sun*, after kidding us for two columns, concluded with a serious statement from Art Young:

"The dissenting five artists were opposed to 'a policy.' They want to run pictures of ash cans and girls hitching up their skirts in Horatio Street—regardless of ideas—and without title. On the other hand a group of us believe that such pictures belong better in exclusive art magazines. Therefore we put an emphasis on the value of constructive cartoons for a publication like *The Masses*. It's a question of emphasis. For my part, I do not care to be connected with a publication that does not try to point the way out of a sordid materialistic world. And it looks unreasonable to me for artists who delight in portraying sordid and bourgeois ugliness to object to a policy."

The New York *World* was jocular throughout:

"Max Eastman met a reporter at the door of his Washington Square apartment last night clad in pajamas, a raincoat and an ample yawn. 'Nothing to it,' said Max. 'It was just our semi-annual scrap.

We live on scraps. Twenty fellows can't get together to paste up a magazine without scrapping about it. I just decided I'd make it up to suit myself after this.'

"At 9 o'clock John Sloan, wearing a vivid green flannel shirt and an even vivider scarlet necktie, was interviewed in his Washington Place studio. 'It just proves that real democracy doesn't work —yet,' he said, adding the 'yet' as he remembered the future Socialist paradise."

O. O. McIntyre, in his syndicated column, pronounced the benediction:

"Eastman, in a letter to Sloan, says that he will regret the loss of his wit and artistic genius as much as he shall enjoy the absence of his cooperation. And thus the brotherhood of man failed to be ushered in by a little group of serious thinkers who finally fought among themselves as hotly as the Ford peace pilgrims that started out to smother the European war with kisses."

Nothing really failed but a pretense. As I have said, my own delusion that *The Masses* was co-operative expired the day I learned I was to be the goat in the matter of money raising and running the business. I had no hesitation after that in editing the magazine, so far as its peculiar organization permitted, according to my own best judgment. Floyd Dell puts it a little extremely when he says in his autobiography: "I, who tried to get up a rebellion against Max Eastman when I first came on the magazine over some high-handed proceeding of his, had soon become his faithful lieutenant in a practical dictatorship." Since Floyd did not have the job of securing contributions, he sensed less keenly than I the limits of this dictatorship. So far as the contents of the magazine went, our power was purely negative. We had a veto only. We could reject what we did not want, but we could not order what we wanted. The magazine had to be created out of what the editor-owners gave. In that sense the magazine was their production, and to that degree it had no policy.

I was forcefully reminded of this a year later, when I did attempt to commit the editors to a joint position on a public question. I wrote a manifesto against America's entrance into the European war and asked them all to sign it. The answer I received from George Bellows shows that the equivocation on this question of policy was never cleared up.

"Dear Max,

"I decidedly will not sign the enclosed paper, although I am in hearty sympathy with the first paragraph. I am also of the opinion that it would be a hell of a situation if Germany succeeded even a little bit.

"*The Masses* has no business with a 'policy.' It is not a political paper and will do better without any platforms. Its 'policy' is the expression of its contributors. They have the right to change their minds continually, looking at things from all angles.

"In the presence of great, ultimate, and universal questions like

Drawn by George Bellows

"By God, Maria! I believe we've busted this umbrella."

these, it is impossible, at least for me, to know quite where I stand. And I will not sign papers which sound well and then learn later to repent. I think this business is unnecessary and foolish and against the spirit and best interests of *The Masses*.

George Bellows.

"If you go ahead and publish this thing as representing *The Masses*, you must also publish what the non-signers have to say and the names of the signers."

My answer to this letter was brusque, but perhaps not so undiplomatic as it sounds:

"March 20, 1917

"Dear George,

"I dislike the imperial tone of your letter. I don't know whether you are conscious of it or not.

"As to a policy, *The Masses* has certainly as pronounced an editorial policy as any paper in the country and as long as I am the editor and raise money for it, it will have.

Sincerely,
Max Eastman."

Notwithstanding this clash, and his increasingly violent pro-war opinions, George Bellows never resigned from *The Masses*. He stuck through and kept on drawing magnificent pictures for the double page until it was suppressed. Henry J. Glintenkamp, although he had joined in the vote for Sloan's millennium, also did not resign. There was surprisingly little change, considering the noise of the revolt, in either the kind or quality of art in *The Masses*.

To replace the missing artists, we elected Boardman Robinson, Robert Minor, the humorist G. S. Sparks, and the gifted painter John Barber. At this time also Arthur B. Davies began to contribute a wealth of poetic drawings to *The Masses*. Bob Brown we did not replace; he had contributed nothing for six months and was due for removal in any case. The magazine continued, perhaps even with a little more vigor, to combine a socialist policy with a many-sided communication of life. Arturo Giovannitti exclaimed in the July number:

"This paper belongs to the proletariat. It is the recording secretary of the Revolution in the making. It is NOT meant as a foray of unruly truant children trying to sneak into the rich orchards of literature and art. It is an earnest and living thing, a battle call, a shout of defiance, a blazing torch running madly through the night to set afire the powder magazines of the world . . ."

Floyd Dell sums up its policy more circumspectly:

"It stood for fun, truth, beauty, realism, freedom, peace, feminism, revolution."

Drawn by Arthur B. Davies

A MELODY

Chapter 64

My Heroic Deed

PHYSICALLY I was rebounding in the spring of 1916, having been cured of my "peaked" condition by a miracle of common sense. My journey among doctors brought me at last to Evan Evans, a conqueror of science and yet a gentle friend of the human body. After a long talk and a thorough examination, he sat down and said:

"I haven't the ghost of an idea what is the cause of your trouble, but one of the effects is quite obvious—you're undernourished. You're not eating because you're sick, but you're also sick because you're not eating. I can cure the latter condition by a very simple prescription: eat six times a day. Take something like buttermilk or kumiss, or if need be a baby food—whatever digests most easily —at eleven and four and before going to bed. Don't try to eat more at your regular meals, but eat *just as much* as you did before. Do you see? And don't be *afraid* to do it. Never mind how sick it makes you. Crowd it down even if it comes up again. You need nourishment and you've got to have it."

That was one of the major events of my history. My father, I think, was undernourished all his life long, caught in that same vicious circle, and I imagine a lot of tired, thin people are. Within three days I was well, and in a month I had gained fifteen pounds.

On the psychic side I was not doing so well. I spent many solitary days in my house in Croton, happy in thinking of it as mine. Over in Harmon Eugen and Inez had charge of Crown Prince, a famous racing stallion belonging to John E. Milholland. Crown Prince needed to be exercised, and I was invited to ride him whenever I would. It added a lusty and reminiscent joy to the days I spent alone. But I did not spend so many as I might, nor was the house altogether mine. For I still kept bringing Ida and the baby up, and it would be *ours* again. We planted trees and shrubs together. A pink dog-wood from which the baby broke off the largest branch had to be specially cherished.

"Years after we'll show it to Dan and tell him why it grew up lopsided."

There seems to be no armature in me, nothing to withhold me from flowing into the mould of eternal love for half a minute. When Dan and his mother were gone, I was not sentimental about the dog-wood. I was sentimental about meditation in solitude, about free-dom to roam the universe, about infinite possibilities kept brightly open as the only redeemer of the soul from the down-drag of the actual.

It was the moment, if ever, for a beautiful, blithe-hearted, and tender woman to cross my path, but none seemed to be lurking near or to be so venturesome. When staying in Croton alone I would take walks up the road past Mabel Dodge's house, and think some-times how convenient it would be for us both if we fell in love. I went in to see her one evening, and we sat on two sides of the fire, and talked about our friends. We might have got to talking about each other if I had stayed longer, but I was ill at ease. I could not get into a flow of conversation with Mabel, and I dreaded the big blocks of silence. By way of mixing a tribute to her with an excuse to myself, I told her she was a witch and went home early to my own house. I knew she would like to be called a witch, but I did not mean exactly all she thought I did. I give ground before witches not because of their occult powers, but because of their unfruitful cerebration. People seem to me to lack zest for living who have to paint up reality with occult notions in order to get a kick out of it. For me the occult is a plaything—or a fringe of the serious to be investigated—but to make life exciting the actual and potential, the classic and romantic, are enough.

In those days, however, I was dangerously overworking the roman-tic. When not actually at home with wife and child, I was dwelling in dreams of young love as steadily as I had during my junior year which ended in the idyl of Frederica and the infirmary. I was under-going a second adolescence. I remember meeting one day on 34th Street a dark-eyed girl like the St. Anne of Leonardo walking rapidly westward, carrying over her head a vivid little Japanese umbrella. I stopped still because the unconventionality of the act pleased me, and because she was so beautiful. She was by far the most beautiful woman I had ever seen. So I sincerely thought, and I turned mechanically as she passed and walked beside her, believing she must look up and give me a chance, or a genuine impulse, to say something. But she quickened her pace and kept her eyes steadfastly down, and I had no words. All that evening I was tormented with sadness because I had seen the most beautiful woman in America, the one sole being I could utterly love, and had lost her in the crowd!

In a like shy, baffled, boyish way I yearned over the beautiful girls I saw on the stage. For weeks I was in love with three at least of Isadora Duncan's pupils, but especially with Lisa, whose lithe golden beauty in motion was as perfect an embodiment of music in its lightly melodious forms as Isadora was of all music. I have stated elsewhere that Isadora Duncan and her five pupils dancing to the music of a great orchestra produced an exaltation in me that nothing else on the stage has ever equaled. She combined art with nature, restraint with abandon, in the very proportions that bring me the feeling of perfection. But I can not pretend that my emotion about the half-naked bodies of those girls, so simple in their little Greek tunics, so dedicated to nature that their hair hung free, their feet were bare, and their armpits unshaven, was what is called purely aesthetic. I was passionately desirous of them. I was sure, moreover, that with the opportunity to choose, I could find a true-love friend in one of them. Irma, Anna, Lisa—it would be one of those three, and probably Lisa.

But when we went one day to their studio and I actually met them, I could not think of a thing to say. They spoke English imperfectly then, and Ida was there, and Mabel was there; a crowd of radicals— the anti-war party—were there. I only murmured a word of congratulation to Lisa and passed on to the high priestess, toward whom my adoration was indeed quite purely aesthetic. That evening I was sad again with a sense of frustration. If I could only meet a girl like Lisa alone by accident, everything, I was very sure, would turn out well. But I did not possess even in this second and adult adolescence the audacity to scheme up such an accident, still less to go to the girl, propelled frankly by the principle of causation, and ask if I might buy her an ice-cream soda, or even perhaps a drink.

So I would drop back from these obsessing dreams to the home life with Ida and to my now surprisingly comfortable affection for the baby, as one returns to sobriety after a debauch. With a great muster of resolution I would be "realistic"—until some new vision of a nubile beauty tempted and tormented me back to the mood of romance.

While I was thus vaguely staggering between a belated adolescence and a premature dotage, Crystal took her life vigorously in hand and changed it. She broke up her home with Bennie, got a divorce, and married a new lover—all in that same year 1916. Of the dates and details of this process, its pains and anxieties, I knew very little; and she knew as little of the conflict in my will. We had drawn so close in the delusion of felicity that the bitter truth drove us apart. Each wanted to protect the other's fragment of a happiness that had been shared. Only so can I explain our remoteness during this eventful year. Crystal was thinking about a new marriage, and was asking my opinion of her proposed husband, before I perfectly realized that she and Bennie were through.

An Englishman, Walter Fuller, was the proposed husband, and my opinion of him, though on other grounds favorable, was considerably warmed up by the presence of his ravishing sisters. For several years these three young girls, Dorothy, Cynthia, and Rosalinde Fuller, with Walter as impresario, had been bringing English folksongs to America. They were lovely in three different ways and brimming with melody like birds in a bush, and their tours were quite an event in the history of song. Now they were brimming also with enthusiasm for peace, and this brought them into close relations with Crystal. English pacifists were then desperately anxious that America stay out of the war, and Walter gave Crystal, together with his love, ingenious, warm, and witty help in promoting the American Union against Militarism. He supplied that companionship in idealism for which, with pleasure-bent Bennie as a husband, she had been starving.

I could not help thinking how neat it would be if I divorced Ida too and fell in love with Rosalinde. Indeed I did fall in love with Rosalinde whenever she stepped forth from the trio to sing "She's gone with the raggle-taggle gipsies, Oh!" That song made me want to go and take her in my arms and carry her to the extreme rim of the universe. Rosalinde became later a distinguished actress, and many have shared my admiration, but at that time she was very young, and her slim, gay, tender, self-confident grace belonged by right of adequate perception to me. I made a sektch of it in my notebook:

> You give so free advancingly,
> And with a sweet eye-gleam,
> Yourself with every melody,

Your singing motions seem
The essence of all liberty
Poured through you like a stream.

But I did not even try to express it to her. Although she was moving right into my family—or perhaps for that very reason—my shyness toward her and my sense of captivity were completely effective. I did nothing about her sweet eye-gleam. What could I do, after all? What can one do about perfection in the best of circumstances, but destroy it? I turned from Rosalinde and the gipsy dream she awakened—as long ago in an earlier adolescence I had turned from the Ascending Moon—to the "blunt comfort of routine."

In this state of inhibition and dividedness, I went with Ida and the baby to spend another summer in Provincetown. It was the famous summer when we organized the Provincetown Players. My own part in that historic beginning was wilfully slight. At the first meeting I was elected to a committee to draft a constitution, but I saw other committees and boards of directors looming behind it. Recalling my boyhood technique of pretending to be impractical, I failed to remember when the committee was to meet. Jack Reed brought the draft to show me, and my contribution consisted of saying: "I think that's swell!" I did play the part of Lancelot in Floyd Dell's charming comedy, *King Arthur's Sox,* but that was later when the Players had moved to MacDougal Street in New York. In Provincetown I did little but pay my dues and stroll around the wharf sometimes at rehearsals.

This almost cost me my life one day—this and the attitude of kid brother that I instinctively took toward Jack Reed's prowess. He came over in a bathing suit and climbed up to the peak of our fish-house theatre, and dived off into the bay. The wharf was high, and the fish house higher, and he reaped quite a reward of admiration for a casual and graceful dive. It became necessary for me to climb up there the next day and dive from the same height. It was only a little higher than I had gone from the rocks in the glen, but at that height a little is a lot, and in my preoccupation with the effort of will, I failed to notice that the tide was running out. My dive, although nobody saw it—for I was not showing off, but only fulfilling an inward necessity—was very artistic. But my joy in the deftly cleft water was brief, for I hit the hard sand bottom in the same position in which I had hit the water. My body floated up only half conscious, drifted dimly for some moments, and finally paddled its way to shore and crawled up the beach like a half-drowned cat. For several days I could not move my head or any muscle in my back without excruciating pain, and I judge that two inches less of water, a few minutes more of pumping up my courage, would have been too much for those muscles.

John Reed was a steadying influence to me—though he would be the most surprised to hear me say it. Not that he had stability, but he was more easefully daring than I, more instinctively belligerent. He did not have to fall back so often, in the class war we were waging, on naked resolution. He actually liked battle; he liked dust and smoke—he liked the town! One day during that year 1916 he called up and asked permission to dedicate a volume of poems to me. I stammered a yes that must have sounded more abashed than complimented. I remember thinking I had been impolite, and wondering if he would understand. His understanding was subtle—his dedication, when it appeared, proved to be a celebration of this very difference between us. He had turned that squeamish timorousness which made me admire him extravagantly into a cause of his admiring me.[1]

Jack lived almost directly across the street from us that summer, he and his red-cheeked, freckled, grey-eyed Irish bride from Oregon, Louise Bryant. Although it was *The Masses* that brought them together—Louise had been sending us prodigious bundles of subscriptions before he ever discovered her—the home they made never seemed to draw me in except as to a spectacle. They employed as "chief cook and bottle washer" the long-haired, owl-eyed, irrepressibly intellectual, and conscientiously irresponsible anarchist, Hippolyte Havel. Another colorful anarchist frequently to be found there was Terry Carlin. These men used their belief in anarchism, as artists often use their talents, to justify a loafer's life. Terry was a thin, dark, handsome, hawklike type, with firm chin and austere cheekbones, who had decided in his penniless youth that he would never do a stroke of work and was sticking to it with the determination of a Navajo brave. Hippolyte was roly-poly by comparison, a tiny large-eyed revolutionary doll with subtle sweetness and a bewitching smile, who outwitted work instead of attacking it head on. Louise herself was no housekeeper, and their place was barnlike in its physical aspect. A large assortment of interesting males was provided with abundant nutrition, however, and beds to sleep on: Bobby Rogers,

[1] The poem seems to me one of his best, and although this book proves that I do not deserve it, I have placed it in the appendix, page 594.

David Carb, red-headed Bobby Jones with his gaunt white saintly face; Eugene O'Neill, darkly handsome but sombre and sallow as a down-and-outer brought to Jesus by the Salvation Army; Fred Boyd, the dry precise little English Marxist who had publicly recanted his extreme words when arraigned for incitement to riot in the Paterson strike. Fred was leading Jack's eager mind beyond *The Masses* editorials into the absolute Calvin-logic of Marxian fundamentalism, getting him ready, though no man knew it then, to understand the bolsheviks in Russia.

Ida and I felt more at home a stone's throw down the street in the other direction, where Jig Cook and Susan Glaspell had just bought a tiny house with a yard. Jig was always to be seen digging or hammering in that yard, while Susan inside with her pen was earning their living. A husky, brown-skinned farmer, you would call Jig Cook, with hotly glowing eyes under his greying hair, and Susan an overtired but sweetly conscientious farmer's wife. An atmosphere of Christian conservatism, a quiet piety, brooded over their white New England house with its pure white little fence. You were surprised to learn that the striped cat on the fencepost was called "Copycat," and still more that his full name was "Carnal Copulation." But they would surprise you all the way to The Temple, this Jig and Susan, they were so good, so sensible, so midwestern, yet so devotedly determined to escape from Davenport, Iowa, and live a high and un-Philistine kind of life. I could not share that zeal for social creativeness that made Jig such a dynamo in the Provincetown Players; it was explained, I thought, by his abstract wish to be a genius combined with an inability to retire into a lonely corner and get down to concrete work. But it made him a lovable and thrilling director, and he created a stage, at least, for the lonely and highly individual art of Eugene O'Neill. Jig's fervent admiration of the ancient Greeks I did share; and I added my bit to the nostalgia that carried him back finally to the mountain slopes near Delphi to end his days teaching the peasants to produce the plays of Aeschylus and Sophocles.[2]

Ida and I lived in a small white house that turned its back on the main street in order to face the bay. I remember that a little flag walk ran along beside the house, close under the windows, to bring you to the front porch. But of the inside of that house, or of anything that

[2] My use of the word "Temple" above was an allusion to the book in which Susan described Jig's life as a mounting toward this act of romantic devotion to the classic age. She called it *The Road to the Temple*.

existed or took place within it, I have no image or recollection. It stands like a sealed vault on the highway as I move back and forth among the brightly peopled memories of that summer. I only know that while living there I finished the poem of rejection which I had begun years ago when Ida and I were first drawing together. I was convinced of its thesis now, and I called it "Fire and Water."

> Flame-Heart, take back your love. Swift, sure
> And poignant as the dagger to the mark,
> Your will is burning ever; it is pure.
> Mine is vague water welling through the dark,
> Holding all substances—except the spark.
>
> Picture the pleasure of the meadow stream
> When some clear striding naked-footed girl
> Cuts swift and lucid as a morning gleam
> Across its bosom, ambling and aswirl
> With mooning eddies and soft lips acurl.
>
> Such was our meeting—fatefully so brief.
> I have no purpose and no power to clutch.
> Gleam onward, maiden, to your goal of grief;
> And I more sadly flow, remembering much,
> Yet doomed to take the form of all I touch.

I know further that as a result of the sorrows of that summer, Ida decided to go away on the first of September. She would visit some friends in Maine before going back to New York, and I could try living alone with Dan. I think she went away to see if she could get a hold on life without me. It was a very quiet decision, a matter-of-fact departure such as one might make if going out on an errand, or if going for good. I experienced a relief as though I were indeed a fluid expanding after having been compressed to an artificial rigidity. But alas, I also experienced, when the night fell, that dizzy and morti-fied fear and wither of self-distrust which never dies, but only sleeps awhile sometimes, in my breast. I wrote Ida a yearningly affection-ate letter, but received no reply, and so poured out my orphaned feelings in another poem:

> You make no answer. You have stolen away
> Deliberately in that twilight sorrow
> Where the dark flame that is your being shines
> So well. Mysterious and deeply tender

In your motion you have softly left me,
And the little path along the house is still.
And I, a child forsaken of its mother,
I, a pilgrim leaning for a friend,
Grow faint, and tell myself in terror that
My love reborn and burning shall yet bring you,
More than friend and slender-bodied mother,
O sweet-passioned spirit, shining home.

I am afraid it was only a short few hours after choking with this sincere emotion that I went over to take a tango lesson from a dark-eyed Beatrice who was pretending to be a sculptor in a near-by studio. The tango lesson had been agreed upon in Ida's presence, but its character was now subtly and completely changed. It was the "accident" I had been yearning for, and Bee was the dream girl fate had been withholding from my arms so long. I can not describe to you how beautiful she became, for this earth contains nothing to compare it with. Suffice it to say that I fell passionately and very superficially in love with Bee, and I have rarely reveled in anything in my life more than I then reveled in being superficial. I was all taken up with it. I wooed her with a declaration of inconstancy, comparing myself again to fluids, to the wind, the waves, the tide—

A mountain in its motion,
Forever homing to the land,
And ever to the ocean.

I called her attention to the way of the ripples with the prows of ships that "slip along so slenderly."

I would as lightly touch your lips,
And your heart as tenderly,
If you would move with all that move,
The flowing and caressing,
Who have no firmness in their love,
No sorrow in its passing.

I sang her a "Rainy Song" when we went walking among the scrub oaks and got caught by a thunderstorm, begging her to laugh with me,

The happy sweet laughter of love without pain,
Young love, the strong love, burning in the rain.

But that was not the way to woo a straying daughter of the American bourgeoisie—not until the next decade. She would not move, she would not laugh. It all seemed wedding-bell serious to her, a sin to kiss a fluid lover even in the rain.

So all I achieved was to stir my adolescent passions up to a painful tension and outrage Ida's feelings. For though I tried to be discreet, she naturally heard from kind friends—and in no kindly light— about my "affair" with "this girl." It was a real friendship, and its honest shallowness enabled me to feel songfully whole-hearted, a thing I could not feel in the delving whirlpools of all-and-forever love.

I was soon back in those whirlpools, however, for Ida, notwith-standing her outraged feelings, had failed to get a hold on life alone. Two things combine to make almost unbreakable the force uniting a man and woman who have made a home together tenderly. Each has become the other's child, and each has become the other's parent. Freudians see only one strand of this double binding-cord. I was held firmly by them both, but more and more it was a feeling of parental responsibility, an acute and probably exaggerated sense of the blank universe in which she would be left a waif if we parted, that bound me to Ida. Sometimes we yearn to live another's sorrow, because it actually pains us more in sympathetic imagination that it would in reality. Reality, to a poet at least, is a kind of sedative.

Moreover, as I grew strong in the determination to be myself, returning to the high mood of my last years in college, Ida was becoming the infirm, the divided one. She it was now who did not know what she wanted. That automatic gear shift from love to hate, first manifested in her letter and telegram from Provincetown in the summer of 1914, was beginning to operate frequently and smoothly. So long as she was having a passion and getting a response from me, she seemed hardly to care, or even to know, whether the passion was love or hate.

She did not return to Provincetown, but went straight to New York where we had taken an apartment at 118 Waverly Place—by chance, or unhappy intention, the very apartment in which Crystal and I had last lived together. I brought the baby there, and rented a little attic study for myself three blocks away on West 10th Street. Ida too had a studio of her own, for she had made a new turn from birth-control agitation to sculpture as her career. I tried earnestly to believe that this was a robust and real decision, and meant for her the surest of life's blessings, an interest that does not depend on any person.

But my wishful belief collapsed dreadfully at our first meeting in that studio, for she had made no stroke or gesture with the clay, and confessed that she had no interest in anything at all. She wept humbly and bitterly—a more terrible thing than her anger—and seemed wholly to have lost the will to live. Hitherto I had done most of the crying, having inherited this much at least of my grandfather's oratorical genius. Indeed I would cry sometimes in solitude, or pour out on paper baby words that were as formless as tears. But they would relieve me, and I would fall asleep and wake up the next morning full of joy in the astonishing gift of an opportunity to live. For her no such healing at dawn. For her to eternity this immovable and implacable black-marble attitude and inward enterprise of grief. It awakened again in me the Sense of Guilt and made me ashamed of that superficiality about which I had been so jauntily singing. I became a child again as well as a parent and, notwithstanding the attic room and the house by the side of the road, 118 Waverly Place became my home. I even learned, to my astonishment, to make up bunny-rabbit stories for my baby, and came within an ace of finding pleasure in this strange and strenuous kind of hard work.

I do not mean to say that my new-found adolescence got lost altogether, but I was absorbed in my writing and not continually yearning for the Divine Accident that should bring a radiantly beautiful girl-friend to my arms. The failure of my seashore songs to get Bee into a state of aqueous motion had rather damped my faith in the fruits of such an accident even if it came. And when it did come, I was not ready with belief. I was not free enough, not juvenile-romantic enough in my heart, to receive it.

It came at *The Masses* ball, which was held in Tammany Hall, of all places, on December 15, 1916. Fate, in preparing its path, made firm in Ida's heart a whimsical decision not to go. Those *Masses* balls were gay and tumultuous affairs where all bars against "Greenwich Villageism" were let down. They were a reflection, within the frame of American morals, of the "Quatz' Arts" ball in Paris, and many curious visitors came down from the upper bourgeoisie to see them. Among the curious on this occasion was John Fox, Jr., whom I had never seen since the dinner at Mrs. Belmont's four years back when he chipped in a thousand dollars toward *The Masses*. He brought with him a rising movie star, Florence Deshón, who had just made a hit in *The Beloved Vagabond*. It was not this time a romantic notion of mine, but a fact—in the opinion, at least, of distinguished authorities—that she was the most beautiful woman in America. And she was vivid-minded too, and though reckless of knowledge, startling in her intelligence. She had the ghost of a pout, the merest suggestion of something sulky and wanton in her beauty, and in her opinions correspondingly a note of mutiny.

We danced together while John Fox sat at a table sipping highballs and looking on in a grandfatherly manner. We talked fervently as we danced, and our minds flowed together like two streams from the same source rejoining. She was twenty-one and was in exactly that state of obstreperous revolt against artificial limitations which I had expressed in my junior and senior essays at college. Even in my impulse against patriotism, a form of idealism that is surprisingly rare in the history of man, she outran me in our conversation, describing with happy laughter how she had almost caused a riot in a theatre by refusing to stand up when they played the "Star Spangled Banner."

"What do I care about a flag? I'm living in the world, not a country!" she exclaimed. And there was no zealotry in the exclamation, just a joyous overflowing of bounds.

I walked rather dizzily home in the dawn from the fourth *Masses* ball. I went to sleep believing that I had miraculously found what all young men forever vainly dream of, the girl who is at once ravishingly beautiful and admirable to what lies deepest in their mind and spirit. At noon, when I woke up in my own home, I realized that this could hardly be true. To prove it was not true, I remembered a certain unmanageable excess and impetuosity in her judgments which troubled what is Greek in my nature. No one person could really fulfill the ideals of another. Besides, she was John Fox's girl, and here was I, the husband of a proud wife, the father and dutiful teller of bunny-rabbit stories to a four-year-old baby. I kept the telephone number at 49 East 34th Street where she lived with her mother—I kept it very carefully—but I did not use it. Shyness, the dread of disillusionment, the inhibiting weight of Ida's emotions, my sense of guilt, my deep affection for Ida—I could not keep on forever going away and then coming back to her—all these things held me in a tight circle that I called "reality." There was no place in it, obviously, for pure romance.

There was, however, one thing in that circle that I rejected with my undivided self—that was the increasingly frequent storms of anger it contained. When two lovers are drifting apart, the rate of movement can rarely be equal, and the one who is moving more slowly, the one who is "getting left," will usually fall madly in love again. It is a love made largely of injured pride and the child's stubborn craving for what is escaping his reach. But it does not so clothe itself in consciousness. It wears the garments of a sublime passion. Hence almost all breakups and separations, no matter how needful to both parties, are one-sided and tragic. It was so with ours.

To the last I think I treasured Ida's qualities more than she mine, but I was the one who was gaining independence, and hence her feelings increased in force.

Not only was my having another address an injury to her amour-propre, but the poise and composure I derived from it was irritating, I imagine, beyond endurance. Her love had to upset that composure and could do it most easily by turning into rage. I remember once when Ida came over to my attic room to ask about some plan for dinner. Sid Wood was there, and as she walked out, she was seized with a sense of the ignominy of her position, that she had to climb up six flights of stairs to ask her husband where he would be living that evening. She left some bitterly sarcastic remark to this effect behind her as she went down the hall, and Sid said:

"Max, we've got to get you out of this!"

It was the first intimation I had that friends were aware of my emotional predicament, the first birth of a feeling that my trouble with Ida had two sides, and that somebody was on my side. Sid had been talking to Crystal; that is what he meant by "we." Though unforgettably affected by this, I made no answer, and it was neither Sid nor Crystal in whom I finally confided.

Once more, and for the last time, my fate was swerved by that of the beautiful Amazon, Inez Milholland. She was a flower of the late spring; her beauty was too lush and large veined, too moistly gorgeous like the bloom of the marsh mallow, to last through the summer's heat. I never could imagine her passing beyond youth—it was something for which nature had neglected to prepare her blood —and I was not overwhelmingly shocked when she died. She had insisted, in spite of a mysterious weakness, on fulfilling a series of lecture engagements across the country. In Los Angeles, in the midst of a lecture, she collapsed and fell to the floor. Eugen was there, and he carried her home to their hotel to die of what was discovered to be pernicious anaemia.

"Shall I come with you?" he asked, sitting by her deathbed.

And she whispered: "No, you go ahead and live another life."

Eugen telegraphed me on his way back to New York, and expressed a desire to see me. I was for some reason the one to whom chiefly he wanted to talk. He told me that after Inez died, her fundamentalist father came in by the bedside and wanted to pray for her soul. To him this was a "sacrilege," and he described how almost by main force he had put the man out of their room. It led to a conversation about all things and all the values of things. I was released from my "sentimental reticence"—the death of truth-telling Inez released me —and I began at last to entrust my inmost preoccupations to another mind.

Eugen did not advise me to leave Ida; he did no more than listen to the deep truth I delved up from my experience, and respond with what he could surely find in his. As I have said, a pseudo-scientific jargon stood between me and Dr. Jelliffe, a mystic notion that knowledge is of something behind and beyond the facts. We never in any simple and real sense came together. But Eugen had, besides an understanding of psychoanalysis and a grateful tolerance of its vagaries, a keen sense of fact, a distaste for mystification, an honesty of mind that seemed to me, and still seems, heroic. To the normally communicative I am only saying, I suppose, that Eugen became my intimate friend. He was, however, my first intimate friend, and I was thirty-three years old.

Eugen took an apartment on the second floor at 12 East 8th Street. It had an extra room, and he proposed that I give up my narrow garret, which was chilly now and less conveniently near to Waverly Place, and come and use that room as my secondary dwelling. It struck me as a most natural, and not in the least revolutionary thing to do. But it was a final blow to Ida's pride.

"It's all right for you to have another room alone," she said very calmly, "but if you are going to live with somebody else, you can't live with me."

I did not argue with her, nor suggest compromise or accommodation. I intended to take the room with Eugen; I was sure of that. A force of character descended into me as surprisingly as on the day when I gathered up my books and ran out of the little schoolhouse on Chapel Street. I said:

"All right, Ida, then I won't come back."

Like other candid heroes, I must confess that I was scared to death. My extremities were cold, my limbs trembling, and in my solar plexus was a vacuum with the weight of lead. Nevertheless, I got my hat and coat, my toothbrush and safety razor, the razor Ida had just given me for Christmas; we said a friendly and even affectionate farewell; and I actually opened the door and, at a concrete, definite, and inexorable moment in time, walked down the stairs and away from my "friend and slender-bodied mother" forever. It took more courage than anything else I ever did.

Chapter 65

My Life Begins . . .

I SAID there are two strong ties binding people who have lived tenderly together, but there is a third: homesickness. I do not know any psychologist who has treated this force adequately. A stall is a mere square of space, yet a horse yearns to it with all his mettle; at any hour he will quicken his pace if you turn his head toward home. And man is more anciently and surely a nesting animal. To be in his nest, and belong there, is to be a part of his safety and self-assurance.

I got the full strength of this gravitative force. For the room I had moved into was vacant of all but a bed, a chair, and a table; Eugen had plunged into a business venture to drown his sorrow and never came home except for a few hours' sleep; and I fell ill with the flu on the first day after my heroic deed. I had to lie abed with a fever in that bare lonely barrack for a week. Crystal would bring or send food over, and Dr. Lorber would drop in to assure me I was not going to die. But otherwise I had to take my heroism straight.

To emphasize my outcast condition, Dan's bland, putty-colored nurse brought him to call on me every afternoon, and I had to rise up in bed and try to explain in words of one syllable why I did not live with him any more. On her second visit she dumped unceremoniously on the bare floor a house-coat and some neckties and other personal odds and ends that I had left at Ida's in my sudden departure. To my febrile eyes those worn things lying on the hard polished floor looked like the refuse of a dead man. I felt that I had been dumped out with the junk. And I knew intuitively—what came to me later by a hundred roads—that Ida's love had turned into hostility. She seemed to regard me with abhorrence from the moment I walked out of her house until she fell in love with someone else. Then I heard that she had spoken kindly of me.

This is perhaps an oversimplification of her soul's workings, and should be taken as a fact in my experience rather than hers. To me her contemptuous hostility, freely enough expressed so that I met echoes of it at every turn, was a horrifying surprise. We had parted with words of understanding affection, on which I relied and in which, more than I knew, my morale rested. It made my hair stand on end—I can hardly express it in less physical terms—to learn that my bosom friend had become an enemy. Nothing in my childhood or youth had prepared me for a world in which such things might happen. Friends tried to comfort me, and I suppose they tried to shake Ida's fixed attitude of fury. An intervention by the warm-hearted poet, Sara Bard Field—her friend more than mine—enabled me to ease my heart of some of its anguish. But it turned out I had said things to Sara which inflamed Ida all the more. Nothing can be said, nothing can be done, no squirming can help you, when love turns to rage. Jonathan Edwards was not crazy when he pictured God, who "so loved the world," holding those who failed to return his love like scorched, writhing spiders on a celestial toaster over the flames of hell, refusing even to drop them in until his wrath was assuaged.

Other futile efforts were made to civilize our separation. I remember Lincoln Steffens coming to my room with his trivial philosophy and large kindness, so large a kindness that I feel compunction now for the harsh truths I spoke about him in a previous chapter.

"Why don't you try hating her, Max?"

"I don't know how, Steff. I honestly don't know how."

Perhaps, at some sacrifice of pride, I can convey this phase of my life, and conclude it, by showing the reader one of those unseemly verbal sobbings that I would pour out sometimes on a sheet of paper within reach of my bed.

> O my sweet mother child
> My slender and impassioned friend of years.
> Body of dark beauty
> Soul of darker flame
> Intolerant and terrible in pain
> And tender as the bending moon
> In beauty over me in friendliness.
> Love I have wounded,
> Hear in your bitter hatred,

Hear my cry for one brief tender memory
Of me.

O Ida, O my love, my mother, my child, my friend,
I am in the last utter anguish of loneliness for you.
Thoughts die in my mind, words on my tongue.
My breast is stifled with the anguish of this black gulf
    of the death of love between us.
O my soul cries to you—there are no words—
Give me some touch, some token of a tender motion in
    your heart.
No, it is dark,
It is the awful blank and bitterness of death that aches
    between us.
We could not live
We could not die together.
There is nothing—
It is done.

These storms of feeling did not have much momentum, and they soon ceased to recur. Shamefully soon, I used to think, but I think otherwise now. I was not a cornfield, but a field of young oats, and the blast could not blow that would lay my tassels down for many days.

Herman Lorber came in one morning with a solemn and very earnest piece of advice. Ida was in such a condition that at whatever cost to my feelings I would have to let her take the baby to herself and give up for a long time trying to see him. His arguments were weighty and would have convinced a more fanatical lover of children than I. To me they brought a sentimental sorrow which stayed with me, or would be wafted over me occasionally, for some years. I expressed it once in a stanza:

Sometimes a child's voice crying on the street
Comes winging like an arrow through the wind
To pierce my breast with you, my baby, and
My pen is weak, and all my thinking dreams
Are mist of yearning for the touch of you.

Aside from these moments, however, I must confess that to learn on the authority of the family physician that parental irresponsibility was to be my moral duty did not overwhelm me. I wanted no connections with Ida after I learned of her hostility; I wanted never to think again about the years we spent together. This impulse of obliteration was a thousand times stronger, how sad soever it may be, than any sense of identity with or attachment to my child.

I wrote Dan a letter and put it away to be delivered when he grew up—one of those ritual performances which emotion demands and time laughs at. The letter will be delivered when he reads it in this book.

"Dear Dan, I have given you up to your mother completely because the fact that I do not love her has hurt her beyond measure, and the only thing I have that I can give her to make up for it is my absence from her life. She can be at peace forgetting me and loving you. And so though I love you and long for you, and I have cried in the night for the sound of your voice, and your wonderful endless questions that I would answer, and for the trusting of your little hand in mine—I have given it up until she is healed. It is more right that her suffering heart should have peace than even that you and I should be the happy friends that we were.

"Someday you will read this—and perhaps you will resent my calling your hand little! But you will understand, and if I am here then, we will be friends. I love you, Dan, and I never forget you.

Max."

Convalescence is a joyous thing, an eager, happy, hungry state like another childhood. And I was convalescing not only from influenza, but from a disease of conflict that for five-and-a-half years had dimmed and damped my soul. I was feeling again, in sudden uncaused waves, the ineffable joy that floods the heart with the thought of times and places still unexplored. No inward arm reached out any longer to strangle this joy. No matter how much or how often I had to pay for it in childish terrors, moral qualms, or the mere frantic hunger to gallop home, I was free. The future was open. I might do anything. Anything might happen. Whether you call it noble or despicable, sin or salvation, health or neurosis, that thought is as needful to me as God is to the devout. Indeed I could not describe except in the language of ecstasy the feeling of being reborn, the freshly kindled verve and ardor that like a visible radiation sharpened the angles of my little square room, making its mere empty dimensions an exciting fact, its plain oak door the entrance to a paradise of possible experience.

If you find it hard to understand this pagan, abstract, unfurnished, and irrational religion of life's adventure, you will find it still harder to believe that pure luck could have brought through that plain oak door and into my heart's open chambers a perfect fulfillment of it, a beautiful and similarly gipsy-hearted friend whom I cherish with romantic ardor after thirty years. I should not say luck, truly, for it was Crystal's unfailing concern to get up happiness for other people that brought it to pass. I had never especially mentioned Rosalinde to Crystal, nor had Rosalinde mentioned me. But she knew us both. She knew that Rosalinde was just on the edge of opening like a tulip into thirsty bloom, and I was lying there tossed between compunction and exaltation. What she did, moreover, was the most innocent thing in the world. She said:

"Rosalinde, won't you go over and find out whether Max is well enough to come to dinner?"

So, after all, it was only my sister-in-law who came through the door; she had walked only two blocks to get there; and the message she brought was most casual. Her eyes, however, were incredibly blue, and their lashes were like petals of an aster; her cheeks glowed brightly against a dark fur, and her lips and teeth as she spoke shone red and white like the halves of a fresh winter apple. My heart was beating violently before she reached my bedside, and she was trembling when she touched my brow.

So many cynical things are said about passionate embraces that do not consecrate themselves in life-union that I feel like advertising, at the expense of modesty, the jewel of inconstant, intermittent, irresponsible, and yet indestructible love that was born that day. Rosalinde was going away two days later on a long tour, and I did not see her again for several years. Our love has been like a mountain brook that trickles a little way glistening from its source, and then disappears under the earth and under a leafy and luxuriant forest, but after a while emerges in the valley and flows with increasing volume, still glistening joyfully, all the way to the sea.

Even in those brief and rather bashful first hours of our friendship, Rosalinde was of great moment to me because her joy in life is unwounded with fear and compunction. I needed to be reassured that my avid thirst of experience, and my belief in the freedom to have it, were not abnormal and base. I needed to find flowerlike beauty and exquisite fineness of stem and of spirit in a friend who shared my thirst and went all the way with me in my belief. It was as though God sent a young angel direct to my bedside to explain how the saints had misunderstood Him.

Even my editorials seemed to take flame and take vital force from my joy in possessing myself again. My own reconquest of freedom fanned up my zeal to extend it to all men. And though my "scientific basis" had got lost, I was still confidently expounding the method of progress towards liberty.

"We are not advocates of violence," I wrote in the January 1917 *Masses,* 'but as between two current misfortunes we much prefer domestic to international violence. For in domestic violence it usually happens that some definite benefit is being fought for, and not infrequently the fighting holds a possibility of gaining the benefit; whereas in international wars the fighting usually arises at the bidding of blind tribal instincts wholly maladjusted to the present real world, and even where concrete ends are aimed at, they are habitually lost in a welter of patriotic emotions before the war ends."

There was enough dynamite in that sentiment, published but three months before our entrance into the First World War, to keep me busy for two years trying to stay out of jail. It lined me up with the IWW and the left wing of the Socialist Party in a war against war which was to be put down ruthlessly—by judicial and police action and action of unpoliced mobs. At the same time, I stood firm in my own struggle with socialist dogma as to the cause of war and its cure.

"War is death to liberty, and death to the struggle for liberty. At whatever cost we must avoid war. . . . There is more than that, however. I think that men's hereditary instinctive reactions are such that they will go to war (even against their economic interest) whenever a plausible war is declared, that our only hope is in *preventing declarations of war,* that this can be accomplished only through international federation, and that the main driving power toward international federation is international capital—the biggest of big business. We ought to support and encourage the capitalistic governments in their new motion toward internationalism because they will get there before we will . . . We ought to help business stop war."

With that heresy to defend on the left, and on the right the war fever rising, and my gorge rising recklessly against it, I was being pushed perilously near to a position of leadership. The impression got abroad that I was a man of consecrated force and singleness of purpose. *The Masses* became a kind of spearhead for the native American resistance to our intervention in the European war. It had not the prestige of *The Nation*, or the literary self-consciousness of *The Seven Arts*, but it had a muscular force and gusto, and a home in the hearts of the downright rebels that gave it another kind of precedence.

Considering the prominence of Karl Marx in my theoretical foundations, there was a good deal of Jesus in my fulminations against war. My gorge rose particularly against bloodthirsty ministers. By some miracle of magnanimity or modesty, our new great cartoonist, Boardman Robinson, enjoyed having me suggest ideas for his drawings, and we cracked down on the war-mongering Christians in hammer blows that Thor himself might have envied. The art of drawing rarely rose higher, in my opinion, than in his *Masses* cartoons of this period. If America has pride of culture, they will never be lost. His double page of January 1917, representing Christ and the disciples at supper, has kinship with the greatest religious pictures of the past. That Judas happens to wear the vestments of a contemporary Episcopal bishop is astonishingly incidental now. In a different way I called it incidental then.

"It is not this rector," I wrote, "but that institution as a whole, both Protestant and Catholic, that has betrayed its Master, and delivered him into the hands of the enemy . . . We say again: the Church is Judas Iscariot."

I will quote one more editorial to show how brash and lusty my opinions were in those days: it was a greeting to the creation in America of an "Academy of Arts and Letters":

"Some time ago Congress passed a law making 100 American men of letters and artists immortal. It was an emergency bill, for most of them would soon have been dead otherwise. President Lowell of Harvard, Hadley of Yale, Butler of Columbia, Professor Brander Matthews, Robert Underwood Johnson, Professor William Milligan Sloane—to mention a few who never wrote a line that the public has any recollection of—and Professor Barrett Wendell who wrote a text book in English Composition, are among the undying.

We can understand the selection of professors and editors and other hangers-on of literature to be rescued from oblivion by process of law. But why the college presidents? If they can not get into the scientific societies on the strength of the money they raise, why call it literary? And why waste a membership on Theodore Roosevelt who will be immortal in spite of his literature, having been the only entirely male citizen in a nation of mollycoddles and college sissies? Why throw a life-belt to a man who is already on the raft? . . ."

Notwithstanding this gay militance, I did not share the illusion that I might become a leader. That tempting notion, first introduced by my mother, has turned up several times in the course of my life, calling me from my natural preoccupations, but I always shut the door quickly when I saw who was there. A leader has to love the battle, not just believe in it. He has to be loyal to an organization, not only to an idea. Purpose must be the core of him—not poetry, not truth-seeking. The sole time when I feel as right as a compass is when I am building reality into a poem, or defining with exactitude my perception of a truth. Every other obligation seems incidental and unimportant then. Truth, more-

The front row at the first meeting of the American Academy of Arts and Letters, at the Ritz-Carlton hotel, New York City, November, 1916. Reading from left to right, Hamlin Garland, John Burroughs, Robert Underwood Johnson, Monsieur Lanson, Member of the French Institute, Edwin Howland Blashfield, and the bravest literary man in the world, author of that classic essay: "If a Man Slaps Your Wife's Face, What Will You Do?"

over, is an embryonic thing to be developed mainly by experiment, and experiment requires suspense of judgment; it requires doubt. Doubt too is ruled out for a man who gets pushed into a position of revolutionary leadership; he must be dead sure he is right. If wrong he may be praised afterward as "the prophet of an unfulfilled hope," who by "battling in a cause never vindicated . . . demonstrated the utility of an enthusiastic error." But he can not himself know or suspect while battling that this may be his justification. In devising that eulogy for Bruno's misdirected ardor in my graduating essay, I had proven my own unfitness for a leader's role. Of this I became more and more clearly aware as I grew in self-knowledge and knowledge of the world.

I began in the days about which I am writing to prepare a new volume of poems, and in its preface, deprecating the fact that most of them reflected "my own too easy taste of freedom rather than my sense of the world's struggle toward an age and universe of it," I wrote:

"That struggle has always occupied my thoughts, and often my energies, and yet I have never identified myself with it or found my undivided being there. I have found that rather in individual experience, and in those moments of energetic idleness when the life of universal nature seemed to come to its bloom of realization in my consciousness. Life is older than liberty. It is greater than revolution. It burns in both camps. And life is what I love. And though I love life for all men and women, and so inevitably stand in the ranks of revolution against the cruel system of these times, I love it also for myself. And its essence—the essence of life—is variety and specific depth. It can not be found in monotonous consecration to a general principle. Therefore I have feared and avoided this consecration, which earnest friends for some reason always expect me to exemplify . . ."

After I got well, and Rosalinde so swiftly disappeared out of the scene, I went up to my house in Croton to live. My room at Eugen's had served its purpose; I could enjoy my freedom better in my own house and in the country. Besides, I had decided finally and once for all to be a poet, a decision which often precedes the birth of a brief poem in my mind. My poem was the very extreme opposite of a love-song. In fancy I saw a woman past her youth reclining under a willow beside a stream where she had been bathing, and in her nakedness longing for a lover. I spoke, to console her, my own disillusionment with love:

THE LONELY BATHER

Loose-veined and languid as the yellow mist
That swoons along the river in the sun,
Your flesh of passion pale and amber-kissed
With years of heat that through your veins have run,

You lie with aching memories of love
Alone and naked by the weeping tree,
And indolent with inward longing move
Your slim and sallow limbs despondently.

If love came warm and burning to your dream,
And filled you all your avid veins require,
You would lie sadly still beside the stream,
Sobbing in torture of that vivid fire;

The same low sky would weave its fading blue,
The river still exhale its misty rain,
The willow trail its waving over you,
Your longing only quickened into pain.

Bed your desire among the pressing grasses;
Lonely lie, and let your thirsting breasts
Lie on you, lonely, till the fever passes,
Till the undulation of your longing rests.

That was my first utterance in solitude. That was the point of view to which my experience with Ida and my new adolescence had brought me. I was not sorry that Rosalinde had been torn so abruptly by circumstance out of my arms; I was glad. I considered myself dedicated to a hermit's life—with occasional interludes—for many years to come. I would marry my art, my science, my evangel of liberty—that would be enough.

Just out of fidelity, however, to the underlying dogma that life must be adventurously lived, I did, in a mood of Calvinistic self-discipline, push myself into a telephone booth and ring the number that had been given me a month before by the radiant movie star, Florence Deshon, at the *Masses* ball. By that act my dedication was disrupted, my point of view exploded, my "misty rain" shattered into starlight, and the whole temper and tenor of my being changed.

Florence had, besides that mixture of the sculpturesque and the wayward which made her beauty so startling, a richly melodious voice. Her laughter was a riotous tumble of jewelly tone-qualities poured out like the colors in a kaleidoscope. I don't know what she said, or I, but she filled the whole telephone booth and filled me with mirthful excitement. We agreed to meet for dinner the next day, and I came from the telephone in a state of credulous wonder. It was true then after all, my masquerade-ball dream of finding a girl utterly beautiful, and yet rich in the qualities of mind and feeling I adore. The whole juvenile and semidrunken invention had been true! Of that large proposition I was convinced by the tones of her voice in the telephone and her few words deftly and joyously spoken.

For journeys to Croton I had bought me a disintegrating Ford car in which I could, with a noise like Gettysburg, and a similar recklessness of human life, go forty miles an hour—almost as fast as a railroad train! It was not the vehicle in which John Fox would have called for a movie heroine, and I was arrogantly aware of that as I drove over to 49 East 34th Street—past the corner where I had been turned around by the girl with the Japanese umbrella and pulled mutely along like an iron filing. That girl had been a wish; this one was a reality, and I was on my way in my own actual self to see her. Perhaps only those tormented as I am by an irrepressible romanticism combined with an obdurate allegiance to fact will understand what was happening to me. I was *believing* that reality might conceivably live up to a dream. I was facing it out with the Ascending Moon. I was giving nature a chance to be divine.

Florence was dressed in a slim gown of heavy black silk that clung softly to her body. She wore no jewelry. Her incomparable colors and precisely carved features, and the lustrous dark waves natural to her hair made ornament superfluous. She introduced me to her bright-eyed Hungarian mother, whom she supported and treated rather as a child. (Her British father, a linotypist, tall, cool, handsome, and self-willed, had quietly walked away some years before.) Florence put on a hat and coat in the living room while I sat talking to her mother, and we went downstairs together and climbed into the old Ford car, admiring its good points with a like laughter and wondering with a like mixture of whim and honest perplexity where it was going to take us.

There is no reason why I should recite these simple steps of our coming together, except that their simplicity was a fact of importance to my emotions. Once again, and even more explicitly than at the *Masses* ball, we seemed to have flowed from a common source. We seemed to be, underneath the thrill of our strangeness to each other, kin.

The old Ford took us across town to Mouquin's famous and not too expensive restaurant in a rambling wooden house opposite the Haymarket at Sixth Avenue and 29th Street. We spent several hours there dining and drinking a little wine, telling each other about ourselves, and finding out to our sustained astonishment how much alike we were. And as though this miracle of downright communion, adjoined to her unutterable beauty, were not enough to unsettle all the points of my compass, luck had to add the one last touch of ideality to it, the coming true of a dream.

She had been expressing petulantly, almost in the language of my college essay "O Mores!" her scorn of men's slavery to custom, and to illustrate their sheeplike stupidity she said:

"You can't do any little thing to please your own taste in this town without starting a riot. I once got a present of a little gay-colored Japanese umbrella. It was becoming to me, and I thought it would be fun to carry it. Do you know I never got farther than Fifth Avenue, and had to turn back home, it caused such a commotion?"

I felt as though I had seen Pan dancing with the dryads, as though lead had been transmuted into gold, as though the moon had come down at last and made the obtruding actual her own.

We could not part when the restaurant closed. We could not say goodbye at a doorjamb and go our separate ways like two ordinary mortals—slaves of custom, all of them. I had told her about the house in Croton. It was waiting. The old Ford car was waiting too, its battered radiator pointing north. It *started* north when I got in after cranking it. Where was the cause, or the will, or the reason, to make it turn?

We slept side-by-side in the corner bed by the big moonlit window, a very tranquil tenderness filling our hearts. Florence was extremely chaste and modest in her instincts; she had been loyal until then to her first lover. And I was still diffident and inexpert at the art of unfamiliar love. But in this relation too, which seemed to me the farthest that magic could reach, we were not unfamiliar. We were kin. The night gave to our bodily union the same instinctive simplicity, that quality of the inevitable, the awaited, which had marked the flowing together of our minds. That sense of having come from the same source, of finding ourselves in each other, that flame of "very ownness" burning in both our hearts, dissolved all the little problems of reticence and self-consciousness. In each of us for the first time the ideal rapture and the physical achievement of love were so perfectly blended as to be undistinguishable.

While we were so happy, the world was plunging in bloodshed toward a doom that no mind could imagine. In one month news would come of the outbreak of revolution in Russia—in another Wilson's high speech to Congress and America's entrance into the European war. We were on the brink of a new epoch in history. Nothing again, after those two ingulfing events, would be the same. As I look back, my whole life up to that point seems to have been introduction—a too tender introduction, politically, to the hard, fierce, bloody, and tyrannical thing that man's life on this planet predominantly has been and is. Like all my radical friends, I had mistaken for final reality the brief paradise of America at the turn of the century. For notwithstanding Ludlow Massacres and wars in West Virginia it was, comparatively, a protected little historic moment of peace and progress that we grew up in. We were children reared in a kindergarten, and now the real thing was coming. . . .

Morally and intellectually, too, I had come to a landing-place in my development. I find inscribed in a notebook of those days the statement: "My life began in January 1917!" I do not remember writing that proclamation, but I can see a truth in what it says. I had won my long war of independence; I had accomplished the feat of confiding in a friend; I had faced loneliness without melancholy; I had outlived that bashfulness which deprived me of the joys of adolescence; I had fallen wholeheartedly in love. After much preaching and philosophizing, and many academic vows of consecration to it, I had at last stepped forth into the enjoyment of living. It was possible for me now to use in a grown-up way whatever wisdoms I possessed.

And I possessed one or two. I had learned in the course of my thirty-three years' introduction to living—as the meditative reader may possibly have noticed—that most of the difficult virtues are essential to its full enjoyment. And I had arrived at an intellectual equilibrium that I have not been moved by the storms which followed to revise. "A liberal mind," I had written in my notes, "is a mind that is able and willing to imagine itself believing anything.

That is the only mind that is capable of judging beliefs, or that can hold strongly without bigotry to a belief of its own." In taking my stand against the pro-war socialists I tried to exemplify that definition of a liberal mind. An editorial from *The Masses* of September 1917 will show the attitude in which I approached those cataclysmic events which divided my life, together with all modern history, in two.

"If this magazine has contributed anything to social revolutionary philosophy in America, its contribution has been a resolute opposition to bigotry and dogmatic thinking of all kinds. It has insisted upon the recognition of variety and change in the facts, and the need for pliancy in the theories of the revolution. It has insisted that the world can no more be saved by a single ism—syndicalism, socialism, single-taxism, anarchism, or whatever—than it was saved by a single God. Along with theology, we have urged the dumping of theological methods of thought. We have asked our readers to use all general ideas as working hypotheses, and not as havens of rest. We have foresworn the absolute and the abstract and the predetermined, and tried to meet each fresh and developing situation with a fresh and developing mind.

"The reason for rehearsing this matter just now is that we wish to bespeak a respectful hearing for those socialists who have resigned from the party in a sincere belief that this war must be fought to a finish for the liberation of the world. We think they are entirely, and somewhat pathetically, wrong. But we also think that there was no antecedent, prima facie, overhead certainty that they *would be* wrong. It was, and is, altogether possible that a situation should arise in which a national war must be fought to a finish for the liberation of the world. Time holds more various wonders in her womb than our intellects can ever prepare for in advance. . . ."

Appendices

I

ABOUT MY FIRST BIRTHDAY
A letter from my mother

Berlin, Prussia
January 4, 1902

Dearest Max,

Is it nineteen years ago—that winter night when I first met you and about an hour after seeing you came very near losing the pleasure of your further acquaintance? You were a "fine boy" they all said, "a beautiful baby," though Morgan did not seem to admire you very much. He was polite, however, and gave you the name of his best beloved hero, Fritz, the oldest son of the Swiss Family Robinson. You had no cradle but slept in your carriage.

The first night of your life the woman who held you by the register fell asleep in her chair, and I was so afraid she would let you roll off her lap—and I was propped up in a very uncomfortable position, with my feet higher than my head, and told not to move a muscle. So all I could do was to wake her up every minute by some sudden sound, and then timidly caution her about the baby on her knees, which she didn't take kindly.

After two or three days of our acquaintance had passed, and I began to feel that the ice was broken, Anstice came home from a long sojourn at the Antes's in which he had learned to read from the New York *Observer* and the letters on the stores—and brought me a bit of candy all gnawed round the edges that he had been *saving* for me—the old darling! What good times we had together, you and I! You had a little mark like a

589

basting thread left in your nose—I guess it is gone now—and you used to look so wise and solemn!

We went to the St. Lawrence River the next summer and Lizzie Tuohy was your slave. I can hear her yet singing you to sleep at the top of a very shrill voice, "Have courage, my boy, to say No!"

Your education was begun right—who can tell how those words helped form your infant mind and give you that adamantine firmness of character which is now one of the bulwarks of Williams College!

She had one other song—"When the myrtle and the iv'ry were in bloom!" But she was a dear good girl and loved you all and managed nicely for a fifteen-year-old. I'd love to have her here this minute to talk over the old days. She was so sorry for us when we passed into the dreadful shadows—never to be the same happy, blessed little company again.

But what an unspeakable comfort you have always been to me, beloved. I didn't see how I could live after my beautiful Morgan slipped away—for oh, so many awful mornings, I *hated* to wake up, and I couldn't bear to have people say to me, "You have so much left to live for." But they were right, and I am so glad I lived to know and love you all as I do tonight.

I'm so sorry for you when I think that you'll *never* be a mother! It seems to me that there can be no other experience that will ever make up to you for the loss of that.

Did you skate on the river without me to watch you from the window?

II

AN ECHO FROM WEST BLOOMFIELD

A further reminder of West Bloomfield's unusual I.Q. came the other day from my little neighbor and schoolmate, Mamie Ashe, who now lives in Rochester—and is now too, I sadly realize, no longer little. Mamie had been reading my *Enjoyment of Laughter* and also a poem of mine called "Diogenes," to which she wrote an answer that I think deserves the light. I will have to quote my own poem first:

DIOGENES

A hut and a tree
And a hill for me,
And a piece of a weedy meadow.
I'll ask no thing
Of God or King,
But to clear away his shadow.

TO MAX EASTMAN

God must enjoy
Laughter in heaven,
Watching his creatures,
The cleverest even,
Using His gifts
With puny might,
To order the Giver
Out of the light.

Mamie was a "Catholic," and therefore a strange being to me, a comely elf who lived up the road a few houses beyond the parsonage.

"I recall so well," she writes, "when your family came to town. The arrival of the Eastman children at school was an event for us. Your names were so unusual, and you were all so dark. You wore your hair in a brush cut, although we did not recognize the style. Crystal and I used to sit together. She had such wonderful pencils! (I had a penny one probably.) She used to ride horseback *astride* and wear *bloomers*. She organized a theatrical company, and we used to rehearse in the Eastman attic. Fancy all that for the country kids! I remember how liked and respected your mother was by both creeds."

III

ALEXANDER TO HIS MUTINOUS SOLDIERS

From *The Williams Literary Monthly*, January 1903

If I were leading into war a troop of pallid citizens, homesick and fagged with walking, I would not ride out here to tell them that I lead them. I lead an army; you are soldiers; I ask you why you sit among your tents.

Amid the hills of Macedonia we rose up and marched away together. Where the cold torrent bursts out of the mountain and leaps down snarling on the cluttered rocks, and where we heard the mountain lion scream, there we learned to march and fight. Since we have marched and fought, and scorched our way this far three thousand miles from those wild brooks, must we on account of that be like the sick and torpid streams that lie upon this country—upon whose banks you seem so prone to sit and mutter? If you have a thing to say, shout it aloud, remembering that you are Northern warriors and not sleeping dogs of this south!

You murmur, "Wherefore do I lead you? Whither do you march?" Ask it of those red plains behind us, ask it of your long swords, ask it of yourselves. I lead you into battle; you can make red your swords;

you can glut yourselves with gold; you can teach these Persians that you are strong. And if I did not lead, and if you did not march, what would you? Slink back along our cindered path like jackals into Greece, and there lift up your heads among our hills? They would start back from you in horror! Or will you sit down here upon these slippery river banks, and turn your dull eyes up to the sun and pray, as do these Persians—who will stick their swords in you, or else stand by and watch you starve? And if you do I hope that no mad god of Greece may come in shame and fell you with some gleaming stroke, but you may rot, while these Persians laugh!

What loathsome oil has poured upon this sea of soldiers that was wont to laugh and gleam and bellow with applause? What foul disease of cowardice has withered you? Can you not remember that wild day when a million of these eastern dogs swarmed forth upon us, and we rose up, and lifted our swords, and turned our eyes upon them, while the battle-blood boiled in us, and we laughed, and ran against them beating on our shields and singing, and we lashed them back into their towns, or left them twisted in the dust?

Is it your leader that dispirits you? Have I become a drudge, a yoke, a lasher of unwilling slaves? Have I not camped with you upon these plains, as I did in bright Greece? Have I not marched with you, and lived with you, and fought with you? Do you say that all the gain is mine, that I am eager to stretch out my hand and see the world kneel down? Yes, I am eager, and you are with me, and I will stretch out my hand, and we need no longer say: "The world and Macedonia!" If you are not eager, then I am your leader and I will fight before you; I am your king, and you shall run behind me into battle. If you must needs be driven in like sheep, I will send for some elected general from Attica, to come and ride behind and whistle at you. Are you not Macedonians?

IV

A BALLAD

From *The Masses* January 1916

The Biggest man in creation?
    It was Joseph the Nazarene.
Joe, the Yiddisher "carpenter stiff,"
    The husband o' Heaven's Queen!
Joe, that was smitten o' Mary,
    Joe, that was game as grit—
When she came weepin' to 'is arms,
    Needin' a father for it.

Joe was as right as the compass,
    Joe was as square as the square.
He knew men's ways with women,
    An' Mary was passin' fair!
Passin' pretty an' helpless,
    She that he loved th' most,
God knows what he told th' neighbors,
    But he knew it warn't no Ghost.

He tuk th' tale as she told it,
    And never th' bat of an eye,
E'en tho' 'is 'eart was breakin'
    Under the load of the lie—
Steady an' game an' tender,
    When she needed a strong man's care,
An' then he saddled the ol' jackass,
    An' took 'er away from there.

Took 'er away from th' neighbors,
    That spoke o' th' fit of 'er gown,
Took 'er away from th' gossips,
    That made 'er th' talk o' the town,
Comforted, soothed and coddled,
    Just as he might ha' done,
If it that was heavy within 'er
    Was Joseph's, the Carpenter's son.

Joe, he was silent an' tender,
    Joe, he was game as grit,
But I'll bet when he walked by Mary,
    To have been the father of it,
He'd a give all 'is 'opes o' heaven,
    He'd a shot like a bat into 'ell,
The minute he knew for certain
    That mother and child was well.

Patience surpassin' the mountains,
    Kindness shamin' the rain,
When th' sickness came upon her,
    An' she cursed 'im in 'er pain;
So he came to the manger,
    With Mary makin' 'er moan,
An' 'e 'eld 'er 'and while she labored
    With a child that wa'n't 'is own!

He looked at th' brat in pity,
An' 'e held it up to 'is breast,
That ached with an awful feeling
That Mary never guessed.
And 'im an' th' brat they 'it it,

(Carn't yer see 'im standin' there in th' shop lookin' at th' brat like 'is
eyes u'd eat 'im up? Carn't yer see th' tenderness when 'e'd show 'im th'
'ow o' th' 'ammer an' saw? Carn't yer see 'im 'ust lookin' at 'im, and
lookin' at 'im, an' a-goin' over an' puttin' 'is arms around 'im an' sayin'
to 'isself underneath 'is breath: "Yer mine, God dam it, yer mine any'ow!"
An' carn't yer 'ear th' brat, lookin' up, an' sayin', "Daddy"? Yes, 'im
an' th' brat, they 'it it.)

An' after th' years had run,
Folks tho't no more o' th' gossip,
But called 'im the Carpenter's Son.

"Williams"*

V

A DEDICATION

To Max Eastman

There was a man, who, loving quiet beauty best
Yet could not rest.
Attuned to the majestic rhythm of whirling suns,
That chimes and runs
Through happy stillnesses—birth in the dawn, and stark
Love in the dark;
The unconquerable semen of the world, that mounts and sings
Through endless springs,
And the dumb death-like sleep of the winter-withered hill
That warms life still;
There was a man, who, loving quiet beauty best,
Yet could not rest
For the harsh moaning of unhappy humankind,
Fettered and blind—
Too driven to know beauty and too hungry-tired
To be inspired.

* The author had signed his name "Williams" in quotation marks, and, oddly
enough, that *was* his name—William Williams. It is the only poem he ever wrote, and
he died in New York, alone and destitute, not long after bringing it to me. Only one
man attended his funeral—Frederick Blossom, who told me these facts twenty-five years
later.

From his high, windy-peaceful hill, he stumbled down
Into the town,
With a child's eyes, clear bitterness, and silver scorn
Of the outworn
And cruel mastery of life by senile death;
And with his breath
Fanned up the noble fires that smoulder in the breast
Of the oppressed.
What guerdon, to forswear for dust and smoke and this
The high-souled bliss
Of poets in walled gardens, finely growing old,
Serene and cold?
A vision of new splendor in the human scheme—
A god-like dream—
And a new lilt of happy trumpets in the strange
Clangor of Change!

John Reed

Index

Set in Linotype Baskerville
Format by A. W. Rushmore
Manufactured by The Haddon Craftsmen
Published by HARPER & BROTHERS
New York and London